W9-BOO-718

Delivering Health Care in America

A Systems Approach

SIXTH EDITION

Leiyu Shi, DrPH, MBA, MPA
Professor, Bloomberg School of Public Health
Director, Johns Hopkins Primary Care Policy Center for the Underserved
Johns Hopkins University
Baltimore, Maryland

Douglas A. Singh, PhD, MBA
Associate Professor Emeritus of Management, School of Business and Economics
Indiana University—South Bend
South Bend, Indiana

JONES & BARTLETT
LEARNING

World Headquarters
Jones & Bartlett Learning
5 Wall Street
Burlington, MA 01803
978-443-5000
info@jblearning.com
www.jblearning.com

Jones & Bartlett Learning books and products are available through most bookstores and online booksellers. To contact Jones & Bartlett Learning directly, call 800-832-0034, fax 978-443-8000, or visit our website, www.jblearning.com.

Substantial discounts on bulk quantities of Jones & Bartlett Learning publications are available to corporations, professional associations, and other qualified organizations. For details and specific discount information, contact the special sales department at Jones & Bartlett Learning via the above contact information or send an email to specialsales@jblearning.com.

Copyright © 2015 by Jones & Bartlett Learning, LLC, an Ascend Learning Company

All rights reserved. No part of the material protected by this copyright may be reproduced or utilized in any form, electronic or mechanical, including photocopying, recording, or by any information storage and retrieval system, without written permission from the copyright owner.

The content, statements, views, and opinions herein are the sole expression of the respective authors and not that of Jones & Bartlett Learning, LLC. Reference herein to any specific commercial product, process, or service by trade name, trademark, manufacturer, or otherwise does not constitute or imply its endorsement or recommendation by Jones & Bartlett Learning, LLC and such reference shall not be used for advertising or product endorsement purposes. All trademarks displayed are the trademarks of the parties noted herein. *Delivering Health Care in America: A Systems Approach, Sixth Edition* is an independent publication and has not been authorized, sponsored, or otherwise approved by the owners of the trademarks or service marks referenced in this product.

There may be images in this book that feature models; these models do not necessarily endorse, represent, or participate in the activities represented in the images. Any screenshots in this product are for educational and instructive purposes only. Any individuals and scenarios featured in the case studies throughout this product may be real or fictitious, but are used for instructional purposes only.

This publication is designed to provide accurate and authoritative information in regard to the Subject Matter covered. It is sold with the understanding that the publisher is not engaged in rendering legal, accounting, or other professional service. If legal advice or other expert assistance is required, the service of a competent professional person should be sought.

03775-3

Production Credits
Executive Publisher: William Brottmiller
Publisher: Michael Brown
Associate Editor: Chloe Falivene
Editorial Assistant: Nicholas Alakel
Production Manager: Tracey McCrea
Senior Marketing Manager: Sophie Fleck Teague

Manufacturing and Inventory Control Supervisor: Amy Bacus
Composition: Cenveo Publisher Services
Cover Design: Kristin E. Parker
Photo Research and Permissions Coordinator: Amy Rathburn
Cover Image: © OrhanCam/ShutterStock, Inc.
Printing and Binding: Edwards Brothers Malloy
Cover Printing: Edwards Brothers Malloy

To order this product, use ISBN: 978-1-284-07463-5

The Library of Congress has cataloged the first printing as follows:
Shi, Leiyu, author.
  Delivering health care in America : a systems approach / Leiyu Shi, Douglas A. Singh.—Sixth edition.
    p. ; cm.
  Includes bibliographical references and index.
  ISBN 978-1-284-03775-3 (pbk.)
  I. Singh, Douglas A., 1946- author. II. Title.
  [DNLM: 1. Delivery of Health Care—United States. 2. Health Policy—United States.
    3. Health Services—United States. W 84 AA1]
  RA395.A3
  362.10973—dc233
                                                                                        2013045774
  6048
Printed in the United States of America
18 17 16 15 14   10 9 8 7 6 5 4 3 2

Contents

Preface

As of this writing, a few weeks after the health insurance exchanges were opened for enrollment on October 1, 2013, millions of Americans across the nation were beginning to get a first-hand experience with the Affordable Care Act (ACA), nicknamed Obamacare. In a country in which people have been divided almost in the middle on their views, there has been no dearth of speculations on both sides ever since the ACA became law. One side has claimed that the ACA is destined to fail, while the other side has reached the grandiose conclusion that, finally, most Americans will have access to affordable, high-quality health care. We think that such prophetic assertions on both sides are premature. The truth perhaps lies somewhere between the two extremes, but it will not be known for at least a year or two.

Some provisions of the ACA went into effect between 2010 and 2012. They included coverage of children and adults under the age of 26 as dependents under their parents' health insurance plans, elimination of lifetime dollar limits in health plans, increases in annual caps on health care use, inclusion of preventive services with no out-of-pocket expenses, temporary credits to small employers to offset health insurance costs, certain discounts on drugs for Medicare beneficiaries, and a requirement that health plans spend no less than a certain proportion of the premiums on providing medical care. These mandates, mainly imposed on insurers, were implemented without much ado as most consumers benefited from them. The additional costs were, of course, borne by the insurers. Eventually, however, increased business costs are always passed on to the consumers.

The eventual success or failure of the ACA, or of any other health care reform efforts in the future, will hinge on several factors. Some critical unanswered questions are: Will a large number of young and healthy people enroll through the exchanges to prevent an upward spiral in premium costs, sometimes referred to as a "death spiral?" Will the employment-based health insurance system survive, and, if so, to what extent? Will private insurance companies continue to participate in the government exchanges, or will they hand over the reins to the government at some point? Will the number of providers be sufficient to care for a large influx of the newly insured population? Will Americans have at least the same level of access to health care services that the insured now have, or will access deteriorate for everyone? Will a heavily indebted nation be able to afford the rising levels of spending without causing serious disloca-tions in the overall economy? Even though there is uncertainty in these areas, this book attempts to inform the readers on these and many other issues based on what is already known and what some of the trends may be pointing to. In most areas, however, we offer known facts so that the readers can apply their critical thinking skills and draw their own conclusions, pro or con.

Reforms under the new law contain several areas aimed at improving the cur-rent health care system. The main areas include a reinvigorated emphasis on pre-vention; incentives for care coordination; incentives for hospitals to improve qual-ity; enhanced quality reporting require-ments; federal assistance to improve the primary care infrastructure, although it is quite inadequate; federal support to autho-rize "generic" (biosimilar) versions of cer-tain biologics; and insurance coverage for low-income citizens and certain vulnerable groups. These reforms have theoretical bases and precedents so that positive out-comes can be expected in the future.

On the flip side, the ACA has created much confusion, uncertainty, and con-troversy. For employers, even though the mandate to provide health insurance has been delayed until January 2015, complex reporting requirements will increase busi-ness costs. Both large and small businesses are juggling with various options in an effort to find optimum solutions. Eventu-ally, many workers will be left with reduced work hours, unaffordable premiums, with-out family coverage altogether, or complete loss of a job because of how the ACA has been crafted. As an example of the burden many working Americans are likely to face, researchers at the Kaiser Family Founda-tion estimated that 3.9 million non-working

dependents were in families in which the worker had employment-based coverage but the family did not. These family members would be excluded from getting federal tax credits to subsidize their purchase of health insurance through the government-run mar-ketplaces. On another front, literally millions of Americans have experienced cancellation of their existing privately-purchased health insurance because the policies do not com-ply with ACA mandates. That these covered individuals were satisfied with their insur-ance is inconsequential as far as ACA com-pliance is concerned. The same individuals are finding premiums to be unaffordable when they sign up for coverage through the government-run marketplaces. A last-min-ute announcement by the Obama admin-istration on November 14, 2013 to allow existing insurance policies to continue for another year under certain conditions seems to have done little to assuage the problem.

The US Supreme Court did not help matters when it upheld half of the law, but let states decide whether they wished to expand their Medicaid programs—as ini-tially intended by the ACA—or opt out. About half the states have opted out, which leaves many vulnerable groups in those states in a state of uncertainty if they are not already covered under Medicaid.

Other issues associated with the ACA include the bulk of the previously unin-sured people still to be left without health insurance (estimated to be around 25 to 30 million), uncertain health care costs, experimentation with untested care deliv-ery models that could create dislocations in access and cost, and controversies and legal actions still in place even after the Supreme Court's ruling that was handed down in June 2012. The latter category includes lawsuits brought by Catholic and other religious groups based on objections to providing contraceptives mandated by the ACA. On December 31, 2013, US Supreme Court justice, Sonia Sotomayor, an Obama appointee, issued a temporary injunction that blocked the Obama administration from enforcing the birth control mandate for certain Catholic groups. Of course, the Obama administration has objected to Sotomayor's injunction. According to one report, more than 90 legal challenges have been filed around the country, and the ACA could once again be reviewed by the Supreme Court. In addition, the forthcoming November 2014 congressional elections have some Democrats worried because they voted for the now unpopular ACA. They are trying their best to distance themselves from the ACA. No doubt, the ACA faces turbulent times ahead. Hence, confusion and uncertainty are likely to prevail for some time to come.

New to This Edition

This *Sixth Edition* has undergone some of the most extensive revisions we have ever undertaken. We have done this while maintaining the book's basic structure and layout which, for more than 15 years, has served quite well in helping readers both at home and overseas understand the complexities of the US health care delivery system. Some basic elements of US health insurance and delivery are intentionally retained to assist the growing number of foreign students in US colleges and universities, as well as those residing in foreign countries.

The major updates reflect on two main areas: (1) Regardless of its future, the ACA will radically change health care delivery in the United States, for better or for worse. Because of its far-reaching scope, different

aspects of the ACA are woven through all 14 chapters (see the Topical Reference Guide to the Affordable Care Act for easy reference). The reader will find a gradual unfolding of this complex and cumbersome law so it can be slowly digested. To aid in this process, every chapter ends with a new feature, "ACA Takeaway," as an overview of what the reader would have encountered in the chapter. Details of the law are confined to the context and scope of this book. (2) US health care can no longer remain isolated from globalization. An integrative process in certain domains has been underway for some time. Hence, it has become increasingly important to provide global perspectives, which the readers will encounter in several chapters.

As in the past, this edition has been updated throughout with the latest pertinent data, trends, and research findings available at the time the manuscript was prepared. Copious illustrations in the form of examples, facts, figures, tables, and exhibits continue to make the text come alive. Following is a list of the main additions and revisions:

- Chapter 1:
  - A basic overview of health care reform and the Affordable Care Act (ACA)
  - Critical global health issues
- Chapter 2:
  - Health insurance under the ACA
  - Measurement of *Healthy People 2020* goals
  - Global health indicators
- Chapter 3:
  - E-health and its current applications for consumers
  - New expanded section: Era of Health Care Reform

- Chapter 4:
  - The ACA and physician supply
  - Updated information on non-physician providers
- Chapter 5:
  - Clinical decision support systems (CDSS) and their benefits
  - Introduction to health information organizations (HIOs)
  - Introduction to nanomedicine
  - Revisions to HIPAA in conjunction with the HITECH law
  - Update on remote monitoring technology
  - New section on biologics and their regulation by the FDA
  - The ACA as it applies to medical devices and biologics
- Chapter 6:
  - Adjusted community rating for insurance underwriting under the ACA
  - New exhibit to spotlight differences between the two main types of high-deductible/savings plans
  - New section, "Private Health Insurance Under the ACA," covering details of the many changes that private insurance plans and employers must comply with
  - Changes in Medicare, including changes in reimbursement, required by the ACA
  - Recent trends affecting the HI and SMI trust funds
  - Ambiguity over Medicaid that creates two different programs and ironies created by the ACA
  - Refined DRGs (MS-DRGs) for reimbursement of acute-care inpatient hospital services, and ACA stipulations for hospital reimbursement
  - Updated current directions and issues in financing
- Chapter 7:
  - Primary Care Assessment Tool
  - Medical home measurement
  - Primary care providers in other countries
  - Current developments in home health care
  - Current developments in community health centers
  - Current developments in alternative medicine
  - Global trends in health care providers
- Chapter 8:
  - New section on hospital utilization and factors that affect hospital employment
  - New section on hospital costs
- Chapter 9:
  - New section on pharmaceutical management as a cost-control mechanism in managed care
  - Introduction to triple-option plans
  - New section on managed care and health insurance exchanges under the ACA
  - Expanded section on accountable care organizations
  - New section on payer–provider integration
- Chapter 10:
  - Limited federal financial incentives to states for additional home- and community-based long-term care services under the ACA
  - New model of continuing care at home
- Chapter 11:
  - The uninsured under the ACA
  - Updated information on the homeless
  - Updated information on mental health
  - Updated information on the chronically ill
  - New section on the migrant populations

- Chapter 12:
  - Current issues in health care cost, access, and quality
  - CMS program related to quality
  - AHRQ quality report card/indicators
  - NCQA and quality measures
- Chapter 13:
  - Current critical policy issues
  - Future health policy issues/challenges in both the US and abroad
- Chapter 14:
  - Expansion of the framework: Forces of Future Change
  - Revised section on the future of health care reform
  - Perspectives on universal coverage and access vs. single-payer system

As in the previous editions, our aim is to continue to meet the needs of both graduate and undergraduate students. We have attempted to make each chapter complete without making it overwhelming for beginners. Instructors, of course, will choose the sections they decide are most appropriate for their courses.

As in the past, we invite comments from our readers. Communications can be directed to either or both authors:

Leiyu Shi
Department of Health Policy and
  Management
Bloomberg School of Public Health
Johns Hopkins University
624 North Broadway, Room 409
Baltimore, MD 21205-1996
lshi@jhsph.edu

Douglas A. Singh
Judd Leighton School of Business and
Economics
Indiana University—South Bend
1800 Mishawaka Avenue
P.O. Box 7111
South Bend, IN 46634-7111
dsingh@iusb.edu

We appreciate the work of Xiaoyu Nie in providing assistance in the preparation of selected chapters of this book.

List of Exhibits

List of Figures

List of Tables

List of Abbreviations/Acronyms

A

AALL—American Association of Labor Legislation

AAMC—Association of American Medical Colleges

AA/PIs—Asian American and Pacific Islanders

AAs—Asian Americans

ACA—Affordable Care Act

ACNM—American College of Nurse-Midwives

ACO—accountable care organization

ACPE—American Council on Pharmaceutical Education

ACS—American College of Surgeons

ADA—American Dental Association

ADA—Americans with Disabilities Act

ADC—adult day care

ADLs—activities of daily living

ADN—associate's degree nurse

AFC—adult foster care

AFDC—Aid to Families with Dependent Children

AHA—American Hospital Association

AHRQ—Agency for Healthcare Research and Quality

AIANs—American Indians and Alaska Natives

AIDS—acquired immune deficiency syndrome

ALF—assisted living facility

ALOS—average length of stay

AMA—American Medical Association

AMDA—American Medical Directors Association

amfAR—Foundation for AIDS Research

ANA—American Nurses Association

APCs—ambulatory payment classifications

APN—advanced practice nurse

ARRA—American Recovery and Reinvestment Act

ASPR—Assistant Secretary for Preparedness

B

BBA—Balanced Budget Act of 1997

BPCI—bundled payments for care improvement

BPHC—Bureau of Primary Health Care

BSN—baccalaureate degree nurse

BWC—Biological Weapons Convention

C

CAH—critical access hospital

CAM—complementary and alternative medicine

CAT—computerized axial tomography

CBO—Congressional Budget Office

CCAH—continuing care at home

CCIP—Chronic Care Improvement Program

CCRC—continuing care retirement community

CDC—Centers for Disease Control and Prevention
CDSS—clinical decision support systems
CEO—chief executive officer
CEPH—Council on Education for Public Health
CF—conversion factor
CHAMPVA—Civilian Health and Medical Program of the Department of Veterans Affairs
CHC—community health center
CHIP—Children's Health Insurance Program
CIA—Central Intelligence Agency
CMGs—case-mix groups
C/MHCs—Community and Migrant Health Centers
CMS—Centers for Medicare & Medicaid Services
CNA—certified nursing assistant
CNM—certified nurse-midwife
CNSs—clinical nurse specialists
COBRA—Consolidated Omnibus Budget Reconciliation Act of 1985
COGME—Council on Graduate Medical Education
CON—certificate-of-need
COPC—community-oriented primary care
COPD—chronic obstructive pulmonary disease
COTA—certified occupational therapy assistant
COTH—Council of Teaching Hospitals and Health Systems
CPI—consumer price index
CPOE—computerized physician order entry
CPT—current procedural terminology
CQI—continuous quality improvement
CRNA—certified registered nurse anesthetist
CT—computed tomography
CVA—cardiovascular accident

D

DC—doctor of chiropractic
DD—developmentally disabled
DDS—Doctor of Dental Surgery
DHHS—Department of Health and Human Services
DHS—Department of Homeland Security
DMD—doctor of dental medicine
DME—durable medical equipment
DoD—Department of Defense
DO—doctor of osteopathy
DPM—doctor of podiatric medicine
DRA—Deficit Reduction Act of 2005
DRGs—diagnostic-related groups
DSM-IV—*Diagnostic and Statistical Manual of Mental Disorders*
DTP—diphtheria-tetanus-pertussis

E

EBM—evidence-based medicine
EBRI—Employee Benefit Research Institute
ECG—electrocardiogram
ECU—extended care unit
ED—emergency department
EHRs—electronic health records
EMT—emergency medical technician
EMTALA—Emergency Medical Treatment and Labor Act
ENP—elderly nutrition program
EPA—Environmental Protection Agency
EPO—exclusive provider organization
ERISA—Employee Retirement Income Security Act
ESRD—end-stage renal disease

F

FBI—Federal Bureau of Investigation
FD&C—Federal Food, Drug, and Cosmetic Act
FDA—Food and Drug Administration
FMAP—Federal Medical Assistance Percentage

FPL—federal poverty level
FQHC—Federally Qualified Health Center
FTE—full-time equivalent
FY—fiscal year

G

GAO—General Accounting Office
GATS—General Agreement on Trade in
 Services
GDP—gross domestic product
GP—general practitioner

H

HAART—highly active antiretroviral
 therapy
HCBS—home- and community-based
 services
HCBW—home- and community-based
 waiver
HCH—Health Care for the Homeless
HDHP—high-deductible health plan
HEDIS—Health Plan Employer Data and
 Information Set
HHRG—home health resource group
HI—hospital insurance
HIAA—Health Insurance Association of
 America
Hib—*Haemophilus influenzae* B
HIO—health information organization
HIPAA—Health Insurance Portability and
 Accountability Act
HIT—health information technology
HITECH— Health Information
 Technology for Economic and Clinical
 Health Act
HIV—human immunodeficiency virus
HMO—health maintenance organization
HMO Act—Health Maintenance
 Organization Act
HPSAs—health professional shortage
 areas
HPV—human papillomavirus
HRQL—health-related quality of life

HRSA—Health Resources and Services
 Administration
HSA—health savings account
HSAs—health system agencies
HTA—health technology assessment
HUD—Department of Housing and Urban
 Development

I

IADL—instrumental activities of daily
 living
ICD-9—International Classification of
 Diseases, version 9
ICF—intermediate care facility
ICF/IID—intermediate care facilities
 for individuals with intellectual
 disabilities
ICF/MR—intermediate care facilities for
 mentally retarded
ID—intellectual disability
IDD—intellectually/developmentally
 disabled
IDEA—Individuals with Disabilities
 Education Act
IDS—integrated delivery systems
IDU—injection drug use
IHR—International Health Regulations
IHS—Indian Health Service
IMGs—international medical graduates
INS—Immigration and Naturalization
 Service
IOM—Institute of Medicine
IPA—independent practice association
IPAB—Independent Payment Advisory
 Board
IRB—Institutional Review Board
IRF—inpatient rehabilitation facility
IRMAA—income related monthly
 adjustment amount
IRS—Internal Revenue Service
IS—information systems
IT—information technology
IV—intravenous

L

LPN—licensed practical nurse
LTC—long-term care
LTCH—long-term care hospital
LVN—licensed vocational nurse

M

MA—Medicare Advantage
MA-PD—Medicare Advantage
　Prescription Drug Plan
MA-SNP—Medicare Advantage Special
　Needs Program
MBA—master of business administration
MCOs—managed care organizations
MD—doctor of medicine
MDS—minimum data set
MedPAC—Medicare Payment Advisory
　Commission
MEPS—Medical Expenditure Panel
　Survey
MFS—Medicare Fee Schedule
MHA—master of health administration
MHS—multihospital system
MHSA—master of health services
　administration
MLP—midlevel provider
MLR—medical loss ratio
MMA—Medicare Prescription Drug,
　Improvement, and Modernization Act
MMR—measles-mumps-rubella vaccine
MPA—master of public administration/
　affairs
MPFS—Medicare Physician Fee Schedule
MPH—master of public health
MR/DD—mentally retarded,
　developmentally disabled
MRHFP—Medicare Rural Hospital
　Flexibility Program
MRI—magnetic resonance imaging
MSA—metropolitan statistical area
MS-DRGs—Medicare severity diagnosis-
　related groups
MSO—management services organization

MUAs—medically underserved areas

N

NAB—National Association of Boards
　of Examiners of Long-Term Care
　Administrators
NADSA—National Adult Day Services
　Association
NAPBC—National Action Plan on Breast
　Cancer
NCCAM—National Center for
　Complementary and Alternative
　Medicine
NCHS—National Center for Health
　Statistics
NCQA—National Committee for Quality
　Assurance
NF—nursing facility
NGC—National Guideline Clearinghouse
NHC—neighborhood health center
NHE—national health expenditures
NHI—national health insurance
NHS—British National Health Service
NHSC—National Health Service Corps
NIAAA—National Institute of Alcohol
　Abuse and Alcoholism
NICE—National Institute for Health and
　Clinical Excellence
NIDA—National Institute on Drug Abuse
NIH—National Institutes of Health
NIMH—National Institute of Mental
　Health
NP—nurse practitioner
NPC—nonphysician clinician
NPP—nonphysician practitioner
NRA—Nurse Reinvestment Act of 2002
NRP— National Response Plan

O

OAM—Office of Alternative Medicine
OBRA—Omnibus Budget Reconciliation
　Act
OD—doctor of optometry

OI—opportunistic infections
OMB—Office of Management and Budget
OPPS—Outpatient Prospective Payment System
OSHA—Occupational Safety and Health Administration
OT—occupational therapist
OWH—Office on Women's Health

P

P4P—pay-for-performance
PA—physician assistant
PACE—Program of All-Inclusive Care for the Elderly
PAHP—Pandemic and All-Hazards Preparedness Act
PASRR—Preadmission Screening and Resident Review
PBMs—pharmacy benefits management companies
PCCM—primary care case management
PCGs—primary care groups
PCIP—Pre-Existing Condition Insurance Plan
PCM—primary care manager
PCP—primary care physician
PDAs—personal digital assistants
PDP—stand-alone prescription drug plan
PERS—personal emergency response systems
PET—positron emission tomography
PFFS—private fee-for-service
PharmD—doctor of pharmacy
PhD—doctor of philosophy
PHI—personal health information
PHO—physician–hospital organization
PhRMA—Pharmaceutical Research and Manufacturers of America
PHS—public health service
PMPM—payment per member per month
POS—point-of-service plan
PPD—per-patient day rate
PPM—physician practice management

PPOs—preferred provider organizations
PPS—prospective payment system
PROs—peer review organizations
PSO—provider-sponsored organization
PSROs—professional standards review organizations
PsyD—doctor of psychology
PTA—physical therapy assistant
PTCA—percutaneous transluminal coronary angioplasty
PTs—physical therapists

Q

QALY—quality-adjusted life year
QI—quality indicator
QIOs—quality improvement organizations

R

R&D—research and development
RAI—resident assessment instrument
RBRVS—resource-based relative value scales
RHIO—Regional Health Information Organization
RICs—rehabilitation impairment categories
RN—registered nurse
RUG-III—Resource Utilization Groups, version 3
RUGs—resource utilization groups
RVUs—relative value units
RWJF—Robert Wood Johnson Foundation

S

SAMHSA—Substance Abuse and Mental Health Services Administration
SARS—severe acute respiratory syndrome
SAV—small area variations
SES—socioeconomic status
SHI—socialized health insurance
SHOP—small business health options program
SMI—supplementary medical insurance

SNF—skilled nursing facility
SPECT—single-photon emission
   computed tomography
SSI—Supplemental Security Income
STDs—sexually transmitted diseases

T

TAH—total artificial heart
TANF—Temporary Assistance for Needy
   Families
TCU—transitional care unit
TEFRA—Tax Equity and Fiscal
   Responsibility Act
TFL—TriCare for Life
TPA—third-party administrator
TQM—total quality management

U

UCR—usual, customary, andreasonable
UR—utilization review

V

VA—Department of Veterans Affairs
VBP—value-based purchasing
VHA—Veterans Health Administration
VISN—Veterans Integrated Service Network
VNA—Visiting Nurses Association

W

WHO—World Health Organization
WIC—Special Supplemental Nutrition
   Program for Women, Infants, and
   Children

Topical Reference Guide to the Affordable Care Act (ACA)

Chapter 1

An Overview of US Health Care Delivery

Learning Objectives

- To understand the basic nature of the US health care system
- To outline the key functional components of a health care delivery system
- To get a basic overview of health care reform and the Affordable Care Act
- To discuss the primary characteristics of the US health care system
- To emphasize why it is important for health care practitioners and managers to understand the intricacies of the health care delivery system
- To get an overview of health care systems in selected countries
- To point out global health challenges and reform efforts
- To introduce the systems model as a framework for studying the health services system in the United States

The US health care delivery system is a behemoth that is almost impossible for any single entity to manage and control.

Introduction

The United States has a unique system of health care delivery unlike any other health care system in the world. Most developed countries have national health insurance programs run by the government and financed through general taxes. Almost all citizens in such countries are entitled to receive health care services. Such is not yet the case in the United States, where not all Americans are automatically covered by health insurance.

The US health care delivery system is really not a system in its true sense, even though it is called a system when reference is made to its various features, components, and services. Hence, it may be somewhat misleading to talk about the American health care delivery "system" because a true system does not exist (Wolinsky 1988). One main feature of the US health care system is that it is fragmented because different people obtain health care through different means. The system has continued to undergo periodic changes, mainly in response to concerns regarding cost, access, and quality.

Describing health care delivery in the United States can be a daunting task. To facilitate an understanding of the structural and conceptual basis for the delivery of health services, this text is organized according to a systems framework presented at the end of this chapter. Also, for the sake of simplicity, the mechanisms of health services delivery in the United States are collectively referred to as a system throughout this text.

The main objective of this chapter is to provide a broad understanding of how health care is delivered in the United States. Examples of how health care is delivered in other countries are also presented. The overview presented here introduces the reader to several concepts treated more extensively in later chapters.

An Overview of the Scope and Size of the System

Table 1–1 demonstrates the complexity of health care delivery in the United States. Many organizations and individuals are involved in health care, ranging from educational and research institutions, medical suppliers, insurers, payers, and claims processors to health care providers. Multitudes of providers are involved in the delivery of preventive, primary, subacute, acute, auxiliary, rehabilitative, and continuing care. An increasing number of managed care organizations (MCOs) and integrated networks now provide a continuum of care, covering many of the service components.

The US health care delivery system is massive, with total employment that reached over 16.4 million in 2010 in various health delivery settings. This included over 838,000 professionally active doctors of medicine (MDs), 70,480 osteopathic physicians (DOs), and 2.6 million active nurses (US Census Bureau 2012). The vast number of health care and health services professionals (5.98 million) work in ambulatory health service settings, such as the offices of physicians, dentists, and other health practitioners, medical and diagnostic laboratories, and home health care service locations. This is followed by hospitals (4.7 million) and nursing and residential care facilities (3.13 million). The vast array of health care institutions includes approximately 5,795 hospitals, 15,700 nursing homes, and 13,337 substance abuse treatment facilities (US Census Bureau 2012).

Table 1–1 The Complexity of Health Care Delivery

Education/Research	Suppliers	Insurers	Providers	Payers	Government
Medical schools	Pharmaceutical companies	Managed care plans	*Preventive Care*	Blue Cross/ Blue Shield plans	Public insurance financing
Dental schools	Multipurpose suppliers	Blue Cross/ Blue Shield plans	Health departments	Commercial insurers	Health regulations
Nursing programs	Biotechnology companies	Commercial insurers	*Primary Care*	Employers	Health policy
Physician assistant programs		Self-insured employers	Physician offices	Third-party administrators	Research funding
Nurse practitioner programs		Medicare	Community health centers	State agencies	Public health
Physical therapy, occupational therapy, speech therapy programs		Medicaid	Dentists		
		VA	Nonphysician providers		
Research organizations		Tricare	*Subacute Care*		
Private foundations			Subacute care facilities		
US Public Health Service (AHRQ, ATSDR, CDC, FDA, HRSA, IHS, NIH, SAMHSA)			Ambulatory surgery centers		
			Acute Care		
			Hospitals		
Professional associations			*Auxiliary Services*		
Trade associations			Pharmacists		
			Diagnostic clinics		
			X-ray units		
			Suppliers of medical equipment		
			Rehabilitative Services		
			Home health agencies		
			Rehabilitation centers		
			Skilled nursing facilities		
			Continuing Care		
			Nursing homes		
			End-of-Life Care		
			Hospices		
			Integrated		
			Managed care organizations		
			Integrated networks		

In 2011, 1,128 federally qualified health center grantees, with 138,403 full-time employees, provided preventive and primary care services to approximately 20.2 million people living in medically underserved rural and urban areas (HRSA 2013). Various types of health care professionals are trained in 159 medical and osteopathic schools, 61 dental schools, over 100 schools of pharmacy, and more than 1,500 nursing programs located throughout the country (US Bureau of Labor Statistics 2011). Multitudes of government agencies are involved with the financing of health care, medical research, and regulatory oversight of the various aspects of the health care delivery system.

A Broad Description of the System

US health care delivery does not function as a rational and integrated network of components designed to work together coherently. To the contrary, it is a kaleidoscope of financing, insurance, delivery, and payment mechanisms that remain loosely coordinated. Each of these basic functional components—financing, insurance, delivery, and payment—represents an amalgam of public (government) and private sources. Thus, government-run programs finance and insure health care for select groups of people who meet each program's prescribed criteria for eligibility. To a lesser degree, government programs also deliver certain health care services directly to certain recipients, such as veterans, military personnel, American Indians/Alaska Natives, and some of the uninsured. However, the financing, insurance, payment, and delivery functions are largely in private hands.

The market-oriented economy in the United States attracts a variety of private entrepreneurs driven by the pursuit of profits obtained by carrying out the key functions of health care delivery. Employers purchase health insurance for their employees through private sources, and employees receive health care services delivered by the private sector. The government finances public insurance through Medicare, Medicaid, and the Children's Health Insurance Program (CHIP) for a significant portion of the low-income, elderly, disabled, and pediatric populations. However, insurance arrangements for many publicly insured people are made through private entities, such as health maintenance organizations (HMOs), and health care services are rendered by private physicians and hospitals. The blend of public and private involvement in the delivery of health care has resulted in:

- a multiplicity of financial arrangements that enable individuals to pay for health care services;
- numerous insurance agencies or MCOs that employ varied mechanisms for insuring against risk;
- multiple payers that make their own determinations regarding how much to pay for each type of service;
- a large array of settings where medical services are delivered; and
- numerous consulting firms offering expertise in planning, cost containment, electronic systems, quality, and restructuring of resources.

There is little standardization in a system that is functionally fragmented, and the various system components fit together only loosely. Such a system is not subject to overall planning, direction, and coordination from a central agency, such as the government. Duplication, overlap, inadequacy, inconsistency, and waste exist, leading to complexity and inefficiency, due to the missing dimension of system-wide planning, direction, and coordination. The system as a whole does not lend itself to standard budgetary methods of cost control. Each individual and corporate entity within a predominantly private entrepreneurial system seeks to manipulate financial incentives to its own advantage, without regard to its impact on the system as a whole. Hence, cost containment remains an elusive goal. In short, the US health care delivery system is like a behemoth or an economic megalith that is almost impossible for any single entity to manage or control. The US economy is the largest in the world, and, compared to other nations, consumption of health care services in the United States represents a greater proportion of the country's total economic output. Although the system can be credited for delivering some of the best clinical care in the world, it falls short of delivering equitable services to every American.

An acceptable health care delivery system should have two primary objectives: (1) it must enable all citizens to obtain needed health care services, and (2) the services must be cost effective and meet certain established standards of quality. The US health care delivery system falls short of both these ideals. On the other hand, certain features of US health care are the envy of the world. The United States leads the world in the latest and the best in medical technology, training, and research. It offers some of the most sophisticated institutions, products, and processes of health care delivery.

Basic Components of a Health Services Delivery System

Figure 1–1 illustrates that a health care delivery system incorporates four functional components—financing, insurance, delivery, and payment, or the *quad-function model*. Health care delivery systems differ depending on the arrangement of these components. The four functions generally overlap, but the degree of overlap varies between a private and a government-run system and between a traditional health insurance and managed care–based system. In a government-run system, the functions are more closely integrated and may be indistinguishable. Managed care arrangements also integrate the four functions to varying degrees.

Financing

Financing is necessary to obtain health insurance or to pay for health care services. For most privately insured Americans, health insurance is employment-based; that is, the employers finance health care as a fringe benefit. A dependent spouse or children may also be covered by the working spouse's or working parent's employer. Most employers purchase health insurance for their employees through an MCO or an insurance company selected by the employer. Small employers may or may not be in a position to afford health insurance coverage for their employees. In public programs, the government functions as the financier; the insurance function may be carved out to an HMO.

Insurance

Insurance protects the insured against catastrophic risks when needing expensive

Figure 1–1 Basic Health Care Delivery Functions.

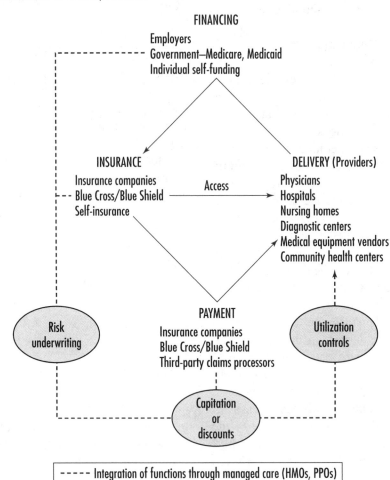

health care services. The insurance function also determines the package of health services the insured individual is entitled to receive. It specifies how and where health care services may be received. The MCO or insurance company also functions as a claims processor and manages the disbursement of funds to the health care providers.

Delivery

The term "delivery" refers to the provision of health care services by various providers.

The term *provider* refers to any entity that delivers health care services and can either independently bill for those services or is tax supported. Common examples of providers include physicians, dentists, optometrists, and therapists in private practices, hospitals, and diagnostic and imaging clinics, and suppliers of medical equipment (e.g., wheelchairs, walkers, ostomy supplies, oxygen). With few exceptions, most providers render services to people who have health insurance. With a few exceptions, even those covered under public insurance programs receive health care services from private providers.

Payment

The payment function deals with *reimbursement* to providers for services delivered. The insurer determines how much is paid for a certain service. Funds for actual disbursement come from the premiums paid to the MCO or insurance company. The patient is usually required, at the time of service, to pay an out-of-pocket amount, such as $25 or $30, to see a physician. The remainder is covered by the MCO or insurance company. In government insurance plans, such as Medicare and Medicaid, tax revenues are used to pay providers.

Insurance and Health Care Reform

In 2009, there were 194.5 million Americans with private health insurance coverage (US Census Bureau 2012). The US government finances health benefits for certain special populations, including government employees, the elderly (people age 65 and over), people with disabilities, some people with very low incomes, and children from low-income families. The program for the elderly and certain disabled individuals is called *Medicare*. The program for the indigent, jointly administered by the federal government and state governments, is named *Medicaid*. The program for children from low-income families, another federal/state partnership, is called the Children's Health Insurance Program (CHIP). In 2009, there were 43.4 million Medicare beneficiaries and 47.8 million Medicaid recipients, but 50.7 million people (16.7%) remained

without any health insurance (US Census Bureau 2012).

Even the predominant employment-based financing system in the United States has left some employed individuals uninsured for two main reasons: (1) In many states, employers are not mandated to offer health insurance to their employees; therefore, some employers, due to economic constraints, do not offer it. Some small businesses simply cannot get group insurance at affordable rates and, therefore, are not able to offer health insurance as a benefit to their employees. (2) In many work settings, participation in health insurance programs is voluntary and does not require employees to join. Some employees choose not to sign up, mainly because they cannot afford the cost of health insurance premiums. Employers rarely pay 100% of the insurance premium; most require their employees to pay a portion of the cost, called *premium cost sharing*. People such as those who are self-employed have to obtain health insurance on their own. Individual rates are typically higher than group rates available to employers. In the United States, working people earning low wages have been the most likely to be uninsured because most cannot afford premium cost sharing and are not eligible for public benefits.

In the US context, *health care reform* refers to the expansion of health insurance to cover the *uninsured*—those without private or public health insurance coverage. The Affordable Care Act (ACA) of 2010 is the most sweeping health care reform in recent US history. How the ACA became law is discussed in Chapters 3 and 13. One of the main objectives of the ACA is to reduce the number of uninsured. This section provides a brief overview of how the ACA plans to accomplish this; more complete details are furnished in Chapter 6.

The ACA was rolled out gradually starting in 2010 when insurance companies were mandated to start covering children and young adults below the age of 26 under their parents' health insurance plans. Most other insurance provisions went into effect on January 1, 2014, except for a mandate for employers to provide health insurance, which is postponed until 2015. The ACA requires that all US citizens and legal residents must be covered by either public or private insurance. The law also relaxed standards to qualify additional numbers of people for Medicaid, although many states have chosen not to implement it based on the US Supreme Court's ruling in 2012 (see Chapter 3 for details). Individuals without private or public insurance must obtain health insurance from participating insurance companies through Web-based, government-run exchanges; failing do so, they must pay a tax. The main function of the exchanges—also referred to as health insurance marketplaces—is to first determine whether an applicant qualifies for Medicaid or CHIP programs. If an applicant does not qualify for a public program, the exchange would enable the individual to compare health plans offered by private insurers and to purchase a suitable health plan. Federal subsidies have been made available to people with incomes up to 400% of the federal poverty level to partially offset the cost of health insurance. Small employers can also obtain health coverage for their employees through the exchanges. The law mandates insurance plans to cover a variety of services referred to as "essential health benefits."

A predictive model developed by Parente and Feldman (2013) estimated that, at best, full implementation of the ACA will reduce the number of uninsured by more than 20 million. If achieved in 2014, this would be the largest coverage expansion in recent US history. Nevertheless, by its own design, the ACA would fail to achieve *universal coverage* that would enable all citizens and legal residents to have health insurance. Possible future scenarios for health care reform are discussed in Chapter 14.

Role of Managed Care

Under traditional insurance, the four basic health delivery functions have been fragmented; that is, the financiers, insurers, providers, and payers have often been different entities, with a few exceptions. During the 1990s, however, health care delivery in the United States underwent a fundamental change involving a tighter integration of the basic functions through managed care.

Previously, fragmentation of the functions meant a lack of control over utilization and payments. The quantity of health care consumed refers to *utilization* of health services. Traditionally, determination of the utilization of health services and the price charged for each service has been left up to the insured individuals and the providers of health care. Due to rising health care costs, however, current delivery mechanisms have instituted some controls over both utilization and price.

Managed care is a system of health care delivery that (1) seeks to achieve efficiencies by integrating the four functions of health care delivery discussed earlier, (2) employs mechanisms to control (manage) utilization of medical services, and (3) determines the price at which the services are purchased and, consequently, how much the providers get paid. The primary financier is still the employer or the government, as the case may be. Instead of purchasing health insurance through a traditional insurance company, the employer contracts with an MCO, such as an HMO or a preferred provider organization (PPO), to offer a selected health plan to its employees. In this case, the MCO functions like an insurance company and promises to provide health care services contracted under the health plan to the enrollees of the plan. The term *enrollee* (member) refers to the individual covered under the plan. The contractual arrangement between the MCO and the enrollee—including the collective array of covered health services that the enrollee is entitled to—is referred to as the *health plan* (or "plan," for short). The health plan uses selected providers from whom the enrollees can choose to receive services.

Compared with health services delivery under fee-for-service, managed care was successful in accomplishing cost control and greater integration of health care delivery. By ensuring access to needed health services, emphasizing preventive care, and maintaining a broad provider network, effective cost-saving measures can be implemented by managed care without compromising access and quality, thus providing health care budget predictability unattainable by other kinds of health care deliveries.

Major Characteristics of the US Health Care System

In any country, certain external influences shape the basic character of the health services delivery system. These forces consist of the political climate of a nation; economic development; technological progress; social and cultural values; physical environment; population characteristics, such as

demographic and health trends; and global influences (Figure 1–2). The combined interaction of these environmental forces influences the course of health care delivery.

Ten basic characteristics differentiate the US health care delivery system from that of most other countries:

1. No central agency governs the system.
2. Access to health care services is selectively based on insurance coverage.
3. Health care is delivered under imperfect market conditions.
4. *Third-party* insurers act as intermediaries between the financing and delivery functions.
5. The existence of multiple payers makes the system cumbersome.
6. The balance of power among various players prevents any single entity from dominating the system.
7. Legal risks influence practice behavior of physicians.
8. Development of new technology creates an automatic demand for its use.
9. New service settings have evolved along a continuum.
10. Quality is no longer accepted as an unachievable goal.

No Central Agency

The US health care system is not administratively controlled by a department or an agency of the government. Most other developed nations have national health care programs in which every citizen is entitled to receive a defined set of health care services. To control costs, these systems use

Figure 1–2 External Forces Affecting Health Care Delivery.

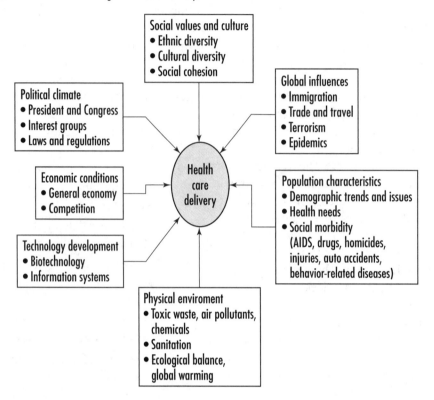

global budgets to determine total health care expenditures on a national scale and to allocate resources within budgetary limits. Availability of services, as well as payments to providers, is subject to such budgetary constraints. The governments of these nations also control the proliferation of health care services, especially costly medical technology. System-wide controls over the allocation of resources determine to what extent government-sponsored health care services are available to citizens. For instance, the availability of specialized services is restricted.

By contrast, the United States has mainly a private system of financing and delivery. Private financing, predominantly through employers, accounts for approximately 53%

of total health care expenditures; the government finances the remaining 47%. Private delivery of health care means that the majority of hospitals and physician clinics are private businesses, independent of the government. No central agency monitors total expenditures through global budgets or controls the availability and utilization of services. Nevertheless, the federal and state governments play an important role in health care delivery. They determine public-sector expenditures and reimbursement rates for services provided to Medicare, Medicaid, and CHIP beneficiaries. The government also formulates *standards of participation* through health policy and regulation, meaning providers must comply with the standards established by the government to be certified to provide services to Medicare, Medicaid, and CHIP beneficiaries. Certification standards are also regarded as minimum standards of quality in most sectors of the health care industry.

Partial Access

Access means the ability of an individual to obtain health care services when needed, which is not the same as having health insurance. Americans can access health care services if they (1) have health insurance through their employers, (2) are covered under a government health care program, (3) can afford to buy insurance with their own private funds, (4) are able to pay for services privately, or (5) can obtain charity or subsidized care. Health insurance is the primary means for ensuring access. Although the uninsured can access certain types of services, they often encounter barriers to obtaining needed health care. Federally supported health centers, for example, provide physician services to anyone regardless of ability to pay. Such centers and other types of free clinics, however, are located only in certain geographic areas and provide limited specialized services. Under US law, hospital emergency departments are required to evaluate a patient's condition and render medically needed services for which the hospital does not receive any direct payments unless the patient is able to pay. Uninsured Americans, therefore, are able to obtain medical care for acute illness. Hence, one can say that the United States does have a form of universal catastrophic health insurance even for the uninsured (Altman and Reinhardt 1996). On the other hand, the uninsured generally have to forego continual basic and routine care, commonly referred to as *primary care*.

Countries with national health care programs provide universal coverage. However, access to services when needed may be restricted because no health care system has the capacity to deliver on demand every type of service for their citizens. Hence, *universal access*—the ability of all citizens to obtain health care when needed—remains mostly a theoretical concept.

The main goal of the ACA is to increase access and make it more affordable. As just mentioned, having coverage does not necessarily equate with access. Cost of insurance, cost of care, availability of services, and a relatively large number of uninsured still cast some doubts on whether the ACA will successfully achieve access for a large segment of the US population.

Imperfect Market

In the United States, even though the delivery of services is largely in private hands, health care is only partially governed by free market forces. The delivery and consumption of health care in the United States does not quite pass the basic test of a *free market*, as subsequently described. Hence, the system is best described as a quasi-market or an imperfect market.

In a free market, multiple patients (buyers) and providers (sellers) act independently, and patients can choose to receive services from any provider. Providers neither collude to fix prices, nor are prices fixed by an external agency. Rather, prices are governed by the free and unencumbered interaction of the forces of supply and demand (Figure 1–3). *Demand*—that is, the quantity of health care purchased—in turn, is driven by the prices prevailing in the free market. Under free market conditions, the quantity demanded will increase as the

Figure 1–3 Relationship Between Price, Supply, and Demand Under Free-Market Conditions.

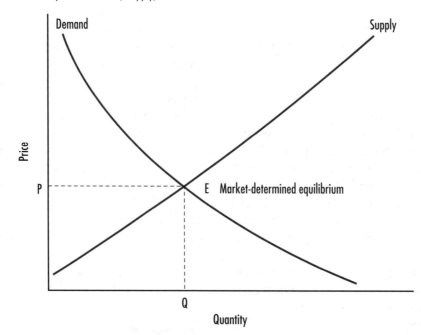

Under free-market conditions, there is an inverse relationship between the quantity of medical services demanded and the price of medical services. That is, quantity demanded goes up when the prices go down and vice versa. On the other hand, there is a direct relationship between price and the quantity supplied by the providers of care. In other words, providers are willing to supply higher quantities at higher prices and vice versa. In a free market, the quantity of medical care that patients are willing to purchase, the quantity of medical care that providers are willing to supply, and the price reach a state of equilibrium. The equilibrium is achieved without the interference of any nonmarket forces. It is important to keep in mind that these conditions exist only under free-market conditions, which are not characterisitic of the health care market.

price is lowered for a given product or service. Conversely, the quantity demanded will decrease as the price increases.

At casual observation, it may appear that multiple patients and providers do exist. Most patients, however, are now enrolled in either a private health plan or government-sponsored program(s). These plans act as intermediaries for the patients, and the consolidation of patients into health plans has the effect of shifting the power from the patients to the administrators of the plans. The result is that the health plans, not the patients, are the real buyers in the health care services market. Private health plans, in many instances, offer their enrollees a limited choice of providers rather than an open choice.

Theoretically, prices are negotiated between the payers and providers. In practice, however, prices are determined by the payers, such as MCOs, Medicare, and Medicaid. Because prices are set by agencies external to the market, they are not governed by the unencumbered forces of supply and demand.

For the health care market to be free, unrestrained competition must occur among providers based on price and quality. The consolidation of buying power in the hands of private health plans, however, has been forcing providers to form alliances and integrated delivery systems (discussed in Chapter 9) on the supply side. In certain geographic sectors of the country, a single giant medical system has taken over as the sole provider of major health care services, restricting competition. As the health care system continues to move in this direction, it appears that only in large metropolitan areas will there be more than one large integrated system competing to get the business of the health plans.

A free market requires that patients have information about the appropriateness of various services. Such information is difficult to obtain because technology-driven medical care has become highly sophisticated. New diagnostic methods, intervention techniques, and more effective drugs fall in the domain of the professional physician. Also, medical interventions are commonly required in a state of urgency. Hence, patients have neither the skills nor the time and resources to obtain accurate information when needed. Channeling all health care needs through a primary care provider can reduce this information gap when the primary care provider acts as the patient's advocate or agent. Conversely, the Internet is becoming a prominent source of medical information, and medical advertising is having an impact on consumer expectations.

In a free market, patients must directly bear the cost of services received. The purpose of insurance is to protect against the risk of unforeseen catastrophic events. Since the fundamental purpose of insurance is to meet major expenses when unlikely events occur, having insurance for basic and routine health care undermines the principle of insurance. When you buy home insurance to protect your property against the unlikely event of a fire, you do not anticipate the occurrence of a loss. The probability that you will suffer a loss by fire is very small. If a fire does occur and cause major damage, insurance will cover the loss, but insurance does not cover routine wear and tear on the house, such as chipped paint or a leaky faucet. Health insurance, however, generally covers basic and routine services that are predictable. Health insurance coverage for minor services, such as colds and coughs, earaches, and so forth, amounts to prepayment for such services. Health insurance has the effect of insulating patients from the full cost of health care. There is a *moral hazard* that, once enrollees have purchased health insurance, they will use health care services to a greater extent than if they were to pay for these services out-of-pocket.

At least two additional factors limit the ability of patients to make decisions. First, decisions about the utilization of health care are often determined by need rather than by price-based demand. *Need* has been defined as the amount of medical care that medical experts believe a person should have to remain or become healthy (Feldstein 1993). Second, the delivery of health care can result in demand creation. This follows from self-assessed need, which, coupled with moral hazard, leads to greater utilization, creating an artificial demand because prices are not taken into consideration. Practitioners who have a financial interest in additional treatments also create artificial demand (Hemenway and Fallon 1985), referred to as *provider-induced demand*, or supplier-induced demand. Functioning as patients' agents, physicians exert enormous influence on the demand for health care services (Altman and Wallack 1996). Demand creation occurs when physicians prescribe medical care beyond what is clinically necessary. This can include practices such as making more frequent follow-up appointments than necessary, prescribing excessive medical tests, or performing unnecessary surgery (Santerre and Neun 1996).

In a free market, patients have information on price and quality for each provider. The current system has other drawbacks that obstruct information-seeking efforts. Item-based pricing is one such hurdle. Surgery is a good example to illustrate item-based pricing, also referred to as fee for service. Patients can generally obtain the fees the surgeon would charge for a particular operation. But the final bill, after the surgery has been performed, is likely to include charges for supplies, use of the hospital's facilities, and services performed by providers, such as anesthesiologists, nurse anesthetists, and pathologists. These providers, sometimes referred to as *phantom providers*, who function in an adjunct capacity, bill for their services separately. Item billing for such additional services, which sometimes cannot be anticipated, makes it extremely difficult to ascertain the total price before services have actually been received. Package pricing can help overcome these drawbacks, but it has made relatively little headway for pricing medical procedures. *Package pricing* refers to a bundled fee for a package of related services. In the surgery example, this would mean one all-inclusive price for the surgeon's fees, hospital facilities, supplies, diagnostics, pathology, anesthesia, and postsurgical follow-up.

Third-Party Insurers and Payers

Insurance often functions as the intermediary among those who finance, deliver, and receive health care. The insurance intermediary does not have the incentive to be the patient's advocate on either price or quality. At best, employees can air their dissatisfactions with the plan to their employer, who has the power to discontinue the current plan and choose another company. In reality, however, employers may be reluctant to change plans if the current plan offers lower premiums compared to a different plan.

Multiple Payers

A national health care system is sometimes also referred to as a *single-payer system*, because there is one primary payer, the government. When delivering services, providers send the bill to an agency of the government that subsequently sends payment to each provider. By contrast, the United States has a multiplicity of health plans. Multiple payers often represent a billing and collection nightmare for the providers of services. Multiple payers make the system more cumbersome in several ways:

• It is extremely difficult for providers to keep tabs on the numerous health plans. For example, it is difficult to keep up with which services are covered under each plan and how much each plan will pay for those services.

• Providers must hire claims processors to bill for services and monitor receipt of payments. Billing practices are not standardized, and each payer establishes its own format.

- Payments can be denied for not precisely following the requirements set by each payer.
- Denied claims necessitate rebilling.
- When only partial payment is received, some health plans may allow the provider to *balance bill* the patient for the amount the health plan did not pay. Other plans prohibit balance billing. Even when the balance billing option is available to the provider, it triggers a new cycle of billings and collection efforts.
- Providers must sometimes engage in lengthy collection efforts, including writing collection letters, turning delinquent accounts over to collection agencies, and finally writing off as bad debt amounts that cannot be collected.
- Government programs have complex regulations for determining whether payment is made for services actually delivered. Medicare, for example, requires that each provider maintain lengthy documentation on services provided. Medicaid is known for lengthy delays in paying providers.

It is generally believed that the United States spends far more on *administrative costs*—costs associated with billing, collections, bad debts, and maintaining medical records—than the national health care systems in other countries.

Power Balancing

The US health services system involves multiple players, not just multiple payers. The key players in the system have been physicians, administrators of health service institutions, insurance companies, large employers, and the government. Big business, labor, insurance companies, physicians, and hospitals make up the powerful and politically active special interest groups represented before lawmakers by high-priced lobbyists. Each set of players has its own economic interests to protect. Physicians, for instance, want to maintain their incomes and have minimum interference with the way they practice medicine; institutional administrators seek to maximize reimbursement from private and public insurers. Insurance companies and MCOs are interested in maintaining their share of the health insurance market; large employers want to contain the costs they incur providing health insurance as a benefit to their employees. The government tries to maintain or enhance existing benefits for those covered under public insurance programs and simultaneously contain the cost of providing these benefits. The problem is that self-interests of different players are often at odds. For example, providers seek to increase government reimbursement for services delivered to Medicare, Medicaid, and CHIP beneficiaries, but the government wants to contain cost increases. Employers dislike rising health insurance premiums. Health plans, under pressure from the employers, may constrain fees for the providers who then resent these cuts.

The fragmented self-interests of the various players produce countervailing forces within the system. In an environment that is rife with motivations to protect conflicting self-interests, achieving comprehensive system-wide reforms has been next to impossible, and cost containment has remained a major challenge. Consequently, the approach to health care reform in the United States has been characterized as incremental or piecemeal, and the focus of reform initiatives has been confined to health insurance coverage and payment cuts to providers rather than how care can be better provided.

Litigation Risks

America is a litigious society. Motivated by the prospects of enormous jury awards, Americans are quick to drag an alleged offender into a courtroom at the slightest perception of incurred harm. Private health care providers have become increasingly susceptible to litigation. Hence, in the United States, the risk of malpractice lawsuits is a real consideration in the practice of medicine. To protect themselves against the possibility of litigation, it is not uncommon for practitioners to engage in what is referred to as *defensive medicine* by prescribing additional diagnostic tests, scheduling return checkup visits, and maintaining copious documentation. Many of these additional efforts may be unnecessary; hence, they are costly and inefficient.

High Technology

The United States has been the hotbed of research and innovation in new medical technology. Growth in science and technology often creates demand for new services despite shrinking resources to finance sophisticated care. People generally equate high-tech care to high-quality care. They want "the latest and the best," especially when health insurance will pay for new treatments. Physicians and technicians want to try the latest gadgets. Hospitals compete on the basis of having the most modern equipment and facilities. Once capital investments are made, costs must be recouped through utilization. Legal risks for

providers and health plans alike may also play a role in discouraging denial of new technology. Thus, several factors promote the use of costly new technology once it is developed.

Continuum of Services

Medical care services are classified into three broad categories: curative (e.g., drugs, treatments, and surgeries), restorative (e.g., physical, occupational, and speech therapies), and preventive (e.g., prenatal care, mammograms, and immunizations). Health care settings are no longer confined to the hospital and the physician's office, where many of the aforementioned services were once delivered. Additional settings, such as home health, subacute care units, and outpatient surgery centers, have emerged in response to the changing configuration of economic incentives. Table 1–2 depicts the continuum of health care services. The health care continuum in the United States remains lopsided, with a heavier emphasis on specialized services than on preventive services, primary care, and management of chronic conditions.

Quest for Quality

Even though the definition and measurement of quality in health care are not as clear-cut as they are in other industries, the delivery sector of health care has come under increased pressure to develop quality standards and demonstrate compliance with those standards. There are higher expectations for improved health outcomes at the individual and broader community levels. The concept of continual quality improvement has also received much emphasis in managing health care institutions.

Table 1–2 The Continuum of Health Care Services

Types of Health Services	Delivery Settings
Preventive care	Public health programs
	Community programs
	Personal lifestyles
	Primary care settings
Primary care	Physician's office or clinic
	Community health centers
	Self-care
	Alternative medicine
Specialized care	Specialist provider clinics
Chronic care	Primary care settings
	Specialist provider clinics
	Home health
	Long-term care facilities
	Self-care
	Alternative medicine
Long-term care	Long-term care facilities
	Home health
Subacute care	Special subacute units (hospitals, long-term care facilities)
	Home health
	Outpatient surgical centers
Acute care	Hospitals
Rehabilitative care	Rehabilitation departments (hospitals, long-term care facilities)
	Home health
	Outpatient rehabilitation centers
End-of-life care	Hospice services provided in a variety of settings

Trends and Directions

Since the final two decades of the 20th century, the US health care delivery system has continued to undergo certain fundamental shifts in emphasis, summarized in Figure 1–4. Later chapters discuss these transformations in greater detail and focus on the factors driving them.

Promotion of health while reducing costs has been the driving force behind these trends. An example of a shift in emphasis is the concept of health itself: The focus is changing from illness to wellness. Such a change requires new methods and settings for wellness promotion, although the treatment of illness continues to be the primary goal of the health services delivery system. The ACA is moving towards that direction, partly by shifting focus from disease treatment to disease prevention (see details in Chapter 2), better health outcomes for individuals and communities, and lower health care costs.

Significance for Health Care Practitioners

An understanding of the intricacies within the health services system would be beneficial to all those who come in contact

Figure 1–4 Trends and Directions in Health Care Delivery.

◊ Illness ⟶ Wellness

◊ Acute care ⟶ Primary care

◊ Inpatient ⟶ Outpatient

◊ Individual health ⟶ Community well-being

◊ Fragmented care ⟶ Managed care

◊ Independent institutions ⟶ Integrated systems

◊ Service duplication ⟶ Continuum of services

with the system. In their respective training programs, health professionals, such as physicians, nurses, technicians, therapists, dietitians, and pharmacists, as well as others, may understand their own individual roles but remain ignorant of the forces outside their profession that could significantly impact current and future practices. An understanding of the health care delivery system can attune health professionals to their relationship with the rest of the health care environment. It can help them understand changes and the impact of those changes on their own practice. Adaptation and relearning are strategies that can prepare health professionals to cope with an environment that will see ongoing change long into the future. For example, many of the ACA's requirements present both opportunities and challenges for health care practitioners. For example, besides increasing the number of the insured who will flock to providers to receive services, the ACA places additional responsibilities on providers to deliver services in a more coordinated manner while also improving the quality of care. However, health care practitioners are concerned that changes in the ACA regarding health care financing may affect the availability of adequate and sustainable funding as they make adjustments to cope with the influx of recently insured consumers who are likely to have greater health care needs than the general population.

Significance for Health Care Managers

An understanding of the health care system has specific implications for health services managers, who must understand the macro environment in which they make critical decisions in planning and strategic

management, regardless of whether they manage a private institution or a public service agency. Such decisions and actions, eventually, affect the efficiency and quality of services delivered. The interactions among the system's key components and the implications of those interactions must be well understood because the operations of health care institutions are strongly influenced, either directly or indirectly, by the financing of health services, reimbursement rates, insurance mechanisms, delivery modes, new statutes and legal opinions, and government regulations.

The environment of health care delivery will continue to remain fluid and dynamic. The viability of delivery settings, and, thus, the success of health care managers, often depends on how the managers react to the system dynamics. Timeliness of action is often a critical factor that can make the difference between failure and success. Following are some more specific reasons why understanding the health care delivery system is indispensable for health care managers.

Positioning the Organization

Managers need to understand their own organizational position within the macro environment of the health care system. Senior managers, such as chief executive officers, must constantly gauge the nature and impact of the fundamental shifts illustrated in Figure 1–4. Managers need to consider which changes in the current configuration of financing, insurance, payment, and delivery might affect their organization's long-term stability. Middle and first-line managers also need to understand their role in the current configuration and how that role might change in the future.

How should resources be realigned to effectively respond to those changes? For example, these managers need to evaluate whether certain functions in their departments will have to be eliminated, modified, or added. Would the changes involve further training? What processes are likely to change and how? What do the managers need to do to maintain the integrity of their institution's mission, the goodwill of the patients they serve, and the quality of care? Well thought-out and appropriately planned change is likely to cause less turbulence for the providers, as well as the recipients of care.

Handling Threats and Opportunities

Changes in any of the functions of financing, insurance, payment, and delivery can present new threats or opportunities in the health care market. Health care managers are more effective if they proactively deal with any threats to their institution's profitability and viability. Managers need to find ways to transform certain threats into new opportunities.

Evaluating Implications

Managers are better able to evaluate the implications of health policy and new reform proposals when they understand the relevant issues and how such issues link to the delivery of health services in the establishments they manage. The expansion of health insurance coverage under the ACA brings more individuals into the health care system, creating further demand for health services. Planning and staffing for the right mix of health care workforce to meet this anticipated surge in demand is critical.

Planning

Senior managers are often responsible for strategic planning regarding which services should be added or discontinued, which resources should be committed to facility expansion, or what should be done with excess capacity. Any long-range planning must take into consideration the current makeup of health services delivery, the evolving trends, and the potential impact of these trends.

Capturing New Markets

Health care managers are in a better position to capture new health services markets if they understand emerging trends in the financing, insurance, payment, and delivery functions. New opportunities must be explored before any newly evolving segments of the market get overcrowded. An understanding of the dynamics within the system is essential to forging new marketing strategies to stay ahead of the competition and often to finding a service niche.

Complying with Regulations

Delivery of health care services is heavily regulated. Health care managers must comply with government regulations, such as standards of participation in government programs, licensing rules, and security and privacy laws regarding patient information, and must operate within the constraints of reimbursement rates. The Medicare and Medicaid programs have, periodically, made drastic changes to their reimbursement methodologies that have triggered the need for operational changes in the way services are organized and delivered. Private agencies, such as the Joint Commission, also play an indirect regulatory role, mainly in the monitoring of quality of services. Health care managers have no choice but to play by the rules set by the various public and private agencies. Hence, it is paramount that health care managers acquaint themselves with the rules and regulations governing their areas of operation.

Following the Organizational Mission

Knowledge of the health care system and its development is essential for effective management of health care organizations. By keeping up to date on community needs, technological progress, consumer demand, and economic prospects, managers can be in a better position to fulfill their organizational missions to enhance access, improve service quality, and achieve efficiency in the delivery of services.

Health Care Systems of Other Countries

By 2012, the 25 wealthiest nations all had some form of universal coverage (Rodin and de Ferranti 2012). Canada and Western European nations have used three basic models for structuring their national health care systems:

1. In a system under *national health insurance* (NHI), such as in Canada, the government finances health care through general taxes, but the actual care is delivered by private providers. In the context of the quad-function model, NHI requires a tighter consolidation of the financing, insurance, and payment functions coordinated by the government. Delivery is characterized by detached private arrangements.

2. In a *national health system* (NHS), such as in Great Britain, in addition to financing a tax-supported NHI program, the government manages the infrastructure for the delivery of medical care. Under such a system, the government operates most of the medical institutions. Most health care providers, such as physicians, are either government employees or are tightly organized in a publicly managed infrastructure. In the context of the quad-function model, NHS requires a tighter consolidation of all four functions.

3. In a *socialized health insurance* (SHI) system, such as in Germany, government-mandated contributions by employers and employees finance health care. Private providers deliver health care services. Private not-for-profit insurance companies, called sickness funds, are responsible for collecting the contributions and paying physicians and hospitals (Santerre and Neun 1996). In a socialized health insurance system, insurance and payment functions are closely integrated, and the financing function is better coordinated with the insurance and payment functions than in the United States. Delivery is characterized by independent private arrangements. The government exercises overall control.

In the remainder of this text, the terms "national health care program" and "national health insurance" are used generically and interchangeably to refer to any type of government-supported universal health insurance program. Following is a brief discussion of health care delivery in selected countries from various parts of the world to illustrate the application of the three models discussed and to provide a sample of the variety of health care systems in the world.

Australia

In the past, Australia had switched from a universal national health care program to a privately financed system. In 1984, it returned to a national program—called Medicare—financed by income taxes and an income-based Medicare levy. The system is built on the philosophy of everyone contributing to the cost of health care according to his or her capacity to pay. In addition to Medicare, approximately 43% of Australians carry private health insurance (Australian Government 2004) to cover gaps in public coverage, such as dental services and care received in private hospitals (Willcox 2001). Although private health insurance is voluntary, it is strongly encouraged by the Australian government through tax subsidies for purchasers and tax penalties for non-purchasers (Healy 2002). Public hospital spending is funded by the government, but private hospitals offer better choices. Costs incurred by patients receiving private medical services, whether in or out of the hospital, are reimbursed in whole or in part by Medicare. Private patients are free to choose and/or change their doctors. The medical profession in Australia is composed mainly of private practitioners, who provide care predominantly on a fee-for-service basis (Hall 1999; Podger 1999).

In 2011 the Council of Australian Governments signed the National Health Reform Agreement, which sets out the architecture of national health reform. In particular, the Agreement provides for more sustainable funding arrangements for Australia's health system. At the same time, the National Health Reform Act 2011 establishes a new Independent Hospital Pricing Authority and the National Health Performance Authority. The Pricing Authority will determine and publish the national price for services provided by public hospitals. The Commonwealth Government will determine its contribution to funding public hospitals on the basis of these prices. The Performance Authority is to monitor, and report on, the performance of local hospital networks, public and private hospitals, primary health care organizations and other bodies or organizations that provide health care services. The Act provides a new statutory framework for the Australian Commission on Safety and Quality in Health Care (Australia Government 2011).

Recent health care reform undertaken by the Australian government has focused mainly on the following aspects: (1) establishing a more sustainable funding framework for public hospitals, (2) reducing emergency department and elective surgery waiting times, (3) improving primary care by establishing more primary care facilities across the country, (4) transferring full policy and funding responsibility for aged care services to the Australian Government, and (5) enhancing transparency and accountability in the health system (Australian Government 2011).

Canada

Canada implemented its national health insurance system—referred to as Medicare—under the Medical Care Act of 1966. Currently, Medicare is composed of 13 provincial and territorial health insurance plans, sharing basic standards of coverage, as defined by the Canada Health Act (Health

Canada 2013). The bulk of financing for Medicare comes from general provincial tax revenues; the federal government provides a fixed amount that is independent of actual expenditures. The health expenditure in the public sector accounts for 70% of the total health care expenditures. The private sector expenditure is composed of household out-of-pocket expenditure, commercial and not-for-profit insurance expenditure and non-consumption expenditure (Canadian Institute for Health Information 2012). Many employers offer private insurance for supplemental coverage.

Provincial and territorial departments of health have the responsibility to administer medical insurance plans, determine reimbursement for providers, and deliver certain public health services. Provinces are required by law to provide reasonable access to all medically necessary services and to provide portability of benefits from province to province. Patients are free to select their providers (Akaho et al. 1998). According to Canada's Fraser Institute, specialist physicians surveyed across 12 specialties and 10 Canadian provinces reported a total waiting time of 18.2 weeks between referral from a general practitioner and delivery of treatment in 2010, an increase from 16.1 weeks in 2009. Patients had to wait the longest to undergo orthopedic surgery (35.6 weeks) (Barua et al. 2010).

Nearly all the Canadian provinces (Ontario being one exception) have resorted to regionalization, by creating administrative districts within each province. The objective of regionalization is to decentralize authority and responsibility to more efficiently address local needs and to promote citizen participation in health care decision making (Church and Barker 1998). The majority of Canadian hospitals are operated as private nonprofit entities run by community boards of trustees, voluntary organizations, or municipalities, and most physicians are in private practice (Health Canada 2013). Most provinces use global budgets and allocate set reimbursement amounts for each hospital. Physicians are paid fee-for-service rates, negotiated between each provincial government and medical association (MacPhee 1996; Naylor 1999).

In 2004 the 10-Year Plan to Strengthen Health Care was created focusing on wait times, health human resources, pharmaceutical management, electronic health records, health innovation, accountability and reporting, public health, and Aboriginal health. Overall, progress has been made in these fields, but the goals have not been fully achieved (Health Council of Canada 2013).

Although most Canadians are quite satisfied with their health care system, how to sustain current health care delivery and financing remains a challenge. Spending on health care has increased from about 7% of program spending at the provincial level in the 1970s to almost 40% today. It is expected to surpass 50% in every province and territory within the next few years.

China

Since the economic reforms initiated in the late 1970s, health care in the People's Republic of China has undergone significant changes. In urban China, health insurance has evolved from a predominantly public insurance (either government or public enterprise) system to a multipayer system. Government employees are covered under government insurance as a part of their benefits. Employees for public enterprises are largely covered through public enterprise insurance, but the actual benefits and payments vary according to the financial well-being of the enterprises. Employees of foreign businesses or joint ventures are typically well insured through private insurance arrangements. Almost all of these plans contain costs through a variety of means, such as experience-based premiums, deductibles, copayments, and health benefit dollars (i.e., pre-allocated benefit dollars for health care that can be converted into income if not fully used). The unemployed, self-employed, and employees working for small enterprises (public or private) are largely uninsured. They can purchase individual or family plans in the private market or pay for services out of pocket. In rural China, the New Cooperative Medical Scheme (NCMS; discussed later) has become widespread, with funds pooled from national and local government, as well as private citizens. Although the insurance coverage rate is high (reaching over 90%), the actual benefits are still very limited.

Similar to the United States, China has been facing the growing problems of a large uninsured population and health care cost inflation. Although health care funding was increased by 87% in 2006 and 2007, the country has yet to reform its health care system into one that is efficient and effective. Employment-based insurance in China does not cover dependents, nor does it cover migrant workers, leading to high out-of-pocket cost sharing in total health spending. Rural areas in China are the most vulnerable because of a lack of true insurance plans and the accompanying comprehensive coverage. Health care cost inflation is also growing at a rate that is 7% faster than the gross domestic product (GDP) growth of 16% per year (Yip and Hsiao 2008).

Health care delivery has undergone significant changes. The former three-tier referral system (primary, second, tertiary) has been largely abolished. Patients can now go to any hospital of their choice as long as they are insured or can pay out of pocket. As a result, large (tertiary) hospitals are typically overutilized, whereas smaller (primary and secondary) hospitals are underutilized. Use of large hospitals contributes to medical cost escalation and medical specialization.

Major changes in health insurance and delivery have made access to medical care more difficult for the poor, uninsured, and underinsured. As a result, wide and growing disparities in access, quality, and outcomes are becoming apparent between rural and urban areas, and between the rich and the poor. Since the severe acute respiratory syndrome (SARS) epidemic in 2003, the government created an electronic disease-reporting system at the district level. In addition, each district in China now has a hospital dedicated to infectious disease. However, flaws still remain, particularly in monitoring infectious disease in the remote localities that comprise some districts (Blumenthal and Hsiao 2005).

To fix some of its problems, the Chinese government has pushed through health reform initiatives in five prominent areas: health insurance, pharmaceuticals, primary care, public health, and public/community hospitals. For example, it created the New Cooperative Medical Scheme to provide rural areas with a government-run voluntary insurance program. It prevents individuals living in these areas from becoming impoverished due to illness or catastrophic health expenses (Yip and Hsiao 2008). A similar program was established in urban areas in 2008, called the Urban Resident Basic

Medical Insurance scheme. The scheme targets the uninsured children, elderly, and other nonworking urban residents and enrolls them into the program at the household level rather than at the individual level (Wagstaff et al. 2009).

To improve access to primary care, China has reestablished community health centers (CHCs) to provide preventive and primary care services to offset the expensive outpatient services at hospitals. The goal is to reduce hospital utilization in favor of CHCs that can provide prevention, home care, and rehabilitative services (Yip and Hsiao 2008; Yip and Mahal 2008). The CHCs have not been very popular among the public because of their perceived lack of quality and reputation. It remains uncertain whether China will restore its previously integrated health care delivery system, aimed at achieving universal access, or continue its current course of medical specialization and privatization.

Another major component of the health reform is to establish an essential drug system which aims at enhancing access to and reducing out-of-pocket spending for essential medicines. The reform policies specified a comprehensive system including selection, procurement, pricing, prescription, and quality and safety standards (Barber et al. 2013). As for public hospitals reform, quality and efficiency as well as hospital governance structure have been emphasized. Several pilot reforms have been launched in various cities in China, but no national implementation plan has been formulated (Yip et al. 2012).

Germany

Health insurance has been made mandatory for all citizens and permanent residents in Germany since 2009 (Blumel 2012). As pointed out earlier, the German health care system is based on the SHI model. In addition, there is voluntary substitutive private health insurance. About 85% of the population has been enrolled in a sickness fund and 10% is covered by private insurance. There are also special programs to cover the rest of the population (Blumel 2012). Sickness funds act as purchasing entities by negotiating contracts with hospitals. However, with an aging population, fewer people in the workforce, and stagnant wage growth during recessions, paying for the increasing cost of medical care has been challenging.

During the 1990s, Germany adopted legislation to promote competition among sickness funds (Brown and Amelung 1999). To further control costs, the system employs global budgets for the hospital sector and places annual limits on spending for physician services. Inpatient care is paid per admission based on diagnosis-related groups (DRGs)—discussed in Chapter 6—which was made obligatory in 2004 (Blumel 2012).

Great Britain

Great Britain follows the national health system (NHS) model. The British health delivery system is also named NHS (National Health Service), and is now more than 65 years old. The NHS is founded on the principles of primary care and has a strong focus on community health services. The system owns its hospitals and employs its hospital-based specialists and other staff on a salaried basis. The primary care physicians, referred to as general practitioners (GPs), are mostly private practitioners. People are required to register with a local GP.

There were on average 6,651 patients per practice and 1,562 patients per GP in 2011 (Harrison 2012).

Delivery of primary care is through primary care trusts (PCTs) in England, local health groups in Wales, health boards in Scotland, and primary care partnerships in Northern Ireland. PCTs have geographically assigned responsibility for community health services, in which each person living in a given geographic area is assigned to a particular PCT. A typical PCT is responsible for approximately 50,000–250,000 patients (Dixon and Robinson 2002). PCTs function independently of the local health authorities and are governed by a consumer-dominated board. A fully developed PCT has its own budget allocations, used for both primary care and hospital-based services. In this respect, PCTs function like MCOs in the United States.

About 82% of the health expenditure in 2009 was in the public sector (Harrison 2012). Private expenditure is mainly for drugs and other medical products as well as private hospital care. Despite having a national health care system, 11.5% of the British population holds private health insurance (Dixon and Robinson 2002). Future "pro-market" reforms in the United Kingdom's NHS would likely shift decision making to general practitioners, let some hospitals become nonprofit, and give patients more control over their health care.

The Health and Social Care Act 2012 demands an extensive reorganization of the structure of the National Health Service. It proposes to abolish the PCTs and to transfer between £60 and £80 billion of health care funds to several hundred "clinical commissioning groups," partly run by the general practitioners (GPs) in England. A new executive agency of the Department of Health, Public Health England, was established in 2013.

Israel

Until 1995, Israel had a system of universal coverage based on the German SHI model, financed through an employer tax and income-based contributions from individuals. When the National Health Insurance (NHI) Law went into effect in 1995, it made insurance coverage mandatory for all Israeli citizens. Adults are required to pay a health tax. General tax revenue supplements the health tax revenue, which the government distributes to the various health plans based on a capitation formula. Each year the government determines how much from the general tax revenue should be contributed toward the NHI. In 2009, public funds accounted for 77% of NHI revenues. The remaining was from individuals' copayments, supplemental health insurance and sale of health products (Zwanziger and Brammli-Greenberg 2011).

Health plans (or sickness funds) offer a predefined basic package of health care services and are prohibited from discriminating against those who have preexisting medical conditions. The capitation formula has built-in incentives for the funds to accept a larger number of elderly and chronically ill members. Rather than relying on a single-payer system, the reform allowed the existence of multiple health plans (today there are four competing, nonprofit sickness funds) to foster competition among funds with the assumption that competition would lead to better quality of care and an increased responsiveness to patient needs. The plans also sell private health insurance to supplement the basic package. The system is believed to provide a high standard of care (Gross et al. 1998; Rosen and Merkur 2009).

Japan

Since 1961, Japan has been providing universal coverage to its citizens through two main health insurance schemes. The first one is an employer-based system, modeled after Germany's SHI program. The second is a national health insurance program. Generally, large employers (with more than 300 employees) have their own health programs. Nearly 2,000 private, nonprofit health insurance societies manage insurance for large firms. Smaller companies either band together to provide private health insurance or belong to a government-run plan. Day laborers, seamen, agricultural workers, the self-employed, and retirees are all covered under the national health care program. Individual employees pay roughly 8% of their salaries as premiums and receive coverage for about 90% of the cost of medical services, with some limitations. Dependents receive slightly less than 90% coverage. Employers and the national government subsidize the cost of private premiums. Coverage is comprehensive, including dental care and prescription drugs, and patients are free to select their providers (Akaho et al. 1998; Babazono et al. 1998). Providers are paid on a fee-for-service basis with little control over reimbursement (McClellan and Kessler 1999).

Several health policy issues have emerged in Japan in the past few years. First, since 2002, some business leaders and economists urged the Japanese government to lift its ban on mixed public/private payments for medical services, arguing that private payments should be allowed for services not covered by medical insurance (i.e., services involving new technologies or drugs). The Japan Medical Association and Ministry of Health, Labor, and Welfare have argued against these recommendations, stating such a policy would favor the wealthy and create disparities in access to care. Although the ban on mixed payments has not been lifted, Prime Minister Koizumi expanded the existing "exceptional approvals system" for new medical technologies in 2004 to allow private payments for selected technologies not covered by medical insurance (Nomura and Nakayama 2005).

Another recent policy development in Japan is the hospitals' increased use of a new system of reimbursement for inpatient care services, called diagnosis-procedure combinations (DPCs). Using DPCs, hospitals receive daily fees for each condition and treatment, regardless of actual provision of tests and interventions, proportionate to patients' length of stay. It is theorized that the DPC system will incentivize hospitals to become more efficient (Nomura and Nakayama 2005).

Japan's economic stagnation in the last several years has led to an increased pressure to contain costs (Ikegami and Campbell 2004). In 2005, Japan implemented reform initiatives in long-term care (LTC) delivery to contain costs in a growing sector of health care with rapidly rising costs. The policy required residents in LTC facilities to pay for room and board. It also established new preventive benefits for seniors with low needs, who are at risk of requiring care in the future. Charging nursing home residents a fee for room and board was a departure from past policies which had promoted institutionalization (Tsutsui and Muramatsu 2007).

Despite its success, Japan's health and long-term care systems face similar sustainability issues to those in the United States, including rising costs and increasing demand. The Japanese government is considering and pursuing several options: preventive services, promotion of community-based services, and increases in taxes, premiums, and fees. In 2011, reform centered on the comprehensive community care model was implemented. This model would ensure access to long-term care, medical or hospital care, preventive services, residential care facilities and "life support" (or legal services) within a community where an elder lives. The focus on prevention and service consolidation is expected to result in decreased use of more expensive services because the population would remain healthier.

Singapore

Prior to 1984, Singapore had a British-style NHS program, in which medical services were provided mainly by the public sector and financed through general taxes. Since then, the nation has designed a system based on market competition and self-reliance. Singapore has achieved universal coverage through a policy that requires mandatory private contributions but little government financing. The program, known as Medisave, mandates every working person, including the self-employed, to deposit a portion of earnings into an individual Medisave account. Employers are required to match employee contributions. These savings can only be withdrawn (1) to pay for hospital services and some selected, expensive physician services or (2) to purchase a government-sponsored insurance plan, called MediShield, for catastrophic (expensive and major) illness. For basic and routine services, people are expected to pay out of pocket. Those who cannot afford to

pay receive government assistance (Hsiao 1995). In 2002, the government introduced ElderShield, which defrays out-of-pocket medical expenses for the elderly and severely disabled requiring long-term care (Singapore Ministry of Health 2004). The fee-for-service system of payment is prevalent throughout Singapore (McClellan and Kessler 1999).

In 2006 the Ministry of Health launched the Chronic Disease Management Program. By November 2011, the program covered 10 chronic diseases, including mental health illnesses. More than 700 GP clinics and GP groups are supported by the Ministry to provide comprehensive chronic disease management to patients. The patients can use their own or their family members' Medisave to pay for outpatient services under the program (Singapore Ministry of Health 2012).

Developing Countries

Developing countries, containing almost 85% of the world's population, claim only 11% of the world's health spending. Yet, these countries account for 93% of the worldwide burden of disease. The six developing regions of the world are East Asia and the Pacific, Europe (mainly Eastern Europe) and Central Asia, Latin America and the Caribbean, the Middle East and North Africa, South Asia, and Sub-Saharan Africa. Of these, the latter two have the least resources and the greatest health burden. On a per capita basis, industrialized countries have six times as many hospital beds and three times as many physicians as developing countries. People with private financial means can find reasonably good health care in many parts of the developing world. However, the majority of the populations have to depend on limited government services that are often of questionable quality, as evaluated by Western standards. As a general observation, government financing for health services increases in countries with higher per capita incomes (Schieber and Maeda 1999).

Global Health Challenges and Reform

There is a huge gap in health care and health status between developing and developed countries. For example, in 2009, the global life expectancy at birth was 68 years of age, while life expectancy in the African region was only 54. Infant mortality rates varied between 2 per 1,000 live births and 114 per 1,000 live births. There were also wide variations in health care for pregnant women, availability of skilled health personnel for childbirth, and access to medicine (World Health Organization 2012).

The poor quality and low efficiency of health care services in many countries, especially services provided by the public sector which is often the main source of care for poor people, have become a serious issue for decision makers in these countries (Sachs 2012). This combined with the rising out-of-pocket costs and high numbers of uninsured forced many governments to launch health care reform efforts. Many low- and middle-income countries are moving toward universal health coverage (Lagomarsino et al. 2012). On the other hand, international health assistance plays a significant role in health care in many developing countries. Global aid increased from $10 billion in 2000 to $27 billion in 2010 (Sachs 2012). However, the total international aid started to fall in 2011 because of a global recession (Organization for Economic Co-operation and Development 2012).

The Systems Framework

A *system* consists of a set of interrelated and interdependent, logically coordinated components designed to achieve common goals. Even though the various functional components of the health services delivery structure in the United States are, at best, only loosely coordinated, the main components can be identified using a systems model. The systems framework used here helps one understand that the structure of health care services in the United States is based on some foundations, provides a logical arrangement of the various components, and demonstrates a progression from inputs to outputs. The main elements of this arrangement are system inputs (resources), system structure, system processes, and system outputs (outcomes). In addition, system outlook (future directions) is a necessary feature of a dynamic system. This systems framework is used as the conceptual base for organizing later chapters in this text (see Figure 1–5).

System Foundations

The current health care system is not an accident. Historical, cultural, social, and economic factors explain its current structure. These factors also affect forces that shape new trends and developments, as well as those that impede change. Chapters 2 and 3 provide a discussion of the system foundations.

System Resources

No mechanism for health services delivery can fulfill its primary objective without deploying the necessary human and nonhuman resources. Human resources consist of the various types and categories of workers directly

Figure 1–5 The Systems Model and Related Chapters.

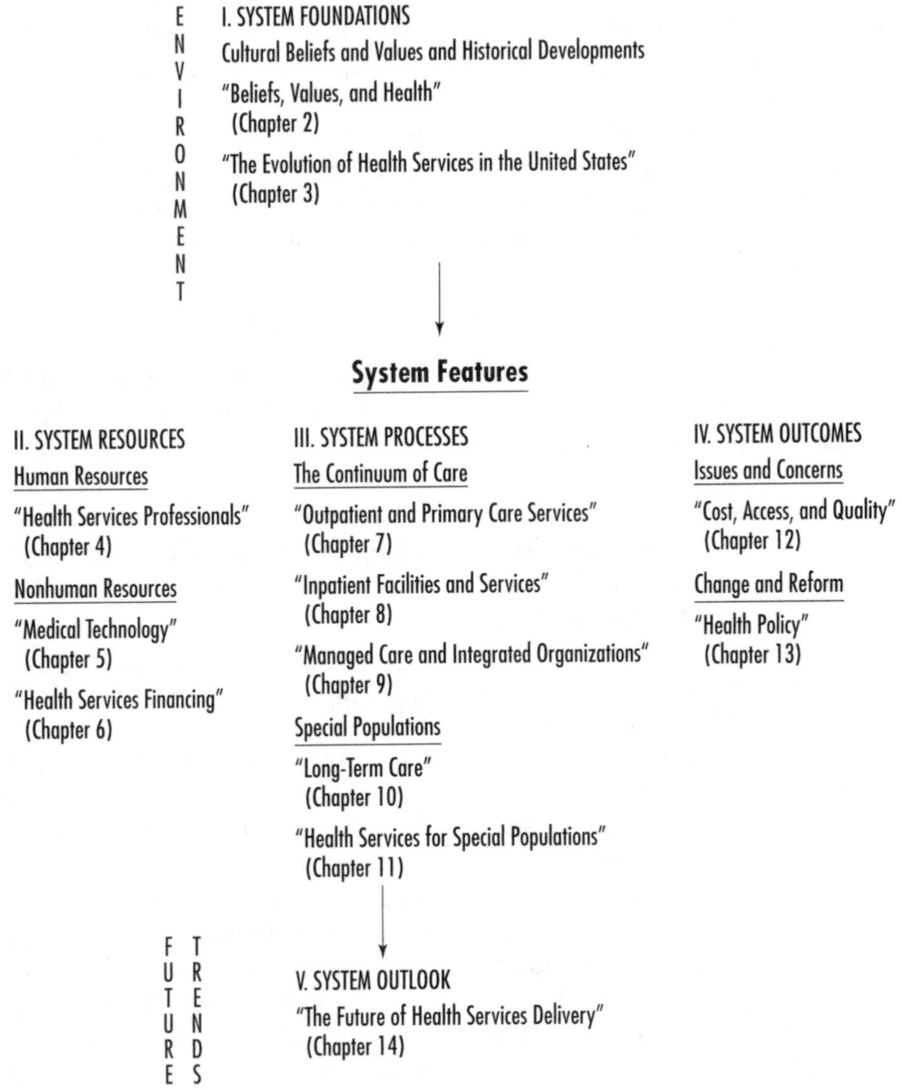

```
E     I. SYSTEM FOUNDATIONS
N     Cultural Beliefs and Values and Historical Developments
V
I     "Beliefs, Values, and Health"
R        (Chapter 2)
O
N     "The Evolution of Health Services in the United States"
M        (Chapter 3)
E
N
T
```

System Features

II. SYSTEM RESOURCES	III. SYSTEM PROCESSES	IV. SYSTEM OUTCOMES
Human Resources	The Continuum of Care	Issues and Concerns
"Health Services Professionals" (Chapter 4)	"Outpatient and Primary Care Services" (Chapter 7)	"Cost, Access, and Quality" (Chapter 12)
Nonhuman Resources	"Inpatient Facilities and Services" (Chapter 8)	Change and Reform
"Medical Technology" (Chapter 5)	"Managed Care and Integrated Organizations" (Chapter 9)	"Health Policy" (Chapter 13)
"Health Services Financing" (Chapter 6)	Special Populations	
	"Long-Term Care" (Chapter 10)	
	"Health Services for Special Populations" (Chapter 11)	

```
F  T
U  R   V. SYSTEM OUTLOOK
T  E
U  N   "The Future of Health Services Delivery"
R  D      (Chapter 14)
E  S
```

engaged in the delivery of health services to patients. Such personnel—physicians, nurses, dentists, pharmacists, other doctoral trained professionals, and numerous categories of allied health professionals—usually have direct contact with patients. Numerous ancillary workers—billing and collection agents, marketing and public relations personnel, and building maintenance employees—often play an important, but indirect, supportive role in the delivery of health care. Health care managers are needed to manage various types of health care services. This text primarily discusses the personnel engaged in the direct delivery of health care services (Chapter 4). The nonhuman resources include medical technology (Chapter 5) and health services financing (Chapter 6).

Resources are closely intertwined with access to health care. For instance, in certain rural areas of the United States, access is restricted due to a shortage of health professionals within certain categories. Development and diffusion of technology also determine the caliber of health care to which people may have access. Financing for health insurance and reimbursement to providers affect access indirectly.

System Processes

System resources influence the development and change in the physical infrastructure—such as hospitals, clinics, and nursing homes—essential for the different processes of health care delivery. Most health care services are delivered in noninstitutional settings, mainly associated with processes referred to as outpatient care (Chapter 7). Institutional health services provided in hospitals, nursing homes, and rehabilitation institutions, for example, are predominantly inpatient services (Chapter 8). Managed care and integrated systems (Chapter 9) represent a fundamental change in the financing (including payment and insurance) and delivery of health care. Special institutional and community-based settings have been developed for long-term care (Chapter 10). Delivery of services should be tailored to meet the special needs of certain vulnerable population groups (Chapter 11).

System Outcomes

System outcomes refer to the critical issues and concerns surrounding what the health services system has been able to accomplish, or not accomplish, in relation to its primary objective, to provide, to an entire nation, cost-effective health services that meet certain established standards of quality. The previous three elements of the systems model play a critical role in fulfilling this objective. Access, cost, and quality are the main outcome criteria to evaluate the success of a health care delivery system (Chapter 12). Issues and concerns regarding these criteria trigger broad initiatives for reforming the system through health policy (Chapter 13).

System Outlook

A dynamic health care system must be forward looking. In essence, it must project into the future the accomplishment of desired system outcomes in view of anticipated social, economic, political, technological, informational, ecological, anthro-cultural, and global forces of change (Chapter 14).

Summary

The United States has a unique system of health care delivery. Its basic features characterize it as a patchwork of subsystems. Health care is delivered through an amalgam of private and public financing, through private health insurance and public insurance programs; the latter programs are for special groups. Contrary to popular opinion, health care delivery in the United States is not governed by free-market principles; at best it is an imperfect market. Yet, the system is not dominated or controlled by a single entity as would be the case in national health care systems.

No country in the world has a perfect system, and most nations with a national health care program also have a private sector that varies in size. Because of resource limitations, universal access remains a theoretical concept even in countries that offer universal health insurance coverage. The developing countries of the world also face serious challenges due to scarce resources and strong underlying needs for services.

Health care managers must understand how the health care delivery system works and evolves. Such an understanding can help them maintain a strategic position within the macro environment of the health care system. The systems framework provides an organized approach to an understanding of the various components of the US health care delivery system.

ACA Takeaway

- The main goal of the ACA is to increase access to health care and make it more affordable, mainly for those who were previously uninsured.
- All US citizens and legal residents are required to have health insurance or pay a fine.
- Two main avenues for covering the uninsured are expansion of Medicaid and purchase of subsidized private health insurance through government-run exchanges.
- Insurance companies are required to include coverage for a variety of health care services.
- The ACA fails to achieve universal coverage; it may also not successfully achieve access for a large segment of the US population.
- The ACA promises to shift focus from disease treatment to disease prevention and improved health outcomes.
- Additional responsibilities are placed on providers to deliver services in a more coordinated manner while also improving the quality of care.

Test Your Understanding

Terminology

access	*Medicare*	*reimbursement*
administrative costs	*moral hazard*	*single-payer system*
balance bill	*national health insurance*	*socialized health insurance*
defensive medicine	*national health system*	*standards of participation*
demand	*need*	*system*
enrollee	*package pricing*	*third party*
free market	*phantom providers*	*uninsured*
global budget	*premium cost sharing*	*universal access*
health care reform	*primary care*	*universal coverage*
health plan	*provider*	*utilization*
managed care	*provider-induced demand*	
Medicaid	*quad-function model*	

Review Questions

1. Why does cost containment remain an elusive goal in US health services delivery?

2. What are the two main objectives of a health care delivery system?

3. Name the four basic functional components of the US health care delivery system. What role does each play in the delivery of health care?

4. What is the primary reason for employers to purchase insurance plans to provide health benefits to their employees?

5. Why is it that, despite public and private health insurance programs, some US citizens are without health care coverage? How will the ACA change this?

6. What is managed care?

7. Why is the US health care market referred to as "imperfect"?

8. Discuss the intermediary role of insurance in the delivery of health care.

9. Who are the major players in the US health services system? What are the positive and negative effects of the often conflicting self-interests of these players?

10. What main roles does the government play in the US health services system?

11. Why is it important for health care managers and policy makers to understand the intricacies of the health care delivery system?

12. What is the difference between national health insurance (NHI) and a national health system (NHS)?

13. What is socialized health insurance (SHI)?

14. Provide a general overview of the Affordable Care Act. What is its main goal?

REFERENCES

Akaho, E., et al. 1998. A proposed optimal health care system based on a comparative study conducted between Canada and Japan. *Canadian Journal of Public Health* 89, no. 5: 301–307.

Altman, S.H., and U.E. Reinhardt. 1996. Introduction: Where does health care reform go from here? An uncharted odyssey. In: *Strategic choices for a changing health care system*. S.H. Altman and U.E. Reinhardt, eds. Chicago: Health Administration Press. p. xxi–xxxii.

Altman, S.H., and S.S. Wallack. 1996. Health care spending: Can the United States control it? In: *Strategic choices for a changing health care system*. S.H. Altman and U.E. Reinhardt, eds. Chicago: Health Administration Press. p. 1–32.

Australian Government, Department of Health and Ageing. May 2004. *Australia: Selected health care delivery and financing statistics*. Available at: http://www.health.gov/au. Accessed December 15, 2010.

Australian Government, Department of Health and Aging. 2011. *Improving Primary Health Care for All Australians*. Available at: http://www.yourhealth.gov.au/internet/yourHealth/publishing

.nsf/Content/improving-primary-health-care-for-all-australians-toc/$FILE/Improving%20Primary%20Health%20Care%20for%20all%20Australians.pdf. Accessed December 16, 2013.

Babazono, A., et al. 1998. The effect of a redistribution system for health care for the elderly on the financial performance of health insurance societies in Japan. *International Journal of Technology Assessment in Health* Care 14, no. 3: 458–466.

Barber, S.L., B. Huang, et al. 2013. The reform of the essential medicines system in China: a comprehensive approach to universal coverage. *Journal of global health* 3, no. 1: 10303.

Barua, B., et al. 2010. *Waiting your turn: Wait times for health care in Canada 2010 report.* Vancouver, Canada: The Fraser Institute.

Blumel, M. 2012. *The German Health Care System, 2012.* Available at: http://www.commonwealthfund .org/~/media/Files/Publications/Fund%20Report/2012/Nov/1645_Squires_intl_profiles_hlt_care_ systems_2012.pdf. Accessed December 16, 2013.

Blumenthal, D., and W. Hsiao. 2005. Privatization and its discontents—The evolving Chinese health care system. *New England Journal of Medicine* 353, no. 11: 1165–1170.

Brown, L.D., and V.E. Amelung. 1999. "Manacled competition": Market reforms in German health care. *Health Affairs* 18, no. 3: 76–91.

Canadian Institute for Health Information. 2012. *National health expenditure trends, 1975 to 2012.* Ottawa, ON: The Institute. Available at: https://secure.cihi.ca/free_products/ NHEXTrendsReport2012EN.pdf. Accessed December 16, 2013.

Church, J., and P. Barker. 1998. Regionalization of health services in Canada: A critical perspective. *International Journal of Health Services* 28, no. 3: 467–486.

Dixon, A., and R. Robinson. 2002. The United Kingdom. In: *Health care systems in eight countries: Trends and challenges.* A. Dixon and E. Mossialos, eds. London: The European Observatory on Health Care Systems, London School of Economics & Political Science. p. 103–114.

Feldstein, P.J. 1993. *Health care economics.* 4th ed. New York: Delmar Publishing.

Gross, R., et al. 1998. Evaluating the Israeli health care reform: Strategy, challenges, and lessons. *Health Policy* 45: 99–117.

Hall, J. 1999. Incremental change in the Australian health care system. *Health Affairs* 18, no. 3: 95–110.

Harrison, A. 2012. *The English Health Care System, 2012.* Available at: http://www.commonwealthfund .org/~/media/Files/Publications/Fund%20Report/2012/Nov/1645_Squires_intl_profiles_hlt_care_ systems_2012.pdf. Accessed December 16, 2013. p. 32–38.

Health Canada. 2013. Available at: http://laws-lois.justice.gc.ca/eng/acts/C-6/index.html. Accessed July 2013.

Health Council of Canada. 2005. *Annual report 2005.* Available at: http://www.healthcouncilcanada. ca/en/index.php?option=com_content&task =view&id=51&Itemid=50. Accessed September 2006.

Health Council of Canada. 2013. Progress report 2013. Available at: http://www.healthcouncilcanada .ca/rpt_det.php?id=481. Accessed July 2013.

Health Resources and Services Administration (HRSA). 2013. Health center snapshot 2011. Available at: http://www.hrsa.gov/data-statistics/health-center-data/index.html. Accessed June 2013.

Healy, J. 2002. Australia. In: *Health care systems in eight countries: Trends and challenges*. A. Dixon and E. Mossialos, eds. London: The European Observatory on Health Care Systems, London School of Economics & Political Science. p. 3–16.

Hemenway, D., and D. Fallon. 1985. Testing for physician-induced demand with hypothetical cases. *Medical Care* 23, no. 4: 344–349.

Hsiao, W.C. 1995. Medical savings accounts: Lessons from Singapore. *Health Affairs* 14, no. 2: 260–266.

Ikegami, N., and J.C. Campbell. 2004. Japan's health care system: Containing costs and attempting reform. *Health Affair* 23: 26–36.

Lagomarsino, G., A. Garabrant, et al. 2012. Moving towards universal health coverage: Health insurance reforms in nine developing countries in Africa and Asia. *Lancet* 380, no. 9845, 933–943.

MacPhee, S. 1996. Reform the watchword as OECD countries struggle to contain health care costs. *Canadian Medical Association Journal* 154, no. 5: 699–701.

McClellan, M., and D. Kessler. 1999. A global analysis of technological change in health care: The case of heart attacks. *Health Affairs* 18, no. 3: 250–257.

Naylor, C.D. 1999. Health care in Canada: Incrementalism under fiscal duress. *Health Affairs* 18, no. 3: 9–26.

Nomura, H., and T. Nakayama. 2005. The Japanese healthcare system. *BMJ* 331: 648–649.

Organization for Economic Co-operation and Development. 2012. *Development: Aid to developing countries falls because of global recession*. Available at: http://www.oecd.org/ development/ developmentaidtodevelopingcountriesfallsbecauseofglobalrecession.htm. Accessed July, 2013.

Parente, S.T., and R. Feldman. 2013. Microsimulation of private health insurance and Medicaid take-up following the U.S. Supreme Court decision upholding the Affordable Care Act. *Health Services Research* 48, no. 2 Pt 2: 826–849.

Podger, A. 1999. Reforming the Australian health care system: A government perspective. *Health Affairs* 18, no. 3: 111–113.

Rodin, J., and D. de Ferranti. 2012. Universal health coverage: The third global health transition? *The Lancet* 380, no. 9845: 861–862.

Rosen, B., and S. Merkur. 2009. Israel: Health system review. *Health Systems in Transition* 11: 1–226.

Sachs, J.D. 2012. Achieving universal health coverage in low-income settings. *The Lancet* 380, no. 9845: 944–947.

Santerre, R.E., and S.P. Neun. 1996. *Health economics: Theories, insights, and industry studies*. Chicago: Irwin.

Schieber, G., and A. Maeda. 1999. Health care financing and delivery in developing countries. *Health Affairs* 18, no. 3: 193–205.

Singapore Ministry of Health. 2004. *Medisave, Medishield and other subsidy schemes: Overview*. Available at: www.moh.gov.sg/corp/financing/overview.do. Accessed September 2006.

Singapore Ministry of Health. 2012. *Medisave for Chronic Disease Management Programme (CDMP) and vaccinations*. Available at: http://www.moh.gov.sg/content/moh_web/home/ policies-and-issues/elderly_healthcare.html. Accessed December 16, 2013.

Tsutsui T., and N. Muramatsu. 2007. Japan's universal long-term care system reform of 2005: Containing costs and realizing a vision. *Journal of the American Geriatrics Society* 55: 1458–1463.

US Bureau of Labor Statistics. 2011. *Occupational outlook handbook, 2010–2011.* Available at: http://www.bls.gov/oco/home.htm. Accessed January 2011.

US Census Bureau. 2012. The 2012 Statistical Abstract. Available at: http://www.census.gov/compendia/statab/cats/health_nutrition/health_care_resources.html. Accessed July 2013.

US Department of Health and Human Services. 2013. About the Law. Retrieved August 1, 2013 from http://www.hhs.gov/healthcare/rights/index.html.

Wagstaff, A., et al. (2009). China's health system and its reform: A review of recent studies. *Health Economics* 18: S7–S23.

Willcox, S. 2001. Promoting private health insurance in Australia. *Health Affairs* 20, no. 3: 152–161.

Wolinsky, F.D. 1988. *The sociology of health: Principles, practitioners, and issues.* 2nd ed. Belmont, CA: Wadsworth Publishing Company.

World Health Organization. 2012. *World Health Statistics 2012.* http://www.who.int/gho/publications/world_health_statistics/2012/en/. Accessed July 2013.

Yip, W., and W.C. Hsiao. (2008). The Chinese health system at a crossroads. *Health Affairs* 27: 460–468.

Yip, W., and A. Mahal. (2008). The health care systems of China and India: Performance and future challenges. *Health Affairs* 27: 921–932.

Yip, W.C., W.C. Hsiao, et al. 2012. Early appraisal of China's huge and complex health-care reforms. *Lancet* 379, no. 9818: 833–842.

Zwanziger, J., and S. Brammli-Greenberg. 2011. Strong government influence over the Israeli health care system has led to low rates of spending growth. *Health affairs (Project Hope)* 30, no. 9: 1779–1785.

PART I

Systems Foundations

Chapter 2

Beliefs, Values, and Health

Learning Objectives

- To study the concepts of health and disease, risk factors, and the role of health promotion and disease prevention
- To summarize the disease prevention requisites under the Affordable Care Act
- To get an overview of public health and appreciate its expanding role in health protection both in the United States and globally
- To explore the determinants of health, and measures related to health
- To understand the American anthro-cultural values and their implications for health care delivery
- To evaluate justice and equity in health care according to contrasting theories
- To explore the integration of individual and population health

"This is the market justice system. Social justice is over there."

Introduction

From an economic perspective, curative medicine appears to produce decreasing returns in health improvement while increasing health care expenditures (Saward and Sorensen 1980). There has also been a growing recognition of the benefits to society from the promotion of health and prevention of disease, disability, and premature death. However, progress in this direction has been slow because of the prevailing social values and beliefs that still focus on curing diseases rather than promoting health. The common definitions of health, as well as measures for evaluating health status, reflect similar inclinations. This chapter proposes a balanced approach to health, although fully achieving such an ideal is not without difficult challenges. The 10-year *Healthy People* initiatives, undertaken by the US Department of Health and Human Services (DHHS) since 1980, illustrate steps taken in this direction, even though these initiatives have been typically strong in rhetoric but weak in actionable strategies and sustainable funding.

Anthro-cultural factors reflected in the beliefs and values ingrained in the American culture have been influential in laying the foundations of a system that has remained predominantly private, as opposed to a tax-financed national health care program. Discussion on this theme begins in this chapter and continues in Chapter 3, where failures of past proposals to create a nationalized health care system are discussed in the context of cultural beliefs and values.

This chapter further explores the issue of equity in the distribution of health services, using the contrasting theories of market justice and social justice. US health care delivery incorporates both principles, which are complementary in some ways and create conflicts in other areas. The Affordable Care Act (ACA) tilts the system more toward a social justice orientation, places a greater emphasis on preventive services, but does not quite promise to achieve equitable access to health care for all Americans.

Significance for Managers and Policymakers

Materials covered in this chapter have several implications for health services managers and policymakers: (1) The health status of a population has tremendous bearing on the utilization of health services, assuming the services are readily available. Planning of health services must be governed by demographic and health trends and initiatives toward reducing disease and disability. (2) The basic meanings of health, determinants of health, and health risk appraisal should be used to design appropriate educational, preventive, and therapeutic initiatives. (3) There is a growing emphasis on evaluating the effectiveness of health care organizations based on the contributions they make to community and population health. The concepts discussed in this chapter can guide administrators in implementing programs of most value to their communities. (4) Quantified measures of health status and utilization can be used by managers and policymakers to evaluate the adequacy and effectiveness of existing programs, plan new strategies, measure progress, and discontinue ineffective services.

Basic Concepts of Health

Health

In the United States, the concepts of health and health care have largely been governed by the medical model, more specifically referred to as the biomedical model. The *medical model* defines health as the absence of illness or disease. This definition implies that optimum health exists when a person is free of symptoms and does not require medical treatment. However, it is not a definition of health in the true sense. This prevailing view of health emphasizes clinical diagnosis and medical interventions to treat disease or symptoms of disease, while prevention of disease and health promotion are not included. Therefore, when the term "health care delivery" is used, in reality it refers to medical care delivery.

Medical sociologists have gone a step further in defining health as the state of optimum capacity of an individual to perform his or her expected social roles and tasks, such as work, school, and doing household chores (Parsons 1972). A person who is unable (as opposed to unwilling) to perform his or her social roles in society is considered sick. However, this concept also seems inadequate because many people continue to engage in their social obligations despite suffering from pain, cough, colds, and other types of temporary disabilities, including mental distress. Then, there are those who shirk from their social responsibilities even when they may be in good health. In other words, optimal health is not necessarily reflected in a person's engagement in social roles and responsibilities.

An emphasis on both physical and mental dimensions of health is found in the definition of health proposed by the Society for Academic Emergency Medicine, according to which health is "a state of physical and mental well-being that facilitates the achievement of individual and societal goals" (Ethics Committee, Society for Academic Emergency Medicine 1992). This view of health recognizes the importance of achieving harmony between the physiological and emotional dimensions.

The World Health Organization's (WHO) definition of health is most often cited as the ideal for health care delivery systems; it recognizes that optimal health is more than a mere absence of disease or infirmity. WHO defines health as "a state of complete physical, mental and social well-being and not merely the absence of disease or infirmity" (WHO 1948). As a biopsychosocial model, WHO's definition specifically identifies social well-being as a third dimension of health. For example, having a social support network is positively associated with life stresses, self-esteem, and social relations. Conversely, many studies show that social isolation is associated with a higher risk for poor health and mortality (Pantell et al. 2013).

WHO has also defined a health care system as all the activities whose primary purpose is to promote, restore, or maintain health (McKee 2001). As this chapter points out, health care should include much more than medical care. Thus, *health care* can be defined as a variety of services believed to improve a person's health and well-being.

There has been a growing interest in *holistic health*, which emphasizes the well-being of every aspect of what makes a person whole and complete. Thus, *holistic medicine* seeks to treat the individual as a whole person (Ward 1995). For example, diagnosis and treatment should take into account the mental, emotional, spiritual, nutritional, environmental, and other factors surrounding the origin of disease (Cohen 2003).

Holistic health incorporates the spiritual dimension as a fourth element—in addition to the physical, mental, and social aspects—necessary for optimal health (Figure 2–1). A growing volume of medical literature, both in the United States and abroad, points to the healing effects of a person's religion and spirituality on morbidity and mortality. The importance of spirituality as an aspect of health care is also reflected in a number of policy documents produced by the WHO (2003) and other bodies.

From an extensive review of literature, Chida et al. (2009) concluded that religious practice/spirituality was associated with reductions in death from all causes and death from cardiovascular diseases. Heart patients who attended regular religious services were found to have a significant survival advantage (Oman et al. 2002). Religious and spiritual beliefs and practices have shown a positive impact on a person's physical, mental, and social well-being. Many studies have shown positive relations between religious practice and protective health behaviors (Chida et al. 2009). Several religious communities promote healthy lifestyles associated with tobacco use, alcohol consumption, and diet. An examination of literature found a reduced risk for cancer in these communities (Hoff et al. 2008). Spiritual well-being has also been recognized as an important internal resource for helping people cope with illness. For instance, a study conducted at the University of Michigan found that 93% of the women undergoing cancer treatment indicated that their religious lives helped them sustain their hope (Roberts et al. 1997). Studies have found that a large percentage of patients want their physicians to consider their spiritual needs, and almost half expressed a desire for the physicians to pray with them if they could (see Post et al. 2000).

The spiritual dimension is frequently tied to one's religious beliefs, values, morals, and practices. Broadly, it is described as meaning, purpose, and fulfillment in life; hope and will to live; faith; and a person's relationship with God (Marwick 1995; Ross 1995; Swanson 1995). A clinically tested scale to measure spiritual well-being included categories such as belief in a power greater than oneself, purpose in life, faith, trust in providence, prayer, meditation, group worship, ability to forgive, and gratitude for life (Hatch et al. 1998).

The Committee on Religion and Psychiatry of the American Psychiatric Association has issued a position statement to emphasize the importance of maintaining respect for a patient's religious/spiritual beliefs. For the first time, "religious or spiritual problem" was included as a

Figure 2–1 The Four Dimensions of Holistic Health.

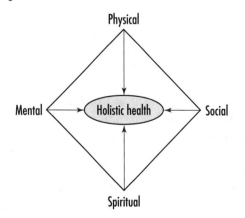

diagnostic category in DSM-5.[1] The holistic approach to health also alludes to the need for incorporating alternative therapies (discussed in Chapter 7) into the predominant medical model.

Quality of Life

The term *quality of life* is used to capture the essence of overall satisfaction with life during and following a person's encounter with the health care delivery system. Thus, the term is employed in two ways. First, it is an indicator of how satisfied a person is with the experiences while receiving health care. Specific life domains, such as comfort factors, respect, privacy, security, degree of independence, decision-making autonomy, and attention to personal preferences are significant to most people. These factors are now regarded as rights that patients can demand during any type of health care encounter. Second, quality of life can refer to a person's overall satisfaction with life and with self-perceptions of health, particularly after some medical intervention. The implication is that desirable processes during medical treatment and successful outcomes would, subsequently, have a positive effect on an individual's ability to function, carry out social roles and obligations, and have a sense of fulfillment and self-worth.

Risk Factors and Disease

The occurrence of disease involves more than just a single factor. For example, the

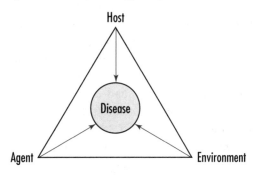

Figure 2–2 The Epidemiology Triangle.

mere presence of tubercle bacillus does not mean the infected person will develop tuberculosis. Other factors, such as poverty, overcrowding, and malnutrition, may be essential for development of the disease (Friedman 1980). Hence, tracing *risk factors*—attributes that increase the likelihood of developing a particular disease or negative health condition in the future—requires a broad approach. One useful explanation of disease occurrence (for communicable diseases, in particular) is provided by the tripartite model, sometimes referred to as the Epidemiology[2] Triangle (Figure 2–2). Of the three entities in this model, the *host* is the organism—generally, a human—that becomes sick. Factors associated with the host include genetic makeup, level of immunity, fitness, and personal habits and behaviors. However, for the host to become sick, an *agent* must be present, although presence of an agent does not ensure that disease will occur. In the previous example, tubercle bacillus is the agent for tuberculosis. Other examples are chemical agents, radiation, tobacco smoke, dietary

---

[1]*Diagnostic and Statistical Manual of Mental Disorders* is the most widely recognized system of classifying mental disorders.

[2]Epidemiology is the study of the nature, cause, control, and determinants of the frequency and distribution of disease, disability, and death in human populations (Timmreck 1994, 2).

indiscretions, and nutritional deficiencies. The third entity, *environment*, is external to the host and includes the physical, social, cultural, and economic aspects of the environment. Examples include sanitation, air pollution, anthro-cultural beliefs, social equity, social norms, and economic status. The environmental factors play a moderating role that can either enhance or reduce susceptibility to disease. Because the three entities often interact to produce disease, disease prevention efforts should focus on a broad approach to mitigate or eliminate risk factors associated with all three entities.

Behavioral Risk Factors

Certain individual behaviors and personal lifestyle choices represent important risk factors for illness and disease. For example, smoking has been identified as the leading cause of preventable disease and death in the United States, because it significantly increases the risk of heart disease, stroke, lung cancer, and chronic lung disease (DHHS 2004). Substance abuse, inadequate physical exercise, a high-fat diet, irresponsible use of motor vehicles, and unsafe sex are additional examples of behavioral risk factors. (Table 2–1 presents the percentage of the US population with selected behavioral risks.)

Acute, Subacute, and Chronic Conditions

Disease can be classified as acute, subacute, or chronic. An *acute condition* is relatively severe, episodic (of short duration),

• •

Table 2–1 Percentage of US Population with Behavioral Risks

Behavioral Risks	Percentage of Population	Year
Alcohol (12 years and over)	51.8	2010
Marijuana (12 years and over)	6.9	2010
Cocaine use (12th graders)	1.1	2011
Cocaine use (10th graders)	0.7	2011
Cocaine use (8th graders)	0.8	2011
Cigarette smoking (18 years and over)	19.0	2011
Hypertension (20 years and over)	31.9	2009–10
Overweight (20–74 years)	68.5	2007–10
Serum cholesterol (20 years and over)	13.6	2009–10

Note: Data are based on household interviews of a sample of the civilian noninstitutionalized population 12 years of age and over in the coterminous United States.

Source: Data from National Center for Health Statistics. *Health, United States*, 2009. Hyattsville, MD: US Department of Health and Human Services, 2012, pp. 276, 281, 283, 292, 293, 301.

• •

and often treatable and subject to recovery. Treatments are generally provided in a hospital. Examples of acute conditions are a sudden interruption of kidney function or a myocardial infarction (heart attack). A *subacute condition* is a less severe phase of an acute illness. It can be a postacute condition, requiring continuity of treatment after discharge from a hospital. Examples include ventilator and head trauma care. A *chronic condition* is one that persists over time, is not severe, but is generally irreversible. A chronic condition may be kept under control through appropriate medical treatment, but if left untreated, the condition may lead to severe and life-threatening health problems. Examples of chronic conditions are hypertension, asthma, arthritis, heart disease, and diabetes. Contributors to chronic disease include ethnic, cultural, and behavioral factors and the social and physical environment, discussed later in this chapter.

In the United States, chronic diseases have become the leading cause of death and disability. Almost 50% of Americans have at least one chronic illness (Robert Wood Johnson Foundation 2010), and 8.7 out of every 10 deaths are attributable to chronic disease (WHO 2011). Among both the younger and older age groups (ages 18 and up), hypertension was ranked the most common chronic condition, followed by cholesterol disorders. Among children up to age 17, respiratory diseases and asthma were the most common chronic conditions (Agency for Healthcare Research and Quality 2006). The incidence of childhood chronic diseases has almost quadrupled over the past four decades, mostly due to a threefold increase in childhood obesity (PFCD 2009). Moreover, 26% of adults aged 18 or older had multiple chronic conditions in 2010. The combination of arthritis and hypertension was the most common dyad, and the combination of arthritis, hypertension, and diabetes was the most common triad (Ward and Schiller 2010).

It is estimated that 75% of total health expenditures in the United States are attributable to the treatment of chronic conditions (PFCD 2009). In 2011, total health care costs associated with the treatment of chronic diseases were approximately $1.7 trillion (PFCD 2009). In addition, health disparities continue to be a serious threat to the health and well-being of some population groups. For example, African American, Hispanic, American Indian, and Alaskan Native adults are twice as likely as white adults to have diabetes (CDC 2010a).

There are three main reasons behind the rise of chronic conditions in the US population: (1) New diagnostic methods, medical procedures, and pharmaceuticals have significantly improved the treatment of acute illnesses, survival rates, and longevity, but these achievements have come at the consequence of a larger number of people living with chronic conditions. The prevalence of chronic disease is expected to continue to rise with an aging population and longer life expectancy. (2) Screening and diagnosis have expanded in scope, frequency, and accuracy (Robert Wood Johnson Foundation 2010). (3) Lifestyle choices, such as high-salt and high-fat diets and sedentary lifestyles, are risk factors that contribute to the development of chronic conditions. To address these issues, the DHHS launched a comprehensive initiative with the aid of $650 million allocated under the American Recovery and Reinvestment Act of 2009. The goal of this initiative—Communities

Putting Prevention to Work—is to "reduce risk factors, prevent/delay chronic disease, promote wellness in children and adults, and provide positive, sustainable health change in communities" (DHHS 2010a).

Health Promotion and Disease Prevention

A program of health promotion and disease prevention is built on three main principles: (1) An understanding of risk factors associated with host, agent, and/or environment. Risk factors and their health consequences are evaluated through a process called *health risk appraisal.* Only when the risk factors and their health consequences are known can interventions be developed to help individuals adopt healthier lifestyles. (2) Interventions for counteracting the key risk factors include two main approaches: (a) behavior modification geared toward the goal of adopting healthier lifestyles and (b) therapeutic interventions. Both are discussed in the next paragraph. (3) Adequate public health and social services, as discussed later in this chapter, include all health-related services designed to minimize risk factors and their negative effects in order to prevent disease, control disease outbreaks, and contain the spread of infectious agents.

Various avenues can be used for motivating individuals to alter behaviors that may contribute to disease, disability, or death. Behavior can be modified through educational programs and incentives directed at specific high-risk populations. In the case of cigarette smoking, for example, health promotion aims at building people's knowledge, attitudes, and skills to avoid or quit smoking. It also involves reducing advertisements and other environmental enticements that promote nicotine addiction. Financial incentives/disincentives, such as a higher cigarette tax, have been used to discourage purchase of cigarettes.

Therapeutic interventions fall into three areas of preventive effort: primary prevention, secondary prevention, and tertiary prevention. *Primary prevention* refers to activities undertaken to reduce the probability that a disease will develop in the future (Kane 1988). Its objective is to restrain the development of a disease or negative health condition before it occurs. Therapeutic intervention would include community health efforts to assist patients in smoking cessation and exercise programs to prevent conditions such as lung cancer and heart disease. Safety training and practices at the workplace can reduce serious work-related injuries. Prenatal care is known to lower infant mortality rates. Immunization has had a greater impact on prevention against childhood diseases and mortality reduction than any other public health intervention besides clean water (Plotkin and Plotkin 1999). Hand washing, refrigeration of foods, garbage collection, sewage treatment, and protection of the water supply are also examples of primary prevention (Timmreck 1994). There have been numerous incidents where emphasis on food safety and proper cooking could have prevented outbreaks of potentially deadly episodes, such as those caused by *E. coli.*

Secondary prevention refers to early detection and treatment of disease. Health screenings and periodic health examinations are just two examples. Screening for hypertension, cancers, and diabetes, for example, have been instrumental in prescribing early treatment. The main objective of secondary prevention is to block the progression of a disease or an injury from developing into an impairment or disability (Timmreck 1994).

Tertiary prevention refers to interventions that could prevent complications from chronic conditions and prevent further illness, injury, or disability. For example, regular turning of bed-bound patients prevents pressure sores; rehabilitation therapies can prevent permanent disability; and infection control practices in hospitals and nursing homes are designed to prevent *iatrogenic illnesses*, that is, illnesses or injuries caused by the process of health care.

As shown in Table 2–2, prevention, early detection, and treatment efforts helped reduce cancer mortality quite significantly between 1991 and 2010. This decrease was the first sustained decline since record keeping was instituted in the 1930s.

Disease Prevention Under Health Care Reform

Prevention and wellness have received a great deal of emphasis in the health reform law. The ACA requires Medicare and private health insurance plans to provide a range of preventive services with no out-of-pocket costs (see Chapter 6). As a result, in 2011 and 2012, an estimated 71 million Americans with private insurance gained access to preventive services (DHHS 2013).

The ACA established the Prevention and Public Health Fund (PPHF) which has distributed almost $3.2 billion toward national preventive efforts and toward improving health outcomes and enhancing quality of health care (American Public Health Association 2013). Grants have been issued to reduce chronic diseases. The Office of the Surgeon General has developed a National Prevention Strategy that encourages partnerships among federal, state, tribal, local, and territorial governments; business, industry, and other private sector partners; philanthropic organizations; community and faith-based organizations; and everyday Americans to improve health through prevention (National Prevention Council 2011). The Centers for Disease Control and Prevention

Table 2–2 Annual Percent Decline in US Cancer Mortality 1991–2010

Type of Cancer	1991–1995	1994–2003	1998–2007	2001–2010
All cancers	3.0	1.1	1.4	1.5
Breast cancer	6.3	2.5	2.2	2.2
Cervical cancer	9.7	3.6	2.6	1.5
Ovarian cancer	4.8	0.5	0.8	2.0
Prostate cancer	6.3	3.5	3.1	2.7

Source: Data from National Center for Health Statistics of the Centers for Disease Control and Prevention, National Cancer Institute, SEER Cancer Statistics Review, 1975–2010.

(CDC) established a National Diabetes Prevention Program. In 2012, six organizations received $6.75 million to develop partnerships that reach a large numbers of individuals with pre-diabetes (CDC 2013a, 2013b).

In 2011, $10 million was made available to establish and evaluate comprehensive workplace wellness programs (DHHS 2011b). Beginning in 2014, $200 million in wellness grant funding will be available to small businesses to encourage the formation of wellness programs and employee incentivizing (Anderko et al. 2012).

Public Health

Public health remains poorly understood by its prime beneficiaries, the public. For some people, public health evokes images of a massive social enterprise or welfare system. To others, the term means health care services for everyone. Still another image of public health is that of a body of knowledge and techniques that can be applied to health-related problems (Turnock 1997). However, none of these ideas adequately reflects what public health is.

The Institute of Medicine (IOM) proposed that the mission of public health is to fulfill "society's interest in assuring conditions in which people can be healthy" (IOM 1988). *Public health* deals with broad societal concerns about ensuring conditions that promote optimum health for the society as a whole. It involves the application of scientific knowledge to counteract any threats that may jeopardize health and safety of the general population. Because of its extensive scope, the vast majority of public health efforts are carried out by

government agencies, such as the CDC in the United States.

Three main distinctions can be seen between the practices of medicine and public health: (1) Medicine focuses on the individual patient—diagnosing symptoms, treating and preventing disease, relieving pain and suffering, and maintaining or restoring normal function. Public health, conversely, focuses on populations (Shi and Johnson 2014). (2) The emphases in modern medicine are on the biological causes of disease and developing treatments and therapies. Public health focuses on (a) identifying the environmental, social, and behavioral risk factors as well as emerging or potential risks that may threaten people's health and safety, and (b) implementing population-wide interventions to minimize those risk factors (Peters et al. 2001). (3) Medicine focuses on the treatment of disease and recovery of health. Public health deals with various efforts to prevent disease and counteract threats that may negatively affect people's health.

Public health activities can range from providing education on nutrition to passing laws that enhance automobile safety. For example, public health includes dissemination to the public and to health professionals timely information about important health issues, particularly when communicable diseases pose potential threats to large segments of a population.

Compared to the delivery of medical services, public health involves a broader range of professionals. The medical sector encompasses physicians, nurses, dentists, therapists, social workers, psychologists, nutritionists, health educators, pharmacists, laboratory technicians, health services administrators, and so forth. In addition to these professionals, public health also involves professionals such as sanitarians, epidemiologists, statisticians, industrial hygienists, environmental health specialists, food and drug inspectors, toxicologists, and economists (Lasker 1997).

Health Protection and Environmental Health

Health protection is one of the main public health functions. In the 1850s, John Snow successfully traced the risk of cholera outbreaks in London to the Broad Street water pump (Rosen 1993). Since then, *environmental health* has specifically dealt with preventing the spread of disease through water, air, and food

(Schneider 2000). Environmental health science, along with other public health measures, was instrumental in reducing the risk of infectious diseases during the 1900s. For example, in 1900, pneumonia, tuberculosis, and diarrhea, along with enteritis, were the top three killers in the United States (CDC 1999); that is no longer the case today (see Table 2–3). With the rapid industrialization during the 20th century, environmental health faced new challenges due to serious health hazards from chemicals, industrial waste, infectious waste, radiation, asbestos, and other toxic substances. In the 21st century, chemical, biological, and nuclear agents in the hands of terrorists and rogue nations has emerged as a new environmental threat.

Table 2–3 Leading Causes of Death, 2010

Cause of Death	Deaths	Percentage
All causes	2,468,435	100.0
Diseases of the heart	597,689	24.2
Malignant neoplasms	574,743	23.3
Chronic lower respiratory diseases	138,080	5.6
Cerebrovascular diseases	129,476	5.2
Unintentional injuries	120,859	4.9
Alzheimer's disease	83,494	3.4
Diabetes mellitus	69,071	2.8
Nephritis, nephrotic syndrome, and nephrosis	50,476	2.0
Influenza and pneumonia	50,097	2.0
Suicide	38,364	1.6

Source: Data from National Center for Health Statistics. *Health, United States, 2012.* Hyattsville, MD: Department of Health and Human Services, 2013, p. 88.

Health Protection During Global Pandemics

Over time, public health has become a complex global undertaking. Its main goal of protecting the health and safety of populations from a variety of old and new threats cannot be achieved without global cooperation (see Chapter 14). In 2003, severe acute respiratory syndrome (SARS)—a contagious disease that is accompanied by fever and symptoms of pneumonia or other respiratory illness—spread from China to Canada. Worldwide over 8,000 people were affected (CDC 2012).

The global threat of avian influenza has also elicited a public health response. The CDC launched a website dedicated to educating the public about avian influenza, how it is spread, and past and current outbreaks. The website contains specific information for health professionals, travelers, the poultry industry, state departments of health, and people with possible exposures to avian influenza (CDC 2007).

After a novel H1N1 influenza virus emerged from Mexico in April 2009, US health officials anticipated and prepared for an influenza pandemic, and it stretched the response capabilities of the public health system. The virus affected every US state, and Americans were left unprotected because of the unavailability of antiviral medications. Since then, a global effort has been undertaken to establish collaborative networks to exchange information and contain global pandemics (WHO 2013).

Health Protection and Preparedness in the United States

Since the horrific events of what is commonly referred to as 9/11 (September 11, 2001),

America has opened a new chapter in health protection. The efforts to protect the health and safety of Americans began in June 2002 when President Bush signed into law the Public Health Security and Bioterrorism Preparedness Response Act of 2002. Subsequently, the Homeland Security Act of 2002 created the Department of Homeland Security (DHS) and called for a major restructuring of the nation's resources with the primary mission of helping prevent, protect against, and respond to any acts of terrorism in the United States. It also provided better tools to contain attacks on the food and water supplies; protect the nation's vital infrastructures, such as nuclear facilities; and track biological materials anywhere in the United States. The term *bioterrorism* encompasses the use of chemical, biological, and nuclear agents to cause harm to relatively large civilian populations.

Now, health protection and preparedness involves a massive operation to deal with any natural or man-made threats. Dealing with such threats requires large-scale preparations, which include appropriate tools and training for workers in medical care, public health, emergency care, and civil defense agencies at the federal, state, and local levels. It requires national initiatives to develop countermeasures, such as new vaccines, a robust public health infrastructure, and coordination among numerous agencies. It requires an infrastructure to handle large numbers of casualties and isolation facilities for contagious patients. Hospitals, public health agencies, and civil defense must be linked together through information systems. Containment of infectious agents, such as smallpox, necessitates quick detection, treatment, isolation, and organized efforts to protect the unaffected population. Rapid cleanup, evacuation of the affected population, and transfer of victims to medical care facilities require detailed plans and logistics.

The United States has confronted major natural disasters, such as hurricane Katrina in 2005, hurricane Sandy in 2012, and tornadoes in Oklahoma in 2013, as well as man-made mass casualties such as the Boston Marathon Bombing on April 15, 2013. Health protection and preparedness have become ongoing efforts through revitalized initiatives such as the Pandemic and All-Hazards Preparedness Act (PAHPA) of 2006 which also authorized a new Assistant Secretary for Preparedness and Response (ASPR) within the DHHS and called for the establishment of a quadrennial National Health Security Strategy (NHSS). The CDC has developed the National Biosurveillance Strategy for Human Health which covers six priority areas: electronic health information exchange, electronic laboratory information exchange, unstructured data, integrated biosurveillance information, global disease detection and collaboration, and biosurveillance workforce. Based on the National Health Security Strategy developed by the DHHS in 2009, *Healthy People 2020* focused on four areas of reinforcement under an overarching goal to "improve the Nation's ability to prevent, prepare for, respond to, and recover from a major health incident": time to release official information about a public health emergency, time for designated personnel to respond to an emergency, Laboratory Response Network (LRN) laboratories, and time to develop after-action reports and improvement plans in states (DHHS 2010b). A progress report shows that most states and localities have strong biological laboratory capabilities and capacities, with nearly 90% of laboratories in the LRN reachable around the clock (CDC 2010b).

In 2011, the Health Alert Network (HAN) was established, which is a nationwide program designed to facilitate communication, information, and distance learning related to health threats, including bioterrorism (DHHS 2011a). When fully established, the network will link together the various local health departments as well as other components of bioterrorism preparedness and response, such as laboratories and state health departments.

One of the key concepts of preparedness is *surge capacity*, defined as "the ability of a healthcare facility or system to expand its operations to safely treat an abnormally large influx of patients" (Bonnett and Peery 2007). The initial response is conducted at a local health care facility, such as a hospital. Strategies for expanding the surge capacity of a hospital include early discharge of stable patients, cancellation of elective procedures and admissions, conversion of private rooms to double rooms, reopening of closed areas, revision of staff work hours to a 12-hour disaster shift, callback of off-duty personnel, and establishment of temporary external shelters for patient holding (Hick et al. 2004).

If the local level response becomes overloaded or incapacitated, it requires activation of a second tier of disaster response—community-level surge capacity. Cooperative regional planning necessitates sharing of staff and supplies across a network of regional healthcare facilities (Hick et al. 2004). An important aspect of disaster planning at the community level focuses on the transportation logistics of the region. The quantity of ambulances in the area and the means of accessing these resources during an event could be crucial to delivering proper care to critical patients (Kearns et al. 2013). The final tier of disaster response involves federal aid under the National Disaster Medical System (NDMS), which actually dates back to the 1980s and was designed to accommodate large numbers of military casualties. Disaster Medical Assistance Teams (DMATs) are a vital component of the NDMS that directly respond to the needs of an overwhelmed community. DMATs deploy with trained personnel (in both medical and ancillary services), equipped with tents, water filtration, generators, and medical supplies (Stopford 2005).

Despite the progress made, disaster preparedness efforts in the United States remain fragmented and underfunded. For example, review, rotation, replacement, and upgrade of equipment and supplies in the system on a regular basis have remained a challenge (Cohen and Mulvaney 2005).

Determinants of Health

Health determinants are major factors that, over time, affect the health and well-being of individuals and populations. An understanding of health determinants is necessary for any positive interventions necessary to improve health and longevity.

Blum's Model of Health Determinants

In 1974, Blum (1981) proposed an "Environment of Health" model, later called the "Force Field and Well-Being Paradigms of Health" (Figure 2–3). Blum proposed four major inputs that contributed to health and well-being. These main influences (called "force fields") are environment, lifestyle, heredity, and medical care, all of which must be considered simultaneously when addressing the health status of an individual or a population. In other words, there is no single pathway to better health, because health determinants interact in complex ways. Consequently, improvement in health requires a multipronged approach.

The four wedges in Figure 2–3 represent the four major force fields. The size of each wedge signifies its relative importance. Thus, the most important force field is environment, followed by lifestyles and heredity. Medical care has the least impact on health and well-being.

Blum's model also explains that the four main forces operate within a much broader context, and are affected by broad national and international factors, such as a nation's population characteristics, natural resources, ecological balance, human satisfactions, and cultural systems. Among these factors, type of health care delivery system can also be included. In the United States, the preponderance of health care expenditures is devoted to the treatment of medical conditions rather than to the prevention and control of factors that produce those medical conditions in the first place. This misdirection can be traced to the conflicts that often result from the beliefs and values ingrained in the American culture.

Environment

Environmental factors encompass the physical, socioeconomic, sociopolitical, and sociocultural dimensions. Among physical environmental factors are air pollution, food and water contaminants, radiation, toxic chemicals, wastes, disease vectors, safety hazards, and habitat alterations.

The relationship of socioeconomic status (SES) to health and well-being may be explained by the general likelihood that people who have better education also have

Figure 2–3 The Force Field and Well-Being Paradigms of Health.

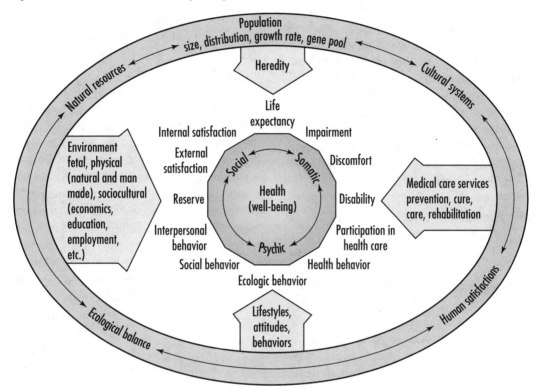

Source: Reproduced from H.L. Blum, *Planning for Health,* © 1981, Human Sciences Press, with kind permission from Springer Science+Business Media B.V.

higher incomes. The greater the economic gap between the rich and the poor in a given geographic area, the worse the health status of the population in that area is likely to be. It has been suggested that wide income gaps produce less social cohesion, greater psychosocial stress, and, consequently, poorer health (Wilkinson 1997). For example, social cohesion—characterized by a hospitable social environment in which people trust each other and participate in communal activities—is linked to lower overall mortality and better self-rated health (Kawachi et al. 1997, 1999). Even countries with national health insurance programs, such as Britain, Australia, Denmark, and Sweden,

experience persistent and widening disparities in health according to socioeconomic status (Pincus et al. 1998). The joint relationship of income inequality and availability of primary care has also been found to be significantly associated with individuals' self-rated health status (Shi et al. 2002).

Lifestyle

Lifestyle, or behavioral risk factors, were previously discussed. This section provides some illustrations of how lifestyle factors are related to health. Studies have shown that diet and foods, for example, play a major role in most of the significant health problems of today. Heart disease, diabetes, stroke, and cancer are but some of the diseases with direct links to dietary choices. Throughout the world, incidence and mortality rates for many forms of cancer are rising. Yet research has clearly indicated that a significant portion of cancer is preventable. Researchers estimated that 40% to 60% of all cancers, and as many as 35% of cancer deaths, are linked to diet (American Institute for Cancer Research 1996). Current research also shows that a diet rich in fruits, vegetables, and low-fat dairy foods, and with reduced saturated and total fat, can substantially lower blood pressure (see, for example, the DASH Eating Plan recommended by DHHS 2006). The role of exercise and physical activity as a potentially useful, effective, and acceptable method is significant in reducing the risk of colon cancer (Macfarlane and Lowenfels 1994) as well as many other health problems.

Heredity

Genetic factors predispose individuals to certain diseases. For example, cancer occurs when the body's healthy genes lose their ability to suppress malignant growth or when other genetic processes stop working properly, although this does not mean that cancer is entirely a disease of the genes (Davis and Webster 2002). A person can do little about the genetic makeup he or she has inherited. However, lifestyles and behaviors that a person may currently engage in can have significant influences on future progeny. Advances in gene therapy hold the promise of treating a variety of inherited or acquired diseases.

Medical Care

Even though the other three factors are more important in the determination of health, medical care is, nevertheless, a key determinant of health. Both individual and population health are closely related to having access to adequate preventive and curative health care services. Despite the fact that medical care, compared to the other three factors, has the least impact on health and well-being, Americans' attitudes toward health improvement focus on more medical research, development of new medical technology, and spending more on high-tech medical care. Yet, significant declines in mortality rates were achieved well before the modernization of Western medicine and the escalation in medical care expenditures.

The availability of primary care may be one alternative pathway through which income inequality influences population-level health outcomes. Research by Shi and colleagues (1999, 2001) suggests that access to primary care, in addition to income inequality, significantly correlates with reduced mortality, increased life expectancy, and improved birth outcomes. In the United States, individuals living in states with a higher primary care physician-to-population ratio are more likely to report good health than those living in states with a lower ratio (Shi et al. 2002).

Contemporary Models of Health Determinants

More recent models have built upon Blum's framework of health determinants. For example, the model proposed by Dahlgren and Whitehead (2006) states that age, sex, and genetic makeup are fixed factors, but other factors in the surrounding layers can be

Figure 2–4 WHO Commission on Social Determinants of Health Conceptual Framework.

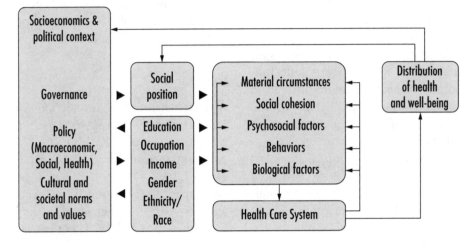

Source: Centers for Disease Control and Prevention. 2010. *Establishing a Holistic Framework to Reduce Inequities in HIV, Viral Hepatitis, STDs, and Tuberculosis in the United States.*

modified to positively influence population health. Individual lifestyle factors have the potential to promote or damage health, and social interactions can sustain people's health; but living and working conditions; food supplies; access to essential goods and services; and the overall economic, cultural, and environmental conditions have wider influences on individual and population health.

Ansari and colleagues (2003) proposed a public health model of the social determinants of health in which the determinants are categorized into four major groups: social determinants, health care system attributes, disease-inducing behaviors, and health outcomes.

The WHO Commission on Social Determinants of Health (2007) concluded that "the social conditions in which people are born, live, and work are the single most important determinant of one's health status." The WHO model provides a conceptual framework for understanding the socioeconomic and political contexts, structural determinants, intermediary determinants (including material circumstances, social-environmental circumstances, behavioral and biological factors, social cohesion, and the health care system), and the impact on health equity and well-being measured as health outcomes.

US government agencies, such as the CDC and DHHS, have recognized the need to address health inequities. CDC's National Center for HIV/AIDS, Viral Hepatitis, STD, and TB Prevention adopted the WHO framework on social determinants of health to use as a guide for its activities (see Figure 2–4).

Measures Related to Health

Certain quantitative measures commonly apply to health, health status, and the utilization of health care. The conceptual approaches for defining health and its distribution help form a vision for the future, and objective measures play a critical role in evaluating the success of various programs, as well as for directing future planning activities. Practical approaches for measuring health are, however, quite limited, and mental health is more difficult to quantify and measure than physical health. An objective evaluation of social and spiritual health is even more obscure.

The concept of population, as it applies to population health, has been borrowed from the disciplines of statistics and epidemiology. The term "population" is not restricted to describing the total population. Although commonly used in that way, the term may also apply to a defined subpopulation, for example, age groups, marital categories, income levels, occupation categories, racial/ethnic groups, people having a common disease, people in a certain risk category, or people in a certain community or geographic region of a country. The main advantage of studying subpopulations is that it helps trace the existence of health problems to a defined group. Doing so avoids concealing serious problems in a minority group within the favorable statistics of the majority. By pinpointing health problems in certain well defined groups, targeted interventions and new policy initiatives can be deployed in the most effective manner.

Measures of Physical Health

Physical health status is often interpreted through *morbidity* (disease and disability) and *mortality* (death) rates. In addition, self-perceived health status is a commonly used indicator of health and well-being. Respondents are asked to rate their health as excellent, very good, good, fair, or poor. Self-perceived health status is highly correlated with many objective measures of health status. It is also a good predictor of patient-initiated physician visits, including general medical and mental health visits.

Longevity

Life expectancy—a prediction of how long a person will live—is widely used as a basic measure of health status. The two common measures are life expectancy at birth (Table 2–4)—or how long a newborn can expect to live—and life expectancy at age 65—expected remaining years of life for someone at age 65. These measures are actuarially determined and published by government agencies such as the National Center for Health Statistics (NCHS). The US Census Bureau (1995) projected that life expectancy in the United States will increase

••••••••••••••••••••••••••••••••••

Table 2–4 US Life Expectancy at Birth—1999, 2003, and 2010

Year	Total	Male	Female
1999	76.7	73.9	79.4
White	77.3	74.6	79.9
Black	71.4	67.8	74.7
2003	77.5	74.8	80.1
White	78.0	75.3	80.5
Black	72.7	69.0	76.1
2010	78.8	76.4	81.1
White	81.2	78.5	83.8
Black	74.7	71.4	77.7

Sources: Data from National Center for Health Statistics, *Health, United States, 1996–1997* and *Injury Chartbook.* Hyattsville, MD: 1997, p. 108; *Health, United States, 2002,* p. 116; *Health, United States, 2006,* p. 176; and *Health, United States, 2012,* p. 77.

••••••••••••••••••••••••••••••••••

from 76.0 years in 1993 to 82.6 years in 2050.

Morbidity

The measurement of morbidity or disease, such as cancer or heart disease, is expressed as a ratio or proportion of those who have the problem and the ***population at risk***. The population at risk includes all the people in the same community or population group who could acquire a disease or condition (Smith 1979). Incidence and prevalence are two widely used indicators for the number of ***cases***, that is, people who end up acquiring a negative health condition. ***Incidence*** counts the number of new cases occurring in the population at risk within a certain period of time, such as a month or a year (Smith 1979; see Formula 2–1). Incidence describes the extent to which, in a given population, people acquire a given disease during a specified time period. Incidence is particularly useful in estimating the magnitude of conditions of relatively short duration. Declining levels of incidence point to success of health promotion and disease prevention efforts, because they prevent new cases (Ibrahim 1985). High levels of incidence may suggest an impending ***epidemic***, that is, a large number of people who get a specific disease from a common source. The second measure of morbidity, ***prevalence***, determines the total number of cases at a specific point in time, in a defined population (see Formula 2–2). Prevalence is useful in quantifying the magnitude of illnesses of a relatively long duration. Decreased prevalence indicates success of treatment programs by shortening the duration of illness (Ibrahim 1985). Both incidence and prevalence rates can apply to disease, disability, or death.

Formula 2–1

Incidence = Number of new cases during a specified period/Population at risk

Formula 2–2

Prevalence = Total number of cases at a specific point in time/Specified population

The calculation of rates often requires dividing a small number by a large number representing a defined population. The result is a fraction. To make the fractions meaningful and interpretable, they are multiplied by 100 (to get a percentage), 1,000 (to get a rate per 1,000 people), 10,000 (to get a rate per 10,000 people), or a higher multiple of 10.

Disability

Disease and injury can lead to temporary or permanent, as well as partial or total, disability. Although the idea of morbidity includes disabilities, as well as disease, there are specific measures of disability. Some common measures are the number of days of bed confinement, days missed from work or school, and days of restricted activity. All measures are in reference to a specific time period, such as a year.

One of the most widely used measures of physical disability among the elderly, in particular, is the ***activities of daily living*** (ADL) scale. The ADL scale is appropriate for evaluating disability in both community-dwelling and institutionalized adults. The classic ADL scale, developed by Katz and Akpom (1979), includes six basic activities: eating, bathing, dressing, using the toilet, maintaining continence, and transferring from bed to chair. To evaluate disability in community-dwelling adults, a modified Katz scale is commonly used. It consists of seven items (Ostir et al. 1999).

Five of these items—feeding, bathing, dressing, using the toilet, and transferring from bed to chair—have been retained from the original Katz scale. The additional two items are grooming and walking a distance of 8 feet. Thus, it includes items measuring self-care and mobility. The ADLs identify personal care functions with which a disabled person may need assistance. Depending on the extent of disability, personal care needs can be met through adaptive devices; care rendered by another individual, such as a family member; or care in a nursing facility.

Another commonly used measure of physical function is the *instrumental activities of daily living* (IADL) scale. This scale measures activities that are necessary for living independently in the community, such as using the telephone, driving a car or traveling alone on a bus or by taxi, shopping, preparing meals, doing light housework, taking medicines, handling money, doing heavy housework, walking up and down stairs, and walking a half-mile without help. IADLs typically require higher cognitive functioning than ADLs and, as such, are not purely physical tests of functional disability. The IADL scale measures the level of functioning in activities that are important for self-sufficiency, such as the ability to live independently.

Mortality

Death rates are computed in different forms as indicators of population health. *Crude rates* refer to the total population; they are not specific to any age group or disease category (Formula 2–3).

Formula 2–3
Crude death rate = Total deaths (usually in 1 year)/ Total population

Specific rates are useful because death rates vary greatly by race, sex, age, and type of disease or condition. Specific rates allow health care professionals to target programs at the appropriate population subgroups (Dever 1984). Examples of specific rates are age-specific mortality rate (Formula 2–4) and cause-specific mortality rate (Formula 2–5). The age-specific mortality rate provides a measure of the risk (or probability) of dying when a person is in a certain age group. The cause-specific mortality rate provides a measure of the risk (or probability) of dying from a specific cause.

Formula 2–4
Age-specific mortality rate = Number of deaths within a certain age group/Total number of persons in that age group

Formula 2–5
Cause-specific mortality rate = Number of deaths from a specific disease/Total population

Infant mortality rate (actually a ratio; Formula 2–6) is an indicator that reflects the health status of the mother and the child through pregnancy and the birth process. It also reflects the level of prenatal and postnatal care (Timmreck 1994).

Formula 2–6
Infant mortality rate = Number of deaths from birth to 1 year of age (in 1 year)/Number of live births during the same year

Demographic Change

In addition to measures of disease and mortality, changes in the composition of a population over time are important in planning health services. Population change involves three components: births, deaths, and migration (Dever 1984). For example, the migration of the elderly to the southern states requires planning of adequate retirement and long-term care services in those states. Longevity is also an important factor that determines demographic change. For example, lower death rates, lower birth rates, and greater longevity, together, indicate an aging population. The next section presents measures of births and migration, whereas measures of death were previously discussed.

Births

Natality and fertility are two measures associated with births. *Natality*, or birth rate, is useful in assessing the influence of births on demographic change and is measured by the crude birth rate (Formula 2–7).

Formula 2–7

Crude birth rate = Number of live births (usually in 1 year)/Total population

Fertility refers to the capacity of a population to reproduce (Formula 2–8). Fertility is a more precise measure than natality, because fertility relates actual births to the sector of the population capable of giving birth.

Formula 2–8

Fertility rate = Number of live births (usually in 1 year)/Number of females aged 15–44

Migration

Migration refers to the geographic movement of populations between defined geographic units and involves a permanent change of residence. The net migration rate (Formula 2–9) defines the change in the population as a result of *immigration* (in migration) and *emigration* (out migration) (Dever 1984, p. 249). The rate is calculated for a specified period, such as 1 year, 2 years, 5 years, and so on.

Formula 2–9

Net migration rate = (Number of immigrants – Number of emigrants)/Total population (during a specific period of time)

Measures of Mental Health

Measurement of mental health is less objective than measurement of mortality and morbidity, because mental health often encompasses feelings that cannot be observed. Physical functioning, by contrast, reflected in behaviors and performances, can be more readily observed. Hence, measurement of mental health more appropriately refers to assessment rather than measurement. Mental health can be assessed by the presence of certain symptoms, including both psychophysiologic and psychological symptoms. Examples of psychophysiologic symptoms are low energy, headache, and upset stomach. Examples of psychological symptoms are nervousness, depression, and anxiety.

Self-assessment of one's own psychological state may also be used for mental health assessment. Self-assessment can be obtained through self-reports of frequency and intensity of psychological distress, anxiety, depression, and psychological well-being.

Measures of Social Health

Measures of social health extend beyond the individual to encompass the extent of social contacts across various facets of life, such as family life, work life, and community life. Breslow (1972) attempted to measure social health along four dimensions: (1) employability, based on educational achievement, occupational status, and job experience; (2) marital satisfaction; (3) sociability, determined by the number of close friends and relatives; and (4) community involvement, which encompassed attendance at religious services, political activity, and organizational membership.

Social health status is sometimes evaluated in terms of social contacts and social resources. *Social contacts* are evaluated in terms of the number of social contacts or social activities a person engages in within a specified period. Examples are visits with friends and relatives, as well as attendance at social events, such as conferences, picnics, or other outings. *Social resources* refer to social contacts that can be relied on for support, such as relatives, friends, neighbors, and members of a religious congregation. Social contacts can be observed, and they represent the more objective of the two categories; however, one criticism of social contact measures is their focus on events and activities themselves, with little consideration of how the events are personally experienced. Unlike social contacts, social resources cannot be directly observed and are best measured by asking the individuals direct questions. Evaluative questions include whether these individuals can rely on their social contacts to provide tangible support and needed companionship and whether they feel cared for, loved, and wanted.

Measures of Spiritual Health

Within a person's individual, social, and cultural context, spiritual well-being can have a large variety of connotations. Such variations make it extremely difficult to propose standardized approaches for measuring the spiritual dimension. Attempts to measure this dimension are illustrated in the General Social Survey, which includes people's self-perceptions about happiness; religious experiences; and their degree of involvement in activities, such as prayer and attending religious services. A wide range of tools for spiritual assessment are now available. Generic methods of spiritual assessment are not associated with any particular religion or practice, and hence do not require a detailed understanding of any particular religious tradition (Draper 2012). An example of a generic scale is one developed by Vella-Brodrick and Allen (1995) which evaluates items such as reaching out for spiritual intervention; engaging in meditation, yoga, or prayer; duration of meditation or prayer for inner peace; frequency of meditation or prayer; reading about one's religious beliefs; and discussions or readings about ethical and moral issues. Several quantitative measurement scales are also available to assess dimensions such as general spirituality, spiritual well-being, spiritual needs, and spiritual coping (Monod et al. 2011), but their use has been confined mainly to clinical research.

Measures of Health Services Utilization

Utilization refers to the consumption of health care services and the extent to which health care services are used. Measures of utilization can be used to determine which individuals in a population group receive certain types of medical services, which do not receive services, and why. A health care provider, such as a hospital, can find out the extent to which its services are used. Measures of utilization can help managers decide whether certain services should be added or eliminated, and health planners can determine whether programs have been effective in reaching their targeted populations. Measures of utilization, therefore, play a critical role in the planning of health care delivery capacity, for example, how many hospital beds are required to meet the acute care needs of a given population (Pasley et al. 1995). Measures of utilization are too numerous to be covered here, but some selected common measures are provided (Formulas 2–10 to 2–16).

Crude Measures of Utilization

Formula 2–10

Access to primary care services = Number of persons in a given population who visited a primary care provider in a given year/Size of the population

(This measure is generally expressed as a percentage, i.e., the fraction is multiplied by 100.)

Formula 2–11

Utilization of primary care services = Number of primary care visits by people in a given population in a given year/Size of the population

(This measure is generally expressed as number of visits per person per year.)

Specific Measures of Utilization

Formula 2–12

Utilization of targeted services = Number of people in a specific targeted population using special services (or visits)/Size of the targeted population group

(The fraction obtained is multiplied by 100, 1000, or a higher multiple of 10 to facilitate interpretation of the result.)

Formula 2–13

Utilization of specific inpatient services = Number of inpatient days/Size of the population

(The fraction obtained is multiplied by 100, 1000, or a higher multiple of 10 to facilitate interpretation of the result.)

Measures of Institution-Specific Utilization

Formula 2–14

Average daily census = Total number of inpatient days in a given time period/Number of days in the same time period

Formula 2–15

Occupancy rate = Total number of inpatient days in a given time period/Total number of available beds during the same time period

or

Average daily census/Total number of beds in the facility

(This measure is expressed as a percentage, i.e., the fraction is multiplied by 100.)

Formula 2–16

Average length of stay = Total number of inpatient days during a given time period/Total number of patients served during the same time period

Measures of Global Health

Global monitoring of changes in the health of various populations requires the use of "tried and true" global health indicators. Global health indicators can be divided into those that directly measure health phenomena (e.g., diseases, deaths, use of services) and indirect measures (e.g., social development, education and poverty indicators); these are also referred to as proximal and distal indicators, respectively. On the basis of population statistics describing levels of education attained and access to safe water and sanitation, it is possible to categorize a country fairly accurately as having a population with high, medium, or low burden of disease (Larson and Mercer 2004).

Anthro-Cultural Beliefs and Values

A value system orients the members of a society toward defining what is desirable for that society. It has been observed that even a society as complex and highly differentiated as in the United States can be said to have a relatively well integrated system of institutionalized common values at the societal level (Parsons 1972). Although such a view may still prevail, American society now has several different subcultures that have grown in size due to a steady influx of immigrants from different parts of the world.

The current system of health services delivery traces its roots to the traditional beliefs and values espoused by the American people. The value and belief system governs the training and general orientation of health care providers, type of health delivery settings, financing and allocation of resources, and access to health care.

Some of the main beliefs and values prevalent in the American culture are outlined as follows:

1. A strong belief in the advancement of science and the application of scientific methods to medicine were instrumental in creating the medical model that primarily governs health care delivery in the United States. In turn, the medical model has fueled the tremendous growth in medical science and technological innovation. As a result, the United States has been leading the world in medical breakthroughs. These developments have had numerous implications for health services delivery:

   a. They increase the demand for the latest treatments and raise patients' expectations for finding cures.

   b. Medical professionals have been preoccupied with clinical interventions, whereas the holistic aspects of health and use of alternative therapies have not received adequate emphasis.

   c. Health care professionals have been trained to focus on physical symptoms rather than the underlying causes of disease.

   d. Integration of diagnosis and treatment with disease prevention has been lagging behind.

   e. Most research efforts have focused on the development of medical technology. Commitment of resources to the preservation and enhancement of health and well-being has lagged behind.

   f. Medical specialists, using the latest technology, are held in higher esteem and earn higher incomes than general practitioners.

   g. The desirability of health care delivery institutions, such as hospitals, is often evaluated by their acquisition of advanced technology.

   h. Whereas biomedicine has taken central stage, diagnosis and treatment of mental health have been relegated to a lesser status.

   i. The biomedical model has neglected the social and spiritual elements of health.

2. America has been a champion of capitalism. Due to a strong belief in capitalism, health care has largely been viewed as an economic good (or service), not as a public resource.

3. A culture of capitalism promotes entrepreneurial spirit and self-determination. Hence, individual capabilities to obtain health services have largely determined the production and consumption of health care—which services will be produced, where and in what quantity, and who will have access to those services. Some key implications are:

   a. Upper-tier access to health care services is available mainly through private health insurance. Those with public insurance fall in a second tier. The uninsured make up a third tier.

   b. A clear distinction exists between the types of services for poor and affluent communities and between those in rural and inner-city locations.

   c. The culture of individualism emphasizes individual health rather than population health. Medical practice, therefore, has been directed at keeping the individual healthy rather than keeping the entire community healthy.

   d. A concern for the most underprivileged classes in society—the poor, the elderly, the disabled, and children—led to the creation of the public programs Medicaid, Medicare, and the Children's Health Insurance Program (CHIP).

4. Principles of free enterprise and a general distrust of big government have kept the delivery of health care largely in private hands. Hence, a separation also exists between public health functions and the private practice of medicine.

Equitable Distribution of Health Care

Scarcity of economic resources is a central economic concept. From this perspective, health care can be viewed as an economic good. Two fundamental questions arise with regard to how scarce health care resources ought to be used: (1) How much health care should be produced? (2) How should health care be distributed? The first question concerns the appropriate combination in which health services ought to be produced in relation to all other goods and services in the overall economy. If more health care is produced, a society may have to do less with some other goods, such as food, clothing, and transportation. The second question affects individuals at a more personal level. It deals with who can receive which type of medical service, and how access to services will be restricted.

The production, distribution, and subsequent consumption of health care must be perceived as equitable by a society. No society has found a perfectly equitable method to distribute limited economic resources. In fact, any method of resource distribution leaves some inequalities. Societies, therefore, try to allocate resources according to some guiding principles acceptable to each society. Such principles are ingrained in a society's value and belief system. It is recognized that not everyone can receive everything medical science has to offer.

A just and fair allocation of health care poses conceptual and practical difficulties; hence, a theory of justice needs to resolve the problem of health care allocation (Jonsen

1986). Even though various ethical principles can be used to guide decisions pertaining to just and fair allocation of health care in individual circumstances, the broad concern about equitable access to health services is addressed by two contrasting theories referred to as market justice and social justice.

Market Justice

The principle of *market justice* ascribes the fair distribution of health care to the market forces in a free economy. Medical care and its benefits are distributed based on people's willingness and ability to pay (Santerre and Neun 1996). In other words, people are entitled to purchase a share of the available goods and services that they value. They are to purchase these valued goods and services by means of wealth acquired through their own legitimate efforts. This is how most goods and services are distributed in a free market. The free market implies that giving people something they have not earned would be morally and economically wrong.

Chapter 1 discussed several characteristics that describe a free market. Those market characteristics are a precondition to the distribution of health care services according to market justice principles. It should be added that health care in the United States is not delivered in a free market; rather it is delivered in a quasi-market (see Chapter 1). Hence, market justice principles are only partially applicable to the US health care delivery system. Distribution of health care according to market justice is based on the following key assumptions:

- Health care is like any other economic good or service, the distribution and consumption of which are determined by free market forces of supply and demand.

- Individuals are responsible for their own achievements. From the rewards of their achievements, people are free to obtain various economic goods and services, including health care. When individuals pursue their own best interests, the interests of society as a whole are best served (Ferguson and Maurice 1970).

- People make rational choices in their decisions to purchase health care products and services. Grossman (1972) proposed that health is also an investment commodity. People consider the purchase of health services as an investment. For example, the investment has a monetary payoff when it reduces the number of sick days, making extra time available for productive activities, such as earning a living. Or it can have a utility payoff—a payoff in terms of satisfaction—when it makes life more enjoyable and fulfilling.

- People, in consultation with their physicians, know what is best for them. This assumption implies that people place a certain degree of trust in their physicians and that the physician–patient relationship is ongoing.

- The marketplace works best with minimum interference from the government. In other words, the market, rather than the government, can allocate health care resources in the most efficient and equitable manner.

Under market justice, the production of health care is determined by how much the consumers are willing and able to purchase at the prevailing market prices. Thus, prices and ability to pay ration the quantity and type of health care services people consume. The uninsured and those who lack sufficient income to pay privately face barriers to obtaining health care. Such limitations to obtaining health care are referred to as "rationing by ability to pay" (Feldstein 1994), *demand-side rationing*, or price rationing. To an extent, barriers faced by the uninsured would be overcome through charitable services.

The key characteristics and their implications under the system of market justice are summarized in Table 2–5. Market justice emphasizes individual, rather than collective, responsibility for health. It proposes private, rather than government, solutions to social problems of health.

Social Justice

The idea of social justice is at odds with the principles of capitalism and market justice. The term "social justice" was invented in the 19th century by the critics of capitalism to describe the "good society" (Kristol 1978). According to the principle of *social justice*, the equitable distribution of health care is a societal responsibility, which is

Table 2–5 Comparison of Market Justice and Social Justice

Market Justice	Social Justice
Characteristics	
• Views health care as an economic good	• Views health care as a social resource
• Assumes free-market conditions for health services delivery	• Requires active government involvement in health services delivery
• Assumes that markets are more efficient in allocating health resources equitably	• Assumes that the government is more efficient in allocating health resources equitably
• Production and distribution of health care determined by market-based demand	• Medical resource allocation determined by central planning
• Medical care distribution based on people's ability to pay	• Ability to pay inconsequential for receiving medical care
• Access to medical care viewed as an economic reward of personal effort and achievement	• Equal access to medical services viewed as a basic right
Implications	
• Individual responsibility for health	• Collective responsibility for health
• Benefits based on individual purchasing power	• Everyone is entitled to a basic package of benefits
• Limited obligation to the collective good	• Strong obligation to the collective good
• Emphasis on individual well-being	• Community well-being supersedes that of the individual
• Private solutions to social problems	• Public solutions to social problems
• Rationing based on ability to pay	• Planned rationing of health care

best achieved by letting the government take over the production and distribution of health care. Social justice regards health care as a social good—as opposed to an economic good—that should be collectively financed and available to all citizens regardless of the individual recipient's ability to pay. The main characteristics and implications of social justice are summarized in Table 2–5.

Canadians and Europeans long ago reached a broad consensus that health care is a social good (Reinhardt 1994). Public health also has a social justice orientation (Turnock 1997). Under the social justice system, inability to obtain medical services because of a lack of financial resources is considered inequitable. Accordingly, a just distribution of health care must be based on need, not simply on one's ability to purchase in the marketplace (demand). Need for health care is determined either by the patient or by a health professional.

The principle of social justice is also based on certain assumptions:

- Health care is different from most other goods and services. Health-seeking behavior is governed primarily by need rather than by ability to pay.
- Responsibility for health is shared. Individuals are not held completely responsible for their condition because factors outside their control may have brought on the condition. Society is held responsible because individuals cannot control certain environmental factors, such as economic inequalities, unemployment, or unsanitary conditions.
- Society has an obligation to the collective good. The well-being of the community is superior to that of the individual. An unhealthy individual is a burden on society. A person carrying a deadly infection, for example, is a threat to society. Society, therefore, is obligated to cure the problem by providing health care to the individual, because, by doing so, the whole society would benefit.
- The government rather than the market can better decide through central planning how much health care to produce and how to distribute it among all citizens.

Just like true market justice does not exist in health care, true social justice also does not exist. This is because no society can afford to provide unlimited amounts of health care to all its citizens (Feldstein 1994). The government may offer insurance coverage to all, but subsequently has to find ways to limit the availability of certain health care services. For example, under social justice, the government decides how technology will be dispersed and who will be allowed access to certain types of costly high-tech services, even though basic services may be available to all. The government engages in *supply-side rationing*, which is also referred to as *planned rationing*, or nonprice rationing. In social justice systems, the government uses the term "health planning" to limit the supply of health care services, although the limited resources are often more equally dispersed throughout the country than is generally the case under a market justice system. It is because of the necessity to ration health care that citizens of a country can be given universal coverage but not universal access (see Chapter 1). Even when a covered individual has a medical need, depending on the nature of health services required, he or she may have to wait until services become available.

Justice in the US Health Delivery System

In a quasi- or imperfect market, which characterizes health care delivery in the United States, elements of both market and social justice exist. In some areas, the principles of market and social justice complement each other. In other areas, the two present conflicts.

The two contrasting principles complement each other with employer-based health insurance for most middle-class working Americans (market justice) and publicly financed Medicare, Medicaid, and CHIP coverage for certain disadvantaged groups (social justice). Insured populations access health care services delivered mainly by private practitioners and private institutions (market justice). Tax-supported county and city hospitals, public health clinics, and community health centers can be accessed by the uninsured in areas where such services are available (social justice).

Market and social justice principles create conflicts when health care resources are not uniformly distributed throughout the United States, and there is a general shortage of primary care physicians (discussed in Chapter 4). Consequently, in spite of having public insurance, many Medicaid-covered patients have difficulty obtaining timely access, particularly in rural and inner-city areas. In part, this conflict is created by artificially low reimbursement from public programs whereas reimbursement from private payers is more generous.

In the past, market justice principles have been dominant in the United States, but the ACA promises to change that and swing the pendulum more toward social justice. Massive new government subsidies are available to many people who would purchase private insurance through government-run exchanges. Medicaid is being expanded significantly for low-income families. These expansions will be paid through a number of new taxes provided for in the ACA. However, as pointed out in Chapter 1, The ACA is not designed to achieve universal coverage; it may also not successfully achieve access for a large segment of the US population, particularly if the providers are unable to meet the law's demands within reimbursement constraints.

Limitations of Market Justice

The principles of market justice work well in the allocation of economic goods when their unequal distribution does not affect the larger society. For example, based on individual success, people live in different sizes and styles of homes, drive different types of automobiles, and spend their money on a variety of things, but the allocation of certain resources has wider repercussions for society. In these areas, market justice has severe limitations:

1. Market justice principles fail to rectify critical human concerns. Pervasive social problems, such as crime, illiteracy, and homelessness, can significantly weaken the fabric of a society. Indeed, the United States has recognized such issues and instituted programs based on social justice to combat the problems through added police protection, publicly supported education, and subsidized housing for many of the poor and elderly. Health care is an important social issue because it not only affects human

productivity and achievement but also provides basic human dignity.

2. Market justice does not always protect a society. Individual health issues can have negative consequences for society because ill health is not always confined to the individual. The AIDS epidemic is an example in which society can be put at serious risk. Initial spread of the SARS epidemic in Beijing, China was largely due to patients with SARS symptoms being turned away by hospitals because they were not able to pay in advance for the cost of the treatment. Similar to clean air and water, health care is a social concern that, in the long run, protects against the burden of preventable disease and disability, a burden that is ultimately borne by society.

3. Market justice does not work well in health care delivery. A growing national economy and prosperity in the past did not materially reduce the number of uninsured Americans. On the other hand, the number of uninsured increases during economic downturns. For example, during the 2007–2009 recession, 5 million Americans lost employment-based health insurance (Holahan 2011).

Integration of Individual and Population Health

It has been recognized that typical emphasis on the treatment of acute illness in hospitals, biomedical research, and high technology has not significantly improved the population's health. Consequently, the medical model should be integrated with a disease-prevention, health-promotion, primary care–based model. Society will always need the benefits of modern science and technology for the treatment of disease, but disease prevention, health promotion, and primary care can prevent certain health problems, delay the onset of disease, and prevent disability and premature death. An integrated approach will improve the overall health of the population, enhance people's quality of life, and conserve health care resources.

The real challenge for the health care delivery system is to incorporate the medical and wellness models within the holistic context of health. The Ottawa Charter for Health Promotion, for instance, mentions caring, holism, and ecology as essential issues in developing strategies for health promotion (de Leeuw 1989). "Holism" and "ecology" refer to the complex relationships that exist among the individual; the health care delivery system; and the physical, social, cultural, and economic environmental factors. In addition, as the increasing body of research points out, the spiritual dimension must be incorporated into the integrated model.

Another equally important challenge for the health care delivery system is to focus on both individual and population health outcomes. The nature of health is complex, and the interrelationships among the physical, mental, social, and spiritual dimensions are not well understood. How to translate this multidimensional framework of health into specific actions that are efficiently configured to achieve better individual and community health is one of the greatest challenges health care systems face.

For an integrated approach to become reality, resource limitations make it necessary to deploy the best American ingenuity toward health-spending reduction, elimination of

Figure 2–5 Integrated Model for Holistic Health.

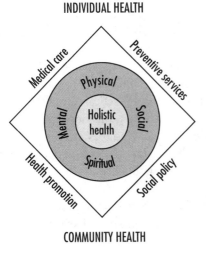

INDIVIDUAL HEALTH

COMMUNITY HEALTH

among public health agencies, hospitals, and other health care providers. Community hospitals, in particular, are increasingly held accountable for the health status of the communities in which they are located. To fulfill this mission, hospitals must first conduct a health assessment of their communities. Such assessments provide broad perspectives of the populations' health and point to specific needs that health care providers can address. These assessments can help pinpoint interventions that should be given priority to improve the populations' health status or address critical issues pertaining to certain groups within the populations.

Healthy People Initiatives

Since 1980, the United States has undertaken 10-year plans outlining certain key national health objectives to be accomplished during each of the 10-year periods. The objectives are developed by a consortium of national and state organizations under the leadership of the US Surgeon General. The first of these programs, with objectives for 1990, provided national goals for reducing premature deaths among all age groups and for reducing the average number of days of illness among those over the age of 65. A final review of this program concluded that positive changes in premature death had been achieved for all age categories except adolescents, and illness among the elderly had not been reduced. However, the review set the stage for development and modification of goals and objectives for the subsequent 10-year program (Chrvala and Bulger 1999).

Healthy People 2000: National Health Promotion and Disease Prevention Objectives identified three main goals to be reached by the year 2000: Increase the span of healthy life for Americans, reduce health disparities,

wasteful care, promotion of individual responsibility and accountability for one's health, and improved access to basic services. In a broad sense, these services include medical care, preventive services, health promotion, and social policy to improve education, lifestyle, employment, and housing (Figure 2–5). The Ottawa Charter has proposed achieving health objectives through social public policy and community action. An integrated approach also necessitates creation of a new model for training health care professionals by forming partnerships with the community (Henry 1993). The subsequent paragraphs describe examples of community partnership reflected in community health assessment and *Healthy People* initiatives.

Community Health Assessment

Community health assessment is a method used to conduct broad assessments of populations at a local or state level. For integrating individual and community health, the assessment is best conducted by collaboration and achieve access to preventive services by all Americans (DHHS 1992). According to the final review, the major accomplishments included surpassing the targets for reducing deaths from coronary heart disease and cancer; meeting the targets for incidence rates for AIDS and syphilis, mammography exams, violent deaths, and tobacco-related deaths; nearly meeting the targets for infant mortality and number of children with elevated levels of lead in blood; and making some progress toward reducing health disparities among special populations.

Healthy People 2010: Healthy People in Healthy Communities continued in the earlier traditions as an instrument to improve the health of the American people in the first decade of the 21st century. It focused on two broad goals: (1) to increase quality and years of healthy life and (2) to eliminate health disparities. It went a step beyond the previous initiatives by emphasizing the role of community partners—businesses; local governments; and civic, professional, and religious organizations—as effective agents for improving health in their local communities (DHHS 1998). The final report revealed that 23% of the targets were met or exceeded and the nation had made progress in 48% of the targets. Specifically, life expectancy at birth, expected years in good or better health, and expected years free of activity limitations all improved, while expected years free of selected chronic diseases decreased. However, the goal of reducing health disparities has not been achieved. Health disparities in about 80% of the objectives have not changed and even increased in another 13% of the objectives (NCHS 2012). Hence, challenges remain in the reduction of chronic conditions and health disparities among population groups.

Launched in 2010, *Healthy People 2020* (DHHS 2010b) has a five-fold mission: (1)

Identify nationwide health improvement priorities. (2) Increase public awareness and understanding of the determinants of health, disease, and disability and the opportunities for progress. (3) Provide measurable objectives and goals that can be used at the national, state, and local levels. (4) Engage multiple sectors to take actions that are driven by the best available evidence and knowledge. (5) Identify critical research and data collection needs. Its four overarching goals are to:

1. Attain high-quality, longer lives free of preventable disease, disability, injury, and premature death.

2. Achieve health equity, eliminate disparities, and improve the health of all groups.

3. Create social and physical environments that promote good health for all.

4. Promote quality of life, healthy development, and healthy behaviors across all life stages.

The overarching goals are in line with the tradition of earlier *Healthy People* initiatives but place particular emphasis on the determinants of health. Figure 2–6 illustrates the Action Model to Achieve *Healthy People 2020* Overarching Goals. This model illustrates that interventions (i.e., policies, programs, information) influence the determinants of health at four levels: (1) individual; (2) social, family, and community; (3) living and working conditions; and (4) broad social, economic, cultural, health, and environmental conditions, leading to improvement in outcomes. Results are to be demonstrated through assessment, monitoring, and evaluation, and the dissemination of findings would provide feedback for future interventions.

Figure 2–6 Action Model to Achieve US *Healthy People 2020* Overarching Goals.

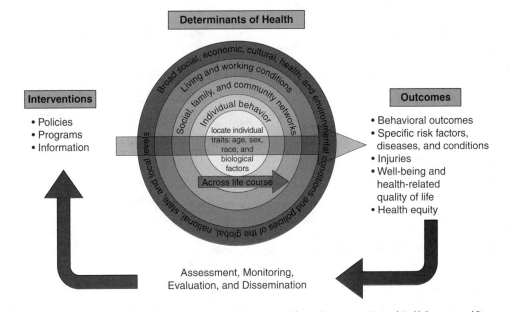

Source: Courtesy of U.S. Department of Health and Human Services. The Secretary's Advisory Committee on National Health Promotion and Disease Prevention Objectives for 2020. 2008. Phase I report: Recommendations for the framework and format of Healthy People 2020. Section IV. Advisory Committee findings and recommendations.

Healthy People 2020 is differentiated from previous *Healthy People* initiatives by including multiple new topic areas to its objective list, such as adolescent health, genomics, global health, health communication and health information technology, and social determinants of health. *Healthy People 2020* has 42 topic areas, with 13 new areas (underlined in Table 2–6).

Measurement of *Healthy People 2020*

Healthy People 2020 establishes four foundational health measures to monitor progress toward achieving its goals. The foundational health measures include general health status, health-related quality of life and well-being, determinants of health, and disparities. Measures of general health status include life expectancy, healthy life expectancy, years of potential life lost, physically and mentally unhealthy days, self-assessed health status, limitation of activity, and chronic disease prevalence. Measures of health-related quality of life and well-being include physical, mental, and social health-related quality of life; well-being/satisfaction; and participation in common activities. *Healthy People 2020* defines determinants of health as "a range of personal, social, economic, and environmental factors that influence health status. Determinants of health include such things as biology, genetics, individual behavior, access to health services, and the environment in which people are born, live, learn, play, work, and age." Measures of disparities and inequity include differences in health status based on race/ethnicity, gender, physical and mental ability, and geography (DHHS 2010b).

Table 2–6 List of *Healthy People 2020* Topic Areas

1. Access to Health Services
2. Adolescent Health
3. Arthritis, Osteoporosis, and Chronic Back Conditions
4. Blood Disorders and Blood Safety
5. Cancer
6. Chronic Kidney Disease
7. Dementias, Including Alzheimer's Disease
8. Diabetes
9. Disability and Health
10. Early and Middle Childhood
11. Educational and Community-Based Programs
12. Environmental Health
13. Family Planning
14. Food Safety
15. Genomics
16. Global Health
17. Health Communication and Health Information Technology
18. Healthcare-Associated Infections
19. Health-Related Quality of Life and Well-Being
20. Hearing and Other Sensory or Communication Disorders

21. Heart Disease and Stroke
22. HIV
23. Immunization and Infectious Diseases
24. Injury and Violence Prevention
25. Lesbian, Gay, Bisexual, and Transgender Health
26. Maternal, Infant, and Child Health
27. Medical Product Safety
28. Mental Health and Mental Disorders
29. Nutrition and Weight Status
30. Occupational Safety and Health
31. Older Adults
32. Oral Health
33. Physical Activity
34. Preparedness
35. Public Health Infrastructure
36. Respiratory Diseases
37. Sexually Transmitted Diseases
38. Sleep Health
39. Social Determinants of Health
40. Substance Abuse
41. Tobacco Use
42. Vision

Note: New areas are underlined.

There has been ongoing review of how well the health care system is working toward achievement of the delineated goals. The findings of these ongoing studies are compared to the baseline data from the beginning of the 10-year period to determine if adequate progress has occurred.

Global health is also an important topic area in *Healthy People 2020*. The measurement of global health focuses on two aspects. The first is to measure the reduction of global diseases in the United States including malaria and tuberculosis (TB). The second is to measure "global capacity in support of the International Health Regulations to detect and contain emerging health threats" (DHHS 2010b). The indicators include the number of Global Disease Detection (GDD) Regional Centers Worldwide, the number of public health professionals trained by GDD programs worldwide, and the number of diagnostic tests established or improved by GDD programs (DHHS 2010b).

Summary

The delivery of health care is primarily driven by the medical model, which emphasizes illness rather than wellness. Holistic concepts of health, along with the integration of medical care with preventive and health promotional efforts, need to be adopted to significantly improve the health of Americans. Such an approach would also require individual responsibility for one's own health-oriented behaviors, as well as community partnerships to improve both personal and community health. An understanding of the determinants of health, health education, community health assessment, and national initiatives, such as *Healthy People*, are essential to accomplishing these goals. *Healthy People 2020*, launched in 2010, continues its goals of improving health and eliminating disparities. Public health has gained increased importance because of a growing recognition of its role in health protection, environmental health, and preparedness for natural disasters and bioterrorism. Public health has now become global in its scope.

The various facets of health and its determinants, and ongoing initiatives in the areas of prevention, health promotion, health protection, and equality are complex undertakings and require substantial financial resources. Objective measures play a critical role in evaluating the success of various programs, as well as for directing future planning activities.

The broad concern about equitable access to health services is addressed by the contrasting theories of market justice and social justice. Countries offering universal coverage have adopted the principles of social justice under which the government finances health care services and decides on the distribution of those services. However, because no country can afford to provide unlimited amounts of health care to all citizens, supply-side rationing becomes inevitable. Many of the characteristics of the US health care system trace back to the beliefs and values underlying the American culture. The principles of market justice have been dominant, but social justice is also apparent in publicly financed programs and in the health reform initiatives under the ACA. Under market justice, not all citizens have health insurance coverage, a phenomenon called demand-side rationing.

ACA Takeaway

- Medicare and private health plans are required to cover a range of recommended preventive services with no out-of-pocket costs.
- The ACA has provided funds to expand preventive national efforts.
- Wellness grants are made available to small businesses to encourage wellness programs.
- The ACA will move US health care toward social justice. Yet, it is unlikely to achieve justice and equity in delivering access to health care for all Americans.

Terminology

Test Your Understanding

activities of daily
    living
acute condition
agent
bioterrorism
cases
chronic condition
community health
    assessment
crude rates
demand-side rationing
emigration
environment
environmental health
epidemic
fertility
health care

health determinants
health risk appraisal
holistic health
holistic medicine
host
iatrogenic illnesses
immigration
incidence
instrumental activities of
    daily living
life expectancy
market justice
medical model
migration
morbidity
mortality
natality

planned rationing
population at risk
prevalence
primary prevention
public health
quality of life
risk factor
secondary prevention
social contacts
social justice
social resources
subacute condition
supply-side rationing
surge capacity
tertiary prevention
utilization

Review Questions

1. What is the role of health risk appraisal in health promotion and disease prevention?

2. Health promotion and disease prevention may require both behavioral modification and therapeutic intervention. Discuss.

3. Discuss the definitions of health presented in this chapter in terms of their implications for the health care delivery system.

4. What are the main objectives of public health?

5. Discuss the significance of an individual's quality of life from the health care delivery perspective.

6. What "preparedness"-related measures have been taken to cope with potential natural and man-made disasters since the tragic events of 9/11? Assess their effectiveness.

7. The Blum model points to four key determinants of health. Discuss their implications for health care delivery.

8. What has been the main cause of the dichotomy in the way physical and mental health issues have traditionally been addressed by the health care delivery system?

9. Discuss the main cultural beliefs and values in American society that have influenced health care delivery and how they have shaped the health care delivery system.

10. Briefly describe the concepts of market justice and social justice. In what way do the two principles complement each other and in what way are they in conflict in the US system of health care delivery?

11. Describe how health care is rationed in the market justice and social justice systems.

12. To what extent do you think the objectives set forth in *Healthy People* initiatives can achieve the vision of an integrated approach to health care delivery in the United States?

13. What are the major differences of *Healthy People 2020* from the previous *Healthy People* initiatives?

14. How can health care administrators and policymakers use the various measures of health status and service utilization? Please illustrate your answer.

15. Using the data given in the table below:
    (a) Compute crude birth rates for 2005 and 2010.
    (b) Compute crude death rates for 2005 and 2010.
    (c) Compute cancer mortality rates for 2005 and 2010.
    (d) Answer the following questions:
        (i) Did the infant death rates improve between 2005 and 2010?
        (ii) What conclusions can you draw about the demographic change in this population?
        (iii) Have efforts to prevent death from heart disease been successful in this population?

Population	2005	2010
Total	248,710	262,755
Male	121,239	128,314
Female	127,471	134,441
Whites	208,704	218,086
Blacks	30,483	33,141
Number of live births	4,250	3,840
Number of infant deaths (birth to 1 year)	39	35
Number of total deaths	1,294	1,324
Deaths from heart disease	378	363
Deaths from cancer	336	342

REFERENCES

Agency for Healthcare Research and Quality. 2006. The Medical Expenditure Panel Survey. Available at: http://www.ahrq.gov/. Accessed December 2008.

American Institute for Cancer Research. 1996. *Food, nutrition and the prevention of cancer: A global perspective.* Washington, DC. Available at: http://www.aicr.org/site/PageServer. Accessed December 2000.

American Public Health Association. 2013. Prevention and Public Health Fund. Updated chart of Prevention and Public Health Fund allocations, FY 2010 enacted through FY 2014 request. Available at: http://www.apha.org/NR/rdonlyres/A448A5CD-6BFE-4AA5-B25D-DF59C195484E/0/PPH2010201441613.pdf. Accessed December 17, 2013.

Anderko, L., et al. 2012. Promoting prevention through the Affordable Care Act: Workplace wellness. *Preventing Chronic Disease* 9:E175.

Ansari, Z., et al. 2003. A public health model of the social determinants of health. *Sozial und Präventivmedizin/Social and Preventive Medicine* 48, no. 4: 242–251.

Blum, H.L. 1981. *Planning for health.* 2nd ed. New York: Human Sciences Press.

Bonnett, C., and B.C. Peery 2007. Surge capacity: A proposed conceptual framework. *The American Journal of Emergency Medicine* 25: 297–306.

Breslow, L. 1972. A quantitative approach to the World Health Organization definition of health: Physical, mental, and social well-being. *International Journal of Epidemiology* 4: 347–355.

Centers for Disease Control and Prevention (CDC). 1999. *Morbidity and mortality weekly report* 48, no. 29.

Centers for Disease Control and Prevention (CDC). 2007. Avian influenza (bird flu). Available at: http://www.cdc.gov/flu/avian/. Accessed January 2007.

Centers for Disease Control and Prevention (CDC). 2010a. Establishing a holistic framework to reduce inequities in HIV, Viral Hepatitis, STDs, and Tuberculosis in the United States. Available at: http://www.cdc.gov/socialdeterminants. Accessed November 2010.

Centers for Disease Control and Prevention (CDC). 2010b. Office of Public Health Preparedness and Response. Public health preparedness: Strengthening the Nation's emergency response state by state. Available at: http://www.bt.cdc.gov/publications/2010phprep. Accessed November 2010.

Centers for Disease Control and Prevention (CDC). 2012. SARS basics fact sheet. Available at: http://www.cdc.gov/sars/about/fs-SARS.html. Accessed October 2013.

Centers for Disease Control and Prevention (CDC). 2013a. National Diabetes Prevention Program. http://www.cdc.gov/diabetes/prevention/about.htm.

Centers for Disease Control and Prevention (CDC). 2013b. National Diabetes Prevention Program. Funded Organizations. Retrieved August 19, 2013 from http://www.cdc.gov/diabetes/prevention/foa/index.htm.

Chida, Y., et al. 2009. Religiosity/spirituality and mortality. *Pshychotherapy and Psychosomatics* 78: 81–90.

Cohen, M.H. 2003. *Future Medicine.* Ann Arbor: University of Michigan Press.

Cohen, S., and K. Mulvaney. 2005. Field observations: Disaster medical assistance team response for Hurricane Charley, Punta Gorda, Florida, 2004. *Disaster Management and Response*, 22–27.

Chrvala, C.A., and R.J. Bulger (Eds.). 1999. *Leading health indicators for Healthy People 2010: Final report*. Washington, DC: National Academy of Sciences.

Dahlgren, G., and M. Whitehead. 2006. European strategies for tackling social inequities in health: Concepts and principles for tackling social inequities in health: Levelling up (part 2). Denmark: World Health Organization: Studies on Social and Economic Determinants of Population Health no. 3. Available at: http://www.euro.who.int/__data/assets/pdf_file/0018/103824/ E89384.pdf. Accessed December 2010.

Davis, D.L., and P.S. Webster. 2002. The social context of science: Cancer and the environment. *The Annals of the American Academy of Political and Social Science* 584, November 13–34.

de Leeuw, E. 1989. Concepts in health promotion: The notion of relativism. *Social Science and Medicine* 29, no. 11: 1281–1288.

Department of Health and Human Services (DHHS). 1992. *Healthy People 2000: National health promotion and disease prevention objectives*. Boston: Jones & Bartlett Publishers.

Department of Health and Human Services (DHHS). 1998. *Healthy People 2010 objectives: Draft for public comment*. Washington, DC: US Government Printing Office.

Department of Health and Human Services (DHHS). 2004. *The health consequences of smoking: A report of the Surgeon General*. Available at: http://www.surgeongeneral.gov/library /smokingconsequences/. Accessed December 2010.

Department of Health and Human Services (DHHS). 2006. DASH Eating Plan. Available at: http://www .nhlbi.nih.gov/health/public/heart/hbp/dash/new_dash.pdf. Accessed December 17, 2013.

Department of Health and Human Services (DHHS). 2010a. *Summary of the prevention and wellness initiative*. Available at: http://http://www.cdc.gov/chronicdisease/recovery/docs/PW_Community_ fact_sheet_final.pdf. Accessed November 2010.

Department of Health and Human Services (DHHS). 2010b. *Healthy People 2020*. Available at: http://healthypeople.gov/2020. Accessed December 2010.

Department of Health and Human Services (DHHS). 2011a. *National Health Security Strategy 2009*. Available at: http://www.phe.gov/Preparedness/planning/authority/nhss/Pages/default.aspx. Accessed August 2013.

Department of Health and Human Services (DHHS). 2011b. $10 million in Affordable Care Act funds to help create workplace health programs. News Release. June 23, 2011. Available at: http://www.hhs.gov/news/press/2011pres/06/20110623a.html. Accessed December 17, 2013.

Department of Health and Human Services (DHHS). 2012. *Medicare Preventive Services*. Available at: http://www.hhs.gov/healthcare/prevention/seniors/medicare-preventive-services.html. Accessed August 2013.

Department of Health and Human Services (DHHS). 2013. Affordable Care Act rules on expanding access to preventive services for women. Available at: http://www.hhs.gov/healthcare/facts/ factsheets/2011/08/womensprevention08012011a.html. Accessed December 17, 2013.

Dever, G.E. 1984. *Epidemiology in health service management*. Gaithersburg, MD: Aspen Publishers, Inc.

Draper, P. 2012. An integrative review of spiritual assessment: Implications for nursing management. *Journal of Nursing Management* 20, no. 8: 970–980.

Ethics Committee, Society for Academic Emergency Medicine. 1992. An ethical foundation for health care: An emergency medicine perspective. *Annals of Emergency Medicine* 21, no. 11: 1381–1387.

Feldstein, P.J. 1994. *Health policy issues: An economic perspective on health reform.* Ann Arbor, MI: AUPHA/HAP.

Ferguson, C.E., and S.C. Maurice. 1970. *Economic analysis.* Homewood, IL: Richard D. Irwin.

Friedman, G.D. 1980. *Primer of epidemiology.* New York: McGraw-Hill.

Grossman, M. 1972. On the concept of health capital and the demand for health. *Journal of Political Economy* 80, no. 2: 223–255.

Hatch, R.L., et al. 1998. The spiritual involvement and beliefs scale: Development and testing of a new instrument. *Journal of Family Practice* 46: 476–486.

Henry, R.C. 1993. Community partnership model for health professions education. *Journal of the American Podiatric Medical Association* 83, no. 6: 328–331.

Hick, J., et al. 2004. Health care facility and community strategies for patient care surge capacity. *Annals of Emergency Medicine, 44*, 253–261.

Hoff, A., et al. 2008. Religion and reduced cancer risk—what is the explanation? A review. *European Journal of Cancer* 44, no. 17: 2573–2579.

Holahan, J. 2011. The 2007-09 recession and health insurance coverage. *Health Affairs* 30, no. 1: 145–152.

Ibrahim, M.A. 1985. *Epidemiology and health policy.* Gaithersburg, MD: Aspen Publishers, Inc.

Institute of Medicine, National Academy of Sciences (IOM). 1988. *The future of public health.* Washington, DC: National Academies Press.

Jonsen, A.R. 1986. Bentham in a box: Technology assessment and health care allocation. *Law, Medicine, and Health Care* 14, no. 3–4: 172–174.

Kane, R.L. 1988. Empiric approaches to prevention in the elderly: Are we promoting too much? In: *Health promotion and disease prevention in the elderly.* R. Chernoff and D.A. Lipschitz, eds. New York: Raven Press. p. 127–141.

Katz, S., and C.A. Akpom. 1979. A measure of primary sociobiological functions. In: *Sociomedical health indicators.* J. Elinson and A.E. Siegman, eds. Farmingdale, NY: Baywood Publishing Co. p. 127–141.

Kawachi, I., et al. 1997. Social capital, income inequality, and mortality. *American Journal of Public Health* 87: 1491–1498.

Kawachi, I., et al. 1999. Social capital and self-rated health: A contextual analysis. *American Journal of Public Health* 89: 1187–1193.

Kearns, R., et al. 2013. Disaster planning: Transportation resources and considerations for managing a burn disaster. *Journal of Burn Care and Research,* 1–12.

Kristol, I. 1978. A capitalist conception of justice. In: *Ethics, free enterprise, and public policy: Original essays on moral issues in business.* R.T. De George and J.A. Pichler, eds. New York: Oxford University Press. p. 57–69.

Lasker, R.D. 1997. *Medicine and public health: The power of collaboration.* New York: The New York Academy of Medicine.

Larson, C., and Mercer A. Global health indicators: An overview. *CMAJ.* no. 171–10: 1199–200.

Macfarlane, G.J., and A.B. Lowenfels. 1994. Physical activity and colon cancer. *European Journal of Cancer Prevention* 3, no. 5: 393–398.

Marwick, C. 1995. Should physicians prescribe prayer for health? Spiritual aspects of well-being considered. *Journal of the American Medical Association* 273, no. 20: 1561–1562.

McKee, M. 2001. Measuring the efficiency of health systems. *British Medical Journal* 323, no. 7308: 295–296.

Monod, S., et al. 2011. Instruments measuring spirituality in clinical research: A systematic review. *Journal of General Internal Medicine* 26, no. 11: 1345–1357.

National Center for Health Statistics (NCHS). 2012. *Healthy People 2010 Final Review.* Hyattsville, MD. Available at: http://www.cdc.gov/nchs/healthy_people/hp2010/hp2010_final_review.htm. Accessed August 2013.

National Prevention Council. 2011. *Nation prevention strategy: America's plan for better health and wellness.* Washington, DC: US Department of Health and Human Services.

Oman, D., et al. 2002. Religious attendance and cause of death over 31 years. *International Journal of Psychiatry and Medicine* 32: 69–89.

Ostir, G.V., et al. 1999. Disability in older adults 1: Prevalence, causes, and consequences. *Behavioral Medicine* 24, no. 4: 147–156.

Pantell, M., et al. 2013. Social isolation: A predictor of mortality comparable to traditional clinical risk factors. *American Journal of Public Health* 103, no. 11: 2056–2062.

Parsons, T. 1972. Definitions of health and illness in the light of American values and social structure. In: *Patients, physicians and illness: A sourcebook in behavioral science and health.* 2nd ed. E.G. Jaco, ed. New York: Free Press.

Partnership to Fight Chronic Disease (PFCD). 2009. *Almanac of Chronic Disease.* Available at: http://www.fightchronicdisease.org/sites/fightchronicdisease.org/files/docs/2009AlmanacofChronicDisease_updated81009.pdf. Accessed December 17, 2013.

Pasley, B.H., et al. 1995. Excess acute care bed capacity and its causes: The experience of New York State. *Health Services Research* 30, no. 1: 115–131.

Peters, K.E., et al. 2001. *Cooperative actions for health programs: Lessons learned in medicine and public health collaboration.* Chicago: American Medical Association.

Pincus, T., et al. 1998. Social conditions and self-management are more powerful determinants of health than access to care. *Annals of Internal Medicine* 129, no. 5: 406–411.

Plotkin, S.L., and S.A. Plotkin. 1999. A short history of vaccination. In: *Vaccines,* 3rd ed. S.A. Plotkin and W.A. Orenstein, eds. Philadelphia, PA: W.B. Saunders.

Post, S.G., et al. 2000. Physicians and patient spirituality: Professional boundaries, competency, and ethics. *Annals of Internal Medicine* 132, no. 7: 578–583.

Reinhardt, U.E. 1994. Providing access to health care and controlling costs: The universal dilemma. In: *The nation's health,* 4th ed. P.R. Lee and C.L. Estes, eds. Boston: Jones & Bartlett Publishers. p. 263–278.

Robert Wood Johnson Foundation. 2010. *Chronic care: Making the case for ongoing care.* Available at: http://www.rwjf.org/pr/product.jsp?id=50968. Accessed April 25, 2011.

Roberts, J.A., et al. 1997. Factors influencing the views of patients with gynecologic cancer about end-of-life decisions. *American Journal of Obstetrics and Gynecology* 176: 166–172.

Rosen, G. 1993. *A history of public health.* Baltimore, MD: Johns Hopkins University Press.

Ross, L. 1995. The spiritual dimension: Its importance to patients' health, well-being and quality of life and its implications for nursing practice. *International Journal of Nursing Studies* 32, no. 5: 457–468.

Santerre, R.E., and S.P. Neun. 1996. *Health economics: Theories, insights, and industry studies.* Chicago: Irwin.

Saward, E., and A. Sorensen. 1980. The current emphasis on preventive medicine. In: *Issues in health services.* S.J. Williams, ed. New York: John Wiley & Sons. p. 17–29.

Schneider, M.J. 2000. *Introduction to public health.* Gaithersburg, MD: Aspen Publishers, Inc.

Shi, L., and J. Johnson, eds. 2014. *Public health administration: Principles for population-based management.* 3rd ed. Burlington, MA: Jones & Bartlett Learning.

Shi, L., and B. Starfield. 2001. Primary care physician supply, income inequality, and racial mortality in US metropolitan areas. *American Journal of Public Health* 91, no. 8: 1246–1250.

Shi, L., et al. 1999. Income inequality, primary care, and health indicators. *Journal of Family Practice* 48, no. 4: 275–284.

Shi, L., et al. 2002. Primary care, self-rated health, and reduction in social disparities in health. *Health Services Research* 37, no. 3: 529–550.

Smith, B.C. 1979. *Community health: An epidemiological approach.* New York: Macmillan Publishing Co. p. 197–213.

Stopford, B. 2005. The National Disaster Medical System—America's medical readiness force. *Disaster Management and Response*, 53–56.

Swanson, C.S. 1995. A spirit-focused conceptual model of nursing for the advanced practice nurse. *Issues in Comprehensive Pediatric Nursing* 18, no. 4: 267–275.

Timmreck, T.C. 1994. *An introduction to epidemiology.* Boston: Jones & Bartlett Publishers.

Turnock, B.J. 1997. *Public health: What it is and how it works.* Gaithersburg, MD: Aspen Publishers, Inc.

US Census Bureau. 1995. Population profile of the United States 1995. Available at: http://www .census.gov/population/pop-profile/p23-189.pdf. Accessed December 17, 2013.

Vella-Brodrick, D.A., and F.C. Allen. 1995. Development and psychometric validation of the mental, physical, and spiritual well-being scale. *Psychological Reports* 77, no. 2: 659–674.

Ward, B. 1995. Holistic medicine. *Australian Family Physician* 24, no. 5: 761–762, 765.

Ward, B.W., and J.S. Schiller. 2010. Prevalence of multiple chronic conditions among US adults: Estimates from the National Health Interview Survey. *Preventing Chronic Diseases* 10: 120203.

Wilkinson, R.G. 1997. Comment: Income, inequality, and social cohesion. *American Journal of Public Health* 87: 1504–1506.

WHO Commission on Social Determinants of Health. 2007. *A Conceptual Framework for Action on the Social Determinants of Health.* Geneva, Switzerland: World Health Organization. Available at: http://www.who.int/social_determinants/resources/csdh_framework_action_05_07.pdf. Accessed November 4, 2009.

World Health Organization (WHO). 1948. *Preamble to the constitution.* Geneva, Switzerland: Author.

World Health Organization (WHO). 2003. *WHO definition of palliative care.* Geneva, Switzerland: Author.

World Health Organization (WHO). 2011. *Noncommunicable diseases country profiles.* Available at: http://www.who.int/nmh/countries/usa_en.pdf. Accessed August 2013.

World Health Organization (WHO). 2013. *Pandemic influenza preparedness framework.* Available at: http://www.who.int/influenza/resources/pip_framework/en/. Accessed August 2013.

Chapter 3

The Evolution of Health Services in the United States

Learning Objectives

- To discover historical developments that have shaped the US health care delivery system
- To evaluate why the system was resistant to national health insurance reforms during the 1900s
- To explore developments associated with the corporatization of health care
- To provide a historical perspective on health care reform under the Affordable Care Act

"Where's the market?"

Introduction

Delivery of health care in the United States evolved quite differently from the systems in Europe. The US health care system has been shaped by anthro-cultural values (discussed in Chapter 2) and the social, political, and economic antecedents. This chapter discusses how these forces have been instrumental in shaping the current structure of medical services and its ongoing evolution. Because social, political, and economic contexts are not static, their shifting influences lend a certain dynamism to the health care delivery system. Conversely, cultural beliefs and values remain relatively stable over time. Consequently, in the American experience, initiatives toward a government-run national health care program have failed to make significant inroads. Rather, the interaction of forces just mentioned led to certain compromises that resulted in incremental changes over time. Incremental changes, both small and large, since 1935 have gradually shifted US health care from mainly a private enterprise to one in which both private and public sectors have a substantial role in financing and insurance of health care for different population groups in the United States.

More recently, the Affordable Care Act (ACA) promises to bring about the most sweeping change in US health care since the creation of Medicare and Medicaid programs in 1965. Historically, traditional American beliefs and values have been instrumental in opposing any attempts to initiate fundamental changes in the financing and delivery of health care. Ironically, the political maneuvering that led to the passage of the ACA in 2010 (see Chapter 13) did not represent consensus among Americans on basic values and ethics in the enactment of a major health system reform. Hence, the nation is deeply divided over issues of health care and its financing. Therefore, the ultimate effects of the ACA are still unknown.

American medicine did not emerge as a professional entity until the beginning of the 20th century, with the progress in biomedical science. Since then, the US health care delivery system has been a growth enterprise. The growth of medical science and technology (discussed in Chapter 5) has also played a key role in shaping the US health care delivery system. Advancement of technology has influenced other factors as well, such as medical education, growth of alternative settings of health services delivery, and corporatization of medicine in both national and global contexts. Many of these are recent developments.

This chapter traces the evolution of health care delivery through historical phases, each demarcating a major change in the structure of the delivery system. The first evolutionary phase is the preindustrial era from the middle of the 18th century to the latter part of the 19th century. The second phase is the postindustrial era beginning in the late 19th century. The third phase—called the corporate era—began in the latter part of the 19th century and is marked by the growth of managed care, organizational integration, the information revolution, and globalization. The fourth phase, which is still in its infancy, is characterized by what is referred to as health care reform, recently brought about by the ACA.

The practice of medicine is central to the delivery of health care; therefore, a portion of this chapter is devoted to tracing the transformations in medical practice from a weak and insecure trade to an independent, highly respected, and lucrative profession.

Developments since the corporatization stage, however, have made a significant impact on practice styles and have compromised the autonomy that physicians had historically enjoyed. Heightened government regulations and oversight under the ACA are likely to put further operational and financial constraints on medical organizations and physicians. Figure 3–1 provides a snapshot of the historical developments in US health care delivery.

Medical Services in the Preindustrial Era

From colonial times to the beginning of the 20th century, American medicine lagged behind the advances in medical science, experimental research, and medical education that were taking place in Britain, France, and Germany. While London, Paris, and Berlin were flourishing as major research centers, Americans had a tendency to neglect research in basic sciences and to place more emphasis on applied science (Shryock 1966). In addition, American attitudes about medical treatment placed strong emphasis on natural history and conservative common sense (Stevens 1971). Consequently, the practice of medicine in the United States had a strong domestic, rather than professional, character. Medical services, when deemed appropriate by the consumer, were purchased out of one's private funds, because there was no health insurance. The health care market

Figure 3–1 Evolution of the US Health Care Delivery System.

Development of science and technology

Mid-18th to late 19th century	Late 19th to late 20th century	Late 20th to 21st century
• Open entry into medical practice	• Scientific basis of medicine	• **Corporatization**
• Intense competition	• Urbanization	Managed care
• Weak and unorganized profession	• Emergence of the modern hospital	Organizational integration
• Apprenticeship training	• Emergence of organized medicine	Diluted physician autonomy
• Undeveloped hospitals	• Reform of medical training	• **Information revolution**
• Almshouses and pesthouses	• Licensing	Telemedicine
• Dispensaries	• Specialization in medicine	E-health
• Mental asylums	• Development of public health	Patient empowerment
• Private payment for services	• Community mental health	• **Globalization**
• Low demand for services	• Birth of workers' compensation	Global telemedicine
• Private medical schools providing only general education	• Emergence of private insurance	Medical tourism
	• Failure of national health insurance	Foreign investment in health care
	• Medicaid and Medicare	Migration of professionals
	• Prototypes of managed care	Spread of infectious diseases
		• **Corporate dominance**
		Era of health care reform
Consumer sovereignty	Professional dominance	Government dominance

Beliefs and values/Social, economic, and political constraints

was characterized by competition among providers, and the consumer decided who the provider would be. Thus, the consumer was sovereign in the health care market and health care was delivered under free-market conditions.

Five main factors explain why the medical profession remained largely an insignificant trade in preindustrial America:

1. Medical practice was in disarray.
2. Medical procedures were primitive.
3. An institutional core was missing.
4. Demand was unstable.
5. Medical education was substandard.

Medical Practice in Disarray

The early practice of medicine could be regarded more as a trade than a profession. It did not require the rigorous course of study, clinical practice, residency training, board exams, or licensing without which it is impossible to practice today. At the close of the Civil War (1861–1865), "anyone who had the inclination to set himself up as a physician could do so, the exigencies of the market alone determining who would prove successful in the field and who would not" (Hamowy 1979). The clergy, for example, often combined medical services and religious duties. The generally well educated clergyman or government official was more learned in medicine than physicians were at the time (Shryock 1966). Tradesmen, such as tailors, barbers, commodity merchants, and those engaged in numerous other trades, also practiced the healing arts by selling herbal prescriptions, nostrums, elixirs, and cathartics. Midwives, homeopaths, and naturalists could also practice medicine without restriction. The red-and-white striped poles (symbolizing blood and bandages) seen outside barbershops are reminders that barbers also functioned as surgeons at one time, using the same blade to cut hair, shave beards, and bleed the sick.

This era of medical pluralism has been referred to as a "war zone" by Kaptchuk and Eisenberg (2001) because it was marked by bitter antagonism among the various practicing sects. Later, in 1847, the American Medical Association (AMA) was founded with the main purpose of erecting a barrier between orthodox practitioners and the "irregulars" (Rothstein 1972).

In the absence of minimum standards of medical training, entry into private practice was relatively easy for both trained and untrained practitioners, creating intense competition. Medicine as a profession was weak and unorganized. Hence, physicians did not enjoy the prestige, influence, and incomes that they later earned. Many physicians found it necessary to engage in a second occupation because income from medical practice alone was inadequate to support a family. It is estimated that most physicians' incomes in the mid-19th century placed them at the lower end of the middle class (Starr 1982). It is estimated that in 1830 there were 6,800 physicians serving primarily the upper classes (Gabe et al. 1994). It was not until 1870 that medical education was reformed and licensing laws were passed in the United States.

Primitive Medical Procedures

Up until the mid-1800s, medical care was based more on primitive medical traditions than science. In the absence of diagnostic tools, a theory of "intake and outgo" served as an explanation for all diseases

(Rosenberg 1979). It was believed that diseases needed to be expelled from the body. Hence, bleeding, use of emetics (to induce vomiting) and diuretics (to increase urination), and purging with enemas and purgatives (to clean the bowels) were popular forms of clinical therapy.

When George Washington became ill with an inflamed throat in 1799, he too was bled by physicians. One of the attending physicians argued, unsuccessfully, in favor of making an incision to open the trachea, which today would be considered a more enlightened procedure. The bleeding most likely weakened Washington's resistance, and historians have debated whether it played a role in his death (Clark 1998).

Surgeries were limited because anesthesia had not yet been developed and antiseptic techniques were not known. Stethoscopes and X-rays had not been discovered, clinical thermometers were not in use, and microscopes were not available for a better understanding of pathology. Physicians relied mainly on their five senses and experience to diagnose and treat medical problems. Hence, in most cases, physicians did not possess any technical expertise greater than that of the mothers and grandparents at home or experienced neighbors in the community.

Missing Institutional Core

In the United States, no widespread development of hospitals occurred before the 1880s. A few isolated hospitals were either built or developed in rented private houses in large cities, such as Philadelphia, New York, Boston, Cincinnati, New Orleans, and St. Louis. By contrast, general hospital expansion began much before the 1800s in France and Britain (Stevens 1971).

In Europe, medical professionals were closely associated with hospitals. New advances in medical science were being pioneered, which European hospitals readily adopted. The medical profession came to be supremely regarded because of its close association with an establishment that was scientifically advanced. In contrast, American hospitals played only a small part in medical practice because most hospitals served a social welfare function by taking care of the poor, those without families, or those who were away from home on travel.

The Almshouse and the Pesthouse

In the United States, the *almshouse,* also called a poorhouse, was the common ancestor of both hospitals and nursing homes. The poorhouse program was adopted from the Elizabethan system of public charity based on English Poor Laws. The first poorhouse in the United States is recorded to have opened in 1660 in Boston (Wagner 2005). Almshouses served, primarily, general welfare functions by providing food and shelter to the destitute of society. Therefore, the main function of the almshouse was custodial. Caring for the sick was incidental because some of the residents would inevitably become ill and would be cared for in an adjoining infirmary. Almshouses were unspecialized institutions that admitted poor and needy persons of all kinds: the elderly, the orphaned, the insane, the ill, and the disabled. Hence, the early hospital-type institutions emerged mainly to take care of indigent people whose families could not care for them.

Another type of institution, the *pesthouse*, was operated by local governments to quarantine people who had contracted a contagious disease, such as cholera, smallpox, typhoid, or yellow fever. Located primarily in seaports, the primary function of a pesthouse was to isolate people with contagious diseases so disease would not spread among the inhabitants of a city. These institutions were the predecessors of contagious-disease and tuberculosis hospitals.

The Dispensary

Dispensaries were established as outpatient clinics, independent of hospitals, to provide free care to those who could not afford to pay. Urban workers and their families often depended on such charity (Rosen 1983).

Starting with Philadelphia in 1786, dispensaries gradually spread to other cities. They were private institutions, financed by bequests and voluntary subscriptions. Their main function was to provide basic medical care and to dispense drugs to ambulatory patients (Raffel 1980). Generally, young physicians and medical students desiring clinical experience staffed these dispensaries, as well as hospital wards, on a part-time basis for little or no income (Martensen 1996), which served a dual purpose. It provided needed services to the poor and enabled both physicians and medical students to gain experience diagnosing and treating a variety of cases. Later, as the practice of specialized medicine, as well as teaching and research, was transferred to hospital settings, many dispensaries were gradually absorbed into hospitals as outpatient departments. Indeed, outpatient or ambulatory care departments became an important locale for specialty consultation services within large hospitals (Raffel 1980).

The Mental Asylum

Mental health care was seen, primarily, as the responsibility of state and local governments. At this time, little was known about what caused mental illness or how to treat it. Although some mental health patients were confined to almshouses, asylums were built by states for patients with untreatable, chronic mental illness. The first such asylum was built around 1770 in Williamsburg, Virginia. When the Pennsylvania Hospital opened in Philadelphia in 1752, its basement was used as a mental asylum. Attendants in these asylums employed physical and psychological techniques in an effort to return patients to some level of rational thinking. Techniques such as bleeding, forced vomiting, and hot and ice-cold baths were also used. Between 1894 and World War I, the State Care Acts were passed, centralizing financial responsibility for mentally ill patients in every state government. Local governments took advantage of this opportunity to send all those with a mental illness, including dependent, older citizens, to the state asylums. The quality of care in public asylums deteriorated rapidly, as overcrowding and underfunding ran rampant (US Surgeon General 1999).

The Dreaded Hospital

Not until the 1850s were hospitals similar to those in Europe developed in the United States. These early hospitals had deplorable conditions due to a lack of resources. Poor sanitation and inadequate ventilation were hallmarks of these hospitals. Unhygienic practices prevailed because nurses were unskilled and untrained. These early hospitals had an undesirable image of being houses of death. The mortality rate among hospital patients, both in Europe and America, stood around 74% in the 1870s (Falk 1999). People went into hospitals because of dire consequences, not by personal choice. It is not hard to imagine why members of the middle and upper classes, in particular, shunned such establishments.

Unstable Demand

Professional services suffered from low demand in the mainly rural, preindustrial society, and much of the medical care was provided by people who were not physicians. The most competent physicians were located in more populated communities (Bordley and Harvey 1976). In the small communities of rural America, a spirit of strong self-reliance prevailed. Families and communities were accustomed to treating the sick, often using folk remedies passed from one generation to the next. It was also common to consult published books and pamphlets that gave advice on home remedies (Rosen 1983).

The market for physicians' services was also limited by economic conditions. Many families could not afford to pay for medical services. Two factors contributed to the high cost associated with obtaining professional medical care: (1) The indirect costs of transportation and the "opportunity cost" of travel (i.e., forgone value of time that could have been used for something more productive) could easily outweigh the direct costs of physicians' fees. (2) The costs of travel often doubled because two people, the physician and an emissary, had to make the trip back and forth. For a farmer, a trip of 10 miles into town could mean an entire day's work lost. Farmers had to cover travel costs and the opportunity cost of time spent traveling. Mileage charges amounted to four or five times the basic fee for a visit if a physician had to travel 5 to 10 miles. Hence, most families obtained only occasional

intervention from physicians, generally for nonroutine and severe conditions (Starr 1982).

Personal health services had to be purchased without the help of government or private insurance. Private practice and *fee for service*—the practice of billing separately for each individual type of service performed—was firmly embedded in American medical care. Similar to physicians, dentists were private entrepreneurs who made their living by private fee-for-service dental practice, but their services were not in great demand because there was little public concern about dental health (Anderson 1990).

Substandard Medical Education

From about 1800 to 1850, medical training was largely received through individual apprenticeship with a practicing physician, referred to as a preceptor, rather than through university education. Many of the preceptors were themselves poorly trained, especially in basic medical sciences (Rothstein 1972). By 1800, only four small medical schools were operating in the United States: College of Philadelphia (whose medical school was established in 1756, and which later became the University of Pennsylvania), King's College (whose medical school was established in 1768, and which later became Columbia University), Harvard Medical School (opened in 1782), and the Geisel School of Medicine at Dartmouth College (started in 1797).

American physicians later initiated the establishment of medical schools in large numbers. This was partly to enhance professional status and prestige and partly to enhance income. Medical schools were inexpensive to operate and often quite profitable. All that was required was a faculty of four or more physicians, a classroom, a back room to conduct dissections, and legal authority to confer degrees. Operating expenses were met totally out of student fees that were paid directly to the physicians (Rothstein 1972). Physicians would affiliate with a local college for the conferral of degrees and use of classroom facilities. Large numbers of men entered medical practice as education in medicine became readily available and unrestricted entry into the profession was still possible (Hamowy 1979). Gradually, as physicians from medical schools began to outnumber those from the apprenticeship system, the Doctor of Medicine (MD) degree became the standard of competence. The number of medical schools tripled between 1800 and 1820 and tripled again between 1820 and 1850, numbering 42 in 1850 (Rothstein 1972). Academic preparation gradually replaced apprenticeship training.

At this point, medical education in the United States was seriously deficient in science-based training, unlike European medical schools. Medical schools in the United States did not have laboratories, and clinical observation and practice were not part of the curriculum. In contrast, European medical schools, particularly those in Germany, were emphasizing laboratory-based medical research. At the University of Berlin, for example, professors were expected to conduct research, as well as teach, and were paid by the state. In American medical schools, students were taught by local practitioners, who were ill-equipped in education and training. Unlike Europe, where medical education was financed and regulated by the government, proprietary medical schools in the United States set their own standards (Numbers and Warner 1985). A year of medical school in the United States generally lasted only 4 months and required only

2 years for graduation. In addition, American medical students customarily repeated the same courses they had taken during their first year again during their second year (Numbers and Warner 1985; Rosner 2001). The physicians' desire to keep their schools profitable also contributed to low standards and a lack of rigor. It was feared that higher standards in medical education would drive enrollments down, which could force the schools into bankruptcy (Starr 1982).

Medical Services in the Postindustrial Era

In the postindustrial period, American physicians, unlike other physicians in the world, were highly successful in retaining private practice of medicine and resisting national health care. Physicians delivered scientifically and technically advanced services to insured patients; became an organized medical profession; and gained power, prestige, and financial success. Notably, much of this transformation occurred in the aftermath of the Civil War. Social and scientific changes in the period following the war were accompanied by a transition from a rural, agricultural economy to a system of industrial capitalism. Mass production techniques used in the war were applied to peacetime industries. Railroads linked the east and west coasts, and small towns became cities (Stevens 1971).

The American system for delivering health care took its current shape during this period. The well defined role of employers in providing workers' compensation for work-related injuries and illnesses, together with other economic considerations, was instrumental in the growth of private health insurance. Even though attempts to pass national health care legislation failed, rising costs of health care prompted Congress to create the publicly financed programs, such as Medicare and Medicaid, for the most vulnerable members of society. Cost considerations also motivated the formation of prototypes for modern managed care organizations (MCOs).

Growth of Professional Sovereignty

The 1920s may well mark the consolidation of physicians' professional power. During and after World War I, physicians' incomes grew sharply, and their prominence as a profession finally emerged. This prestige and power, however, did not materialize overnight. Through the years, several factors interacted in the gradual transformation of medicine from a weak, insecure, and isolated trade into a profession of power and authority. Seven key factors contributed to this transformation:

1. Urbanization
2. Science and technology
3. Institutionalization
4. Dependency
5. Autonomy and organization
6. Licensing
7. Educational reform

Urbanization

Urbanization created increased reliance on the specialized skills of paid professionals. First, it distanced people from their families and neighborhoods where family-based care was traditionally given. Women began working outside the home and could no longer care for sick members of the family. Second, physicians became less expensive to consult as telephones, automobiles, and paved roads reduced the opportunity cost of time and travel and medical care became more affordable. Urban development attracted more and more Americans to the growing towns and cities. In 1840, only 11% of the US population lived in urban areas; by 1900, the proportion of the US population living in urban areas grew to 40% (Stevens 1971). The trend away from home visits to office practice also began to develop around this time (Rosen 1983). Physicians moved to cities and towns in large numbers to be closer to their growing markets. Better geographic proximity of patients enabled physicians to see more patients in a given amount of time. Whereas physicians in 1850 only saw an average of 5 to 7 patients a day, by the early 1940s, the average patient load of general practitioners had risen to 18 to 22 patients a day (Starr 1982).

Science and Technology

Exhibit 3–1 summarizes some of the groundbreaking scientific discoveries in medicine. Advances in bacteriology, antiseptic surgery, anesthesia, immunology, and diagnostic techniques, along with an expanding repertoire of new drugs, gave medicine an aura of legitimacy and complexity, and the therapeutic effectiveness of scientific medicine became widely recognized.

When advanced technical knowledge becomes essential to practice a profession and the benefits of professional services are widely recognized, a greater acceptance and a legitimate need for the services of that profession are simultaneously created. *Cultural authority* refers to the general acceptance of and reliance on the judgment of the members of a profession (Starr 1982) because of their superior knowledge and expertise. Cultural authority legitimizes a profession in the eyes of common people.

Exhibit 3–1 Groundbreaking Medical Discoveries

- The discovery of anesthesia was instrumental in advancing the practice of surgery. Nitrous oxide (laughing gas) was first employed as an anesthetic around 1846 for tooth extraction by Horace Wells, a dentist. Ether anesthesia for surgery was first successfully used in 1846 at the Massachusetts General Hospital. Before anesthesia was discovered, strong doses of alcohol were used to dull the sensations. A surgeon who could do procedures, such as limb amputations, in the shortest length of time was held in high regard.
- Around 1847, Ignaz Semmelweis, a Hungarian physician practicing in a hospital in Vienna, implemented the policy of handwashing. Thus, an aseptic technique was born. Semmelweis was concerned about the high death rate from puerperal fever among women after childbirth. Even though the germ theory of disease was unknown at this time, Semmelweis surmised that there might be a connection between puerperal fever and the common practice by medical students of not washing their hands before delivering babies and right after doing dissections. Semmelweis's hunch was right.
- Louis Pasteur is generally credited with pioneering the germ theory of disease and microbiology around 1860. Pasteur demonstrated sterilization techniques, such as boiling to kill microorganisms and withholding exposure to air to prevent contamination.
- Joesph Lister is often referred to as the father of antiseptic surgery. Around 1865, Lister used carbolic acid to wash wounds and popularized the chemical inhibition of infection (antisepsis) during surgery.
- Advances in diagnostics and imaging can be traced to the discovery of X-rays in 1895 by Wilhelm Roentgen, a German professor of physics. Radiology became the first machine-based medical specialty. Some of the first training schools in X-ray therapy and radiography in the United States attracted photographers and electricians to become doctors in Roentgenology (from the inventor's name).
- Alexander Fleming discovered the antibacterial properties of penicillin in 1929.

Advances in medical science and technology bestowed this legitimacy on the medical profession because medical practice could no longer remain within the domain of lay competence.

Scientific and technological change also required improved therapeutic competence of physicians in the diagnosis and treatment of disease. Developing these skills was no longer possible without specialized training. Science-based medicine created an increased demand for advanced services that were no longer available through family and neighbors.

Physicians' cultural authority was further bolstered when medical decisions became necessary in various aspects of health care delivery. For example, physicians decide whether a person should be admitted to a hospital or nursing home and for how long, whether surgical or nonsurgical treatments should be used, and which medications should be prescribed. Physicians' decisions have a profound impact on other providers and nonproviders alike. The judgment and opinions of physicians even affect aspects of a person's life outside the delivery of health care. For example, physicians often evaluate the fitness of persons for jobs during pre-employment physicals many employers demand. Physicians assess the disability of the ill and the injured in workers' compensation cases. Granting of medical leave for sickness and release back to work require authorizations from physicians. Payment of medical claims requires physicians' evaluations. Other health care professionals, such as nurses, therapists, and dietitians, are expected to follow physicians' orders for treatment. Thus, during disease and disability, and sometimes even in good health, people's lives have become increasingly governed by decisions made by physicians.

Institutionalization

The evolution of medical technology and the professionalization of medical and nursing staff enabled advanced treatments that necessitated the pooling of resources in a common arena of care (Burns 2004). Rapid urbanization was another factor that necessitated the institutionalization of medical care. As had already occurred in Europe, in the United States, hospitals became the core around which the delivery of medical services was organized. Thus, development of hospitals as the center for the practice of scientific medicine and the professionalization of medical practice became closely intertwined.

Indeed, physicians and hospitals developed a symbiotic relationship. For economic reasons, as hospitals expanded, their survival became increasingly dependent on physicians to keep the beds filled because the physicians decided where to hospitalize their patients. Therefore, hospitals had to make every effort to keep the physicians satisfied, which enhanced physicians' professional dominance, even though they were not employees of the hospitals. This gave physicians enormous influence over hospital policy. Also, for the first time, hospitals

began conforming to both physician practice patterns and public expectations about medicine as a modern scientific enterprise. The expansion of surgery, in particular, had profound implications for hospitals, physicians, and the public. As hospitals added specialized facilities and staff, their regular use became indispensable to physicians and surgeons, who earlier had been able to manage their practices with little reference to hospitals (Martensen 1996).

Hospitals in the United States did not expand and become more directly related to medical care until the late 1890s. However, as late as the 1930s, hospitals incurred frequent deaths due to infections that could not be prevented or cured. Nevertheless, hospital use was on the rise due to the great influx of immigrants into large American cities (Falk 1999). From only a few score in 1875, the number of general hospitals in the United States expanded to 4,000 by 1900 (Anderson 1990) and to 5,000 by 1913 (Wright 1997).

Dependency

Patients depend on the medical profession's judgment and assistance. First, dependency is created because society expects a sick person to seek medical help and try to get well. The patient is then expected to comply with medical instructions. Second, dependency is created by the profession's cultural authority because its medical judgments must be relied on to (1) legitimize a person's sickness; (2) exempt the individual from social role obligations, such as work or school; and (3) provide competent medical care so the person can get well and resume his or her social role obligations. Third, in conjunction with the physician's cultural authority, the need for hospital services for critical illness and surgery also creates dependency when patients are transferred from their homes to a hospital or surgery center.

Once physicians' cultural authority became legitimized, the sphere of their influence expanded into nearly all aspects of health care delivery. For example, laws were passed that prohibited individuals from obtaining certain classes of drugs without a physician's prescription. Health insurance paid for treatments only when they were rendered or prescribed by physicians. Thus, beneficiaries of health insurance became dependent on physicians to obtain covered services. The referral role (gatekeeping) of primary care physicians in managed care plans has also increased patients' dependency on primary care physicians for referral to specialized services.

Autonomy and Organization

For a long time, physicians' ability to remain free of control from hospitals and insurance companies remained a prominent feature of American medicine. Hospitals and insurance companies could have hired physicians on salary to provide medical services, but individual physicians who took up practice in a corporate setting were castigated by the medical profession and pressured to abandon such practices. In some states, courts ruled that corporations could not employ licensed physicians without engaging in the unlicensed practice of medicine, a legal doctrine that became known as the "corporate practice doctrine" (Farmer and Douglas 2001). Independence from corporate control enhanced private entrepreneurship and put American physicians in an enviable strategic position in relation to hospitals and insurance companies. Later, a formally organized medical profession was

in a much better position to resist control from outside entities.

The AMA was formed in 1847, but it had little strength during its first half-century of existence. Its membership was small, with no permanent organization and scant resources. The AMA did not attain real strength until it was organized into county and state medical societies and until state societies were incorporated, delegating greater control at the local level. As part of the organizational reform, the AMA also began, in 1904, to concentrate attention on medical education (Bordley and Harvey 1976). Since then, it has been the chief proponent for the practitioners of conventional medicine in the United States. Although the AMA often stressed the importance of raising the quality of care for patients and protecting the uninformed consumer from "quacks" and "charlatans," its principal goal—like that of other professional associations—was to advance the professionalization, prestige, and financial well-being of its members. The AMA vigorously pursued its objectives by promoting the establishment of state medical licensing laws and the legal requirement that, to be licensed to practice, a physician must be a graduate of an AMA-approved medical school. The concerted activities of physicians through the AMA are collectively referred to as *organized medicine*, to distinguish them from the uncoordinated actions of individual physicians competing in the marketplace (Goodman and Musgrave 1992).

Licensing

Under the Medical Practice Acts established in the 1870s, medical licensure in the United States became a function of the states (Stevens 1971). By 1896, 26 states had enacted medical licensure laws (Anderson 1990). Licensing of physicians and upgrading of medical school standards developed hand in hand. At first, licensing required only a medical school diploma. Later, candidates could be rejected if the school they had attended was judged inadequate (Starr 1982). Through both licensure and upgrading of medical school standards, physicians obtained a clear monopoly on the practice of medicine (Anderson 1990). The early licensing laws served to protect physicians from the competitive pressures posed by potential new entrants into the medical profession. Physicians led the campaign to restrict the practice of medicine. As biomedicine gained political and economic ground, the biomedical community expelled providers such as homeopaths, naturopaths, and chiropractors from medical societies; prohibited professional association with them; and encouraged prosecution of such providers for unlicensed medical practice (Rothstein 1972). In 1888, in a landmark Supreme Court decision, *Dent v. West Virginia*, Justice Stephen J. Field wrote that no one had the right to practice "without having the necessary qualifications of learning and skill" (Haber 1974). In the late 1880s and 1890s, many states revised laws to require all candidates for licensure, including those holding medical degrees, to pass an examination (Kaufman 1980).

Educational Reform

Reform of medical education started around 1870, with the affiliation of medical schools with universities. In 1871, Harvard Medical School, under the leadership of a new university president, Charles Eliot, completely revolutionized the system of medical education. The academic year was extended from 4 to 9 months, and the length of medical education was increased from 2 to 3 years. Following the European model, laboratory instruction and clinical subjects, such as chemistry, physiology, anatomy, and pathology, were added to the curriculum.

Johns Hopkins University took the lead in further reforming medical education when it opened its medical school in 1893, under the leadership of William H. Welch, who trained in Germany. Medical education, for the first time, became a graduate training course, requiring a college degree, not a high school diploma, as an entrance requirement. Johns Hopkins had well equipped laboratories, a full-time faculty for the basic science courses, and its own teaching hospital (Rothstein 1972). Standards at Johns Hopkins became the model of medical education in other leading institutions around the country. The raising of standards made it difficult for proprietary schools to survive, and, in time, proprietary schools were closed.

The Association of American Medical Colleges (AAMC) was founded in 1876 by 22 medical schools (Coggeshall 1965). Later, the AAMC set minimum standards for medical education, including a 4-year curriculum, but it was unable to enforce its recommendations. In 1904, the AMA created the Council on Medical Education, which inspected the existing medical schools and found that less than half provided acceptable levels of training. The AMA did not publish its findings but obtained the help of the Carnegie Foundation for the Advancement of Teaching to provide a rating of medical schools (Goodman and Musgrave 1992). The Foundation appointed Abraham Flexner to investigate medical schools located in both the United States and Canada. The Flexner Report, published in 1910, had a profound effect on medical education reform.

The report was widely accepted by both the profession and the public. Schools that did not meet the proposed standards were forced to close. State laws were established, requiring graduation from a medical school accredited by the AMA as the basis for a license to practice medicine (Haglund and Dowling 1993).

Once advanced graduate education became an integral part of medical training, it further legitimized the profession's authority and galvanized its sovereignty. Stevens (1971) noted that American medicine moved toward professional maturity between 1890 and 1914, mainly as a direct result of educational reform.

Specialization in Medicine

Specialization has been a key hallmark of American medicine. As a comparison, in 1931, 17% of all physicians in the United States were specialists, whereas today, the proportion of specialists to generalists is approximately 58:42 (Bureau of Labor Statistics 2011), and many generalists also have a subspecialty focus. The growth of allied health care professionals has also diversified, both in medical specialization—such as laboratory and radiological technologists, nurse anesthetists, and physical therapists—as well as in new or expanded specialized fields—such as occupational therapists, psychologists, dietitians, and medical social workers (Stevens 1971).

Lack of a rational coordination of medical care in the United States has been one consequence of the preoccupation with specialization. The characteristics of the medical profession in various countries often shape and define the key attributes of their health care delivery systems. The role of the primary care physician (PCP),

the relationship between generalists and specialists, the ratio of practicing generalists to specialists, the structure and nature of medical staff appointments in hospitals, and the approach to group practice of medicine have all been molded by the evolving structure and ethos of the medical profession. In Britain, for example, the medical profession has divided itself into general practitioners (GPs) practicing in the community and consultants holding specialist positions in hospitals. This kind of stratification did not develop in American medicine. PCPs in America were not assigned the role that GPs had in Britain, where patients could consult a specialist only by referral from a GP. Unlike Britain, where GPs hold a key intermediary position in relation to the rest of the health care delivery system, the United States has lacked such a gatekeeping role. Only since the early 1990s, under health maintenance organizations (HMOs), has the *gatekeeping* model requiring initial contact with a generalist and the generalist's referral to a specialist gained prominence. The distinctive shaping of medical practice in the United States explains why the structure of medicine did not develop around a nucleus of primary care.

From the Asylum to Community Mental Health

At the turn of the 20th century, the scientific study and treatment of mental illnesses, called neuropathology, had just begun. Later, in 1946, federal funding was made available under the National Mental Health Act for psychiatric education and research. This Act led to the creation, in 1949, of the National Institute of Mental Health (NIMH). Early treatment of mental disorders was championed, and the concept of community mental health was born. By this time, new drugs for treating psychosis and depression had become available. Reformers of the mental health system argued that long-term institutional care had been neglectful, ineffective, and even harmful (US Surgeon General 1999). Passage of the Community Mental Health Centers Act of 1963 lent support to the joint policies of "community care" and "deinstitutionalization." From 1970 to 2000, state-run psychiatric hospital beds dropped from 207 to 21 beds per 100,000 population (Manderscheid et al. 2004). The deinstitutionalization movement further intensified after the 1999 US Supreme Court decision in *Olmstead v. L.C.* that directed US states to provide community-based services to people with mental illness. Today, state mental institutions provide long-term treatment to people with severe and persistent mental illness (Patrick et al. 2006).

Development of Public Health

Historically, public health practices in the United States have concentrated on sanitary regulation, the study of epidemics, and vital statistics. The growth of urban centers for the purpose of commerce and industry, unsanitary living conditions in densely populated areas, inadequate methods of sewage and garbage disposal, limited access to clean water, and long work hours in unsafe and exploitative industries led to periodic epidemics of cholera, smallpox, typhoid, tuberculosis, yellow fever, and other diseases. Such outbreaks led to arduous efforts to protect the public interest. For example, in 1793, the national capital had to be moved out of Philadelphia due to a devastating outbreak of yellow fever. This epidemic prompted the city to develop its first board of health that same year. In 1850, Lemuel Shattuck outlined the blueprint for the development of a public health system in Massachusetts. Shattuck also called for the establishment of state and local health departments. A threatening outbreak of cholera in 1873 mobilized the New York City Health Department to alleviate the worst sanitary conditions within the city. Previously, cholera epidemics in 1832 and 1848–1849 had swept through American cities and towns within a few weeks, killing thousands (Duffy 1971). Until about 1900, infectious diseases posed the greatest health threat to society. The development of public health played a major role in curtailing the spread of infection among populations. Simultaneously, widespread public health measures and better medical care reduced mortality and increased life expectancy.

By 1900, most states had health departments that were responsible for a variety of public health efforts, such as sanitary inspections, communicable disease control, operation of state laboratories, vital statistics, health education, and regulation of food and water (Turnock 1997; Williams 1995). Public health functions were later extended to fill gaps in the medical care system. Such functions, however, were limited mainly to child immunizations, care of mothers and infants, health screening in public schools, and family planning. Federal grants were also made available to state and local governments for programs in substance abuse, mental health, and community prevention services (Turnock 1997).

Public health has remained separate from the private practice of medicine because of the skepticism of private physicians that the government could use the boards of health to control the supply of physicians and to regulate the private practice of medicine

(Rothstein 1972). Fear of government intervention, loss of autonomy, and erosion of personal incomes created a wall of separation between public health and private medical practice. Under this dichotomous relationship, medicine has concentrated on the physical health of the individual, whereas public health has focused on the health of whole populations and communities. The extent of collaboration between the two has been largely confined to the requirement by public health departments that private practitioners report cases of contagious diseases, such as sexually transmitted diseases, human immunodeficiency virus (HIV) infection, and acquired immune deficiency syndrome (AIDS), and any outbreaks of cases such as West Nile virus and other types of infections.

Health Services for Veterans

Shortly after World War I, the government started to provide hospital services to veterans with service-related disabilities and for nonservice-related disabilities if the veteran declared an inability to pay for private care.

At first, the federal government contracted for services with private hospitals, but, over time, the Department of Veterans Affairs (formerly called Veterans Administration) built its own hospitals, outpatient clinics, and nursing homes. The current health system for veterans is discussed in Chapter 6.

Birth of Workers' Compensation

The first broad-coverage health insurance in the United States emerged in the form of workers' compensation programs initiated in 1914 (Whitted 1993). The theory underlying workers' compensation is that all accidents that occur during the course of employment and all illnesses directly attributable to the workplace must be regarded as risks of industry. In other words, the employer is financially liable for the full cost of such injuries and illnesses regardless of who is at fault.

Workers' compensation was originally concerned with cash payments to workers for wages lost due to job-related injuries and disease. Compensation for medical expenses and death benefits to the survivors were later added. Looking at the trend, some reformers believed that, since Americans had been persuaded to adopt compulsory insurance against industrial accidents, they could also be persuaded to adopt compulsory insurance against sickness. Workers' compensation served as a trial balloon for the idea of government-sponsored, universal health insurance in the United States. However, the growth of private health insurance, along with other key factors discussed later, has prevented any proposals for a national health care program from taking hold.

Rise of Private Health Insurance

Private health insurance was commonly referred to as *voluntary health insurance*, in contrast to proposals for a government-sponsored compulsory health insurance system. Some private insurance coverage limited to bodily injuries was available since approximately 1850. By 1900, health insurance policies became available, but their initial role was to protect against loss of income during sickness and temporary disability (Whitted 1993). Later, coverage was added for surgical fees, but emphasis remained on replacing lost income. Thus, the coverage was, in reality, disability insurance rather than health insurance (Mayer and Mayer 1984).

As detailed in subsequent sections, technological, social, and economic factors created a general need for health insurance. However, economic conditions that prompted private initiatives, self-interests of a well organized medical profession, and the momentum of a successful health insurance enterprise gave private health insurance a firm footing in the United States. Coverage for hospital and physician services began separately and was later combined under the auspices of Blue Cross and Blue Shield. Later, economic conditions during the World War II period laid the foundations for health insurance to become an employment-based benefit.

Technological, Social, and Economic Factors

The health insurance movement of the early 20th century was the product of three converging developments: the technological, the social, and the economic. From a technological perspective, medicine offered new and better treatments. Because of its well established healing values, medical care had become individually and socially desirable, which created a growing demand for medical services. From an economic perspective, people could predict neither their future needs for medical care nor the costs, both of which had been gradually increasing. In short, scientific and technological advances made health care more desirable but less affordable. These developments pointed to the need for some kind of insurance that could spread the financial risks over a large number of people.

Early Blanket Insurance Policies

In 1911, insurance companies began to offer blanket policies for large industrial populations, usually covering life insurance, accidents and sickness, and nursing services. A few industrial and railroad companies set up their own medical plans, covering specified medical benefits, as did several unions and fraternal orders; however, the total amount of voluntary health insurance was minute (Stevens 1971).

Economic Necessity and the Baylor Plan

The Great Depression, which started at the end of 1929, forced hospitals to turn from philanthropic donations to patient fees for support. Patients now faced not only loss of income from illness but also increased debt from medical care costs when they became sick. People needed protection from the economic consequences of sickness and hospitalization. Hospitals also needed protection from economic instability (Mayer and Mayer 1984). During the Depression, occupancy rates in hospitals fell, income from endowments and contributions dropped sharply, and the charity patient load almost quadrupled (Richardson 1945).

In 1929, the blueprint for modern health insurance was established when Justin F. Kimball began a hospital insurance plan for public school teachers at the Baylor University Hospital in Dallas, Texas. Kimball was able to enroll more than 1,200 teachers, who paid 50 cents a month for a maximum of 21 days of hospital care. Within a few years, it became the model for Blue Cross plans around the country (Raffel 1980). At first, other independent hospitals copied Baylor and started offering single-hospital plans. It was not long before community-wide plans, offered jointly by more than one hospital, became popular because they provided consumers a choice of hospitals. The hospitals agreed to provide services in exchange for a fixed monthly payment by the plans.

Hence, in essence, these were prepaid plans for hospital services. A *prepaid plan* is a contractual arrangement under which a provider must provide all needed services to a group of members (or enrollees) in exchange for a fixed monthly fee paid in advance.

Successful Private Enterprise— The Blue Cross Plans

A hospital plan in Minnesota was the first to use the name Blue Cross in 1933 (Davis 1996). The American Hospital Association (AHA) lent support to the hospital plans and became the coordinating agency to unite these plans into the Blue Cross network (Koch 1993; Raffel 1980). The Blue Cross plans were nonprofit—that is, they had no shareholders who would receive profit distributions—and covered only hospital charges, as not to infringe on the domain of private physicians (Starr 1982).

Later, control of the plans was transferred to a completely independent body, the Blue Cross Commission, which subsequently became the Blue Cross Association (Raffel 1980). In 1946, Blue Cross plans in 43 states served 20 million members. Between 1940 and 1950 alone, the proportion of the population covered by hospital insurance increased from 9% to 57% (Anderson 1990).

Self-Interests of Physicians— Birth of Blue Shield

Voluntary health insurance had received the AMA's endorsement, but the AMA had also made it clear that private health insurance plans should include only hospital care. It is, therefore, not surprising that the first Blue Shield plan designed to pay for physicians' bills was started by the California Medical Association, which established the California Physicians' Service in 1939 (Raffel 1980). By endorsing hospital insurance and by actively developing medical service plans, the medical profession committed itself to private health insurance as the means to spread the financial risk of sickness and to ensure that its own interests would not be threatened.

From the medical profession's point of view, voluntary health insurance, in conjunction with private fee-for-service practice by physicians, was regarded as a desirable feature of the evolving health care system (Stevens 1971). Throughout the Blue Shield movement, physicians dominated the boards of directors not only because they underwrote the plans but also because the plans were, in a very real sense, their response to the challenge of national health insurance. In addition, the plans met the AMA's stipulation of keeping medical matters in the hands of physicians (Raffel and Raffel 1994).

Combined Hospital and Physician Coverage

Even though Blue Cross and Blue Shield developed independently and were financially and organizationally distinct, they often worked together to provide hospital and physician coverage (Law 1974). In 1974, the New York Superintendent of Insurance approved a merger of the Blue Cross and Blue Shield plans of Greater New York (Somers and Somers 1977). Since then, similar mergers have occurred in most states, and in nearly every state Blue Cross and Blue Shield plans are joint corporations or have close working relationships (Davis 1996).

The for-profit insurance companies were initially skeptical of the Blue Cross plans and adopted a wait-and-see attitude.

Their apprehension was justified because no actuarial information was available to predict losses. But within a few years, lured by the success of the Blue Cross plans, commercial insurance companies also started offering health insurance.

Employment-Based Health Insurance

Between 1916 and 1918, 16 state legislatures, including New York and California, attempted to enact legislation mandating employers to provide health insurance, but these efforts were unsuccessful (Davis 1996). Subsequently, three main developments pushed private health insurance to become employment based in the United States: (1) To control high inflation in the economy during the World War II period, Congress imposed wage freezes. In response, many employers started offering health insurance to their workers in lieu of wage increases. (2) In 1948, the US Supreme Court ruled that employee benefits, including health insurance, were a legitimate part of union–management negotiations. Health insurance then became a permanent part of employee benefits in the postwar era (Health Insurance Association of America 1991). (3) In 1954, Congress amended the Internal Revenue Code to make employer-paid health coverage nontaxable. In economic value, employer-paid health insurance was equivalent to getting additional salary without having to pay taxes on it, which provided an incentive to obtain health insurance as an employer-furnished benefit.

Employment-based health insurance expanded rapidly. The economy was strong during the postwar years of the 1950s, and employers started offering more extensive benefits. This led to the birth of "major medical" expense coverage to protect against prolonged or catastrophic illness or injury (Mayer and Mayer 1984). Thus, private health insurance became the primary vehicle for the delivery of health care services in the United States.

Failure of National Health Care Initiatives During the 1990s

Starting with Germany in 1883, compulsory sickness insurance had spread throughout Europe by 1912. Health insurance in European countries was viewed as a natural outgrowth of insurance against industrial accidents. Hence, it was considered logical that Americans would also be willing to support a national health care program to protect themselves from the high cost of sickness and accidents occurring outside employment.

The American Association of Labor Legislation (AALL) was founded in 1906. Its relatively small membership was mainly academic—including some leading economists and social scientists—and some prominent labor leaders. Their all-important agenda was to bring about social reform through government action. The AALL was primarily responsible for leading the successful drive for workers' compensation. It then spearheaded the drive for a government-run health insurance system for the general population (Anderson 1990) and supported the Progressive movement headed by former President Theodore Roosevelt, who was again running for the presidency in 1912 on a platform of social reform. Roosevelt, who might have been a national political sponsor for compulsory health insurance, was defeated by Woodrow Wilson, but the Progressive movement for national health insurance did not die.

The AALL continued its efforts toward a model for national health insurance by appealing to both social and economic concerns. The reformers argued that national health insurance would relieve poverty because sickness usually brought wage loss and high medical costs to individual families. Reformers also argued that national health insurance would contribute to economic efficiency by reducing illness, lengthening life, and diminishing the causes of industrial discontent (Starr 1982). Leadership of the AMA, at the time, showed outward support for a national plan, and the AALL and the AMA formed a united front to secure legislation. A standard health insurance bill was introduced in 15 states in 1917 (Stevens 1971).

As long as compulsory health insurance was only under study and discussion, potential opponents paid no heed to it; but, once bills were introduced into state legislatures, opponents expressed vehement disapproval. Eventually, support for the AMA's social change proved only superficial.

Historically, repeated attempts to pass national health insurance legislation in the United States have failed for several reasons, which can be classified under four broad categories: political inexpediency, institutional dissimilarities, ideological differences, and tax aversion.

Political Inexpediency

Before embarking on their national health programs, countries in Western Europe, notably Germany and England, were experiencing labor unrest that threatened political stability. Social insurance was seen as a means to obtain workers' loyalty and ward off political threats. Conditions in the United States were quite different. There was no real threat to political stability. Unlike countries in Europe, the American

government was highly decentralized and engaged in little direct regulation of the economy or social welfare. Although Congress had set up a system of compulsory hospital insurance for merchant seamen as far back as 1798, it was an exceptional measure.* Matters related to health and welfare were typically left to state and local governments, and as a general rule, these levels of government left as much as possible to private and voluntary action.

The entry of America into World War I in 1917 provided a final political blow to the health insurance movement as anti-German feelings were aroused. The US government denounced German social insurance, and opponents of health insurance called it a Prussian menace, inconsistent with American values (Starr 1982).

After attempts to pass compulsory health insurance laws failed at the state levels in California and New York, by 1920, the AALL itself lost interest in an obviously lost cause. Also in 1920, the AMA's House of Delegates approved a resolution condemning compulsory health insurance that would be regulated by the government (Numbers 1985). The main aim of this resolution was to solidify the medical profession against government interference with the practice of medicine.

Institutional Dissimilarities

The preexisting institutions in Europe and America were dissimilar. Germany and England had mutual benefit funds to

---

*Important seaports, such as Boston, were often confronted with many sick and injured seamen, who were away from their homes and families. Congress enacted a law requiring that 20 cents a month be withheld from the wages of each seaman on American ships to support merchant marine hospitals (Raffel and Raffel 1994).

provide sickness benefits. These benefits reflected an awareness of the value of insuring against the cost of sickness among a sector of the working population. Voluntary sickness funds were less developed in the United States than in Europe, reflecting less interest in health insurance and less familiarity with it. More important, American hospitals were mainly private, whereas in Europe they were largely government operated (Starr 1982).

Dominance of private institutions of health care delivery was seen to be inconsistent with national financing and payment mechanisms. For instance, compulsory health insurance proposals of the AALL were regarded by individual members of the medical profession as a threat to their private practice because such proposals would shift the primary source of income of medical professionals from individual patients to the government (Anderson 1990). Any efforts that would potentially erode the fee-for-service payment system and let private practice of medicine be controlled by a powerful third party—particularly the government—were opposed.

Other institutional entities were also opposed to government-sponsored universal coverage. The insurance industry feared losing the income it derived from disability insurance, some insurance against medical services, and funeral benefits* (Anderson 1990). The pharmaceutical industry feared the government as a monopoly buyer, and retail pharmacists feared that hospitals would establish their own pharmacies under a government-run national health

---

*Patients admitted to a hospital were required to pay a burial deposit so the hospital would not have to incur a burial expense if they died (Raffel and Raffel 1994). Therefore, many people bought funeral policies from insurance companies.

care program (Anderson 1990). Employers also saw the proposals as contrary to their interests. Spokespersons for American business rejected the argument that national health insurance would add to productivity and efficiency. It may seem ironic, but the labor unions—the American Federation of Labor in particular—also denounced compulsory health insurance at the time. Union leaders were afraid they would transfer over to the government their own legitimate role of providing social benefits, thus weakening the unions' influence in the workplace. Organized labor was the largest and most powerful interest group at that time, and its lack of support is considered instrumental in the defeat of national health insurance (Anderson 1990).

Ideological Differences

The American value system has been based largely on the principles of market justice (discussed in Chapter 2). Individualism and self-determination, distrust of government, and reliance on the private sector to address social concerns as typical American values have stood as a bulwark against anything perceived as an onslaught on individual liberties. The beliefs and values have represented the sentiments of the American middle class, whose support was necessary for any broad-based health care reform. Conversely, during times of national distress, such as the Great Depression, pure necessity may have legitimized the advancement of social programs, such as the New Deal programs of the Franklin Roosevelt era (for example, Social Security legislation providing old-age pensions and unemployment compensation).

In the early 1940s, during Roosevelt's presidency, several bills on national health insurance were introduced in Congress, but they all failed to pass. Perhaps the most notable bill was the Wagner-Murray-Dingell bill, drafted in 1943 and named after the bill's congressional sponsors. However, this time, World War II diverted the nation's attention to other issues, and without the president's active support the bill died quietly (Numbers 1985).

In 1946, Harry Truman became the first president to make an appeal for a national health care program (Anderson 1990). Unlike the Progressives, who had proposed a plan for the working class, Truman proposed a single health insurance plan that would include all classes of society. At the president's behest, the Wagner-Murray-Dingell bill was redrafted and reintroduced. The AMA was vehement in opposing the plan. Other interest groups, such as the AHA, also opposed it. By this time, private health insurance had expanded. Initial public reaction to the Wagner-Murray-Dingell bill was positive; however, when a government-controlled medical plan was compared to private insurance, polls showed that only 12% of the public favored extending Social Security to include health insurance (Numbers 1985).

During this era of the Cold War,* any attempts to introduce national health insurance were met with the stigmatizing label of *socialized medicine*, a label that has since become synonymous with any large-scale government-sponsored expansion of health insurance or intrusion in the private practice of medicine. The Republicans took control of Congress in 1946, and any interest in enacting national health insurance was put to rest. However, to the surprise of many, Truman was reelected in 1948, promising

national health insurance if the Democrats would be returned to power (Starr 1982). Fearing the inevitable, the AMA levied a $25 fee on each of its members toward a war chest of $3.5 million (Anderson 1990), which was a substantial sum of money at the time. The AMA hired the public relations firm of Whitaker and Baxter and spent $1.5 million, in 1949 alone, to launch one of the most expensive lobbying efforts in American history. The campaign directly linked national health insurance with Communism until the idea of socialized medicine was firmly implanted in the public's minds. Republicans proposed a few compromises in which neither the Democrats nor the AMA were interested. By 1952, the election of a Republican president, Dwight Eisenhower, effectively ended any further debate over national health insurance.

Tax Aversion

An aversion to increased taxes to pay for social programs is another reason middle-class Americans, who are already insured, have opposed national initiatives to expand health insurance coverage. According to polls, Americans have been found to support the idea that the government ought to help people who are in financial need to pay for their medical care. However, most Americans have not favored an increase in their own taxes to pay for such care. This is perhaps why health care reform failed in 1993.

While seeking the presidency in 1991, Governor Bill Clinton made health system reform a major campaign issue. Not since Harry Truman's initiatives in the 1940s had such a bold attempt been made by a presidential candidate. In the Pennsylvania US Senate election in November 1991,

---

*Rivalry and hostility after World War II between the United States and the then Soviet Union.

the victory of Democrat Harris Wofford over Republican Richard Thornburgh sent a clear signal that the time for a national health care program might be ripe. Wofford's call for national health insurance was widely supported by middle-class Pennsylvanians. Election results in other states were not quite as decisive on the health reform issue, but various public polls seemed to suggest that the rising cost of health care was a concern for many people. Against this backdrop, both Bill Clinton and the running incumbent, President George (Herbert Walker) Bush, advanced health care reform proposals.

After taking office in 1992, President Clinton made health system reform a top priority. Policy experts and public opinion leaders have debated over what went wrong. Some of the fundamental causes for the failure of the Clinton plan were no doubt historical in nature, as discussed previously in this chapter. One seasoned political observer, James J. Mongan, however, remarked that reform debates in Congress were not about the expansion of health care services but rather were about the financing of the proposed services. Apparently, avoiding tax increases took priority over expanding health insurance coverage and caused the demise of Clinton's health care reform initiatives (Mongan 1995).

Creation of Medicare and Medicaid

The year 1965 marks a major turning point in US health policy. Up to this point, private health insurance was the only widely available source of payment for health care, and it was available primarily to middle-class working Americans and their families. Many of the elderly, the unemployed, and the poor had to rely on their own resources,

on limited public programs, or on charity from hospitals and individual physicians. Often, when charity care was provided, private payers were charged more to make up the difference, a practice referred to as *cost-shifting* or *cross-subsidization*. In 1965, Congress passed the amendments to the Social Security Act and created the Medicare and Medicaid programs. Thus, for the first time in US history, the government assumed direct responsibility to pay for some of the health care on behalf of two vulnerable population groups—the elderly and the poor (Potter and Longest 1994).

Through the debates over how to protect the public from rising costs of health care and the opposition to national health insurance, one thing had become clear: Government intervention was not desired insofar as it pertained to how most Americans received health care, with one exception. Less opposition would be encountered if reform initiatives were proposed for the underprivileged and vulnerable classes. In principle, the poor were considered a special class who could be served through a government-sponsored program. The elderly—those 65 years of age and over—were another group who started to receive increased attention in the 1950s. On their own, most of the poor and the elderly could not afford the increasing costs of health care. Also, because the health status of these population groups was significantly worse than that of the general population, they required a higher level of health care services. The elderly, particularly, had higher incidence and prevalence of disease compared to younger groups. It was also estimated that less than one-half of the elderly population was covered by private health insurance. By this time, the growing elderly middle class was also becoming a politically active force.

Government assistance for the poor and the elderly was sought once it became clear that the market alone would not ensure access for these vulnerable population groups. A bill introduced in Congress by Aime Forand in 1957 provided momentum for including necessary hospital and nursing home care as an extension of Social Security benefits for the elderly (Stevens 1971). The AMA, however, undertook a massive campaign to portray a government insurance plan as a threat to the physician–patient relationship. The bill was stalled, but public hearings around the country, which were packed by the elderly, produced an intense grassroots support to push the issue onto the national agenda (Starr 1982). A compromised legislation, the Medical Assistance Act (Public Law 86–778), also known as the Kerr-Mills Act, went into effect in 1960. Under the Act, federal grants were given to the states to extend health services provided by the state welfare programs to those low-income elderly who previously did not qualify (Anderson 1990). Since the program was based on a *means test* that confined eligibility to people below a predetermined income level, it was opposed by liberal congressional representatives as a source of humiliation to the elderly (Starr 1982). Within 3 years, the program was declared ineffective because many states did not even implement it (Stevens 1971). In 1964, health insurance for the aged and the poor became top priorities of President Johnson's Great Society programs.

During the debate over Medicare, the AMA developed its own "Eldercare" proposal, which called for a federal–state program to subsidize private insurance policies for hospital and physician services. Representative John W. Byrnes introduced yet another proposal, dubbed "Bettercare."

It proposed a federal program based on partial premium contributions by the elderly, with the remainder subsidized by the government. Other proposals included tax credits and tax deductions for health insurance premiums.

In the end, a three-layered program emerged. The first two layers constituted Part A and Part B of *Medicare*, or *Title XVIII* of the Social Security Amendment of 1965 to provide publicly financed health insurance to the elderly. Based on Forand's initial bill, the administration's proposal to finance hospital insurance and partial nursing home coverage for the elderly through Social Security became *Part A* of Medicare. The Byrnes proposal to cover physicians' bills through government-subsidized insurance became *Part B* of Medicare. An extension of the Kerr-Mills program of federal matching funds to the states, based on each state's financial needs, became *Medicaid*, or *Title XIX* of the Social Security Amendment of 1965. The Medicaid program was for the indigent, based on means tests established by each state, but it was expanded to include all age groups, not just the poor elderly (Stevens 1971).

Although adopted together, Medicare and Medicaid reflected sharply different traditions. Medicare was upheld by broad grassroots support and, being attached to Social Security, had no class distinction. Medicaid, however, was burdened by the stigma of public welfare. Medicare had uniform national standards for eligibility and benefits; Medicaid varied from state to state in terms of eligibility and benefits. Medicare allowed physicians to *balance bill*, that is, charge the patient the amount above the program's set fees and recoup the difference. Medicaid prohibited balance billing and, consequently, had limited participation from physicians (Starr 1982). Medicaid, in essence, has created a two-tier system of medical care delivery because, even today, many physicians refuse to accept Medicaid patients due to low fees set by the government.

Not long after Medicare and Medicaid were in operation, national spending for health services began to rise, as did public outlays of funds in relation to private spending for health services (Anderson 1990). For example, national health expenditures (NHE), which had increased by 50% from 1955 to 1960, and again from 1960 to 1965, jumped by 78% from 1965 to 1970, and by 71% from 1970 to 1975. Similarly, public expenditures for health care, which were stable at 25% of NHE for 1955, 1960, and 1965, increased to 36.5% of NHE in 1970, and to 42.1% of NHE in 1975 (based on data from Bureau of the Census 1976).

Regulatory Role of Public Health Agencies

With the expansion of publicly financed Medicare and Medicaid programs, the regulatory powers of government have increasingly encroached upon the private sector. This is because the government provides financing for the two programs, but services are delivered by the private sector. After the federal government developed the standards for participation in the Medicare program, states developed regulations in conjunction with the Medicaid program. The regulations often overlapped, and the federal government delegated authority to the states to carry out the monitoring of regulatory compliance. As a result, the regulatory powers assigned to state public health agencies increased dramatically. Thus, most institutions of health care delivery are subject to annual scrutiny by public health agencies

under the authority delegated to them by the federal and state governments.

Prototypes of Managed Care

Even though the early practice of medicine in the United States was mainly characterized by private solo practice, three subsequent developments in medical care delivery are noteworthy: contract practice, group practice, and prepaid group practice. All three required some sort of organizational integration, which was a departure from solo practice. These innovative arrangements can also be regarded as early precursors of managed care and integrated organizations which, a few decades later, paved the way for the corporate era in medical care.

Contract Practice

In 1882, Northern Pacific Railroad Beneficial Association was one of the first employers to provide direct medical care (Davis 1996). Between 1850 and 1900, other railroad, mining, and lumber enterprises developed extensive employee medical services. Such companies conducted operations in isolated areas where physicians were unavailable. Inducements, such as a guaranteed salary, were commonly offered to attract physicians. Another common arrangement was to contract with independent physicians and hospitals at a flat fee per worker per month, referred to as *capitation*. The AMA recognized the necessity of contract practice in remote areas, but elsewhere contract practice was regarded as a form of exploitation because it was assumed that physicians would bid against each other and drive down the price. Offering services at reduced rates was regarded by the AMA as an unethical invasion of private practice. When employer-based health insurance became common in the 1940s, the medical profession was freed from the threat of direct control by large corporations. Health insurance also enabled workers to go to physicians and hospitals of their choice (Starr 1982).

Corporate practice of medicine—that is, delivery of medical care by for-profit corporations—was generally prohibited by law. It was labeled as commercialism in medicine. In 1917, however, Oregon passed the Hospital Association Act, which permitted for-profit corporations to provide medical services. Whereas health insurance companies, functioning as insurers and payers, acted as intermediaries between patients and physicians, the hospital associations in Oregon contracted directly with physicians and exercised some control over them. Utilization was managed by requiring second opinions for major surgery and by reviewing length of hospital stays. The corporations also restricted medical fees, refusing to pay prices deemed excessive. In short, they acted as a countervailing power in the medical market to limit physicians' professional autonomy. Even though physicians resented controls, they continued to do business with the hospital associations in return for guaranteed payments (Starr 1982).

Later, in the 1980s and 1990s, MCOs used contractual arrangements with providers and were successful in replacing the traditional fee-for-service payment arrangements by capitation and discounted fees. Mechanisms to control excessive utilization are another key feature of managed care.

Group Practice

Group medicine represented another form of corporate organization for medical care. Group practice changed the relationship among physicians by bringing them together with business managers and technical assistants in a more elaborate division of labor (Starr 1982). The Mayo Clinic, started in Rochester, Minnesota, in 1887, is regarded as a prototype of the consolidation of specialists into group practice. The concept of a multispecialty group presented a threat to the continuation of general practice. It also presented competition to specialists who remained in solo practice. Hence, the development of group practice met with widespread professional resistance (Stevens 1971), however, sharing of expenses and incomes and other economic advantages caused group practices to grow.

Prepaid Group Plans

In time, the efficiencies of group practice led to the formation of prepaid group plans, in which an enrolled population received comprehensive services for a capitated fee. Prepaid group practice plans first became popular in some large urban markets in the United States. The American Medical Association (AMA) opposed the first plan, the Group Health Association of Washington (started in 1937 in Washington, DC), but the AMA was found guilty of restraint of trade, violating the Sherman Antitrust Act. This verdict may have been crucial in paving the way for the growth of other prepaid group practice plans.

The HIP Health Plan of New York, started in 1947, stands as one of the most successful programs, providing comprehensive medical services through organized medical groups of family physicians and specialists (Raffel 1980). Similarly, Kaiser-Permanente, started in 1942, has grown on the West Coast. Other examples are the

Group Health Cooperative of Puget Sound in Seattle, operating since 1947, which is a consumer-owned cooperative prepaid group practice (Williams 1993), and the Labor Health Institute in St. Louis, started in 1945, which is a union-sponsored group practice scheme (Stevens 1971).

The idea of prepaid group practice had limitations. It required the sponsorship of large organizations. HIP, for example, was created by New York's Mayor Fiorello La Guardia for city employees. Industrialist Henry Kaiser initially set up his prepaid plan to provide comprehensive health care services to his own workers, but the health plan was later extended to other employers.

The HMO Act of 1973

Health care expenditures in the United States started to explode after the creation of Medicare and Medicaid, which enrolled over 35 million people who then had access to health care services financed by the government. The HMO Act of 1973 was passed during the Nixon Administration, with the objective of stimulating growth of HMOs by providing federal funds for the establishment and expansion of new HMOs (Wilson and Neuhauser 1985). The underlying reason for supporting the growth of HMOs was the belief that prepaid medical care, as an alternative to traditional fee-for-service practice, would stimulate competition among health plans, enhance efficiency, and slow the rate of increase in health care expenditures. The HMO Act required employers with 25 or more employees to offer an HMO alternative if one was available in their geographic area. The objective was to create 1,700 HMOs to enroll 40 million members by 1976 (Iglehart 1994). However, the HMO Act failed to achieve

this objective. By 1976, only 174 HMOs had formed, with an enrollment of 6 million (Public Health Service 1995). Employers did not take the HMO option seriously and continued to offer traditional fee-for-service insurance until their own health insurance expenses started to grow rapidly during the 1980s.

Medical Care in the Corporate Era

The latter part of the 20th century and dawning of the 21st century were marked by the growth and consolidation of large business corporations and tremendous advances in global communications, transportation, and trade. These developments have been changing the way health care is delivered in the United States and, indeed, around the world. The rise of multinational corporations, the information revolution, and globalization have been interdependent phenomena. The World Trade Organization's General Agreement on Trade in Services (GATS), which became effective in 1995, aims to gradually remove all barriers to international trade in various services. In health care services, GATS may regulate health insurance, hospital services, telemedicine, and acquisition of medical treatment abroad. GATS negotiations, however, have faced controversy as various countries fear that it may interfere with their domestic health care systems (Belsky et al. 2004).

Corporatization of Health Care Delivery

Corporatization here refers to the ways in which health care delivery in the United States has become the domain of large organizations. These organizations have the financial resources to deliver sophisticated modern health care in comfortable and pleasant surroundings. But, one main expectation of maintaining quality of health care while reducing its cost remains largely unrealized.

On the supply side, until the mid-1980s, physicians and hospitals clearly dominated the medical marketplace. Since then, managed care has emerged as a dominant force by becoming the primary vehicle for insuring and delivering health care to the majority of Americans. The rise of managed care consolidated immense purchasing power on the demand side. To counteract this imbalance, providers began to consolidate, and larger, integrated health care organizations began forming. More recently, with the passage of the ACA, many of these organizations are morphing into accountable care organizations (discussed in Chapter 9). A second, influential factor behind health care integration was reimbursement cuts for inpatient acute care hospital services since the mid-1980s. To make up for lost revenues in the inpatient sector, hospitals developed their own alternative settings to deliver primary care, outpatient surgery, home health care, long-term care, and specialized rehabilitation. Together, managed care and integrated health services organizations have, in reality, corporatized the delivery of health care in the United States.

In a health care landscape that has been increasingly dominated by corporations, individual physicians have struggled to preserve their autonomy. As a matter of survival, many physicians consolidated into large clinics, formed strategic partnerships with hospitals, or started their own specialty hospitals. There is a growing trend of physicians choosing to become employees of hospitals and other medical corporations.

Corporatization has shifted marketplace power from individuals to corporations.

It is too early to tell whether the health insurance marketplaces, or exchanges, established under the ACA, would move the power pendulum toward the consumer.

Information Revolution

The delivery of health care is being transformed in unprecedented and irreversible ways by telecommunications, information technology, and informatics (see Chapter 5). Their use in clinical care, education, and research has become indispensable.

Medical information technologies were first developed in the 1950s. In the postwar period, the United States was the leader in the field of computer science and developed the first uses of computers in medicine. Information and communication technologies were later applied to the fields of telemedicine (Masic 2007). Telemedicine dates back to the 1920s, when shore-based medical specialists were radio linked to address medical emergencies at sea (Winters 1921). Telemedicine came to the forefront in the 1990s, with the technological advances in the distant transmission of image data and the recognition that there was inequitable access to medical care in rural America. Federal dollars were poured into rural telemedicine projects. E-health (discussed in Chapter 5) has also become an unstoppable force that is driven by consumer demand for health care information and services offered over the Internet. The Internet has led to patient empowerment, which in some ways has led to a dilution of the dependent role of the patient.

Since its inception in 2001, eHealth Initiative (eHI), a private nonprofit organization, has emerged as a national leader in research, education, and advocacy activities pertaining to the use of information technology in health care organizations. It has attracted a broad membership from among the various stakeholders in the health care industry. Adoption of information technology in health care has been slow, yet the need for its widespread adoption is clear. An organization such as eHI is playing an important role in helping health care organizations navigate through the many challenges that information technology presents.

Globalization

Globalization refers to various forms of cross-border economic activities. It is driven by global exchange of information, production of goods and services more economically in developing countries, and increased interdependence of mature and emerging world economies. Without corporatization and information revolution, it is doubtful that globalization would have become a growing phenomenon in health care.

From the standpoint of cross-border trade in health services, Mutchnick and colleagues (2005) identified four different modes of economic interrelationships: (1) Advanced telecommunication infrastructures in telemedicine enable cross-border transfer of information for instant answers and services. For example, teleradiology (the electronic transmission of radiological images over a distance) now enables physicians in the United States to transmit radiological images to Australia, where they are interpreted and reported back the next day (McDonnell 2006). Innovative telemedicine consulting services in pathology and radiology are being delivered to other parts of the world by cutting-edge US medical institutions, such as Johns Hopkins. (2) Consumers travel abroad to receive elective, nonemergency medical care, referred to as *medical tourism*. The Centers for Disease

Control and Prevention (CDC) estimated that as many as 750,000 US residents travel abroad each year to receive medical and dental care (CDC 2012). Specialty hospitals, such as the Apollo chain in India and Bumrungrad International Hospital in Thailand, offer state-of-the-art medical facilities to foreigners at a fraction of the cost for the same procedures done in the United States or Europe. Physicians and hospitals outside the United States have clear competitive advantages: reasonable malpractice costs, minimum regulation, and lower costs of labor. As a result of these efficiencies, Indian specialty hospitals can do quality liver transplants for one-tenth of the cost in US hospitals (Mutchnick et al. 2005). Some health insurance companies have also started to explore cheaper options for their covered members to receive certain costly services overseas. Conversely, dignitaries and other wealthy foreigners come to multispecialty centers in the United States, such as the Mayo Clinic, to receive highly specialized services. (3) Foreign direct investment in health services enterprises benefits foreign citizens. For example, Chindex International, a US corporation, provides medical equipment, supplies, and medical services in China. Chindex's United Family Healthcare serves Beijing, Shanghai, and Guangzhou. (4) Health professionals move to other countries that present high demand for their services and better economic opportunities than their native countries. For example, nurses from other countries are moving to the United States to relieve the existing personnel shortage. Migration of physicians from developing countries helps alleviate at least some of the shortage in underserved locations in the developed world.

To the above list, we can add two more: (1) Corporations based in the United States have increasingly expanded their operations overseas. As a result, an increasing number of Americans are now working overseas as expatriates. Health insurance companies based in the United States are, in turn, having to develop benefit plans for these expatriates. According to a survey of 87 insurance companies, health care is also becoming one of the most sought-after employee benefits worldwide, even in countries that have national health insurance programs. Also, the cost of medical care overseas is rising at a faster rate than the rate of inflation in the general economy (Cavanaugh 2008). Hence, the cost-effective delivery of health care is becoming a major challenge worldwide. (2) Medical care delivery by US providers is in demand overseas. American providers, such as Johns Hopkins, Cleveland Clinic, Mayo Clinic, Duke University, and several others, are now delivering medical services in various developing countries.

Cross-border collaborations in health care are also on the rise, mainly triggered by worldwide health care budget constraints. For example, the United States and Japan are collaboratively developing and testing medical devices (Uchida et al. 2013). India's Apollo Group is exporting telemedicine services from its Apollo Gleneagles Hospital in Kolkata (India) to patients in Bangladesh, Nepal, Bhutan, and Myanmar. It provides telediagnostic and teleconsultation from its center in Karaganda Oblastu in Kazakhstan to the region, and partners with Health Services America and Medstaff International in the United States for billing, documentation of clinical and administrative records, coding of medical processes, and insurance claim processing (Smith et al. 2009).

Globalization has also produced some negative effects. The developing world pays a price when emigration leaves these countries with shortages of trained professionals. The burden of disease in these countries is often greater than it is in the developed world, and emigration only exacerbates the inability of these countries to provide adequate health care to their own populations (Norcini and Mazmanian 2005). As developing countries become more prosperous, they acquire Western tastes and lifestyles. In some instances, negative health consequences follow. For example, increased use of motorized vehicles results in a lack of physical exercise, which, along with changes in diet, greatly increases the prevalence of chronic diseases, such as heart disease and diabetes, in the developing world. Conversely, better information about health promotion and disease prevention, as well as access to gyms and swimming pools, in developing countries is making a positive impact on the health and well-being of their middle-class citizens. Globalization has also posed some new threats. For instance, the threat of infectious diseases has increased, as diseases appearing in one country can spread rapidly to other countries. HIV/AIDS, hepatitis B, and hepatitis C infections have spread worldwide.

Era of Health Care Reform

Although incremental reforms through government action have periodically dotted the US health care landscape since Franklin Roosevelt's Social Security Act of 1935 (the Old Age Assistance program to provide government funding for health-related social programs was part of this legislation), the ACA represents the most sweeping reform since the creation of Medicare and Medicaid in 1965. At the national level, other small-scale incremental steps in the interim were the expansion of Medicare in 1972 to cover younger than 65 disabled individuals on Social Security and people with end-stage renal disease, creation of the Children's Health Insurance Program (CHIP) under the Balanced Budget Act of 1997, and creation of Medicare Part D that added prescription drug benefits under the Medicare Prescription Drug, Improvement, and Modernization Act of 2003. Details on Medicare, Medicaid, CHIP, and the ACA are covered in Chapter 6.

State Precedents of the Affordable Care Act

Expansion of health insurance under the ACA is based on two major historical state-based initiatives—the Oregon Health Plan and the Massachusetts Health Plan—both of which have been perceived as successful in many respects.

The Oregon Health Plan

The state of Oregon embarked on a bold initiative in the late 1980s to extend health insurance coverage to uninsured Oregonians. At that time, the uninsured rate in Oregon was 18%. The Oregon Health Plan was formed over several years through successive pieces of legislation. In the end, reform incorporated three main components: (1) Expansion of Medicaid to cover people who previously did not qualify. Delivery of services was mainly through managed care, which now covers roughly 75% of Medicaid clients in Oregon. The cost for Medicaid expansion was to be paid by implementing supply-side rationing (see

Chapter 2). Oregon's model of rationing revolved around the creation of a list of medical services. A state-appointed Health Services Commission reduced over 10,000 medical procedures to a list of 709 medical conditions and their related treatments. The list was prioritized, according to the "net benefit" of each condition/treatment pair (Oberlander et al. 2001). (2) The Oregon Medical Insurance Pool was established as a state agency with state funding to offer health insurance to people who could not buy coverage because of previous health conditions. (3) An *employer mandate* in which employers are legally required to help pay for their employees' coverage was installed. The Oregon Plan required employers to provide medical insurance to all employees working 17.5 hours or more per week and to cover their dependents as well. The law had a *play-or-pay* provision in which employers must either provide their employees health insurance (play) or pay into a public health insurance program. In Oregon's case, the latter was envisioned as a special state insurance fund that would offer coverage to workers not covered by their employers. This play-or-pay provision, however, never materialized because the federal Employee Retirement Income Security Act (ERISA) of 1974 exempts self-insured businesses from state insurance regulations and taxes. ERISA prevents states from requiring employers to provide health coverage or to spend any particular amount on health coverage (Steuerle and Van de Water 2009). Obtaining exemption from ERISA has proven very difficult. Oregon, for one, was unable to obtain federal exemption. Hawaii is the only state to have this exemption for its employer mandate. The state passed its employer mandate (not a true play-or-pay) law in 1974 and was able to get a limited exemption from ERISA. In Hawaii, employers must provide most employees with health insurance and must make a prescribed contribution to that insurance rather than pay a tax (Steuerle and Van de Water 2009).

The Massachusetts Health Plan

In April 2006, Massachusetts became the first state to pass a bipartisan plan that intended to achieve nearly universal coverage in the state. The reform has four main features: (1) The individual mandate (implemented at the end of 2007) requires all state residents to have health insurance or face legal penalties. (2) The employer mandate requires all employers with more than 10 workers to offer, at a minimum, a Section 125 cafeteria plan that permits workers to purchase health insurance with pretax dollars (Henry J. Kaiser Family Foundation 2006). Employers are mandated to make a "fair and reasonable" contribution to their employees' insurance or pay a fee called a "fair share provision" (RAND 2011). By playing (pun intended) around play or pay, but without calling it as such, it appears that Massachusetts has been able to skirt around ERISA. (3) Government subsidies enable low-income individuals to buy insurance under a feature called Commonwealth Care. People whose incomes are less than the federal poverty level (FPL) have their premiums paid by the state. Those earning up to 300% of the FPL pay a subsidized premium. (4) At the core of the plan is the reorganization of a large part of the state's private insurance system into a "single market" structure with uniform rules and a central clearinghouse, called a Connector, to facilitate the purchase and administration of private health insurance plans.

Passage of the Affordable Care Act

Despite the obstacles to national health insurance, discussed previously in this chapter, on March 21, 2010, the House Democrats in Congress passed, by a narrow majority of 219–212 vote, the Patient Protection and Affordable Care Act, which was signed into law 2 days later by President Obama. A week later, on March 30, the President signed the Health Care and Education Reconciliation Act of 2010, which amended certain provisions of the first law, mainly to raise additional revenues through taxation to pay for expanded health care services. Together the two laws comprise the principal features of what is called the Affordable Care Act, also commonly known as Obamacare. Not a single Republican voted in favor of these legislations.

Unlike the defeat of Clinton's reform proposals, which were criticized by some congressional leaders in his own party, Obama was able to maneuver the passage of his health care agenda by uniting his party behind a common cause. Support for the bill required backroom deals with waffling members of the Democratic Party and with interest groups representing the hospital and pharmaceutical industries. Surprisingly, the AMA sheepishly pledged its support for the legislation, which was a complete reversal of its historic stance toward national health insurance. According to one commentator, the AMA has tried to protect itself. The AMA is no longer the powerful organization it once was; it now represents only 17% of the physicians in the United States. It is plausible that the AMA's primary motivation was to protect its monopoly over the medical coding system that health care providers must use to get paid, which generated an annual income of over $70 million for the organization (Scherz 2010). The American public was also kept in the dark about the details buried in the 2,700 pages filled by the final legislation.

The Supreme Court's Ruling

After its passage, the law had remained controversial and unpopular in many circles. Polls showed that nearly two-thirds of Americans opposed the legislation as too ambitious and too costly (Page 2010). A later Gallup poll showed that 46% of Americans were in favor of repealing the law; 40% opposed repealing it (Jones 2011).

Over one-half of the states and some private parties filed lawsuits challenging the constitutionality of the ACA. The main issue in these suits was whether the federal government had the constitutional authority to mandate people that they either purchase health insurance or pay an income tax penalty (referred to as the "individual mandate"). Federal courts in Virginia and Florida had already ruled against the law on constitutional grounds.

The constitutional issues finally came before the US Supreme Court. On June 28, 2012, the ACA cleared a major hurdle to its survival when the Court, in a 5–4 decision, ruled that the majority of ACA provisions— including the individual mandate—were constitutional under Congress' power to tax. The Court, however, struck down a major provision of the law. The Court held that the federal government could not coerce states to expand their state Medicaid programs by threatening to eliminate funding for the existing Medicaid programs in states that would choose not to expand Medicaid coverage under the ACA (Anderson 2012).

The Aftermath

The controversy over the ACA lives on. The majority of Americans continues to have unfavorable opinions about the ACA. Republicans, who gained control of the House of Representatives in 2010, voted numerous times to repeal the ACA, either completely or in part (Grant 2013), but they also failed to propose any alternatives. Even under threats from the Republicans to defund the ACA, the Democrats have not budged, and have asserted that the law must stand as is, without any revisions. Yet, on July 2, 2013, the Obama administration announced that the mandate for employers to provide health insurance to their employees would be delayed until 2015, although the individual mandate would go forward. In the meantime, the main stakeholders— states, consumers, insurers, providers, and employers—have been making efforts to try to comply with the numerous rules and regulations issued by the Department of Health and Human Services, the Department of the Treasury, and other federal agencies. On other fronts, legal battles have not abated. Some institutions affiliated with religious groups and other private groups have contended that certain contraceptive drugs and devices that must be provided under employer health plans may cause abortions. Some states have refused to implement other provisions of the ACA, such as expanding their existing Medicaid programs.

Several requirements of the ACA have been implemented since 2010. The main provisions, however, particularly those dealing with expansion of health insurance coverage are slated for implementation in 2014. The complex and confusing law still faces thorny challenges for its implementation across the country. States that fully espouse and implement the law may, in the future, serve as a case study for its eventual success or failure.

Summary

The evolution of health care services in the United States, in approximately 150 years, has come a long way from the delivery of primitive care to technologically advanced services delivered by small and large medical corporations that have increasingly crossed national boundaries. The need for health insurance arose during the Great Depression. Unlike in Europe where government-sponsored health insurance took roots, in the United States health insurance began mainly as a private endeavor because of circumstances that did not parallel those in Europe. Yet, social, political, and economic exigencies and opportunities led to the creation of two major government health insurance programs, Medicare and Medicaid, in 1965. Since then, small-scale incremental reforms were undertaken because they were politically and socially more acceptable than large-scale changes in how most middle-class Americans obtained health care services. Historically, traditional American beliefs and values have acted as strong forces against attempts to initiate fundamental changes in the financing and delivery of health care. The ACA was passed through political maneuvering, without seeking consensus among Americans on basic values and ethics. Hence, the nation is deeply divided over issues of health care and its financing. To become uniform national policy, the ACA still faces legal and implementation challenges. Much will depend on its future success or failure.

ACA Takeaway

- The Patient Protection and Affordable Care Act of 2010 as amended by the Health Care and Education Reconciliation Act of 2010 is known as the Affordable Care Act.
- The ACA is patterned after two state-based reforms, the Oregon Health Plan and the Massachusetts Health Plan.
- The 2012 US Supreme Court's ruling validated the constitutionality of the individual mandate, but left Medicaid expansion up to each state's discretion.
- The ACA opens a new era of health care reform at the national level in the United States, but its ultimate effects will not be known for some time.
- Americans remain divided over health care reform under the ACA.

Test Your Understanding

Terminology

almshouse   gatekeeping   Part B
balance bill   globalization   pesthouse
capitation   means test   play or pay
cost-shifting   Medicaid   prepaid plan
cross-subsidization medical tourism   socialized medicine
cultural authority   Medicare   Title XVIII
employer mandate   organized medicine   Title XIX
fee for service   Part A   voluntary health insurance

Review Questions

1. Why did the professionalization of medicine start later in the United States than in some Western European nations?

2. Why did medicine have a domestic, rather than professional, character in the preindustrial era? How did urbanization change that?

3. Which factors explain why the demand for the services of a professional physician was inadequate in the preindustrial era? How did scientific medicine and technology change that?

4. How did the emergence of general hospitals strengthen the professional sovereignty of physicians?

5. Discuss the relationship of dependency within the context of the medical profession's cultural and legitimized authority. What role did medical education reform play in galvanizing professional authority?

6. How did the organized medical profession manage to remain free of control by business firms, insurance companies, and hospitals until the latter part of the 20th century?

7. In general, discuss how technological, social, and economic factors created the need for health insurance.

8. Which conditions during the World War II period lent support to employer-based health insurance in the United States?

9. Discuss, with particular reference to the roles of (a) organized medicine, (b) the middle class, and (c) American beliefs and values, why reform efforts to bring in national health insurance have historically been unsuccessful in the United States.

10. Which particular factors that earlier may have been somewhat weak in bringing about national health insurance later led to the passage of Medicare and Medicaid?

11. On what basis were the elderly and the poor regarded as vulnerable groups for whom special government-sponsored programs needed to be created?

12. Discuss the government's role in the delivery and financing of health care, with specific reference to the dichotomy between public health and private medicine.

13. Explain how contract practice and prepaid group practice were the prototypes of today's managed care plans.

14. Discuss the main ways in which current delivery of health care has become corporatized.

15. In the context of globalization in health services, what main economic activities are discussed in this chapter?

16. What were the two main aspects of the Supreme Court's ruling in lawsuits filed against the Affordable Care Act?

REFERENCES

Anderson, D., and the Health Policy Institute of Ohio. 2012. *The Supreme Court's ruling on the Affordable Care Act: A review of the decision and its impact on Ohio.* Available at: http://a5e8c023c8899218225edfa4b02e4d9734e01a28.gripelements.com/pdf/publications/scotus_brief.pdf. Accessed January 2013.

Anderson, O.W. 1990. *Health services as a growth enterprise in the United States since 1875.* Ann Arbor, MI: Health Administration Press.

Belsky, L., et al. 2004. The general agreement on trade in services: Implications for health policymakers. *Health Affairs* 23, no. 3: 137–145.

Bordley, J., and A.M. Harvey. 1976. *Two centuries of American medicine 1776–1976.* Philadelphia, PA: W.B. Saunders Company.

Bureau of the Census. 1976. *Statistical abstract of the United States, 1976.* Washington, DC: US Department of Commerce.

Bureau of Labor Statistics. 2011. *Occupational outlook handbook, 2010-11.* Available at: http://www.bls.gov/oco/home.htm. Accessed January 2011.

Burns, J. 2004. Are nonprofit hospitals really charitable? Taking the question to the state and local level. *Journal of Corporate Law* 29, no. 3: 665–683.

Cavanaugh, B.B. 2008. Building the worldwide health network. *Best's Review* 108, no. 12: 32–37.

Centers for Disease Control and Prevention (CDC). 2012. *Medical tourism—getting medical care in another country.* Available at: http://www.cdc.gov/Features/MedicalTourism. Accessed July 2013.

Clark, C. 1998. A bloody evolution: Human error in medicine is as old as the practice itself. *The Washington Post,* 20 October, Z10.

Coggeshall, L.T. 1965. *Planning for medical progress through education.* Evanston, IL: Association of American Medical Colleges.

Davis, P. 1996. The fate of Blue Shield and the new blues. *South Dakota Journal of Medicine* 49, no. 9: 323–330.

Duffy, J. 1971. Social impact of disease in the late 19th century. *Bulletin of the New York Academy of Medicine* 47: 797–811.

Falk, G. 1999. *Hippocrates assailed: The American health delivery system*. Lanham, MD: University Press of America, Inc.

Farmer, G.O., and J.H. Douglas. 2001. Physician "unionization"—A primer and prescription. *Florida Bar Journal* 75, no. 7: 37–42.

Gabe, J., et al. 1994. *Challenging medicine*. New York: Routledge.

Goodman, J.C., and G.L. Musgrave. 1992. *Patient power: Solving America's health care crisis*. Washington, DC: CATO Institute.

Grant, D. 2013. House Republicans repeal Obamacare again. Why do they keep doing it? *Christian Science Monitor*, May 16.

Haber, S. 1974. The professions and higher education in America: A historical view. In: *Higher education and labor markets*. M.S. Gordon, ed. New York: McGraw-Hill Book Co.

Haglund, C.L., and W.L. Dowling. 1993. The hospital. In: *Introduction to health services*. 4th ed. S.J. Williams and P.R. Torrens, eds. New York: Delmar Publishers. pp. 135–176.

Hamowy, R. 1979. The early development of medical licensing laws in the United States, 1875–1900. *Journal of Libertarian Studies* 3, no. 1: 73–119.

Health Insurance Association of America. 1991. *Source book of health insurance data*. Washington, DC: Health Insurance Association of America.

Henry J. Kaiser Family Foundation. 2006. *Massachusetts health care reform plan*. Available at: http://www.kff.org. Accessed April 2006.

Iglehart, J.K. 1994. The American health care system: Managed care. In: *The nation's health*. 4th ed. P.R. Lee and C.L. Estes, eds. Boston: Jones & Bartlett Publishers. pp. 231–237.

Jones, J.M. 2011. In U.S., 46% favor, 40% oppose repealing healthcare law. Available at: http://www.gallup.com/poll/145496/Favor-Oppose-Repealing-Healthcare-Law.aspx. Accessed April 2011.

Kaptchuk, T.J., and D.M. Eisenberg. 2001. Varieties of healing 1: Medical pluralism in the United States. *Annals of Internal Medicine* 135, no. 3: 189–195.

Kaufman, M. 1980. American medical education. In: *The education of American physicians: Historical essays*. R.L. Numbers, ed. Los Angeles: University of California Press.

Koch, A.L. 1993. Financing health services. In: *Introduction to health services*. 4th ed. S.J. Williams and P.R. Torrens, eds. New York: Delmar Publishers. pp. 299–331.

Law, S.A. 1974. *Blue Cross: What went wrong?* New Haven, CT: Yale University Press.

Manderscheid, R.W., et al. 2004. Highlights of organized mental health services in 2000 and major national and state trends. In: *Mental health, United States, 2002*. R.W. Manderscheid and M.J. Henderson, eds. Washington, DC: US Government Printing Office.

Martensen, R.L. 1996. Hospital hotels and the care of the "worthy rich." *Journal of the American Medical Association* 275, no. 4: 325.

Masic, I. 2007. A review of informatics and medical informatics history. *Acta Informatica Medica* 15, no. 3: 178–188.

Mayer, T.R., and G.G. Mayer. 1984. *The health insurance alternative: A complete guide to health maintenance organizations*. New York: Putnam Publishing Group.

McDonnell, J. 2006. Is the medical world flattening? *Ophthalmology Times* 31, no. 19: 4.

Mongan, J.J. 1995. Anatomy and physiology of health reform's failure. *Health Affairs* 14, no. 1: 99–101.

Mutchnick, I.S., et al. 2005. Trading health services across borders: GATS, markets, and caveats. *Health Affairs* – Web Exclusive 24, suppl. 1: W5-42–W5-51.

Norcini, J.J., and P.E. Mazmanian. 2005. Physician migration, education, and health care. *Journal of Continuing Education in the Health Professions* 25, no. 1: 4–7.

Numbers, R.L. 1985. The third party: Health insurance in America. In: *Sickness and health in America: Readings in the history of medicine and public health.* J.W. Leavitt and R.L. Numbers, eds. Madison, WI: The University of Wisconsin Press.

Numbers, R.L., and J.H. Warner. 1985. The maturation of American medical science. In: *Sickness and health in America: Readings in the history of medicine and public health.* J.W. Leavitt and R.L. Numbers, eds. Madison, WI: The University of Wisconsin Press.

Oberlander, J., et al. 2001. Rationing medical care: Rhetoric and reality in the Oregon health plan. *Canadian Medical Association Journal* 164, no. 11: 1583–1587.

Page, S. 2010. Health care law too costly, most say (USA Today). Available at: http://www .usatoday.com/news/washington/2010-03-29-health-poll_N.htm. Accessed January 2011.

Patrick, V., et al. 2006. Facilitating discharge in state psychiatric institutions: A group intervention strategy. *Psychiatric Rehabilitation Journal* 29, no. 3: 183–188.

Potter, M.A., and B.B. Longest. 1994. The divergence of federal and state policies on the charitable tax exemption of nonprofit hospitals. *Journal of Health Politics, Policy and Law* 19, no. 2: 393–419.

Public Health Service. 1995. *Health United States, 1994.* Washington, DC: Government Printing Office.

Raffel, M.W. 1980. *The U.S. health system: Origins and functions.* New York: John Wiley & Sons.

Raffel, M.W., and N.K. Raffel. 1994. *The U.S. health system: Origins and functions.* 4th ed. Albany, NY: Delmar Publishers.

RAND. 2011. *Overview of employer mandate.* The RAND Corporation. Available at: http://www .randcompare.org/policy-options/employer-mandate. Accessed March 2011.

Richardson, J.T. 1945. The origin and development of group hospitalization in the United States, 1890–1940. *University of Missouri Studies* XX, no. 3.

Rosen, G. 1983. *The structure of American medical practice 1875–1941.* Philadelphia, PA: University of Pennsylvania Press.

Rosenberg, C.E. 1979. The therapeutic revolution: Medicine, meaning, and social change in nineteenth-century America. In: *The therapeutic revolution.* M.J. Vogel, ed. Philadelphia, PA: The University of Pennsylvania Press.

Rosner, L. 2001. The Philadelphia medical marketplace. In: *Major problems in the history of American medicine and public health.* J.H. Warner and J.A. Tighe, eds. Boston: Houghton Mifflin Company.

Rothstein, W.G. 1972. *American physicians in the nineteenth century: From sect to science.* Baltimore, MD: Johns Hopkins University Press.

Scherz, H. 2010. Why the AMA wants to muzzle your doctor (*The Wall Street Journal*). Available at: http://online.wsj.com/article/SB10001424052748703961104575226323909364054.html. Accessed April 2011.

Shryock, R.H. 1966. *Medicine in America: Historical essays.* Baltimore, MD: The Johns Hopkins Press.

Smith, R.D., et al. 2009. Trade in health-related services. *The Lancet* 373, no. 9663: 593–601.

Somers, A.R., and H.M. Somers. 1977. *Health and health care: Policies in perspective.* Germantown, MD: Aspen Systems.

Starr, P. 1982. *The social transformation of American medicine.* Cambridge, MA: Basic Books.

Steuerle, C.E., and P.N. Van de Water. 2009. *Administering health insurance mandates.* Available at: http://www.nasi.org/usr_doc/Administering_Health_Insurance_Mandates.pdf. Accessed March 2011.

Stevens, R. 1971. *American medicine and the public interest.* New Haven, CT: Yale University Press.

Turnock, B.J. 1997. *Public health: What it is and how it works.* Gaithersburg, MD: Aspen Publishers, Inc. pp. 3–38.

Uchida, T., et al. 2013. Global cardiovascular device innovation: Japan-USA synergies. *Circulation Journal: Official Journal of the Japanese Circulation Society* 77, no. 7: 1714–1718.

US Surgeon General. 1999. *Mental health: A report of the Surgeon General. Overview of mental health services.* Available at: http://www.surgeongeneral.gov/library/mentalhealth/chapter2/sec2.html. Accessed February 2011.

Wagner, D. 2005. *The poorhouse: America's forgotten institution.* Lanham, MD: Rowman & Littlefield Publishers.

Whitted, G. 1993. Private health insurance and employee benefits. In: *Introduction to health services.* 4th ed. S.J. Williams and P.R. Torrens, eds. New York: Delmar Publishers. pp. 332–360.

Williams, S.J. 1993. Ambulatory health care services. In: *Introduction to health services.* 4th ed. S.J. Williams and P.R. Torrens, eds. New York: Delmar Publishers.

Williams, S.J. 1995. *Essentials of health services.* Albany, NY: Delmar Publishers. pp. 108–134.

Wilson, F.A., and D. Neuhauser. 1985. *Health services in the United States.* 2nd ed. Cambridge, MA: Ballinger Publishing Co.

Winters, S.R. 1921. Diagnosis by wireless. *Scientific American* 124: 465.

Wright, J.W. 1997. *The New York Times almanac.* New York: Penguin Putnam, Inc.

PART II

System Resources

Chapter 4

Health Services Professionals

Learning Objectives

- To become familiar with the various types of health services professionals and their training, practice requirements, and practice settings
- To differentiate between primary care and specialty care and identify the causes for an imbalance between primary care and specialty care in the United States
- To learn about the extent of maldistribution in the physician labor force and to comprehend the reasons for such maldistribution
- To outline initiatives under the Affordable Care Act to relieve shortages of primary care providers and coordinated care delivery in team settings
- To appreciate the role of nonphysician providers in health care delivery
- To understand the role of allied health professionals in health care delivery
- To discuss the functions and qualifications of health services administrators
- To assess global health workforce challenges

"Hmm, they're all beginning to look like me."

Introduction

The US health care industry is the largest and most powerful employer in the nation. It constitutes more than 3% of the total labor force in the United States. In terms of total economic output, in 2011, the health care sector in the United States contributed 17.9% to the gross domestic product (World Bank 2013). Although the number of jobs in many areas of the US economy shrank since the beginning of an economic recession in December 2007, the health care sector continued its growing trend. The growth has been most pronounced in the hospital industry. Overall demand for all types of health care services will increase with the aging of the population. Hence, several health care and related occupations are projected to grow substantially. The Bureau of Labor Statistics projected the "healthcare practitioners and technical occupations" to grow by 21.4% and the "healthcare support occupations" by 28.8% during 2008–2018, whereas the entire US workforce was projected to grow by 10.1% during this period (US Bureau of Labor Statistics 2009).

Health professionals are among the most well educated and diverse of all labor groups. Almost all of these practitioner groups are now represented by their respective professional associations, which are listed in Appendix 4–A at the end of this chapter.

Health services professionals work in a variety of health care settings that include hospitals, managed care organizations (MCOs), nursing care facilities, mental health institutions, insurance firms, pharmaceutical companies, outpatient facilities, community health centers, migrant health centers, mental health centers, school clinics, physicians' offices, laboratories, voluntary health agencies, professional health associations, colleges of medicine and allied health professions, and research institutions. Most health professionals are employed by hospitals (40.5%), followed by nursing and personal care facilities (12.1%) and physicians' offices and clinics (10.0%) (Table 4–1).

The expansion of the number and types of health services professionals closely follows population trends, advances in research and technology, disease and illness trends, and changes in health care financing and delivery of services. New and complex medical techniques, equipment, and advanced computer-based information systems are constantly introduced, and health services professionals must continually learn how to use these innovations. Specialization in medicine has contributed to the proliferation of different types of medical technicians. The changing patterns of disease, from acute to chronic, and a greater emphasis on prevention create a greater need for professionals who are formally trained to address the consequences of behavioral risk factors and the delivery of primary care. Increased insurance coverage under the Affordable Care Act (ACA) will also increase the demand for health services professionals.

This chapter provides an overview of the large array of health services professionals employed in a vast assortment of health delivery settings. It briefly discusses the training and practice requirements for the various health professionals, their major roles, the practice settings in which they are employed, and some critical issues concerning their professions. Emphasis is placed on physicians because they play a leading role in the delivery of health care. There has been increased recognition of the role nonphysician practitioners (NPPs) play in boosting the nation's primary care infrastructure.

Table 4–1 Persons Employed in Health Service Sites (139,887 employed civilians in 2009)

Site	2000		2009	
	Number of Persons (in thousands)	Percentage Distribution	Number of Persons (in thousands)	Percentage Distribution
All employed civilians	136,891	100.0	139,887	100.0
All health service sites	12,211	100.0	15,478	100.0
Offices and clinics of physicians	1,387	11.4	1,555	10.0
Offices and clinics of dentists	672	5.5	801	5.2
Offices and clinics of chiropractors	120	1.0	136	0.9
Offices and clinics of optometrists	95	0.8	117	0.8
Offices and clinics of other health practitioners	143	1.2	220	1.4
Outpatient care centers	772	6.3	1,102	7.1
Home health care services	548	4.5	967	6.2
Other health care services	1,027	8.4	1,747	11.3
Hospitals	5,202	42.6	6,265	40.5
Nursing care facilities	1,593	13.0	1,869	12.1
Residential care facilities, without nursing	652	5.3	699	4.5

Source: Data from *Health, United States, 2009,* Table 105.

Physicians

In the delivery of health services, physicians play a central role by evaluating a patient's health condition, diagnosing abnormalities, and prescribing treatment. Some physicians are engaged in medical education and research to find new and better ways to control and cure health problems. Many are involved in the prevention of illness.

All states require physicians to be licensed to practice. The licensure requirements include graduation from an accredited medical school that awards a Doctor of Medicine (MD) or Doctor of Osteopathic Medicine (DO) degree, successful completion of a licensing examination, governed by either the National Board of Medical Examiners or the National Board of Osteopathic Medical Examiners, and completion of a supervised internship/residency program (Stanfield et al. 2009) The term *residency* refers to graduate medical education in a specialty that takes the form of paid on-the-job training, usually in a hospital. Before entering a residency, which may last 2 to 6 years, most DOs serve a 12-month rotating internship after graduation.

The number of active physicians, both MDs and DOs, has steadily increased from 14.1 physicians per 10,000 population in 1950 to 27.3 per 10,000 population in 2009 (Table 4–2). Of the 159 medical schools in the United States, 133 teach allopathic medicine and award a Doctor of Medicine (MD) degree; 29 teach osteopathic medicine and award the Doctor of Osteopathic Medicine (DO) degree (US Bureau of Labor Statistics 2011).

Similarities and Differences Between MDs and DOs

Both MDs and DOs use accepted methods of treatment, including drugs and surgery. The two differ mainly in their philosophies and approaches to medical treatment. *Osteopathic medicine*, practiced by DOs, emphasizes the musculoskeletal system of the body, such as correction of joints or tissues. In their treatment plans, DOs stress preventive medicine, and how factors such as diet and environment, might influence natural resistance. They take a holistic approach to patient care. MDs are trained in *allopathic medicine*, which views medical treatment as active intervention to produce a counteracting reaction in an attempt to neutralize the effects of disease. MDs, particularly generalists, may also use preventive medicine, along with allopathic treatments. About 5% of all active physicians are osteopaths (American Association of Colleges of Osteopathic Medicine 2007). About 42% of MDs and more than one-half of DOs work in primary care (US Bureau of Labor Statistics 2011).

Generalists and Specialists

Most DOs are generalists and most MDs are specialists. In the US, physicians trained in family medicine/general practice, general internal medicine, and general pediatrics are considered primary care physicians (PCPs) or *generalists* (Rich et al. 1994). In general, PCPs provide preventive services (e.g., health examinations, immunizations, mammograms, Papanicolaou smears) and treat frequently occurring and less severe problems. Problems that occur less frequently or that require complex diagnostic or therapeutic approaches are referred to specialists after an initial evaluation.

Physicians in nonprimary care specialties are referred to as *specialists*. Specialists must seek certification in an area of medical specialization, which commonly requires additional years of advanced residency training, followed by several years of practice in the specialty. A specialty board examination is often required as the final step in becoming a board-certified specialist. The common medical specialties, along with brief descriptions, are listed in Exhibit 4–1. Medical specialties may be divided into six major functional groups: (1) the subspecialties of internal medicine; (2) a broad group of medical specialties; (3) obstetrics and gynecology; (4) surgery of all types; (5) hospital-based radiology, anesthesiology, and pathology; and (6) psychiatry (Cooper 1994). The distribution of physicians by specialty appears in Table 4–3.

Work Settings and Practice Patterns

Physicians practice in a variety of settings and arrangements. Some work in hospitals as medical residents or staff physicians. Others work in the public sector, such as federal government agencies, public health departments, community and migrant health centers, schools, and prisons. Most physicians,

Table 4–2 Active US Physicians, According to Type of Physician and Number per 10,000 Population

Year	All Active Physicians	Doctors of Medicine	Doctors of Osteopathy	Active Physicians per 10,000 Population
1950	219,900	209,000	10,900	14.1
1960	259,500	247,300	12,200	14.0
1970	326,500	314,200	12,300	15.6
1980	427,122	409,992	17,130	19.0
1990	567,610	539,616	27,994	22.4
1995	672,859	637,192	35,667	25.0
2000	772,296	727,573	44,723	27.0
2001	793,263	751,689	41,574	27.4
2009	838,453	972,400	70,480	27.3

Source: Data from *Health, United States, 1995,* p. 220; *Health, United States, 2002,* p. 274; *Health, United States, 2006,* p. 358; and *Health, United States, 2012,* p.308.

however, are office-based practitioners, and most physician contacts occur in physician offices. An increasing number of physicians are partners or salaried employees, working in both hospitals and various outpatient settings, such as group practices, freestanding ambulatory care clinics, and diagnostic imaging centers.

Figure 4–1 shows that, in 2010, physicians in general/family practice accounted for the greatest proportion of ambulatory care visits, followed by those in internal medicine and pediatrics. Physicians in obstetrics and gynecology tend to spend the most hours in patient care per week, even exceeding those in surgery. Surgeons, however, have the highest average annual net income. Operating expenses and malpractice insurance premiums are the highest in obstetrics/gynecology.

Differences Between Primary and Specialty Care

Primary care may be distinguished from *specialty care*, according to the time, focus, and scope of the services provided to patients. The five main areas of distinction are as follows:

1. In linear time sequence, primary care is first-contact care and is regarded as the portal to the health care system (Kahn et al. 1994). Specialty care, when needed, generally follows primary care.

2. In a managed care environment in which health services functions are integrated, PCPs serve as gatekeepers, an important role in controlling cost, utilization, and the rational allocation of resources. In the gatekeeping

Exhibit 4–1 Definitions of Medical Specialties and Subspecialties

Allergists	Treat conditions and illnesses caused by allergies or related to the immune system
Anesthesiologists	Use drugs and gases to render patients unconscious during surgery
Cardiologists	Treat heart diseases
Dermatologists	Treat infections, growths, and injuries related to the skin
Emergency Medicine	Work specifically in emergency departments, treating acute illnesses and emergency situations, for example, trauma
Family Physicians	Are prepared to handle most types of illnesses and involve the care of the patient as a whole
General Practitioners	Similar to family physicians — examine patients or order tests and have X-rays done to diagnose illness and treat the patient
Geriatricians	Specialize in problems and diseases that accompany aging
Gynecologists	Specialize in the care of the reproductive system of women
Internists	Treat diseases related to the internal organs of the body, for example, conditions of the lungs, blood, kidneys, and heart
Neurologists	Treat disorders of the central nervous system and order tests necessary to detect diseases
Obstetricians	Work with women throughout their pregnancy, deliver infants, and care for the mother after the delivery
Oncologists	Specialize in the diagnosis and treatment of cancers and tumors
Ophthalmologists	Treat diseases and injuries of the eye
Otolaryngologists	Specialize in the treatment of conditions or diseases of the ear, nose, and throat
Pathologists	Study the characteristics, causes, and progression of diseases
Pediatricians	Provide care for children from birth to adolescence
Preventive Medicine	Includes occupational medicine, public health, and general preventive treatments
Psychiatrists	Help patients recover from mental illness and regain their mental health
Radiologists	Perform diagnosis and treatment by the use of X-rays and radioactive materials
Surgeons	Operate on patients to treat disease, repair injury, correct deformities, and improve the health of patients
General Surgeons	Perform many different types of surgery, usually of relatively low degree of difficulty
Neurologic Surgeons	Specialize in surgery of the brain, spinal cord, and nervous system
Orthopaedic Surgeons	Specialize in the repair of bones and joints
Plastic Surgeons	Repair malformed or injured parts of the body
Thoracic Surgeons	Perform surgery in the chest cavity, for example, lung and heart surgery
Urologists	Specialize in conditions of the urinary tract in both sexes and of the sexual/reproductive system in males

Source: Data from Stanfield, P.S. 1995. *Introduction to the Health Professions*, 2nd ed. Boston, MA: Jones & Bartlett Learning.

Table 4–3 US Physicians, According to Activity and Place of Medical Education, 2010

Activity and Place of Medical Education	Numbers	Percentage	Distribution
Doctors of medicine (professionally active)*	794,862	100.0	
Place of medical education:			
US medical graduates	595,908	75.0	
International medical graduates	198,954	25.0	
Activity			
Patient care	752,572	100.0	
Office-based practice	565,024	76.9	100.0
General and family practice	77,098		13.6
Cardiovascular diseases	17,454		3.1
Dermatology	9,272		1.6
Gastroenterology	10,466		1.0
Internal medicine	110,612		19.6
Pediatrics	53,054		9.4
Pulmonary diseases	7,846		1.4
General surgery	24,327		4.3
Obstetrics and gynecology	34,083		6.0
Ophthalmology	15,723		2.8
Orthopaedic surgery	19,325		3.4
Otolaryngology	7,964		1.4
Plastic surgery	6,180		1.1
Urological surgery	8,606		1.5
Anesthesiology	31,819		5.6
Diagnostic radiology	17,503		3.1
Emergency medicine	20,654		3.7
Neurology	10,547		1.9
Pathology, anatomical/clinical	10,688		1.9
Psychiatry	25,690		4.5
Radiology	7,032		1.2
Other specialty	39,081		6.9
Hospital-based practice	187,548	23.1	100.0
Residents and interns	108,142		57.7
Full-time hospital staff	79,406		42.3

*Excludes inactive, not classified, and address unknown.
Source: Data from *Health, United States, 2012*, p. 309.

Figure 4–1 Ambulatory Care Visits to Physicians According to Physician Specialty, 2010.

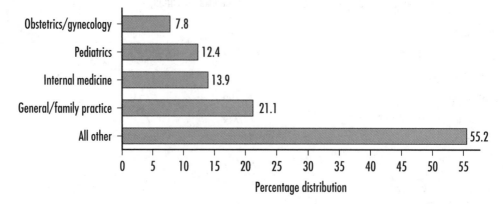

Percentage distribution

Source: Data from *Health, United States, 2012,* pp. 278–279.

model, specialty care requires referral from a primary care physician.

3. Primary care is longitudinal. In other words, primary care providers follow through the course of treatment and coordinate various activities, including initial diagnosis, treatment, referral, consultation, monitoring, and follow-up. Primary care providers serve as patient advisors and advocates. Their coordinating role is especially important in continuity of care for chronic conditions. Specialty care is episodic and, thus, more focused and intense.

4. Primary care focuses on the person as a whole, whereas specialty care centers on particular diseases or organ systems of the body. Patients often have multiple problems, a condition referred to as *comorbidity*, which requires balancing of the multiple requirements, addressing changes in health conditions over time, and drug and disease interactions. Specialty care tends to be limited to illness episodes, the organ system, or the disease process involved. Comorbidities may necessitate referrals to multiple specialists, which present challenges in care coordination by PCPs.

5. The difference in scope is reflected in how primary and specialty care providers are trained. Primary care students spend a significant amount of time in ambulatory care settings, familiarizing themselves with a variety of patient conditions and problems. Students in medical subspecialties spend significant time in inpatient hospitals, where they are exposed to state-of-the–art medical technology.

The Expanding Role of Hospitalists

Since the mid-1990s, an increasing amount of inpatient medical care in the United States has been delivered by *hospitalists*, physicians who specialize in the care of hospitalized patients (Schneller 2006). Hospitalists do not usually have a relationship with the patient prior to hospitalization. Essentially, the patient's primary care provider entrusts the oversight of the patient's care to a hospitalist upon admission, and the patient returns to the regular physician after discharge (Freed 2004). Approximately 21,100 to 22,900 hospitalists practice in the United States (Association of American Medical College 2012).

The growth of the number of hospitalists is influenced by the desire of hospital executives, HMOs, and medical groups to reduce inpatient costs and increase efficiency, without compromising quality or patient satisfaction. Published research shows that using hospitalists does, in fact, achieve these goals (Wachter 2004). Research findings have also put to rest initial concerns from PCPs, who were accustomed to the traditional method of rounding on their hospitalized patients. The debate over hospitalists has largely shifted from quality and efficiency to optimizing hospitalists' skills and expanding their roles (Sehgal and Wachter 2006). The American Board of Hospital Medicine (ABHM), founded in 2009 as a member board of the American Board of Physician Specialists (ABPS), is the only board of certification for hospital medicine.

Issues in Medical Practice, Training, and Supply Medical Practice

Research has shown that the way physicians practice medicine and prescribe treatments for similar conditions varies significantly. Physicians have at their disposal an increasing number of therapeutic options because of the exponential growth in medical science and technology. Conversely, increasing health care costs continue to threaten the viability of the health care delivery system. The responsibilities placed on physicians to perform difficult balancing acts between the availability of the most advanced treatments, uncertainties about their potential benefits, and whether the higher costs of treatment are justified have created a confusing environment. Hence, support has been growing for the development and refinement of standardized clinical guidelines to streamline clinical decision making and improve quality of care (discussed in Chapter 12). However, there have been some criticisms about the applicability, flexibility, and objectivity of some guidelines. Although the number of conditions for which guidelines are available is steadily increasing, guidelines for combinations of conditions are not often available. Furthermore, many of the recommendations incorporated in the most well accepted clinical guidelines permit much flexibility to practicing physicians, making it difficult to determine whether the care physicians decide to give complies with recommendations in the guidelines (Garber 2005). In addition, the changing nature of chronic diseases and comorbidities is creating new challenges in the disease-centered reactive practice patterns (Starfield 2011). A better care model such as the Chronic Care Model requires patient-centered, longitudinal, coordinated, evidence-based, and information system–supported care, which could facilitate physician–patient interaction and patient self-management (Coleman et al. 2009).

Medical Training

The principal source of funding for graduate medical education is the Medicare program, which provides explicit payments to teaching hospitals for each resident in training. The government, however, does not mandate how these physicians should be trained.

Emphasis on hospital-based training in the United States has produced more specialists than PCPs. Meanwhile, the health care delivery system is evolving toward primary care orientation. The increasing prevalence of chronic diseases further highlights the deficiency of the medical training model in the United States, which focuses mainly on acute interventions. Medical training in primary care needs to be refocused on patient-centered care (see Chapter 7), general internal medicine, and longitudinal clinical experiences (Julian et al. 2011).

Health Care Reform and Supply of Health Care Professionals

Aided by tax-financed subsidies, the United States has experienced a steady increase in its physician labor force (see Table 4–2 and Figure 4–2). In 2009, for example, there were 273 physicians per 100,000 population (US Census Bureau 2012). The number of active physicians under age 75 is expected to grow from approximately 817,500 in 2005 to 951,700 by 2020 (HRSA/BHP 2006).

The growth, however, has been mainly for specialists.

The ACA places significant emphasis on the delivery of preventive care and coordination of services. A large influx of newly insured individuals seeking care will strain the existing primary care infrastructure and result in personnel shortages in primary care (Schwartz 2011). By 2025, an additional 52,000 PCPs would be needed (Petterson et al. 2012). The problem is that the primary care workforce is shrinking. Only 32% of physicians currently practice primary care, much below the recommended minimum of 40% (COGME 2010). Moreover, almost one-quarter of the primary care workforce are 56 or older and "near retirement," and less than one-quarter of medical students are choosing primary care (COGME 2010).

To alleviate the shortages, the ACA will invest $230 million to increase the number of medical residents, nurse practitioners, and physician assistants trained in

Figure 4–2 Supply of US Physicians, Including International Medical Graduates (IMGs), per 100,000 Population, 1985–2010.

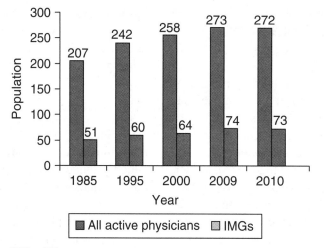

Source: Health, United States, 2012, p. 327.

primary care (The White House 2012). In July 2013, $12 million in ACA funding was awarded to train more than 300 new primary care residents during the 2013–2014 academic year; 32 teaching health centers in 21 states received funding (U.S. Department of Health and Human Services 2013).

Maldistribution

Maldistribution refers to either a surplus or a shortage of the type of physicians needed to maintain the health status of a given population at an optimum level. Even surpluses are not desirable because they result in increased health care expenditures without a positive return in health outcomes. The United States faces maldistributions in terms of both geography and specialty.

Geographic Maldistribution

One of the ironies of excess physician supply is that localities outside metropolitan areas (that is, counties with < 50,000 residents) continue to have physician shortages. Non-metropolitan areas have 59 PCPs/100,000 population compared to 94 PCPs/100,000 population in metropolitan areas (General Accounting Office 2003). Rural areas, particularly, lack an adequate supply of both PCPs and specialists even though residents in rural areas are sicker, older, and poorer than those in nonrural areas. Whereas 20% of the US population lives in rural areas, only 9% of physicians practice there (AHRQ 2005).

Health Professional Shortage Areas (HPSAs) are designations by the Department of Health and Human Services (DHHS) for urban or rural areas, population groups, or medical or other public facilities that have a shortage of providers in primary care, dental care, and mental health care. As of January 2013, there were approximately 5,900 designated primary care HPSAs, 4,600 dental HPSAs, and 3,800 mental health HPSAs (DHHS 2013).

Several federal programs have demonstrated success in increasing the supply of primary care services in rural areas. Some of these programs are discussed in Chapter 11. They include the National Health Service Corps, which makes scholarship support conditional on a commitment to future service in an underserved area; the Migrant and Community Health Center Programs, designated to provide primary care services to the poor and underserved using federal grants; and the support of primary care training programs and Area Health Education Centers.

Specialty Maldistribution

Besides geographic maldistribution of physicians, a considerable imbalance exists between primary and specialty care in the United States. Approximately 42% of physicians work in primary care; the remaining 58% are specialists (US Bureau of Labor Statistics 2011). In other industrialized countries, only 25% to 50% of physicians are specialists (Schroeder 1992).

Figure 4–3 illustrates trends in the supply of PCPs. The proportion of active PCPs has been continually declining since 1949 and has reached its lowest point in recent years. Also, a decreasing number of physicians have been entering primary care. According to one study, only 21.5% of third-year internal medicine graduating residents reported general internal medicine as their ultimate career plan. Most of the residents reported subspecialty career plans (West and Dupras 2012). Moreover, about one in six general internists leave their

Figure 4–3 Trend of US Primary Care Generalists of Medicine.

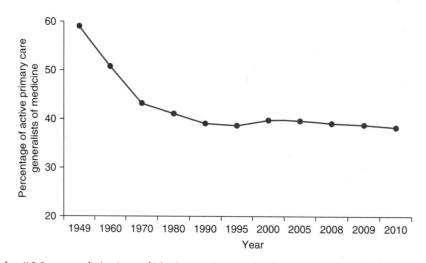

Source: Data from U.S. Department of Labor, Bureau of Labor Statistics. Occupational Employment and Wages – May 2012. http://www.bls .gov/oes/current/oes_stru.htm

practice by midcareer either due to dissatisfaction or by moving into a subspecialty of internal medicine (Bylsma et al. 2010). An increasing number of international medical graduates (IMGs) practicing in the United States have helped alleviate PCPs shortages to some extent.

Growth of new medical technology is one major driving force behind the increasing number of specialists. Because the population increases at a significantly slower rate than technological advancements, the gap between primary and specialty care workforces continues to expand.

Higher incomes of specialists relative to PCPs have also contributed to an oversupply of specialists. In recent years, reimbursement systems designed to increase payments to PCPs have been implemented, but wide disparities between the incomes of generalists and specialists continue (Table 4–4). Specialists also have more predictable work hours and enjoy higher prestige among their

colleagues and the public at large (Rosenblatt and Lishner 1991; Samuels and Shi 1993). High status and prestige are accorded to specialties engaged in employing the

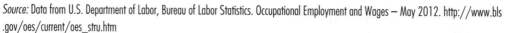

Table 4–4 Mean Annual Compensation of US Physicians by Specialty, May 2012

Anesthesiologists	232,830
Family and general practitioners	180,850
Internists, general	191,520
Obstetricians and gynecologists	216,760
Pediatricians, general	167,640
Psychiatrists	177,520
Surgeons	230,540
Physicians and surgeons, all other	184,820

Source: US Department of Labor, Bureau of Labor Statistics. *Occupational Employment and Wages* – May 2012. http://www. gov/oes/current/oes_stru.htm (accessed August 14, 2013).

Table 4–5 Percentage of Total Enrollment of Students for Selected Health Occupations, 2008–2009

Race	Allopathic	Osteopathic	Dentistry	Pharmacy	Nursing Baccalaureate
All races	100.0	100.0	100.0	100.0	100.0
White, non-Hispanic	61.7	70.0	59.9	58.9	75.2
Black, non-Hispanic	7.1	3.5	5.8	6.4	12.4
Hispanic	8.1	3.7	6.2	4.1	5.4
American Indian	0.8	0.7	0.7	0.5	0.7
Asian	21.7	17.1	23.4	22.1	6.3

Data from *Health, United States, 2010*, p. 352.

latest advances in medical technology. Such considerations influence medical students' career decisions.

The medical education environment in the United States is organized according to specialties and controlled by those who have achieved leadership positions by demonstrating their abilities in narrow scientific or clinical areas. Medical education in the United States emphasizes technology, intensive procedures, and tertiary care settings, which are generally more appealing to medical students than the more rudimentary primary care.

The imbalance between generalists and specialists has several undesirable consequences. Having too many specialists has contributed to the high volume of intensive, expensive, and invasive medical services, as well as to the rise in health care costs (Greenfield et al. 1992; Rosenblatt 1992; Schroeder and Sandy 1993; Wennberg et al. 1993). Seeking care directly from specialists is often less effective than using primary care because the latter attempts to provide early intervention before complications develop (Starfield 1992; Starfield and Simpson 1993). Higher levels of primary care professionals are associated with lower overall death and lower mortality rates due to diseases of the heart and cancer (Shi 1992, 1994). PCPs have been the major providers of care to minorities, the poor, and people living in underserved areas (Ginzberg 1994; Starr 1982), and can play a major role in overcoming disparities in health. Hence, the underserved populations suffer the most from PCP shortages.

International Medical Graduates

The ratio of IMGs to population has steadily grown over time (Figure 4–2) and so has the proportion of IMGs to total active physicians practicing in the United States (Figure 4–4). About 25% of professionally active physicians in the United States are IMGs, also known as foreign medical graduates (Cohen 2006). This translates to more than 150,000 active IMGs in the US physician workforce (Gastel 2006). An estimated one-fourth of all

Figure 4–4 MG Physicians As a Proportion of Total Active Physicians.

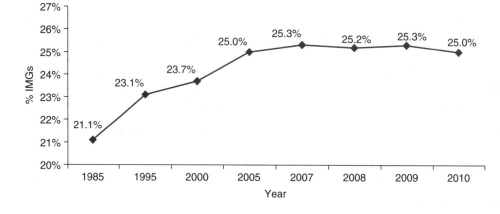

Source: Data from Health, United States, 2012, p. 309.

residency positions are filled by IMGs (AMA 2013), and an increasing number of IMGs are filling family practice residency slots (Koehn et al. 2002). In 1995, only 6.3% of IMGs entered family practice residencies; by 2003, the number had increased to 15.8% (Boulet et al. 2006). IMGs comprise 37% of total physicians in internal medicine, 28% anesthesiology, 32% in psychiatry, and 28% in pediatrics (AMA 2013).

Dentists

Dentists diagnose and treat dental problems related to the teeth, gums, and tissues of the mouth. All dentists must be licensed to practice. The licensure requirements include graduation from an accredited dental school that awards a Doctor of Dental Surgery (DDS) or Doctor of Dental Medicine (DMD) degree and successful completion of both written and practical examinations. Some states require dentists to obtain a specialty license before practicing as a specialist in that state (Stanfield et al. 2009). Nine specialty areas are recognized by the American Dental Association: orthodontics (straightening teeth), oral and maxillofacial surgery (operating on the mouth and jaws), oral and maxillofacial radiology (producing and interpreting images of the mouth and jaws), pediatric dentistry (dental care for children), periodontics (treating gums), prosthodontics (making artificial teeth or dentures), endodontics (root canal therapy), public health dentistry (community dental health), and oral pathology (diseases of the mouth). The growth of dental specialties is influenced by technological advances, including implant dentistry, laser-guided surgery, orthognathic surgery (surgery performed on the bones of the jaw) for the restoration of facial form and function, new metal combinations for use in prosthetic devices, new bone graft materials in "tissue-guided regeneration" techniques, and new materials and instruments.

Many dentists are involved in the prevention of dental decay and gum disease.

Dental prevention includes regular cleaning of patients' teeth and educating patients on proper dental hygiene. Dentists also spot symptoms that require treatment by a physician. Dentists employ dental hygienists and assistants to perform many of the preventive and routine care services.

Dental hygienists work in dental offices and provide preventive dental care, including cleaning teeth and educating patients on proper dental care. Dental hygienists must be licensed to practice. The licensure requirements include graduation from an accredited school of dental hygiene and successful completion of both a national board written examination and a state or regional clinical examination. Many states require further examination on legal aspects of dental hygiene practice.

Dental assistants work for dentists in the preparation, examination, and treatment of patients. Dental assistants do not have to be licensed to work; however, formal training programs that offer a certificate or diploma are available. Dental assistants typically work alongside dentists.

Most dentists practice in private offices as solo or group practitioners. As such, dental offices are operated as private businesses, and dentists often perform business tasks, such as staffing, financing, purchasing, leasing, and work scheduling. Some dentists are employed in clinics operated by private companies, retail stores, or franchised dental outlets. Group dental practices, offering lower overhead and increased productivity, have slowly grown. The federal government also employs dentists, mainly in the hospitals and clinics of the Department of Veterans Affairs and the US Public Health Service. Mean annual earnings of salaried dentists were $166,910 in 2012 (US Bureau of Labor Statistics 2012).

The emergence of employer-sponsored dental insurance caused an increased demand for dental care because it enabled a greater segment of the population to afford dental services. The demand for dentists will continue to grow with an increase in populations having high dental needs, such as the elderly, and an increase in public awareness of the importance of dental care toward general health status. Demand will also be affected by the fairly widespread appeal of cosmetic and esthetic dentistry, the prevalence of dental insurance plans, and the inclusion of dental care as part of many public-funded programs, such as Head Start, Medicaid, community and migrant health centers, and maternal and infant care.

Pharmacists

The traditional role of *pharmacists* has been to dispense medicines prescribed by physicians, dentists, and podiatrists and to provide consultation on the proper selection and use of medicines. All states require a license to practice pharmacy. The licensure requirements include graduation from an accredited pharmacy program that awards a Bachelor of Pharmacy or Doctor of Pharmacy (PharmD) degree, successful completion of a state board examination, and practical experience or completion of a supervised internship (Stanfield et al. 2009). After 2005, the bachelor's degree was phased out, and a PharmD, requiring 6 years of postsecondary education, became the standard. The mean annual earnings of pharmacists in 2011 were $114,950 (US Bureau of Labor Statistics 2012).

Although most pharmacists are generalists, dispensing drugs and advising providers and patients, some become specialists. Pharmacotherapists specialize in drug therapy and work closely with physicians. Nutrition-support pharmacists determine and prepare drugs needed for nutritional therapy. Radiopharmacists, or nuclear pharmacists, produce radioactive drugs used for patient diagnosis and therapy.

Most pharmacists hold salaried positions and work in community pharmacies that are independently owned or are part of a national drugstore, discount store, or department store chain. Pharmacists are also employed by hospitals, MCOs, home health agencies, clinics, government health services organizations, and pharmaceutical manufacturers.

The role of pharmacists has expanded from primarily preparing and dispensing prescriptions to include drug product education and serving as experts on specific drugs, drug interactions, and generic drug substitution.

Under the Omnibus Budget Reconciliation Act of 1990, pharmacists are required to give consumers information about drugs and their potential misuse. This educating and counseling role of pharmacists is broadly referred to as *pharmaceutical care*. The American Council on Pharmaceutical Education (ACPE; 1992) defined pharmaceutical care as "a mode of pharmacy practice in which the pharmacist takes an active role on behalf of patients, by assisting prescribers in appropriate drug choices, by effecting distribution of medications to patients, and by assuming direct responsibilities collaboratively with other health care professionals and with patients to achieve the desired therapeutic outcome." This concept entails a high level of drug knowledge, clinical skill, and independent judgment and requires that pharmacists share with other health professionals the responsibility for optimizing the outcome of patients' drug therapy, including health status, quality of life, and satisfaction (Helper and Strand 1990; Schwartz 1994; Strand et al. 1991). Pharmacists are often consulted by physicians to identify and prevent potential drug-related problems and resolve actual drug-related problems (Morley and Strand 1989).

Certain provisions within the ACA could impact pharmacists either directly or indirectly. For Medicare recipients in particular, the ACA emphasizes medical care delivery by teams of health care professionals in a coordinated delivery environment. As a result, accountable care organizations (ACOs) are emerging in certain parts of the country (see Chapter 9). Pharmacists are expected to be an integral part of the team environment of care delivery, not just as dispensers of prescriptions.

Other Doctoral-Level Health Professionals

In addition to physicians, dentists, and some pharmacists, other health professionals have doctoral education, including optometrists, psychologists, podiatrists, and chiropractors.

Optometrists provide vision care, such as examination, diagnosis, and correction of vision problems. They must be licensed to practice. The licensure requirements include the possession of a Doctor of Optometry (OD) degree and passing a written and clinical state board examination. Most optometrists work in solo or group practices. Some work for the government, optical stores, or vision care centers as salaried employees.

Psychologists provide patients with mental health care. They must be licensed or certified to practice. The ultimate recognition is the diplomate in psychology, which requires a Doctor of Philosophy (PhD) or Doctor of Psychology (PsyD) degree, a minimum of 5 years' postdoctoral experience, and the successful completion of an examination by the American Board of Examiners in Professional Psychology. Psychologists may specialize in several areas, such as clinical, counseling, developmental, educational, engineering, personnel, experimental, industrial, psychometric, rehabilitation, school, and social domains (Stanfield et al. 2009).

Podiatrists treat patients with diseases or deformities of the feet, including performing surgical operations, prescribing medications and corrective devices, and administering physiotherapy. They must be licensed to practice. Requirements for licensure include completion of an accredited program that awards a Doctor of Podiatric Medicine (DPM) degree and passing a national examination by the National Board of Podiatry. Most podiatrists work in private practice, but some are salaried employees of health service organizations.

Chiropractors provide treatment to patients through chiropractic (done by hand) manipulation, physiotherapy, and dietary counseling. They typically help patients with neurological, muscular, and vascular disturbances. Chiropractic care is based on the belief that the body is a self-healing organism. Chiropractors do not prescribe drugs or perform surgery. Chiropractors must be licensed to practice. Requirements for licensure include completion of an accredited program that awards a 4-year Doctor of Chiropractic (DC) degree and passing an examination by the state chiropractic board. Most chiropractors work in private solo or group practice.

Nurses

Nurses constitute the largest group of health care professionals. The nursing profession developed around hospitals after World War I, primarily attracting women. Before that time, more than 70% of nurses worked in private duty, either in patients' homes or for private-pay patients in hospitals. Hospital-based nursing flourished after the war as the effectiveness of nursing care became apparent. Federal support of nursing education increased after World War II, represented by the Nursing Training Act of 1964, the Health Manpower Act of 1968, and the Nursing Training Act of 1971; however, state funding remains the primary source of financial support for nursing schools.

Nurses are the major caregivers of sick and injured patients, addressing their physical, mental, and emotional needs. All states require nurses to be licensed to practice. Nurses can be licensed in more than one state through examination or endorsement of a license issued by another state. The licensure requirements include graduation from an approved nursing program and successful completion of a national examination. Educational preparation distinguishes between two levels of nurses. *Registered nurses* (RNs) must complete an associate's degree (ADN), a diploma program, or a baccalaureate degree (BSN). ADN programs take about 2 to 3 years and are offered by community and junior colleges. Diploma programs take 2 to 3 years and are still offered by a few hospitals. BSN programs take 4 to 5 years and are offered by colleges and universities (Stanfield et al. 2009). *Licensed practical nurses* (LPNs)—called licensed vocational nurses (LVNs) in some states—must complete a state-approved program in practical nursing and a national written examination. Most practical nursing programs last about 1 year and include classroom study, as well as supervised clinical practice. Head nurses act as supervisors of other nurses. RNs supervise LPNs.

Nurses work in a variety of settings listed in the introduction to this chapter. In addition, they also work in home health care, hospice care, and a variety of long-term care settings. A few work as private-duty nurses in patients' homes. Nurses are often classified according to the settings in which they work: hospital nurses, long-term care nurses, public health nurses, private-duty nurses, office nurses, and occupational health or industrial nurses. With the remarkable growth in various types of outpatient settings (see Chapter 7), hospitals and nursing homes now treat much sicker patients than before. Hence, the ratio of nurses to patients has increased, and nurses' work has become more intensive. The growing opportunities for RNs in supportive roles, such as case management, utilization review, quality assurance, and prevention counseling, have also expanded the demand for their services.

Between 2001 and 2011, the total full-time equivalent (FTE) RN workforce increased by 506,580. In 2011, registered nurse was one of the largest occupations in the United States, with more than 2.6 million RNs earning an average salary of $67,930 per year. Projections of the future need for nurses indicate there will be a deficit of 340,000 nurses in 2020 (Auerbach et al. 2007). To make the nursing profession more attractive, health services organizations need to initiate measures, such as creating incentive packages to attract new nurses, increasing pay and benefits of current nurses, introducing more flexible work schedules, awarding tuition reimbursement

for continuing education, and providing on-site daycare assistance.

A nationwide shortage of primary care providers inspired the Advanced Nursing Education Expansion Program, an ACA component that allocates $30 million to support academic training programs for nurse practitioners and certified nurse midwives. The funds help pay for instructors and for students' housing and living expenses.

Advanced Practice Nurses

The term *advanced practice nurse* (APN) is a general classification of nurses who have education and clinical experience beyond that required of an RN. APNs include four areas of specialization (Cooper et al. 1998): clinical nurse specialists (CNSs), certified registered nurse anesthetists (CRNAs), nurse practitioners (NPs), and certified nurse midwives (CNMs). NPs and CNMs are also categorized as NPPs and will be discussed in the next section. Besides being direct caregivers, APNs perform other professional activities, such as collaborating and consulting with other health care professionals; educating patients and other nurses; collecting data for clinical research projects; and participating in the development and implementation of total quality management programs, critical pathways, case management, and standards of care (Grossman 1995).

The main difference between CNSs and NPs is that CNSs work in hospitals, whereas NPs work mainly in primary care settings. CNSs can specialize in specific fields, such as oncology, neonatal health, cardiac care, or psychiatric care. Examples of their functions in an acute care hospital include taking social and clinical history at the time of admission, conducting physical assessment after admission, adjusting IV infusion rates, managing pain, managing resuscitation orders, removing intracardiac catheters, and ordering routine laboratory tests and radiographic examinations. They generally do not have the legal authority to prescribe drugs. NPs, on the other hand, may prescribe drugs in most states. CRNAs are trained to manage anesthesia during surgery, and CNMs deliver babies and manage the care of mothers and healthy newborns before, during, and after delivery. The requirements for becoming an APN vary greatly from state to state. In general, the designation requires a graduate degree in nursing or certification in an advanced practice specialty area.

Nonphysician Practitioners

The terms *nonphysician practitioners* (NPPs), nonphysician clinicians (NPCs), and midlevel providers (MLPs) refer to clinical professionals who practice in many of the areas similar to those in which physicians practice but who do not have an MD or a DO degree. NPPs receive less advanced training than physicians but more training than RNs. They are also referred to as *physician extenders* because in the delivery of primary care, they can, in many instances, substitute for physicians. However, they do not engage in the entire range of primary care or deal with complex cases requiring the expertise of a physician (Cooper et al. 1998). Hence, NPPs often work in close consultation with physicians. Efforts to formally establish the NPP role began in the late 1960s, in recognition of the fact that they could improve access to primary care, especially in rural areas.

NPPs include physician assistants (PAs), NPs, and CNMs. The expansion of health insurance coverage and the growth of the nation's population will continue to drive the demand for NPPs (Jacobson and Jazowski 2011). As of 2010, the rate of new NPs is increasing at 9.44% per capita compared to 1.7% for physicians. Approximately 12,600 NPs and PAs graduated in 2008, up from 11,200 in 2006.

Nurse Practitioners

The American Nurses Association defines *nurse practitioners* as individuals who have completed a program of study leading to competence as RNs in an expanded role. NPs constitute the largest group of NPPs. As of 2011, the United States had approximately 105,780 NPs (US Bureau of Labor Statistics 2012).

Close to 6,000 new NPs are trained every year in 325 colleges and universities (American Association of Nurse Practitioners 2013). The training of NPs may be a certificate program (at least 9 months in duration) or a master's degree program (2 years of full-time study). States vary with regard to licensure and accreditation requirements. Most NPs are now trained in graduate or postgraduate nursing programs. In addition, NPs must complete clinical training in direct patient care. Certification examinations are offered by the American Nurses Credentialing Center, the American Academy of Nurse Practitioners, and specialty nursing organizations.

NPs work predominantly in primary care, whereas PAs are evenly divided between primary care and specialty care. Another main difference between the practice orientation of NPs and PAs is that NPs are oriented toward health promotion and education; PAs are oriented more toward a practice model that focuses on disease (Hooker and McCaig 2001). NPs spend extra time with patients to help them understand the need to take responsibility for their own health.

NP specialties include pediatric, family, adult, psychiatric, and geriatric programs. NPs have statutory prescribing authority in almost all states. NPs can also receive direct reimbursement as providers under the Medicaid and Medicare programs.

Physician Assistants

The American Academy of Physician Assistants (1986) defines *physician assistants* "as part of the healthcare team . . . [who] work in a dependent relationship with a supervising physician to provide comprehensive care." In 2011, there were approximately 83,640 jobs available for PAs in the United States (US Bureau of Labor Statistics 2012). The number of PA jobs exceed the number of PAs and about 15% of PAs work more than one job.

PAs are licensed to perform medical procedures only under the supervision of a physician who may be on site or off site. The major services provided by PAs include evaluation, monitoring, diagnostics, therapeutics, counseling, and referral (Fitzgerald et al. 1995). As of 2011, 165 accredited PA training programs were operating in the United States, with a steady growth in enrollment (US Bureau of Labor Statistics 2011). PA programs award bachelor's degrees, certificates, associate degrees, or master's degrees. The mean length of the program is 26 months (Hooker and Berlin 2002). PAs are certified by the National Commission on Certification of Physician Assistants. In most states, PAs have the authority to prescribe medications.

Certified Nurse Midwives

Certified nurse midwives are RNs with additional training from a nurse midwifery program, in areas such as maternal and fetal procedures, maternity and child nursing, and patient assessment (Endicott 1976). CNMs deliver babies, provide family planning education, and manage gynecological and obstetric care and can substitute for obstetricians/gynecologists in prenatal and postnatal care. They are certified by the American College of Nurse-Midwives (ACNM) to provide care for normal expectant mothers. They refer abnormal or high-risk patients to obstetricians or jointly manage the care of such patients. There are approximately 45 ACNM-accredited nurse-midwifery education programs in the United States (US Bureau of Labor Statistics 2007).

Midwifery has never assumed the central role in the management of pregnancies in the United States that it has in Europe (Wagner 1991). Physicians, mainly obstetricians, attend most deliveries in the United States, but some evidence indicates that, for low-risk pregnancies, CNMs are much less likely to use available technical tools to monitor or modify the course of labor. Patients of CNMs are less likely to be electronically monitored, have induced labor, or receive epidural anesthesia. These differences are associated with lower Caesarean section rates and less resource use, such as hospital stay, operating room costs, and use of anesthesia staff (Rosenblatt et al. 1997).

Allied Health Professionals

The term *allied health* is used loosely to categorize several different types of professionals in a vast number of health-related technical areas. Among these professionals are technicians, assistants, therapists, and technologists. These professionals receive specialized training, and their clinical interventions complement the work of physicians and nurses. Certain professionals, however, are allowed to practice independently, depending on state law.

In the early part of the 20th century, the health care provider workforce consisted of physicians, nurses, pharmacists, and optometrists. As knowledge in health sciences expanded and medical care became more complex, physicians found it difficult to spend the necessary time with their patients. Time constraints, as well as the limitations in learning new skills, created a need to train other professionals who could serve as adjuncts to or as substitutes for physicians and nurses.

Section 701 of the Public Health Service Act defines an ***allied health professional*** as someone who has received a certificate; associate's, bachelor's, or master's degree; doctoral-level preparation; or post-baccalaureate training in a science related to health care and has responsibility for the delivery of health or related services. These services may include those associated with the identification, evaluation, and prevention of diseases and disorders, dietary and nutritional services, rehabilitation, or health system management. Further, these professionals are other than those who have received a degree in medicine, dentistry, veterinary medicine, optometry, podiatry, chiropractic, or pharmacy; a graduate degree in health administration; a degree in clinical psychology; or a degree equivalent to one of these.

Allied health professionals can be divided into two broad categories: technicians/assistants and therapists/technologists. The main allied health professions in the United States are listed in Exhibit 4–2.

Formal requirements for these professionals range from certificates gained in postsecondary educational programs to postgraduate degrees for some professions.

Exhibit 4–2 Examples of Allied Health Professionals

Activities Coordinator
Audiology Technician
Cardiovascular Technician
Cytotechnologist
Dental Assistant
Dietary Food Service Manager
Exercise Physiologist
Histologic Technician
Laboratory Technician
Legal Services
Medical Records Technician
Medical Technologist
Mental Health Worker
Nuclear Medicine
Occupational Therapist
Occupational Therapy Assistant
Optician
Pharmacist
Physical Therapist
Physical Therapy Assistant
Physician Assistant
Radiology Technician
Recreation Therapist
Registered Dietitian
Registered Records Administrator
Respiratory Therapist
Respiratory Therapy Technician
Social Services Coordinator
Social Worker
Speech Therapist
Speech Therapy Assistant

Typically, technicians and assistants receive less than 2 years of postsecondary education. They require supervision from therapists or technologists to ensure that treatment plans are followed. Technicians and assistants include physical therapy assistants (PTAs), certified occupational therapy assistants (COTAs), medical laboratory technicians, radiologic technicians, and respiratory therapy technicians.

Technologists and therapists receive more advanced training. They evaluate patients, diagnose problems, and develop treatment plans. Many technologists and therapists have independent practices. For example, physical therapy is practiced in most US states without the requirement of a prescription or referral from a physician. Many states also allow occupational therapists and speech therapists to see patients without referral from a physician.

Therapists

Physical therapists (PTs) provide care for patients with movement dysfunction. Educational programs in physical therapy are accredited by the Commission on Accreditation of Physical Therapy Education. Of the 212 physical therapist education programs in the United States, in 2009, 12 awarded master's degrees and 200 awarded doctoral degrees. Currently, only graduate degree physical therapy programs are accredited. Master's degree programs typically are 2 to 3 years in length, while doctoral degree programs last 3 years. To obtain a license, PTs must also pass the National Physical Therapy Examination or a similar state-administered exam (US Bureau of Labor Statistics 2013).

Occupational therapists (OTs) help people of all ages improve their ability to perform tasks in their daily living and working environments. They work with individuals who have conditions that are mentally, physically, developmentally, or emotionally disabling. A master's degree in occupational therapy is the typical minimum requirement for entry into the field. In 2009, 150 master's degree programs or combined bachelor's and master's degree programs were accredited, and 4 doctoral degree programs were accredited by the Accreditation Council for Occupational Therapy Education (US Bureau of Labor Statistics 2011).

Speech–language pathologists treat patients with speech and language problems. Audiologists treat patients with hearing problems. The American Speech-Language-Hearing Association is the credentialing association for audiologists and speech–language pathologists.

Other Allied Health Professionals

Medical dietetics includes dietitians or nutritionists and dietetic technicians who ensure that institutional foods and diets are prepared in accordance with acceptable nutritional standards. Dietitians are registered by the Commission on Dietetic Registration of the Academy of Nutrition and Dietetics. Dispensing opticians fit eyeglasses and contact lenses. They are certified by the American Board of Opticianry and the National Contact Lens Examiners. Social workers help patients and families cope with problems resulting from long-term illness, injury, and rehabilitation. The Council on Social Work Education accredits baccalaureate and master's degree programs in social work in the United States.

Many programs are accredited by the Committee on Allied Health Education and Accreditation under the American Medical

Association, including anesthesiologist assistants, cardiovascular technologists, cytotechnologists (study changes in body cells under a microscope), diagnostic medical sonographers (work with ultrasound diagnostic procedures), electroneurodiagnostic technologists (work with procedures related to the electrical activity of the brain and nervous system), emergency medical technician–paramedics (provide medical emergent care to acutely ill or injured persons in prehospital settings), histologic technicians/technologists (analyze blood, tissue, and fluids), medical assistants (perform a number of administrative and clinical duties in physicians' offices), medical illustrators, medical laboratory technicians, medical record administrators (direct the medical records department), medical record technicians (organize and file medical records), medical technologists (perform clinical laboratory testing), nuclear medicine technologists (operate diagnostic imaging equipment and use radioactive drugs to assist in the diagnosis of illness), ophthalmic medical technicians, perfusionists (operate life support respiratory and circulatory equipment), radiologic technologists (perform diagnostic imaging exams, such as X-rays, computed tomography, magnetic resonance imaging, and mammography), respiratory therapists and technicians (treat patients with breathing disorders), specialists in blood bank technology, surgeon's assistants, and surgical technologists (prepare operating rooms and patients for surgery).

Certain health care workers are not required to be licensed, and they usually learn their skills on the job; however, their roles are limited to assisting other professionals in the provision of services. Examples include dietetic assistants, who assist dietitians or dietetic technicians in the provision of nutritional care;

electroencephalogram technologists or technicians, who operate electroencephalographs; electrocardiogram technicians, who operate electrocardiographs; paraoptometrics, including optometric technicians and assistants, who perform basic tasks related to vision care; health educators, who provide individuals and groups with facts on health, illness, and prevention; psychiatric/mental health technicians, who provide care to patients with mental illness or developmental disabilities; and sanitarians, who collect samples for laboratory analysis and inspect facilities for compliance with public health regulations. Increasingly, these practitioners seek their credentials through certifications, registrations, and training programs.

As the number of older people continues to grow and as new developments allow for the treatment of more medical conditions, more allied health professionals will be needed. For example, home health aides will be needed as more individuals seek care outside of traditional institutional settings. Jobs for LPNs, LVNs, and pharmacy technicians are also expected to increase by a substantial number, roughly 168,500 and 108,300, respectively (US Bureau of Labor Statistics 2013).

To meet the growing demand for allied health professionals, the ACA has provisions for the forgiveness of existing education loans. The program includes allied health professionals who are employed full-time in a federal, state, local, or tribal public health agency or other qualified employment location, including acute care and ambulatory care facilities, settings located in Health Professional Shortage Areas, or medically underserved areas (Redhead and Williams 2010). The law also includes Mid-career Training Grants (Section 5206) for the Health Resources and Services Administration (HRSA) to support scholarships for mid-career professionals in public health or allied health working in federal, state, tribal, or local public health agencies or clinical health care settings to further their education in health.

Health Services Administrators

Health services administrators are employed at the top, middle, and entry levels of various types of organizations that deliver health services. Top-level administrators provide leadership and strategic direction, work closely with the governing boards (see Chapter 8), and are responsible for an organization's long-term success. They are responsible for operational, clinical, and financial outcomes of their entire organization. Middle-level administrators may have leadership roles for major service centers, such as outpatient, surgical, and nursing services, or they may be departmental managers in charge of single departments, such as diagnostics, dietary, rehabilitation, social services, environmental services, or medical records. Their jobs involve major planning and coordinating functions, organizing human and physical resources, directing and supervising, operational and financial controls, and decision making. They often have direct responsibility for implementing changes, creating efficiencies, and developing new procedures with respect to changes in the health care delivery system. Entry-level administrators may function as assistants to middle-level managers. They may supervise a small number of operatives. For example, their main function may be to oversee and assist with operations critical to the efficient operation of a departmental unit.

Today's medical centers and integrated delivery organizations are among the most complex organizations to manage. Leaders in health care delivery face some unique challenges, including changes in financing and payment structures, as well as having to work with reduced levels of reimbursement. Other challenges include pressures to provide uncompensated care, greater responsibility for quality, accountability for community health, separate contingencies imposed by public and private payers, uncertainties created by new policy developments, changing configurations in the competitive environment, and maintaining the integrity of an organization through the highest level of ethical standards.

Health services administration is taught at the bachelor's and master's levels in a variety of settings, and the programs lead to several different degrees. The settings for such academic programs include schools of medicine, public health, public administration, business administration, and allied health sciences. Bachelor's degrees prepare students for entry-level positions. Mid- and senior-level positions require a graduate degree. The most common degrees are the Master of Health Administration (MHA) or Master of Health Services Administration (MHSA), Master of Business Administration (MBA, with a health care management emphasis), Master of Public Health (MPH), or Master of Public Administration (or Affairs; MPA). The schools of public health that are accredited by the Council on Education for Public Health (CEPH) play a key role in training health services administrators in their MHA (or MHSA) and MPH programs (CEPH 2011). The MHA programs, however, compared to the MPH programs, have more course requirements to furnish skills in business management (both theory and applied management) and quantitative/analytical areas, considered crucial for managing today's health services organizations. This disparity has been viewed as a concern that the schools of public health need to address (Singh et al. 1996).

Educational preparation of nursing home administrators is a notable exception to the MHA model. The training of nursing home administrators has largely been influenced by government licensing regulations. Even though licensure of nursing home administrators dates back to the mid-1960s, regulations favoring a formal postsecondary academic degree are more recent. Passing a national examination administered by the National Association of Boards of Examiners of Long-Term Care Administrators (NAB) is a standard requirement; however, educational qualifications needed to obtain a license vary significantly from one state to another. Although about one-third of the states still require less than a bachelor's degree as the minimum academic preparation, an increasing number of practicing nursing home administrators have at least a bachelor's degree. The problem is that most state regulations call for only general levels of education rather than specialized preparation in long-term care administration. General education does not furnish adequate skills in all the domains of practice relevant to nursing home management (Singh et al. 1997). However, various colleges and universities offer specialized programs in nursing home administration.

Global Health Workforce Challenges

A 2006 World Health Organization (WHO) Report identified 57 countries that were facing a health workforce crisis, meaning that each country had less than 23 health workers per 10,000 people (WHO 2006). Most of these countries are poor and predominately in sub-Saharan Africa. The report also pointed out that a provider shortage of 4.3 million doctors, midwives, nurses, and support workers existed (WHO 2006). Another publication emphasized that the shifting from acute to chronic health problems is placing different demands on the health care workforce, as addressing chronic diseases requires different resources and skill sets (WHO 2005). The increased prevalence of chronic conditions globally introduces the need for the workforce to adopt a patient-centered approach, improve communication skills, ensure safety and quality of patient care, monitor patients across time, use available technology, and consider care from a population perspective (WHO 2005).

In Europe, while the number of physicians per capita is increasing, it appears to be insufficient to accommodate the growing needs of an aging population (Lang 2011). In addition, there are far more specialists than generalists in recent years, as well as projected shortages of nurses, physiotherapists, and occupational therapists (Lang 2011). The situation is similar in the United States, where the number of older adults is expected to double between 2005 and 2030 (Institute of Medicine 2008). An aging health workforce is also an important issue to consider. The United States is hoping to enhance the geriatric workforce, as well as the retention of geriatric specialists (Institute of Medicine 2008). There is a growth in the number of non-MDs providing care in order to address these shortages (Riegel et al. 2012).

A growing public health concern is the migration of health professionals from developing countries to the United States,

United Kingdom, Canada, and Australia. For example, IMGs make up 25% of the US physician population (this includes US citizens who go to medical schools abroad) (AMA 2010). WHO has developed the Global Code of Practice on the International Recruitment of Health Personnel, which sets principles and voluntary standards for countries to consider in workforce development and recruitment. Components of the code are (WHO 2013):

- greater commitment to assist countries facing critical health worker shortages with their efforts to improve and support their health workforce;
- joint investment in research and information systems to monitor the international migration of health workers in order to develop evidence-based policies;
- member states should meet their health personnel needs with their own human resources as far as possible and thus take measures to educate, retain, and sustain their health workforce; and
- migrant workers' rights are enshrined and equal to domestically trained health workers.

The opposite of this migration appears to be another growing trend in the form of medical tourism (see Chapter 3). The industry and economic impacts of medical tourism remain unknown, and this is a field for increased research (Connell 2006).

Summary

Health services professionals in the United States constitute the largest labor force.

The development of these professionals is influenced by demographic trends, advances in research and technology, disease and illness trends, and the changing environment of health care financing and delivery. Physicians play a leading role in the delivery of health services. The United States has a maldistribution of physicians both by specialty and by geography. The current shortage of health care workforce, especially PCPs, is likely to continue into the future, considering the growth and aging of the population, the growing burden of chronic diseases and the implementation of ACA. Various policies and programs have been used or proposed to address both physician imbalance and maldistribution, including regulation of health care professions, reimbursement initiatives targeting suitable incentives, targeted programs for underserved areas, changes in medical school curricula, changes in the financing of medical training, and a more rational referral system.

In addition to physicians, many other health services professionals contribute significantly to the delivery of health care, including nurses, dentists, pharmacists, optometrists, psychologists, podiatrists, chiropractors, NPPs, and other allied health professionals. These professionals require different levels of training. They work in a variety of health care settings as complements to or substitutes for physicians. Health services administrators face new challenges in the leadership of health care organizations. These challenges call for some reforms in the educational programs designed to prepare adequately trained managers for the various sectors of the health care industry.

ACA Takeaway

- A large influx of newly insured individuals seeking care will strain the existing primary care infrastructure.
- $230 million will be invested to increase the number of medical residents, nurse practitioners, and physician assistants trained in primary care.
- For Medicare recipients in particular, the ACA emphasizes medical care delivery by teams of health care professionals in a coordinated delivery environment.
- The Advanced Nursing Education Expansion Program allocates funds to support academic training programs for nurse practitioners and certified nurse midwives.
- To meet the growing demand for allied health professionals, the ACA provides for loan forgiveness for individuals who choose to work in certain locations.

Test Your Understanding

Terminology

advanced practice nurse
allied health
allied health professional
allopathic medicine
certified nurse midwives
chiropractors
comorbidity
dental assistants
dental hygienists
dentists
generalist

hospitalist
licensed practical nurses
maldistribution
nonphysician practitioners
nurse practitioners
occupational therapists
optometrists
osteopathic medicine
pharmaceutical care
pharmacists
physical therapists

physician assistants
physician extenders
podiatrists
primary care
psychologists
registered nurses
residency
specialist
specialty care

Review Questions

1. Describe the major types of health services professionals (physicians, nurses, dentists, pharmacists, physician assistants, nurse practitioners, certified nurse midwives), including their roles, training, practice requirements, and practice settings.

2. What factors are associated with the development of health services professionals in the United States?

3. What are the major distinctions between primary care and specialty care?

4. Why is there a geographic maldistribution of the physician labor force in the United States?

5. Why is there an imbalance between primary care and specialty care in the United States?

6. What measures have been or can be employed to overcome problems related to physician maldistribution and imbalance?

7. Who are nonphysician primary care providers? What are their roles in the delivery of health care?

8. In general, who are allied health professionals? What role do they play in the delivery of health services?

9. Provide a brief description of the roles and responsibilities of health services administrators.

REFERENCES

Agency for Healthcare Research and Quality (AHRQ). 2005. *Health care disparities in rural areas: Selected findings from the 2004 National Healthcare Disparities Report*. Available at: http://www.ahrq.gov/research/ruraldisp/ruraldispar.htm. Accessed October 2010.

American Academy of Physician Assistants. 1986. *PA fact sheet*. Arlington, VA: Author.

American Association of Colleges of Osteopathic Medicine. 2007. Available at: http://www.aacom.org/om.html. Accessed January 2007.

American Association of Nurse Practitioners. 2013. Available at: http://www.aanp.org/. Accessed December 2013.

American Council on Pharmaceutical Education. 1992. *The proposed revision of accreditation standards and guidelines*. Chicago: National Association of Boards on Pharmacy.

American Medical Association (AMA). 2010. International Medical Graduates in American Medicine: Contemporary challenges and opportunities. Available at: http://www.ama-assn.org/resources/doc/img/img-workforce-paper.pdf. Accessed December 2013.

American Medical Association (AMA). 2013. IMGs in the United States. http://www.ama-assn.org//ama/pub/about-ama/our-people/member-groups-sections/international-medical-graduates/imgs-in-united-states.page. Accessed August 21, 2013.

Association of American Medical Colleges. 2012. Estimating the number and characteristics of hospitalist physicians in the United States and their possible workforce implications. *Analysis in Brief* 12, no. 3.

Auerbach, D.I., et al. 2007. Better late than never: Workforce supply implications of later entry into nursing. *Health Affairs* 26, no. 1: 178–185.

Boulet, J.R., et al. 2006. The international medical graduate pipeline: Recent trends in certification and residency training. *Health Affairs* 25, no. 6: 469–477.

Bylsma, W.H., et al. 2010. Where have all the general internists gone? *Journal of General Internal Medicine* 25, no. 10: 1020–1023.

Cohen, J.J. 2006. The role and contribution of IMGs: A US perspective. *Academic Medicine* 81, no. 12 (suppl): S17–S21.

Coleman, K., et al. 2009. Evidence on the chronic care model in the new millennium. *Health Affairs* 28, no. 1: 75–85.

Connell J. 2006. Contemporary medical tourism: Conceptualisation, culture and commodification. *Tourism Management*, 34, 1–13.

Cooper, R.A. 1994. Seeking a balanced physician workforce for the 21st century. *Journal of the American Medical Association* 272, no. 9: 680–687.

Cooper, R.A., et al. 1998. Current and projected workforce of nonphysician clinicians. *Journal of the American Medical Association* 280, no. 9: 788–794.

Council on Education for Public Health (CEPH). 2011. *ASPH graduate training programs*. Available at: http://www.asph.org/document.cfm?page=752. Accessed January 2011.

Council on graduate Medical Education (COGME). 2010. *Twentieth report: Advancing primary care*. Available at: http://www.hrsa.gov/advisorycommittees/bhpradvisory/cogme/Reports/twentiethreport.pdf. Accessed August 2013.

Department of Health and Human Services (DHHS). 2013. *Shortage designation: Health professional shortage areas & medically underserved areas/populations*. Available at: http://www.hrsa.gov/shortage/. Accessed August 2013.

Endicott, K.M. 1976. Health and health manpower. In: *Health in America: 1776–1976*. Health Resources Administration, US Public Health Service. DHEW Pub. No. 76616. Washington, DC: US Department of Health, Education, and Welfare: pp. 138–165.

Fitzgerald, M.A., et al. 1995. The midlevel provider: Colleague or competitor? *Patient Care* 29, no. 1: 20.

Freed, D.H. 2004. Hospitalists: Evolution, evidence, and eventualities. *The Health Care Manager* 23, no. 3: 238–256.

Garber, A.M. 2005. Evidence-based guidelines as a foundation for performance incentives. *Health Affairs* 24, no.1: 174–179.

Gastel, B. 2006. Concurrent sessions: Exploring issues relating to international medical graduates. *Academic Medicine* 81, no. 12 (suppl): S63–S68.

General Accounting Office. 2003. *Physician workforce: Physician supply increased in metropolitan and nonmetropolitan areas but geographic disparities persisted*. Available at: http://www.gao.gov/new.items/d04124.pdf. Accessed October 2010.

Ginzberg, E. 1994. Improving health care for the poor. *Journal of the American Medical Association* 271, no. 6: 464–467.

Greenfield, S., et al. 1992. Variation in resource utilization among medical specialties and systems of care. *Journal of the American Medical Association* 267, no. 12: 1624–1630.

Grossman, D. 1995. APNs: Pioneers in patient care. *American Journal of Nursing* 95, no. 8: 54–56.

Health Resources and Services Administration, Bureau of Health Professions (HRSA/BHP). 2006. *Physician supply and demand: Projections to 2020*. Available at: http://bhpr.hrsa.gov/healthworkforce/supplydemand/medicine/physician2020projections.pdf. Accessed December 2013.

Helper, C., and L. Strand. 1990. Opportunities and responsibilities in pharmaceutical care. *American Journal of Hospital Pharmacy* 47, no. 3: 533–543.

Hooker, R.S., and L.E. Berlin. 2002. Trends in the supply of physician assistants and nurse practitioners in the United States. *Health Affairs* 21, no. 5: 174–181.

Hooker, R.S., and L.F. McCaig. 2001. Use of physician assistants and nurse practitioners in primary care, 1995–1999. *Health Affairs* 20, no. 4: 231–238.

Institute of Medicine. 2008. Retooling for an Aging America: Building the Health Care Workforce. April. Available at: http://www.iom.edu/~/media/Files /Report%20Files/2008/Retooling-for-an-Aging-America-Building-the-Health-Care-Workforce/ReportBriefRetoolingforanAgingAmerica BuildingtheHealthCareWorkforce.pdf. Accessed December 2013.

Jacobson, P.D., and S.A. Jazowski. 2011. Physicians, the Affordable Care Act, and primary care: Disruptive change or business as usual? *Journal of General Internal Medicine* 26, no. 8: 934–937.

Julian, K., et al. 2011. Creating the next generation of general internists: A call for medical education reform. *Academic Medicine* 86, no. 11: 1443–1447.

Kahn, N.B., et al. 1994. AAFP constructs definitions related to primary care. *American Family Physician* 50, no. 6: 1211–1215.

Koehn, N.N., et al. 2002. The increase in international medical graduates in family practice residency programs. *Family Medicine* 34, no. 6: 429–435.

Lang, R. 2011. Future challenges to the provision of health care in the 21st century. University College London. Available at: http://www.ucl.ac.uk/lc-ccr/downloads/presentations/R_LANG_COHEHRE_LISBON_PRESENTATION.pdf. Accessed December 2013.

Morley, P., and L. Strand. 1989. Critical reflections of therapeutic drug monitoring. *Journal of Clinical Pharmacy* 2, no. 3: 327–334.

Petterson, S.M., et al. 2012. Projecting US primary care physician workforce needs: 2010–2025. *Annals of Family Medicine* 10, no. 6: 503–509.

Redhead, C.S., and E.D. Williams. 2010. *Public health, workforce, quality, and related provisions in PPACA: Summary and timeline.* Congressional Research Service.

Rich, E.C., et al. 1994. Preparing generalist physicians: The organizational and policy context. *Journal of General Internal Medicine* 9 (suppl 1): S115–S122.

Riegel, B., et al. 2012. Meeting global needs in primary care with nurse practitioners. *The Lancet* 380, no. 9840; 449–450.

Rosenblatt, R.A. 1992. Specialists or generalists: On whom should we base the American health care system? *Journal of the American Medical Association* 267, no. 12: 1665–1666.

Rosenblatt, R.A., et al. 1997. Interspecialty differences in the obstetric care of low-risk women. *American Journal of Public Health* 87: 344–351.

Rosenblatt, R.A., and D.M. Lishner. 1991. Surplus or shortage? Unraveling the physician supply conundrum. *Western Journal of Medicine* 154, no. 1: 43–50.

Samuels, M.E., and L. Shi. 1993. *Physician recruitment and retention: A guide for rural medical group practice.* Englewood, CO: Medical Group Management Press.

Schneller, E.S. 2006. The hospitalist movement in the United States: Agency and common agency issues. *Health Care Management Review* 31, no. 4: 308–316.

Schroeder, S., and L.G. Sandy. 1993. Specialty distribution of U.S. physicians: The invisible driver of health care costs. *New England Journal of Medicine* 328, no. 13: 961–963.

Schroeder, S.A. 1992. Physician supply and the U.S. medical marketplace. *Health Affairs* 11, no. 1: 235–243.

Schwartz, M. 1994. Creating pharmacy's future. *American Pharmacy* NS34: 44–45, 59.

Schwartz, M.D. 2011. Health care reform and the primary care workforce bottleneck. *Journal of General Internal Medicine* 27, no. 4: 469–472.

Sehgal, N.J., and R.M. Wachter. 2006. The expanding role of hospitalists in the United States. *Swiss Medical Weekly* 136: 591–596.

Shi, L. 1992. The relation between primary care and life chances. *Journal of Health Care for the Poor and Underserved* 3, no. 2: 321–335.

Shi, L. 1994. Primary care, specialty care, and life chances. *International Journal of Health Services* 24, no. 3: 431–458.

Singh, D.A., et al. 1996. A comparison of academic curricula in the MPH and the MHA-type degrees in health administration at the accredited schools of public health. *The Journal of Health Administration Education* 14, no. 4: 401–414.

Singh, D.A., et al. 1997. How well trained are nursing home administrators? *Hospital and Health Services Administration* 42, no. 1: 101–115.

Stanfield, P.S., et al. 2009. *Introduction to the health professions.* 2nd ed. Sudbury, MA: Jones and Bartlett Publishers.

Starfield, B. 1992. *Primary care: Concepts, evaluation, and policy.* New York: Oxford University Press.

Starfield, B., and L. Simpson. 1993. Primary care as part of US health services reform. *Journal of the American Medical Association* 269, no. 24: 3136–3139.

Starfield, B. 2011. Point: The changing nature of disease implications for health services. *Medical Care* 49, no. 11: 971–972.

Starr, P. 1982. *The social transformation of American medicine: The rise of a sovereign profession and the making of a vast industry.* New York: Basic Books.

Strand, L.R., et al. 1991. Levels of pharmaceutical care: A needs-based approach. *American Journal of Hospital Pharmacy* 48, no. 3: 547–550.

The White House. (2012). Fact sheet: Creating health care jobs by addressing primary care workforce needs. Available at: http://www.whitehouse.gov/the-press-office/2012/04/11/fact-sheet-creating-health-care-jobs-addressing-primary-care-workforce-n. Accessed December 2013.

US Bureau of Labor Statistics. 2007. *Occupational outlook handbook, 2006–2007.* Available at: http://www.bls.gov/oco/home.htm. Accessed January 2007.

US Bureau of Labor Statistics. 2009. *Occupational employment and wages.* Available at: http:// www.bls.gov/oes/2009/may/figure1.pdf. Accessed December 2010.

US Bureau of Labor Statistics. 2012. *Occupational employment and wages – May 2012.* Available at: http://www.bls.gov/oes/current/oes_stru.htm. Accessed August 2013.

US Bureau of Labor Statistics. 2011. *Occupational outlook handbook, 2010–11.* Available at: http:// www.bls.gov/oco/home.htm. Accessed January 2011.

US Bureau of Labor Statistics. 2013. *Occupational outlook handbook, 2012–13.* Available at: http:// www.bls.gov/oco/home.htm. Accessed August 2013.

US Census Bureau. 2012. *Statistical abstract of the United States, 2011.* Washington, DC: US Census Bureau.

US Department of Health and Human Services. 2013. HHS awards $12 million to help teaching health centers train primary care providers. Available at: http://www.hhs.gov/news/press/2013pres/07/20130719a.html. Accessed December 2013.

Wachter, R.M. 2004. Hospitalists in the United States—Mission accomplished or work in progress? *New England Journal of Medicine* 350, no. 19: 1935–1936.

Wagner, M. 1991. Maternal and child health services in the United States. *Journal of Public Health Policy* 12, no. 4: 443–449.

West, C.P., and Dupras D.M. 2012. General medicine vs subspecialty career plans among internal medicine residents. *JAMA* 308, no. 21: 2241–2247.

Wennberg, J.E., et al. 1993. Finding equilibrium in U.S. physician supply. *Health Affairs* 12, no. 2: 89–103.

World Bank. 2013. Health expenditure, total (% of GDP). Available at: http://data.worldbank.org/indicator/SH.XPD.TOTL.ZS. Accessed August 21, 2013.

World Health Organization (WHO). 2006. The World Health Report 2006: Working together for health. Available at: http://www.who.int/whr/2006/en/index.html. Accessed December 2013.

World Health Organization (WHO). 2005. Preparing a health care workforce for the 21st century. The challenge of chronic conditions. Available at: http://www.who.int/chp/knowledge/publications /workforce_report.pdf. Accessed December 2013.

World Health Organization (WHO). 2013. Migration of health workers. Available at: http://www .who.int/mediacentre/factsheets/fs301/en/. Accessed December 2013.

Appendix 4–A

List of Professional Associations

Academy of Nutrition and Dietetics
American Academy of Nurse Practitioners
American Academy of Physician Assistants
American Art Therapy Association, Inc.
American Association for Practical Nurse Education and Service
American Association for Rehabilitation Therapy
American Association for Respiratory Care
American Association of Colleges of Nursing
American Association of Colleges of Osteopathic Medicine
American Association of Colleges of Pharmacy
American Association of Dental Schools
American Association of Homes and Services for the Aging
American Association of Medical Assistants
American Chiropractic Association
American College of Emergency Physicians
American College of Health Care Administrators
American College of Healthcare Executives
American College of Nurse-Midwives
American Corrective Therapy Association
American Council on Pharmaceutical Education
American Dance Therapy Association
American Dental Assistants Association
American Dental Association
American Dental Association SELECT Program
American Dental Hygienists' Association

American Health Care Association
American Hospital Association
American Medical Association
American Medical Technologists
American Nurses Association
American Occupational Therapy Association
American Optometry Association
American Organization of Nurse Executives
American Osteopathic Association
American Pharmaceutical Association
American Physical Therapy Association
American Psychiatric Association
American Psychological Association
American Public Health Association
American Registry of Radiologic Technologists
American School Health Association
American Society of Clinical Pathologists
American Society of Hospital Pharmacists
American Society of Radiologic Technologists
American Speech–Language–Hearing Association
American Therapeutic Recreation Association
Association of American Medical Colleges
Association of Physician Assistant Programs
Association of Schools and Colleges of Optometry
Association of Schools of Public Health
Association of Surgical Technologists
Association of University Programs in Health Administration

Council on Podiatry Education
Council on Social Work Education
Dental Assisting National Board, Inc.
Environmental Management Association
Healthcare Financial Management Association
International Society for Clinical Laboratory Technology
National Academy of Opticianry
National Association for Music Therapy
National Association of Boards of Pharmacy
National Association of Chain Drug Stores
National Association of Emergency Medical Technicians
National Association of Social Workers
National Board for Respiratory Care
National Board of Podiatry
National Certification Agency for Medical Laboratory Personnel

National Commission for Health Certifying Agencies
National Council for Therapeutic Recreational Certification
National Council for Therapy and Rehabilitation through Horticulture
National Environmental Health Association
National League for Nursing
National Nursing Centers Consortium
National Registry of Emergency Medical Technicians
National Society of Cardiovascular Technology
National Society of Pulmonary Technology
National Therapeutic Recreation Association
Opticians Association of America
Society of Nuclear Medicine

Chapter 5

Medical Technology

Learning Objectives

- To understand the meaning and role of medical technology in health care delivery
- To appreciate the growing applications of information technology and informatics in the delivery of health care
- To survey the factors influencing the creation, dissemination, and utilization of technology
- To discuss the government's role in technology diffusion
- To examine the impact of technology on various aspects of domestic and global delivery of health care
- To study the various facets of health technology assessment, and its current and future directions
- To become familiar with provisions in the Affordable Care Act that pertain to medical technology

"This must be high technology."

Introduction

Drake and colleagues (1993) labeled technology as "the boon and bane of medicine." In one respect, medical technology has been a great blessing to modern civilization. Sophisticated diagnostic procedures have reduced complications and disability, new medical cures have increased longevity, and new drugs have helped stabilize chronic conditions. However, most new technology comes at a price that society must ultimately pay. A tremendous amount of costly research is necessary to produce most modern breakthroughs. Once technology is developed and put into use, even more costs are generated. Yet, issues surrounding the unrestrained development and use of new technology have received little attention from policymakers.

Chapter 3 pointed out that developments in science and technology were instrumental in transforming the nature of health care delivery during the postindustrial era. Since then, the ever-increasing proliferation of new technology has continued to profoundly alter many facets of health care delivery. Besides its role in medical cost inflation, technology has triggered other changes: (1) Technology has raised consumer expectations that the latest may also be the best. These expectations have led to increased demand and utilization of new technology once it becomes available. (2) Technology has changed the organization of medical services. Specialized services that previously could be offered only in hospitals are now available in outpatient settings and patients' homes. (3) Technology has driven the scope and content of medical training and the practice of medicine, fueling specialization in medicine. (4) Technology has influenced the way status is imputed to various medical workers. Specialization is held in higher regard than primary care and public health. (5) Technology assessment is becoming a growing activity because new drugs, devices, and procedures are not always useful or safe. Their effectiveness and potential negative consequences must be evaluated using scientific methods. (6) Technology has raised complex social and ethical concerns that defy straightforward solutions. Perplexing social and ethical controversies pertaining to modern innovations raise such questions as: Who should be subjected to the experimental evaluations of technological breakthroughs to assess their safety and effectiveness? Who should and who should not receive high-tech interventions? To what extent should life-supporting procedures be continued? Is it moral to use human embryos in biomedical research? How can safety and effectiveness be assured for experimental technologies, such as nanomedicine.

Globalization has also enveloped biomedical knowledge and technology. In both developed and developing nations, physicians have access to the same scientific knowledge through medical journals and the Internet. Most drugs and medical devices available in the United States are also available in almost all parts of the world. However, depending on the extent of supply-side rationing (see Chapter 2), the adoption of new technology often differs widely from one country to another. Thus, even in developed nations, people do not always have adequate access to the latest high-tech therapies. Conversely, in almost all parts of the world, people who possess adequate means can gain access to the latest and best in medicine regardless of the type of health care delivery system in their country.

This chapter discusses medical technology from multiple angles. Highlights from the American Recovery and Reinvestment Act of 2009 and the Affordable Care Act (ACA) are also incorporated.

What Is Medical Technology?

At a fundamental level, *medical technology* is the practical application of the scientific body of knowledge for the purpose of improving health and creating efficiencies in the delivery of health care. Medical science benefited from rapid developments in other applied sciences, such as chemistry, physics, engineering, and pharmacology. For example, advances in organic chemistry made it possible to identify and extract the active ingredients in plants to produce drugs and anesthetics, which then became available in purer forms that were better adapted to controlled dosages than their earlier botanical forms. Magnetic resonance imaging (MRI), a technology that had its origins in basic research on the structure of the atom, was later transformed into a major diagnostic tool (Gelijns and Rosenberg 1994). The disciplines of computer science and communication systems find their application in information technology and telemedicine (Tan 1995).

Nanomedicine is an emerging area, still in its infancy, which involves the application of nanotechnology for medical use. Nanotechnology is not confined to a single field, but requires an intense collaboration between disciplines to manipulate materials on the atomic and molecular level (one nanometer is one-billionth of a meter; Taub 2011). Nonomedicine has potential applications in both diagnostics and therapeutics. For example, a screening test has been developed to identify lung cancer in its very early stages (Taub 2011). Nanoparticles are being developed as effective carriers of drugs to target regions of the body that have been hard to reach using traditional drug formulations (Thorley and Tetley 2013).

Medical technology runs across many facets of health care delivery. Table 5–1 gives examples of some of the main applications of medical technology.

Information Technology and Informatics

Information technology (IT) deals with the transformation of data into useful information. IT involves determining data needs, gathering appropriate data, storing and analyzing the data, and reporting the information in a format desired by its end users. Different types of information are made available for specific uses to health care professionals, managers, payers, patients, researchers, and the government.

Many health care organizations have IT departments and managers to handle the continually increasing flow of information (Tan 1995). IT departments play a critical role in decisions to adopt new information technologies to improve health care delivery, increase organizational efficiency, and comply with various laws and regulations. Health care IT includes medical records systems to collect, transcribe, and store clinical data; radiology and clinical laboratory reporting systems; pharmacy data systems to monitor medication use and avoid errors, adverse reactions, and drug interactions; scheduling systems for patients, space (such as surgery suites), and personnel; and financial systems for billing and collections, materials management, and many other aspects of organizational management (Cohen 2004a).

• •

Table 5–1 Examples of Medical Technologies

Type	Examples
Diagnostic	CAT scanner
	Fetal monitor
	Computerized electrocardiography
	Automated clinical laboratories
	Magnetic resonance imaging
	Blood pressure monitor
Survival (life saving)	Intensive care unit (ICU)
	Cardiopulmonary resuscitation (CPR)
	Bone marrow transplant
	Liver transplant
	Autologous bone marrow transplant
Illness management	Renal dialysis
	Pacemaker
	PTCA (angioplasty)
	Stereotactic cingulotomy (psychosurgery)
Cure	Hip joint replacement
	Organ transplant
	Lithotripter
Prevention	Implantable automatic cardioverter defibrillator
	Pediatric orthopedic repair
	Diet control for phenylketonuria
	Vaccines for immunization
System management	Health information systems
	Telemedicine
Facilities and clinical settings	Hospital satellite centers
	Clinical laboratories
	Subacute care units
	Modern home health
Organizational delivery structure	Managed care
	Integrated delivery networks

Adapted from Rosenthal, G. *Anticipating the costs and benefits of new technology: A typology for policy. Medical technology: The culprit behind health care costs?* Washington, DC: Department of Health and Human Services, 1979.

• •

In health care organizations, IT applications fall into three general categories (Austin 1992):

1. *Clinical information systems* involve the organized processing, storage, and retrieval of information to support patient care delivery. Electronic medical records, for example, provide quick and reliable information necessary to guide clinical decision making and produce timely reports on quality of care delivered. Computerized physician order entry (CPOE) enables physicians to electronically transmit orders from a patient's bedside, which increases efficiency and reduces errors.

2. *Administrative information systems* assist in carrying out financial and administrative support activities, such as payroll, patient accounting, billing, materials management, budgeting and cost control, and office automation. For medical clinics, CPOE technology can interface with the billing system to minimize rejected claims by pinpointing errors in billing codes.

3. *Decision support systems* provide information and analytical tools to support managerial and clinical decision making. Hence, there are two types of decision support systems. Managerial decision support systems can be used to forecast patient volume, project staffing requirements, and schedule patients to optimize utilization of patient care and surgical facilities. Clinical decision support systems (CDSS) encompass a range of applications, from general references, through treatment protocols, to recommendations that are tailored to a patient's unique clinical data.

CDSSs are found to be effective in improving the way health care is delivered, but their widespread use needs to be promoted (Bright et al. 2012). Both CPOE and CDSS technologies have been shown to reduce harmful medical errors (Shekelle et al. 2006).

Health informatics is broadly defined as the application of information science to improve the efficiency, accuracy, and reliability of health care services. Health informatics requires the use of IT but goes beyond IT by emphasizing the improvement of health care delivery. For example, designing CDSSs falls in the domain of health informatics. Applications of informatics are also found in electronic health records and telemedicine.

Electronic Health Records and Systems

Electronic health records (EHRs) are IT applications that enable the processing of any electronically stored information pertaining to individual patients for the purpose of delivering health care services (Murphy et al. 1999). EHRs replace the traditional paper medical records, which include a patient's demographic information, problems and diagnoses, plan of care, progress notes, medications, vital signs, past medical history, etc. An EHR system with basic features should incorporate the ability to update patient demographics, view test results, maintain problem lists, compile clinical notes, and manage prescription ordering (Decker et al. 2012).

Fully Developed EHR Systems

According to the Institute of Medicine (2003), a fully developed EHR system includes four key components: (1) collection

and storage of health information on individual patients over time; (2) immediate electronic access to person- and population-level information by authorized users; (3) availability of knowledge and decision support that enhances the quality, safety, and efficiency of patient care; and (4) support of efficient processes for health care delivery.

Benefits of EHRs

It is generally believed that widespread adoption of EHR systems will lead to major savings in health care costs, reduced medical errors, and improved health (Hillestad et al. 2005). As an example, nurses working in a fully implemented EHR environment are less likely to report poor patient safety, medication errors, poor quality of care, and unfavorabe patient outcomes compared to their peers working in environments that do not have fully implemented EHR systems (Kutney-Lee and Kelly 2011).

Interoperability

Interoperability makes it possible to access individual records online from many separate, automated systems within an electronic network, eliminating the need for older methods, such as letters and faxes, for sharing a patient's clinical information among providers. Physicians, for example, need timely information on test results. Care needs to be coordinated when patients receive services from multiple providers, such as physicians, pharmacists, and hospitals.

Health Information Organizations

A *health information organization* (HIO) is an independent organization that brings together health care stakeholders within a defined geographic area and facilitates electronic information exchange among these stakeholders with the objective of improving the delivery of health care in the community. The stakeholders often include not only health care providers, but also payers, laboratories, and sometimes public health departments. The HIO is managed by a board of directors comprised of representatives from the various stakeholder organizations. Apart from managing the actual exchange of information, HIOs assist providers in setting up protocols for information exchange and in building consensus on what type of information should be exchanged.

So far in the United States, the exchange of health information across provider organizations has received support for local or regional systems, rather than national systems. HIOs are still at an early stage although there is widespread interest in their development. In 2012, 29% of hospitals were participating in an HIO (Furukawa et al. 2013).

Adoption of EHRs

Both physician clinics and hospitals have been slow to adopt EHRs mainly because of a lack of capital and uncertain return on investment (DesRoches et al. 2008), but rapid progress is being made. Over half of the physicians in the United States now use EHR systems, which the Department of Health and Human Services (DHHS) referred to as a "tipping point" (Conn 2013). On the other hand, only 44% of US hospitals reported having even a basic EHR system (DesRoches et al. 2013a). Purchase and implementation of EHRs in large institutions can take 2 years to complete. Also, implementation is not a one-time event, but an ongoing process of testing and modifying to make the system more effective. A survey by the American Hospital

Association found that 85% of US hospitals intend to adopt EHRs by taking advantage of financial incentives from the federal government (Silow-Carroll et al. 2012), discussed in the next section.

Financial Incentives Under the HITECH Law

To accelerate the adoption of EHRs, some major policy initiatives were launched during the George W. Bush administration. These initiatives culminated in the enactment of the Health Information Technology for Economic and Clinical Health (HITECH) Act, which became part of the American Recovery and Reinvestment Act of 2009—the $787 billion plan to stimulate the economy—passed shortly after the Obama administration took office. This Act earmarked an estimated $19 billion in direct grants and financial incentives to promote the adoption of EHRs by hospitals and physicians (Wang et al. 2013). Beginning in 2011, Medicare and Medicaid started offering financial incentives of up to $44,000 for Medicare providers and $63,750 for Medicaid providers for "meaningful use" of health information technology (CDC 2012). To demonstrate "meaningful use," health care providers have to meet a range of metrics in areas such as quality, safety, efficiency, reduction of health disparities, patient engagement, care coordination, and security of health information (Halamka 2010). Meaningful use criteria are being phased in over three stages between 2011 and 2015. To qualify for incentive payments, eligible providers must meet a set of objectives at each meaningful use stage (CMS 2013). Starting in 2015, hospitals that fail to meet the meaningful use criteria will be subject to financial penalties (DesRoches et al. 2013b).

HITECH also established the State Health Information Exchange Cooperative Agreement Program, which awarded more than $540 million to states to establish mechanisms that would facilitate the exchange of clinical information (Blumenthal 2011). One approach states are employing is to establish HIOs.

Confidentiality Under the HIPAA Law

To alleviate concerns by patients and providers about the confidentiality of patient information, the Health Insurance Portability and Accountability Act (HIPAA) of 1996 makes it illegal to gain access to a patient's personal health information (PHI) for reasons other than health care delivery, operations, and reimbursement. HIPAA legislation mandated strict controls on the transfer of personally identifiable health data between two entities, provisions for disclosure of protected information, and penalties for violation (Clayton 2001). In January 2013, the DHHS issued revisions to HIPAA in conjunction with the HITECH law. More stringent rules now apply to disclosure of breaches of confidential PHI, inclusion of vendors and subcontractors as "business associates" who must comply with HIPAA requirements, restrictions on the use of PHI for marketing purposes, patient authorization related to the use of PHI for research purposes, use of genetic information for underwriting purposes by health insurance companies, and the patients' right to receive electronic copies of their PHI (Thompson Coburn LLP 2013).

Smart Card Technology

Pocket-size smart cards that are embedded with a microchip have found applications in other industries for access control, but adoption of their use in health care delivery has been slow. A *smart card* that is designed for medical use holds personal medical information that can be accessed and updated at hospitals or physicians' offices (Ellis 2000). Privacy concerns have been the main drawback in realizing the full potential and use of smart cards in medical care. However, as such hurdles are overcome, the use of smart card technology is expected to grow.

The Internet, E-Health, M-Health, and E-Therapy

With the growth of the Internet and proliferation of mobile devices for online access, patients are becoming active participants in their own health care. A number of websites offer physician consultations, and others sell prescription medications. Patients are also forming online support communities to help themselves through discussion groups and bulletin boards. Consequently, patients are becoming active participants in their own health care. Information empowers patients, which leads to changes in the traditional patient–physician dynamics. Even though the vast majority of patients rely on and trust their physicians or other health care professionals for information, care, or support (Fox 2013), for specific health conditions, the Internet is often the first source of information (Marrie et al. 2013).

Patients' reliance on the Internet for health information seems to be associated with their satisfaction with the care they receive from their physicians. Those satisfied with care tend to rely more on their physician than on the Internet, using the physician as the primary source of health information. Conversely, dissatisfied patients turn to the

Internet as their primary source of information, regarding it as a more credible and more authoritative information source than their physicians. Dissatisfied patients may also be less likely to comply with treatments prescribed by their physicians (Tustin 2010).

E-health, m-health, and e-therapy are related terms, sometimes used interchangeably. There are, however, slight differences between them.

"*E-health* refers to all forms of electronic health care delivered over the Internet, ranging from informational, educational, and commercial 'products' to direct services offered by professionals, nonprofessionals, businesses, or consumers themselves" (Maheu et al. 2001). The use of e-health has grown as many providers have created secure Internet portals to enable patients to access their EHRs, allow patient–provider email messaging, and use mobile apps for smartphones and tablets (Ricciardi et al. 2013).

The term "mobile health," or *m-health*, refers to "the use of wireless communication devices to support public health and clinical practice" (Kahn et al. 2010). These devices facilitate communication among researchers, clinicians, and patients. Physicians are also recognizing the potential utility of mobile computing. The most common current use is for EHR access (Sclafani et al. 2013).

E-therapy has emerged as an alternative to face-to-face therapy for behavioral health support and counseling (Skinner and Latchford 2006). Also referred to as online therapy, e-counseling, teletherapy, or cyber-counseling, *e-therapy* refers to any type of professional therapeutic interaction that makes use of the Internet to connect qualified mental health professionals and their clients (Rochlen et al. 2004). Although e-therapy is not widely used at this point, many Internet mental health interventions have reported

early results that are promising. Both therapist-led and self-directed online therapies indicate significant alleviation of disorder-related symptomatology (Ybarra and Eaton 2005). E-therapy has the potential of reaching a significant number of clients who need mental health services yet do not receive them (Wodarski and Frimpong 2013). Nevertheless, e-therapy remains controversial. Issues and problems potentially best suited for online therapy include personal growth and fulfillment; adult children of alcoholics; anxiety disorders, including agoraphobia and social phobias; and body image and shame/guilt issues. Clients not appropriate for online therapy include those who have suicidal ideation, thought disorders, borderline personality disorder, or unmonitored medical issues (Stofle 2001).

Another emerging application of communication technology is *virtual physician visits*, which are online clinical encounters between a patient and physician. One research study found that patients regarded virtual visits with primary care physicians to be similar to face-to-face visits on measures that included time spent and interaction with the physicians. Physicians were also highly satisfied with the virtual visit modality (Dixon and Stahl 2009). Virtual visits are a type of telemedicine practice, described in the next section.

Telemedicine, Telehealth, and Remote Monitoring

The terms "telemedicine" and "telehealth" are often used interchangeably. Both employ telecommunication systems for the purpose of promoting health, but there is a technical difference between the two. *Telemedicine*, or distance medicine, employs the use of telecommunications technology for medical diagnosis and patient care when the provider and client are separated by distance. Similar to a virtual visit, it eliminates the requirement for face-to-face contact between the examining physician and the patient. Unlike virtual visits, however, telemedicine has applications in the delivery of specialized medical services. Examples include teleradiology, the transmission of radiographic images and scans; telepathology, the viewing of tissue specimens via video-microscopy; telesurgery, controlling robots from a distance to perform surgical procedures; and clinical consultation provided by a wide range of specialists. With the exception of teleradiology, however, the use of telemedicine in other areas has not become widespread (Zanaboni and Wootton 2012).

The term *telehealth* is broader in scope. It encompasses telemedicine, as traditionally known, and educational, research, and administrative uses, as well as clinical applications that involve a variety of caregivers, such as physicians, nurses, psychologists, and pharmacists (Field and Grigsby 2002).

Telemedicine can be synchronous or asynchronous. *Synchronous technology* allows telecommunication to occur in real time. For example, interactive videoconferencing allows two or more professionals to see and hear each other and even share documents in real time. The technology allows a specialist located at a distance to directly interview and examine a patient. *Asynchronous technology* employs store-and-forward technology that allows users to review the information later. Interpretation of scans in teleradiology is one example where asynchronous technology is employed.

Newer applications of telemedicine are in home monitoring of patients. Vital signs, blood pressure, and blood glucose levels can be monitored remotely, using video technology, which has been shown to be effective, well received by patients, and capable of maintaining quality of care and to have the potential for cost savings (Johnston et al. 2000). Recently, remote monitoring of cardiac implantable electronic devices, such as pacemakers and implantable cardioverter defibrillators, in the United States and Europe has been gaining acceptance. The technology has been found to be highly effective in managing clinical events, such as arrhythmias, cardiovascular disease progression, and device malfunction, with remarkably low manpower and resource use (Ricci et al. 2013; Slotwiner and Wilkoff 2013). In 2012, the Federal Communications Commission allocated spectrum bands specifically for medical body area networks (MBAN). Some of this spectrum has been set aside for monitoring patients at home (Lee 2013). An MBAN is a low-power wideband network that can transmit patient data to a control device wirelessly through body-worn sensors (American Hospital Association 2012).

Rural populations, in particular, face various types of barriers in access to quality health care. Barriers, such as shortage of providers, long travel distances, physical and social isolation, and weather-related difficulties can be overcome with appropriate telehealth services. The Nebraska Statewide Telehealth Network—a collaborative effort of hospitals, health departments, the Nebraska Hospital Association, and other organizations—has demonstrated increased access to health care by rural residents (Meyers et al. 2012).

The largest barrier to telemedicine adoption is the lack of a reimbursement model, according to a survey of 75 health care executives (Smith 2010). Also, the cost effectiveness of most telemedicine applications remains unsubstantiated. Conversely, diagnostic and consultative teleradiology is almost universally reimbursed and has been proven cost effective (Field and Grigsby 2002). The American Recovery and Reinvestment Act of 2009 provides funding for not only improving the IT infrastructure in health care institutions but also for implementing telehealth networks designed to serve patients in rural areas and to integrate telehealth into the delivery of home health care (Singh et al. 2010).

Innovation, Diffusion, and Utilization of Medical Technology

In the context of medical technology, innovation is the creation of a product, technique, or service perceived to be new by members of a society. The spread of technology into society once it is developed is referred to as *technology diffusion* (Luce 1993). Rapid diffusion of a technology occurs when the innovation is perceived to be of benefit that can be evaluated or measured, is compatible with the adopter's values and needs, and is covered through third-party payment. Once technology is acquired, its use is almost ensured. Hence, the diffusion and utilization of technology are closely intertwined. The desire to have state-of-the-art technology available and to use it despite its cost or established health benefit is called the *technological imperative*.

High-tech procedures are more readily available in the United States than in most other countries, and little is done to limit the expansion of new medical technology. Compared to most European hospitals, American hospitals perform a far greater number of catheterizations, angioplasties, and bypass heart surgeries. In 2009, the rate of knee replacement in the United States was about 75% greater than the median rate in countries belonging to the Organization for Economic Cooperation and Development (OECD 2011).

The United States also has more high-tech equipment, such as magnetic resonance imaging (MRI) and computed tomography (CT) scanners, available to its population than most other countries. In 2009, the United States had more than twice the number of MRI units and 1.5 times the number of CT scanners per million population than the average for OECD countries (OECD 2011). Other nations have tried to limit, mainly through central planning, the diffusion and utilization of high-tech procedures to control medical costs. The British government, for instance, established the National Institute for Health and Clinical Excellence (NICE) in 1999 to decide whether the National Health Service should make select health technologies available (Milewa 2006). Hence, the availability of MRI and CT scanners in the United Kingdom is lower than it is in most OECD nations (OECD 2011). Conversely, in many other European countries, technology diffusion has grown at a rapid pace.

Factors That Drive Innovation and Diffusion

The rate and pattern by which a technology diffuses is often governed by multiple forces (Cohen 2004b). For example, public and private financing for research and development (R&D) can promote or inhibit innovation; government regulations, such as the US Food and Drug Administration (FDA) approval process, can promote or hinder the availability of new drugs and devices; marketing and promotion by the manufacturers can have an impact on the decisions of both providers and consumers about the adoption and use of technology.

Some of the main forces that have shaped the innovation, diffusion, and utilization of technology in the United States are:

- Anthro-cultural beliefs and values
- Medical specialization
- Financing and payment
- Technology-driven competition
- Expenditures on research and development
- Supply-side controls
- Government policy

Anthro-Cultural Beliefs and Values

Studies have shown that, when technology becomes available for a particular indication, it is used at significantly different intensities in various countries and among regions within countries (Wennberg 1988). American beliefs and values have been instrumental in determining the nature of health care delivery in the United States (discussed in Chapter 2). Based on these beliefs and values, Americans have much higher expectations of what medical technology can do to cure illness than, for instance, Canadians and Germans. In an opinion survey, a significantly higher number of Americans (35%) than Germans (21%) indicated that it was absolutely essential for them to be able to get the most advanced tests, drugs, medical procedures, and equipment (Kim et al. 2001). In another survey, 91% of Americans indicated that their ability to get the most advanced tests, drugs, medical equipment, and procedures was very important to improving the quality of health care (Schur and Berk 2008). As a case in point, in 2007, the Centers for

Medicare and Medicaid Services (CMS) proposed to sharply restrict payment for computer tomography angiography for Medicare patients. Even though this newer imaging technology had not been shown to have any remarkable improvements in diagnosing heart disease, there was a barrage of outrage over Medicare's proposed ruling from radiologists and cardiologists, technology development firms such as General Electric, and 79 members of the House of Representatives. Finally, the CMS announced that it would not impose its proposed determination despite continued uncertainty about the test's usefulness (Appleby 2008).

The primacy of technology can also be traced to the medical model that has dominated medical practice in the United States (see Chapter 2), and is reinforced by American beliefs and values. Consequently, the emphasis on specialty care, rather than primary care and preventive services, raises the expectations of both physicians and patients for the use of all available technology.

Medical Specialization

Evidence of the technological imperative is most apparent in acute care hospitals, especially those affiliated with medical schools, because they are the main centers for specialty residency training programs in which physicians are trained to use the latest medical advances. Broad exposure to technology early in training affects not only clinical preferences but also future professional behavior and practice patterns (Cohen 2004c). Both patients and practitioners also equate high-quality care with high-intensity care.

Financing and Payment

Evidence from several countries suggests that fixed provider payments, such as salaried physicians, and strong limits on payments to hospitals, such as stringent use of global budgets, curtail the incentive to use high-tech procedures. Hence, payment incentives can place limitations on how quickly and widely new treatments are diffused into medical practice (McClellan and Kessler 1999).

Traditionally, the US health care delivery system has lacked internal checks and balances to determine when high-cost services are appropriate. Health insurance promotes the phenomenon referred to as moral hazard and provider-induced demand (see Chapter 1), unless mechanisms to limit utilization of high-cost services are put in place. Insurance insulates both patients and providers from any personal accountability for the utilization of high-cost services. Generally, both patients and physicians want to use everything that medical science has to offer as long as out-of-pocket costs are of little concern.

There is likely a two-way relationship between technology diffusion and insurance coverage. Increasingly generous insurance coverage causes increases in spending for new products. Conversely, the development of beneficial but costly new technology puts pressure on insurers to cover those technologies (Danzon and Pauly 2001). In coverage decisions, private insurance companies follow Medicare's lead, which is by far the largest and most influential payer in the United States. The current direction in reimbursement decisions is to seek *value*, that is, the most benefits possible for the price to pay.

In Europe, research has suggested that higher levels of reimbursement do not always promote technology diffusion (Cappellaro et al. 2011). This is mainly because European national health care programs have the means to suppress unintended diffusion of technology through central planning.

Technology-Driven Competition

Despite the fact that health care delivery in the United States is not characterized by true market conditions (see Chapter 1), providers of health care services do compete. Paradoxically, however, competition in health care often increases costs. Hospitals, as well as outpatient centers, compete to attract insured patients. Well insured patients look for quality, and institutions create perceptions of higher quality by acquiring and advertising state-of-the-art technology. Specialists have also been responsible for stimulating competition. Many physicians, for example, have opened their own specialty hospitals, diagnostic imaging facilities stocked with next-generation scanners, and same-day surgery centers that have hotel-like facilities—these developments have fueled a de facto medical arms race. In response, hospitals are adding new service lines—such as cancer, heart, and brain centers—and are acquiring costly CT scanners and high-field MRI machines (Kher 2006), fueling more technology-based competition. To recruit specialists, medical centers often have to obtain new technology and offer high-tech procedures. When hospitals develop new services and invest heavily in modernization programs, other hospitals in the area are often forced to do the same. Such practices result in a tremendous amount of duplication of services and equipment.

Self-Referral and Stark Laws

Investment interests by physicians in various types of facilities prompted Congress to pass regulations against *self-referrals*. These laws prohibit physicians from sending patients to facilities in which the referring physician or a family member has an ownership interest or some kind of compensation arrangement. Prohibition of self-referrals is based on the theory of provider-induced demand which would create overutilization and result in increased health care costs.

The Ethics in Patient Referrals Act of 1989 (commonly known as Stark I after Representative Pete Stark, author of the original bill) prohibited the referral of Medicare patients to laboratories in which the referring physician had an ownership interest. Provisions of this law expanded under the Omnibus Budget Reconciliation Act of 1993 (OBRA-93). Commonly referred to as Stark II, the statute covers both Medicare and Medicaid referrals. It also expanded the categories of services to include clinical laboratory services; rehabilitation services; radiology services, including MRI, CT scans, and ultrasound; radiation therapy services and supplies; durable medical equipment and supplies; prosthetics, orthotics, and prosthetic devices and supplies; home health services; outpatient prescription drugs; and inpatient and outpatient hospitalization services. Nearly half the states also have self-referral prohibitions that apply to privately insured patients (Mitchell 2007). There are some exceptions to the laws, however, such as in-office ancillary services (Wachler and Avery 2011), which allow physicians to own or lease imaging equipment for their office-based practices. Hence, a significant amount of self-referral still exists (Mitchell 2007).

Expenditures on Research and Development

Innovation is driven by spending on research and development (R&D). The American Recovery and Reinvestment Act of 2009 allocated $10.4 billion in new funding to the National Institutes of Health (NIH),

mainly to support research (Steinbrook 2009). This funding, however, ended in 2011 with the passage of the Budget Control Act. In 2011, both government and private sources of funding for biomedical research in the United States amounted to 136.2 billion (or 5% of total health care expenditures; Bronstein 2012), which represents an increase of 35% over the $101.1 billion spent in 2007 (or 4.5% of total health care expenditures; Dorsey et al. 2010). The biggest share of R&D spending is attributed to private pharmaceutical, biotechnology, and medical device industries, which together accounted for 57% of R&D spending in 2011 (Figure 5–1). Although R&D spending in other countries has continued to increase, the United States spends the most.

Supply-Side Controls

In the United States, supply-side controls have met with stiff resistance, as the early experiences with health maintenance organizations (HMOs) demonstrated in the 1990s (see Chapter 9). Managed care may have had some early impact on slowing the adoption of high-cost technologies (Baker 2002). For example, high levels of market penetration by HMOs were associated with reduced levels of availability and use of MRI (Baker and Wheeler 1998).

Rationing curtails costs, but it also restricts access to critically needed care. Canada, which restricts specialist services and limits expensive medical equipment to control health care spending, is a case in point. For a number of years, the Fraser Institute has researched access to care issues in Canada. The institute found, for example, that in 2012, Canadians had to wait an estimated 3.7 weeks for a CT scan or an ultrasound, and 8.4 weeks for an MRI. Although, lately, these waiting times have

Figure 5–1 Sources of funding for biomedical research, 2007.

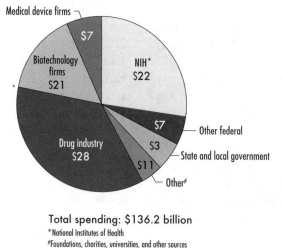

Total spending: $136.2 billion
*National Institutes of Health
#Foundations, charities, universities, and other sources

Source: Data from Dorsey, E.R. et al. 2010. Funding of US biomedical research, 2003–2008. *Journal of the American Medical Association* 303, no. 2: 137–143.

decreased somewhat, physicians themselves have indicated that their patients face medically unreasonable wait times (Barua 2013). Because of unreasonable waits, approximately one in five Canadians reported adverse effects, including worry, stress, and pain (Sanmartin and Berthelot 2006). Several studies have reported deaths resulting from delayed heart surgery due to waiting times in Canada, even in cases classified as nonurgent (Sobolev et al. 2013). Medical tourism (see Chapter 3) is partly driven by waiting lines to receive high-technology health care in developed nations that use supply-side controls.

Government Policy

Unlike most other developed countries, in the United States, direct controls over the innovation, diffusion, and utilization of technology through government policy have not been possible. Nevertheless, public policy does play a significant role in deciding which drugs, devices, and biologics are made available to Americans. The US government is also one of the largest sources of funding for biomedical research. By controlling the amount of funding, public policy indirectly influences medical innovation.

The Government's Role in Technology Diffusion

The growth of technology has been accompanied by issues of cost, safety, benefits, and risks. Federal legislation has been aimed primarily at addressing the concerns related to safety. The government plays a minor role in health care organizations' decisions to acquire new technology. As previously indicated, the government is also an important source of funding for biomedical research.

Regulation of Drugs, Devices, and Biologics

The FDA is an agency under the DHHS that is responsible for ensuring that drugs and medical devices are safe and effective for their intended use. It also controls access to drugs by deciding whether a certain drug will be available by prescription only or as an over-the-counter purchase. The FDA may also stipulate standards on how certain over-the-counter products may be purchased and sold. For example, under the Combat Methamphetamine Epidemic Act of 2005 (incorporated into the USA PATRIOT Act and signed by President Bush in March 2006), certain cold and allergy medicines containing pseudoephedrine are required to be kept behind pharmacy counters and sold in only limited quantities to consumers, who must present photo identification and sign a logbook. This action was taken because pseudoephedrine is used in making methamphetamine—a highly addictive drug—in home laboratories.

Regulation of Drugs and Evolution of Approval Processes

The FDA's regulatory functions have evolved over time (Table 5–2). The first piece of drug legislation in the United States was the Food and Drugs Act of 1906. The purpose of the law was to prevent the manufacture, sale, or transportation of adulterated, misbranded, poisonous, or deleterious foods, drugs, medicines, and liquors

(FDA 2009a). It authorized the Bureau of Chemistry (predecessor of the FDA) to take action only after drugs had been marketed to consumers. It was assumed that the manufacturer would conduct safety tests before marketing the product. If innocent consumers were harmed, however, the Bureau of Chemistry could act only after such harm had been done (Bronzino et al. 1990). The law was strengthened by the passage of the Federal Food, Drug, and Cosmetic Act of 1938 (FD&C Act) in response to the infamous Elixir Sulfanilamide disaster, which caused almost 100 deaths in Tennessee due to poisoning from a toxic solvent used in the liquid preparation (Flannery 1986). According to the revised law, a new drug could not be marketed without first notifying the FDA and allowing the agency time to assess the drug's safety (Merrill 1994).

The drug approval system was further transformed by the drug amendments of 1962, after thalidomide (a sleeping pill that was distributed in the United States as an experimental drug but had been widely marketed in Europe) was shown to cause birth defects (Flannery 1986). The 1962 amendments (Kefauver-Harris Drug Amendments) essentially stated that premarket notification was inadequate. The amendments put a premarket approval system in force, giving the FDA authority to review the effectiveness and safety of a new drug before it could be marketed. Its consumer protection role enabled the FDA to prevent harm before it occurred. However, the drug approval process was criticized for slowing down the introduction of new drugs and, consequently, denying patients early benefit of the latest treatments. Drug manufacturers essentially "became prisoners of the agency's [FDA's] indecision, its preoccupation

· ·

Table 5–2 Summary of FDA Legislation

1906   Food and Drugs Act
The FDA was authorized to take action only after drugs sold to consumers caused harm.

1938   Food, Drug, and Cosmetic Act
Required premarket notification to the FDA so the agency could assess the safety of a new drug or device.

1962   Kefauver-Harris Amendments
Premarket notification was inadequate. The FDA took charge of reviewing the efficacy and safety of new drugs, which could be marketed only once approval was granted.

1976   Medical Devices Amendments
Authorized premarket review of medical devices and classified devices into three classes.

1983   Orphan Drug Act
Drug manufacturers were given incentives to produce new drugs for rare diseases.

1990   Safe Medical Devices Act
Health care facilities must report serious or potentially serious device-related injuries, illness, or death of patients and/or employees.

1992   Prescription Drug User Fee Act
The FDA received authority to collect application fees from drug companies to provide additional resources to shorten the drug-approval process.

1997   Food and Drug Administration Modernization Act
Provides for fast-track approvals for life-saving drugs when expected benefits exceed those of current therapies.

2012   Food and Drug Administration Safety Innovations Act
Allows the FDA to use markers that are thought to predict or that are reasonably likely to predict clinical benefit to qualify a drug for accelerated approval if the drug is indicated for a serious condition and fills an unmet medical need.

· ·

with other issues, or its lack of resources" (Merrill 1994).

The Orphan Drug Act of 1983 and subsequent amendments were passed to provide incentives for pharmaceutical firms to develop new drugs for rare diseases and conditions. Incentives, such as grant funding to defray the expenses of clinical testing and exclusive marketing rights for seven years, were necessary because a relatively small number of people are afflicted by rare conditions, creating a relatively small market. As a result of the Orphan Drug Act, certain new drug therapies, called *orphan drugs*, have become available for conditions that affect fewer than 200,000 people in the United States.

In the late 1980s, pressure on the FDA from those wanting rapid access to new drugs for the treatment of the human immunodeficiency virus (HIV) infection called for a reconsideration of the drug review process (Rakich et al. 1992). For example, Saquinavir, a protease inhibitor indicated for patients with advanced HIV infection, received accelerated approval in late 1995; however, its manufacturer, Roche Laboratories, was subsequently required to show that the drug prolonged survival or slowed clinical progression of HIV.

In 1992, Congress passed the Prescription Drug User Fee Act, which authorized the FDA to collect fees from biotechnology and pharmaceutical companies to review their drug applications. The additional funds provided needed resources, and, according to the General Accounting Office (GAO), the fees allowed the FDA to make new drugs available more quickly. From 1993 to 2001, the median approval time for standard new drugs dropped from 21 months to approximately 14 months. In 2004, the approval time dropped even further to 12.9 months.

In 1997, Congress passed the Food and Drug Administration Modernization Act. The law provides for increased patient access to experimental drugs and medical devices. It provides for "fast-track" approvals when the potential benefits of new drugs for serious or life-threatening conditions are considered significantly greater than those for current therapies. In addition, the law provides for an expanded database on clinical trials, which is accessible to the public. Under a separate provision, when a manufacturer plans to discontinue a drug, patients who are heavily dependent on the drug receive advance notice.

The Food and Drug Administration Safety and Innovation Act of 2012 allows the FDA to either use a marker that is thought to predict clinical benefit (surrogate endpoint) or use a marker that is considered reasonably likely to predict clinical benefit (intermediate clinical endpoint). These markers allow for faster approval of drugs. For example, the FDA may approve a drug based on evidence that the drug shrinks tumors, because tumor shrinkage is considered reasonably likely to predict a real clinical benefit (FDA 2013).

There has been ample criticism of the FDA. On the one hand, faster reviews have allowed unsafe drugs to be brought to market. On the other hand, it is contended that the drug approval process has slowed drastically. Some observers have referred to it as the "regulatory paradox," which increases costs, stifles innovation, and indirectly prevents some people in dire need from getting the benefits of new technology. A panel of experts from the medical industry suggested that some technologies developed in the United States were approved in Singapore, Europe, and Japan, but would not be available in the United States for some time to come mainly because of the inefficiencies at the FDA (Katz 2011).

Regulation of Medical Devices and Equipment

The FDA first received jurisdiction over medical devices under the FD&C Act of 1938. However, such jurisdiction was confined to the sale of products believed to be unsafe or that made misleading claims of effectiveness (Merrill 1994). In the 1970s, several deaths and miscarriages were attributed to the Dalkon Shield, which had been marketed as a safe and effective contraceptive device (Flannery 1986). In 1976, the Medical Device Amendments extended the FDA's authority to include premarket review of medical devices divided into three classes. Devices in Class I are subject to general controls regarding misbranding, that is, fraudulent claims regarding the therapeutic effects of certain devices. Class II devices are subject to special requirements for labeling, performance standards, and postmarket surveillance. The most stringent requirements of premarket approval regarding safety and effectiveness apply to Class III devices that support life, prevent health impairment, or present an unreasonable risk of illness or injury. For most Class III devices, premarket approval is required to ensure their safety and effectiveness. The Safe Medical Devices Act of 1990 strengthened the FDA's hand in controlling entry of new products and in monitoring use of marketed products (Merrill 1994). Under this Act, health care facilities must report serious or potentially serious device-related injuries or illness of patients and/or employees to the manufacturer of the device and, if death is involved, to the FDA as well. In essence, the Act is intended to serve as an "early warning" system through which the FDA can obtain important information on device problems.

Regulation of Biologics

Biologics, or biological products, include a wide range of products such as vaccines, blood and blood components, allergenics, somatic cells, gene therapy, tissues, and recombinant therapeutic proteins, particularly when they are used for prevention or treatment of a disease or health condition. Biologics are isolated from a variety of natural sources—human, animal, or microorganism. In contrast to most drugs that are chemically synthesized and have a known chemical structure, most biologics are complex mixtures that are not easily identified or characterized (FDA 2009b). The FDA regulates biologics under the Public Health

Service Act of 1944, the Food, Drug, and Cosmetic Act of 1938, the Biologics Price Competition and Innovation Act of 2009, and the Biosimilar User Fee Act of 2012. The first two legislations mainly deal with the safety of biologics by requiring licensing of these products. The last two are part of the ACA and are discussed in the next section.

The Affordable Care Act and Medical Technology

In the area of medical technology, the ACA mainly affects devices and biologics. A 2.3% excise tax on the sale of certain medical devices by manufacturers and importers of these devices became effective on January 1, 2013. Products such as eyeglasses, contact lenses, and hearing aids are exempt. The higher costs associated with the tax will, of course, be passed on to the purchasers, mainly hospitals and physicians, and will eventually filter down to consumers through higher health insurance premiums.

The ACA also affects the regulation of biologic medications. First, the Biologics Price Competition and Innovation Act of 2009 was incorporated into the ACA. In a nutshell, the law allows the FDA to approve "biosimilars" under a process similar to the approval of generic drugs. Because of their complexity, the term "generic" cannot apply to biologics; hence, the term "biosimilar" was created to apply to products that are highly similar to, or are interchangeable with, an already approved biological product (referred to as the reference product). Secondly, the Biosimilar User Fee Act of 2012 authorizes the FDA to charge biopharmaceutical firms a user fee to pay for the review of applications for biosimilar products before the products can be marketed.

It is believed that the introduction of bio-similars will create competition and drive down the cost of biologics.

Developers of an original reference product are protected by law because no biosimilar license can be granted until the reference product has been licensed for at least 12 years. Also, the law requires a biosimilar applicant to disclose to the reference product license holder its application, a description of its manufacturing process, and any other requested information so that the license holder can engage in an efficient process of patent assertion against the bio-similar applicant, if necessary. Forthcoming FDA regulations may help create a process through which biosimilar products can quickly and efficiently be introduced and create savings for consumers. However, the nature of the market for biological products is such that examples of competitive bio-logics will be few and far between. This is because most biologics are the result of a highly complex scientific process. Still, the new laws are a step in the right direction and may help strike a balance between innovation and competition (Johnson 2010).

Certificate of Need

The National Health Planning and Resources Development Act of 1974 designated a regional network of health systems agencies (HSAs) for the planning and allocation of health resources, including technology. States were required to enact certificate of need (CON) laws to obtain federal funds for planning functions under this Act. These activities were intended to influence the diffusion of technology by requiring hospitals to seek state approval before acquiring major equipment or embarking on new construction or modernization projects (Iglehart 1982). Effective January 1, 1987, the federal law was repealed and funding for HSAs was terminated. Although some states have abandoned CON requirements, approximately 36 states retain some control over planning and construction of new health care facilities (National Conference of State Legislatures 2011). Hence, the government still exercises a limited amount of control over technology diffusion.

States that have retained CON laws are facing controversies and, in some cases, legal challenges (Carlson 2012). For example, CON laws have had no effect in the adoption of robotic prostatectomy (Jacobs et al. 2013). Also, CON laws may not be effective in reducing costs, at least for some medical technologies (Ho et al. 2013), nor do they have a direct effect on reducing per capita health care expenditures (Hellinger 2009).

Research on Technology

The Agency for Healthcare Research and Quality (AHRQ) was established in 1989 under the Omnibus Budget Reconciliation Act of 1989 and was originally the Agency for Health Care Policy and Research. AHRQ, a division of the DHHS, is the lead federal agency charged with supporting research that focuses on improving the quality of health care, reducing health care cost, and improving access to essential services. For instance, the agency's Center for Outcomes and Evidence (formerly the Center for Outcomes and Effectiveness Research) conducts and supports studies of the outcomes and effectiveness of diagnostic, therapeutic, and preventive health services and procedures. The agency's technology assessments are available to medical practitioners, consumers, and others.

Funding for Research

The NIH—a division of the DHHS—both conducts and supports basic and applied biomedical research in the United States. Funding through NIH provided much of the impetus for medical schools to undertake research in the medical subspecialties, which led to the growth of specialty departments within academic medical centers (Rakich et al. 1992). These institutions have produced many specialists, which is reflected in the sustained imbalance between the number of general practitioners, compared to specialists.

The Impact of Medical Technology

Health care technology involves the practical application of scientific discoveries in many disciplines. The deployment of scientific knowledge has had far-reaching and pervasive effects, as the various examples in Table 5–1 would suggest. The effects of technology often overlap, making it difficult to pinpoint technology's impact in a single area of health care delivery.

Impact on Quality of Care

When advanced techniques can provide more precise medical diagnoses than before, quicker and more complete cures than previously available, or reduce risks in a cost-effective manner, the result is improved quality. Technology can also provide new remedies where none existed before. More effective, less invasive, and safer therapeutic and preventive remedies can increase longevity and decrease morbidity.

Numerous examples illustrate the role of technology in enhancing the quality of care.

Coronary angioplasty has become a common procedure for opening blocked or narrowed coronary arteries. Before this treatment became available, patients suffering a heart attack were prescribed prolonged bed rest and treated with morphine and nitroglycerin (CBO 2008). Angioplasty has reduced the need for open-heart bypass surgery. A total artificial heart (TAH), approved by the FDA in 2005 for implantation in patients with end-stage heart failure, can be a life saver for those awaiting heart transplantation. Implantable cardioverter defibrillators prolong the lives of people who have life-threatening irregular heartbeats.

Laser technology reduces trauma in patients undergoing surgery and shortens the period for postsurgical recovery. Laser applications are widely used in medical specialties for both medical and cosmetic procedures. For example, advanced laser procedures are available for high-precision eye surgery.

Robot-assisted surgeries have gained significant momentum in areas such as urology. For example, in the United States, more than 70% of all radical prostatectomies are performed using the da Vinci robot (Rassweiler et al. 2010). The robotic approach allows improved dexterity and precision of the instruments.

Advanced bioimaging methods have opened new ways to see the body's inner workings, while minimizing invasive procedures. Modern imaging technologies include MRI, positron emission tomography (PET), single-photon emission computed tomography (SPECT), computed tomography (CT), and 3-D fluorescence imaging. PET has important applications in cardiology, neurology, and oncology. For example, it can spot tumors and other problems that may not be detectable with traditional MRI or CT scans. SPECT is of great value in imaging the brain.

SPECT imaging could also reduce inappropriate use of invasive procedures through a more accurate diagnosis of coronary artery disease (Shaw et al. 2000).

Molecular and cell biology has opened a new era in clinical medicine. Screening for genetic disorders, gene therapy, and powerful new drugs for cancer and heart disease promise to radically improve the quality of medical care. Genetic research might even help overcome the critical shortage of transplantable organs. On a parallel track, regenerative medicine and tissue engineering hold the promise of creating other biological and bioartificial substitutes that will restore and maintain normal function in a variety of diseased and injured tissues. Products such as bioartificial kidneys, artificial implantable livers, and insulin-producing cells to replace damaged pancreatic cells are examples of what biomedical science might be able to accomplish. Treatment of disease using stem cells that can be derived from discarded human embryos (human embryonic stem cells), fetal tissue, or adult sources (bone marrow, fat, or skin) is another example of regenerative medicine.

Amid all the enthusiasm emerging technologies might generate, some degree of caution must prevail. Experience shows that greater proliferation of technology may not necessarily equate with higher quality. Unless the effect of each individual technology is appropriately assessed, some innovations may be wasteful and others may be harmful.

Impact on Quality of Life

Thanks to new scientific developments, thousands of people are able to live normal lives, which otherwise would not be possible. People with disabling conditions have been able to overcome their limitations in speech, hearing, vision, and movement through prosthetic devices and therapies. Long-term maintenance therapies have enabled people suffering from conditions such as diabetes and end-stage renal disease to engage in activities that they otherwise would not be able to do. Major pharmaceutical breakthroughs enable people suffering from heart disease, cancer, HIV/AIDS, and preterm birth to have a much longer life expectancy and improved health (Kleinke 2001).

Modern technology has also been instrumental in relieving pain and suffering, and pain management is being recognized as a new subspecialty in medicine. For example, in cancer pain management, new opioids have been developed for transdermal, nasal, and nebulized administration, which allow needleless means of controlling pain (Davis 2006). Apart from new drugs, patient-controlled analgesia allows patients to determine when and how much medication they receive, which gives patients more independence and control. HIV/AIDS was recognized as a killer disease in the early 1980s, but modern treatments, such as protease inhibitors and nonnucleoside reverse transcriptase inhibitors (known as antiretroviral agents), have suppressed the disease's ability to proliferate and damage organs. Thanks to these treatments, HIV/AIDS has become a chronic disease, not a death sentence (Komaroff 2005). Clinical trials have been under way to evaluate the effectiveness and safety of inhaled and oral administration of insulin for patients with Type II diabetes. A substitute for injectable insulin could greatly enhance the quality of life for diabetic patients, particularly the elderly, who require assistance with insulin injections.

Impact on Health Care Costs

Technological innovations have been the single most important factor in medical cost inflation. They have accounted for about one-half of the total rise in real (after eliminating the effects of general inflation) health care spending during the past several decades (CBO 2008; Sorenson et al. 2013). Nevertheless, the impact of technology on costs differs across technologies, in that some—such as, cancer drugs and invasive medical devices—have significant cost implications, while others are cost-neutral or cost-saving (Sorenson et al. 2013).

Three main cost drivers are associated with the adoption of medical technology. First, there is the cost of acquiring the new technology and equipment. Second, specially trained physicians and technicians are often needed to operate the equipment and to analyze the results, which often leads to increases in labor costs. Third, new technology may require special housing and setting requirements, resulting in facility costs (McGregor 1989). Hence, widespread adoption of technology has a multiplier effect as costs increase in these three main areas. A second set of cost drivers is associated with utilization. As discussed previously, perceptions of quality and expectations of better cure along with insurance coverage fuel demand for utilization. On the supply side, once technology is adopted by hospitals and physicians, the volume of use must be maintained to recover the investment. Hence, it turns out that technology's purchase price has a minimal effect on system-wide health care costs (Littell and Strongin 1996); costs associated with utilization of technology, once it becomes available, become more important. For example, each additional MRI unit incurs approximately

733 additional MRI procedures (Baker et al. 2008). Also, many of the most notable medical advances in recent decades involve ongoing treatments for the management of chronic conditions, such as diabetes and coronary artery disease (CBO 2008), where costs continue to aggregate over time.

Although it is true that many new technologies increase costs, some have been found to reduce costs. For example, antiretroviral therapies have been largely credited with the dramatic reduction in hospitalization of AIDS patients (Centers for Disease Control and Prevention 1999). Thanks to technology, the initially estimated cost burden of the AIDS epidemic has not materialized. Technology should also be credited for an overall reduction in the average length of inpatient hospital stays. Many services that previously could be provided only in hospitals can now be delivered in less costly home and outpatient settings without adversely affecting health outcomes. Whereas many new technologies may increase labor costs, some actually produce labor cost savings. For example, when Northwestern University Medical Center in Chicago automated its lab, it dropped the human handling steps from 14 to 1.5, and the turnaround time from 8 hours to 90 minutes. Largely because of a significant drop in labor costs, a saving of 30% was realized. Not only that, but the error rate dropped to zero since the system was installed (Flower 2006).

Instead of focusing solely on the excessive costs that new technologies may produce, increasing attention needs to be given to the value or worth of the advances in medical care. In a groundbreaking study, Cutler and colleagues (2006) addressed this issue by examining how medical spending has translated into additional years of life saved, based on the assumption that 50% of the improvements in life expectancy have resulted from medical care. These researchers concluded that the increases in medical spending in the 1960 to 2000 period, in terms of increased life expectancy, have rendered reasonable value for the money spent. For example, for a 45-year-old American who has a remaining life expectancy of 30 years, the value of remaining life is more than $200,000 per year (Murphy and Topel 2003). For this 45-year-old person, the average annual spending in health care for each year of life gained was $53,700 (Cutler et al. 2006).

Impact on Access

Geography is an important factor in access to technology. If a technology is not physically available to a patient population living in remote areas, access is limited. Geographic access can improve for many technologies by providing mobile equipment or by employing new communications technologies to allow remote access to centralized equipment and specialized personnel. For example, GPS (global positioning system) technology significantly improves emergency medical services response time to the scene of motor vehicle crashes and other emergencies (Gonzalez et al. 2009).

Mobile equipment can be transported to rural and remote sites, making it accessible to those populations. Mobile cardiac catheterization laboratories, for example, can provide high technology in rural settings. Cardiac catheterizations can be performed safely in a mobile laboratory at rural hospitals, provided immediate transfer is available for those in need of urgent intervention or revascularization (Peterson and Peterson 2004). As discussed earlier, access to specialized medical care for rural

and other hard-to-reach populations has been transformed through innovations in telemedicine.

Impact on the Structure and Processes of Health Care Delivery

Medical technology has transformed large urban hospitals into medical centers, where the latest diagnostic and therapeutic remedies are offered. Recent growth in alternative settings (home health and outpatient surgery centers) has also been made possible primarily by technology. For example, numerous surgical procedures are now performed in same-day outpatient settings. Earlier, in many cases, the patients would have required hospital stays. Extensive home health services have brought many hospital and nursing home services to the patient's home, reducing the need for institutionalization. Apart from telehealth, home care technology includes kidney dialyzers, feeding pumps, ultrasound, ventilators, and pulse oximeters.

The growth of managed care, integrated delivery systems, and emerging accountable care organizations (discussed in Chapter 9) all require robust IT systems and information exchange capabilities. Certain technologies adopted from other industries have improved health care delivery. For example, the bar-coding system has found several new applications in hospitals, including automation of drug dispensing, which drastically reduces medication errors. Scanning of information on nurses' badges, patients' wristbands, and drugs administered ensures that the right drug is given in the right dose to the right patient (Nicol and Huminski 2006). In some applications, radio frequency identification (RFID) has started to replace bar-coding technology in the areas of patient identification, equipment management, inventory control, and automatic supply and equipment billing (Roark and Miguel 2006).

Telecommunications technology used in telemedicine is also used for administrative teleconferencing and continuing medical education. For example, interactive compressed videoconferencing allows for an almost face-to-face meeting in which vendors can demonstrate new products or services and discuss their utilization, costs, and delivery schedules. Eliminating airfares, hotel expenses, and other travel-related costs can achieve significant savings. Interactive videoconferencing is also used for continuing education in the United States and abroad, with a high degree of satisfaction from participants. Recently, videoconferencing applications have been tried to provide language interpretation to translate physician orders and medication regimens for patients who have limited English proficiency (Hamblen 2006).

Impact on Global Medical Practice

Technology developed in the United States has significantly impacted the practice of medicine worldwide. More than half of the leading medical device companies, for example, are based in the United States. It is one of the few American manufacturing industries that consistently exports more than it imports (Holtzman 2012). Many nations wait for the United States to develop new technologies, which can then be introduced into their systems in a more controlled and manageable fashion. This process gives them access to high-technology medical care with less national investment. Although the United States is expected to continue to maintain its lead in technological innovation, Europe, Japan, and, more recently,

developing nations are also focusing their attention and resources on advances in medical technology (Tripp et al. 2012).

Impact on Bioethics

Increasingly, technological change is raising serious ethical and moral issues. For example, when in vitro fertilization is applied in medical practice and leads to the production of spare embryos, the moral question is what to do with these embryos. Gene mapping of humans, genetic cloning, stem cell research, and other areas of growing interest to scientists may hold potential benefits, but they also present serious ethical dilemmas. Life support technology raises serious ethical issues, especially in medical decisions regarding continuation or cessation of mechanical support, particularly when a patient exists in a permanent vegetative state. Attention to ethical issues is also critical in medical research involving human subjects and in the evaluation of experimental technologies, such as nanomedicine.

The Assessment of Medical Technology

Technology assessment, or more specifically, *health technology assessment* (HTA), refers to "any process of examining and reporting properties of a medical technology used in health care, such as safety, effectiveness, feasibility, and indications for use, cost, and cost-effectiveness, as well as social, economic, and ethical consequences, whether intended or unintended" (Institute of Medicine 1985). HTA seeks to contribute to clinical decision making by providing evidence about the efficacy, safety, and cost effectiveness of medical technologies. It also informs decision makers, clinicians, patients, and the public about the ethical, legal, and social implications of medical technologies (Lehoux et al. 2009).

Technology assessment can play a critical role in distinguishing between services that are appropriate and those that are not. According to the Congressional Budget Office, roughly $700 billion each year goes to health care spending that cannot show improved health outcomes (Orszag 2008). In 2008, $700 billion spent on ineffective care represented 32% of the total expenditures on health services and supplies. Hence, HTA presents a tremendous opportunity to reduce waste and improve health outcomes. Questions related to the adoption of new technology and decisions to control its diffusion should be governed by HTA (Garber 1994).

Efficacy and safety are the basic starting points in evaluating the overall utility of medical technology. Cost effectiveness and cost benefit go a step further in evaluating the safety and efficacy in relation to the cost of using technology. Efficacy and safety are evaluated through clinical trials. A *clinical trial* is a carefully designed research study in which human subjects participate under controlled observations. Clinical trials are carried out over three or four phases, starting with a small number of subjects to evaluate the safety, dosage range, and side effects of new treatments. Subsequent studies using larger groups of people are carried out to confirm effectiveness and further evaluate safety. Compliance with rigid standards is required under HIPAA to protect the rights of study participants and to ensure that the experimentation protocols are ethical. Every institution that conducts or supports biomedical or behavioral research involving human subjects must establish an Institutional Review Board (IRB),

which initially approves and periodically reviews the research.

Efficacy

Efficacy or *effectiveness* is defined simply as health benefit derived from the use of technology. If a product or service actually produces some health benefit, it can be considered efficacious or effective. Decisions about efficacy require that one ask the right questions. For example, are the current diagnostic capabilities satisfactory? What is the likelihood that the new procedure would result in a better diagnosis? If the problem is more accurately diagnosed, what is the likelihood of a better cure?

The question of benefit is not as simple as it first seems because health outcomes have traditionally been measured in terms of mortality and morbidity. Increasingly, improvement in one's quality of life has been viewed as an important outcome. Reliable measures of improvement in quality of life, however, are difficult to obtain because they are not nearly as objective as mortality rates and are subject to bias (Fuchs 2004). Moreover, the same technology employed by different caregivers can sometimes yield different results, although such variations can be minimized by education and training.

Safety

Safety considerations are designed to protect patients against unnecessary harm from technology. As a primary benchmark, benefits must outweigh any negative consequences; however, negative consequences cannot always be foreseen. Hence, clinical trials involving patients who may stand to gain the most from a technology are employed to obtain a reasonable consensus on safety. Subsequently, outcomes from the wider use of the technology are closely monitored to identify any problems related to safety.

Cost Effectiveness

Cost efficiency (or cost effectiveness) is a step beyond the determination of efficacy. Whereas efficacy is concerned only with the benefit derived from the technology, cost effectiveness evaluates the additional (marginal) benefits derived in relation to the additional (marginal) costs incurred. Thus, cost efficiency weighs benefits against costs, which is difficult in actual practice. Hence, cost effectiveness for the vast majority of technologies has not been evaluated.

Figure 5–2 presents a conceptual understanding of cost effectiveness. At the start of medical treatment, each unit of technology utilization is likely to provide benefits in excess of its costs. At some point (Point A in Figure 5–2), an additional unit of technology utilization would result in parity between benefits and costs. This is where the slopes of the benefit and cost lines are equal, as illustrated by the parallel lines. From an economic standpoint, this is the optimum point of health resource inputs. From this point on, it is highly unlikely that additional technological interventions would result in benefits equal to or in excess of the additional costs. As costs continue to increase, the health benefit curve becomes flatter. At Point B (Figure 5–2), the marginal benefits from additional care approach zero, which is referred to as the *flat of the curve*.

A considerable amount of the care delivered in the United States is at the flat of the curve, referring to a level of intensity of care that provides no incremental health benefit

Figure 5–2 Cost Effectiveness and Flat of the Curve.

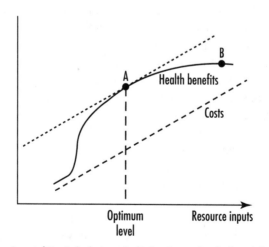

Source: Adapted from T.A. Massaro, Impact of New Technologies on Health Care Costs and on the Nation's Health, *Clinical Chemistry*, Vol. 36, no. 8B, p. 1612, © 1990, The American Association for Clinical Chemistry, Inc.

(Fuchs 2004). Hence, high-intensity care is often wasteful. Yet, in many cases, it is difficult for a physician to determine at what point additional use of technology should be curtailed. Legal ramifications play a role in medical decision making (see "legal risks" and "defensive medicine" in Chapter 1).

Conversely, a more expensive procedure may actually be more cost efficient when used appropriately. For instance, CT scans are more expensive than traditional X-ray images, but the use of CT scans has markedly reduced the need for exploratory surgery (Nitzkin 1996). When CT scan use is warranted, the benefits can outweigh their cost. Their use also bypasses the risks associated with exploratory surgery that may otherwise be necessary.

A *cost-effectiveness analysis* incorporates the elements of both costs and benefits, especially when the costs and benefits are not expressed in terms of dollars (Wan 1995). If costs cannot be monetarily measured, they may be evaluated in terms of resource inputs, such as staff time, number of service units, space requirements, and degree of specialization needed (specialist versus generalist, physician versus allied health professional). Benefits, evaluated in terms of health outcomes, include elements such as efficacy of treatment, prognosis or expected outcomes, number of cases of a certain disease averted, years of life saved, increase in life expectancy, hospitalization and sick days avoided, early return to work, patient satisfaction, and quality of life. Benefits are then evaluated in relation to resource inputs.

Risk is another type of nonmonetary cost. Most medical procedures are not totally safe, and are accompanied by certain levels of risk. Medical care can also result in undesired side effects, iatrogenic illnesses,

medical complications, injuries, or death, all of which carry a cost that is often difficult to measure. Hence, the effectiveness of medical interventions should be evaluated not only in terms of costs but also in terms of risks. Thus, Figure 5–2 can also be used to determine the optimum point at which the benefits equal the risks. Beyond that point, the risks from additional technological interventions are likely to exceed the benefits. An example is overutilization of imaging procedures, such as CT scans, which carry potentially harmful radiation exposure. When used for the wrong reason, such as whole body CT scans for asymptomatic patients, they contribute to unnecessary costs and potential harm (Roberts and Keene 2008).

Cost Benefit

In contrast to cost-effectiveness analysis, *cost-benefit analysis* evaluates benefits in relation to costs, when both are expressed in dollar terms (Seidel et al. 1995; Wan 1995). Hence, cost-benefit analysis is subject to a more rigorous quantitative analysis compared to cost-effectiveness analysis. Cost-benefit analysis is based on four main assumptions: (1) The problem or health condition can be identified or diagnosed. (2) The problem can be controlled or eradicated using an appropriate intervention. (3) The benefit or outcome can be assigned a dollar value. (4) The cost of intervention can be determined in dollars.

The same principles that apply to cost effectiveness are also used for assessing cost benefit. If the estimated benefits exceed costs, the additional spending on medical care is worth the extra costs. As a measure of health benefit, the *quality-adjusted life year (QALY)* is commonly used in the United States,

Canada, Europe, and Australia. Analyses that include the use of QALYs are referred to as *cost-utility analyses* (Neumann and Weinstein 2010). QALY is defined as the value of 1 year of high-quality life. Cutler and McClellan (2001) assigned a value of $100,000 per QALY and demonstrated that, at least in the case of four selected conditions, namely, heart attacks, low birth-weight infants, depression, and cataracts, the estimated benefit of technology was much greater than the cost. For breast cancer treatment, the costs and benefits were found to be equal in magnitude. The value of $100,000 per QALY is debatable. Moreover, there is no standard method for the calculation of QALY.

The ACA prohibits the Patient-Centered Outcomes Research Institute (created under the Act) from placing a dollar value on QALY for the purpose of determining cost effectiveness. The law also prohibits other measures that discount the value of a life because of an individual's disability (Saver 2011).

Directions and Issues in Health Technology Assessment

Private Sector Initiatives

In the United States, HTA is conducted predominantly in the private sector, unlike many European nations that have centralized technology assessment agencies. In the public sector, the Department of Veterans Affairs and the Department of Defense mainly conduct the clinical trials and other evaluations of technology. Hence, much of the talent needed to assess medical technology is also located, organized, and financed in the private sector. Private

agencies, including the Blue Cross and Blue Shield Association, Kaiser Permanente, the American Medical Association, and other professional societies, have undertaken technology assessment.

Need for Coordinated Effort

At present, efforts in HTA remain fragmented and poorly funded, with little or no coordination between public or private sector groups to deliberately address the assessment and diffusion of technologies. Also, information garnered from HTA studies is not efficiently shared among medical organizations, health care systems, and policy makers. The response has been a demand for broad regional and national HTA programs that would study the effects of health care technology more systematically and involve providers, policy makers, patient advocacy groups, and government representatives (Bozic et al. 2004).

Need for Standardization

HTA methods used by the various organizations still lack standardization, which makes it difficult to compare efficacy and cost-effectiveness results. Once methods are standardized, there will be a need for benchmarking HTA organizations to ensure adherence to the standards (Drummond et al. 2012).

Balance Between Clinical Efficacy and Economic Worth

Achieving a balance between efficacy and economic worth will require a change in the American mindset, which will not be forthcoming in the near future. As just mentioned, the stance taken toward QALY in the ACA seems to promote the use of technology without regard to cost benefit. Even the CMS does not allow cost effectiveness to be used in rendering care to Medicare and Medicaid patients. In contrast, European countries, Canada, and Australia use cost effectiveness openly and explicitly in their centralized health planning decisions (Neumann and Sullivan 2006). In the United States, the predominant fear is that an organization risks being sued if it denies access to treatments that are known to be medically effective even when their cost effectiveness is questionable (Bryan et al. 2009). Without malpractice reform, overuse of technology will continue to rack up costs. At some point, the United States may have no choice but to restrict the use of medical technologies on the basis of their economic worth.

Ethical Issues

With the rapid pace of innovation, concerns in HTA transcend the traditional questions about safety, effectiveness, and economic value. New technologies also raise social, ethical, and legal concerns. These issues raise complex questions but provide few answers. Yet, in an era of resource constraints, HTA will have to take into account social, ethical, economic, and legal concerns.

How to provide the latest and best in health care within limited resource parameters has become a major concern for all developed countries. In the United States, insurers, pharmaceutical companies, medical device manufacturers, MCOs, and physician advocacy institutions often act and advocate out of their own self-interests. For example, physicians' representatives, such as medical associations, and the

medical device and pharmaceutical industries frequently argue in favor of increasing resource inputs in delivering health care (Wild 2005). They often claim that quality would deteriorate and/or harm would ensue unless new innovations are funded. When these same groups assume major roles in HTA, a conflict of interest is likely to occur. Biases might also arise in studies funded by sources that have a financial stake in the results. Such concerns have stimulated interest in developing standards for assessments, perhaps under the aegis of a governmental body.

Within social, ethical, and legal constraints, public and private insurers face the problem of deciding whether to cover novel treatments. Recent challenges include, for example, decisions about new reproductive techniques, such as intracytoplasmic sperm injection in vitro fertilization (ICSI IVF), new molecular genetic predictive tests for hereditary breast cancer, and new drugs such as sildenafil (Viagra) for erectile dysfunction (Giacomini 2005). The question arises as to whether society should even bear the cost of infertility treatments, genetic tests, and lifestyle remedies that do not affect people's health and longevity.

Therapies classified as experimental are, generally, not covered by insurance. When new treatments promise previously unattainable health benefits, decisions about assessment of such treatments are often surrounded by controversy. Critical to the debate, but defying easy answers, is the availability of and payment for treatments considered experimental that may be needed by critically ill patients who could possibly benefit from the treatment (Reiser 1994). Concerns about withholding treatment from patients are not easily juxtaposed against equally valid concerns about exposing these same patients to unjustified risk.

Ethical issues also surround the conduct of clinical research. Emanuel and colleagues (2000) contended that ethical clinical research must fulfill seven requirements: (1) The research must have social or scientific value for improving health or enhancing knowledge. (2) The study must be scientifically valid and methodologically rigorous. (3) The selection of subjects in clinical trials must be fair. (4) The potential benefits to patients and the knowledge gained for further scientific work must outweigh the risks. (5) Independent review of the research methods and findings must be conducted by unaffiliated individuals. (6) Informed, voluntary consent must be obtained from subjects. (7) The privacy of enrolled subjects must be protected, they must be offered the opportunity to withdraw, and their well-being must be maintained throughout the trial.

Summary

Medical technology has produced many benefits by making positive changes in the quality of medical care delivered to patients who often end up enjoying a better quality of life. Medical technology can be credited with increased longevity and decreased mortality for people around the world. Much of this technology has been developed through the application of scientific knowledge that was discovered in fields other than medicine. For example, applications of computer science and telecommunications have been adapted for use in the delivery of medical services. The application of information technology and informatics is becoming indispensable in efficient delivery of care and in the effective management of modern health care organizations. The fields of e-health, m-health, e-therapy, telemedicine, and telehealth will continue to expand. Nanotechnology is a cutting-edge advancement within science and engineering which is beginning to find applications in health care on an experimental basis.

On the downside, the development and diffusion of technology are closely intertwined with its utilization. Although cost-saving technology is also widely used, the uncontrolled use of most medical technology has prompted deep concerns about rising costs. Unlike other countries, the United States has not found a way to limit the use of high-cost medical technology. However, health policy in the United States does play a role through the FDA's drug and device approval process and government funding for biomedical research. Uncontrolled use of technology also raises bioethical concerns because human lives are involved.

Given the costs and risks associated with the use of technology, its assessment has become an area of growing interest. The focus of health technology assessment in the United States has been on safety and efficacy. Although cost-effectiveness is widely used in other countries as a criterion for making coverage decisions, in the United States, litigation risks have presented the main barrier for the adoption of delivering services on the basis of economic worth. As escalating health care expenditures reach a critical point, appropriateness of medical treatments may have to be based on their incremental health value at a given cost.

ACA Takeaway

- A 2.3% excise tax is applied to the sale of certain medical devices by manufacturers and importers of these devices. The additional costs will eventually filter down to the consumers.
- The FDA has been given authority to approve the "generic" (biosimilar) versions of biologics, and to charge biopharmaceutical firms a user fee to pay for the review of applications for biosimilar products.
- The ACA prohibits the Patient-Centered Outcomes Research Institute (created under the Act) from placing a dollar value on quality-adjusted life years for the purpose of determining cost effectiveness of medical technology.

Test Your Understanding

Terminology

administrative information systems
asynchronous technology
biologics
clinical information systems
clinical trial
cost-benefit analysis
cost-effectiveness analysis
cost efficiency
cost-utility analysis
decision support systems
effectiveness
efficacy

e-health
electronic health records
e-therapy
flat of the curve
health informatics
health information organization
health technology assessment
information technology
medical technology
m-health
nanomedicine

orphan drugs
quality-adjusted life year (QALY)
self-referrals
smart card
synchronous technology
technological imperative
technology diffusion
telehealth
telemedicine
value
virtual physician visits

Review Questions

1. Medical technology encompasses more than just sophisticated equipment. Discuss.
2. What role does an IT department play in a modern health care organization?
3. Provide brief descriptions of clinical information systems, administrative information systems, and decision support systems in health care delivery.
4. Distinguish between information technology (IT) and health informatics.
5. According to the Institute of Medicine, what are the four main components of a fully developed electronic health record (EHR) system?

6. What are the main provisions of HIPAA with regard to the protection of personal health information? What provisions were added to HIPAA under the HITECH Act?

7. What is telemedicine? How do the synchronous and asynchronous forms of telemedicine differ in their applications?

8. Which factors have been responsible for the low diffusion and low use of telemedicine?

9. Generally speaking, why is medical technology more readily available and used in the United States than in other countries?

10. How does technology-driven competition lead to greater levels of technology diffusion? How does technological diffusion, in turn, lead to greater competition? How does technology-driven competition lead to duplication of services?

11. Summarize the government's role in technology diffusion.

12. What does the ACA propose regarding the development of biosimilars? What is this proposal intended to accomplish?

13. Provide a brief overview of how technology influences the quality of medical care and quality of life.

14. Discuss the relationship between technological innovation and health care expenditures.

15. What impact has technology had on access to medical care?

16. Discuss the roles of efficacy, safety, and cost effectiveness in the context of health technology assessment.

17. Why is it important to achieve a balance between clinical efficacy and economic worth (cost effectiveness) of medical treatments?

18. What are some of the ethical issues surrounding the development and use of medical technology?

REFERENCES

American Hospital Association. 2012. FCC adopts MBAN rule. *AHA News* May 28: 1.

Appleby, J. 2008. The case of CT angiography: How Americans view and embrace new technology. *Health Affairs* 27, no. 6: 1515–1521.

Austin, C.J. 1992. *Information systems for health services administration.* 4th ed. Ann Arbor, MI: AUPHA Press/Health Administration Press.

Baker, L. 2002. Managed care, medical technology, and the well-being of society. *Topics in Magnetic Resonance Imaging* 13, no. 2: 107–113.

Baker, L.C., and S.K. Wheeler. 1998. Managed care and technology diffusion: The case of MRI. *Health Affairs* 17, no. 5: 195–207.

Baker, L.C., et al. 2008. Expanded use of imaging technology and the challenge of measuring value. *Health Affairs* 27, no. 6: 1467–1478.

Barua, B. 2013. *Diagnosis: Medically unreasonable.* Vancouver, British Columbia: The Fraser Institute.

Blumenthal, D. 2011. Implementation of the federal health information technology initiative. *New England Journal of Medicine* 365, no. 25: 2426–2431.

Bozic, K.J., et al. 2004. Health care technology assessment: Basic principles and clinical applications. *The Journal of Bone and Joint Surgery* 86A, no. 6: 1305–1314.

Bright, T.J., et al. 2012. Effect of clinical decision-support systems: A systematic review. *Annals of Internal Medicine* 157, no. 1: 29–43.

Bronstein, M. 2012. *U.S. investment in health research: 2011.* Alexandria, VA: Research America.

Bronzino, J.D., et al. 1990. *Medical technology and society: An interdisciplinary perspective.* Cambridge, MA: MIT Press.

Bryan, S., et al. 2009. Has the time come for cost-effectiveness analysis in U.S. health care? *Health Economics, Policy, and Law* 4, no. 4: 425–443.

Cappellaro, G., et al. 2011. Diffusion of medical technology: The role of financing. *Health Policy* 100, no. 1: 51–59.

Carlson, J. 2012. Targeting constitutionality. Providers going to court over state CON laws. *Modern Healthcare* 42, no. 37: 18.

Centers for Disease Control and Prevention. 1999. *New data show AIDS patients less likely to be hospitalized.* Available at: http://www.cdc.gov/media/pressrel/r990608.htm. Accessed December 2013.

Centers for Disease Control and Prevention (CDC). 2012. Meaningful use. Available at: http://www.cdc.gov/ehrmeaningfuluse/introduction.html. Accessed July 2013.

Centers for Medicare and Medicaid Services (CMS). 2013. Meaningful use. Available at: http://www.cms.gov/Regulations-and-Guidance/Legislation/EHRIncentivePrograms/Meaningful_Use.html. Accessed July 2013.

Clayton, P.D. 2001. Confidentiality and medical information. *Annals of Emergency Medicine* 38, no. 3: 312–316.

Cohen, A.B. 2004a. The adoption and use of medical technology in health care organizations. In: *Technology in American healthcare: Policy directions for effective evaluation and management.* A.B. Cohen and R.S. Hanft, eds. Ann Arbor, MI: The University of Michigan Press. pp. 105–147.

Cohen, A.B. 2004b. Critical questions regarding medical technology and its effects. In: *Technology in American healthcare: Policy directions for effective evaluation and management.* A.B. Cohen and R.S. Hanft, eds. Ann Arbor, MI: The University of Michigan Press. pp. 15–42.

Cohen, A.B. 2004c. The diffusion of new medical technology. In: *Technology in American healthcare: Policy directions for effective evaluation and management.* A.B. Cohen and R.S. Hanft, eds. Ann Arbor, MI: The University of Michigan Press. pp. 79–104.

Congressional Budget Office (CBO). 2008. *Technological change and the growth of health care spending.* Washington, DC: Congressional Budget Office.

Conn, J. 2013. Tipping point. *Modern Healthcare* 43, no. 25: 14–15.

Cutler, D.M., and M. McClellan. 2001. Is technological change in medicine worth it? *Health Affairs* 20, no. 5: 11–29.

Cutler, D.M., et al. 2006. The value of medical spending in the United States, 1960–2000. *The New England Journal of Medicine* 355, no. 9: 920–927.

Danzon, P.M., and M.V. Pauly. 2001. Insurance and new technology: From hospital to drugstore. *Health Affairs* 20, no. 5: 86–100.

Davis, M.P. 2006. Management of cancer pain: Focus on new opioid analgesic formulations. *American Journal of Cancer* 5, no. 3: 171–182.

Decker, S.L., et al. 2012. Physicians in nonprimary care and small practices and those age 55 and older lag in adopting electronic health record systems. *Health Affairs* 31, no. 5: 1108–1114.

DesRoches, C.M., et al. 2008. Electronic health records in ambulatory care—a national survey of physicians. *New England Journal of Medicine* 359, no. 1: 50–60.

DesRoches, C.M., et al. 2013a. Adoption of electronic health records grows rapidly, but fewer than half of US hospitals had at least a basic system in 2012. *Health Affairs* 32, no. 8: 1478–1485.

DesRoches, C.M., et al. 2013b. Some hospitals are falling behind in meeting 'meaningful use' criteria and could be vulnerable to penalties in 2015. *Health Affairs* 32, no. 8: 1355–1360.

Dixon, R.F., and J.E. Stahl. 2009. A randomized trial of virtual visits in a general medicine practice. *Journal of Telemedicine and Telecare* 15, no. 3: 115–117.

Dorsey, E.R., et al. 2010. Funding of US biomedical research, 2003–2008. *Journal of the American Medical Association* 303, no. 2: 137–143.

Drake, D., et al. 1993. *Hard choices: Health care at what cost?* Kansas City, MO: Andrews and McMeel.

Drummond, M., et al. 2012. Can we reliably benchmark health technology assessment organizations? *International Journal of Technology Assessment in Health Care* 28, no. 2: 159–165.

Ellis, D. 2000. *Technology and the future of health care: Preparing for the next 30 years.* San Francisco, CA: Jossey-Bass Publishers.

Emanuel, E.J., et al. (2000). What makes clinical research ethical? *Journal of the American Medical Association* 283, no. 20: 2701–2711.

Field, M.J., and J. Grigsby. 2002. Telemedicine and remote patient monitoring. *Journal of the American Medical Association* 288, no. 4: 423–425.

Flannery, E.J. 1986. Should it be easier or harder to use unapproved drugs and devices? *Hastings Center Report* 16, no. 1: 17–23.

Flower, J. 2006. Imagining the future of health care. *The Physician Executive* 32, no. 1: 64–66.

Food and Drug Administration (FDA). 2009a. *Federal Food and Drugs Act of 1906.* Available at: http://www.fda.gov/regulatoryinformation/legislation/ucm148690.htm. Accessed January 2010.

Food and Drug Administration (FDA). 2009b. What are "biologics" questions and answers. Available at: http://www.fda.gov/AboutFDA/CentersOffices/OfficeofMedicalProductsandTobacco/CBER/ucm133077.htm. Accessed July 2013.

Food and Drug Administration (FDA). 2013. Fast track, breakthrough therapy, accelerated approval and priority review. Available at: http://www.fda.gov/ForConsumers/ByAudience/ForPatientAdvocates/SpeedingAccesstoImportantNewTherapies/ucm128291.htm#fast. Accessed July 2013.

Fox, S. 2013. *Pew Internet: Health.* Available at: http://www.pewinternet.org/Commentary/2011/November/Pew-Internet-Health.aspx. Accessed July 2013.

Fuchs, V.R. 2004. More variation in use of care, more flat-of-the-curve medicine. *Health Affairs* 23 (Variations Suppl): 104–107.

Furukawa, M.F., et al. 2013. Hospital electronic health information exchange grew substantially in 2008-12. *Health Affairs* 32, no. 8: 1346–1354.

Garber, A.M. 1994. Can technology assessment control health spending? *Health Affairs* 13, no. 3: 115–126.

Gelijns, A., and N. Rosenberg. 1994. The dynamics of technological change in medicine. *Health Affairs* 13, no. 3: 28–46.

Giacomini, M. 2005. One of these things is not like the others: The idea of precedence in health technology assessment and coverage decisions. *The Milbank Quarterly* 83, no. 2: 193–223.

Gonzalez, R.P., et al. 2009. Improving rural emergency medical service response time with global positioning system navigation. *The Journal of Trauma* 67, no. 5: 899–902.

Halamka, J.D. 2010. Making the most of federal health information technology regulations. *Health Affairs* 29, no. 4: 596–600.

Hamblen, M. 2006. Hospitals expand videoconferencing. *Computerworld* 40, no. 23: 21.

Hellinger, F.J. 2009. The effect of certificate-of-need laws on hospital beds and healthcare expenditures: An empirical analysis. *American Journal of Managed Care* 15, no. 10: 737–744.

Hillestad, R., et al. 2005. Can electronic medical record systems transform health care? Potential health benefits, savings, and costs. *Health Affairs* 24, no. 5: 1103–1117.

Ho, V., et al. 2013. State deregulation and Medicare costs for acute cardiac care. *Medical Care Research & Review* 70, no. 2: 185–205.

Holtzman, Y. 2012.*The U.S. medical device industry in 2012: Challenges at home and abroad.* Available at: http://www.mddionline.com/article/medtech-2012-SWOT. Accessed July 2013.

Iglehart, J.K. 1982. The cost and regulation of medical technology: Future policy directions. In: *Technology and the future of health care.* J.B. McKinlay, ed. Cambridge, MA: MIT Press. pp. 69–103.

Institute of Medicine. 1985. *Assessing medical technologies.* Washington, DC: National Academies Press.

Institute of Medicine. 2003. *Key capabilities of an electronic health records system.* Washington, DC: National Academies Press.

Jacobs, B.L., et al. 2013. Certificate of need legislation and the dissemination of robotic surgery for prostate cancer. *The Journal of Urology* 189, no. 1: 80–85.

Johnson, C. 2010. *Generic biologics: A regulatory pathway, but who can afford the tolls?* Available at: http://wtnnews.com/articles/7486/. Accessed July 2013.

Johnston, B. et al. 2000. Outcomes of the Kaiser Permanente tele-home health research project. *Archives of Family Medicine* 9: 40–45.

Kahn, J.G., et al. 2010. "Mobile" health needs and opportunities in developing countries. *Health Affairs* 29, no. 2: 252–258.

Katz, J. 2011. FDA regulations stifle medical device innovation. *Industry Week*, October 3. Available at: http://www.industryweek.com/articles/fda_regulations_stifle_medical_device_innovation_25713. aspx. Accessed October 2013.

Kher, U. 2006. The hospital wars. *Time* 168, no. 24: 64–68.

Kim, M., et al. 2001. How interested are Americans in New Medical Technologies? A multicountry comparison. *Health Affairs* 20, no. 5: 194–201.

Kleinke, J.D. 2001. The price of progress: Prescription drugs in the health care market. *Health Affairs* 20, no. 5: 43–60.

Komaroff, A.L. 2005. Beyond the horizon. *Newsweek* 146, no. 24: 82–84.

Kutney-Lee, A., and D. Kelly. 2011. The effect of hospital electronic health record adoption on nurse-assessed quality of care and patient safety. *Journal of Nursing Administration* 41, no. 11: 466–472.

Lee, J. 2013. A new sensory system. *Modern Healthcare* 43, no. 19: 30–31.

Lehoux, P., et al. 2009. What medical specialists like and dislike about health technology assessment reports. *Journal of Health Services Research & Policy* 14, no. 4: 197–203.

Littell, C.L., and R.J. Strongin. 1996. The truth about technology and health care costs. *IEEE Technology and Society Magazine* 15, no. 3: 10–14.

Luce, B.R. 1993. Medical technology and its assessment. In: *Introduction to health services*. 4th ed. S.J. Williams and P.R. Torrens, eds. Albany, NY: Delmar Publishers. pp. 245–268.

Maheu, M.M., et al. 2001. *E-health, telehealth, and telemedicine: A guide to start-up and success*. San Francisco, CA: Jossey-Bass.

Marrie, R.A., et al. 2013. Preferred sources of health information in persons with multiple sclerosis: Degree of trust and information sought. *Journal of Medical Internet Research* 15, no. 4: e67.

McClellan, M., and D. Kessler. 1999. A global analysis of technological change in health care: The case of heart attacks. *Health Affairs* 18, no. 3: 250–257.

McGregor, M. 1989. Technology and the allocation of resources. *The New England Journal of Medicine* 320, no. 2: 118–120.

Merrill, R.A. 1994. Regulation of drugs and devices: An evolution. *Health Affairs* 13, no. 3: 47–69.

Meyers, L., et al. 2012. Building a telehealth network through collaboration: The story of the Nebraska Statewide Telehealth Network. *Critical Care Nursing Quarterly* 35, no. 4: 346–352.

Milewa, T. 2006. Health technology adoption and the politics of governance in the UK. *Social Science and Medicine* 63, no. 12: 3102–3112.

Mitchell, J.M. 2007. The prevalence of physician self-referral arrangements after Stark II: Evidence from advanced diagnostic imaging. *Health Affairs* 26, no. 3: w415–w424.

Murphy, G.F., et al. 1999. EHR vision, definition, and characteristics. In: *Electronic health records: Changing the vision*. G.F. Murphy, M.A. Hanken, and K.A. Waters, eds. Philadelphia, PA: Saunders. pp. 3–26.

Murphy, K.M., and R.H. Topel. 2003. The economic value of medical research. In: *Measuring the gains from medical research: An economic approach*. K.M. Murphy and R.H. Topel, eds. Chicago: University of Chicago Press. pp. 41–73.

National Conference of State Legislatures. 2011. *Certificate of need: State health laws and programs*. Available at: http://www.ncsl.org/default.aspx?tabid=14373. Accessed January 2011.

Neumann, P.J., and S.D. Sullivan. 2006. Economic evaluation in the US: What is the missing link? *Pharmacoeconomics* 24, no. 11: 1163–1168.

Neumann, P.J., and M.C. Weinstein. 2010. Legislation against use of cost-effectiveness information. *The New England Journal of Medicine* 363, no. 16: 1495–1497.

Nicol, N., and L. Huminski. 2006. How we cut drug errors. *Modern Healthcare* 36, no. 34: 38.

Nitzkin, J.L. 1996. Technology and health care—Driving costs up, not down. *IEEE Technology and Society Magazine* 15, no. 3: 40–45.

Organization for Economic Cooperation and Development (OECD). 2011. *OECD health data: 2011*. Paris, OECD.

Orszag, P.R. 2008. *Opportunities to increase efficiency in health care*. Washington, DC: Congressional Budget Office.

Peterson, L.F., and L.R. Peterson. 2004. The safety of performing diagnostic cardiac catheterizations in a mobile catheterization laboratory at primary care hospitals. *Angiology* 55, no. 5: 499–506.

Rakich, J.S., et al. 1992. *Managing health services organizations*. Baltimore, MD: Health Professions Press.

Rassweiler, J., et al. 2010. The role of laparoscopic radical prostatectomy in the era of robotic surgery. *European Urology Supplements* 9, no. 3: 379–387.

Reiser, S.J. 1994. Criteria for standard versus experimental therapy. *Health Affairs* 13, no. 3: 127–136.

Ricci, R.P., et al. 2013. Effectiveness of remote monitoring of CIEDs in detection and treatment of clinical and device-related cardiovascular events in daily practice: The HomeGuide Registry. *Europace* 15, no. 7: 970–977.

Ricciardi, L., et al. 2013. A national action plan to support consumer engagement via e-health. *Health Affairs* 32, no. 2: 376–384.

Roark, D.C., and K. Miguel. 2006. Replacing bar coding: Radio frequency identification. *Nursing* 36, no. 12: 30.

Roberts, J., and S. Keene. 2008. Asymptomatic CT scans: A health assessment or a health risk? *Internet Journal of Radiology* 9, no. 1: 18.

Rochlen, A.B., et al. 2004. Online therapy: Review of relevant definitions, debates, and current empirical support. *Journal of Clinical Psychology* 60, no. 3: 269–283.

Sanmartin, C., and J.M. Berthelot. 2006. *Access to health care services in Canada, January to December 2005*. Ottawa, Ontario: Statistics Canada.

Saver, R.S. 2011. The new era of comparative effectiveness: Will public health end up left behind? *Journal of Law, Medicine & Ethics* 39, no. 3: 437–449.

Schur, C.L., and M.L. Berk. 2008. Views on health care technology: Americans consider the risks and sources of information. *Health Affairs* 27, no. 6: 1654–1664.

Sclafani, J., et al. 2013. Mobile tablet use among academic physicians and trainees. *Journal of Medical Systems* 37, no. 1: 1–6.

Seidel, L.F., et al. 1995. *Applied quantitative methods for health services management*. Baltimore, MD: Health Professions Press.

Shaw, L.J., et al. 2000. Clinical and economic outcomes assessment in nuclear cardiology. *Quarterly Journal of Nuclear Medicine* 44, no. 2: 138–152.

Shekelle, P.G., et al. 2006. *Costs and benefits of health information technology*. Rockville, MD: Agency for Healthcare Research and Quality.

Silow-Carroll, S., et al. 2012. *Using electronic health records to improve quality and efficiency: The experiences of leading hospitals*. New York: The Commonwealth Fund.

Singh, R., et al. 2010. Sustainable rural telehealth innovation: A public health case study. *Health Services Research* 45, no. 4: 985–1004.

Skinner, A.E.G., and G. Latchford. 2006. Attitudes to counselling via the Internet: A comparison between in-person counselling client and Internet support group users. *Counseling and Psychotherapy Research* 6, no. 3: 92–97.

Slotwiner, D., and B. Wilkoff. 2013. Cost efficiency and reimbursement of remote monitoring: A US perspective. *Europace* 15, Suppl. 1: i54–i58.

Smith, B.D. 2010. Reimbursement, implementation seen as barriers to telemedicine. *PT in Motion* 2, no. 10: 41–42.

Sobolev, B.G., et al. 2013. The occurrence of adverse events in relation to time after registration for coronary artery bypass surgery: A population-based observational study. *Journal of Cardiothoracic Surgery* 8, no. 1 (special section): 1–14.

Sorenson, C., et al. 2013. Medical technology as a key driver of rising health expenditures: Disentangling the relationship. *ClinicoEconomics and Outcomes Research* 5: 223–234.

Steinbrook, R. 2009. The NIH stimulus—The Recovery Act and biomedical research. *The New England Journal of Medicine* 360, no. 15: 1479–1481.

Stofle, G.S. 2001. *Choosing an online therapist.* Harrisburg, PA: White Hat Communications.

Taub, J. 2011. The smallest revolution: 5 recent breakthroughs in nanomedicine. *Scientific American*, September 30. Availabe at: http://blogs.scientificamerican.com/guest-blog/2011/09/30/the-smallest-revolution-five-recent-breakthroughs-in-nanomedicine. Accessed July 2013.

Tan, J.K.H. 1995. *Health management information systems: Theories, methods, and applications.* Gaithersburg, MD: Aspen Publishers, Inc.

Thompson Coburn LLP. 2013. *2013 HIPAA changes.* Available at: http://www.thompsoncoburn.com/Libraries/Alerts/2013_HIPAA_Changes.pdf. Accessed July 2013.

Thorley, A.J., and T.D. Tetley. 2013. New perspectives in nanomedicine. *Pharmacology & Therapeutics* 140, no. 2: 176–185.

Tripp, S., et al. 2012. *The economic impact of the U.S. advanced medical technology industry.* Cleveland, OH: Battelle Technology Partnership Practice.

Tustin, N. 2010. The role of patient satisfaction on online health information seeking. *Journal of Health Communication* 15, no. 1: 3–17.

Wachler, A.B., and P.A. Avery. 2011. *Stark II proposed regulations: Rule offers additional guidance while regulators seek more input from health care community.* Available at: http://www.wachler.com/CM/Publications/Publications17.asp. Accessed January 2011.

Wan, T.T.H. 1995. *Analysis and evaluation of health care systems: An integrated approach to managerial decision making.* Baltimore, MD: Health Professions Press.

Wang, T., et al. 2013. Funding alternatives in EHR adoption beyond HITECH incentives and traditional approaches. *Healthcare Financial Management* 67, no. 5: 86–91.

Wennberg, J.E. 1988. Improving the medical decision-making process. *Health Affairs* 7, no. 1: 99–106.

Wild, C. 2005. Ethics of resource allocation: Instruments for rational decision making in support of a sustainable health care. *Poiesis & Praxis* 3, no. 4: 296–309.

Wodarski, J., and J. Frimpong. 2013. Application of e-therapy programs to the social work practice. *Journal of Human Behavior in the Social Environment* 23, no. 1: 29–36.

Ybarra, M.L., and W.W. Eaton. 2005. Internet-based mental health interventions. *Mental Health Services Research* 7, no. 2: 75–87.

Zanaboni, P., and R. Wootton. 2012. Adoption of telemedicine: from pilot stage to routine delivery. *BMC Medical Informatics and Decision Making* 12, no. 1: 1–9.

Chapter 6

Health Services Financing

Learning Objectives

- To study the role of health care financing and its impact on the delivery of health care
- To understand the basic concept of insurance and how general insurance terminology applies to health insurance
- To differentiate between group insurance, self-insurance, individual health insurance, managed care, high-deductible plans with savings, and Medigap plans
- To explore trends in employer-based health insurance
- To examine the distinctive features of public insurance programs, such as Medicare, Medicaid, CHIP, Department of Defense, Veterans Health Administration, and Indian Health Service
- To understand the various methods of reimbursement and developing trends
- To discuss national health care and personal health care expenditures and trends in private and public financing
- To become familiar with the requirements of the Affordable Care Act and their likely effects on financing and insurance
- To assess current directions and issues in health care financing

"I have comprehensive insurance."

Introduction

Complexity of financing is one of the primary characteristics of medical care delivery in the United States. Single-payer systems in countries such as Australia, Canada, and Great Britain simplify health care financing; taxes are raised by the government to provide health insurance to the citizens, and private financing plays a minor role for those who want more extensive coverage than what the government offers. In the United States, both public and private financing play substantial roles. In the public sector, the government has created a multitude of tax-financed programs; each program serves a defined category of citizens provided they meet the established qualifications. Insurance overlap is also relatively common. For example, a significant number of Medicare beneficiaries either qualify for Medicaid or have purchased private supplementary insurance to pay for expenses not covered by Medicare. Under the Affordable Care Act (ACA), the public sector's role in providing health insurance will increase considerably. In the private sector, financing for health insurance is shared between the employer and the employee; the employer provides the bulk of financing. Self-employed people purchase health insurance in the open market. For the unemployed, the underemployed (those working part-time who do not qualify for employer-sponsored health insurance), and those who lose their private insurance thanks to the ACA, the government is expected to facilitate the purchase of health insurance starting in 2014. The actual payment to providers of care is also handled in numerous ways. Patients generally pay a portion of the costs directly, but the bulk is paid through a variety of insurance plans

and government programs. The government and some large employers use the services of third-party administrators (TPAs) to process payment claims from providers.

In this chapter, financing is discussed in broad terms that include the concepts of financing, insurance, and payment. This does not mean, however, that the three functions are structurally integrated. For example, government-financed programs, such as Medicare and Medicaid, integrate the functions of financing and insurance, but contracted TPAs make the actual payments to the providers after services have been delivered. Traditional insurance plans integrate the functions of insurance and payment, whereas both employers and employees provide the financing. Managed care has gone one step further in integrating all four functions of health care delivery—financing, insurance, delivery, and payment.

This chapter focuses on financing for both private and public health insurance, points out trends, discusses health care expenditures, explains various payment methods to reimburse providers, and incorporates the main provisions of the ACA along with their likely impact. Two main sections of the chapter present details of the ACA as they apply to private insurance and Medicaid. The ACA had envisioned Medicaid to have some degree of uniformity throughout the country, but has been left in a muddled state as a result of the June 2012 US Supreme Court decision. Hence, the "old" Medicaid and Medicaid under the ACA are discussed in this chapter. Differences in benefits for Medicaid beneficiaries living in different states are likely to be significant. The chapter concludes with current directions and issues in health insurance and financing.

The Role and Scope of Health Services Financing

As its central role, health services financing pays for health insurance premiums. Providers generally rely on the patients' insurance status to be assured that they will receive payment for the services they deliver. The various methods used to determine how much providers should be paid (i.e., reimbursement) for their services are also closely intertwined with the broad financing function.

To a large extent, financing determines who has access to health care and who does not, although many uninsured have access to charitable care, and despite the ACA, charity will continue to play a noteworthy role mainly for the many who remain uninsured. Illegal immigrants, young healthy individuals who choose not to buy insurance, those who do not pay any income taxes and yet do not qualify for Medicaid, and those who will be exempt from having to purchase health insurance under the ACA will constitute the estimated 25 to 30 million uninsured.

The demand for health care is mostly related to its financing. Health insurance increases the demand for covered services; the demand would be less if those same services were paid out of pocket. Increased demand means greater utilization of health services, given adequate supply. According to economic theory, insurance lowers the out-of-pocket cost of medical care to consumers; hence, they will consume more medical services than if they had to pay the entire price out of their own pockets. Consumer behavior that leads to a higher utilization of health care services when the services are covered by insurance is referred to as ***moral hazard*** (Feldstein 1993).

Financing also exerts powerful influences on supply-side factors, such as how much health care is produced in the private sector. Health care services and technology proliferate when services are covered by insurance. Even new services and technologies may start emerging, and new models of organization may form. When reimbursement is cut, supply can also curtail.

Issues pertaining to reimbursement for services are critical in health services management decision making. Demand-side factors, including reimbursement, typically guide health services managers in evaluating the type and extent of services to offer. The amount of reimbursement needed to recoup capital costs over time also heavily influences decisions such as acquisition of new equipment, renovation or expansion of facilities, and launching of new services.

Financing can also influence the supply and distribution of health care professionals. As an example, employer financing for dental insurance has spawned the growth of dentists and dental hygienists. Mechanisms for reimbursing physicians, such as the resource-based relative value scale (RBRVS) used by Medicare, directly affect physicians' incomes. One of the main intents of RBRVS, implemented in 1992, was to entice more medical residents into general practice by increasing the reimbursement for services provided by generalists. Due to other factors, however, the imbalance between generalists and specialists continues (see Chapter 4).

Financing eventually affects, directly as well as indirectly, the total health care expenditures incurred by a health care delivery system. The subsequent section discusses the relationship between financing and health care expenditures and provides a general framework for controlling health care costs.

Financing and Cost Control

Health care financing and cost control are closely intertwined. Figure 6–1 presents a conceptual model of cost control. In the US health care delivery system, insurance is the main factor that determines the level of demand for medical services. Restricting financing for health insurance (see demand-side rationing in Chapter 2) eventually controls total health care expenditures. Conversely, extension of health insurance to the uninsured, without supply-side rationing (discussed in Chapter 2), will increase total health care expenditures (E). Apart from the extent of insurance coverage, the cost of health insurance also affects system-wide health care expenditures.

Insurance, along with payment (price = P), influences the supply or availability of health services. Reducing reimbursement for providers has a direct influence on E, as well as an indirect influence through shrinkage in supply. Cuts in reimbursement have been used in the United States, as well as in other countries, to contain the growth of health care expenditures.

As discussed in Chapter 5, diffusion of technology and other types of services can be directly restricted through health planning, which is commonly used in countries that have national health insurance. When supply of technology is rationed, people may be insured but do not have free access to those services. Reduced utilization of expensive technology results in direct savings. Nations that have national health care also achieve indirect savings by having fewer specialist physicians and specialized technicians and by spending less on research and development (R&D).

Insurance and supply of health care services together determine access and, eventually, the utilization of services (quantity of services consumed = Q). Utilization can also be directly controlled. For example, private health insurance, as well as Medicare and Medicaid, contain utilization by specifying which services are noncovered. Managed care directly controls utilization using various mechanisms (discussed in Chapter 9).

Because $E = P \times Q$, rising health care costs can be controlled by managing the numerous factors that influence P and Q. Many of these factors are external to the health care delivery system. P, for example, includes general economy-wide inflation,

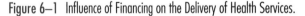

Figure 6–1 Influence of Financing on the Delivery of Health Services.

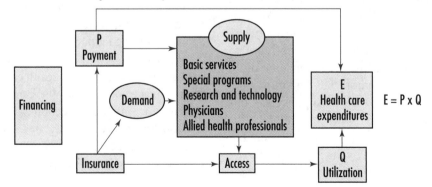

as well as medical inflation that exceeds general inflation. In addition to the intrinsic factors discussed in this section, Q is also a function of changes in the size and demographic composition (i.e., age, sex, and racial mix) of the population (Levit et al. 1994). Chapter 12 discusses these factors more extensively.

The Insurance Function

Insurance is a mechanism for protection against risk; that is its primary purpose. In this context, *risk* refers to the possibility of a substantial financial loss from an event of which the probability of occurrence is relatively small (at least in a given individual's case). For example, even though auto accidents are common in the United States, the likelihood is quite small that a specific individual will have an auto accident in a given year. Even when the risk is small, people buy insurance to protect their assets against catastrophic loss.

The insuring agency that assumes risk is called the *insurer*, or underwriter. *Underwriting* is a systematic technique for evaluating, selecting (or rejecting), classifying, and rating risks. Medical underwriting, for example, would take into account the health status of people to be insured. Four fundamental principles underlie the concept of insurance (Health Insurance Institute 1969; Vaughn and Elliott 1987): (1) Risk is unpredictable for the individual insured. (2) Risk can be predicted with a reasonable degree of accuracy for a group or a population. (3) Insurance provides a mechanism for transferring or shifting risk from the individual to the group through the pooling of resources. (4) All members of the insured group share actual losses on some equitable basis.

Technically, health care services for all Americans 65 and over (the elderly population) are provided through Medicare. For those below the age of 65, private insurance—either employment-based or self-financed—is the predominant avenue for receiving health care. Medicaid and Children's Health Insurance Program (CHIP) cover many of the poor, including children in low-income households. Other public programs cover a small number of people, such as the Department of Veterans Affairs (VA) and the military health system. The remainder, without any coverage, are the uninsured.

Because of overlaps in coverage, however, it is almost impossible to neatly categorize people into specific types of health insurance. Figure 6–2 broadly categorizes the US population into privately insured, publicly insured, and uninsured categories. Although private insurance is dominant in US health care delivery, between 2005 and 2011, there has been a significant shift between private and public insurance. Private insurance declined from covering

Figure 6–2 Health Insurance Status of the Total US Resident Population, 2011.

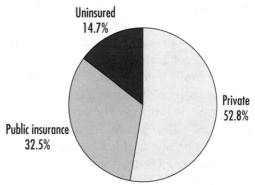

Source: Data from *Health, United States, 2012.* National Center for Health Statistics.

almost 66% of the nonelderly population to 61% while Medicaid increased from covering almost 12.6% of the nonelderly population to 17.5% based on data from the National Center for Health Statistics (NCHS 2012).

Health insurance, particularly private health insurance, comes in the form of a *plan*, which specifies, among other details, information pertaining to costs, covered services, and how to obtain health care when needed. There are numerous plans. Anyone covered by health insurance is called the *insured* or a *beneficiary*. Two types of employer-sponsored plans are single coverage plans and family coverage plans. The latter cover the spouse and dependent children of the working employee. Medicare and Medicaid plans recognize only individual beneficiaries. In the case of married couples, for instance, Medicare and Medicaid recognize each spouse as an independent beneficiary.

Private Health Insurance

Private health insurance has also been called "voluntary health insurance." Most private health insurance is employment-based, but workers are not mandated to buy in. Private insurance includes many different types of health plan providers, such as commercial insurance companies (e.g., United Health Group, Well Point, Cigna, and Aetna), Blue Cross/Blue Shield, and managed care organizations (MCOs). The nonprofit Blue Cross and Blue Shield Associations are similar to private health insurance companies, and the companies named here operate their own MCOs. Many businesses are self-insured, using insurance companies for stop-loss coverage.

Basic Health Insurance Terminology

Premiums

A *premium* is the amount charged by the insurer to insure against specified risks. An employer may offer more than one health insurance plan, in which case premiums can vary depending on the plan selected by the employee. Employment-based health insurance is heavily subsidized by the employer, and the employee is asked to share in the cost of premiums. Cost trends are discussed later under "Health Insurance Costs."

Risk Rating

Premiums are determined by the actuarial assessment of risk. Three different methods have been used to determine premiums. The first, called *experience rating*, is based on a group's own medical claims experience. Under this method, premiums differ from group to group because different groups have different risks. For example, people working in various industries are exposed to various levels and types of hazards, people in certain occupations are more susceptible to certain illnesses or injuries, and older groups represent higher risks than younger groups. High-risk groups are expected to incur high utilization of medical care services, so these groups are charged higher premiums compared to preferred or favorable risk groups. The main issue with experience rating is that it makes premiums unaffordable for high-risk groups. *Community rating* spreads the risk among members of a larger population. Premiums are based on the utilization experience of the entire population covered by the same type of health insurance. Under pure community rating, the same rate applies to everyone regardless of age, gender, occupation, or any other indicator of health risk (Goodman and Musgrave 1992). For example, a person who has a life-threatening condition would pay the same premium as someone who does not. When premiums are based on community rating, the good risks, that is, healthy people, actually subsidize the insurance cost for the poor risks (Somers and Somers 1977). In other words, costs shift from people in poor health to people in good health and make health insurance less affordable for those who are healthy. *Adjusted community rating*, also known as modified community rating, overcomes the main drawbacks of experience rating and pure community rating. Under this method, price differences take into account demographic factors such as age, gender, geography, and family composition, while ignoring other risk factors. In the past, state laws have governed health insurance, including premium rate setting, with different states adopting one of the three methods discussed earlier. The ACA requires the use of adjusted community rating as the method to determine premiums for individuals and small groups. Only age, family composition (individual or family), geography, and tobacco use may be used to adjust premiums.

Cost Sharing

In addition to paying a share of the cost of premiums through payroll deductions, insured individuals pay a portion of the actual cost of medical services out of their own pockets. These out-of-pocket expenses are in the form of deductibles and copayments and are incurred only if and when medical services are used. A *deductible* is the amount the insured must first pay each year before any benefits are payable by the plan. For example, suppose a plan requires the insured to pay a $1,000 deductible. When the insured receives medical care, the plan starts paying only after the cost of medical services received by the insured has exceeded $1,000 in a given year. Not all health plans have a deductible. Many HMO plans, for example, do not have deductibles.

The second type of cost sharing is a *copayment*, which is a flat amount the insured must pay each time health services are received. Health plans may also use *coinsurance*, which is a set proportion of the medical costs that the insured must pay out of pocket. As an example, for a certain health care product or service covered by a health plan, a copayment of $30 or an 80/20 coinsurance may be required. In the latter case, once the deductible has been met, the plan pays 80% of the costs; the insured pays the remaining 20%.

In case of a catastrophic illness or injury, the deductible and copayment/coinsurance amounts can add up to a substantial sum. Hence, health plans generally have an annual maximum limit on cost sharing. Once the maximum cost sharing amount has been reached, the plan pays 100% of any additional expenses.

The rationale for cost sharing is to control utilization of health care services. Since insurance creates moral hazard by insulating the insured against the cost of health care, making the insured share in the cost promotes more responsible behavior in health care utilization. A comprehensive study employing a controlled experimental design conducted in the 1970s, commonly referred to as the Rand Health Insurance Experiment, demonstrated that cost sharing had a material impact on lowering utilization, without any significant negative health consequences (see details in Chapter 12).

Covered Services

Services covered by an insurance plan are referred to as *benefits*. Each health insurance plan spells out in a contract the type of medical services it covers and also services that it does not cover. The insured is entitled to a copy of the contract. A typical disclaimer included in most contracts states that only "medically necessary" services are covered regardless of whether or not such services are provided by a physician. Almost all plans include medical and surgical services, hospitalizations, emergency services, prescriptions, maternity care, and delivery of a baby. Within specified limits, most plans also provide mental health services, substance abuse services, home health care, skilled nursing care, rehabilitation, supplies, and equipment. Services such as eyeglasses and dental care are generally not covered by health insurance; vision and dental insurance plans can be purchased separately. Services most commonly excluded are those not ordered by a physician, such as self-care and over-the-counter products. Other services commonly excluded from health insurance coverage are cosmetic and reconstructive surgery, work-related illness and injury (covered under workers' compensation—see Chapter 3), rest cures, genetic counseling, and the like.

Types of Private Insurance

Group Insurance

Group insurance can be obtained through an employer, a union, or a professional organization. A *group insurance* program anticipates that a substantial number of people in the group will purchase insurance through its sponsor. Because risk is spread out among the many insured, group insurance provides the advantage of lower costs than if the same type of coverage was purchased in the individual insurance market.

Unlike monetary wages, health insurance benefits are not subject to income tax. Consequently, a dollar of health insurance received from the employer is worth more than the same amount received in taxable wages or an after-tax dollar spent out of pocket for medical care. The tax policy provides an incentive to obtain health insurance as a benefit that is largely paid by the employer.

Starting in the 1950s, major medical insurance became common. Major medical was designed to cover catastrophic situations that could subject families to substantial financial hardships, such as hospitalization, extended illness, and expensive surgery. Since the 1970s, health insurance plans have become comprehensive in coverage, and include basic and routine physician office visits and diagnostic services. Hence, health insurance today is an anomaly to the fundamental concept behind insurance.

Self-Insurance

In a *self-insured plan*, the employer acts as its own insurer instead of obtaining insurance through an insurance company. In 2013, 61% of all covered workers in private and public organizations were covered by a self-insured plan; 94% of workers employed in businesses with 5,000 or more employees were in self-insured plans (Kaiser/HRET 2013).

Both large and small employers can self-insure, but most are large businesses. Rather than pay insurers a dividend to bear the risk, many employers simply assume the risk by budgeting a certain amount to pay medical claims incurred by their employees. Self-insured employers can protect themselves against any potential risk of high losses by purchasing *reinsurance*, also called stop-loss coverage, from a private insurance company. Being self-insured gives such employers a greater degree of control, and costs are contained through a slower rise in premiums during periods of rapid inflation (Gabel et al. 2003).

Self-insurance was spurred by government policies. Self-insured employers are exempt from a premium tax that insurance companies have to pay, the cost of which is passed on to customers through higher premiums. Further, the Employee Retirement Income Security Act (ERISA) of 1974 exempts self-insured plans from certain mandatory benefits that regular health insurance plans are required to provide in many states. Self-insured plans also avoid other types of state insurance regulations, such as reserve requirements and consumer protection requirements. Because of the many advantages, employers that are large enough to make it feasible for themselves have viewed self-insurance as a better economic alternative. Self-insured plans are also exempt from some of the requirements imposed by the ACA (Yee et al. 2012).

Individual Private Health Insurance

Individually purchased private health insurance (nongroup plans) has been a relatively small, but important, source of coverage for some Americans. In 2011, almost 19 million Americans (11.5% of all privately insured individuals) had individual private insurance (Fronstin 2012). The family farmer, the early retiree, the self-employed, and the employee of a business that does not offer health insurance make up most of those relying on individual health insurance. For underwriting purposes, the risk indicated

by each individual's health status and demographics are taken into account. Consequently, high-risk individuals are often unable to obtain privately purchased health insurance. As the implementation of the ACA drew closer, starting October 2013, a large proportion of the insured who had coverage under individual plans were seeing their coverage dropped by the insurers. Hence, the ACA will play a significant role in insuring these individuals.

Managed Care Plans

MCOs, such as HMOs and preferred provider organizations (PPOs), emerged in the 1980s in response to the rapid escalation of health care costs. At first, managed care plans were different and were cheaper than those offered by traditional insurance companies. However, several factors over time (discussed in Chapter 9) converged on MCOs, and traditional insurance companies started offering managed care plans. Today, the vast majority of health insurance exists in the form of managed care plans.

High-Deductible Health Plans and Savings Options

High-deductible health plans (HDHPs) combine a savings option with a health insurance plan carrying a high deductible. A relatively new health insurance product on the market, HDHPs have been gaining popularity. In 2013, HDHPs covered 20% of the workers in employment-based plans, up from just 4% in 2006 (Kaiser/HRET 2013). Because of the high deductibles, premiums for HDHP plans are generally lower than for other types of health plans.

Savings options give consumers greater control over how to use the funds. Hence, these plans are also referred to as *consumer-driven health plans*. There are two main types of HDHPs/savings options which have different guidelines under US tax law. Differences between the two are shown in Exhibit 6–1. Because of the rules proposed under the ACA, availability of HDHPs is in jeopardy (Andrews 2013), although they could be offered by self-insured employers protected under ERISA.

Medigap

Medigap, also called Medicare supplement insurance, is private health insurance that can be purchased only by those enrolled in the original Medicare program which has high out-of-pocket costs (discussed later under "Medicare"). It is illegal for an insurance company to sell a Medigap plan to someone who is covered by Medicaid or Medicare

Exhibit 6–1   Key Differences Between a Health Reimbursement Arrangement and a Health Savings Account

Health Reimbursement Arrangement (HRA)	Health Savings Account (HSA)
Established solely by the employer. Self-employed individuals cannot establish an HRA. The account is owned by the employer.	Established by the individual. The employer can assist in establishing an HSA. The account is owned by the employee.
Having an HDHP is not mandatory. Employers may offer HRAs in addition to or in place of health insurance, which may include an HDHP. Funds are used for deductibles, copayments, insurance premiums, and other medical and related expenses authorized by the Internal Revenue Service.	The individual must have a "qualified health plan" that meets federal standards and is an HDHP. Minimum annual deductible for 2013 was $1,250 for a single plan ($2,500 for a family plan). In 2013, the maximum annual out-of-pocket expenses for deductibles and copayments were capped at $6,250 for a single plan ($12,500 for a family plan). Funds cannot be used for HDHP premiums.
Funded solely by the employer; employees are not allowed to contribute. There is no limit on the amount of contribution. Contributions are tax free.	The individual must fund the HSA. Employers may contribute, but are not required to do so. The maximum contribution for 2013, which is fully tax deductible, was $3,250 for a single plan ($6,450 for a family plan). Enrollees who are 55 years and older can contribute an extra $1,000 to either plan.
An employer may offer an HRA to a retiree even after age 65, or allow a retiree or terminated employee to keep an existing HRA. Conversely, an employer may terminate the account.	The individual must be under the age of 65 and not have any other health insurance (dental, vision, and long-term care insurance do not count). When a person becomes eligible for Medicare at age 65, the remaining balance in an HSA can be used, but no funds can be added.
An employer may offer an HRA and an HSA. In this case, funds from the HRA can be used to pay the premiums for an HDHP which is required with the HSA.	

Advantage. Medigap plans cover all or a portion of Medicare deductibles and copayments/coinsurance. Federal law requires the sale of only standardized plans, each containing uniform benefits to help consumers decide which plan would best suit their needs. In 2014, 10 standard plans were approved; not all states have all the plans available. These plans are labeled A through D, F, G, and K through N. The most common out-of-pocket costs covered by most plans include hospital deductibles and copayments, skilled nursing facility copayments, and Part B deductibles and copayments/coinsurance. Medigap plans do not cover long-term care, vision care, dental care, hearing aids, or private-duty nursing. Premiums vary according to the plan selected and the insurance company selling the plan.

Trends in Employment-Based Health Insurance

In 2011, 89% of private health insurance coverage for people under the age of 65 was employment based; it covered 54% of the nonelderly US population. In 2005, 91.6% of private health insurance for the nonelderly was employment-based (data from NCHS 2012). The overall trends show that a declining number of small businesses are offering health insurance, workers are paying an increasing share of the total health insurance costs (that is, decreasing subsidies from the employers), and out-of-pocket costs have been increasing.

Because the majority of health insurance in the United States is job based, changes in insurance coverage follow the patterns of economic growth and decline. Economic downturns affect not only the level of employment but also health insurance coverage. Layoffs and plant closures negatively affect people's ability to have health insurance. Certain small employers may drop coverage altogether. The US economy experienced a recession from 2000 to 2004, modest economic growth from 2004 to 2007, and a severe recession from 2007 to 2009. Subsequently, the ACA was signed into law in March 2010, and some of its requirements went into effect the same year.

Changing job situations disrupt the continuity of health insurance coverage. In response, Congress passed the Consolidated Omnibus Budget Reconciliation Act of 1985 (COBRA), which allows workers to keep their employer's group coverage for 18 months after leaving a job. The individuals are required to pay 102% of the group rate to continue health benefits, but because employer subsidy is no longer available, the high cost of premiums prevents many from keeping their health insurance during periods of unemployment. The Health Insurance Portability and Accountability Act (HIPAA) of 1996 provided for continued coverage beyond the original COBRA provisions. Extended coverage of up to 29 months is available if the insured or a family member is determined by the Social Security Administration to be disabled at any time during the first 60 days of COBRA coverage. Extended coverage of up to 36 months is available to the spouse and dependent children if the former employee dies, enrolls in Medicare, or gets divorced or legally separated. The ACA does not affect the COBRA legislation.

Trends in Coverage

From 2000 to 2004, 4.1 million Americans lost employer-based health insurance. Coverage increased by 1.2 million from 2004 to 2007, and it declined by 8.3 million from

2007 to 2009. In 2009, 50 million non-elderly Americans were uninsured, compared to 38.2 million in 2000, an increase of almost 31% (Holahan 2011).

Health insurance coverage offered by large firms that employ 200 or more workers has remained relatively unchanged (at between 97% and 99%) during good and bad economic times. Smaller firms of 200 employees or fewer, however, employ nearly 40% of workers who are more likely to be affected by economic trends (Claxton et al. 2010). Recent data show that there is some relationship between the nation's economic performance and the proportion of small businesses offering health insurance. Ironically, since the passage of the ACA, there has been a dramatic decline in the proportion of small businesses offering health insurance, despite the fact that the ACA provides tax credits to small businesses until 2015 (Figure 6–3).

Because not all workers take health insurance even when it is offered by their employers, there is a difference between the offer rates and take-up rates. Hence, in spite of variations in the offer rates, the number of Americans under the age of 65 who have employment-based health insurance has steadily declined. See Figure 6–4, which shows a sharp decline during the 2007–2009 recession.

Trends in Premium Costs

The average cost of premiums in 2013 was $5,884 per year for single coverage and $16,351 per year for family coverage, but there are considerable variations in premium costs. For example, the cost of most of the single plans ranged between $3,000 and $9,000 per year. Between 2008 and 2013, the average cost of single coverage increased by 25% and the cost of family coverage increased by 29%. The employee's share has gradually risen from an average of 15% of the total premium cost for a single plan in 2008 to 17% in 2013, and from 26.5% of the total premium cost for a family plan in 2008 to 28% in 2013. Hence,

Figure 6–3 Percentage of Small Businesses Offering Health Insurance, Selected Years.

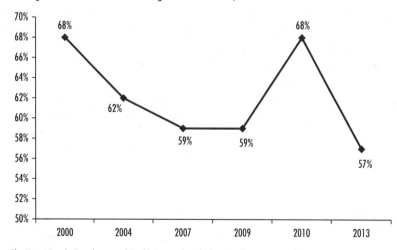

Source: Data from The Kaiser Family Foundation and Health Research and Educational Trust (Kaiser/HRET). 2013. *Employer health benefits: 2013 annual survey.* Menlo Park, CA: The Kaiser Family Foundation.

Figure 6–4 Number of Americans Under the Age of 65 Who Had Employment-Based Health Insurance, Selected Years.

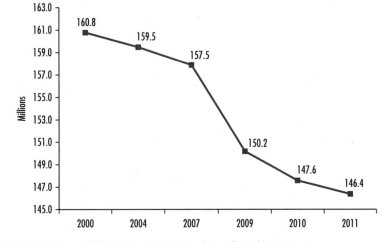

Source: Data from *Health, United States, 2009, 2011, and 2012.* National Center for Health Statistics.

in 2013, an employee would have paid, on average, approximately $1,000 during the year to obtain single coverage, compared to $700 in 2008 (Kaiser/HRET 2013). Clearly, health insurance premium costs have been rising faster than the rate of inflation in the general economy. In fact, rising cost of health insurance is the most cited reason by workers who do not purchase employment-based health insurance (EBRI 2013).

Trends in Utilization Costs: Cost Sharing

Over time, an increasing number of plans have required deductibles. In 2013, 78% of the workers covered by employment-based plans had a deductible, compared with 59% in 2008. The average annual deductible in 2013 was $1,135, up from $735 in 2008. Depending on the type of plan, the average deductible for a single plan varied between $729 and $2,003 in 2013. A $1,000 deductible has become common; still, 59% of workers enrolled in HMO plans did not have a deductible. Most family plans have an aggregate

deductible for the whole family; it amounted to an average of $4,079 in 2013, an increase of 15% over 2008 (Kaiser/HRET 2013).

As for copayments/coinsurance, only 6% of covered workers had none for office visits in 2013. The average was $23 for primary care office visit and $35 for specialty care office visits. Also, 12% of covered workers had no maximum limits on cost sharing, which is scheduled to change under the ACA (Kaiser/HRET 2013).

Private Health Insurance Under the Affordable Care Act

Private health insurance is still intended to be the main source of coverage for Americans. Toward this end, the ACA incorporates two major mandates—the individual mandate and the employer mandate.[1] In addition, the ACA specifies certain requirements that health insurance plans must comply with.

---

[1] The employer mandate was postponed until January 2015.

Some plans may be exempt from some of these requirements under a "grandfathered" clause, as long as these plans do not make any changes to covered benefits, cost sharing, or employer contributions to premiums. The grandfathered plans had to be in existence before March 23, 2010, when the ACA was signed into law. A significant controversy has arisen over the publication of rules by the Department of Health and Human Services (DHHS) in the *Federal Register,* because according to the government's own mid-range estimates "66 percent of small employer plans and 45 percent of large employer plans will relinquish their grandfather status by the end of 2013" (*Federal Register* 2010). If the displacement of several million insured Americans materializes, it is hoped that they would be able to find comparable health insurance through the exchanges established under the ACA.

The ACA also imposes a flat fee on health insurance companies that sell non-ERISA plans, that is, plans that fall outside the self-insurance market. An additional fee is imposed on insurers that sell plans through the exchanges. These costs, of course, will add to the health insurance premiums (Mulvany 2013).

Compliance Requirements for Health Plans

Certain plan requirements have been in effect since 2010. Other requirements become effective in 2014 and beyond.

Coverage for Young Adults

Although the new law does not require that a health plan cover dependents, a plan that provided dependent coverage had to enroll young adults under the age of 26, married or unmarried, under their parents' plan. This requirement applies even if a young adult is not living with his or her parents, is not financially dependent on the parents, and is eligible to enroll in an employer's plan. There is no requirement to enroll the spouse or children of a young adult who thus qualifies. Mandatory enrollment of young adults went into effect with insurance plan renewals starting September 23, 2010. In 2010, 716,000 young adults gained coverage under this ACA requirement, according to Cantor et al. (2012), who also note that this gain in coverage comes with costs; in particular, family premiums increase as more young adults are enrolled. Also, businesses that employ primarily young adults may become less likely to offer coverage as fewer young workers seek their own health benefits.

Coverage for Preexisting Medical Conditions

A *preexisting condition* is any significant health problem that a person has prior to obtaining health insurance; examples include diabetes, cancer, severe heart disease, and HIV/AIDS. Roughly 82 million Americans with preexisting conditions were already covered by employer-based plans (DHHS 2012). In the individual health insurance market, people either could not obtain health insurance or the premiums were unaffordable if the prospective insured had a preexisting condition. To address this problem, approximately 35 states had created high-risk pools to make insurance available to people who otherwise would have been uninsurable. Premiums for these state-based plans were typically set at 150% of the average medically underwritten rate within a state. A substantial share of the funding to run the insurance pools came from the federal government, and approximately 200,000 Americans were able to get insurance through these pools in 2009 (Gruber 2009). Conversely, a number of states did not create these pools, leaving many without the ability to obtain affordable health insurance. The ACA first created a temporary federal program—the Pre-Existing Condition Insurance Plan (PCIP)—which took effect in July 2010 as a stop-gap measure to enroll people who otherwise would be uninsurable. As of January 2014, when the ACA becomes fully implemented, insurers are legally required to cover people with preexisting health conditions without charging high-risk individuals more than anyone else in the same plan. Even though charging more to people with poor health status can be criticized on equity grounds, a disregard of medical underwriting principles will make insurance premiums go up for everyone, and healthy people will subsidize health insurance for the unhealthy.

Coverage for Preventive Services

As of September 23, 2010, all new health insurance plans have been required to include recommended preventive services and immunizations to which no cost sharing applies. The required preventive services fall in four main areas:

1. Services that have a high certainty of providing substantial or moderate net health benefits (graded as "A" and "B" respectively) as determined by the US Preventive Services Task Force.

2. Immunizations that are determined as routine by the Advisory Committee on Immunization Practices.

3. Preventive services recommended for infants, children, and adolescents by

Health Resources and Services Administration's (HRSA) Bright Futures Project. Preventive services also include behavioral and developmental assessments, iron and fluoride supplements, and screening for autism, vision impairment, lipid disorders, tuberculosis, and certain genetic diseases.

4. A range of preventive services for women recommended by the Institute of Medicine. Services required under the law include contraceptives approved by the Food and Drug Administration; well-woman visits; screening for gestational diabetes; screening for human papillomavirus; counseling for sexually transmitted infections; counseling and screening for human immune-deficiency virus (HIV); breastfeeding support, supplies, and counseling; and screening and counseling for interpersonal and domestic violence.

Benefit Limits and Out-of-Pocket Costs

Previously, health plans could establish lifetime benefits limits such as $2 to $5 million. As of 2014, insurers cannot put annual dollar limits or lifetime limits on health care benefits. This provision helps the small number of people who have catastrophic illnesses, and is unlikely to have any noticeable effect on insurance premium costs. The ACA also put limits on out-of-pocket costs for deductibles and copayments/coinsurance to $6,350 for individual plans and $12,700 for family plans. The implementation of this requirement has been delayed until 2015 for employers who use separate plans for health care services and prescription drugs. In 2014, the out-of-pocket limits would apply to each of the two separate plans, so that many people will have their out-of-pocket costs exceed the set limits. In 2015, employers will be required to combine any separate plans into one.

Medical Loss Ratios

The percentage of premium revenue spent on medical expenses is called *medical loss ratio* (MLR). The remainder of the money is used for administration, marketing, and profits. Effective since 2011, the ACA required a minimum MLR of 85% for large-group insurance plans and 80% for individual or small-group plans to pay medical claims. Health plans that do not meet these requirements must give rebates to enrollees. In 2011, insurers paid more than $1 billion in rebates, which amounted to less than 1% of premiums. Rebates per insured member varied between $23 and $176 for the year depending on the type of health plan (Hall and McCue 2013). Hence, savings to the consumers are miniscule at best.

The actual effects of this requirement will not be known for some time, but at least two likely outcomes have been conjectured (Harrington 2013): (1) The MLR rule adds uncertainty to the unpredictable nature of medical costs that a health plan would incur. Consequently, it may lead to higher upfront premiums as a safety cushion. (2) The regulation could lead to consolidation and greater market concentration as smaller insurers that are likely to face greater difficulty in meeting the MLR targets are acquired by larger insurers. If that happens, it would be at odds with the intent of promoting greater choice and competition in the insurance markets.

The Individual Mandate

As of January 2014, legal residents of the United States are mandated to have what is referred to as "minimum essential coverage." If a person fails to comply with this mandate, he or she must either qualify for an exemption or pay a penalty tax, referred to as "individual shared responsibility." Those without health insurance can purchase a plan through "health insurance marketplaces," a term used for health insurance exchanges. Some people will qualify for premium subsidies from the government.

Minimum Essential Coverage

Broadly, minimum essential coverage can be employment-based coverage (including COBRA—discussed previously), individual private health insurance (discussed previously), or public health insurance, such as Medicare, Medicaid, or CHIP. (discussed later under "Public Health Insurance"). The ACA mandates all insurance plans to provide comprehensive coverage which must include Essential Health Benefits (EHBs) in at least 10 categories (Exhibit 6–2). In the absence of details from the federal government on the scope of EHBs, at least for 2014 and 2015, each state must choose what is referred to as a benchmark plan by comparing other plans offered in the state. Plans offered by exchanges would have to provide coverage that is substantially equal to or better than what is included in the benchmark plan. This allows for some variation in plan design from state to state.

Exemptions From Individual Shared Responsibility

There are several exceptions to the mandate. Unaffordability, that is, having to spend more than 8% of one's household income or facing some other financial hardship is one major exception. Exemptions can also

Exhibit 6–2 Mandated Essential Health Benefits under the ACA

1. Ambulatory patient services
2. Emergency services
3. Hospitalization
4. Maternity and newborn care
5. Mental health and substance use disorder services, including behavioral health treatment
6. Prescription drugs
7. Rehabilitative and habilitative services and devices
8. Laboratory services
9. Preventive and wellness services and chronic disease management
10. Pediatric services, including oral and vision care

be granted on the basis of recognized religious opposition to insurance, for example, the Amish people; being a member of a recognized Indian tribe; being exempt from filing income taxes; or having a coverage gap of less than 3 months. Apart from these and other minor exemptions, individuals, their spouses, dependent children, and the elderly, all must have health insurance under the ACA mandate.

Penalty Tax

The penalty tax is the greater of a flat dollar amount per person that starts at $95 in 2014 and rises to $695 in 2016, and is indexed by inflation thereafter, or a percentage of the household's income that starts at 1% in 2014 and rises to 2.5% for 2016 and subsequent years, and is subject to a cap. The penalty for children is half the amount that an adult would pay. The total penalty for a family is also subject to a cap. The first penalty becomes due when income tax returns are filed in 2015 for 2014.

The key question is: Will the penalty be a strong enough incentive that would drive people to buy insurance? Some preliminary research suggests that it may not provide sufficient incentive, even with premium subsidies (discussed later under "Premium Subsidies"). Healthy individuals in particular may choose to pay the penalty instead of buying health insurance (Eastman and Eastman 2013).

Health Insurance Marketplaces

The ACA requires each state to establish health insurance exchanges, online marketplaces which can be either a state-run government agency or a nonprofit organization (Krajnak 2013). On the supply side, an exchange would have several private health insurance companies and MCOs offering plans, each of which must comply with the ACA and must be certified as a "qualified health plan." The DHHS has nominated the National Committee for Quality Assurance (NCQA), a private nonprofit organization, as an accrediting agency for qualified health plan issuers. On the demand side, individuals and small businesses would be able to compare health insurance options and purchase insurance. States can either have one combined exchange or separate exchanges for individual and small-group markets. A separate small-group exchange is called a Small Business Health Options Program (SHOP). Exchanges are also required to have "navigators" that meet prescribed qualifications to assist individuals and small businesses compare and choose health plans and help them enroll.

As the deadline for filing applications to establish exchanges passed by on February 15, 2013, 26 states had opted out, which left the job of establishing exchanges in these states to the federal government (Andersen 2013). According to the ACA, exchanges in all states were to be operational by October 1, 2013 and to start enrollment. The rollout, however, did not proceed as anticipated. Consequently, the enrollment numbers are not likely to meet the government's targeted projection of 7 million by the end of March 2014 (Coombs 2013). Success of the exchanges, and, hence, of enrollment, also depends on the extent of participation from insurers.

Plan Choices

The exchanges must offer four tiers of standardized plans: bronze, silver, gold, and platinum. The four plans differ according to actuarial value, that is, the percentage of medical expenses incurred by an average population that a plan would cover. In simple terms, each plan category provides a certain level of protection against medical expenses. The bronze plan would cover 60% of medical expenses that an average population might incur. It does not mean, however, that this plan will cover 60% of the expenses for a certain individual. Similarly, the actuarial values are 70% for a silver plan; 80% for gold; and 90% for platinum. Because all health plans must include the same essential health benefits, the plans differ mainly by premium costs and out-of-pocket cost sharing. The platinum plan will carry the highest premium, and the bronze plan will have maximum cost sharing. However, as pointed out previously, the ACA puts caps on out-of-pocket costs for deductibles and copayments/coinsurance, but the caps have been set quite high.

Premium Subsidies

To purchase health insurance through the exchanges, premium subsidies in the form of tax credits are made available to people with incomes between 100% and 400% of the federal poverty level (FPL),[2] provided these people do not qualify for Medicaid or employment-based coverage. For people whose incomes fall below 250% of the FPL, government subsidies are also available to pay a portion of the deductibles and copayments. Qualification for the subsidies is based solely on income, without regard to a person's assets or net worth. Hence, theoretically, a millionaire, such as an early retiree, could qualify for the subsidies as long as the individual meets the income thresholds.

The Employer Mandate

Also referred to as "employer shared responsibility," this mandate was required by the ACA to go into effect on January 2014, but it has been delayed until January 2015. Conventionally referred to as a *play-or-pay* mandate, it requires employers to either

---

[2]In 2013 and 2014, 100% of FPL was an annual income of $11,490 for a single person and $23,550 for a family of four ($29,440 in Alaska and $27,090 in Hawaii).

provide their employees with health insurance (play) or pay a penalty for not doing so. The ACA mandate applies to employers with 50 or more full-time equivalent employees, referred to as "large employers" under the ACA. If the employer provides health insurance, the plan must comply with the ACA requirements, as discussed previously. Full time is defined as 30 or more hours per week. Part-time employees' hours are converted to full-time equivalent to determine whether or not the employer is a large employer.

Employment-based health plans must satisfy a "minimum value" test and an "affordability" test. To pass the "minimum value" test, a plan must pay for at least 60% of covered medical costs that an average population might incur. In other words, it must be equivalent to the bronze plan, discussed previously. To pass the "affordability" test, the employee's share of the premium cost for a single plan (the lowest cost option if the employer offers more than one plan) must not exceed 9.5% of the employee's household income (Kopp et al. 2013). This rule actually leaves plenty of room for an employer to shift more of the premium costs to their employees.[3] The plans that meet these two criteria are to be made available to all full-time employees and their biological, step, adopted, or foster children under the age of 26. The employer may, but is not obligated to, provide health insurance to part-time workers.

Employer Penalties

The ACA levies two types of penalties. The first penalty applies if a large employer, as

defined in the previous section, has even one full-time employee receiving government subsidy to buy health insurance through an exchange. The employer must pay an annual tax of $2,000 per full-time employee minus the first 30 full-time employees. The second penalty applies when the employer's health insurance plan fails the tests of "minimum value" and "affordability." The penalty is $3,000 per full-time employee who purchases insurance through an exchange, with a maximum penalty of $2,000 per full-time employee minus the first 30 employees.

In response to the employer mandate and associated penalties, employers may reduce employee hours either to escape being categorized as large employers or to offer health insurance to fewer employees. Of critical concern to businesses will be achieving the delicate balance between cost and compliance factors imposed by the ACA on the one hand, and achieving production objectives on the other hand. In a recent survey of employers of all sizes, industries, and geographic locations, 51% indicated that they would have fewer employees work 30 or more hours (full-time) per week (Watts and Gaertner 2013). Based on this finding, there are likely to be some negative repercussions for employment and health insurance in the United States. If a large number of currently insured workers are forced into exchanges, first, these workers will be less well off to buy insurance on their own, and second, it will impact the cost of the ACA because a larger segment of the population will qualify for subsidies. In fact, a joint report by the Congressional Budget Office and the Joint Commission on Taxation projected that between 3 and 5 million fewer people would obtain employment-based coverage each year from 2019 through 2022 (CBO 2012b). Workers obtaining health insurance

---

[3]Example: An individual who makes 400% of the FPL ($45,960) and does not qualify for government subsidy can be made to pay up to $4,366 per year for employer-based health insurance.

through self-insured employers are more likely to retain their existing plans, but very likely at a higher cost.

Public Health Insurance

Since 1965, government financing has played a significant role in expanding services, mainly to those who otherwise would not be able to afford them. Today, a significant proportion of health services in the United States are supported through public programs. In 2011, almost one-third of the US population was covered under various public insurance programs (see Figure 6–2). Chapter 3 discusses the inception of the two major public insurance programs, Medicare and Medicaid. This section discusses the financing, eligibility requirements, and services covered under the various public health insurance programs and the effects of the ACA on these services.

Public financing supports *categorical programs*, each designed to benefit a certain category of people. Examples are Medicare for the elderly and certain disabled individuals, Medicaid for the indigent, Department of Defense programs for active service people and their families, and VA health care for war veterans. Even though the government finances public insurance, for the most part, health care services are obtained through the private sector. In contrast, financing and delivery functions are largely integrated in the VA program.

Medicare

The Medicare program, also referred to as Title 18 of the Social Security Act, finances medical care for three groups of people: (1) persons 65 years and older, (2) disabled individuals who are entitled to Social Security benefits, and (3) people who have end-stage renal disease (permanent kidney failure, requiring dialysis or a kidney transplant). People in these three categories can enroll regardless of income status.

Shortly after creation of the program, it had 19.5 million beneficiaries in 1967 (NCHS 1996, p. 263). Of the 50.7 million beneficiaries in 2012, 83% of the beneficiaries were 65 years and older; 17% were under the age of 65 (CMS 2013a). With the aging of the population, the number of beneficiaries will continue to rise.

Medicare is a federal program operated under the administrative oversight of the Centers for Medicare and Medicaid Services (CMS), a branch of the DHHS. Because it is a federal program, eligibility criteria and benefits are consistent throughout the United States.

The Balanced Budget Act of 1997 established an independent federal agency, the Medicare Payment Advisory Commission (MedPAC), to advise the US Congress on various issues affecting the Medicare program. MedPAC's statutory mandate includes analysis of payments to private health care providers participating in Medicare, access to care, and quality of care.

For almost 30 years after its inception, Medicare had a dual structure comprising two separate insurance programs referred to as Part A and Part B. It subsequently became a four-part program.

Part A (Hospital Insurance)

Part A, the Hospital Insurance (HI) portion of Medicare is a true *entitlement* program. Throughout their working lives, people contribute to Medicare through special payroll taxes; hence, they are entitled to Part A benefits regardless of the amount of income and assets they may have. The employer and employee share equally in financing the HI trust fund. All working individuals, including those who are self-employed, pay the mandatory taxes. Since 1994, all earnings have become subject to Medicare tax.

To qualify for Part A, a person or the person's spouse must have worked, earned a minimum specified amount, and paid Medicare taxes for at least 40 quarters (10 years) to earn at least 40 credits. People who have earned less than 40 credits can get Part A by paying a monthly premium.

Part A covers inpatient services for acute care hospitals, psychiatric hospitals, inpatient rehabilitation facilities, skilled nursing facility (SNF) services, home health visits, and hospice care. Following is an overview of the type of benefits:

1. A maximum of 90 days of inpatient hospital care is allowed per benefit period. Once the 90 days are exhausted, a lifetime reserve of 60 additional hospital inpatient days remains. A *benefit period* is a spell of illness beginning with hospitalization and ending when a beneficiary has not been an inpatient in a hospital or an SNF for 60 consecutive days. The number of benefit periods is unlimited. These rules apply to acute care hospitals and inpatient rehabilitation facilities. Inpatient psychiatric care in a freestanding psychiatric hospital has a lifetime limit of 190 days.

2. Medicare pays for up to 100 days of care in a Medicare-certified SNF, subsequent to inpatient hospitalization for at least 3 consecutive days, not including the day of discharge. Admission to the SNF must occur within 30 days of hospital discharge.

3. Medicare pays for home health care obtained from a Medicare-certified home health agency when a person is homebound and requires intermittent or part-time skilled nursing care or rehabilitation. Payment is made for 60-day episodes of care. A beneficiary can have unlimited episodes.

4. For terminally ill patients, Medicare pays for care provided by a Medicare-certified hospice.

A deductible applies to each benefit period (except to home health and hospice), and copayments are based on the duration of services (except for home health). Exhibit 6–3 gives details on the Part A program.

Part B (Supplementary Medical Insurance)

Part B, the supplementary medical insurance (SMI) portion of Medicare, is a voluntary program financed partly by general tax revenues and partly by required premium contributions. It is estimated that the beneficiaries bear approximately 25% of the cost of premiums; generally taxes subsidize the remaining 75%. Effective since 2007, CMS implemented income-based Part B premiums as mandated by the Medicare Prescription Drug, Improvement, and Modernization Act (MMA) of 2003. Those whose incomes exceed a threshold amount pay a higher income-based premium—known as Income Related Monthly Adjustment Amount (IRMAA). For 2014, the income threshold that triggers IRMAA is $85,000 per year ($170,000 per couple). The intent of this legislation is to reduce tax-financed premium subsidies for higher income individuals. Hence, for example, an individual earning more than $214,000 in

Exhibit 6–3 Medicare Part A Financing, Benefits, Deductible, and Copayments for 2014

Financing

The Hospital Insurance trust fund is financed by a payroll tax of 1.45% from the employee and 1.45% from the employer on all income. Self-employed individuals must pay the full 2.9%. Starting in 2013, single taxpayers earning $200,000 or more and married couples earning $250,000 or more pay an additional 0.9%, as mandated by the ACA.

Premiums	None (Those who do not qualify for premium-free coverage can buy coverage at a monthly premium of up to $426.)
Deductible	$1,216 per benefit period

Benefits	Copayments
Inpatient hospital (room, meals, nursing care, operating room services, blood transfusions, special care units, drugs and medical supplies, laboratory tests, rehabilitation therapies, and medical social services)	None for the first 60 days [benefit period] $304 per day for days 61–90 [benefit period] $608 per day for days 91–150 [nonrenewable lifetime reserve days] 100% of costs after 150 days
Skilled nursing facility (after a 3-day hospital stay)	None for the first 20 days in a benefit period $152 per day for days 21–100 in a benefit period
Home health services (part-time skilled nursing care, home health aide, rehabilitation therapies, medical equipment, social services, and medical supplies)	None for home health visits 20% of approved amount for medical equipment
Hospice care	A small copayment for drugs
Inpatient psychiatric care (190-day lifetime limit)	Same as for inpatient hospital

Noncovered Services

Long-term care

Custodial services

Personal convenience services (televisions, telephones, private-duty nurses, private rooms when not medically necessary)

Source: Data from Centers for Medicare and Medicaid Services and Social Security Administration.

2014 pays $335.70 in monthly premiums, whereas someone earning less than or equal to $85,000 pays $146.90.

Almost all persons entitled to HI also choose to enroll in SMI because they cannot get similar coverage at the same price from private insurers. The main services covered by SMI are listed in Exhibit 6–4. Part B also covers limited home health services under certain conditions.

Effective January 2011, the ACA provided for an annual physical exam (called

Exhibit 6–4 Medicare Part B Financing, Benefits, Deductible, and Coinsurance for 2014

Financing

The general tax revenues of the federal government support approximately 75% of the program costs. The remaining 25% is financed through monthly premiums paid by persons enrolled in Part B.

Standard premium	$104.90 per month
Income-adjusted premium*	$146.90 to $335.70 annually
Deductible	$147 annually
Coinsurance	80/20 (50/50 for outpatient mental health)

Main Benefits

Physician services
Emergency department services
Outpatient surgery
Diagnostic tests and laboratory services
Outpatient physical therapy, occupational therapy, and speech therapy
Outpatient mental health services
Limited home health care under certain conditions
Ambulance
Renal dialysis
Artificial limbs and braces
Blood transfusions and blood components
Organ transplants
Medical equipment and supplies
Rural health clinic services
Annual physical exam

- Wellness exam
- Preventive services (as medically needed): alcohol misuse screening and counseling, bone mass measurement, mammography, cardiovascular screening, Pap smears, colorectal cancer screening, depression screening, diabetes screening, glaucoma tests, HIV screening, nutritional counseling for diabetes and renal disease, obesity screening and counseling, prostate cancer screening, sexually transmitted infections screening, shots (flu, pneumococcal, Hepatitis B), and tobacco use cessation counseling

Noncovered Services

Dental services
Hearing aids
Eyeglasses (except after cataract surgery)
Services not related to treatment or injury

*For single beneficiaries whose annual incomes exceed $85,000.

Source: Data from Centers for Medicare and Medicaid Services.

a Wellness Exam) for all Part B enrollees, without any cost sharing. The main purpose of the wellness exam is to do a risk assessment and develop an individualized prevention plan. Exhibit 6–4 provides a summary of the Part B program.

Part C (Medicare Advantage)

Part C is, in reality, not a new benefit program because it does not add specifically defined new services. It merely provides some additional choices of health plans, with the objective of channeling a greater number of beneficiaries into managed care plans. The Balanced Budget Act (BBA) of 1997 authorized the Medicare+Choice program, which took effect on January 1, 1998. Medicare+Choice was renamed Medicare Advantage (MA) through the passage of the MMA of 2003. Beneficiaries have the option to remain in the original Medicare fee-for-service program, and if the CMS has contracted with an MCO that serves a beneficiary's geographic area, the beneficiary has the option to join the Medicare Advantage plan. If they join the plan, the beneficiaries receive both Part A and Part B services through the MCO.

In 2013, enrollment in Medicare Advantage plans was 14.4 million, or 28% of all Medicare beneficiaries. Enrollment in Medicare Advantage plans has steadily increased since 2004 when only 5.3 million had used this option (Gold et al. 2013).

Premiums for Medicare Advantage are in addition to those paid to Medicare for Part B coverage. As a trade-off, the beneficiary gets additional benefits that are not available in the original Medicare Plan, and there is no need to purchase Medigap coverage. Part C enrollees also have lower out-of-pocket costs. Hence, it is a cost-effective option, particularly for lower income Medicare beneficiaries.

The MMA of 2003 required that Medicare Advantage include special needs plans. These plans were first offered in 2005 to meet the special needs of people who were institutionalized, enrolled in both Medicare and Medicaid, or had chronic or disabling conditions. Medicare Advantage Special Needs Plans (MA-SNP) are available in limited areas. In 2013, 1.6 million beneficiaries were enrolled in these plans. Unless reauthorized by Congress, the MA-SNP program will end in January 2015.

The ACA aims to reduce payment to MA plans with the goal of achieving some level of parity between the expenditures for Part C compared to expenditures in the original Medicare program. The government has contended that MA plans have been overpaid. The effect of payment cuts and fees imposed on insurers is estimated to reduce payments to MA plans by 8% in 2014 (Zigmond 2013). As an incentive, the ACA authorized payment of quality-based financial bonuses to MA plans effective 2012. Some observers do not think that payment cuts under the ACA will affect MCOs' participation in Part C. However, it is likely that at least some MCOs may stop participating, or they may have to increase premiums, increase cost sharing, reduce benefits that are not mandated by Medicare, or achieve better efficiencies.

Part D (Prescription Drug Coverage)

Part D was added to the existing Medicare program under the MMA of 2003 and was fully implemented in January 2006. Part D is available to anyone who has coverage under Part A or Part B. The prescription drug program requires payment of a monthly premium to Medicare, which is in addition to the premium for Part B. Certain low-income beneficiaries are automatically enrolled without having to pay a premium. As of January 2011, the ACA imposed income-based IRMAA so that people in various income categories pay additional premiums.

Coverage is offered through two types of private plans approved by Medicare: (1) Stand-alone Prescription Drug Plans (PDPs) that offer only drug coverage are used mainly by those who want to stay in the original Medicare fee-for-service program. (2) Medicare Advantage Prescription Drug Plans (MA-PDs) are available to those who are enrolled in Part C if the MCO provides prescription drug coverage; most do.

The average monthly premium expected for 2014 was $39.90, an increase of 5% from $38.14 in 2013 (Hoadley et al. 2013). In 2012, 63% of Medicare beneficiaries (32 million) were enrolled in Part D; 37% of these (11.8 million) were enrolled in MA-PDs (Henry J. Kaiser Family Foundation 2012). Most others have drug coverage through retiree health benefits from previous employers, Department of Defense health programs, or VA.

The Part D program requires payment of a deductible, following which a basic level of coverage becomes available. After that, there is a coverage gap or "doughnut hole," which requires the beneficiary to pay the full cost of drugs (at a discount) until a defined level of spending is reached. The gap is then followed by a catastrophic level of coverage (see Exhibit 6–5). Special provisions in the program are designed to help low-income enrollees by keeping their out-of-pocket costs to a minimum.

Effective 2011, under the ACA, all Part D drugs must be covered under a manufacturer discount agreement with the CMS. Under the provisions of the new law, beneficiaries are to receive discounts on drugs while in the coverage gap. The discounts amount to 50% on brand name drugs and 7% on generic drugs. The ACA also requires a phase-out of the coverage gap until it is eliminated by 2020.

Medicare Out-of-Pocket Costs

Medicare carries relatively high deductibles, copayments, and premiums (see Exhibits 6–3, 6–4, and 6–5). Eyeglasses, dental care, and many long-term care services are not covered, and there is no limit on out-of-pocket expenses, except that about half of Medicare Advantage plans have cost sharing limits. Hence, most Medicare beneficiaries are left with high out-of-pocket costs. Medicaid (provided the beneficiary qualifies), employer retirement benefits, and purchase of private supplement insurance plans (Medigap—discussed previously) are some of the ways to pay for most of these out-of-pocket costs. Still, it is estimated that the typical beneficiary spends nearly 20% of his or her income in out-of-pocket costs; the average being approximately $4,600 per year (AARP 2012).

Medicare Financing and Spending

Medicare consumes over one-fifth of national health expenditures. Data on the sources of financing appear in Figure 6–5. Medicare has established two main trust funds: The HI trust fund provides the money pool for Part A services, and the SMI trust fund provides the money pool for Parts B and D. Each trust fund accounts for incomes and expenditures. Taxes, premiums, and other revenues are credited to the respective trust funds, and benefit payments and

Exhibit 6–5 Medicare Part D Benefits and Individual Out-of-Pocket Costs for 2014

Premiums	$39.90 per month (estimated national average)*
	IRMAA ranging from $12.10 to $69.30
Deductible	$310 annually

Three levels of benefits and out-of-pocket costs beyond the $310 deductible:

Basic level	Medicare pays 75% of the cost of drugs until the combined total payments by the plan and the beneficiary reach $2,850
Coverage gap	Beneficiary pays 97.5% of the cost for brand name drugs, and 72% of the cost for generic drugs after the manufacturers have discounted the drugs by 50%
	Coverage gap ends when the beneficiary has spent $4,550 out of pocket
Catastrophic level	Minimum cost sharing: $2.55 for generic and preferred drugs, $6.35 for brand name drugs

The Extra Help Program

A special part of the Medicare drug coverage program called Extra Help is designed to serve people who have low incomes and savings. This group of beneficiaries includes those who receive Medicaid or Supplemental Security Income. For those who qualify, the out-of-pocket costs are minimal.

*Actual premium varies according to income and the plan selected by the beneficiary

Source: Data from Centers for Medicare and Medicaid Services. Available at:

http://www.cms.gov/Medicare/Health-Plans/MedicareAdvtgSpecRateStats/Downloads/Announcement2014.pdf. Accessed October 2013.

Figure 6–5 Sources of Medicare Financing, 2012.

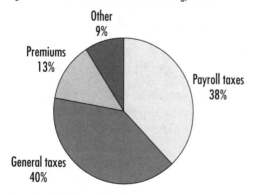

Source: Data from Centers for Medicare and Medicaid Services.
2013 Annual report of the boards of trustees of the federal hospital insurance and federal supplementary medical insurance trust funds. Available at: http://downloads.cms.gov/files/TR2013.pdf. Accessed September 2013.

administrative costs are the only purposes for which disbursements from the funds can be made. Table 6–1 compares the trust fund results for 2009 and 2012.

Note that in the HI trust fund expenditures exceeded revenues for both 2009 and 2012, and the revenue shortfall accelerated. The SMI trust fund showed a surplus in 2009, but incurred a deficit in 2012. Consequently, the assets held in both trust funds are being depleted. In short, Medicare is financially sick and is headed toward insolvency unless it can be steered around. The Medicare trustees have stressed that a sense of urgency exists to address the looming depletion of the trust funds (CMS 2013a).

Table 6–1 Status of HI and SMI Trust Funds, 2009–2012 (billions of dollars)

	HI		SMI	
	2009	2012	2009	2012
Assets at the beginning of year	$321.3	$244.2	$60.3	$80.7
Revenues	225.4	243.0	282.8	293.9
Expenditures	242.5	266.8	266.5	307.4
Difference between revenues and expenditures	−17.1	−23.8	16.3	−13.5
Assets at the end of year	304.2	220.4	76.6	67.2

Source: Social Security Administration. 2010. *A summary of the 2010 annual reports: Social Security and Medicare Board of Trustees.* Available at: http://www.ssa.gov/OACT/TRSUM/index.html. Accessed January 2011; Centers for Medicare and Medicaid Services. *2013 Annual report of the boards of trustees of the federal hospital insurance and federal supplementary medical insurance trust funds.* Available at: http://downloads.cms.gov/files/TR2013.pdf. Accessed September 2013.

In 2012, close to one-third of the total Medicare expenditures were attributed to hospitals, followed by payments to MCOs for Medicare Advantage (24%), physicians (12.1%), prescription drugs (12%), and miscellaneous (12%; CMS 2013a). The miscellaneous category includes payments for services such as hospice, laboratory, durable medical equipment, outpatient rehabilitation, and inpatient psychiatric care. Data on enrolled population and expenditures are given in Table 6–2. Over the years, policy efforts have been made, mainly through payment cuts and enrollment in MCOs, to slow down the rate of growth in expenditures. But, dire efforts are needed to avert insolvency.

Table 6–2 Medicare: Enrolled Population and Expenditures in Selected Years

Population Covered (in millions)				
1970	1980	1990	2000	2010
20.4	28.4	34.3	39.7	47.7
Expenditures (in billions)				
$7.5	$36.8	$111.00	$221.8	$522.9
Proportion of Total US Health Care Expenditures				
10.0%	14.5%	15.5%	16.4%	20.2%
Average Annual Increase in Expenditures From the Previous Year Shown (per decade)				
	17%	12%	7%	9%

Source: Data from *Health, United States, 2012,* pp. 323, 356. National Center for Health Statistics.

A combination of three main factors raises concerns about the future solvency of Medicare: (1) The cost of delivering health care continues to grow at a rate faster than the rate of inflation in the general economy. (2) An aging population will consume a greater quantity of health care services. (3) The workforce is shrinking, and wage increases to support payroll tax revenues are smaller than the rise in medical inflation.

Reduction in fees to MCOs participating in Medicare Advantage was pointed out previously. The ACA envisions reductions in physician payments by as much as 25% starting January 2014. The Medicare trustees have shown skepticism about how realistic these cuts would be, especially because Congress has overridden such reductions since 2003. The ACA also envisions reduced payments for many other providers in accordance with improvements in economy-wide productivity (CMS 2013a). The ACA provides for a new agency, the Independent Payment Advisory Board (IPAB), to be responsible for containing the growth in Medicare spending. The new law also established the Center for Medicare and Medicaid Innovation and provided $10 billion over 10 years for the center to test innovative payment and service delivery models to reduce program expenditures, while preserving or enhancing the quality of care furnished to Medicare and Medicaid beneficiaries. Of course, the achievements of these initiatives will not be known for several years.

Medicaid

Medicaid, also referred to as Title 19 of the Social Security Act, was originally designed to finance health care services for the indigent. Just before 2014, it served approximately 60 million low-income Americans who also had limited assets. Hence, since its inception, Medicaid has always been a *means-tested program* in which eligibility depends on financial resources. Each state has administered its own Medicaid program under federal guidelines.

Medicaid continues to be jointly financed by the federal and state governments. The federal government provides matching funds to the states based on the per capita income in each state. By law, federal matching—known as the Federal Medical Assistance Percentage (FMAP)—cannot be less than 50% nor greater than 83% of total state Medicaid program costs. Wealthier states have a smaller share of their costs reimbursed by the federal government.

Medicaid Under the ACA

The ACA had envisioned expanding Medicaid by establishing a minimum income eligibility standard across the nation, which was previously left up to each state. The law mandated the states to cover any legal US resident under the age of 65 with income up to 138% of the FPL (after an adjustment of 5 percentage points applied to 133% of FPL based on Modified Adjusted Gross Income), starting January 2014. The ACA authorized federal matching at 100% for newly eligible individuals for 3 years (2014–2016), with a gradual reduction each year to 90% in 2020. On the other hand, if a state failed to comply, the DHHS was given the authority to withhold the federal share of financing as a penalty. The US Supreme Court, however, struck down this mandate, giving states a choice to either expand or not expand their Medicaid programs without any penalty from the federal government. As of September 2013, 16 states had decided not to expand their existing Medicaid programs; another 7 were leaning toward not participating (The Advisory Board Company 2013). Hence, coverage and benefits for Medicaid remain in a state of uncertainty for many people.

The ACA has made another critical change to Medicaid. Previously, Medicaid eligibility had depended not only on income, but also on assets as determined by each state. To qualify for Medicaid, states required that assets be "spent down" to a predetermined level. It appears that under the ACA, states can no longer use the assets test; perhaps it applies only to states that decide to expand their Medicaid programs. It is theoretically possible that a millionaire could qualify for Medicaid based solely on low income.

Another irony pertains to preventive services that have been mandated by the ACA for nearly all private plans and Medicare. Regardless of a state's decision to expand Medicaid, for beneficiaries who were already in the Medicaid program, coverage for preventive services is at the discretion of the state. The law provides a 1% increase in federal matching funds if a state chooses to cover all grade "A" and "B" preventive services without cost sharing. Hence, not all Medicaid enrollees even within the same state will be eligible for the same level of preventive services (Wilensky and Gray 2013).

The ACA gives states the option to establish Health Homes (not to be confused with home health care) for Medicaid beneficiaries who have chronic conditions, including serious and persistent mental health conditions. The main function of Health Homes is to undertake comprehensive care management that includes care coordination, follow-up, patient and family support, and referral to social support agencies.

Old Medicaid Option

States that decide not to expand their existing Medicaid programs will follow the old federal guidelines for eligibility. Three main categories of people are automatically eligible: (1) families with children receiving support under the Temporary Assistance for Needy Families (TANF) program; (2) people receiving Supplemental Security Income (SSI), which includes many of the elderly, the blind, and the disabled with low incomes; and (3) children and pregnant women whose family income is at or below 133% of the FPL. States, at their discretion, have defined other "medically needy" categories based on people's income and assets. Most important of these are individuals who are institutionalized in nursing or psychiatric facilities and individuals

who are receiving community-based services but would otherwise be eligible for Medicaid if institutionalized. All of these people have to qualify based on income and assets, which must be below the threshold levels established by each state. In these states, most of those who would have been eligible for Medicaid under the ACA will be eligible for federal subsidies through the health insurance marketplace (exchanges) discussed previously.

Dual-Eligible Beneficiaries

Approximately 9 million people are dual-eligible beneficiaries. They are low-income elderly and disabled young adults who are entitled to Medicare, but also become eligible for some level of assistance under Medicaid. The "full duals" qualify for all benefits under both Medicare and Medicaid. For "partial duals," Medicaid pays some of the costs such as Medicare premiums, deductibles, and copayments. Dual-eligible beneficiaries generally have extensive health care needs because of chronic conditions, disability, or need for long-term care services. Under the ACA, Medicaid will become the new vehicle for health care services for this population group; both income and asset tests will apply.

The ACA calls for a 3-year demonstration project to integrate Medicare's and Medicaid's financing for "full duals." Approximately 15 states are participating in the demonstration projects. Known as the Financial Alignment Initiative, the projects will integrate primary, acute, behavioral, and long-term care needs of the beneficiaries by using two different models. In the capitated model, the state, federal government, and a private health plan will enter into a three-way contract to deliver all services for a fixed payment. In the managed fee-for-service model, the state and federal government will share costs and let the state design a program of coordinated care.

Medicaid Enrollment and Spending

The uncertainty surrounding Medicaid makes enrollment and expenditure projections highly speculative. According to estimates by the Congressional Budget Office, 7 million new beneficiaries would be added to Medicaid in 2014 (CBO 2012a). However, reliable data on the number and characteristics of beneficiaries and how much the program will cost the US taxpayers will not be available until well into 2015.

Children's Health Insurance Program (CHIP)

The CHIP program, codified as Title 21 of the Social Security Act, was initiated under the BBA of 1997 in response to the plight of uninsured children, who were estimated to number 10.1 million (nearly one-quarter of all uninsured) in 1996 and whose families' incomes exceeded the Medicaid threshold levels, which made them ineligible for Medicaid coverage.

The program offers federal funds in the form of set block grants to states. To cover children up to 19 years of age, a state can expand its existing Medicaid program, establish a separate program for children, or use a combined approach. Federal law requires that ineligibility for Medicaid be established before approval for CHIP coverage. Within federal guidelines, each state establishes eligibility criteria for CHIP. There is no federal income threshold, but many states cover children in families with incomes up to 200% of the FPL, provided the children are not covered under another private or public health insurance program. Several states have established income criteria above 200% of FPL. CHIP does not cover parents or adults.

The ACA extends the authorization of CHIP through September 30, 2015. The law requires states to maintain current income eligibility levels through September 30, 2019. States are prohibited from implementing eligibility standards, methodologies, or procedures that are more restrictive than those in place as of March 23, 2010.

Research has shown that CHIP has had a significant impact in reducing uninsurance among children (Hudson 2005). CHIP has also been credited with improved access, continuity of care, and quality of care for all racial/ethnic groups, as well as a reduction in racial/ethnic disparities in access, unmet need, and continuity of care (Shone et al. 2005).

Health Care for the Military

The US Department of Defense (DOD) operates a large and complex health care program to provide medical services to active duty and retired members of the armed forces, their dependents, survivors, and former spouses. The program has also been extended to National Guard/Reserve members. Approximately 150,000 military, civilian, and contract personnel are employed in hospitals and clinics operated by the military. Each of the military departments—Army, Navy, and Air Force—operates its own medical facilities. In 2011, DOD's health care budget was over $52 billion, and it provided services to 9.7 million beneficiaries (GAO 2013).

TRICARE is the insurance arm of military health care. The beneficiaries may obtain health care either through DOD's medical facilities or through services purchased from civilian providers.

TRICARE offers three main plans, but additional options are available. Active duty personnel are automatically enrolled at no cost in TRICARE Prime, a comprehensive managed care plan. Dependents of active duty personnel and retirees may choose TRICARE Prime by paying a premium and subject to cost sharing when services are used. The other option for them is to enroll in TRICARE Standard which is a fee-for-service plan. TRICARE Extra is a plan that has lower coinsurance when in-network providers are used. Retirees age 65 and older are covered by TRICARE for Life, a plan that works in conjunction with Medicare—the enrollee must enroll in Parts A and B. TRICARE for Life pays for certain services not covered by Medicare. All TRICARE plans meet the test of ACA's "minimum essential coverage."

Veterans Health Administration

Veterans Health Administration (VHA), the health services branch of the US Department of Veterans Affairs (VA), operates the largest integrated health services system in the United States, with approximately 153 hospitals, 956 outpatient clinics, 134 community living centers (nursing homes), and various other facilities. In all, the VHA provides care to nearly 6 million veterans through more than 1400 sites throughout the nation. VHA employs a staff of 255,000 and maintains affiliations with 107 academic health systems. Apart from delivering health care services, the VHA system also actively participates in medical education and research. More than 65% of all physicians in the United States have received their training in VHA facilities (VA 2010).

The VHA was originally established to treat veterans with war-related injuries and to help rehabilitate past service members with war-related disabilities. This original mission was expanded so that nonservice-related conditions now account for the bulk of the care provided as poor veterans with medical conditions unrelated to military combat increasingly use the system. More than half of the veterans served by VHA have no service-connected disabilities (NCHS 2012). However, Congress requires VHA to provide services on a priority basis to veterans with service-connected illnesses and disabilities, low incomes, or special health care needs. Eligible veterans are classified into one of eight priority groups upon enrollment. Priority Group 1 receives the highest priority: These veterans have service-connected disabilities rated as 50% or more disabling.

Many veterans who have nonservice-related conditions, do not qualify for enrollment in the VHA program. They may qualify for TRICARE (discussed in the previous section) or Medicaid. Otherwise, they should purchase private health insurance. Although many low-income veterans are eligible for VHA health care, an estimated 2 million veterans and their dependents were uninsured during the 2008–2010 period (Haley and Kenney 2013). Many of them will be able to obtain coverage through the exchanges established under the ACA.

Funding for the VHA program is appropriated in the annual presidential budget approved by Congress. The structure of VHA funding is patterned after the global budget model in which budget appropriations are determined in advance for the entire system. The VHA then distributes the funds to its organizational units having oversight for the delivery of health care.

The organizational units comprise 23 geographically distributed Veterans Integrated Service Networks (VISNs). Each VISN is responsible for coordinating the activities of the hospitals, outpatient clinics, nursing homes, and other facilities located within its jurisdiction. Apart from allocating resources among the health care facilities, VISNs are responsible for improving efficiency. The system also focuses on health promotion and disease prevention and on meeting the chronic care needs of an aging veteran population (VA 2010). Despite its many successes, however, the system suffers from capacity and financing constraints, which result in lack of access and timely care for many veterans.

The VHA also operates the Civilian Health and Medical Program of the Department of Veterans Affairs (CHAMPVA) which covers dependents of permanently and totally disabled veterans. The VHA shares the cost of covered health care services and supplies with eligible beneficiaries.

Indian Health Service

The federal program administered by the Indian Health Service (IHS), a division of the DHHS, provides comprehensive health care services directly to members of federally recognized American Indian and Alaska Native Tribes and their descendants.

American Indians and Alaska Natives (AIANs), as citizens of the United States, are eligible to participate in all public, private, and state health programs available to the general population. However, for many Indians, IHS-supported programs are the only source of health care because no alternative sources of medical care are available, especially in isolated areas. IHS programs serve almost 2 million AIANs residing on or near reservations and in rural communities. The 2010 budget for services was over $4 billion.

Besides medical and dental care, services include health promotion and disease prevention and programs in substance abuse, maternal and child health, sanitation, and nutrition. The IHS system includes 29 hospitals, 59 health centers, and 28 health stations. Additional services are contracted from tribally operated health programs and private providers (IHS 2010). Further details on IHS are presented in Chapter 11.

The Payment Function

Insurance companies, MCOs, Blue Cross/Blue Shield, and the government (for Medicare and Medicaid) are referred to as *third-party payers*, the other two parties being the patient and the provider. The payment function has two main facets: (1) the determination of the methods and amounts of reimbursement for the delivery of services and (2) the actual payment after services have been rendered. The set fee for each different type of service is commonly referred to as a charge or rate. Technically, a *charge* is a fee set by the provider, which is akin to price in general commerce.

A *rate* is a price set by a third-party payer. An index of charges listing individual fees for each type of service is referred to as a *fee schedule*. In general, to receive payment for services rendered, the provider must file a *claim* with the third-party payer. For the sake of simplicity, in this section, we refer to the determination of rates as "reimbursement" and to the payment of claims as "disbursement."

Various methods for determining how much providers should be paid are in use. Historically, providers have preferred the fee-for-service method, which has fallen out of favor with payers because of cost escalations. The Medicare program, in particular, has been at the forefront of devising innovative reimbursement methods; private payers have followed suit. Today, numerous reimbursement methods exist and are used for different types of services. Physicians, dentists, optometrists, therapists, hospitals, nursing facilities, and so on may be paid according to different reimbursement mechanisms.

Fee for Service

Fee for service is the oldest method of reimbursement and is still in existence, although its use has been greatly reduced. Fee for service is based on the assumption that health care is provided in a set of identifiable and individually distinct units of services, such as examination, X-ray, urinalysis, and a tetanus shot, in the case of physician services. For surgery, such individual services may include an admission kit, numerous medical supplies each accounted for separately, surgeon's fees, anesthesia, anesthesiologist's fees, recovery room charges, and so forth. Each of these services is separately itemized on one bill, and there can be more than one bill. For example, the hospital, the surgeon, the pathologist, and the anesthesiologist bill for their services separately.

Initially, providers established their own fee-for-service charges and insurers passively paid the claims. Later, insurers started to limit reimbursement to a usual, customary, and reasonable (UCR) amount. Each insurer determined on its own what the UCR charge should be, through community or statewide surveys of what providers were charging. If the actual charges exceeded the UCR amount, then reimbursement from insurers was limited to the UCR amount. Providers then *balance billed*, that is, asked the patients to pay the difference between the actual charges and the payments received from third-party payers.

The main problem under fee-for-service arrangements is that providers have an incentive to deliver additional services that are not essential. Providers can increase their incomes by increasing the volume of services. However, dentists, therapists, and some physicians continue to receive payment according to fee for service.

Bundled Payments (Package Pricing)

Fee for service essentially pays for unbundled services. Bundled fee, or package pricing, includes a number of related services in one price. For example, optometrists sometimes advertise package prices that include the charges for eye exams, frames for eyeglasses, and corrective lenses. The various prospective payment methods of reimbursement are also examples of payments for bundled services. Package pricing reduces the incentive for providing nonessential services. There is evidence that bundled payment methods, especially when they are prospectively set, are effective in reducing health care spending without significantly affecting quality of care (Hussey et al. 2012).

Medicare is currently testing bundled payment methodologies per episode of care under a Bundled Payments for Care Improvement (BPCI) initiative. Different payment models include hospitals, physicians, and post-acute care providers (CMS 2013b). The BPCI initiative is based on the theory that various providers collaborating to deliver services to a patient through an entire episode will result in coordinated care and improved quality.

Resource-Based Relative Value Scale

Under the Omnibus Budget Reconciliation Act of 1989 (OBRA-89), Medicare developed a new initiative to reimburse physicians according to a "relative value" assigned to each physician service. The resource-based relative value scale (RBRVS) was implemented in 1992. Subsequently, third-party payers adopted the RBRVS system.

RBRVS incorporates *relative value units* (RVUs) based on the time, skill, and intensity (physician work) it takes to provide a service. Hence, RVUs reflect resource inputs—time, effort, and expertise—to deliver a service. RVUs are established for different types of services that are identified by their *Current Procedural Terminology* (CPT) codes—a standard coding system for physician services developed by the American Medical Association. RVUs, therefore, provide a means for comparing resource use among a variety of services that physicians provide.

For reimbursement purposes, in addition to RVUs associated with physician work, separate RVUs are included for the cost of practice (overhead costs) and for malpractice insurance. Because of geographic cost variations, each of the RVU categories is multiplied by its own geographic adjustment factor (Geographic Practice Cost Index). Finally, for each year's Medicare budget for physician payments, a conversion factor (CF) is established based on what Medicare calls a "sustainable growth rate" (SGR). The payment for each CPT equals its RVU × CF. Medicare establishes a national *Medicare Physician Fee Schedule* (MPFS), a price list for physician services, based on which individual payments are made when physicians file their claims.

In essence, RBRVS is a variation of fee for service, therefore it has not addressed the issue of volume-driven payment. The number of RVUs can be increased by increasing the volume of services delivered, thus increasing practice throughput and boosting the number of billable services per patient (Jessee 2011).

Managed Care Approaches

MCOs have concentrated on three main approaches. The first is the preferred-provider approach, which may be regarded as a variation of fee for service. The main distinction is that an MCO contracts with certain "preferred providers" and negotiates discounts off the charges to establish fee schedules. In the second approach, called *capitation,* the provider is paid a set monthly fee per enrollee (sometimes referred to as per member per month, or PMPM, rate). The fixed monthly fee (PMPM rate × number of enrollees) is paid to the provider regardless of how often the enrollees receive medical services from the provider. Capitation removes the incentive for providers to increase the volume of services to generate additional revenues. It also makes providers prudent in providing only necessary services. Salary, combined with productivity-related bonuses, is the third method used by some MCOs that employ their own physicians.

Cost-Plus Reimbursement

Cost-plus was the traditional method used by Medicare and Medicaid to establish *per diem* (daily) rates for inpatient stays in hospitals, nursing homes, and other institutions. Under the cost-plus method, reimbursement rates for institutions are based on the total costs incurred in operating the institution. The institution is required to submit a cost report to the third-party payer. Complex formulas are developed, designating certain costs as "nonallowable" and placing cost ceilings in other areas. The formulas are used to calculate the *per diem* reimbursement rate, also referred to as a per-patient-day (PPD) rate. The method is called *cost-plus* because, in addition to the total operating costs, the reimbursement formula also allows a portion of the capital costs in arriving at the PPD rate. Because the reimbursement methodology sets rates after evaluating the costs retrospectively (by looking back), this mechanism is broadly referred to as *retrospective reimbursement*.

Under the cost-plus system, total reimbursement is directly related to length of stay, services rendered, and cost of providing the services. Providers have an incentive to provide services indiscriminately, thus increasing costs. There is little motivation for efficiency and cost containment in the delivery of services. Paradoxically, health care institutions could increase their profits by increasing costs. Because of the perverse financial incentives inherent in retrospective cost-based reimbursement, it has been largely replaced by various prospective reimbursement methods, except the federal critical access hospital program (see Chapter 8), which continues to allow certain rural hospitals to be paid under the cost-plus reimbursement system.

Prospective Reimbursement

In contrast to retrospective reimbursement, where historical costs are used to determine the amount to be paid, *prospective reimbursement* uses certain established criteria to determine the amount of reimbursement in advance (looking forward), before services are delivered. Prospective reimbursement not only minimizes some of the abuses inherent in cost-plus approaches, but it also enables providers, such as Medicare, to better predict future health care spending. It also provides strong incentives to health care organizations to reduce costs. The organization makes a profit only if it can keep its costs below the prospective reimbursement amount. Inability to control costs jeopardizes the organization's financial health.

Medicare has been using the prospective payment system (PPS) to reimburse inpatient hospital acute care services under Medicare Part A since 1983. Subsequently, the BBA of 1997 mandated implementation of a PPS for hospital outpatient services and postacute care providers, such as SNFs, home health agencies, and inpatient rehabilitation facilities.

The ACA includes several provisions that direct the CMS to reduce reimbursement to these providers and to develop plans for "value-based purchasing" (Linehan 2012). Value-based purchasing incorporates *pay-for-performance* (P4P) as a component in the reimbursement formulas used by Medicare to pay providers. The objective of P4P initiatives is to link reimbursement to quality and efficiency as an incentive to improve the quality of health care, as well as reduce systemwide costs. Starting in 2014, most organizations are required to report quality data to the CMS, failing which they face penalties in reimbursement. New payment models, such as BPCI, are still in their infancy, hence current methods of reimbursement will continue to remain in effect for some time to come. Reimbursement based on P4P can actually have negative repercussions (see Chapter 12).

Depending on the type of service setting, the prospective reimbursement methods discussed in the subsequent sections are based on diagnosis-related groups (DRGs), ambulatory payment classification (APC), case-mix methods, and home health resource groups (HHRGs).

Diagnosis-Related Groups (DRGs)

Overview of DRG-Based Reimbursement

The PPS for acute-care hospital inpatient reimbursement was enacted under the Social Security Amendments of 1983. The predetermined reimbursement amount is set according to DRGs. Each DRG groups together principal diagnoses that are expected to require similar amounts of hospital resources in the delivery of care.

The primary factor governing the amount of reimbursement is the type of case (a DRG classification), but additional factors can create differences in reimbursement for the same DRG. DRG-based rates are adjusted for geographic differences (wage levels in various areas and location of the hospital in urban versus rural areas);

whether or not the institution is a teaching hospital, that is, it has residency programs for medical graduates; and whether a hospital treats a disproportionate share of low-income patients, as determined by the volume of patients receiving Supplemental Security Income or Medicaid benefits. The latter provision was authorized by Congress to give extra financial support to "safety net" hospitals (called disproportionate share hospitals), which are mainly located in inner cities and rural areas, and serve a large number of poor people. Additional payments are also made for cases that involve extremely long hospital stays or are extremely expensive, which are referred to as *outliers*.

The hospital receives a predetermined fixed rate per discharge (i.e., per case) based on the patient's DRG classification and adjustment factors just pointed out. The bundle of services consists of whatever medical care the patient requires for a given principal diagnosis.

Refined Medicare Severity DRGs

In 2007, the CMS adopted a refined DRG-based PPS method that includes patient severity to better reflect hospital resource use. The new system has 335 base DRGs, most of which are further split into 2 or 3 MS-DRGs (Medicare severity diagnosis-related groups) based on comorbidities (secondary conditions) or complications (developed during hospital stay). This new payment system had 751 MS-DRGs in use in 2012. Each MS-DRG carries a relative weight that reflects how costly it would be to take care of a patient in a given MS-DRG category relative to other categories. The process remains dynamic with an annual review of MS-DRGs, and adjustments are made as necessary. A new type of adjustment to the reimbursement method is for the use of certain technologies. Also added to the reimbursement is 65% of bad debts resulting from nonpayment of deductibles and copayments. Because DRG-based PPS pays a fixed amount per discharged patient, hospitals have a financial incentive for keeping the length of stay as short as possible. To counteract this practice, under the refined policy, the CMS now reduces the reimbursement for certain early discharges (MedPAC 2012).

ACA Stipulations for Hospital Reimbursement

Starting in October 2012, the ACA required reduction in payments to hospitals that incurred excessive Medicare readmissions for selected conditions (MedPAC 2012). The benchmark used by the CDC is a readmission to the same or another hospital that is related to the same medical condition for which the patient was previously hospitalized and that occurs within 30 days of discharge. An example would be a patient who is readmitted to the hospital because of an infection that is related to a surgical procedure for which the patient was initially hospitalized. One study found that 20% of Medicare patients were rehospitalized within 30 days, and the cost to Medicare from unplanned rehospitalizations was $17.4 billion in 2004 (Jencks et al. 2009). Hence, policymakers have viewed rehospitalizations as a quality issue, even though some rehospitalizations may be unavoidable. For example, readmissions among homeless patients are strikingly high (Doran et al. 2013), likely because the homeless lack post-illness social support. Despite such noncontrollables, however,

there is evidence that hospitals are having success in reducing the number of readmissions (Goozner 2013).

Under the ACA, the CMS also implemented value-based incentive payments starting in October 2012 based on performance on a set of quality measures. These value-based payments will increase each year through 2017 (MedPAC 2012).

Psychiatric DRG-Based Payment

Inpatient psychiatric facilities receive a *per diem* rate rather than a case-specific rate, based on psychiatric DRGs. The program also includes a stop-loss provision to protect psychiatric hospitals against significant losses. In other respects, the factors considered in arriving at reimbursement rates are similar to those used for reimbursing acute-care hospitals.

Outpatient Prospective Payment System

In August 2000, Medicare's Outpatient Prospective Payment System (OPPS) was implemented to pay for services provided by hospital outpatient departments. Main services included in OPPS are outpatient surgeries, radiology and other diagnostic procedures, clinic visits, and emergency services. Ambulatory payment classification (APC) divides all outpatient services into more than 300 procedural groups. In addition, the CMS has created new technology APCs. The services within each group are clinically similar and require comparable resources. Each APC is assigned a relative weight based on the median cost of services within the APC. The reimbursement rates are adjusted for geographic variation in wages. APC reimbursement is a bundled rate that includes services such as anesthesia, certain drugs, supplies, and recovery room charges in a packaged price established by Medicare.

In January 2008, Medicare implemented the OPPS to pay for facility services, such as nursing, recovery care, anesthetics, drugs, and other supplies, in freestanding (i.e., nonhospital) ambulatory surgery centers. The most common procedures performed in these centers are eye procedures, such as cataract removal and lens replacement, and colonoscopy. Physician services are reimbursed separately under the Physician Fee Schedule based on RBRVS (MedPAC 2009).

Case-Mix Methods

Case mix is an aggregate of the severity of conditions requiring clinical intervention. Case-mix categories are mutually exclusive and differentiate patients according to the extent of resource use. On a case-mix index, higher score categories comprise patients who have more severe conditions than those in lower score categories. A comprehensive assessment of each patient's condition determines the case mix for an inpatient facility. Patients who require similar levels of services are then categorized into groups that are relatively uniform according to resource consumption.

Resource Utilization Groups

This method is used for paying SNFs. Implemented in 1998, the PPS provides for a *per diem* prospective rate based on the intensity of care needed by patients in an SNF. The case mix is determined through a comprehensive assessment of each patient, using an assessment instrument called the Minimum Data Set (MDS). The MDS consists of a core set of screening elements used to assess the clinical, functional, and psychosocial needs of each patient admitted to an SNF. Each patient's day of care is assigned to one of 66 resource utilization groups (RUGs). The RUG categories differentiate between patients according to expected resource use. Among the variables used to differentiate resource utilization are patient characteristics, such as principal diagnosis, functional limitations, cognitive patterns, psychological condition, skin problems, bladder and bowel function, nutritional status, and special treatments and procedures needed. The aim of RUG–based PPS is to ensure that Medicare payments are related to the care requirements of the patient and are made equitably to SNFs with different patient caseloads. The *per diem* rate is all-inclusive, meaning it includes payment for all covered SNF services provided in a nursing facility. Adjustments to the PPS rate are made for differences in wages prevailing in various geographic areas and for facility location in urban versus rural areas.

Case-Mix Groups

Since 2002, inpatient rehabilitation facilities (rehabilitation hospitals and distinctly certified rehabilitation units in general hospitals) have been reimbursed according to case-mix groups (CMGs). Each patient must undergo a patient assessment at admission and discharge. Based on information from the assessment, the patient is assigned to one of the intensive rehabilitation categories, based on the primary reason for rehabilitation, such as stroke or burns, age, functional level, or cognitive impairment. Patients are further categorized into one of four tiers, based on any comorbidities. Each tier has a specific reimbursement rate associated with it. Length of stay is also taken into account in determining the level of reimbursement (MedPAC 2008a).

Home Health Resource Groups

Implemented in 2000, the PPS for home health pays a fixed, predetermined rate for each 60-day episode of care regardless of the specific services delivered. All services provided by a home health agency are bundled under one payment made on a per-patient basis, except the costs of any durable medical equipment (DME) are not included in the bundled rate. To capture the expected resource use, patients are assigned to one of the 153 HHRGs, based on clinical and functional status and service use, which is measured by the Outcome and Assessment Information Set (OASIS). The HHRGs range from groups of relatively uncomplicated patients to those who have severe medical conditions, severe functional limitations, or need extensive therapy. If a patient received fewer than five visits during a 60-day episode, the home health agency is paid per visit based on the type of visit (MedPAC 2008b).

Disbursement of Funds

After services have been delivered, some agency has to perform the administrative task of verifying and paying the claims received from the providers. Disbursement of funds (claims processing) is carried out in accordance with the reimbursement policy adopted by the particular program. Commercial insurance companies and MCOs either have their own claims departments to process payments to providers or they may outsource it. Self-insured employers typically contract the services of a *third-party administrator* (TPA) to process and pay claims. The TPA may also monitor utilization and perform other oversight functions. The government contracts with third parties in the private sector to process Medicare and Medicaid claims. These contractors include Blue Cross/Blue Shield and commercial insurance companies. While *fiscal intermediaries* process Part A claims, Medicare refers to claims processors for Part B services as *carriers*. Even though Medicare makes a technical distinction between the two, fundamentally, fiscal intermediaries and carriers are the same.

National Health Care Expenditures

In 2010, national health expenditures (NHE), also referred to as health care spending, in the United States amounted to almost $2.6 trillion, or an average per capita spending of $8,402 for each American. It represented 17.9% of the gross domestic product (GDP; see Table 6–3). The *GDP* is the total value of goods and services produced in the United States and is an indicator of total economic production (or total consumption). Hence, 17.9% of GDP refers to the share of the total economic output consumed by health care products and services. Because of the 2007–2009 recession and a slow economic growth since then, the share of GDP is somewhat higher than would otherwise be expected. Nevertheless, the data leave little doubt that health care continues to consume an ever-rising share of the nation's total economic production. Total spending grew at an average annual rate of 6.7% from 1990 to 2000, and at 7.3% from 2000 to 2010. According to projections by the CMS, national spending is expected to grow by 7.4% in 2014

Table 6–3 US National Health Expenditures, Selected Years

Year	Amount (in billions)	% of GDP	Amount per capita
1960	$27.4	5.2	$147
1970	74.9	7.2	356
1980	255.8	9.2	1,110
1990	724.3	12.5	2,854
2000	1,377.2	13.8	4,878
2010	2,593.6	17.9	8,402
2020 (projected)	4,416	19.2	13,142

Source: Modified from National Center for Health Statistics. 2013. Health, United States, 2012: With Special Feature on Emergency Care. Hyattsville, MD.

when the main provisions of the ACA would have taken effect. This is 2.1% faster than in the absence of reform (CMS 2012). Chapter 12 discusses projected health care expenditures, the reasons for the growth in spending, international comparisons, and cost-containment measures.

Difference Between National and Personal Health Expenditures

National health expenditures are an aggregate of the amount the nation spends for all health services and supplies, public health services, health-related research, administrative costs, and investment in structures and equipment during a calendar year. The proportional distribution of NHE into the various categories of health services appears in Table 6–4.

Personal health expenditures are a component of national health expenditures, and comprise the total spending for services and goods related directly to patient care. Personal health expenditures constitute the amount remaining after subtracting from NHE, spending for research, structures

Table 6–4 Percentage Distribution of US National Health Expenditures, 2000 and 2010

	2000	2010
NHE	100.0	100.0
Personal health care	84.6	84.3
hospital care	30.2	31.4
physician and clinical services	21.1	19.9
dental services	4.5	4.0
nursing home care	6.2	5.5
other professional services	2.7	2.6
home health	2.4	2.7
prescription drugs	8.8	10.0
other personal health care	4.7	5.0
other medical products	4.1	3.2
Govt administration and net cost of private health insurance	5.9	6.8
Govt public health activities	3.1	3.2
Investment	6.4	5.7
noncommercial research	1.8	1.9
structures & equipment	4.5	3.8
Total NHE (billions)	$1,377.2	$2,593.6
Personal health expenditures (billions)	$1,165.4	$2,186.0

Source: Modified from National Center for Health Statistics. 2013. Health, United States, 2012: With Special Feature on Emergency Care. Hyattsville, MD.

(construction, additions, alterations, etc.) and equipment, administrative expenses incurred in private and public health insurance programs, and costs of government public health activities. In 2010, 84.3% of the total health spending was attributed to the various services classified under personal health expenditures. As a share of national health expenditures in percentage terms, the biggest rise between 2000 and 2010 has been for hospital care and prescription drugs, both rising 1.2 percentage points (see Table 6–4).

The Nation's Health Care Dollar

Figure 6–6 illustrates the shift from private financing to public financing from federal, state, and local governments since 1960. In 1960, private funds, including out-of-pocket payments, private health insurance premiums, and other private funds, paid for 75% of all health care expenditures. The introduction of Medicare and Medicaid in

1966 transferred a large portion of the private expenditures to the public sector, while increasing access for many who previously could not afford the growing costs of health care. A few years later, in 1972, when Medicare began coverage of the disabled population, the proportion of health care expenditures from private sources declined to 62%. The shift from private to public sources of financing has continued as additional government programs, such as CHIP and Part D of Medicare, have been created along the way. The share of private financing reached its lowest point in 2008 when 52.7% of the nation's health dollars came from private sources and 47.3% came from public sources; this ratio has remained stable through 2011. Without doubt, the ACA will significantly shift the ratio toward public financing starting in 2014. Figure 6–7 summarizes the sources of financing and the proportionate consumption of health care dollars by various services.

Figure 6–6 Proportional Distribution of US Private and Public Shares of National Health Expenditures.

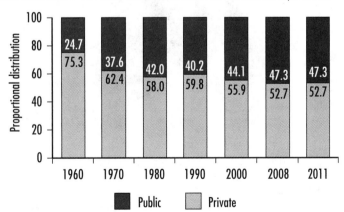

Source: Data from *Health, United States, 2010*, p. 366, National Center for Health Statistics; CMS, Office of the Actuary, National Health Statistics Group.

Figure 6–7 The Nation's Health Dollar: 2011.

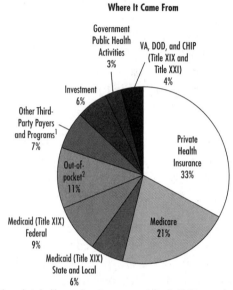

Where It Came From

¹ Includes work-site health care, other private revenues, Indian Health Service, workers' compensation, general assistance, maternal and child health, vocational rehabilitation, Substance Abuse and Mental Health Services Administration, school health, and other federal and state local programs.

² Includes copayments, deductibles, and any amounts not covered by health insurance.

Note: Sum of pieces may not equal 100% due to rounding.

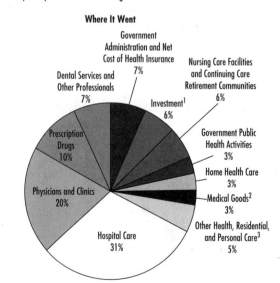

Where It Went

¹ Includes research and structures and equipment.

² Includes durable and nondurable goods.

³ Includes expenditures for residential care facilities, ambulance providers, medical care delivered in nontraditional settings (such as community centers, senior citizens centers, schools, and military field stations), and expenditures for Home and Community Waiver programs under Medicaid.

Note: Sum of pieces may not equal 100% due to rounding.

Total National Health Expenditures = $2,700.7 billion

Current Directions and Issues

The Supreme Court's split ruling on the ACA adds to the uncertainty as states have been given more decision-making power and say in the ACA's implementation, and employers are still weighing the pros and cons of how the law would affect them. Microsimulation economic models predict relatively small declines in employer-sponsored coverage (Buchmueller et al. 2013), but there is considerable controversy about how employers will react to the ACA's implementation (Austin et al. 2013). Moreover, the extent of Medicaid enrollment remains uncertain. Delay in the implementation of the employer mandate, a major provision of the ACA, only compounds the ambiguity. Hence, even the best current estimates on coverage and costs are likely to be far off.

Value and Affordability

Estimates by the CBO in May 2013 project the number of uninsured to drop from 55 million to 44 million in 2014 and to about 30 million in 2017 and beyond (CBO 2013a). The irony is that in spite of all the good intentions of the ACA, the law will still leave at least 25 million uninsured. The revised costs (net cost) to be borne by the federal government are estimated to be $1,375 billion over the 10-year period, 2014 to 2023 (CBO 2013b). The estimate leaves out the additional costs to be borne by the states and the employers. Also left out in CBO's projections is the growth in NHE attributable to increased utilization as a result of the expansion of health insurance. Hence, it is almost impossible to assess whether the ACA represents "value-based purchasing" that it advocates.

For individual consumers, affordability should be measured not only by premium costs, but also by the out-of-pocket costs incurred through cost sharing. The various ACA-mandated benefits—such as coverage of young adults under their parents' plans, coverage of pre-existing conditions, and essential health benefits—will be inflationary for health insurance premiums. For a substantial number of exchange-purchased plans, government subsidies will pass a proportion of the costs on to the taxpayers.

Without health care rationing in the future, moral hazard alone can have a serious impact on costs, provided the millions of newly insured can obtain health care services, a question that is dealt with in Chapter 14. Table 6–3 shows that runaway cost escalations became the norm for several decades after Medicaid and Medicare extended health insurance to millions of Americans. It is true that since then the health care system has become more efficient. Still, the questions surrounding value and affordability will not be answered for a few years when real data will become available.

Favorable Risk Selection and Adverse Selection

Risk selection and adverse selection are the opposite sides of the same coin. Favorable risk selection, or, simply, *risk selection*, occurs when healthy people disproportionately enroll into a health plan. *Adverse selection* occurs when high-risk individuals, that is, people who are likely to use more health care services than others because of their poor health status, enroll in health insurance plans in greater numbers, compared to people who are healthy. When adverse selection occurs, premiums have to be raised for everyone, which makes health insurance less affordable for those in good health. Risk selection and adverse selection distort the true function of insurance, but adjusting premiums to reflect health status and making potential high-cost enrollees pay more, a practice called *risk rating*, is criticized on equity grounds. Premiums based on risk rating makes it almost impossible for very high-risk individuals to obtain health insurance at affordable prices. This function was previously served by the state-based high-risk pools. Because these very high-risk individuals will get insurance through the exchanges under the ACA, a relatively large number of healthy individuals will need to sign up to prevent insurance cost escalation through adverse selection. These healthy individuals may find it more advantageous to pay the penalty tax than buy health insurance. Of course, until data become available, such issues remain hypothetical.

It is yet unknown how small employers will navigate their way through added requirements and regulations emanating from the ACA. One plausible scenario proposed by Yee at al. (2012) is that small employers with 100 or fewer workers whose workforce is relatively healthy may resort to self-insurance. As discussed previously, self-insurance gives employers a number of advantages. The unknown risks that small employers can face when they self-insure can be mitigated if stop-loss coverage can be obtained at reasonable prices, a trend that has been underway in the reinsurance market. The modified community rating required by the ACA may draw employers with younger workforces toward self-insuring. By doing so, these employers can also offer less generous benefits, thus reducing their cost of health insurance. This type of risk selection could adversely affect

small-group plans outside self-insurance. Those plans could face adverse selection, raising the premiums in the small-group market (Yee at al. 2012).

Intentional Churning

Churning refers to a phenomenon in which people gain and lose health insurance periodically. Under the ACA, this can occur intentionally. Mulvany (2013) assumes that one potential unintended consequence of the ACA could be individuals purchasing insurance only after they have a health care need and, subsequently, cancelling coverage once the need no longer exists.

Cost Shifting

When the amount of reimbursement from some payer becomes inadequate or when uncompensated services are rendered without payment from some source, cost shifting is a mechanism used to make up for revenue shortfalls. Providers resort to *cost shifting* by charging extra to payers who do not exercise strict cost controls. A study on cost shifting by hospitals (Robinson 2011) reported that hospitals in less competitive markets raise prices to private insurers when faced with shortfalls between Medicare payments and their projected costs. Conversely, in competitive markets hospitals focus on cutting costs when faced with reimbursement shortfalls from public payers. The ACA coverage expansion will be paid in part by reducing payments to hospitals and other providers. Hence, cost shifting will likely occur, which would have the effect of premium increases for health insurance in both employment-based and exchange-based plans.

Fraud and Abuse

Health care fraud and program abuse are troubling aspects of health care financing. The full extent of health care fraud is almost impossible to measure. However, the Federal Bureau of Investigation (FBI) estimated that fraudulent billings to public and private insurance amounted to 3% to 10% of total health care spending (Morris 2009). Fraud is difficult to detect for lack of routine monitoring and control procedures. Fiscal intermediaries who process and pay claims presume that claims are submitted for medically necessary services, and there is limited verification that services are actually provided (Morris 2009).

HIPAA established a national Health Care Fraud and Abuse Control Program designed to coordinate federal, state, and local law enforcement activities with respect to health care fraud and abuse. This collaborative approach has resulted in identifying and prosecuting the most egregious instances of health care fraud. During the fiscal year 2010, the federal government recovered approximately $2.5 billion in health care fraud judgments and settlements. The Medicare trust funds recovered over $18.0 billion since the program began in 1997 (DHHS and the Department of Justice 2011).

The ACA provides additional funding to fight fraud and abuse in the Medicare, Medicaid, and CHIP programs. The law calls for penalties for delaying or refusing the DHHS access to information in connection with audits and investigations. The DHHS has also been granted authority to suspend payments when fraud is suspected. A new area of fraud is likely to be associated with eligibility for Medicaid and insurance subsidies, even though the taxation powers of the Internal Revenue Service (IRS) have been greatly expanded under the ACA.

Summary

Financing is the lifeblood of any health care delivery system. Fundamentally, it determines who pays for health care services for whom. Secondarily, financing also determines who produces what types of health care services. A significant amount of financing is attributed to the government, mainly to provide health insurance or direct services to defined categories of people. Because most publicly financed services are obtained in the private sector, the government also has a sizable interest in setting the amount of reimbursement to providers.

The ACA has added several requirements that health plans must comply with: Coverage of young adults (under the age of 26) under their parents' plans; coverage for people with preexisting medical conditions; coverage for preventive services without cost sharing; elimination of yearly or lifetime benefit dollar limits; caps on annual cost sharing; and targets for medical loss ratios.

With some exceptions, all legal residents must have "minimum essential coverage" or pay a tax penalty. The minimum essential coverage must include "essential health benefits" in 10 categories. Private insurers sell four main types of plans, with different premium costs and cost sharing, through health insurance exchanges. Federal subsidies are available to people with incomes between 100% and 400% of the FPL.

The employer mandate (play or pay) applies to employers with 50+ full-time equivalent employees (full time = 30+ hours per week). Employer plans must pass both a "minimum value test" and an "affordability test." Penalties apply if an employer's plan fails these two tests or if a full-time worker gets subsidized health insurance through an exchange.

Medicare trust funds are running deficits and are headed toward insolvency unless the trend can be reversed. The ACA proposes payment cuts in Medicare Advantage and hospital reimbursement. It will be some time before value-based purchasing mechanisms can be developed and implemented. Medicaid faces an uncertain future as several states are opting out of the expansion provisions of the ACA.

Health care expenditures have continued to shift from the private sector to the public sector. This trend will accelerate under the ACA. Until actual data become available in the future, the questions of coverage and costs attributable to the ACA will not be known.

ACA Takeaway

- A relatively large number, but not all, of previously uninsured populations will gain coverage under the ACA, but national health care expenditures will also increase.

- The ACA's insurance expansion rests on a three-legged stool—an employer mandate (postponed until 2015), an individual mandate, and expansion of Medicaid (some states have chosen not to comply).

- The ACA specifies numerous rules governing health insurance, for example, rules pertaining to eligibility, risk rating, mandated benefits, and cost sharing. These rules affect both private and public insurance, but employer self-insured plans are exempt from some of the requirements. The various rules will displace a number of currently insured people. They will also have an inflationary effect.

- A relatively large segment of the US population is expected to get government subsidies to purchase health insurance. To qualify for subsidies and Medicaid under the ACA, an asset test does not apply.

- The ACA enhances prevention benefits under Medicare and reduces out-of-pocket costs for prescription drugs. It also cuts payments to insurance companies participating in Medicare Advantage and to physicians. On the other hand, not all Medicaid recipients may receive preventive services.

- The ACA calls for reforming the reimbursement systems, such as integration of services and financing for dual eligibles, BPCI, and value-based purchasing.

- Adverse selection and cost shifting are likely to occur, which will have an inflationary effect on health insurance premiums.

Test Your Understanding

Terminology

adverse selection

adjusted community
    rating

balance bill

beneficiary

benefit period

benefits

capitation

carriers

case mix

categorical programs

charge

churning

claim

coinsurance

community rating

consumer-driven health
    plan

copayment

cost-plus

cost shifting

Current Procedural
    Terminology

deductible

entitlement

experience rating

fee schedule

fiscal intermediaries

GDP

group insurance

high-deductible
    health plan

insurance

insured

insurer

means-tested
    program

medical loss ratio

Medicare Physician Fee
    Schedule

Medigap

moral hazard

national health
    expenditures

outliers

pay-for-performance

personal health
    expenditures

plan

play-or-pay

preexisting
    condition

premium

prospective
    reimbursement

rate

reinsurance

relative value units

retrospective
    reimbursement

risk

risk rating

risk selection

self-insured plan

third-party
    administrator

third-party payers

underwriting

Review Questions

1. What is meant by health care financing in its broad sense? What impact does financing have on the health care delivery system?

2. Discuss the general concept of insurance and its general principles. Describe the various types of private health insurance options, pointing out the differences among them.

3. Discuss how the concepts of premium, covered services, and cost sharing apply to health insurance.

4. What is the difference between experience rating and community rating?

5. What is Medicare Part A? Discuss the financing and cost-sharing features of Medicare Part A. What benefits does Part A cover? What benefits are not covered?

6. What is Medicare Part B? Discuss the financing and cost-sharing features of Medicare Part B. What main benefits are covered under Part B? What services are not covered?

7. Briefly describe the Medicare Advantage program.

8. Briefly explain the prescription drug program under Medicare Part D. What provisions does the ACA have to reduce cost sharing?

9. What are Medicare trust funds? Discuss the current state and the future challenges faced by the Medicare trust funds. What main factors pose these challenges?

10. How does the Supreme Court ruling on the ACA affect Medicaid? How does the ACA affect the program?

11. What provisions has the federal government made for providing health care to military personnel and to veterans of the US armed forces?

12. What are the major methods of reimbursement for outpatient services?

13. What are the differences between the retrospective and prospective methods of reimbursement?

14. Discuss the concept of value-based purchasing, as required by the Affordable Care Act.

15. Discuss the prospective payment system under DRGs.

16. Distinguish between national health expenditures and personal health expenditures.

17. What is adverse selection? What are its consequences?

18. What is risk rating? Why is it criticized?

19. What is the relationship between reimbursement cuts and cost shifting? How do hospitals react in different markets to cuts in reimbursement?

20. Summarize the provisions under HIPAA and the ACA as they apply to fraud and abuse.

REFERENCES

AARP. 2012. *Medicare: Get the facts*. Available at: http://www.aarp.org/health/medicare-insurance/info-02-2012/medicare-get-the-facts.html. Accessed September 2013.

The Advisory Board Company. 2013. Beyond the pledges: Where the states stand on Medicaid. Available at: http://www.advisory.com/Daily-Briefing/Resources/Primers/MedicaidMap. Accessed September 2013.

Andersen, K. 2013. 26 states opt out of ObamaCare's state-run insurance exchanges. *LifeSiteNews*, February 18. Available at: http://www.lifesitenews.com/news/26-states-opt-out-of-obamacares-state-run-insurance-exchanges. Accessed August 2013.

Andrews, M. 2013. Low-premium, high-deductible health plans are endangered by Affordable Care Act. *The Washington Post*. Available at: http://articles.washingtonpost.com/2013-08-12/national/41318345_1_grandfathered-plan-affordable-care-act-high-deductible-health-plans. Accessed October 2013.

Austin, D.R., et al. 2013. Small increases to employer premiums could shift millions of people to the exchanges and add billions to federal outlays. *Health Affairs* 32, no. 9: 1531–1537.

Buchmueller, T., et al. 2013. Will employers drop health insurance coverage because of the Affordable Care Act? *Health Affairs* 32, no. 9: 1522–1530.

Cantor, J.C., et al. 2012. Early impact of the Affordable Care Act on health insurance coverage of young adults. *Health Services Research* 47, no. 5: 1773–1790.

Centers for Medicare and Medicaid Services (CMS). 2012. National health expenditure projections 2011–2021. Available at: http://www.cms.gov/Research-Statistics-Data-and-Systems/Statistics-Trends-and-Reports/NationalHealthExpendData/Downloads/Proj2011PDF.pdf. Accessed September 2013.

Centers for Medicare and Medicaid Services (CMS). 2013a. *2013 Annual report of the boards of trustees of the federal hospital insurance and federal supplementary medical insurance trust funds.* Available at: http://downloads.cms.gov/files/TR2013.pdf. Accessed September 2013.

Centers for Medicare and Medicaid Services (CMS). 2013b. Bundled Payments for Care Improvement (BPCI) initiative: General information. Available at: http://innovation.cms.gov/initiatives/bundled-payments/index.html. Accessed October 2013.

Claxton, G., et al. 2010. *Employer health benefits: 2010 annual survey.* Menlo Park, CA: The Kaiser Family Foundation.

Congressional Budget Office (CBO). 2012a. *CBO and JCT's estimates of the effects of the Affordable Care Act on the number of people obtaining employment-based health insurance.* Washington, DC: Congressional Budget Office.

Congressional Budget Office (CBO). 2012b. Estimates for the insurance coverage provisions of the Affordable Care Act updated for the recent Supreme Court decision. Available at: http://cbo.gov/sites/default/files/cbofiles/attachments/43472-07-24-2012-CoverageEstimates.pdf. Accessed September 2013.

Congressional Budget Office (CBO). 2013a. Table 1. CBO's May 2013 estimate of the effects of the Affordable Care Act on health insurance coverage. Available at: http://www.cbo.gov/sites/default/files/cbofiles/attachments/44190_EffectsAffordableCareActHealthInsuranceCoverage_2.pdf. Accessed September 2013.

Congressional Budget Office (CBO). 2013b. Analysis of the Administration's announced delay of certain requirements under the Affordable Care Act. Available at: http://www.cbo.gov/sites/default/files/cbofiles/attachments/44465-ACA.pdf. Accessed September 2013.

Coombs, B. 2013. Obamacare's biggest test: How many enroll? NBR, CNBC. Available at: http://nbr.com/2013/09/18/obamacares-biggest-test-how-many-enroll. Accessed October 2013.

Department of Health and Human Services (DHHS) and the Department of Justice. 2011. *Health care fraud and abuse control program annual report for fiscal year 2010.* Available at: http://oig.hhs.gov/publications/docs/hcfac/hcfacreport2010.pdf. Accessed January 2011.

Department of Health and Human Services (DHHS). 2012. *At risk: Pre-existing conditions could affect 1 in 2 Americans: 129 million people could be denied affordable coverage without health reform.* Available at: http://aspe.hhs.gov/health/reports/2012/pre-existing/index.pdf. Accessed September 2013.

Department of Veterans Affairs (VA). 2010. *2010 organizational briefing book.* Available at: http://www.osp.va.gov/docs/2010_organizational_briefing_bookfinal.docx. Accessed January 2011.

Doran, K.M., et al. 2013. The revolving hospital door: Hospital readmissions among patients who are homeless. *Medical Care* 51, no. 9: 767–773.

Eastman, A.D., and K.L. Eastman. 2013. Person federal tax issues and the Affordable Care Act: Can tax penalties and subsidized premiums provide sufficient incentives for health insurance purchases. *Journal of Business & Economic Research* 11, no. 7: 315–324.

Employee Benefit Research Institute (EBRI). 2013. *Fast facts: why uninsured? Most workers cite cost. No. 243.* Washington, DC: Employee Benefit Research Institute.

Federal Register. 2010. Part II, Thursday, June 17, 2010 (p. 34552). National Archives and Records Administration. Available at: http://www.gpo.gov/fdsys/pkg/FR-2010-06-17/pdf/2010-14488. pdf. Accessed October 2013.

Feldstein, P.J. 1993. *Health care economics*. 4th ed. New York: Delmar Publishers.

Fronstin, P. 2012. *Sources of health insurance and characteristics of the uninsured: Analysis of the March 2012 Current Population Survey*. Issue Brief No. 376. Washington, DC: Employee Benefit Research Institute.

Gabel, J.R., et al. 2003. Self-insurance in times of growing and retreating managed care. *Health Affairs* 22, no. 2: 202–210.

Government Accountability Office (GAO). 2013. *Defense health care: Department of Defense needs a strategic approach to contracting for health care professionals* (Report to Congressional Committees). Washington, DC: Government Accountability Office.

Gold, M., et al. 2013. *Medicare Advantage 2013 spotlight: Enrollment market update*. Issue Brief. Menlo Park, CA: Henry J. Kaiser Family Foundation.

Goodman, J.C., and G.L. Musgrave. 1992. *Patient power: Solving America's health care crisis*. Washington, DC: CATO Institute.

Goozner, M. 2013. Readmission penalties at work. *Modern Healthcare* 43, no. 33: 25.

Gruber, L.R. 2009. *How state health insurance pools are helping Americans*. National Association of State Comprehensive Health Insurance Plans. Available at: http://www.naschip.org/Position%20Paper%20NJRv25.pdf. Accessed August 2013.

Haley, J., and G.M. Kenney. 2013. Uninsured veterans and family members: State and national estimates of expanded Medicaid eligibility under the ACA. Robert Wood Johnson Foundation and the Urban Institute. Available at: http://www.urban.org/uploadedpdf/412775-Uninsured-Veterans-and-Family-Members.pdf. Accessed September 2013.

Hall, M.A., and M. J. McCue. 2013. *Insurers' medical loss ratios and quality improvement spending in 2011*. Issue Brief, March 2013. Washington, DC: The Commonwealth Fund.

Harrington, S.E. 2013. Medical loss ratio regulation under the Affordable Care Act. *Inquiry* 50, no. 1: 9–26.

Health Insurance Institute. 1969. *Modern health insurance*. New York: Health Insurance Institute.

The Henry J. Kaiser Family Foundation. 2012. *The Medicare prescription drug benefit fact sheet*. Available at: http://kff.org/medicare/fact-sheet/the-medicare-prescription-drug-benefit-fact-sheet. Accessed September 2013.

Hoadley, J., et al. 2013. *Medicare Part D: A first look at plan offerings in 2014*. Available at: http://kff.org/medicare/issue-brief/medicare-part-d-a-first-look-at-plan-offerings-in-2014. Accessed October 2013.

Holahan, J. 2011. The 2007–09 recession and health insurance coverage. *Health Affairs* 30, no. 1: 145–152.

Hudson, J.L. 2005. The impact of SCHIP on insurance coverage of children. *Inquiry* 42, no. 3: 232–254.

Hussey, P.S., et al. 2012. *Bundled payment: Effects on health care spending and quality*. Rockville, MD: Agency for Healthcare Research and Quality.

Indian Health Service (IHS). 2010. *IHS fact sheets*. Available at: http://www.ihs.gov/newsroom/factsheets/. Accessed December 2013.

Jencks, S.F., et al. 2009. Rehospitalizations among patients in the Medicare fee-for-service program. *New England Journal of Medicine* 360, no. 14: 1418–1428.

Jessee, W.F. 2011. Is there an ACO in your future? *MGMA Connexion* 11, no. 1: 5–6.

The Kaiser Family Foundation and Health Research and Educational Trust (Kaiser/HRET). 2013. *Employer health benefits: 2013 annual survey.* Menlo Park, CA: The Kaiser Family Foundation.

Kopp, B., et al. 2013. What's new with the Affordable Care Act? *Employee Benefit Plan Review* 68, no. 2: 7–11.

Krajnak, P. 2013. Navigators and exchanges. *Benefits Magazine* 50, no. 8: 12–13.

Levit, K.R., et al. 1994. National health spending trends, 1960–1993. *Health Affairs* 13, no. 5: 14–31.

Linehan, K. 2012. *Medicare's post-acute care payment: A review of the issues and policy proposals.* Issue Brief No. 847. Washington, DC: National Health Policy Forum.

MedPAC. 2008a. *Rehabilitation facilities (inpatient) payment system.* Available at: http://www.medpac.gov/documents/MedPAC_Payment_Basics_08_IRF.pdf. Accessed January 2011.

MedPAC. 2008b. *Home health care services payment system.* Available at: http://www.medpac.gov/documents/MedPAC_Payment_Basics_08_HHA.pdf. Accessed January 2011.

MedPAC. 2009. *Ambulatory surgical centers payment system.* Available at: http://www.medpac.gov/documents/MedPAC_Payment_Basics_09_ASC.pdf. Accessed January 2011.

MedPAC. 2012. *Hospital acute inpatient services payment system.* http://medpac.gov/documents/MedPAC_Payment_Basics_12_hospital.pdf. Accessed September 2013.

Morris, L. 2009. Combating fraud in health care: An essential component of any cost containment strategy. *Health Affairs* 28, no. 5: 1351–1356.

Mulvany, C. 2013. Insurance market reform: the grand experiment. *Healthcare Financial Management* 67, no. 4: 82–86, 88.

National Center for Health Statistics (NCHS). 1996. *Health, United States, 1995.* Hyattsville, MD: US Department of Health and Human Services.

National Center for Health Statistics (NCHS). 2012. *Health, United States, 2012.* Hyattsville, MD: US Department of Health and Human Services.

Robinson, J. 2011. Hospitals respond to Medicare payment shortfalls by both shifting costs and cutting them, based on market concentration. *Health Affairs* 30, no. 7: 1265–1271.

Shone, L.P., et al. 2005. Reduction in racial and ethnic disparities after enrollment in the State Children's Health Insurance Program. *Pediatrics* 115, no. 6: e697–e705.

Somers, A.R., and H.M. Somers. 1977. *Health and health care: Policies in perspective.* Germantown, MD: Aspen Systems.

Vaughn, E.J., and C.M. Elliott. 1987. *Fundamentals of risk and insurance.* New York: John Wiley & Sons.

Watts, T., and S. Gaertner. 2013. Health care reform and the hourly challenge. *Benefits Quarterly* 29, no. 2: 26–29.

Wilensky, S.E., and E. A. Gray. 2013. Existing Medicaid beneficiaries left off the Affordable Care Act's prevention bandwagon. *Health Affairs* 32, no. 7: 1188–1195.

Yee, T., et al. 2012. Small employers and self-insured health benefits: Too small to succeed? *Issue Brief No. 138.* Washington, DC: Center for Studying Health System Change.

Zigmond, J. 2013. Crushing blow. *Modern Healthcare* 43, no. 8: 0008.

PART III

System Processes

Chapter 7

Outpatient and Primary Care Services

Learning Objectives

- To understand the meanings of outpatient, ambulatory, and primary care
- To explore the main principles behind patient-centered medical homes and community-based primary care
- To identify the reasons behind the dramatic growth in outpatient services
- To survey the various types of outpatient settings and services
- To describe the role of complementary and alternative medicine in health care
- To appreciate primary care delivery in other countries
- To understand the various provisions in the Affordable Care Act that apply to outpatient services

"I suppose a system based on primary care is more robust."

Introduction

The terms "outpatient" and "ambulatory" have been used interchangeably, as they are in this book. Historically, outpatient care has been independent from services provided in health care institutions. In earlier days, physicians saw patients in their clinics, and most physicians also made home visits to treat patients within the limitations of medical science prevalent in those days. Institutions for inpatient care, such as hospitals and nursing homes, developed later. With advances in medical science, the locus of health care delivery concentrated around the institutional core of community hospitals. As the range of services that could be provided on an outpatient basis continued to expand, hospitals gradually became the dominant players in providing the vast majority of outpatient care as well, with the exception of basic diagnostic care provided in physicians' offices (Barr and Breindel 1995). Hospitals were better equipped to provide such services because they had the resources to capitalize on technological innovation. Hospital laboratories and diagnostic units, for example, were better equipped to perform most tests and diagnostic procedures. Independent providers, on the other hand, faced capital constraints and competitive pressures in the health care marketplace.

Later, health care delivery increasingly shifted outside of expensive acute care hospitals to various alternative outpatient settings. Although basic primary care has traditionally been the foundation of outpatient services, certain intensive procedures are increasingly being performed on an outpatient basis. Consumer demand has also fueled the growth of complementary and alternative medicine.

Today, a large variety of outpatient services are available in the United States, yet many Americans face inadequate access because of maldistribution and/or shortages of both providers and services. Hospital emergency care and community health centers constitute the main safety net for primary care services. Delivery of outpatient care by public agencies has been limited in scope and detached from the dominant private system of health services delivery. State and local government agencies sponsor limited outpatient services such as child immunizations, care of mothers and infants, health screening in public schools, monitoring for certain contagious diseases like tuberculosis, family planning, and prevention of sexually transmitted diseases.

The Affordable Care Act has provisions to address some of the issues of access for poor and vulnerable populations. These initiatives, however, may turn out to be inadequate.

What Is Outpatient Care?

Outpatient services do not require an overnight inpatient stay in an institution of health care delivery, such as a hospital or long-term care facility, although certain outpatient services may be offered by a hospital or nursing home. Many hospitals, for instance, have emergency departments (EDs) and other outpatient service centers, such as outpatient surgery, rehabilitation, and specialized clinics.

Outpatient services are also referred to as *ambulatory care*. Strictly speaking, ambulatory care constitutes diagnostic and therapeutic services and treatments provided to the "walking" (ambulatory) patient. Hence, in a restricted sense, the term "ambulatory care" refers to care rendered to patients who come to physicians' offices, hospital outpatient departments, and health centers to receive care. The term is also used synonymously with "community medicine" (Wilson and Neuhauser 1985) because the geographic location of ambulatory services is intended to serve the surrounding community, providing convenience and easy accessibility.

Patients do not always walk to the service centers to receive ambulatory care, however. For example, in a hospital ED, patients may arrive by land or air ambulance. EDs, in most cases, are equipped to provide secondary and tertiary care services rather than primary care. In other instances, such as mobile diagnostic units and home health care, services are transported to the patient, instead of the patient coming to receive the services. Hence, the terms "outpatient" and "inpatient" are more precise, and the term *outpatient services* refers to any health care services that are not provided on the basis of an overnight stay in which room and board are incurred.

The Scope of Outpatient Services

Since the 1980s, extraordinary growth has occurred in the volume and variety of outpatient services and the emergence of new settings in which outpatient services are now delivered (see examples in Table 7–1). Hospital-based medical systems and integrated delivery organizations (see Chapter 9) now offer a range of health care services that include a variety of outpatient services. In other situations, the growth of nonhospital-based ambulatory services has intensified competition for outpatient services between hospitals and community-based providers. Examples of such competition include home health care, freestanding clinics for routine and urgent care, retail clinics, outpatient rehabilitation, and freestanding imaging centers. Other services, such as dental care and optometric services, remain independent of other types of health care services. Financing is the main reason, because medical insurance plans are generally separate from dental and vision care plans. Philosophical and technical differences account for other variations. Chiropractic care, for instance, is generally covered by most health plans but remains isolated from the mainstream practice of medicine. Complementary and alternative therapies and self-care are not covered by insurance, yet continue to experience remarkable growth.

Primary care is the foundation for ambulatory health services, but not all ambulatory care is primary care. For example, hospital ED services are not intended to be primary in nature. Conversely, services other than primary care have now become an integral part of outpatient services. Thanks to the technological advances in medicine, many advanced treatments are now provided in ambulatory care settings. Examples include conditions requiring urgent treatment, outpatient surgery, renal dialysis, and chemotherapy.

Primary Care

Primary care plays a central role in a health care delivery system. Other essential levels of care include secondary and tertiary care (distinct from primary, secondary, and tertiary prevention discussed in Chapter 2). Compared to primary care, secondary and tertiary care services are more complex and specialized.

Table 7–1 Owners, Providers, and Settings for Ambulatory Care Services

Past	Present
Owners/Providers	
• Independent physician practitioners	• Independent physician practitioners
• Hospitals	• Hospitals
• Community health agencies	• Community health agencies
• Home health agencies	• Managed care organizations
	• Insurance companies
	• Corporate employers
	• Group practices
	• National physician chains
	• Home health companies
	• National diversified health care companies
Service Settings	
• Hospital outpatient departments	• Physicians' offices
• Physicians' offices	• Walk-in clinics/urgent care centers
• Outpatient surgery centers	• Retail clinics
• Hospital emergency departments	• Outpatient surgery centers
• Home health agencies	• Chemotherapy and radiation therapy centers
• Neighborhood health centers	• Dialysis centers
	• Community health centers
	• Diagnostic imaging centers
	• Mobile imaging centers
	• Fitness/wellness centers
	• Occupational health centers
	• Psychiatric outpatient centers
	• Rehabilitation centers
	• Sports medicine clinics
	• Hand injury rehab clinics
	• Women's health clinics
	• Wound care centers

Source: Data from Barr, K.W., and C.L. Breindel. 1995. Ambulatory care. In: *Health care administration: Principles, practices, structure, and delivery.* Gaithersburg, MD: Aspen Publishers, Inc.

Primary care is distinguished from secondary and tertiary care according to its duration, frequency, and level of intensity. *Secondary care* is usually short term, involving sporadic consultation from a specialist to provide expert opinion and/or surgical or other advanced interventions that primary care physicians (PCPs) are not equipped to perform. Secondary care thus includes hospitalization, routine surgery, specialty consultation, and rehabilitation. *Tertiary care* is the most complex level of care for conditions that are relatively uncommon. Typically, tertiary care is institution based, highly specialized, and technology driven. Much of tertiary care is rendered in large teaching hospitals, such as university hospitals. Examples include trauma care, burn treatment, neonatal intensive care, tissue transplants, and open heart surgery. In some instances, tertiary treatment may be extended, and the tertiary care physician may assume long-term responsibility for the bulk of the patient's care. It has been estimated that 75% to 85% of people in a general population require only primary care services in a given year, 10% to 12% require referrals to short-term secondary care services, and 5% to 10% use tertiary care specialists (Starfield 1994). These proportions vary in populations with special health care needs.

Definitions of primary care often focus on the type or level of services, such as prevention, diagnostic and therapeutic services, health education and counseling, and minor surgery. Although primary care specifically emphasizes these services, many specialists also provide the same spectrum of services. For example, the practice of most ophthalmologists has a large element of prevention, as well as diagnosis, treatment, follow-up, and minor surgery. Similarly, most cardiologists are engaged in health education and counseling. Hence, primary care should be more appropriately viewed as an approach to providing health care rather than as a set of specific services (Starfield 1994).

World Health Organization Definition

Traditionally, primary care has been the cornerstone of ambulatory care services. The World Health Organization (WHO) describes *primary health care* as:

> Essential health care based on practical, scientifically sound, and socially acceptable methods and technology made universally accessible to individuals and families in the community by means acceptable to them and at a cost that the community and the country can afford to maintain at every stage of their development in a spirit of self-reliance and self-determination. It forms an integral part of both the country's health system of which it is the central function and the main focus of the overall social and economic development of the community. It is the first level of contact of individuals, the family, and the community with the national health system, bringing health care as close as possible to where people live and work and constitutes the first element of a continuing health care process (WHO 1978).

Three elements in this definition are particularly noteworthy for an understanding of primary care: point of entry, coordination of care, and essential care.

Point of Entry

Primary care is the point of entry into the health services system in which health care delivery is organized around primary care

(Starfield 1992). Primary care is the first contact a patient makes with the health care delivery system. This first contact feature is closely associated with the "gatekeeper" role of the primary care practitioner. *Gatekeeping* implies that patients do not visit specialists and are not admitted to a hospital without being referred by their PCPs. The interposition of primary care protects patients from unnecessary procedures and overtreatment (Franks et al. 1992).

The British National Health Service (NHS) is an example of a health care delivery system founded on the principles of gatekeeping. In the NHS, primary care is the single portal of entry to secondary care and acts as a filter so that 90% of care is provided outside hospitals in ambulatory care settings (Orton 1994). General practitioners (GPs) are primary care gatekeepers in the British system. In the United States, under certain managed care gatekeeping arrangements, patients initiate care with their PCPs and obtain authorization when specialized services are needed.

Coordination of Care

One of the main functions of primary care is to coordinate the delivery of health services between the patient and the myriad of delivery components of the system. Hence, in addition to providing basic services, primary care professionals serve as patient advisors and advocates. Coordination of an individual's total health care needs is meant to ensure continuity and comprehensiveness. These desirable goals of primary care are best achieved when the patient and provider have formed a close mutual relationship over time. Primary care can be regarded as the hub of the health care

delivery system wheel. The various components of the health care delivery system are located around the rim, and the spokes signify the coordination of continuous and comprehensive care (see Figure 7–1).

Countries whose health systems are oriented more toward primary care achieve better health levels, higher satisfaction with health services among the populations, and lower expenditures in the overall delivery of health care (Starfield 1994, 1998). Even in the United States, better health outcomes are achieved in states with higher ratios of PCPs and better availability of primary care (Shi 1994; Shi and Starfield 2000, 2001; Shi et al. 2002). Higher ratios of family and general physicians in the population are associated with lower hospitalization rates for conditions treatable with good primary care (Parchman and Culler 1994). Having a regular source of primary care also leads to lower ED visits and inappropriate specialty

Figure 7–1 The Coordination Role of Primary Care in Health Care Delivery.

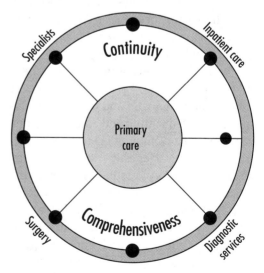

consults. It also provides a setting to manage chronic conditions so individuals can stay healthier over time (Sepulveda et al. 2008). Adults who have PCPs as their regular source of care experience lower mortality (Franks et al. 1998). Research has also shown that primary care may play an important role in mitigating the adverse health effects of income inequality (Shi et al. 1999). A higher proportion of PCPs in a given area has been shown to lead to lower spending on health care (Chernew et al. 2009).

Coordination of health care has certain definite advantages. Studies have shown that both the appropriateness and the outcomes of health care interventions are better when PCPs refer patients to specialists, as opposed to being self-referred (Bakwin 1945; Roos 1979).

Essential Care

Primary health care is regarded as essential health care. The goal of the health care delivery system is to optimize population health, not just the health of individuals who have the means to access health services. Achieving this goal requires that disparities across population subgroups be minimized to ensure equal access. Because financing of health care is a key element in determining access, universal access to primary care services is better achieved under a national health care program.

Institute of Medicine Definition

The Institute of Medicine (IOM) Committee on the Future of Primary Care recommended that primary care be the usual and preferred, but not the only, route of entry into the health care system. As part of this emphasis, the IOM defined primary care

as "the provision of integrated, accessible health care services by clinicians who are accountable for addressing a large majority of personal health care needs, developing a sustained partnership with patients, and practicing in the context of family and community" (Vanselow et al. 1995, 192).

The term "integrated" embodies the concepts of comprehensive, coordinated, and continuous services that provide a seamless process of care. Primary care is *comprehensive* because it addresses any health problem at any given stage of a patient's life cycle. *Coordination* ensures the provision of a combination of health services to best meet the patient's needs. *Continuity* refers to care over time by a single provider or a team of health care professionals. The IOM definition goes further to emphasize accessibility and accountability as key characteristics of primary care. *Accessibility* refers to the ease with which a patient can initiate an interaction with a clinician for any health problem. It includes efforts to eliminate barriers, such as those posed by geography, financing, culture, race, and language. The IOM Committee recognizes that both clinicians and patients have **accountability**. The clinical system is accountable for providing quality care, producing patient satisfaction, using resources efficiently, and behaving in an ethical manner. On the other hand, patients are responsible for their own health to the extent that they can influence it. Patients are also responsible for judicious use of resources when they need health care. Partnership between a patient and a clinician is based on mutual trust, respect, and responsibility.

Various countries have started to institute policies that hold primary care practices accountable for managing chronic conditions and meeting clinical standards. These include financial incentives and primary care practice redesign, with an emphasis on IT and teams to support effective, safe, patient-centered, coordinated, and efficient care.

The IOM definition recognizes that primary care clinicians must consider the influence of the family on a patient's health status and be aware of the patient's living conditions, family dynamics, and cultural background. Finally, exemplary primary care requires an understanding of and a responsibility for the community's health (Vanselow et al. 1995).

Primary Care and the Affordable Care Act

Provisions in the ACA related to primary care include: (1) increasing Medicare and Medicaid payments to primary care providers, (2) creating new incentives such as funding for scholarships and loan repayment for primary care providers working in underserved areas, (3) expanding the health center program and bolstering the capacity of health centers, and (4) establishing additional training programs such as establishing 11 Teaching Health Centers for training primary care providers. These measures are aimed at enhancing the primary care workforce and strengthening the primary care system, especially in underserved areas (Ku et al. 2011).

On the surface, the above measures may appear to be steps in the right direction, but, given the critical shortages in primary care (see Chapter 4), building a workforce cannot be accomplished in a short period of time. Current and prospective physicians will also evaluate factors other than the proposed incentives. For example, physicians may feel burdened by new regulatory demands and may feel frustrated if they end up spending a large share of their time complying with added regulations rather than seeing patients. Besides, increased reimbursement for PCPs proposed under the ACA is temporary and may not turn out to be a significant factor in their decisions to stay in practice, or to sway future medical students to enter primary care. Hence, the primary care system in the United States is expected to be overburdened with an influx of newly insured patients. If that happens, many of the goals of primary care just discussed may remain unrealized for a large segment of the US population. Moreover, gatekeeping is not a requirement of the ACA, which is also likely to create bottlenecks in specialty care.

New Directions in Primary Care
Patient-Centered Medical Home

The term "medical home" was first coined in 1967 and established for special-needs children whose health care needs required constant coordination. A *medical home* consists of an interdisciplinary team of physicians and allied health professionals who partner with patients and their families, taking responsibility for ongoing patient care using a team approach, technology, and evidence-based protocols to deliver and coordinate care. PCPs serve as advocates for patients to help them access services across the wide variety of health care services, ensuring that the patient's values, wishes, and directives are honored (Caudill et al. 2011).

There appear to be conflicting views on how to transform an existing practice into a medical home. Also, the principles behind medical homes bolster primary care's role, but evaluating and rewarding commitment to those principles have been a challenge (Dohan et al. 2013). Evaluation of medical homes varies across the board, but generally adopts the 2007 Joint Principles of the Patient-Centered Medical Home, which include having a personal physician, a physician-directed medical practice, whole person orientation, coordinated and/or integrated care, quality and safety, enhanced access to care, and payment for added value (American Academy of Family Physicians et al. 2007). A 2012 Report compared 10 provider survey tools designed to measure the extent to which a practice is a "patient-centered medical home." This report revealed that the top five content domains that received the most emphasis were care coordination, health information technology, quality measurement, patient engagement and self-management, and presence of policies (Burton et al. 2013).

A cross-national survey of seven countries with medical homes showed positive feedback from patients. The medical home could be a better setting to manage chronic care, especially if the chronic care model (CCM) is used. CCM is based on the idea that chronic conditions are best managed with multidisciplinary practice-based teams in productive interaction with an informed and motivated patient. Despite its potential, the idea of a medical home has been met with much hesitancy from physicians, who are skeptical of change and prefer the fee-for-service structure that pays more for acute care than preventive care (Berenson et al. 2008). Hence, medical homes remain more a concept than an actual system of care delivery. Implementation of this model is discussed in Chapter 14.

Community-Oriented Primary Care

Current thoughts about primary care delivery have extended beyond the traditional biomedical paradigm, which focuses on medical care for the individual in an encounter-based system. The broader biopsychosocial paradigm emphasizes the health of the population, as well as that of the individual (Lee 1994). *Community-oriented primary care* (COPC) is based on the concept of "ecology of medical care," which emphasizes the relations between the population and community, on the one hand, and personal health care, on the other (Van Weel et al. 2008). COPC incorporates the elements of good primary care delivery and adds a population-based approach to identifying and addressing community health problems. The main challenge has been how to bring together individual health needs in the larger context of community health needs.

COPC incorporates the ideals of both WHO and IOM in the delivery of primary care. The 1978 International Conference on Primary Health Care (held at Alma-Ata in the former Soviet Union, under the auspices of WHO) declared a philosophical vision of an affordable community-based primary health care system (WHO 1978). More recently, the WHO (2010) has offered some additional guidelines that encompass five key elements: (1) reducing exclusion and social disparities in health through universal coverage reforms, (2) organizing health services around people's needs and expectations, (3) integrating health into all sectors, (4) pursuing collaborative models of policy dialogue, and (5) increasing stakeholder participation. The application and adoption of these principles in actual practice, however, has not materialized in the United States. One fundamental problem is a lack of consensus on what a community is or should be. Hence, the very foundation appears to be missing. Assuming that a consensus on community can be reached, technological advances at their current stage of development can adequately reflect a community's health. Information technology (IT) can also assist in prioritizing and developing a course of action. Perhaps the biggest hurdles are workforce shortages and financial incentives. COPC requires a major transformation of the current system and faces the same implementation problems as medical homes. Nevertheless, some thoughts on implementing COPC are presented in Chapter 14.

Primary Care Providers

Physicians in general family practice are most commonly the providers of primary care in Europe. In the United States, primary care practitioners are not restricted to physicians trained in general and family practice. Providers of primary care include physicians trained in internal medicine, pediatrics, and obstetrics and gynecology. One cannot assume, however, that these various types of practitioners are equally skilled in rendering primary care services (Starfield 1994). Unless a medical training program is dedicated to providing instruction in primary care, significant differences are likely to exist (Noble et al. 1992). In fact, some controversy and competition have arisen among practitioners as to which specialists should be providing primary care. The specialty of family practice, in particular, represents a challenge to internal medicine in providing adult primary care and to pediatrics in providing child primary care.

As discussed in Chapter 4, it is also important to note the expanded role that nonphysician practitioners (NPPs) play in the delivery of primary care. In view of the increasing emphasis on health care cost containment, NPPs, such as nurse practitioners (NPs), physician assistants (PAs), and certified nurse midwives (CNMs), are in great demand in primary care delivery settings, particularly in medically underserved areas. Data from Medicaid MCOs demonstrate that patients receiving care from NPs at nurse-managed health centers experience significantly fewer emergency room visits, hospital inpatient days, and specialist visits and are at a significantly lower risk of giving birth to low-birth-weight infants, compared to patients in conventional health care (National Nursing Centers Consortium 2003). The expert role of PCPs, however, cannot be minimized.

Growth in Outpatient Services

The proportion of total surgeries performed in outpatient departments of community hospitals increased from 16.3% in 1980 to 63.6% in 2010 (Figure 7–2). The fact that it is not a simple trade-off is of some concern. The decline in inpatient procedures has actually been outweighed by the growth of ambulatory procedures. Also, for patients older than 65 years of age, the rate of inpatient surgeries has not decreased (Kozak et al. 1999). According to Russo et al. (2010), the 10 most common ambulatory surgeries performed in community hospitals in 28 states were colonoscopy and biopsy (18.1% of all ambulatory surgeries); upper gastrointestinal endoscopy and biopsy (10.8%); lens and cataract procedures (5.5%); diagnostic cardiac catheterization, coronary arteriography (3.8%); debridement of wound, infection, or burn (2.6%); excision of semilunar cartilage

Figure 7–2 Percentage of Total Surgeries Performed in Outpatient Departments of US Community Hospitals, 1980–2010.

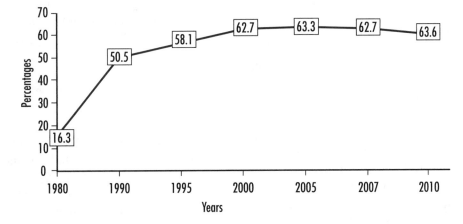

Source: Data from *Health, United States, 2012,* p. 307, National Center for Health Statistics, US Department of Health and Human Services.

of knee (2.5%); cholecystectomy and common duct exploration (2.5%); tonsillectomy and/or adenoidectomy (2.5%); inguinal and femoral hernia repair (2.1%); and other excisions of the cervix and uterus (2.1%).

Over the years, several noteworthy changes have been instrumental in shifting the delivery of health care from inpatient to outpatient settings. These changes can be broadly classified as reimbursement, technological factors, utilization control factors, physician practice factors, and social factors.

Reimbursement

Until the 1980s, health insurance coverage was usually more generous for inpatient services than for outpatient services. For years, many interventions that could have been performed safely and effectively on an outpatient basis remained inpatient procedures, because third-party reimbursement for outpatient care was limited. These payment policies began to change during the 1980s. In response, hospitals aggressively developed outpatient services to offset declining inpatient income.

In the mid-1980s, Medicare substituted a prospective payment system (PPS) for the cost-plus system to reimburse inpatient hospital services (see Chapter 6). PPS reimbursement based on diagnosis-related groups (DRGs) provides fixed case-based payment to hospitals. The outpatient sector, on the other hand, had no payment restrictions. Hospitals, therefore, had a strong incentive to minimize inpatient lengths of stay and to provide continued treatment in outpatient settings. To contain costs in the mushrooming outpatient sector, in 2000, Medicare implemented prospective reimbursement mechanisms, such as the Medicare Outpatient Prospective Payment System (OPPS) for services provided in hospital outpatient departments and home health resource groups (HHRGs) for home health care (see Chapter 6). Cost-containment strategies adopted by managed care also stress lower inpatient use, with a corresponding emphasis on outpatient services.

Technological Factors

Development of new diagnostic and treatment procedures and less invasive surgical methods has made it possible to provide services in outpatient settings that previously required hospital stays. Shorter acting anesthetics are now available. The diffusion of arthroscopes, laparoscopes, lasers, and other minimally invasive technologies has made many surgical procedures less traumatic. These modern procedures have dramatically curtailed recuperation time, which has made same-day surgical procedures very common. Many office-based physicians have expanded their capacity to perform outpatient diagnostic, treatment, and surgical services because acquisition of technology has become more feasible and cost effective.

Utilization Control Factors

To discourage lengthy hospital stays, payers have instituted prior authorization policies for inpatient admission, as well as close monitoring during hospitalization. Chapter 9 discusses the common utilization control methods.

Physician Practice Factors

The growth of managed care and the consolidation by large hospital-centered institutions weakened physician autonomy and professional control over the delivery of medical care. Physicians also lost income. To counter these forces, an increasing number of physicians have broken their ties with hospitals and started their own specialized care centers, such as ambulatory surgery centers and cardiac care centers. In specialized ambulatory care centers, physicians find that they can perform more procedures

in less time and earn higher incomes (Jackson 2002). Higher volumes may also be associated with better quality. Such factors may be behind the growth in specialized centers of excellence for cataract and hernia surgeries and cardiac procedures.

Social Factors

Patients have a strong preference for receiving health care in home- and community-based settings. Unless absolutely necessary, most patients do not want to be institutionalized. Staying in their own homes gives people a strong sense of independence and control over their lives, elements considered important for quality of life.

Large hospitals have traditionally been located in congested urban centers. Increasing numbers of suburbanites have perceived these locations as inconvenient. Hence, many freestanding outpatient centers and satellite clinics operated by inner city hospitals are now located in the suburbs.

Types of Outpatient Care Settings and Methods of Delivery

The services described in this section are not always operated independent of each other. For example, a hospital may operate physician clinics as well as some of the freestanding facilities described here. Also, in a constantly evolving system, new settings and methods are likely to emerge. The various settings for outpatient service delivery found in the US health care delivery system can be grouped as:

• Private practice
• Hospital-based services

- Freestanding facilities
- Retail clinics
- Mobile medical, diagnostic, and screening services
- Home health care
- Hospice services
- Ambulatory long-term care services
- Public health services
- Community health centers
- Free clinics
- Telephone access
- Complementary and alternative medicine

Private Practice

Physicians, as office-based practitioners, are the backbone of ambulatory care and constitute the vast majority of primary care services. Most visits entail relatively limited examination and testing, and encounters with the physician are generally brief. Office waiting time is typically longer than the actual time spent with the physician.

In the past, the solo practice of medicine and small partnerships attracted the most practitioners. Self-employment offered a degree of independence not generally available in large organizational settings. Today, most physicians are affiliated with group practices or institutions, such as hospitals and MCOs. Several factors account for this shift, including uncertainties created by rapid changes in the health care delivery system, contracting by MCOs with consolidated rather than solo entities, competition from large health care delivery organizations, high cost of operating a solo practice, complexity of billings and collections in a multiple-payer system, and increased external demands, such as the necessity of having up-to-date IT systems. Group practice and other organizational arrangements offer the benefits of a patient referral network, negotiating leverage with MCOs, sharing overhead expenses, ease of obtaining coverage from colleagues for personal time off, and attractive starting salaries, with benefits and profit-sharing plans.

Group practice of medicine in the United States has experienced a sharp increase (Figure 7–3). An estimated one-fourth of all US physicians now practice in a group clinic (SMG Solutions 2000). Most of these groups are small, with about 69% having no more than 6 physicians. Of these, 27% have 7 to 25 physicians. Only 4% have 26 or more physicians; however, nearly one-half of all physicians working in

Figure 7–3 Growth in the Number of Medical Group Practices.

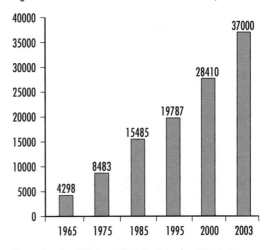

Source: Data from VHA Inc. and Deloitte & Touche, *1997 Environmental assessment: Redesigning health care for the millennium*, Irving, TX: VHA Inc.; SMG Solutions, *2000 Report and directory: Medical group practices*, Chicago, IL: SMG Solutions; Medical Group Management Association. Medical Group Fast Facts. http://www.mgma.com/uploadedFiles/Store_Content/Surveys_and_Benchmarking/8523-Table-of-Content-MGMA-Performance-and-Practices-of-Successful-Medical-Groups.pdf. Accessed January 2014.

group practices have 26 or more partners. In other words, roughly 4% of group practices employ nearly one-half of all physicians.

Group practice clinics also offer important advantages to patients. In many instances, patients can receive up-to-date diagnostic, treatment, pharmaceutical, and certain surgical services. All but the most advanced secondary and tertiary procedures can be performed within these large clinics. Patients also often see cross-referrals among partner physicians located near each other as an added convenience. Apart from physicians, other private practitioners often work in solo or group practice settings, for example, dentists; optometrists; podiatrists; psychologists; and physical, occupational, and speech therapists.

Figure 7–4 shows the distribution of total ambulatory visits among physicians' offices, hospital-based outpatient departments, and hospital EDs. In 2009, approximately 80.4% of all ambulatory

care visits occurred in physicians' offices. Hospitals have made substantial strides gaining market share for outpatient services.

Hospital-Based Outpatient Services

Only a few years ago, hospital administrators regarded outpatient departments of urban hospitals with certain contempt. The outpatient department was often viewed as the "stepchild" of the institution and the least popular area of the hospital in which to work. Even today, certain hospital outpatient clinics in inner city areas may function as the community's safety net, providing primary care to medically indigent and uninsured populations. For the most part, however, outpatient services are now a key source of profit for hospitals. Consequently, hospitals have expanded their outpatient departments, and utilization has grown (see Figure 7–4). This trend is the result of fierce competition in the health care industry in which MCOs

Figure 7–4 Ambulatory care visits in the United States.

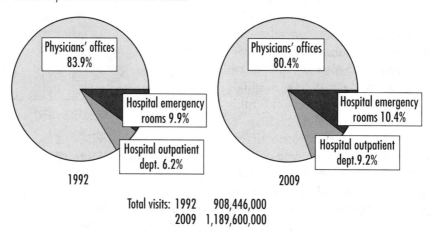

Total visits: 1992   908,446,000
                2009 1,189,600,000

Source: Data from National Center for Health Statistics, United States Department of Health and Human Services. *Statistical Abstracts of United States,* 2001, p. 108; and *Statistical Abstracts of United States,* 2012, p. 117.

emphasizing preventive and outpatient care have waged a relentless drive to cut costs. As hospitals have seen inpatient revenues steadily erode, they have begun sprucing up and expanding outpatient services.

A continuum of inpatient and outpatient services developed by a hospital offers opportunities for cross-referral among services to keep patients within the same delivery system. A hospital providing both inpatient and outpatient services can enhance its revenues by referring postsurgical cases to its affiliated units for rehabilitation and home care follow-up. Patients receiving various types of outpatient services constitute an important source of referrals back to hospitals for inpatient care. A hospital can thus expand its patient base.

Prior to 1985, outpatient care had less than 15% of the total gross patient revenue for all US hospitals. This ratio has now grown to nearly 40% (AHA 2006). Given the growing competition in the delivery of outpatient services, hospitals and hospital systems have launched specialized services, such as sports medicine, women's health, and renal dialysis. Many hospitals have also developed health promotion/disease prevention and health fitness programs as outreaches to the communities they serve.

Most hospital-based outpatient services can be broadly classified into five main types: clinical, surgical, emergency, home health, and women's health.

Clinical Services

Acquisition of group practices has enabled hospitals to increase their market share for outpatient care. Downstream referrals for inpatient, surgical, and other specialized services have generated additional revenues

for these hospitals. Both public and private nonprofit hospitals located in inner city locations provide uncompensated care to patients who do not have access to private practitioners' offices for routine care. The amount of uncompensated care should decrease as more people gain access under the ACA. Teaching hospitals operate various clinics, offering highly specialized, research-based services.

Surgical Services

Hospital-based ambulatory surgery centers provide same-day surgical care; patients are sent home after a few hours of recovery time following surgery. Follow-up care generally continues in the physician's office. In outpatient medical procedures, hospitals have the upper hand over freestanding centers (see Figure 7–5).

Figure 7–5 Medical Procedures by Location.

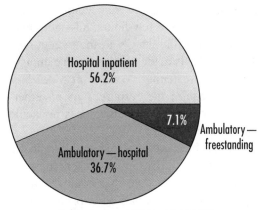

Total procedures (1996) = 71,904,000

Source: Data from Vital and Health Statistics: *Ambulatory and Inpatient Procedures in the United States, 1996,* p. 25, November 1998, National Center for Health Statistics, US Department of Health and Human Services.

Emergency Services

The ED has been a vital outpatient component of many community hospitals. The main purpose of this department is to have services available around the clock for patients who are acutely ill or injured, particularly those with serious or life-threatening conditions requiring immediate attention. When deemed medically appropriate, prompt hospitalization can occur directly from the ED. The department is commonly staffed by physicians who have specialized training in emergency medicine, and various specialists are on call. In small hospitals, the staff may be members of the regular medical staff in rotation. Another option is to contract ED staffing to physician groups specializing in emergency medicine.

Weinerman and colleagues (1966) defined three categories of conditions for which patients present themselves to the ED: *emergent conditions* are critical and require immediate medical attention, time delay is harmful to the patient, and the disorder is acute and potentially threatening to life or function. *Urgent conditions* require medical attention within a few hours, a longer delay presents possible danger to the patient, and the disorder is acute but not severe enough to be life threatening. *Nonurgent conditions* do not require the resources of an emergency service, and the disorder is nonacute or minor in severity.

It has been well documented that, in the United States, EDs are overused for nonurgent or routine care that could be more appropriately addressed in a primary care setting. Actually, fewer than one-half of the visits are for emergency conditions (McCaig and Burt 2002). Reasons for nonurgent use of the ED include unavailability of primary care, erroneous self-assessment of severity of ailment or injury, the 24-hour open-door policy, convenience, socioeconomic stress, psychiatric comorbidities, and a lack of social support (Liggins 1993; Padgett and Brodsky 1992). Moreover, the Emergency Medical Treatment and Active Labor Act of 1986 (EMTALA) requires screening and evaluation of every patient, necessary stabilizing treatment, and admitting when necessary, regardless of ability to pay. Thus, EDs often function as a public "safety net."

The uninsured and people on Medicaid use disproportionately more ED services than those who have private insurance coverage (McCaig and Burt 2002). Many private physicians do not provide services to Medicaid enrollees because of low reimbursement, which leaves people on Medicaid without a regular source of primary care (McNamara et al. 1993).

Crowding in EDs has also been exacerbated by hospital and ED closings nationwide. In 1992, approximately 6,000 hospitals had EDs; less than 4,000 remain today. Yet, the demand for ED visits has increased considerably, as reflected by the growth in the annual number of ED visits from 93.4 million to 110.2 million between 1994 and 2004 (McCaig and Newar 2006). Because of overcrowding, EDs must use triage mechanisms to screen patients according to the level of severity.

Because EDs require high-tech facilities and highly trained personnel and must be accessible 24 hours a day, the costs are high and services are not designed for nonurgent care (Williams 1993). Inappropriate use of emergency services wastes precious resources. Hence, alternatives to the ED for nonurgent and routine care are critically needed, a problem that reverts back to the nation's inadequate primary care infrastructure. Precisely for this reason, the ACA is unlikely to have any material impact on the overuse of EDs for nonurgent conditions.

Home Health Care

Many hospitals have opened separate home health departments, which provide mainly postacute care and rehabilitation therapies. Hospitals have entered the home health business to keep discharged patients within the hospital system. Hospitals operate about 24% of all Medicare-certified home health agencies in the United States (National Association for Home Care and Hospice 2004). Home health care is discussed in detail later in this chapter.

Women's Health Centers

Emerging recognition in the 1980s of the prominence of women as a major health market led medical institutions to develop specialized women's health centers in hospital-based and/or hospital-affiliated settings. Women's health is discussed in greater detail in Chapter 11. Following are some of the reasons behind the growth of women's centers:

- Women are the major users of health care. They seek health care more often than men do. Morbidity is greater among women than among men, even after childbearing-related conditions are factored out.

- A change in philosophy in American culture toward women, including gender equality.

- A recognition that the female majority in the United States will continue to grow, as the aging population includes more females. Table 7–2 shows current population trends.

Hospital-sponsored women's health centers have a variety of service delivery models on a continuum that includes telephone information and referral, educational programs, health screening and diagnostics, comprehensive primary care for women, and mental health services. In addition to services in obstetrics, gynecology, and primary care, women's health centers offer mammography, ultrasound, osteoporosis screening, and other health screenings.

Freestanding Facilities

Freestanding medical clinics include walk-in clinics; urgent care centers; surgicenters;

Table 7–2 Growth in Female US Resident Population by Age Groups Between 1980 and 2011 (in thousands)

	<15	15 to 44	45 to 64	65 to 74	75 to 84	85+	Total
				Age Groups			
1980	25,073	52,833	23,342	8,824	4,862	1,559	116,493
2011	29,931	62,516	42,403	12,005	7,602	3,843	158,301
Growth	4,858	9,683	19,061	3,181	2,740	2,284	41,808

Source: Data from *Health, United States, 2012*, p. 45.

and other outpatient facilities, such as outpatient rehabilitation centers, optometric centers, and dental clinics. These clinics, which are often owned or controlled by private corporations, commonly employ practitioners on salary.

Walk-in clinics provide ambulatory services, ranging from basic primary care to urgent care, but they are used on a nonroutine, episodic basis. The main advantages of these clinics are convenience of location, evening and weekend hours, and availability of services on a "walk-in" (no appointment) basis. *Urgent care centers* offer extended hours; many are open 24 hours a day, 7 days a week and accept patients with no appointments. These centers offer a wide range of routine services for basic and acute conditions on a first-come, first-served basis, but they are not comparable to hospital EDs. *Surgicenters* are freestanding ambulatory surgery centers independent of hospitals. They usually provide a full range of services for the types of surgery that can be performed on an outpatient basis and do not require overnight hospitalization.

Outpatient rehabilitation centers provide physical therapy, occupational therapy, and speech pathology services. In the past, generous Medicare reimbursement attracted various operators to open outpatient rehabilitation centers, but caps were instituted under the Balanced Budget Act of 1997. Therapy caps are determined on a calendar year basis. For physical therapy and speech–language pathology services combined, the annual cap per patient was $1,870 for 2011. For occupational therapy services, the cap was $1,870 for 2011. Deductible and coinsurance amounts applied to therapy services count toward the amount accrued before a cap is reached (CMS 2011b).

Neighborhood optical centers providing vision services have been replacing many office-based opticians. Other freestanding facilities include audiology clinics, dental centers, hemodialysis centers, pharmacies, and suppliers of *durable medical equipment* (DME). DME suppliers furnish ostomy supplies, hospital beds, oxygen tanks, walkers, wheelchairs, and many other types of supplies and equipment. A growing number of the various types of freestanding facilities are part of large regional and nationwide chains, which are opening new facilities at an unprecedented rate in new geographic locations.

Retail Clinics

Opening of small clinics, staffed mostly by nonphysician practitioners, in shopping malls and large retail stores has been a relatively recent phenomenon. Once viewed as a threat to PCPs, retail clinics are increasingly viewed as complementary services that are conveniently available to people for minor ailments. Because of their low cost of operation, even most of the uninsured can pay for the services out of pocket. Because of their low cost, payers have also started to establish contracts with retail clinics. By 2015, the number of retail clinics is expected to double to more than 2,800 (Health Facilities Management 2013).

Mobile Medical, Diagnostic, and Screening Services

Ambulance service and first aid treatment provided to the victims of severe illness, accidents, and disasters by trained emergency medical technicians (EMTs) are the most commonly encountered mobile medical services. Such services are also referred to as prehospital medicine. Early attention following traumatic injury is often lifesaving. EMTs are specially trained to provide such attention at the site and in transit to the hospital. Most ambulance personnel have a Basic-EMT rating. Advanced training can lead to EMT-Paramedic certification. Paramedics are trained to administer emergency drugs and provide advanced life support emergency medical services. Examples include intravenous administration of fluids and drugs, treatment for shock, electrocardiograms, electrical interventions to support cardiac function, and endotracheal intubation (insertion of a tube as an air passage through the trachea).

To provide a speedy response to emergencies, most urban centers have developed formal emergency medical systems that incorporate all area hospital EDs, along with transportation and communication systems. Most such communities have established 911 emergency phone lines to provide immediate access to those needing emergency care. An ambulance is dispatched by a central communications center, which also identifies and alerts the hospital most appropriately equipped to deal with the type of emergency and located closest to the site where the emergency has occurred. Specialized ambulance services or advanced life support ambulances include mobile coronary care units, shock-trauma vans, and disaster relief vans. They are staffed by paramedics and EMTs who have advanced training.

Mobile medical services also constitute an efficient and convenient way to provide certain types of routine health services. Mobile eye care, podiatric care, and dental care units, for example, can be brought to a nursing home or retirement center where they can efficiently serve many patients residing in the facility. They are a convenient service for the patients, many of whom are frail elderly, who can then avoid an often difficult and tiring trip to a regular clinic.

Mobile diagnostic services include mammography and magnetic resonance imaging (MRI). Such mobile units take advanced diagnostic services to small towns and rural communities. They offer the advantages of convenience to patients and cost efficiency in the delivery of diagnostic care.

Health screening vans, staffed by volunteers who are trained professionals and operated by various nonprofit organizations, are often seen at malls and fair sites. Various types of health education and health promotion services and screening checks, such as blood pressure and cholesterol screening, are commonly performed for anyone who walks in.

Home Health Care

Home health care brings certain types of services to patients in their own homes. Without home services, the only alternative for most such patients would be institutionalization in a hospital or nursing home. Home health is consistent with the philosophy of maintaining people in the least restrictive environment possible.

Before the home health boom, the Visiting Nurse Associations (VNAs) provided nursing and other services in patients' homes. The first VNAs were established in Buffalo, Boston, and Philadelphia in 1885 and 1886 (Wilson and Neuhauser 1985). In 2009, VNAs accounted for only 5% of all Medicare-certified agencies (National Association for Home Care and Hospice 2010).

Following a lawsuit in 1989, Medicare rules for home health care were clarified, making it easier for Medicare beneficiaries to receive home health services. Home health care is no longer restricted as a post-acute service following discharge from a hospital. Patients are eligible to receive services under Medicare if they are homebound, have a plan of treatment and periodic review by a physician, and require intermittent or part-time skilled nursing care and/or rehabilitation therapies (Klees 2010).

Home health services typically include nursing care, such as changing dressings, monitoring medications, and providing help with bathing, and short-term rehabilitation, such as physical therapy, occupational therapy, and speech therapy. Other services include homemaker services, such as meal preparation, shopping, transportation, and some specific household chores. Not every home health agency provides all of these services, however. For example, home health agencies often assume responsibility for arranging for DME, but private DME companies actually furnish the equipment.

Under Medicare, home health benefits do not include full-time nursing care, food, blood, and drugs. Since the early 1980s, specialized high-technology home therapies have also proliferated. Before that, those services could only be delivered in hospitals. Such specialized services include intravenous antibiotics, oncology therapy, hemodialysis, parenteral and enteral nutrition, and ventilator care (Evashwick 1993). For specialized services, home health care is cost effective and enhances the patient's quality of life. For example, home hemodialysis costs about one-third of what in-center dialysis costs. Especially for younger patients, the option of dialyzing at home provides greater independence and flexibility, such as the ability to dialyze at night. Overall costs were reduced, on average,

by more than $13,000 per patient when a pulmonary specialty team managed the in-home health care of patients suffering from advanced chronic obstructive pulmonary disease (COPD) because of decreased use of hospital, emergency department, and skilled nursing facility resources (Steinel and Madigan 2003).

Figure 7–6 shows the demographic characteristics of home health care patients in 2000. According to the 2007 National Home and Hospice Care Survey, 1.46 million home health care patients were in the United States (National Center for Health Statistics 2010). Home health care patients tended to be aged

Figure 7–6 Demographic Characteristics of US Home Health Patients, 2000 and 2007.

Gender

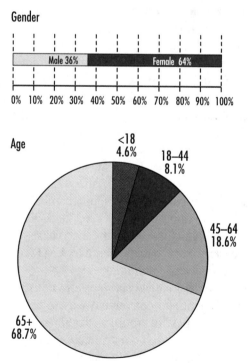

Source: Data from National Center for Health Statistics, *2000 National Home and Hospice Care Survey.*

65 and over (69%), female (64%), and white (82%). Because of variations in data sources, national expenditures for home health care are difficult to calculate. However, estimates from the Centers for Medicare and Medicaid Services (2011b) indicate that total expenditures for home health were $70.2 billion in 2010. Medicare is the largest single payer for home care services. It financed approximately $31.5 billion of home health care expenditures in 2010, compared to $26.2 billion for Medicaid, $4.5 billion for private insurance, and $5.0 billion for out-of-pocket payments (CMS 2011a). Payments to home health agencies were sharply cut under the Balanced Budget Act of 1997. As a result, home health expenditures accounted for 4.2% of total Medicare spending in 2004, compared to 9% in 1997 (National Association for Home Care and Hospice 2004, 2010).

Medicaid payments for home care are divided into three main categories: the traditional home health benefit, which is a federally mandated service provided by all states, and two optional programs—the personal care option and home and community-based waivers. Together, these three home health services represent a relatively small but growing portion of total Medicaid payments.

Various private payers also prefer to minimize the high costs associated with hospital inpatient care and opt for home health services wherever possible. Private home health care is increasingly financed through MCOs. Hence, home health care is no longer synonymous with long-term, home-based care for the elderly, although the elderly are the largest users of home health care.

Reimbursement cuts implemented under the Balanced Budget Act had a marked impact on the home health industry. Between 1997 and 2000, the number of home health agencies in the United States declined from

15,069 to 13,067 (Aventis Pharmaceuticals 2001; Hoechst Marion Roussel 1999). This trend continued through 2007 (CDC 2011b). Thirty percent of Medicare-certified agencies are hospital based, 40% are proprietary, and the remaining 24% have other types of ownership. Figure 7–7 shows sources of revenue and average distribution of revenues from these sources for home health care. Tables 7–3 and 7–4 provide additional statistics.

The ACA made significant changes to home health care, beginning in 2014. A proposed rule was issued in July 2013 to update Medicare's Home Health Prospective Payment System payment rates and wage index for 2014. Payments to home health agencies are expected to decrease in 2014. It is estimated that funding will be cut by 14%

Figure 7–7 Estimated Payments for Home Care by Payment Source, 2010.

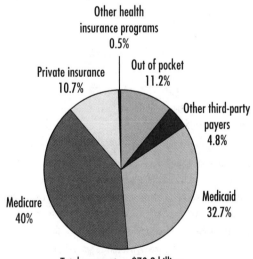

Other health insurance programs 0.5%

Private insurance 10.7%

Out of pocket 11.2%

Other third-party payers 4.8%

Medicaid 32.7%

Medicare 40%

Total payments = $70.2 billion

Source: Data from Centers for Medicare & Medicaid Services, Office of the Actuary, *National Health Expenditures Projections: 2011–2021.* https://www.cms.gov/NationalHealthExpendData/downloads/proj2009.pdf. Accessed January 2014.

Table 7–3 Selected Organizational Characteristics of US Home Health and Hospice Care Agencies: United States, 2007

Characteristic	Home Health Care[1]	Hospice Care[1]
	Number (standard error)	
All agencies[2]	12,300 (746)	3,700 (250)
	Percent distributions (standard error)	
All agencies[2]	100.0 …	100.0 …
Ownership		
Proprietary	69.7 (3.2)	34.0 (3.9)
Voluntary nonprofit	23.5 (2.9)	55.5 (4.0)
Government and other	6.9 (1.2)	10.6 (2.9)
Chain affiliation		
Part of a chain	30.5 (3.8)	23.7 (3.3)
Not part of a chain	69.5 (3.8)	76.3 (3.3)
Medicare certification status		
Certified as home health care agency	81.6 (4.0)	… …
Certified as hospice care agency	… …	93.4 (2.9)
Medicaid certification status		
Certified as home health care agency	80.7 (3.9)	… …
Certified as hospice care agency	… …	86.4 (3.4)
Geographic region		
Northeast	13.5 (3.3)	14.8 (2.5)
Midwest	22.1 (3.2)	22.6 (2.5)
South	50.3 (4.2)	44.5 (4.0)
West	14.1 (2.6)	18.2 (3.3)
Location		
Metropolitan statistical area (MSA)[3]	73.6 (1.9)	66.8 (2.5)
Micropolitan statistical area[4]	13.8 (1.2)	19.5 (1.7)
Neither	12.6 (1.2)	13.7 (1.2)

…Category not applicable.

[1]Include agencies that provide both home health and hospice care services (mixed).

[2]Include agencies that provide home health care services, hospice care services, or both types of services and currently or recently served home health and/or hospice care patients. Agencies that provided only homemaker services or housekeeping services, assistance with instrumental activities of daily living (IADLs), or durable medical equipment and supplies were excluded from the survey.

[3]A metropolitan statistical area is a county or group of contiguous counties that contains at least one urbanized area of 50,000 or more population. May also contain other counties that are economically and socially integrated with the central county as measured by commuting.

[4]A micropolitan statistical area is a nonmetropolitan county or group of contiguous nonmetropolitan counties that contains an urban cluster of 10,000 to 49,999 persons. May include surrounding counties if there are strong economic ties among the counties, based on commuting patterns.

Note: Numbers may not add to totals because of rounding and/or because estimates and percent distributions include a category of unknowns not reported in the table. Percentages are based on the unrounded numbers.

Source: Reproduced from National Center for Health Statistics. 2010. Comparison of Home and Hospice Care Agencies by Organizational Characteristics and Services Provided: United States, 2007. National Health Statistics Reports; no 30. Hyattsville, MD.

Table 7–4 Home Health and Hospice Care Patients Served at the Time of the Interview, by Agency Type and Number of Patients: United States, 2007

Number of Patients	Home Health Care Only	Home Health and Hospice Care (Mixed)
	Mean (standard error)	
Number of home health care patients	109.0 (9.2)	177.7 (17.7)
	Percent distributions (standard error)	
Total	100.0 ...	100.0 ...
0–25	†16.0 (4.3)	†9.8 (2.4)
26–50	†21.3 (4.2)	†25.1 (6.4)
51–100	29.0 (4.0)	18.4 (3.1)
101–150	†10.8 (2.3)	†9.4 (1.9)
151 or more	23.0 (3.5)	37.4 (4.8)

Number of Patients	Hospice Care Only	Home Health and Hospice Care (Mixed)
	Mean (standard error)	
Number of hospice care patients	78.1 (6.4)	39.1 (5.7)
	Percent distributions (standard error)	
Total..	100.0 ...	100.0 ...
0–25	29.5 (5.4)	57.6 (5.6)
26–50	22.1 (4.9)	24.5 (5.9)
51–100	21.2 (4.0)	†6.3 (1.4)
101–150..	†9.9 (2.5)	* (*)
151 or more..	†11.6 (2.3)	* (*)

...Category not applicable.

†Estimate does not meet standards of reliability or precision because the sample size is between 30 and 59 or the sample size is greater than 59 but has a relative standard error of 30% or more.

*Estimate does not meet standards of reliability or precision because the sample size is fewer than 30.

Note: Unknowns are excluded when calculating estimates. There was 1 (unweighted) case with unknown number of home health care patients and 19 (unweighted) cases with unknown number of hospice care patients. Percentages are based on the unrounded numbers.

Source: Reproduced from National Center for Health Statistics. 2010. Comparison of Home and Hospice Care Agencies by Organizational Characteristics and Services Provided: United States, 2007. *National Health Statistics Reports*, no 30. Hyattsville, MD.

between 2014 and 2017, and will save the Medicare program approximately $290 million. Under the ACA, quality reporting is associated with payment to home health agencies (Caron and Isbey 2013; CMS 2013a; National Association for Home Care & Hospice 2013). This is one example of cuts in Medicare that will partially fund health insurance expansion under the ACA. The effects on home health services and the elderly users of these services will not be known for some time. The Medicare Independence at Home Demonstration Program, created by the ACA, is testing a service delivery and payment incentive model that uses home-based primary care teams for Medicare beneficiaries with multiple chronic conditions, with the objective of improving health outcomes and reducing expenditures. These home-based primary care teams are directed by physicians and nurse practitioners. The demonstration will award incentives to providers who succeed in reducing Medicare expenditures and meet specified quality measures (CMS 2013d, Federal Register 2013).

Hospice Services

The term *hospice* refers to a cluster of comprehensive services for the terminally ill with a medically determined life expectancy of 6 months or less. Over one-half of the patients are diagnosed with cancer upon admission. Hospice, whose programs provide services that address the special needs of dying persons and their families, is a method of care, not a location, and services are taken to patients and their families wherever they are located. Thus, hospice can be a part of home health care when the services are provided in the patient's home. In other instances, hospice services are taken to patients in nursing homes, retirement centers, or hospitals. Services can be organized out of a hospital, nursing home, freestanding hospice facility, or home health agency. The dollar outlays in these four types of hospice operations give a fair indication of the volume of services provided through each setting (see Figure 7–8).

Hospice regards the patient and family as the unit of care. This special kind of care includes:

- meeting the patient's physical needs, with an emphasis on pain management and comfort;
- meeting the patient's and family's emotional and spiritual needs;
- support for the family members before and after the patient's death; and
- focus on maintaining the quality of life rather than prolonging life (Miller 1996).

The two primary areas of emphasis in hospice care are (1) pain and symptom management, which is referred to as *palliation*,

Figure 7–8 Medicare Dollar Outlays by Type of Hospice, 2003.

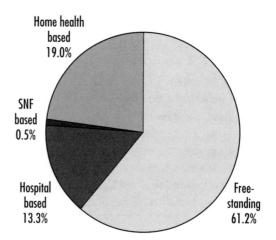

Source: Data from Centers for Medicare & Medicaid Services 2005.

and (2) psychosocial and spiritual support according to the holistic model of care (see Chapter 2). Counseling and spiritual help are made available to relieve anguish and help the patient deal with his or her death. Social services include help with arranging final affairs. Apart from medical, nursing, and social services staff, hospice organizations rely heavily on volunteers.

The idea of providing comprehensive care to terminally ill patients was first promoted by Dame Cicely Saunders in the 1960s in England. In the United States, the first hospice was established in 1974 by Sylvia Lack in New Haven, Connecticut (Beresford 1989). Hospice organizations expanded after Medicare extended hospice benefits in 1983. Hospice is a cost-effective option for both private and public payers. It is estimated that for every dollar spent on hospice, Medicare saves $1.52 in Part A and Part B expenditures (National Hospice and Palliative Care Organization 2003). The difference in cost mainly reflects services that are not medically intensive. Many states now provide hospice benefits under Medicaid.

To receive Medicare certification, a hospice must meet these basic conditions:

- Physician certification that the patient's prognosis is for a life expectancy of 6 months or less
- Make nursing services, physician services, and drugs and biologics available on a 24-hour basis
- Provide nursing services under the supervision of a registered nurse
- Make arrangements for inpatient care when necessary
- Provide social services by a qualified social worker under the direction of a physician

- Make counseling services available to both the patient and the family, including bereavement support after the patient's death
- Provide needed medications, medical supplies, and equipment for pain management and palliation
- Provide physical, occupational, and speech therapy services when necessary
- Provide home health aide and homemaker services when needed

Under the provisions of the Balanced Budget Act of 1997, Medicare provides for two 90-day benefit periods. Subsequently, an unlimited number of 60-day periods are available, based on recertification by a physician that a patient has 6 months or less to live. Figure 7–9 shows the sources of coverage for hospice services.

In 2011, 1.65 million patients received hospice services; the average length of service was 69.1 days (National Hospice and Palliative Care Organization 2012). The majority of hospice patients were 65 years or older (83.3%), female (56.4%), and white (82.8%). The top diagnoses were cancer (37.7%), debility unspecified (13.9%), dementia (12.5%), heart disease (11.4%), and lung disease (8.5%).

There are approximately 5,300 hospice programs in the United States (National Hospice and Palliative Care Organization 2012). The majority of hospices are independent (57.5%), followed by hospital based (20.3%), home health agency based (16.8%), and nursing home based (5.2%). Medicare is the largest source of financing. Tables 7–3 and 7–4 provide additional statistics.

The ACA mandates a Hospice Quality Reporting Program for all Medicare-certified hospices. Beginning with fiscal year 2014,

Figure 7–9 Coverage of Patients for Hospice Care at the Time of Admission.

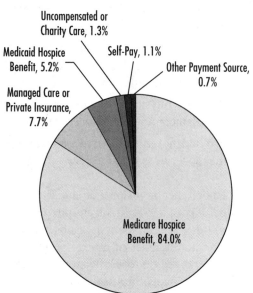

Uncompensated or Charity Care, 1.3%

Medicaid Hospice Benefit, 5.2%

Self-Pay, 1.1%

Other Payment Source, 0.7%

Managed Care or Private Insurance, 7.7%

Medicare Hospice Benefit, 84.0%

Source: Data from the National Hospice and Palliative Care Organization, *NHPCO Facts and Figures, Hospice Care in America.* 2012. http://www.nhpco.org/files/public/Statistics_Research/Hospice_Facts_Figures_Oct-2010.pdf.

failure to report results in a penalty of 2 percentage points reduction in the Annual Payment Update. Quality measures that must be reported are patients treated with an opioid who are given a bowel regimen, pain screening, pain assessment, dyspnea treatment, dyspnea screening, treatment preferences, and beliefs/values addressed (CMS 2013b, 2013c).

Ambulatory Long-Term Care Services

Long-term care has typically been associated with care provided in nursing homes, but two main types of settings—case management and adult day care—deliver

outpatient services. *Case management* provides coordination and referral among a variety of health care services. The objective is to find the most appropriate setting to meet a patient's health care needs. *Adult day care* complements informal care provided at home by family members with professional services available in adult day care centers during the normal workday. Chapter 10 discusses both services in more detail.

Public Health Services

Public health services in the United States are typically provided by local health departments, and the range of services offered varies greatly by locality. Generally, public health services are limited to well-baby care, venereal disease clinics, family planning services, screening and treatment for tuberculosis, and ambulatory mental health. Inner city, poor, and uninsured populations are the main beneficiaries of these services. School health programs in public schools fall under the public health domain and are limited to vision and hearing screening and assistance with dysfunctions that prevent learning. Ambulatory clinics in prisons also fall in the public health domain.

The public school setting is a growing area of practice for physical therapists, occupational therapists, and speech–language pathologists. They help children with special physical and emotional dysfunctions. The Individuals with Disabilities Education Act (IDEA) of 1975 (subject to reauthorization every 3 years) has been instrumental in allowing children with special needs to receive services in public schools so that they can obtain optimum access to education.

Community Health Centers

Creation of community health centers (CHCs)—formerly called neighborhood health centers—was authorized during the 1960s, under the Johnson Administration's war on poverty program, mainly to address health care needs in the medically underserved regions of the United States. The federal government determines the *medically underserved* designation to indicate a dearth of primary care providers and delivery settings, as well as poor health indicators for the populace. Such areas are often characterized by economic, geographic, or cultural barriers that limit access to primary health care for a large segment of the population. CHCs are required by law to locate in medically underserved areas and provide services to anyone seeking care, regardless of insurance status or ability to pay. Hence, CHCs are a primary care safety net for the nation's poor and uninsured in both inner city and rural areas.

CHCs are private, nonprofit organizations, but they operate under the auspices of the federal government. Section 330 of the Public Health Service Act provides federal grant funding for CHCs. They also heavily depend on funding through the Medicaid program. Private-pay patients are charged on sliding-fee scales, determined by the patient's income.

CHCs tailor their services to family-oriented primary and preventive health care and dental services (Shi et al. 2007). These centers have developed considerable expertise managing the health care needs of underserved populations. Many have developed systems of care that include outreach programs, case management, transportation, translation services, alcohol and drug abuse screening and treatment, mental health services, health education, and social services.

In 2009, CHCs served 21.1 million patients through 83.8 million patient visits. The majority of groups that utilize CHCs are vulnerable populations—93% of the patients were below the 200% federal poverty level and 36% were uninsured. Among special populations, more than 1.1 million homeless individuals, 903,089 agricultural workers, and 219,220 residents from public housing received services under this program (HRSA 2012).

Studies have shown that CHCs provide accessible quality care that is cost effective (NACHC 2013a, 2013b, 2013c). Because the majority of the population served belongs to vulnerable groups (i.e., low income, minorities, homeless), CHCs play an important role in reducing health disparities among these populations (NACHC 2013d).

CHCs formed the central element of President Bush's plan for expanding health care access to the uninsured and underserved. In 2002, the Bush Administration proposed a $1.5 billion budget to continue a long-term strategy that would add 1,200 new and expanded CHC sites over 5 years and serve an additional 6.1 million patients (Shi et al. 2007). The Obama Administration continued this trend of support. The American Recovery and Reinvestment Act of 2009 allocated $2 billion to CHCs to expand patient population, create new jobs, and meet the demands for primary care services (US DHHS 2011).

Components of the ACA that affect CHCs involve maintaining adequate funding and developing teaching health centers. In 2011, the ACA provided $1 billion to CHCs to expand primary care to nearly 11 million underserved Americans who did not have a regular source of care. The law also allows for a Title VII grant program to develop residency programs in CHCs to train the next generation of primary care providers (NACHC 2011).

The National Association of Community Health Centers' ACCESS for All Americans plan envisions reaching a total of 30 million patients by 2015 (NACHC 2013e). However, CHCs are likely to face future funding challenges. For example, Medicaid funding anticipated in the ACA may not be forthcoming in states that have chosen not to expand their Medicaid programs following the 2012 Supreme Court's ruling (see Chapter 3). In addition, the expected shortage of primary care physicians will limit the ability of CHCs to accomplish their expanded mission (NACHC 2013e).

Free Clinics

Modeled after the 19th century dispensary (see Chapter 3), the *free clinic* is a general ambulatory care center, serving primarily the poor, the homeless, and the uninsured. Free clinics have three main characteristics: (1) services are provided at no charge or at a very nominal charge, (2) they are not directly supported or operated by a government agency or health department, and (3) services are delivered mainly by trained volunteer staff. Free clinics focus on the delivery of primary care. Other services vary, depending on the number and training of their volunteer staff.

The number of free clinics has continued to grow nationally and is estimated at more than 1,200 (NAFC 2011). Although mainly a voluntary effort, it has taken the form of an organized movement. The National Association of Free Clinics focuses on the issues and needs of the free clinics and the people they serve in the United States.

Other Clinics

Federal funding is used to operate migrant health centers that serve transient farmworkers in agricultural communities, and rural health centers in isolated underserved rural areas. The Community Mental Health Center program was established to provide ambulatory mental health services in underserved areas.

Telephone Access

Telephone access is a means of bringing expert opinion and advice to the patient, especially during the hours when physicians' offices are closed. Referred to as *telephone triage*, this type of access has expanded under managed care. The example of the Park Nicollet Clinic of the Minneapolis, Minnesota Health System illustrates how such a system functions. The telephone call-in system operates 7 days a week, 24 hours a day. The system is staffed by specially trained nurses who receive patients' calls. Using a computer-based clinical decision support system (see Chapter 5), the nurse can access a patient's medical history and view the most recent radiology and laboratory test results. The decision support system enables the nurse to give instructions on how to deal with the patient's problem. Consultation with a primary care physician is done when necessary (Appleby 1995). The nurse can direct patients to appropriate medical services, such as an ED or a physician's office. The URAC Organization accredits telephone triage and health information programs.

Complementary and Alternative Medicine

Because of their tremendous growth, the role of complementary and alternative medicine (CAM)—also referred to as "nonconventional therapies," or "natural medicine"— in the delivery of health care cannot be ignored. Although the terms "complementary medicine" and "alternative medicine" are used synonymously, as they are here, technically there is a distinction between the two: Complementary treatments are used together with conventional medicine; alternative interventions are used instead of conventional medicine (Barnes et al. 2008).

In the United States, the dominant health care practice is the biomedicine-based allopathic medicine, which is also referred to as conventional medicine. Complementary and *alternative medicine*, or CAM, refers to the broad domain of all health care resources other than those intrinsic to biomedicine (CAM Research Methodology Conference 1997) and covers a heterogeneous spectrum of ancient to new approaches that purport to prevent or treat disease (Barnes et al. 2008).

CAM therapies include a wide range of treatments, such as homeopathy, herbal formulas, use of other natural products as preventive and treatment agents, acupuncture, meditation, yoga exercises, biofeedback, and spiritual guidance or prayer. Chiropractic is also largely regarded as a CAM treatment.

No particular settings of health care delivery are involved in CAM treatments. With few exceptions, most therapies are self-administered or at least require active patient participation. The types of trained and licensed health care professionals discussed in Chapter 4 are, generally, not involved in the delivery of unconventional care. A doctor of naturopathic medicine (ND) degree and Diplomate of the Homeopathic Academy of Naturopathic Physicians (DHANP) are offered in the United States. Also,

natural medicine–based private clinics are emerging across the United States. Even though the efficacy of most CAM treatments has not been scientifically established, their use has exploded. CAM's growth has happened mainly for these reasons:

- Most people who seek CAM therapies believe that they have already explored conventional Western treatments but have not been helped. Most have chronic disorders, such as persistent pain, for which Western medicine can usually offer only symptomatic relief rather than definitive treatment.

- People who want to avoid or delay certain complex surgeries or toxic allopathic treatments are persuaded that at least there is no harm in trying alternative treatments first.

- Most people feel empowered by access to a vast amount of medical and health-related information available through the Internet and feel in control to pursue what they think is best for their own health.

- Many patients report that they seek alternative therapies and individuals who practice them because they want practitioners to take the time to listen to them, understand them, and deal with their personal life, as well as their pathology. They believe that alternative practitioners will meet those needs (Gordon 1996).

Use of CAM therapies has been growing for several years in the United States. A landmark study by Eisenberg and colleagues (1998) estimated that between

1990 and 1997, the proportion of the US adult population over 18 years of age using alternative therapies increased from 33.8% (60 million) to 42.1% (83 million). Although the estimated number of visits to regular PCPs remained stable, visits to alternative medical practitioners increased by 47% (39 million in 1997 vs. 22 million in 1990). CAM use of provider-based therapies such as chiropractic care, massage, and acupuncture, grew significantly from 2002 to 2007, more so for whites than minorities (Su and Li 2011). The most common reasons given for seeking alternative therapies were back problems, allergies, fatigue, arthritis, and headaches. Approximately 38% of adults and 12% of children use at least one type of CAM. Use is most common among women with higher levels of education and income. Among the top three CAM therapies are natural products (e.g., fish oil, flaxseed, Echinacea), deep breathing, and meditation (Barnes et al. 2008). As a general rule, CAM therapies are not covered by health insurance, with the exception of chiropractic. Total expenditures on CAM for 2007 were $33.9 billion in out-of-pocket expenses, which amounted to 11.2% of total out-of-pocket expenditures for health care and 1.5% of total health care expenditures. The majority of CAM expenditures were for natural products, at $15.4 billion (Nahin et al. 2009).

Effective coordination of conventional medical services and CAM has the potential to save money, as well as improve quality. This is because, for some chronic problems, conventional medicine offers few proven benefits. Examples include psychosomatic ailments and cases in which patients have recurring complaints of unexplained painful symptoms or spells of dizziness. Such nagging complaints can rack up high costs and compromise an individual's quality of life. Lower cost therapies, such as stress management and meditation classes, can save numerous trips to physicians and costly diagnostic tests. One study found median expenditures to be $39 for CAM care, compared to $74.40 for conventional outpatient care (Lafferty et al. 2006).

CAM also appears to be popular in Europe, Canada, and other industrialized countries. Even though most of these countries provide universal access to medical care, a significant number of people try alternative treatments.

Given the growing public demand for complementary medicine and its claims for health promotion, disease prevention, and promise for certain chronic conditions, mainstream medicine has shown a growing interest in better understanding the value of alternative treatments. On the other hand, skepticism is justifiable because alternative medicine is predominantly unregulated. Also, the efficacy of most treatments and the safety of some have not been scientifically evaluated. Some recent findings suggest that cranberry juice cocktail has no effect on preventing recurrent urinary tract infections (Barbosa-Cesnik et al. 2011), but white tea extract has potential anti-cancer benefits (Mao et al. 2010), and Echinacea does not reduce the duration and severity of the common cold (Barrett et al. 2010). Only rigorous scientific inquiry and research-based evidence will bring about a genuine integration of alternative therapies into the conventional practice of medicine. A 2013 publication in the *Natural Medicine Journal* noted that published research studies have revealed that CAM therapies are cost-effective and may present cost savings, but more research is necessary on individual treatments (Tais and Oberg 2013).

Nevertheless, some developments are noteworthy. In 1993, Congress established the Office of Alternative Medicine (OAM), which became the National Center for Complementary and Alternative Medicine (NCCAM) in 1998. Budget allocations for the center have increased from $2 million in 1993 to $128.3 million in 2012 (NCCAM 2013). The center has three main objectives: (1) explore complementary and alternative healing practices in the context of rigorous science, (2) train complementary and alternative medicine researchers, and (3) disseminate authoritative information to the public and professionals. A few US medical schools now include instruction in alternative medicine.

Section 2706 of the ACA states that insurance companies may not discriminate against health providers with a state-recognized license (ACA 2013; Rao 2013). Some observers have interpreted this to mean that a licensed chiropractor or naturopath, for example, must be reimbursed the same as a medical doctor. At present, this area remains ambiguous. Nevertheless, the Patient-Centered Outcomes Research Institute (PCORI; 2013) is engaging in trials of alternative therapies to test their effectiveness.

Utilization of Outpatient Services

In 2010, Americans made approximately 1,008.803 million visits, or three visits per person, to office-based physicians (Table 7–5). Physicians in general and family practice accounted for the largest share of these visits (21.2%), followed by physicians in internal medicine (13.9%), pediatrics (13.1%), and obstetrics and gynecology (7.9%). Doctors of osteopathy accounted for 6.7% of the visits. The South led the nation in the proportion of physician visits (38.0%), followed by the Midwest (21.6%), the West (20.9%), and the Northeast (19.5%). Most physician office visits (88.5%) took place in metropolitan areas.

Table 7–6 presents the most frequently mentioned principal reasons for visiting a physician in 2007. The top 10 reasons were progress visit, general medical examination, cough, postoperative visit, medication, knee symptoms, prenatal examination, gynecological examination, well-baby examination, and other and unspecified test results. Table 7–7 shows the most frequent principal diagnoses cared for by office-based physicians.

Primary Care in Other Countries

Around the world, there is little consistency in how primary care services are accessed and how physicians get paid. Patients register with a primary care doctor in the United Kingdom, Netherlands, and New Zealand. In Australia, the Netherlands, New Zealand, Norway, Sweden, Iceland, Italy, Denmark, and the United Kingdom, patients go through primary care for referrals to specialists and are often required to register with primary care practices (except in Australia). Canada, France, and Germany use financial incentives to encourage registration with primary care practices and coordinated referrals (Schoen et al.

Table 7–5 US Physician Characteristics

Physician Characteristics	Number of Visits (1000)
All visits..	1,008,802
Physician specialty[1]	
General and family practice	213,770
Internal medicine..	139,843
Pediatrics...	132,247
Obstetrics and gynecology......................................	80,076
Orthopedic surgery	63,391
Ophthalmology...	55,530
Dermatology...	39,698
Cardiovascular diseases..	29,061
Psychiatry..	26,164
Oncology..	25,197
Otolaryngology...	20,762
Urology..	19,763
General surgery	19,201
Neurology...	13,995
All other specialties	130,148
Professional degree	
Doctor of medicine..	941,149
Doctor of osteopathy...	67,653
Specialty type[1]	
Primary care	560,295
Medical specialty	237,458
Surgical specialty	211,049
Geographic region	
Northeast	196,974
Midwest..	218,301
South...	382,932
West...	210,595
Metropolitan status	
MSA[2]...	893,217
Non-MSA[2]..	115,585

[1]Physician specialty and specialty type are defined in the "Technical Notes" of the source document.
[2]MSA is metropolitan statistical area.
Note: Numbers may not add to totals because of rounding.
Source: Reproduced from National Ambulatory Medical Care Survey: 2010 Summary Tables. http://www.cdc.gov/nchs/data/ahcd/namcs_summary/2010_namcs_web_tables.pdf.

2012; Thomson et al. 2012). The German "sickness funds" (insurance plans) offer an enrollment option.

The United Kingdom offers the most comprehensive coverage with little or no patient cost sharing. Canada covers physician visits in full, but medication coverage varies by province. Australia, New Zealand, and Germany include varying degrees of cost sharing (Schoen et al. 2012).

Table 7–6 Principal Reason for Visit

Principal Reason for Visit	Number of Visits
All visits	1,008,802
Progress visit, not otherwise specified	93,196
General medical examination	82,986
Cough	30,981
Postoperative visit	26,581
Medication, other and unspecified kinds	22,031
Knee symptoms	18,624
Prenatal examination, routine	18,595
Gynecological examination	17,713
Well-baby examination	16,628
For other and unspecified test results	16,340
Stomach pain, cramps, and spasms	15,028
Counseling, not otherwise specific	14,958
Diabetes mellitus	13,633
Symptoms referable to throat	13,251
Back symptoms	13,226
Hypertension	12,513
Earache, or ear infection	12,023
Skin rash	11,626
Shoulder symptoms	11,488
Vision dysfunction	10,556
All other reasons	536,826

Note: Numbers may not add to totals because of rounding.

Source: Modified from National Ambulatory Medical Care Survey: 2010 Summary Tables. http://www.cdc.gov/nchs/data/ahcd/namcs_summary/2010_namcs_web_tables.pdf.

Table 7–7 Primary Diagnosis Group

Primary Diagnosis Group[1]	Number of Visits	Percent Distribution
All visits.	1,008,802	100.0
Routine infant or child health check	44,634	4.4
Essential hypertension	38,916	3.9
Arthropathies and related disorders	36,130	3.6
Acute upper respiratory infections, excluding pharyngitis	32,207	3.2
Spinal disorders	31,593	3.1
Diabetes mellitus	30,560	3.0
Malignant neoplasms	29,155	2.9
Rheumatism, excluding back	21,835	2.2
Normal pregnancy	20,879	2.1
General medical examination	19,705	2.0
Gynecological examination	16,345	1.6
Follow-up examination	15,603	1.5
Otitis media and eustachian tube disorders.	14,650	1.5
Specific procedures and aftercare	14,286	1.4
Asthma.	14,232	1.4
Heart disease, excluding ischemic	12,405	1.2
Disorders of lipoid metabolism	12,350	1.2
Cataract	11,266	1.1
Allergic rhinitis	11,057	1.1
Benign neoplasms	10,663	1.1
All other diagnoses[2]	570,331	56.5

[1]Based on the International Classification of Diseases, Ninth Revision, Clinical Modification (ICD–9–CM).

[2]Includes all other diagnoses not listed above, as well as unknown and blank diagnoses.

Note: Numbers may not add to totals because of rounding.

Source: Modified from National Ambulatory Medical Care Survey: 2010 Summary Tables. http://www.cdc.gov/nchs/data/ahcd/namcs_summary/2010_namcs_web_tables.pdf.

Other countries may use moderate cost sharing (Schoen et al. 2012).

In Australia, Canada, France, Germany, Switzerland, and the United States, payers typically use fee-for-service payments and employ performance incentives (Schoen et al. 2012; Thomson et al. 2012). Conversely, the Netherlands, New Zealand, Norway, Denmark, and the United Kingdom use a combination of capitation, fee for service, and incentives (Schoen et al. 2012; Thomson et al. 2012).

Approximately, 59% of doctors in France, the Netherlands, New Zealand, and Switzerland reported that their patients could get same- or next-day appointments when sick, which was only true for 22% in Canada. In Australia, Canada, France, Germany, New Zealand, and Norway, over 60% of providers reported long waits to see specialists. In the United States physicians complained that they spent a significant amount of time with insurance-related issues which limited access to care for their patients (Schoen et al. 2012).

Primary care is mostly privatized in all the countries noted above, with the exception of Iceland (mostly public) and Sweden (mixed). Physicians in Australia, Canada, Norway, the United Kingdom, and the United States are more likely to be in group practices of five or more doctors. Physicians in the Netherlands, France, Germany, and Switzerland are more likely to work in smaller practices.

Summary

In the history of health care delivery, the main settings for ambulatory services have come full circle. First came a shift from outpatient settings to hospitals. Now, ambulatory services outside the hospital have mushroomed. The reasons for this shift are mainly economic, social, and technological. Many physicians have broken their ties with hospitals and have started their own specialized care centers, such as ambulatory surgery centers and cardiac care centers. A variety of general medical and surgical interventions are provided in ambulatory care settings. Thus, ambulatory services now transcend the basic and routine primary care services. Conversely, primary care itself has become "specialized." Primary care is no longer concerned simply with the treatment of simple ailments; primary care physicians must coordinate a plethora of services to maintain the long-term viability of a patient's health. Application of principles to establish patient-centered medical homes and delivery of community-based primary care is slow in taking shape.

In response to the changing economic incentives within the health care delivery system, numerous types of outpatient services have emerged, and a variety of settings for the delivery of services has developed. The growing interest in complementary and alternative medicine is largely consumer driven. Compared to our complex health care system, alternative medicine, with its emphasis on self-care, is one area where many patients feel more in control of their own destiny.

The Affordable Care Act has a number of provisions that apply to different types of outpatient services. However, some existing problems in health care delivery are not likely to go away anytime soon.

ACA Takeaway

- The ACA includes several provisions in the hope of bolstering the nation's primary care capacity. For several reasons, however, primary care, specialty care, and hospital emergency departments are expected to be overburdened with an influx of newly insured patients.

- The need for providing uncompensated care by hospitals is expected to decrease.

- The ACA reduces overall payments to Medicare-certified home health agencies and mandates quality reporting.

- The ACA mandates a Hospice Quality Reporting Program for all Medicare-certified hospices. Payments are linked to quality reporting, failing which reimbursement will be reduced.

- Components of the ACA that affect community health centers involve maintaining adequate funding and developing teaching health centers. Health centers located in states that do not expand Medicaid could face fiscal shortfalls.

- The nondiscrimination clause pertaining to health providers with a state-recognized license remains vague regarding payments for providers of alternative treatments.

Test Your Understanding

Terminology

accountability
adult day care
alternative medicine
ambulatory care
case management
community-oriented
   primary care
durable medical equipment
emergent conditions

free clinic
gatekeeping
home health care
hospice
medical home
medically underserved
nonurgent conditions
outpatient services
palliation

primary health care
secondary care
surgicenter
telephone triage
tertiary care
urgent care centers
urgent conditions
walk-in clinic

Review Questions

1. Describe how some of the changes in the health services delivery system have led to a decline in hospital inpatient days and a growth in ambulatory services.

2. What implications has the decline in hospital occupancy rates had for hospital management?

3. All primary care is ambulatory, but not all ambulatory services represent primary care. Discuss.

4. What are the main characteristics of primary care?

5. Critique the gatekeeping role of primary care.

6. Discuss how the patient-centered medical home advances primary care.

7. What is community-oriented primary care? Explain.

8. Discuss the two main factors that determine what should be an adequate mix between generalists and specialists.

9. What are some of the reasons solo practitioners are joining group practices?

10. Why is it important for hospital administrators to regard outpatient care as a key component of their overall business strategy?

11. Discuss the main hospital-based outpatient services.

12. What are some of the social changes that led to the creation of specialized health centers for women?

13. Why is the hospital emergency department sometimes used for nonurgent conditions? What are the consequences?

14. What are mobile health care services? Discuss the various types of mobile services.

15. What is the basic philosophy of home health care? Describe the services it provides.

16. What are the conditions of eligibility for receiving home health services under Medicare?

17. Explain the concept of hospice care and the types of services a hospice provides.

18. What are some of the main requirements for Medicare certification of a hospice program?

19. Describe the scope of public health ambulatory services in the United States.

20. Describe the main public and voluntary outpatient clinics and the main problems they face.

21. Why do both Republican and Democrat presidents support the community health center program?

22. What is alternative medicine? What role does it play in the delivery of health care?

23. Briefly explain how a telephone triage system functions.

24. Discuss the global trend in primary care.

REFERENCES

American Academy of Family Physicians, American Academy of Pediatrics, American College of Physicians, & American Osteopathic Association. 2007. Joint principles of the patient-centered medical home, March 2007. Available at: http://www.acponline.org/running_practice/pcmh/demonstrations/jointprinc_05_17.pdf. Accessed January 2014.

American Hospital Association (AHA). 2006. *TrendWatch Chartbook*. Washington, DC: AHA.

Appleby, C. 1995. Boxed in? *Hospitals and Health Networks* 69, no. 18: 28–34.

Aventis Pharmaceuticals. 2001. *Managed care digest series, 2001: Institutional highlights digest*. Bridgewater, NJ: Aventis Pharmaceuticals.

Bakwin, H. 1945. Pseudodoxia pediatrica. *New England Journal of Medicine* 232: 691–697.

Barbosa-Cesnik C., et al. 2011. Cranberry juice fails to prevent recurrent urinary tract infection: Results from a randomized placebo-controlled trial. *Clinical Infectious Diseases* 52: 23–30.

Barnes P.M., et al. 2008. *Complementary and alternative medicine use among adults and children: United States, 2007*. Hyattsville, MD: National Center for Health Statistics.

Barr, K.W., and C.L. Breindel. 1995. Ambulatory care. In: *Health care administration: Principles, practices, structure, and delivery*. 2nd ed. L.F. Wolper, ed. Gaithersburg, MD: Aspen Publishers, Inc. pp. 547–573.

Barrett B., et al. 2010. Echinacea for treating the common cold *Annals of Internal Medicine* 153: 769–777.

Berenson, R., et al. 2008. A house is not a home: Keeping patients at the center of practice redesign. *Health Affairs* 27, no. 5: 1219–1230.

Beresford, L. 1989. *History of the National Hospice Organization*. Arlington, VA: The National Hospice Organization.

Burton R.A., et al. 2012. Patient-centered medical home recognition tools: A comparison of ten surveys' content and operational details. Available at: http://www.urban.org/publications/412338.html. Accessed January 2014.

CAM Research Methodology Conference. 1997. Defining and describing complementary and alternative medicine. *Alternative Therapies* 3, no. 2: 49–56.

Caron, J.B., and E.K. Isbey. 2013. CMS Releases Proposed Calendar Year 2014 Updates to Home Health Prospective Payment System. Available at: http://www.mwe.com/CMS-Releases-Proposed-Calendar-Year-2014-Updates-to-Home-Health-Prospective-Payment-System-07-09-2013/. Accessed January 2014.

Caudill, T., et al. 2011. Health care reform and primary care: Training physicians for tomorrow's challenges. *Academic Medicine* 86, no. 2: 158–160.

Centers for Disease Control and Prevention (CDC). 2011. National home and hospice care survey. Available at: http://www.cdc.gov/nchs/nhhcs.htm. Accessed January 2011.

Centers for Medicare & Medicaid Services (CMS). 2011a. Extension of therapy cap exceptions process. Available at: http://www.cms.gov/TherapyServices. Accessed May 2011.

Centers for Medicare & Medicaid Services (CMS). 2011b. National health expenditures projections: 2011-2021. Table 10: Home health care expenditures. Available at: http://www.cms.gov/Research-Statistics-Data-and-Systems/Statistics-Trends-and-Reports/NationalHealthExpendData/Downloads/Proj2011PDF.pdf. Accessed August 2013.

Centers for Medicare & Medicaid Services (CMS). 2013a. Details for Regulation No.: CMS-1450-P. Available at: http://www.cms.gov/Medicare/Medicare-Fee-for-Service-Payment/Home-HealthPPS/Home-Health-Prospective-Payment-System-Regulations-and-Notices-Items/CMS-1450-P.html. Accessed January 2014.

Centers for Medicare & Medicaid Services (CMS). 2013b. Hospice quality reporting. Available at: http://www.cms.gov/Medicare/Quality-Initiatives-Patient-Assessment-Instruments/Hospice-Quality-Reporting/index.html?redirect=/Hospice-Quality-Reporting/. Accessed January 2014.

Centers for Medicare & Medicaid Services (CMS). 2013c. FY2014 Hospice wage index and payment rate update; Hospice quality reporting requirements; and updates on payment reform. Final Rule. Available at: http://www.gpo.gov/fdsys/pkg/FR-2013-08-07/pdf/2013-18838.pdf. Accessed January 2014.

Centers for Medicare & Medicaid Services (CMS). 2013d. Independence at home demonstration fact sheet. Available at: http://innovation.cms.gov/Files/fact-sheet/IAH-Fact-Sheet.pdf. Accessed January 2014.

Chernew, M.E., et al. 2009. Would having more primary care doctors cut health spending growth? *Health Affairs* 28: 1327–1335.

Dohan, D., et al. 2013. Recognition as a patient-centered medical home: Fundamental or incidental? *Annals of Family Medicine* 11, Suppl. 1: S14–S18.

Eisenberg, D.M., et al. 1998. Trends in alternative medicine use in the United States, 1990–1997. *Journal of the American Medical Association* 280, no. 18: 1569–1575.

Evashwick, C.J. 1993. The continuum of long-term care. In: *Introduction to health services*. 4th ed. S.J. Williams and P.R. Torrens, eds. Albany, NY: Delmar Publishers. pp. 177–218.

Federal Register. 2013. Vol. 76, No. 245. Available at: http://www.gpo.gov/fdsys/pkg/FR-2011-12-21/pdf/2011-32568.pdf. Accessed January 2014.

Franks, P., et al. 1992. Gatekeeping revisited: Protecting patients from overtreatment. *New England Journal of Medicine* 327, no. 4: 424–429.

Franks, P., et al. 1998. Primary care physicians and specialists as personal physicians: Health care expenditures and mortality experience. *Journal of Family Practice* 47: 105–109.

Gordon, J.S. 1996. Alternative medicine and the family practitioner. *American Family Physician* 54, no. 7: 2205–2212.

Health Facilities Management. 2013. Will retail medical clinics return to 'save the day'? *Health Facilities Management* 26, no. 26: 7.

Health Resources and Services Administration (HRSA). 2012. Health center data. Available at: http://bphc.hrsa.gov/healthcenterdatastatistics/index.html. Accessed August 2013.

Hoechst Marion Roussel. 1999. *Managed care digest series 1999: Institutional digest*. Kansas City, MO: Hoechst Marion Roussel, Inc.

Jackson, C. 2002. Cutting into the market: Rise of ambulatory surgery centers. *American Medical News* (April 15). Available at: www.amednews.com/2002/bisa0415. Accessed December 2002.

Klees, B.S., et al. 2010. Brief summary of Medicare and Medicaid. CMS. Available at: http://www.cms.gov/Research-Statistics-Data-and-Systems/statistics-Trends-and-Reports/MedicareProgramRatesStats/downloads/MedicareMedicaisSummaries2010.pdf. Accessed January 2014.

Kozak, L.J., et al. 1999. Changing patterns of surgical care in the United States, 1980–1995. *Health Care Financing Review* 21, no. 1: 31–49.

Ku, L., et al. 2011. The states next challenge—securing primary care for expanded Medicaid populations. *New England Journal of Medicine* 364: 493–495.

Lafferty, W.E., et al. 2006. Insurance coverage and subsequent utilization of complementary and alternative medicine providers. *The American Journal of Managed Care* 12, no. 7: 397–404.

Lee, P.R. 1994. Models of excellence. *The Lancet* 344, no. 8935: 1484–1486.

Liggins, K. 1993. Inappropriate attendance at accident and emergency departments: A literature review. *Journal of Advanced Nursing* 18, no. 7: 1141–1145.

Mao J.T., et al. 2010. White tea extract induces apoptosis in non-small cell lung cancer cells: The role of peroxisome proliferator-activated receptor-γ and 15-lipoxygenases. *Cancer Prevention Research* 3, no. 9: 1132–1140.

McCaig, L.F., and C.W. Burt. 2002. *National hospital ambulatory medical care survey: 1999 emergency department summary*. Atlanta, GA: Centers for Disease Control and Prevention/National Center for Health Statistics.

McCaig, L.F., and E.W. Newar. 2006. *National hospital ambulatory medical care survey: 2004 emergency department summary*. Atlanta, GA: Centers for Disease Control and Prevention, National Center for Health Statistics.

McNamara, P. et al. 1993. Pathwork access: Primary care in EDs on the rise. *Hospitals* 67, no. 10: 44–46.

Miller, G. 1996. Hospice. In: *The continuum of long-term care: An integrated systems approach*. C.J. Evashwick, ed. Albany, NY: Delmar Publishers. pp. 98–108.

Nahin R.L. et al. 2009. *Costs of complementary and alternative medicine (CAM) and frequency of visits to CAM practitioners: United States, 2007*. National health statistics reports no 18. Hyattsville, MD: National Center for Health Statistics.

National Association for Home Care & Hospice. 2013. Home health leaders: Medicare proposed rule could result in nearly $100 billion in total cuts to home health benefit. Available at: http://www.nahc.org/NAHCReport/nr130828_1/. Accessed January 2014.

National Association for Home Care and Hospice. 2004. *Basic statistics about home care*. Available at: http://www.homehealth4america.org/media-center/160. Accessed January 2014.

National Association for Home Care and Hospice. 2010. *Basic statistics about home care*. Available at: http://www.nahc.org/assets/1/7/10HC_Stats.pdf. Accessed August 2013.

National Association of Community Health Centers (NACHC). 2011. *Community health centers and health reform*. Available at: http://www.nachc.com/client/Summary%20of%20Final%20Health%20Reform%20Package.pdf. Accessed January 2014.

National Association of Community Health Centers (NACHC). 2013a. *Studies on health centers improving access to care*. Available at: http://www.nachc.com/client/documents/HC%20access%20to%20care%20studies%2006.13.pdf. Accessed August 2013.

National Association of Community Health Centers (NACHC). 2013b. *Studies on health centers quality of care*. Available at: http://www.nachc.org/client/documents/HC%20Quality %20Studies%2007.13.pdf. Accessed August 2013.

National Association of Community Health Centers (NACHC). 2013c. *Studies on health centers cost effectiveness*. Available at: http://www.nachc.org/client/documents/HC_Cost_Effectiveness_0513.pdf. Accessed August 2013.

National Association of Community Health Centers (NACHC). 2013d. *Studies on health centers and disparities*. Available at: http://www.nachc.org/client/documents/HC%20Disparities%20Studies%2006.13.pdf. Accessed August 2013.

National Association of Community Health Centers. (NACHC). 2013e. The challenges. Available at: http://www.nachc.com/health-center-challenges.cfm. Accessed January 2014.

National Association of Free Clinics (NAFC). 2011. Comparison of safety net providers free clinics to federally funded clinics. Available at: http://www.freeclinics.us. Accessed May 2011.

National Center for Complementary and Alternative Medicine (NCCAM). 2013. Available at: http://nccam.nih.gov/about/budget/congressional/2014#His. Accessed January 2014.

National Center for Health Statistics. 2010. Home health care patients and hospice care discharges—2007 National home and hospice care survey fact sheet. Available at: http://www.cdc.gov/nchs/data/nhhcs/2007hospicecaredischarges.pdf. Accessed January 2014.

National Hospice and Palliative Care Organization. 2003. NHPCO facts and figures, January 2003. Available at: http://www.nhpco.org. Accessed January 2014.

National Hospice and Palliative Care Organization. 2012. NHPCO facts and figures: Hospice care in America. Available at: http://www.nhpco.org/sites/default/files/public/Statistics_Research/2011_Facts_Figures.pdf. Accessed January 2014.

National Nursing Centers Consortium. 2003. *Nurse-managed health centers briefing*. May 2003: 1–4.

Noble, J., et al. 1992. Career differences between primary care and traditional trainees in internal medicine and pediatrics. *Annals of Internal Medicine* 116, no. 7: 482–487.

Orton, P. 1994. Shared care. *The Lancet* 344, no. 8934: 1413–1415.

Padgett, D.K., and Brodsky B. 1992. Psychosocial factors influencing non-urgent use of the emergency room: A review of the literature and recommendations for research and improved service delivery. *Social Science & Medicine* 35, no. 9: 1189–1197.

Parchman, M., and S. Culler. 1994. Primary care physicians and avoidable hospitalization. *Journal of Family Practice* 39: 123–128.

Patient Protection and Affordable Care Act (ACA). 2013. Non-discrimination in health care. Available at: http://www.law.cornell.edu/uscode/text/42/300gg-5. Accessed January 2014.

Patient-Centered Outcomes Research Institute. Draft National Priorities for Research and Research Agenda. Version 1. Available at: http://pcori.org/assets/PCORI-Draft-National-Priorities-and-Research-Agenda1.pdf. Accessed January 2014.

Rao, A. 2013. Affordable care act boosts status of alternative medicine – At least on paper. Available at: http://www.huffingtonpost.com/2013/08/05/affordable-care-act-alternative-medicine_n_3707366.html. Accessed January 2014.

Roos, N. 1979. Who should do the surgery? Tonsillectomy and adenoidectomy in one Canadian province. *Inquiry* 16, no. 1: 73–83.

Russo, A., et al. 2010. Hospital-based ambulatory surgery, 2007. Available at: http://www.hcup-us.ahrq.gov/reports/statbriefs/sb86.jsp. Accessed January 2014.

Schoen C., et al. 2012. A survey of primary care doctors in ten countries shows progress in use of health information technology, less in other areas. *Health Affairs* 31 no. 12: 2805–2816.

Sepulveda, M.-J., et al. 2008. Primary care: Can it solve employers' health care dilemma? *Health Affairs* 27: 151–158.

Shi, L. 1994. Primary care, specialty care, and life chances. *International Journal of Health Services* 24, no. 3: 431–458.

Shi, L., et al. 1999. Income inequality, primary care, and health indicators. *The Journal of Family Practice* 48: 275–284.

Shi, L., et al. 2002. Primary care, self-rated health care, and reduction in social disparities in health. *Health Services Research* 37, no. 3: 529–550.

Shi, L., et al. 2007. Health center financial performance: National trends and state variation, 1998–2004. *Journal of Public Health Management and Practice* 13, no. 2: 133–150.

Shi, L., and B. Starfield. 2000. Primary care, income inequality, and self-related health in the US: Mixed-level analysis. *International Journal of Health Services* 30: 541–555.

Shi, L., and B. Starfield. 2001. Primary care physician supply, income inequality, and racial mortality in US metropolitan areas. *American Journal of Public Health* 91: 1246–1250.

SMG Solutions. 2000. *2000 report and directory: Medical group practices*. Chicago, IL: SMG Solutions.

Starfield B. 1998. *Primary care: Balancing health needs, services and technology*. New York: Oxford University Press.

Starfield, B. 1992. *Primary care: Concept, evaluation, and policy*. New York: Oxford University Press.

Starfield, B. 1994. Is primary care essential? *The Lancet* 344, no. 8930: 1129–1133.

Steinel, J.A., and E.A. Madigan. 2003. Resource utilization in home health chronic obstructive pulmonary disease management. *Outcomes Management* 7, no. 1: 23–27.

Su, D., and L. Li. 2011. Trends in the use of complementary and alternative medicine in the United States: 2002-2007. *Journal of Health Care for the Poor and Underserved* 22: 295–309.

Tais, S., and E. Oberg. 2013. The economic evaluation of complementary and alternative medicine. *Natural Medicine Journal*. Available at: http://www.naturalmedicinejournal.com/article_content.asp?article=402. Accessed January 2014.

Thomson, S., et al., eds. 2012. International profiles of health care systems, New York (NY): Commonwealth Fund. Available at: http://www.commonwealthfund.org/~/media/Files/Publications/Fund%20Report/2012/Nov/1645_Squires_intl_profiles_hlt_care_systems_2012.pdf. Accessed January 2014.

US Department of Health and Human Services (US DHHS). 2011. Recovery Act (ARRA): Community health centers. Available at: http://www.hhs.gov/recovery/hrsa/healthcenter grants.html. Accessed January 2011.

Van Weel, C., et al. 2008. Integration of personal and community health care. *Lancet* 372, no. 9642: 871–872.

Vanselow, N.A., et al. 1995. From the Institute of Medicine. *Journal of the American Medical Association* 273, no. 3: 192.

Weinerman, E.R., et al. 1966. Yale studies in ambulatory medical care. V. Determinants of use of hospital emergency services. *American Journal of Public Health* 56, no. 7: 1037–1056.

Williams, S.J. 1993. Ambulatory health care services. In: *Introduction to Health Services*. 4th ed. S.J. Williams and P.R. Torrens, eds. Albany, NY: Delmar Publishers.

Wilson, F.A., and D. Neuhauser. 1985. *Health services in the United States*. 2nd ed. Cambridge, MA: Ballinger Publishing Co.

World Health Organization (WHO). 1978. *Primary health care*. Geneva, Switzerland: WHO.

World Health Organization (WHO). 2010. *Primary health care*. Geneva, Switzerland: WHO.

Chapter 8

Inpatient Facilities and Services

Learning Objectives

- To get a functional perspective on the evolution of hospitals
- To survey the factors that contributed to the growth of hospitals prior to the 1980s
- To understand the reasons for the subsequent decline of hospitals and their utilization
- To learn some key measures pertaining to hospital operations and inpatient utilization
- To differentiate among various types of hospitals
- To learn how the Affordable Care Act affects physician-owned specialty hospitals and nonprofit hospitals
- To comprehend some basic concepts in hospital governance
- To understand and differentiate between licensure, certification, and accreditation and the Magnet Recognition Program of the American Nurses Credentialing Center
- To get a perspective on some key ethical issues

"We have the inpatient sector under control."

Introduction

The term *inpatient* is used in conjunction with an overnight stay in a health care facility, such as a hospital, whereas outpatient refers to services provided while the patient is not lodged in a health care facility. Although the primary function of hospitals is to deliver inpatient acute care services, many hospitals have expanded their scope of services to include nonacute and outpatient care.

According to the American Hospital Association (AHA), a *hospital* is an institution with at least six beds whose primary function is "to deliver patient services, diagnostic and therapeutic, for particular or general medical conditions" (AHA 1994). In addition, a hospital must be licensed, have an organized physician staff, and provide continuous nursing services under the supervision of registered nurses. Other characteristics of a hospital include an identifiable governing body that is legally responsible for the conduct of the hospital, a chief executive with continuous responsibility for the operation of the hospital, maintenance of medical records on each patient, pharmacy services maintained in the institution and supervised by a registered pharmacist, and food service operations to meet the nutritional and therapeutic requirements of the patients (Health Forum 2001). The construction and operation of the modern hospital is governed by federal laws; state health department regulations; city ordinances; standards of the Joint Commission; and national codes for building, fire protection, and sanitation.

In the past 200 years or so, hospitals have gradually evolved from ordinary institutions of refuge for the homeless and poor to ultramodern facilities providing the latest medical services to the critically ill and injured. The term "medical center" is used by some

hospitals, reflecting their high level of specialization and wide scope of services, which may include teaching and research. Growth of multihospital chains, especially those providing a variety of health care services in addition to acute care, has led to the nomenclature "hospital system" or "health system."

Hospital care consumes the biggest share of national health care spending. Hence, the hospital inpatient sector was the first to be targeted by prospective reimbursement methods, during the 1980s. Subsequently, as new technologies emerged to treat patients outside the hospital setting, outpatient services for various types of medical procedures and treatments mushroomed. Managed care also played a significant role in curtailing inpatient utilization.

This chapter describes institutional care delivery with specific reference to acute care—mostly characterized by secondary and tertiary levels of care—in community hospitals. It also discusses various ways to classify hospitals and points out important trends and critical issues that will continue to shape the delivery of inpatient services.

Hospital Transformation in the United States

From about 1840 to 1900, hospitals underwent a drastic change in purpose, function, and number. From supplying merely food, shelter, and meager medical care to the pauper sick, armies, those infected with contagious diseases, the insane, and those requiring emergency treatment, they began to provide skilled medical and surgical attention and nursing care to all classes of people (Raffel 1980). Subsequently, hospitals became centers of medical training and research. More recent transformations are mainly organizational in nature, as hospitals have consolidated into medical systems, delivering a broad range of health care services. These transformations can be neatly categorized according to five significant functions in the evolution of hospitals:

1. Primitive institutions of social welfare
2. Distinct institutions of care for the sick
3. Organized institutions of medical practice
4. Advanced institutions of medical training and research
5. Consolidated systems of health services delivery

Primitive Institutions of Social Welfare

As discussed in Chapter 3, except for a few hospitals that were located in some of the major US cities, municipal almshouses (or poorhouses) and pesthouses existed during the 1800s. Financed through charitable gifts and local government funds, these institutions essentially served a social welfare function. Almshouses served primarily the destitute of society who needed food and shelter. They also took care of the sick who received limited nursing care when needed. People generally stayed in these institutions for months rather than days. Pesthouses were used to quarantine people who were sick with contagious diseases, such as smallpox and yellow fever, so the rest of the community would be protected.

Distinct Institutions of Care for the Sick

Not until the late 1800s did infirmaries or hospital departments of city poorhouses break away to become independent medical care institutions. These were the first public hospitals (Haglund and Dowling 1993), in this case operated by local governments. For example, the Kings County Almshouse and Infirmary, organized in Brooklyn in 1830, later became the Kings County Hospital (Raffel 1980), but these first public hospitals still served mainly the poor. Hospitals at this stage often had poor hygiene, inadequate ventilation, and care provided by untrained nurses.

In Europe, the first hospitals were established predominantly by religious orders. Nurses, who were primarily monks and nuns, attended to both the physical and spiritual needs of the patients. Later, many of these hospitals became tax-financed public institutions as less church money became available for hospitals and monasteries. In England, private donations and taxes supported the "royal hospitals." Other British hospitals were voluntary hospitals, which served as a model for such hospitals in the United States (Raffel and Raffel 1994). Later, creation of the National Health Service in 1948 brought the British voluntary hospitals under public (government) ownership.

In the United States, the founding of *voluntary hospitals*—nonprofit community hospitals financed through local philanthropy as opposed to taxes—was often inspired by influential physicians, with the financial backing of local donors and philanthropists. These hospitals accepted both indigent and paying patients, but to cover their operating expenses, they required charitable contributions from private citizens.

The first voluntary hospital in the United States established specifically to care for the sick was the Pennsylvania Hospital in Philadelphia, opened in 1752.

The city already had an almshouse. However, Dr. Thomas Bond, a London-trained physician, brought to prominence the need for a hospital to care for the sick poor of the city. Benjamin Franklin, who was a friend and advisor of Dr. Bond, was instrumental in promoting the idea and in raising voluntary contributions. According to the charter, the contributors had the right to make all laws and regulations relating to the hospital's operation. The contributors also elected members to form the governing board, or the board of trustees. Thus, the control of voluntary hospitals was in the hands of influential community laypeople rather than physicians (Raffel and Raffel 1994).

Other prominent voluntary hospitals included the New York Hospital in New York, which was completed in 1775 but, due to the Revolutionary War, was not opened to civilian patients until 1791. The Massachusetts General Hospital in Boston was incorporated in 1812 and opened in 1821. During this period, the almshouses continued to serve an important function by receiving overflow patients who could not be admitted to the hospitals because of the unavailability of beds or who had to be discharged from hospitals because they were declared incurable (Raffel and Raffel 1994). Later hospitals in the United States were modeled after Pennsylvania, New York, and Massachusetts General.

Organized Institutions of Medical Practice

Social and demographic change, but above all, the advances in medical science, transformed hospitals into institutions of medical practice. From the latter half of the 19th century, new technology, facilities, and personnel training all became centered in the hospital.

Improvements in hygiene, advanced medical care, and surgical services made hospitals more acceptable to the middle and upper classes. Hospitals actually began to attract affluent patients who could afford to pay privately. Thus, the hospital transformed from a charitable institution into one that could generate a profit. In many instances, physicians started opening small hospitals, financed by wealthy and influential sponsors. These facilities were the first proprietary hospitals.

In the early 20th century, the field of hospital administration became a discipline in its own right. Hospitals needed administrators with expertise in financial management and organizational skills to manage them. The administrative structure of the hospital was organized into departments, such as food service, pharmacy, X-ray, and laboratory. It became necessary to employ professional staff to manage the delivery of services. Efficiency began to emerge as an important element in the management of hospitals. This early emphasis on efficiency foreshadowed two main issues that continue to affect health policy and hospital management: the pressure on hospitals to introduce new technology while containing cost and the assumption that hospitals should act like businesses (Arndt and Bigelow 2006). With greater pressure for cost containment, and availability of advanced medical care in outpatient settings, hospitals began to limit care to the more acute periods of illness rather than the full course of a disease.

Hospital accreditation was another notable development in the early 20th century. The American College of Surgeons (ACS) began inspecting hospitals in 1918 and developed standards for hospital equipment and hospital wards. Until 1951, the ACS single-handedly worked to improve hospital-based medical practice. This effort evolved into the formation of the Joint Commission on Accreditation of Hospitals, a private nonprofit body formed in 1951 with joint effort of the ACS, the American College of Physicians, the AHA, and the American Medical Association (AMA). The organization changed its name in 1987 to the Joint Commission on Accreditation of Healthcare Organizations, which more accurately describes the variety of health facilities it accredits. Since 2007, its official name is The Joint Commission.

Advanced Institutions of Medical Training and Research

The hospital had a profound influence on medical education in the United States. With advances in biomedical knowledge, it became necessary for physicians to receive their training in hospitals.

Recognition of the critical role hospitals played in medical education led to collaborations between hospitals and universities. The Pennsylvania Hospital, for example, taught courses required by the College of Philadelphia's medical school, which later became the University of Pennsylvania School of Medicine. Similarly, New York Hospital served as a teaching hospital for medical students of Columbia Medical School, and Massachusetts General Hospital provided practical clinical instruction for Harvard Medical School (Raffel and Raffel 1994). The Johns Hopkins Hospital (opened in 1889), with its adjoining medical school (opened in 1893), inaugurated a new era, combining clinical practice with teaching and the promotion of scientific inquiry in medicine. From the 1920s, the hospital's teaching role became even more prominent as specialization in medicine led

to a proliferation of internships and residencies (Haglund and Dowling 1993). In affiliation with university-based medical schools, many hospitals became centers of medical research. The vast number of clinical records and a large array of medical conditions among hospital patients have provided a wealth of data to conduct investigative studies to advance medical knowledge. Even today, large hospitals play an important role in clinical studies. To a lesser extent, some aspects of medical training have shifted to outpatient settings, such as nursing homes, hospices, and community health centers.

Consolidated Systems of Health Services Delivery

Hospitals have been the major cost centers in the health care delivery system. During the 1980s and 1990s, concerns over rising costs were met with prospective and capitated payment methods and aggressive utilization review practices that brought about drastic reductions in the length of inpatient stays. The declining utilization of acute care beds had left most hospitals with excess capacity in the form of empty beds. As the acute inpatient care sector of health care delivery became less profitable, hospitals used a number of consolidation strategies. Multihospital systems formed through mergers and acquisitions; hospital systems diversified into nonacute services, such as outpatient centers, home health care, long-term care, and subacute care; and some hospitals affiliated with networks through contractual arrangements. Intense consolidation in certain hospital markets diluted competition, which benefited hospitals. Research suggests that hospital consolidation in the 1990s raised prices by at least

5% as competition eroded (Vogt and Town 2006).

The Expansion Phase: Late 1800s to Mid-1980s

Hospitals grew in numbers when they became a necessary local adjunct of medical practice. Growth in medical technology increased the volume of surgical work, almost all of which was performed in hospitals. The number of hospitals grew from 178 (35,604 beds) in 1872 to 4,359 (421,065 beds) in 1909. By 1929, 6,665 hospitals provided 907,133 beds (Haglund and Dowling 1993). As new beds were built, their availability almost ensured that they would be used. This phenomenon led Milton Roemer (1916–2001) to proclaim, "a built bed is a filled bed," known popularly as Roemer's Law (Roemer 1961).

Haglund and Dowling (1993) pointed to six significant factors in the growth of hospitals: advances in medical science, development of specialized technology, advances in medical education, development of professional nursing, growth of health insurance, and the role of government. The first three factors were discussed in the previous section; this section covers the last three.

Development of Professional Nursing

During the latter half of the 19th century, Florence Nightingale was instrumental in transforming nursing into a recognized profession in Britain. Following the founding of the Nightingale School of Nursing in England, nursing schools in the United States were established at Bellevue Hospital (New York City), New Haven Hospital (New Haven, Connecticut), and Massachusetts General Hospital (Boston). The benefits of

having trained nurses in hospitals became apparent as increased efficacy of treatment and hygiene improved patient recovery (Haglund and Dowling 1993). As a result, hospitals increasingly came to be regarded as places of healing and found acceptance with the middle and upper classes.

Growth of Private Health Insurance

During and after the Great Depression of the 1930s, many hospitals were forced to close, and the financial solvency of many more was threatened. Thus, the number of hospitals in the United States dropped from 6,852 in 1928 to 6,189 in 1937. Subsequently, the growth of private health insurance became a vehicle for enabling people to pay for hospital services, and the flow of insurance funds helped revive the financial stability of hospitals. Historically, insurance plans provided generous coverage for inpatient care. Consequently, there were few restrictions on patients and physicians opting for more expensive hospital services (Feldstein 1971). Note that private health insurance in the United States first began as a hospital insurance plan (see Chapter 3).

Role of Government

Government funding for hospital construction perhaps played the most important role in the expansion of hospitals. Subsequently, Medicare and Medicaid provided indirect funding to the hospital industry by vastly expanding public-sector health insurance.

The Hill-Burton Act

Relatively little hospital construction took place during the Great Depression and World War II, so, by the end of the war, there was a severe shortage of hospital beds. The Hospital Survey and Construction Act of 1946, commonly referred to as the Hill-Burton Act, provided federal grants to states for the construction of new community hospital beds; however, the hospitals would not be under federal control. This legislation required that each state develop and upgrade, annually, a plan for health facility construction—based on bed-to-population ratios—that would serve as a basis for allocation of federal construction grants to the states (Raffel 1980).

In 1946, after the war, 3.2 community hospital beds were available per 1,000 civilian population. The objective of Hill-Burton was to reach 4.5 beds per 1,000 population (Teisberg et al. 1991). The Hill-Burton program assisted in the construction of nearly 40% of the beds in the nation's short-stay general hospitals and was the greatest single factor that increased the nation's bed supply during the 1950s and 1960s (Haglund and Dowling 1993). Hill-Burton made it possible for even small, remote communities to have their own hospitals (Wolfson and Hopes 1994). By 1980, the United States had reached its goal of 4.5 community hospital beds per 1,000 civilian population (DHHS 2002) even though the Hill-Burton program terminated in 1974.

Hill-Burton was also instrumental in promoting the growth of nonprofit community hospitals because it required that hospitals constructed with federal funds must provide a certain amount of charitable care. Competition from these new hospitals led to the closure of many smaller proprietary for-profit hospitals. Most of the remaining proprietary hospitals began delivering free or discounted services to those who could not afford to pay (Muller 2003). Thanks to Hill-Burton, even today, nonprofit community hospitals in the United States far outnumber all other types of hospitals.

Public Health Insurance

The creation of Medicare and Medicaid programs in 1965 also had a significant, although indirect, impact on the increase in the number of hospital beds and their utilization (Feldstein 1993), as government-funded health insurance became available to a large number of elderly and poor Americans. Between 1965 and 1980, the number of community hospitals in the United States increased from 5,736 (741,000 beds) to 5,830 (988,000 beds); total admissions per 1,000 population increased from 130 to 154; and total inpatient days per 1,000 population increased from 1,007 to 1,159. The percentage of occupied beds also remained relatively stable at around 76% (AHA 1990). Figure 8–1 shows trends from 1940 to 2010 in the number of beds per 1,000 resident population.

The Downsizing Phase: Mid-1980s Onward

The mid-1980s marked a turning point in the growth and use of hospital beds. After a sharp decline in 1985, the number of community hospitals and the total number of beds have continued to decline (Figure 8–2). The average bed capacity of a community hospital also declined from 169.5 beds in 1980 to 161.5 beds in 2010 (DHHS 2013).

Even as the numbers of hospitals and beds contracted, further declines have occurred in the actual utilization of the shrunken capacity. Occupancy rates (percentage of beds occupied) in community hospitals declined from 75.6% in 1980 to approximately 63.9% in 2000. Since then, occupancy rates have

Figure 8–1 Trends in the Number of US Community Hospital Beds per 1,000 Resident Population.

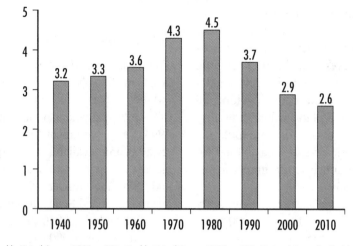

Source: Data from *Health, United States, 2002*, p. 281; *Health, United States, 2012*, p. 315; National Center for Health Statistics.

Figure 8–2 The Decline in the Number of US Community Hospitals and Beds.

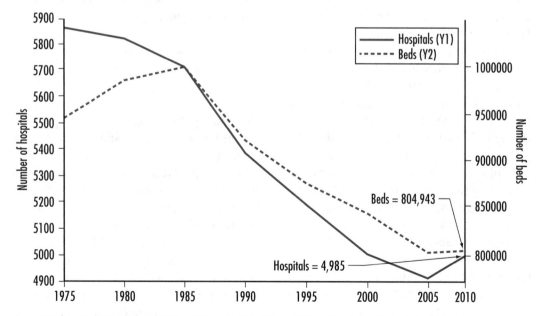

Source: Data from *Health, United States, 2002*, p. 279; *Health, United States, 2012*, p. 314. National Center for Health Statistics.

increased slightly (64.5% in 2010), mainly because capacity (number of available beds) has steadily declined, from 823,560 total community hospital beds in 2000 to 804,943 in 2010. Similarly, the average length of stay (ALOS) in community hospitals has declined from 7.6 days in 1980 to 5.4 days in 2010 (DHHS 2013).

Within hospitals, a tremendous shift from inpatient to outpatient utilization has occurred (as illustrated in Figure 8–3) in the form of increasing ratios between hospital outpatient visits and inpatient days. Along with this shift in the use of hospital services, the share of personal health expenditures for hospital care had declined until 2005, but has slowly crept up since then (see Table 8–1).

The downward pressures on hospital utilization have been exerted by three main forces: changes in hospital reimbursement, the impact of managed care, and hospital closures. Of these three, hospital reimbursement had the most dramatic effect on hospital utilization.

Changes in Reimbursement

The Tax Equity and Fiscal Responsibility Act (TEFRA) of 1982 required the conversion of hospital Medicare reimbursement from cost-plus to a prospective payment system (PPS) based on diagnosis-related groups (DRGs) (see Chapter 6). Under PPS, hospitals are paid a fixed amount per admission according to the patient's principal diagnosis, regardless of how long the patient stays in the hospital. To make a profit, the hospital must keep its costs below the fixed reimbursement amount, which creates an incentive to minimize the patient's length of stay. Following Medicare's lead, other payers adopted prospective methods to reimburse hospitals. Private payers also resorted

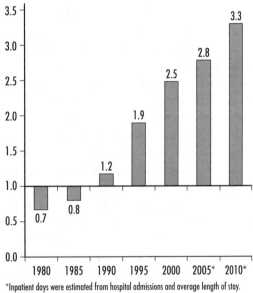

Figure 8–3 Ratio of Hospital Outpatient Visits to Inpatient Days for All US Hospitals, 1980–2010 (selected years).

*Inpatient days were estimated from hospital admissions and average length of stay.

Source: Data from *Statistical Abstract of the United States, 2002,* p. 110; *Health, United States, 2012,* p. 307.

Table 8–1 US Share of Personal Health Expenditures Used for Hospital Care

	Personal Health Expenditures	Hospital Expenditures	% Share
1980	217.2	100.5	46.3%
1990	616.8	250.4	40.6%
2000	1,165.4	415.5	35.7%
2005	1,697.1	609.4	35.9%
2010	2,190.0	815.9	37.3%
2011	2,279.3	850.6	37.3%

Note: Expenditures are in billions of dollars.
Source: Modified from National Health Expenditure Data (Historical). CMS, Office of the Actuary.

to competitive pricing and discounted fees and closely monitored when patients would be hospitalized and for how long. As PPS reimbursement exerted pressure on hospitals to reduce the length of stay after admission, early discharge from hospitals became practical only as alternative services, such as home health care and subacute long-term care, were developed to provide postacute continuity of care.

The effect of PPS on hospitals was dramatic. In the 1980s, 550 hospitals closed and 159 mergers and acquisitions occurred (Balotsky 2005). Since then, the number of community hospital beds per 1,000 resident population has continued to decline, reaching 2.6 in 2010 (Figure 8–1). Notably, since 1998, the nation's hospital capacity per 1,000 resident population has remained below what it was in 1946 when the Hill-Burton Act was passed. In those days, the additional hospital bed capacity may have been necessary because the settings for post-discharge continuity of care were not developed. Technological advances enabled the development of these alternative delivery settings. Hence, technology has played a major role in the tremendous advances in efficiency of the health care system.

Impact of Managed Care

In the 1990s, managed care became a growing force transforming the delivery of health services. Managed care has emphasized cost containment and the efficient delivery of services by stressing the use of alternative delivery settings whenever appropriate. It has been demonstrated that market penetration of health maintenance organizations (HMOs) played a significant role in lowering hospital utilization and profitability (Clement and Grazier 2001).

Hospital Closures

Between 1990 and 2000, a little over 200 rural hospitals (8% of all rural hospitals) and nearly 300 urban hospitals (11% of all urban hospitals) had to close for economic reasons (Office of Inspector General 2003). As a result, the total number of community hospitals declined by 9%; the total number of beds in community hospitals declined by 11% (DHHS 2013). Hospitals of all sizes throughout the country either closed entire wings or converted those beds for alternative uses, such as outpatient care, long-term care, or rehabilitation services. Low utilization was the primary reason, in addition to competition that affected many urban hospitals (Office of Inspector General 2003).

Some Key Utilization Measures and Operational Concepts

Discharges

The total number of patient discharges per 1,000 population is one indicator of access to hospital inpatient services and of the extent of utilization. Because babies born in the hospital are not included in admissions, discharges provide a more accurate count of inpatients served by a hospital. *Discharge* refers to the total number of patients discharged from a hospital's acute care beds in a given period. Deaths in hospitals are counted as discharges. Discharge rates per 1,000 population (see Table 8–2) are important because all other inpatient use patterns depend on them.

Inpatient Days

An *inpatient day* (also called a patient day) is a night spent in the hospital by a patient.

Table 8–2 Discharges, Days of Care, and Average Length of Stay per 1,000 Population in Nonfederal Short-Stay Hospitals, 2009–2010

Characteristics	Discharges	Days of Care	Average Length of Stay
Total	116.0	559.9	4.8
Age			
Under 18 years	33.6	148.0	4.4
18–44 years	86.7	314.7	3.6
45–64 years	120.0	605.8	5.0
65–74 years	248.7	1,350.5	5.4
75–84 years	398.3	2,288.4	5.7
85+ years	566.8	3,184.9	5.6
Gender*			
Male	97.5	515.8	5.3
Female	128.4	563.1	4.4
Geographic Region*			
Northeast	130.0	707.3	5.4
Midwest	114.7	493.3	4.3
South	113.6	551.4	4.9
West	93.3	408.4	4.4

*Age adjusted.

Source: Data from *Health, United States, 2009*, Web update, 2012. National Center for Health Statistics.

The cumulative number of patient days over a certain period is known as *days of care*. Days of care per 1,000 population over 1 year reflect utilization of inpatient services. Hospital utilization increases with age, as indicated by discharges and days of care (see Table 8–2). Among younger age groups, children under 1 year of age have the highest utilization. In general, females incur higher use of hospital services than men do, even after childbirth-related utilization is factored out. Generally, hospital use is higher among people of lower socioeconomic status (SES) than the more affluent because poorer population groups are generally in poorer health and have less access to routine primary care. Lower SES patients also have higher levels of trust in the technical quality of hospital services compared to primary care (Kangovi et al. 2013).

In the western United States, hospital utilization is much lower than in other parts of the country. A high rate of managed care penetration is believed to be primarily responsible for the lower utilization. The utilization patterns also suggest that overall hospital use is higher among Medicare and Medicaid recipients than among the rest of the population.

Average Length of Stay

Average length of stay (ALOS) is calculated by dividing the total days of care by the total number of discharges. It provides a measure of how many days a patient, on average, spends in the hospital. Hence, this measure, when applied to individuals or specific groups of patients, is an indicator of severity of illness and resource use. Figure 8–4 illustrates ALOS trends in community hospitals.

Figure 8–5 shows trends in ALOS by type of hospital ownership. Government-owned hospitals have higher lengths of stay, compared to private hospitals. Federal hospitals mainly include those in the Veterans Health Administration system, which serve a population that is getting older. State and local government hospitals disproportionately serve the poor and uninsured. Both nonprofit and for-profit hospitals had the same ALOS in 2010.

Capacity

The number of beds set up and staffed for inpatient use determines the size or capacity of a hospital. Among all community hospitals in the United States, 84% have fewer than 300 beds (see Figure 8–6). The average size of a community hospital was approximately 161 beds in 2010. The number of hospitals with fewer than 50 beds increased by 33% (from 1,198 to 1,591) between

Figure 8–4 Trends in Average Length of Stay in Nonfederal Short-Stay Hospitals, Selected Years.

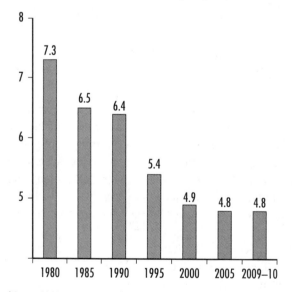

Source: Data from *Health, United States, 2012,* p. 293. National Center for Health Statistics.

Figure 8–5 Average Lengths of Stay by US Hospital Ownership: 2000 and 2010.

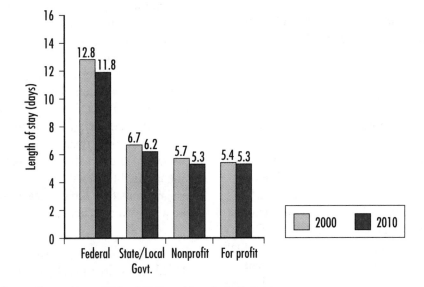

Source: Data from *Health, United States, 2012,* p. 307, National Center for Health Statistics.

Figure 8–6 Breakdown of US Community Hospitals by Size, 2010.

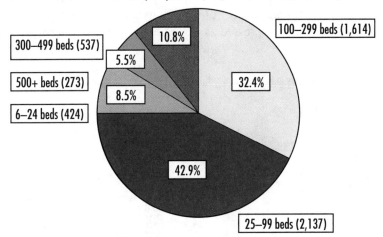

Source: Data from *Health, United States, 2012,* p. 314, National Center for Health Statistics.

2000 and 2010 (DHHS 2013), primarily because of a dramatic rise in the number of physician-owned specialty hospitals (discussed later under the section "Specialty Hospitals").

Average Daily Census

The average number of inpatients receiving care each day in a hospital is referred to as *average daily census*. Hence, it is one of the common measures used to define occupancy of inpatient beds in hospitals and other inpatient facilities. The total inpatient days during a given period (days of care) are divided by the number of days in that period to arrive at the average daily census. For example, if the number of total inpatient days for July is 3,131, then the average daily census for July is 101 (3,131/31).

Occupancy Rate

The *occupancy rate* for a given period is derived by dividing the average daily census for that period by the average number of beds (capacity). The fraction is expressed as

a percentage (percent of beds occupied). It indicates the proportion of a hospital's total inpatient capacity actually utilized. Occupancy rate is also used for other types of inpatient facilities, such as nursing homes, and is often used as a measure of performance. Figure 8–7 shows the change in aggregate occupancy rates for US community hospitals from 1960 to 2010. Individual hospitals can compare their own occupancy rates against industry benchmarks. In a competitive environment, facilities with higher occupancy rates are considered more successful than those with lower occupancy rates.

Hospital Utilization and Employment

Employment in hospitals is influenced by a number of factors; utilization is only one of them. Also, various factors affect hospital utilization and employment in ways that are not always easily decipherable.

Changes in the size and nature of the US population, advances in medical technology, and changes in health insurance are among the long-term factors that affect

Figure 8–7 Change in Occupancy Rates in US Community Hospitals, 1960–2010 (selected years).

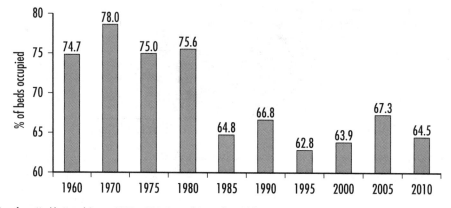

Source: Data from *Health, United States, 2012,* p.314, National Center for Health Statistics.

hospital employment (Goodman 2006). As can be deduced from Table 8–2, aging of the population increases demand for hospital services. Other demographic elements include overall population growth, which increases demand. Demand also varies by the health status of a population. Demand for services is the most important factor that affects hospital employment. New medical technology also increases the demand for hospital staffing. Conversely, certain pharmaceutical developments have substantially reduced the need for hospitalization. The mental health field is especially noted for new pharmaceutical products that shorten hospital stays (Goodman 2006). Hospital utilization is also significantly reduced for HIV/AIDS patients who adhere to antiretroviral therapies (Nachega et al. 2010). After the creation of Medicare and Medicaid in 1965, employment in community hospitals grew by 73% between 1965 and 1975, even though utilization grew by 48% (based on data from the *Statistical Abstract of the United States*, 1985). Clearly, utilization alone does not impact job growth.

Other factors have had a downward influence on hospital jobs. For example, a shift toward treatment from inpatient to outpatient settings has increased employment in various outpatient settings. Starting around 1995, various outpatient care settings started employing more workers than hospitals. In 2010, 36.4% of all employment in health care and social assistance was in outpatient care settings; 28.5% of the employment was in hospitals (US Census Bureau 2012). Changes in reimbursement policy can also affect employment. Hospital employment declined by 2.3%, to about 4 million workers over the 1983 to 1986 period when the hospital downsizing trend started with DRG-based PPS.

Staff cuts, hiring freezes, and the increased use of contract services were part of a belt-tightening effort in response to declining inpatient admissions (Kahl and Clark 1986). But, as hospitals chased more liberal reimbursement in outpatient markets, employment in hospitals in 1989 rose to 4.3 million workers, an increase of 6.9% from 1986 (Anderson and Wootton 1991). This trend has continued even though more recently the rate of job growth in hospitals appears to be moderating (Figure 8–8).

Patterns in hospital employment are quite unlike those in other industries. Changes in hospital employment are opposite to those of gross domestic product (GDP) and of total US nonfarm employment. When unemployment in the general economy rises, so does the rate of job growth in hospitals. While the trend of employment in all hospitals combined is consistently upward, the rate of growth may be described as countercyclical; that is, when general business conditions are weak, hospital employment exhibits greater growth (Goodman 2006). In the most recent 2007–2009 recession, for example, hospitals added an average of 10,000 jobs per month between December 2007 and July 2008 (Wood 2011).

Hospital Costs

As pointed out earlier, inpatient hospital services constitute the largest share of total health care expenditures in the United States. In 2010, the aggregate cost for all hospital inpatient stays was $376 billion; the average cost per stay was $9,700. Adults ages 45–64 and 65–84 had the highest average cost per stay ($12,100 and $12,300 respectively). These two age groups accounted

Figure 8–8 Recent Trends in US Hospital Employment.

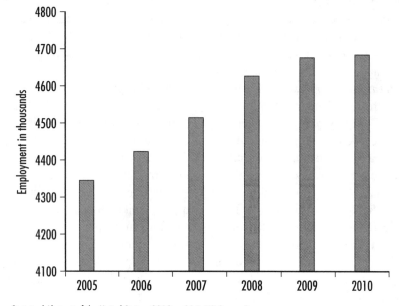

Source: Data from *Statistical Abstract of the United States, 2012,* p. 114, US Census Bureau.

for nearly two-thirds of aggregate hospital costs and about half of all hospital stays. It is surprising that the elderly age 85 and over incurred $9,600 per stay, about the average for all age groups. Death after discharge is not the likely reason because their ALOS is comparable to the other older groups (see Table 8–2). Medicare and Medicaid paid for 61% of the aggregate hospital costs. Medicare was responsible for 45% of the costs; Medicaid accounted for 16%; private insurance covered nearly one-third; and uninsured hospitalizations accounted for 5% (Pfuntner et al. 2013).

After adjusting for inflation, hospital costs increased by 4.4% between 1997 and 2008. The primary cost driver was cost per day or intensity of services provided, followed by growth in the population (Stranges et al. 2011).

Types of Hospitals

The United States has a variety of institutional forms, with both private and government-owned institutions. Most hospitals are private nonprofit, short-stay, general hospitals. State and local government-owned hospitals are next in predominance. Then come the private for-profit (investor-owned) hospitals and, finally, federal hospitals. Figure 8–9 shows the distribution of hospitals, and Figure 8–10 shows the distribution of beds among various hospital types.

The endless variations in hospital characteristics defy any simple classification. The following classification arrangements have been commonly used to differentiate among the various types of hospitals. It is important to keep in mind, however, that these classifications are not mutually exclusive.

Figure 8–9 Proportion of Total US Hospitals by Type of Hospital, 2009.

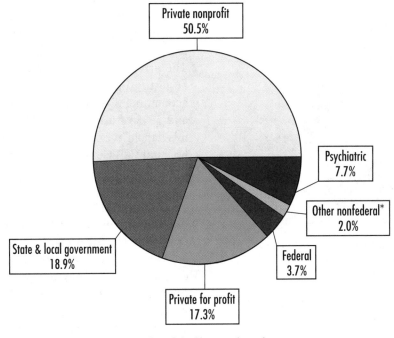

* Mainly nonfederal long-term hospitals.
All hospitals = 5,780 (hospital units of institutions have been excluded).

Source: Data from *Statistical Abstract of the United States, 2012,* p. 119, US Census Bureau.

Classification by Ownership

Public Hospitals

Public hospitals are owned by agencies of federal, state, or local governments. It should be noted that here the word "public" does not carry its ordinary meaning. A public hospital, for instance, is not necessarily a hospital that is open to the general public.

Federal hospitals serve special groups of federal beneficiaries, such as Native Americans, military personnel, and veterans, rather than the common population. Veterans Affairs (VA) hospitals constitute the largest group among federal hospitals.

State governments operate some of the largest mental health institutions. Local governments, such as counties and cities, operate hospitals to serve the general population. Many of these hospitals are located in large urban areas, where they function as an important safety net for the inner city indigent and disadvantaged populations. Hence, Medicare, Medicaid, and state and local tax dollars pay for a large portion of the services these hospitals provide. Because of increasing financial pressures, many public hospitals had to privatize or close. Out of 1,444 state and local government-owned hospitals in 1990, 1,092 remained in 2009 (US Census Bureau 2012). Most hospitals operated by city and county governments are small to moderate size. Some large public hospitals are affiliated with medical schools; they play

Figure 8–10   Proportion of Total US Hospital Beds by Type of Hospital, 2009.

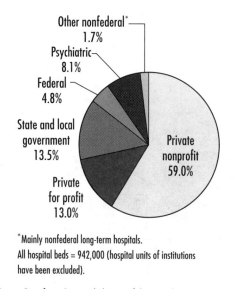

Other nonfederal*
1.7%

Psychiatric
8.1%

Federal
4.8%

State and local
government
13.5%

Private
for profit
13.0%

Private
nonprofit
59.0%

*Mainly nonfederal long-term hospitals.
All hospital beds = 942,000 (hospital units of institutions
have been excluded).

Source: Data from Statistical Abstract of the United States, 2012,
p. 119, US Census Bureau.

a significant role in training physicians and other health care professionals.

Compared to private hospitals, public hospitals incur higher utilization, at least in terms of ALOS (see Figure 8–5). ALOS is the highest in federal hospitals (11.8 days in 2010), and veterans are the biggest users of these hospitals. Of the 22.7 million veterans living in 2011, 41% were age 65 and older (Department of Veterans Affairs 2013), compared to 13.3% of the general US population. The number of discharges in VA hospitals increased from 579,000 in 2000 to 653,000 in 2011 (DHHS 2013).

Private Nonprofit Hospitals

Nonprofit hospitals are owned and operated by community associations or other nongovernment organizations. Their primary mission is to benefit the community in which they are located. Patient fees, third-party reimbursement, donations, and endowments cover their operating expenses. The private nonprofit sector constitutes the largest group of hospitals (Figure 8–9), accounting for 50.5% of all US hospitals and 59% of all beds in 2009. These hospitals had an average capacity of 190 beds per hospital (US Census Bureau 2012).

Private For-Profit Hospitals

For-profit *proprietary hospitals*—also referred to as *investor-owned hospitals*—are owned by individuals, partnerships, or corporations. They are operated for the financial benefit of the entity that owns the institution, that is, the stockholders. At the beginning of the 20th century, more than one-half of the nation's hospitals were proprietary. Most of these hospitals were small and were established by physicians who wanted to hospitalize their own patients (Stewart 1973). Later, most of these institutions were closed or acquired by community organizations or hospital corporations, due to population shifts, increased costs, and the necessities of modern clinical practice (Raffel and Raffel 1994). Even though the nonprofit hospital sector has maintained its market dominance, the number of for-profit hospitals and beds has increased (Table 8–3). Greater increase in the number of hospitals compared to the number of beds and a significant reduction in the average size reflects the growth of physician-owned specialty hospitals (discussed later under "Specialty Hospitals"), which are smaller in size than other community hospitals. Private nonprofit hospitals continue to enjoy greater occupancy rates than for-profit hospitals.

Table 8–3 Changes in Number of US Hospitals, Beds, Average Size, and Occupancy Rates

	2000	2010	Change
Private Nonprofit			
Number of hospitals	3,003	2,904	−3.3%
Number of beds	582,988	555,768	−4.7%
Average size	194	191	−1.4%
Occupancy rate	65.5%	66.2%	1.1%
Private For Profit			
Number of hospitals	749	1,013	35.2%
Number of beds	109,883	124,652	13.4%
Average size	147	123	−16.1%
Occupancy rate	55.9%	57.1%	2.1%

Source: Data from *Health, United States, 2012*, p. 314. National Center for Health Statistics.

Classification by Public Access

Community hospitals are the most common type of hospital in the United States. A *community hospital* is a nonfederal, short-stay hospital, whose services are available to the general public. Its primary mission is to serve the general community. These hospitals are not restricted to serving a certain category of people. A community hospital may be private for profit, private nonprofit, or owned by the state or local government (but not by the federal government). It can be a general hospital or a specialty hospital. The larger the community served, the larger the hospital, range of specialties, and range of supporting equipment and services (Raffel and Raffel 1994). Noncommunity hospitals include hospitals operated by the federal government, such as VA hospitals to serve veterans; hospital units of institutions, such as prisons and infirmaries in colleges and universities; and long-stay hospitals.

Almost 87% of US hospitals are community hospitals. Figure 8–11 shows the breakdown of community hospitals by ownership type.

Figure 8–11 Breakdown of US Community Hospitals by Type of Ownership, 2010.

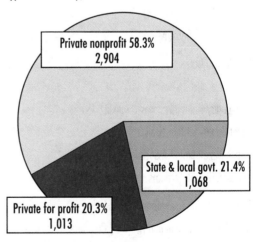

Private nonprofit 58.3%
2,904

State & local govt. 21.4%
1,068

Private for profit 20.3%
1,013

Source: Data from *Health, United States, 2013*, p. 314, National Center for Health Statistics.

Classification by Multiunit Affiliation

Hospitals are part of a multihospital chain (referred to as a *multihospital system* [MHS]) when two or more hospitals are owned, leased, sponsored, or contractually managed by a central organization (AHA 1994). MHSs exist in all three ownership types discussed earlier. The number of hospitals in MHSs has grown annually since 2004, and the pace of consolidation has accelerated and is likely to continue. In 2011, 61% of US hospitals were affiliated with MHSs, up from 52% in 2005 (Sanofi-Aventis 2013). Most MHSs are operated by nonprofit corporations, but three for-profit corporations are the largest (Table 8–4). Some of the advantages

Table 8–4   The Largest US Multihospital Chains, 2011 (Ranked by Staffed Beds in Each Category)

Name of Hospital System (Location)	Number of Owned Hospitals	Number of Staffed Beds
Nonprofit Chains		
Ascension Health (St. Louis, MO)	53	10,587
Dignity Health (San Francisco, CA)	37	9,071
Catholic Health Initiatives (Englewood, CO)	63	8,657
Kaiser Permanente (Oakland, CA)	35	8,149
Trinity Health (Novi, MI)	40	7,880
Adventist Health System (Altamonte Springs, FL)	38	6,736
North Shore-Long Island Jewish Health System (Great Neck, NY)	13	5,678
Providence Health and Services (Renton, WA)	24	5,579
Christus Health (Irving, TX)	23	5,346
Sutter Health (Sacramento, CA)	29	5,144
For-Profit Chains		
HCA (Nashville, TN)	156	33,568
Community Health Systems (Franklin, TN)	133	17,857
Tenet Health System (Dallas, TX)	49	11,709
Health Management Associates (Naples, FL)	62	7,919
Vanguard Health Systems (Nashville, TN)	21	5,861
State and Local Government—Owned Chains		
New York City Health and Hospitals Corporation (New York, NY)	11	4,731

Source: Data from *Managed Care Digest Series: Hospital/Systems Digest, 2013,* Bridgewater, NJ: Sanofi-Aventis.

of multihospital chain affiliation include economies of scale, the ability to provide a wide spectrum of care, the ability to reach a variety of markets, increased access to capital, greater participation in managed care contracting, and access to management resources and expertise. Hospitals not affiliated with an MHS incur higher costs of operation ($5,709 per patient day vs. $5,188 for all hospitals; Sanofi-Aventis 2013).

The VA operates the single largest MHS in the country, with 152 medical centers owned by the federal government. In 2011, VA hospitals had a total of 653,000 inpatient hospital discharges (DHHS 2013).

Classification by Type of Service

General Hospitals

A *general hospital* provides a variety of services, including general and specialized medicine, general and specialized surgery, and obstetrics, to meet almost all medical needs of the community it serves. It provides diagnostic, treatment, and surgical services for patients with a variety of medical conditions. Most hospitals in the United States are general hospitals.

The term "general hospital" does not imply that these hospitals are less specialized or that their care is inferior to that of specialty hospitals. The difference lies in the nature of services, not their quality. General hospitals provide a broader range of services for a larger variety of conditions, whereas specialty hospitals provide a narrow range of services for specific medical conditions or patient populations.

Specialty Hospitals

According to the North American Industry Classification System of the US Census Bureau, *specialty hospitals* are establishments that primarily engage in providing diagnostic and medical treatment to inpatients with a specific type of disease or medical condition, except services for psychiatric care or substance abuse. Specialty hospitals forge a distinct service niche. Traditionally, the two most common specialty hospitals have been rehabilitation hospitals and children's hospitals. With increasing competition, however, other types of specialty hospitals have emerged to provide treatments that are also available in many general hospitals. Examples include orthopedic hospitals, cardiac hospitals, cancer (oncology) hospitals, and women's hospitals. Physicians find such specialized hospitals more efficient, and in many instances, physicians are full or part owners of these hospitals. Affiliation with such hospitals gives physicians control over hospital operations, flexibility with their time, and opportunity to enhance their incomes.

Physician-owned facilities have raised legal and ethical issues with regard to self-referrals without full disclosure. Stark Laws that prohibit self-referrals (see Chapter 5) do not apply when physicians self-refer to a "whole hospital." Under this exception, physicians may refer patients to a facility if their ownership interest is in the whole hospital rather than a part or subdivision of the hospital.

Physician-owned specialty hospitals have been the subject of much controversy, which has invited congressional reviews. In a report to Congress, the Medicare Payment Advisory Commission (MedPAC 2006) pointed out that these hospitals (1) had lower shares of Medicaid patients (2% to 3% of discharges) than community general hospitals (13% of discharges) in the same markets; (2) admitted less severe, more profitable cases; (3) drew patients from community general hospitals, although general hospitals were able to compensate for the revenue loss; and (4) did not have lower costs per severity-adjusted discharge than competing general hospitals in the same markets. Also, the entrance of a physician-owned cardiac hospital was associated with a 6% increase in the number of cardiac surgeries, which suggests that these hospitals may be engaging in creating provider-induced demand. Another issue, emergency care, is at the heart of the controversy between specialty hospitals and community general hospitals. Administrators of general hospitals argue that specialty hospitals are "cream-skimming" insured patients and leaving costly emergency and uncompensated cases to general hospitals (Snyder 2003). Physician-owned specialty hospitals derive approximately 50% of their revenue from Medicare (Weaver 2010).

The Affordable Care Act (ACA) closed the door on future physician-owned hospitals effective January 1, 2011 if they want to participate in Medicare. New or existing hospitals had to be certified by December 31, 2010, failing which they would be barred from participating in the Medicare program (Weaver 2010). Existing physician-owned facilities also faced immediate restrictions on expansion. Many observers view this as an assault on the long-standing American entrepreneurial system. Conversely, when the government pays for health care, it also ends up controlling health care through regulations that may be viewed as unfair. Hence, in response, some of the country's roughly 275 physician-owned hospitals are expanding their operating hours, adding room for MRIs and other imaging tests, launching into same-day surgeries that do not require an inpatient stay, and rejecting Medicare patients to bypass the law (Mundy 2013).

Psychiatric Hospitals

The primary function of a psychiatric inpatient facility is to provide diagnostic and treatment services for a variety of severe mental conditions, such as bipolar disorder, schizophrenia, severe depression, dual diagnosis (mental illness compounded by chemical dependency), and serious emotional disturbances in children and adolescents. The main services include psychiatric, psychological, and social work programs. A psychiatric hospital must also have a written agreement with a general hospital for the transfer of patients who may require medical, obstetric, or surgical services (Health Forum 2001). Inpatient psychiatric facilities can be either freestanding hospitals or specialized psychiatric units in a general hospital.

Historically, state governments have taken the primary responsibility for establishing facilities for the care of the mentally ill. Trends during the 1970s and 1980s resulted in significant deinstitutionalization of the inpatient population who resided in state mental hospitals. As a result, the responsibility for much psychiatric care shifted to psychiatric units in general hospitals, private psychiatric hospitals, other types of residential facilities, and community care programs (Mechanic 1998). However, state mental institutions continue to provide treatment to people with severe and persistent mental illness (Patrick et al. 2006). Between 2000 and 2009, the number of freestanding psychiatric hospitals declined from 496 (87,000 beds) to 444 (76,000 beds; US Census Bureau 2012).

Rehabilitation Hospitals

Rehabilitation hospitals specialize in therapeutic services to restore the maximum level of functioning in patients who have suffered recent disability due to an episode of illness or an accident. According to Medicare rules, to be classified as a rehabilitation hospital, 75% of a hospital's inpatients must require intensive rehabilitation for conditions such as stroke, spinal cord injury, major multiple trauma, and brain injury (Grimaldi 2002). Intensive rehabilitation refers to at least 3 hours of therapy per day. Rehabilitation hospitals also serve amputees, victims of accident or sports injuries, and those needing intensive cardiac rehabilitation. Facilities and staff are available to provide physical therapy, occupational therapy, and speech-language pathology. Most rehabilitation hospitals have special arrangements for psychological, social work, and vocational services and are required to have written arrangements with a general hospital for the transfer of patients who need medical, obstetrical, or surgical care not available at the institution (Health Forum 2001). Inpatient rehabilitation facilities can be either freestanding hospitals or specialized rehab units in a general hospital. Approximately 80% of these facilities are hospital-based units (MedPAC 2012a).

In 2012, approximately 1,140 inpatient rehabilitation facilities (IRFs) were Medicare certified. Medicare accounts for about 60% of the caseload in these facilities (MedPAC 2012a). Medicare has developed a separate IRF prospective payment system that was implemented in 2002. It pays a per discharge prospective rate according to case-mix groups (see Chapter 6).

Children's Hospitals

Children's hospitals are community hospitals that typically have specialized facilities to deal mainly with complex, severe, or chronic illnesses among children. Nearly all children's hospitals provide neonatal intensive care units, pediatric intensive care units, trauma centers, and transplant services. Thus, these hospitals provide a wide range of high-intensity services for children, such as pediatric surgery, cardiology, orthopedic surgery, cancer treatment, HIV/AIDS treatment, and rehabilitation services (DelliFraine 2006). Some specialize in services such as orthopedics or cancer treatment.

Children's hospitals can be freestanding or they can be pediatric centers located in major hospitals. Specialized pediatric departments of major medical centers are run with their own staffs, operating rooms, laboratories, and other facilities as if they were a separate hospital within a hospital (Leonard 2013). In most communities no specialty children's hospitals exist, hence, general acute care hospitals serve as de facto children's hospitals (DelliFraine 2006).

Classification by Length of Stay

Short-Stay Hospitals

A *short-stay hospital* is one in which the average length of stay is 25 days or less. Most hospitals fall in this category. Patients admitted to these hospitals suffer from acute conditions. Hospitals with average stays of more than 25 days are long-stay hospitals. These include state-run, as well as private, psychiatric hospitals; long-term care hospitals providing subacute care; and chronic disease hospitals.

Long-Term Care Hospitals

The majority of long-stay hospitals in the United States are *long-term care hospitals* (LTCHs). A long-term care hospital is a special type of long-stay hospital described in section 1886(d)(1)(B)(iv) of the Social Security Act. LTCHs must meet Medicare's conditions of participation for acute care hospitals and must have an ALOS greater than 25 days. LTCHs serve patients who have complex medical needs and may suffer from multiple chronic problems requiring long-term hospitalization. Many LTCH patients are admitted directly from short-stay hospital intensive care units with respiratory/ventilator-dependent or other complex medical conditions. The number of LTCHs in the United States grew rapidly from 105 facilities in 1993 to 318 in 2003 (MedPAC 2004). In 2010, there were 412 LTCH facilities, but they were not distributed evenly throughout the nation. Medicare accounted for about two-thirds of the revenues for these hospitals (MedPAC 2012b).

The Balanced Budget Refinement Act of 1999 (BBRA) mandated a discharge-based PPS, which was implemented in 2003. The LTCH PPS replaced the previous cost-based reimbursement. The PPS uses the Medicare Severity Long-Term Care Diagnosis-Related Groups (MS-LTC-DRGs) as a patient classification system in which each patient stay is grouped into an MS-LTC-DRG based on diagnoses (including secondary diagnoses), procedures performed, age, gender, and discharge status. Each MS-LTC-DRG has a predetermined ALOS, which is updated annually based on the latest available LTCH discharge data. The hospital receives payment for each Medicare patient based on the MS-LTC-DRG to which that patient's stay is grouped.

This grouping reflects the typical resources used for treating such a patient. Cases assigned to an MS-LTC-DRG are paid based on the Federal Payment Rate, including facility and case-level adjustments. One type of case-level adjustment is an interrupted stay (CMS 2010).

Classification by Location

Based on location, hospitals can be classified as urban or rural. *Urban hospitals* are located in a county that is part of a metropolitan statistical area (MSA). The US Census Bureau has defined an MSA as a geographic area that includes at least (1) one city with a population of 50,000 or more or (2) an urbanized area of at least 50,000 inhabitants and a total MSA population of at least 100,000. *Rural hospitals* are located in a county that is not part of an MSA. Roughly 2,000 hospitals (40% of all community hospitals) are located in rural America (AHA 2008). It is estimated that rural hospitals deliver health care to 54 million Americans, including 9 million Medicare beneficiaries (Slusky 2006).

Compared to rural hospitals, urban hospitals have higher costs because they pay higher salaries in more competitive markets, offer a broader scope of more sophisticated services, and treat patients requiring more complex care. Urban hospitals are located either in inner cities or in the suburbs. Because suburbs of metropolitan areas are more affluent than inner cities or rural areas, both inner city urban hospitals and rural hospitals treat a patient mix that is disproportionately poor and elderly, compared to suburban hospital patients (HCIA, Inc. and Deloitte & Touche 1997). Because of the disproportionate numbers of the elderly and poor in rural areas, small rural community hospitals often find themselves in financial trouble. Conversion to a facility that provides nonacute health care services, such as a primary care clinic, a long-term care facility, or a specialty hospital, is sometimes a viable alternative when closure threatens these hospitals. For example, adoption of long-term care strategies has demonstrated to improve profitability of rural hospitals (Stuart et al. 2006).

Swing-Bed Hospitals

Subsequent to demonstration projects during the 1970s, the swing bed program for rural hospitals was authorized under the Omnibus Reconciliation Act of 1980. A hospital *swing bed* can be used for acute care or skilled nursing care as needed. The program enabled many rural hospitals to survive during a period of declining occupancy rates. The program also enabled rural residents to access post-acute nursing care services which were not available in many rural communities. Because the swing bed program operates under two distinct payment systems, for acute hospital stays and skilled nursing facility (SNF) stays, Medicare rules require discharge of a patient from acute care in accordance with the rules that apply to SNFs, that is, a 3-day inpatient acute care stay is necessary to qualify for an SNF. In July 2002, CMS brought hospital swing beds under the existing SNF PPS reimbursement (discussed in Chapter 6), which has created financial pressures for rural hospitals. To overcome this drawback, many rural hospitals have switched to critical access hospital status.

Critical Access Hospitals

To save some of the very small rural hospitals, the Balanced Budget Act of 1997 created the Medicare Rural Hospital Flexibility Program (MRHFP). Under this program, a rural hospital, upon meeting certain conditions, can file an application with Medicare to be classified as a *critical access hospital* (CAH). To qualify as a CAH, the hospital should have no more than 25 acute care and/or swing beds and it must provide 24-hour emergency medical services. It must also meet a distance test in relation to other hospitals. A CAH is also allowed to have a 10-bed psychiatric unit, a 10-bed rehabilitation unit, and a distinct SNF. If a hospital elects CAH status and meets the criteria for CAH designation, it can receive cost-plus reimbursement (see Chapter 6) for inpatient, outpatient, laboratory, therapy, and most postacute services in swing beds. Total payment to the hospital is fixed at 101% of cost. Because of their many financial advantages, the number of CAHs jumped from 850 in 2003 (Mantone 2005) to over 1,300 in 2012 (MedPAC 2012c).

Classification by Size

There is no standard way to classify hospitals by size. According to one classification scheme, hospitals with fewer than 100 beds would be classified as small, those with 100 to 500 beds as medium, and those with 500-plus beds as large. Others may classify by size a little differently. Less than half (49%) of the community hospitals in the United States have 100 beds or more (see Figure 8–6).

Experience in the manufacturing and retail sectors of the economy suggests that large enterprises often realize economies of scale. The reason is that certain overhead costs are fixed or semifixed—they do not increase proportionately as the size of the enterprise increases. Examples are administrative costs and plant maintenance costs.

In the hospital industry, the reverse may be happening. Coyne and colleagues (2009) showed that cost per adjusted patient day was significantly higher in hospitals exceeding 150 beds compared to hospitals between 40 and 150 beds, regardless of ownership type. Costs in larger hospitals are likely attributable to a more extensive array of specialized and resource-intensive services that these hospitals must be equipped to provide. Such services require sophisticated technology and personnel with advanced training. Large teaching hospitals incur the additional costs of residency training and medical research. Higher costs in much smaller CAHs are likely attributable to cost-based reimbursement which does not provide any incentives for cost control.

Other Types of Hospitals

Teaching Hospitals

To be designated as a *teaching hospital*, a hospital must have one or more graduate residency programs approved by the AMA. The mere presence of nursing programs or training affiliations for other health professionals, such as therapists and dietitians, does not make an institution a teaching hospital.

The term *academic medical center* is commonly used when one or more hospitals, with or without affiliated outpatient clinics, are organized around a medical school. Apart from the training of physicians, research activities and clinical investigations become an important undertaking.

Among the largest and most prestigious teaching hospitals are the members of the Council of Teaching Hospitals and Health Systems (COTH), which has approximately 400 members in both the United States (including 64 VA medical centers) and Canada. They usually have substantial teaching and research programs and are affiliated with medical schools of large universities. The COTH member institutions train more than 100,000 new physicians each year (AAMC 2013).

Three main traits separate teaching and nonteaching hospitals:

1. Teaching hospitals provide medical training to physicians, research opportunities to health services researchers, and specialized care to patients. These hospitals receive separate payments from Medicare (up to 140% of the national average) for the direct costs incurred in operating training programs for medical, dental, or podiatric residents. As part of the prospective DRG rates, these hospitals also receive add-on payments to reflect the additional indirect costs of patient care associated with the training of medical residents (MedPAC 2012d).

2. Teaching hospitals have a broader and more complex scope of services than nonteaching hospitals. These hospitals often operate several intensive care units, possess the latest medical technologies, and attract a diverse group of physicians representing most specialties and many subspecialties. Major teaching hospitals also offer many unique tertiary care services not generally found in other institutions, such as burn care, trauma care, and organ transplantation. Hence, teaching hospitals attract patients who frequently have more complicated diagnoses or need

more complex procedures. Because of the greater case-mix complexity of teaching hospitals, greater resources are required for treatment.

3. Many of the major teaching hospitals are located in economically depressed, older inner city areas and are generally owned by state or local governments. Consequently, these hospitals often provide disproportional amounts of uncompensated care to uninsured patients. For example, COTH member institutions provide nearly one-half of all hospital charity care nationwide (AAMC 2013).

Church-Affiliated Hospitals

Various churches established hospitals mainly during the latter half of the 19th and the early 20th centuries. Various Catholic sisterhoods established the first church-sponsored hospitals in the United States. Later, protestant denominations organized hospitals in accord with their missions of service, and Jewish philanthropic organizations opened hospitals so that Jewish patients could observe their dietary laws more faithfully and Jewish physicians could more easily find sites for training and work opportunities (Raffel 1980).

Church-affiliated hospitals are often community general hospitals. They may be large or small, teaching or nonteaching. Affiliation with a medical school may also vary. Church-affiliated hospitals do not discriminate in rendering care; however, they are generally sensitive to the sponsoring denomination's special spiritual and/or dietary emphasis (Raffel and Raffel 1994).

Osteopathic Hospitals

Chapter 4 points out the main differences between allopathic and osteopathic medicine. For all practical purposes, osteopathic hospitals are community general hospitals. In 1970, osteopathic hospitals became eligible to apply for registration with the AHA (1994). For many years after osteopathy was established as a separate branch of medicine in 1874, osteopaths had to develop their own hospitals because of antagonism from the established allopathic medical practitioners. Since then, both groups have inspected each other's medical schools and satisfied themselves that each is worth associating with and that each could serve on the other's faculties and practice side by side in the same hospitals (Raffel and Raffel 1994). Many osteopathic hospitals today are part of hospital systems and maintain their osteopathic identity within the context of these larger systems. An independent osteopathic hospital is no longer a necessity and seems to be economically out of place in today's market (Hilsenrath 2006). Also, the operation of osteopathic hospitals has been found to be more costly and less productive in comparison to their counterparts (Sinay 2005). Consequently, a number of these hospitals have closed.

Expectations from Nonprofit Hospitals

Lay people make a common assumption that nonprofit (sometimes called not-for-profit) health care corporations are driven by the mission to meet the health care needs of patients regardless of their ability to pay. It is further assumed that these corporations do not make a profit. The fact is that every corporation, regardless of whether it is for profit or nonprofit, has to make a profit (surplus of revenues over expenses) to survive over the long term. No business can survive for long if it continually spends more than it takes in. That is true for both the nonprofit and the for-profit sectors (Nudelman and Andrews 1996).

The Internal Revenue Code, Section 501(c)(3), grants tax-exempt status to nonprofit organizations. As such, these institutions are exempt from federal, state, and local taxes, such as income taxes, sales taxes, and property taxes. In general, these organizations must (1) provide some defined public good, such as service, education, or community welfare and (2) not distribute any profits to any individuals. A major goal for a for-profit corporation, on the other hand, is to provide its shareholders with a return on their investment, but it achieves this goal primarily by excelling at its basic mission. For any health services provider, the basic mission is to deliver the highest quality care at the most reasonable price possible.

Since 1969, a community-benefit standard has been applied to nonprofit hospitals. It broadly refers to services that the government would otherwise have to undertake (Owens 2005). Also, Section 4958 of the IRS code prohibits executive compensation that may be deemed unreasonable for tax-exempt organizations. Nonprofit hospitals have to be prepared to demonstrate not only that they are paying salaries within some reasonable range of industry standards but also that executives are bringing measurable value in key areas of operations, including community benefits (Appleby 2004). Hence, it is recommended that some portion of hospital chief executive officers' salaries directly hinge on their performance in two critical areas (Newman

et al. 2001): (1) organizational effectiveness (financial performance, market share, quality, daily operations, and achievement of strategic objectives) and (2) community health (charitable care, health promotion and education, and overall state of the community's health).

The problem is that nonprofit hospitals, in many instances, compete head-on with for-profit hospitals. For example, nonprofit hospitals frequently engage in the same kinds of aggressive marketplace behaviors that for-profit hospitals pursue. Generally, nonprofit hospitals operate in locations with higher average incomes, lower poverty rates, and lower rates of uninsurance than for-profit hospitals (CBO 2006).

Institutional theory actually predicts such behavior. When for-profit and nonprofit organizations face similar regulatory, legal, and professional constraints, they will imitate each other, according to institutional theory (O'Connell and Brown 2003). In the hospital industry, competition commonly occurs in the same communities for the same patients, with revenues coming from the same public and private third-party sources, and often involving the same physician providers who have admitting privileges at more than one hospital.

Empirical evidence has indicated that for-profit and nonprofit hospitals provide similar levels of charity and uncompensated care (Thorpe et al. 2000), but a later report by the Congressional Budget Office (2006) showed mixed results. Nevertheless, lingering concerns over the issue of tax exemption in exchange for community benefits prompted the Internal Revenue Service (IRS) to require detailed financial documentation from nonprofit hospitals on their community benefit expenditures starting in 2009.

A study based on the initial IRS tax returns found that community benefits by tax-exempt hospitals varied widely from 1% of operating expenses used for community benefits to as high as 20% (Young et al. 2013). In a 2010 decision by the Illinois Supreme Court, pertaining to *Provena v. Department of Revenue*, the court ruled that the medical center was not entitled to charitable exemption for property taxes because it did not provide sufficient community benefits (Supreme Court of the State of Illinois 2010). However, the debate continues, particularly over what is and what is not a community benefit.

Nonprofit institutions face new demands to deliver community benefits under the ACA. The law requires nonprofit hospitals to (1) assess community health needs and implement plans and strategies to meet those needs, (2) establish written financial assistance and emergency care policies, (3) limit charges for individuals who are eligible for assistance under the hospital's financial assistance policy, (4) limit certain billing and collection actions against those who fall within the guidelines of financial assistance, and (5) report on community health needs and provide annual audited financial statements to the IRS. An excise tax will be imposed for failure to comply with the community health assessment mandate (Betbeze 2011; Internal Revenue Service 2013).

Some Management Concepts

From a management standpoint, hospitals are complex organizations. Compared to other business enterprises of similar size, both external and internal environments of hospitals are more complex. A hospital is responsible to numerous stakeholders in its external environment. These stakeholders include the community, the government, insurers, managed care organizations (MCOs), and accreditation agencies. A hospital's organizational structure also differs substantially from that of other large organizations in the business world.

Hospital Governance

Hospital governance has traditionally followed a tripartite structure (see Figure 8–12). The three major sources of authority are the chief executive officer (CEO), the board of trustees, and the chief of staff. In earlier periods, when physicians operated their own hospitals, trustees dominated the hospitals. Trustees were often the source of capital investment, and their influence in the community brought prestige to the hospital. Later, as voluntary hospitals increased in number, the balance of power shifted into the hands of physicians because they played a critical role in bringing patients to the hospitals. As changes in the health care environment made the management of hospitals more complex, considerable power shifted from physicians to senior managers.

The medical staff constitute a separate organizational structure parallel to the administrative structure. Such a dual structure is rarely seen in other businesses and presents numerous opportunities for conflict between the CEO and the medical staff. Matters are further complicated when the lines of authority cross between the two structures. For example, nursing service, pharmacists, diagnostic technicians, and dietitians are administratively accountable to the CEO (via the vertical chain of command) but professionally accountable to the medical staff (Raffel and Raffel 1994). Although most of the medical staff are not

Figure 8–12 Hospital Governance and Operational Structures.

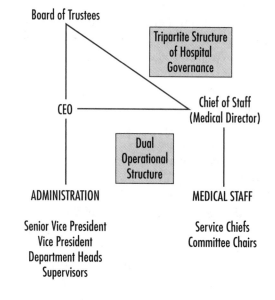

paid employees of the hospital, physicians' interest in employment has been growing as they seek ways to stabilize their incomes and achieve a better work-life balance in a changing health care landscape (Shoger 2011). Regardless of whether the physicians are independent practitioners or contracted employees of the hospital, they play a significant role in the hospital's success. It requires special skills on the part of the CEO to manage the dual structure to achieve the organization's overall objectives.

Board of Trustees

The *board of trustees* (also referred to as the governing body or board of directors) consists of influential business and community leaders. The board is legally responsible for the operations of the hospital. The board has specific responsibilities for defining the hospital's mission and long-range direction; evaluating, from a strategic standpoint, major decisions such as incurring capital expenditures for building and equipment; approving annual budgets; and monitoring performance against plans and budgets. The CEO is a member of the board. One or more physicians also sit on the board as voting members. One of the most important responsibilities of the board is to appoint and evaluate the performance of the CEO, who is charged with providing the board with timely reports on the institution's progress toward achieving its mission and objectives. The board has the power to remove the CEO. In most hospitals, the board also approves the appointment of physicians and other professionals to the hospital's medical staff.

Boards often function through committees. Standing committees usually include executive, medical staff, human resources, finance, planning, quality improvement, and ethics. Special, or ad hoc, committees are established as needed. The two most important committees, from a governance standpoint, are the executive committee and the medical staff committee. The *executive committee* has continuing monitoring responsibility and authority over the hospital. Usually, it receives reports from other committees, monitors policy implementation, and makes recommendations. The *medical staff committee* is charged with medical staff relations. For example, it reviews admitting privileges and the performance of the medical staff. There is also increased emphasis on the legal and ethical obligations of the hospital regarding patient safety, quality improvement, and patient satisfaction.

Chief Executive Officer

Formerly, the titles of "superintendent" and later "administrator" were commonly used for a hospital's chief executive. Now, "chief executive officer" and "president" are the common titles used. The CEO's job is to accomplish the organization's mission and objectives through leadership within the organization. He or she has the ultimate responsibility for day-to-day operations.

The CEO receives delegated authority from the board and is responsible for managing the organization with the help of senior managers. In large hospitals, these senior managers often carry the title of senior vice president or vice president for various key service areas, such as nursing services, rehabilitation services, human resources, finance, and so forth.

Medical Staff

The hospital's medical staff is an organized body of physicians who provide medical services to the hospital's patients and perform related clinical duties. Most physicians are in private practice outside the hospital. The hospital grants them admitting privileges that enable them to admit and care for their patients in the hospital. Other clinicians, such as dentists and podiatrists, may also be granted admitting privileges. Appointment to the medical staff is a formal process outlined in the hospital's medical staff bylaws. The medical staff use a framework of self-governance, which represents the strong tradition of physician independence. The medical staff are formally accountable to the board. Lines of communication to the CEO and the board of trustees are established through various committee representations.

A medical director, or *chief of staff*, heads the medical staff. In all but the smallest hospitals, the medical staff are organizationally divided by major specialties into departments, such as anesthesiology, internal medicine, obstetrics and gynecology, orthopedic surgery, pathology, cardiology, and radiology. A *chief of service*, such as chief of cardiology, heads each specialty.

The medical staff generally have their own executive committee that sets general policies and is the main decision-making body in medical matters. Most hospitals have additional committees. The *credentials committee* grants and reviews admitting privileges for those already credentialed and for new doctors whose skills are yet untested. The *medical records committee* ensures that accurate documentation is maintained on the entire regimen of care given to each patient. This committee also oversees confidentiality issues related to medical records. The *utilization review committee* performs routine checks to ensure that inpatient placements, as well as the lengths of stay, are clinically appropriate. The *infection control committee* is responsible for reviewing policies and procedures for minimizing infections in the hospital. The *quality improvement committee* is responsible for overseeing the program for continual quality improvement.

Licensure, Certification, and Accreditation

A license to operate a certain number of hospital beds is a basic regulatory requirement. State governments oversee the *licensure* of health care facilities, and each state sets its own standards for licensure. A state's department of health carries out licensure functions. State licensure standards strongly emphasize the physical plant's compliance with building codes, fire safety, climate control, space allocations, and sanitation. Minimum standards are also established for equipment and personnel. State licensure is not directly tied to the quality of care a health care facility actually delivers. All facilities must be licensed to operate, but they do not have to be certified or accredited.

Certification gives a hospital the authority to participate in Medicare and Medicaid. The Department of Health and Human Services (DHHS) has developed health, safety, and quality standards referred to as *conditions of participation*, and has the authority to enforce those standards for hospitals that participate in Medicare or Medicaid. Conditions, as currently revised, are intended to focus primarily on the actual quality of care furnished to patients and the outcomes of that care. Each state's department of health verifies the actual compliance with the standards through periodic inspections.

In contrast with licensure and certification, which are government regulatory mechanisms, *accreditation* is a private undertaking designed to assure that accredited health care facilities meet certain basic standards. Seeking accreditation is voluntary, but the passage of Medicare in 1965 specified that accredited facilities were eligible for purposes of Medicare reimbursement. Accreditation of a hospital by the Joint Commission confers *deemed status* on the hospital, meaning the hospital is deemed to have met Medicare and Medicaid certification standards. Thus, an accredited hospital does not need to go through the certification process. Private organizations that have been approved by the CMS to confer deemed status are said to have "deeming authority." In addition to the Joint Commission, the American Osteopathic Association also has deeming authority to accredit hospitals.

The Joint Commission also sets standards for and accredits long-term care facilities, psychiatric hospitals, substance abuse programs, outpatient surgery centers, urgent care clinics, group practices, community health centers, hospices, and home health agencies. Different sets of standards apply to each category of health care organization. Some facilities, such as nursing homes, do not receive deemed status as a result of accreditation and must also be certified by DHHS to receive Medicare and Medicaid reimbursement. Over the years, the Joint Commission has refined its accreditation standards and process of verifying compliance. Since 2006, the Joint Commission has moved from scheduled to unannounced inspections, with the objective that hospitals will attempt to comply with all the standards all the time.

The Magnet Recognition Program[®1]

Magnet hospital is a special designation by the American Nurses Credentialing Center, an affiliate of the American Nurses Association, to recognize quality patient care, nursing excellence, and innovations in professional nursing practice in hospitals. The designation was created after a study of 163 hospitals was undertaken in 1983 by the American Academy of Nursing's Task Force on Nursing Practice in Hospitals. The study found that 41 of these hospitals had an environment that attracted and retained well qualified nurses and promoted quality patient care. These hospitals were labeled as "magnet" hospitals because of their ability to attract and retain professional nurses. The characteristics that seemed to distinguish "magnet" organizations from others became known as the Forces of Magnetism. The Forces of Magnetism have been incorporated into quality indicators and standards of nursing practice as defined in the *ANA Nursing Administration: Scope & Standards of Practice*. The Magnet designation is granted after a thorough and lengthy process that includes data on quality indicators. Studies show that visionary leadership, empowerment, and collaboration have an impact on development and maintenance of healthy work environments and that quality of patient care is related to quality of the nurses' work environment (Kramer et al. 2011).

Ethical and Legal Issues in Patient Care

Ethical issues arise in all types of health services organizations, but the most significant

occur in acute care hospitals. Increasing levels of technology create situations requiring decision making under complex circumstances. For example, life-sustaining therapies in intensive care and dealing with life and death issues commonly raise ethical concerns. Ethical issues also arise in health care research and in experimental medicine.

Principles of Ethics

Ethics requires judgment. Clear-cut rules are often not available. Hence, medical practitioners and managers have to rely on certain well established principles as guides to ethical decision making.

Four important principles of ethics are respect for others, beneficence, nonmaleficence, and justice. The principle of respect for others has four elements: autonomy, truth-telling, confidentiality, and fidelity. Autonomy allows people to govern themselves by choosing and pursuing a course of action without external coercion. In health care delivery, it refers to patient empowerment: obtain consent for treatment, explain the various treatment alternatives, allow the patients and their families to participate in decision making and selection of treatment options, and treat the patients with respect and dignity. Constant tension exists between autonomy and paternalism, the view that someone else must direct what the patient must undergo without the patient's involvement. Truth-telling requires a caregiver to be honest. This principle often needs to be balanced with nonmaleficence because a tension is created when truth-telling would result in harm to the patient. The principle of confidentiality sometimes comes into conflict when the legal system requires

[1]The Magnet Recognition Program® is a registered trademark of the American Nurses Credentialing Center.

disclosure of patient information. Fidelity means performing one's duty, keeping one's word, and keeping promises.

The principle of beneficence means that hospitals and caregivers have a moral obligation to benefit others. A health services organization is ethically obligated to do all it can to alleviate suffering caused by ill health and injury. This obligation includes providing the financially needy with certain types of charitable services.

The principle of nonmaleficence means that medical professionals have a moral obligation not to harm others, but many health care interventions, including certain preventive measures, such as immunization, often carry risks. Hence, in health care, nonmaleficence requires that the potential benefits from medical treatment sufficiently outweigh the potential harm.

The principle of justice encompasses fairness and equality. It denounces discrimination in the delivery of health care.

Legal Rights

Legal issues arise in areas of patient competency and the patient's right to refuse treatment. Although the right of mentally competent patients to refuse medical care is well established, the desires of incompetent or comatose patients present ethical challenges. Unless such patients have expressed their wishes in advance, family members or legal guardians end up making decisions regarding sustained medical treatment, or state laws may govern such decisions. Medical and legal experts and family members may differ, often bitterly, on the controversial issue of withdrawing nutrition and other life support means for dying patients, as the case of Theresa Schiavo, which made national news in 2004, demonstrated in the state of Florida. However, certain legal mechanisms have been established to deal with the issues of patients' rights.

Bill of Rights and Informed Consent

The Patient Self-Determination Act of 1990 applies to all health care facilities participating in Medicare or Medicaid. The law requires hospitals and other facilities to provide all patients, upon admission, with information on patients' rights. Most hospitals and other inpatient institutions have developed what is referred to as the *patient's bill of rights*. This document reflects the law concerning issues such as confidentiality and consent. Other rights include the right to make decisions regarding medical care, be informed about diagnosis and treatment, refuse treatment, and formulate advance directives.

Based on the principle of autonomy, *informed consent* refers to the patient's right to make an informed choice regarding medical treatment. The current climate in medical ethics supports honest and complete disclosure of medical information. In 1972, the Board of Trustees of the AHA affirmed a Patient's Bill of Rights, which states that patients have the right to obtain from their physicians complete current information concerning their diagnosis, treatment, and prognosis, in terms the patients can be reasonably expected to understand (Rosner 2004). Informed consent is customarily obtained via a signature on preprinted forms and becomes part of the patient's medical record.

Certain principles governing patients' rights are being incorporated into provider mindsets and organizational culture creating, what is referred to as *patient-centered care*. Patients' involvement in their own treatment, grounding treatment decisions in patients' preferences, and creating a caregiving environment in which staff solicit patients' inputs and meet their needs for information and education collectively promote patient-centered care (Cross 2004).

Advance Directives

Advance directives refer to the patient's wishes regarding continuation or withdrawal of treatment when the patient lacks decision-making capacity. Advance directives are intended to ensure that the patient's end-of-life wishes are carried out.

Three types of advance directives are in common use: do-not-resuscitate orders, living wills, and durable powers of attorney. A *do-not-resuscitate order* directs medical caregivers not to administer any artificial means to resuscitate the person when his or her heart or breathing stops. It is based on the theory that a patient may prefer to die rather than live when strong odds are against a good quality of life after cardiopulmonary resuscitation, because severe disabilities would likely remain. A *living will* communicates a patient's wishes regarding medical treatment when he or she is unable to make decisions due to terminal illness or incapacitation. The main drawback of a living will is that it is general in nature and does not cover all possible situations. A *durable power of attorney* for health care is a written legal document in which the patient appoints another individual to act as the patient's agent for purposes of health care decision making in the event that the patient is unable or unwilling to make such decisions. Although a durable power of attorney can cover most circumstances, its main drawback is that the appointed person may not act in the same manner in which the patient would have acted had he or she remained competent.

Mechanisms for Ethical Decision Making

Many health care organizations, especially large acute care hospitals, have *ethics committees* charged with developing guidelines and standards for ethical decision making in the delivery of health care (Paris 1995). Ethics committees are also responsible for resolving issues related to medical ethics. Such committees are multidisciplinary, including physicians, nurses, clergy, social workers, legal experts, ethicists, and administrators. Although physicians and other caregivers have moral responsibilities on the clinical side, the health care executive who leads the health services organization must also assume the role of a moral agent. As a *moral agent*, the manager morally affects and is morally affected by actions taken. Although executives are entrusted with the fiduciary responsibility to act prudently in managing the affairs of the organization, their responsibilities to patients must take precedence. In governing the affairs of an organization, health care executives must also recognize that ethics is much more than obeying the law. The law represents only the minimum standard of morality established by society. Similarly, health care professionals must recognize that, even though they are bound by the law, they also have a higher calling, one that includes numerous positive duties to patients, society, and each other (Darr 1991).

Summary

Hospitals are institutions engaged primarily in the delivery of inpatient acute care services. However, they have increasingly branched out to provide postacute and outpatient services. In the United States, almshouses and pesthouses first evolved into public hospitals to serve the poor. Subsequently, voluntary hospitals were patterned after British hospitals to serve all classes of people. Advances in medical science, and improvements in hygiene and nursing transformed hospitals into institutions of medical practice, many of which then became important centers of medical training and research. Since the 1980s, economic pressures have led many hospitals to consolidate. Health systems that offer a full continuum of health care services now exist in many locations.

Hospitals in the United States went through an expansion phase until the mid-1980s. The Hill-Burton Act of 1946 stands as the greatest single factor contributing to the increase in the nation's bed supply. The government played an equally important role in reducing inpatient utilization by means of the prospective payment system. The growth of managed care has been significant in reducing inpatient utilization. Some of the key measures of inpatient utilization are discharges, inpatient days, average length of stay, capacity, average daily census, and occupancy rates.

Hospitals can be classified in numerous ways, and the various classification schemes help differentiate one hospital from another. Performance statistics by hospital type can help executives compare their hospital to others in the same category. Although most US hospitals are general community hospitals, various specialty hospitals treat specific types of patients or conditions. Roughly half of the community hospitals are nonprofit, but physician-owned specialty hospitals have proliferated in recent years.

Most public and voluntary hospitals are nonprofit, and, as such, these institutions enjoy some tax advantages. They are expected to provide community benefits that are equivalent in value to the tax subsidies received; however, many nonprofit hospitals emulate the behavior of their for-profit counterparts. Ongoing concerns have invited greater scrutiny and reporting requirements from the Internal Revenue Service.

The ACA puts restrictions on opening new physician-owned specialty hospitals and from expanding existing ones if these hospitals want to participate in Medicare. The law also places new demands on nonprofit hospitals to engage in providing community benefits.

Hospitals are among the most complex organizations to manage; they must satisfy numerous external stakeholders and manage a complex internal governance structure. A hospital cannot legally operate unless licensed by the state in which it is located. To participate in Medicare and Medicaid, a hospital can voluntarily apply for accreditation by the Joint Commission. Hospitals designated as Magnet hospitals are able to recruit and retain qualified nurses and demonstrate a high level of quality in delivering patient care.

Ethical decision making has been a special area of concern for hospitals. From a medical standpoint, ethical issues often pertain to patient privacy, confidentiality, informed consent, and end-of-life treatment. Bills of rights and advance directives are two of the legal means to address these issues. Active ethics committees develop policies and standards, and deal with ethical issues as they arise.

ACA Takeaway

- No more physician-owned hospitals can be opened or expanded if they want to participate in Medicare.
- Several new requirements are imposed on nonprofit hospitals to engage in community health assessments and implement strategies and develop written policies to assist the financially needy. An excise tax is imposed for failure to comply.

Test Your Understanding

Terminology

academic medical center
accreditation
advance directives
average daily census
average length of stay
board of trustees
certification
chief of service
chief of staff
community hospital
conditions of participation
credentials committee
critical access hospital
days of care
deemed status
discharge
do-not-resuscitate order

durable power of attorney
ethics committees
executive committee
general hospital
hospital
infection control committee
informed consent
inpatient
inpatient day
investor-owned hospitals
licensure
living will
long-term care hospital
Magnet hospital
medical records committee
moral agent
multihospital system

occupancy rate
patient-centered care
patient's bill of rights
proprietary hospitals
public hospitals
quality improvement committee
rehabilitation hospital
rural hospital
short-stay hospital
specialty hospital
swing bed
teaching hospital
urban hospital
utilization review committee
voluntary hospital

Review Questions

1. What is the difference between inpatient and outpatient services?
2. As hospitals evolved from rudimentary custodial and quarantine facilities to their current state, how did their purpose and function change?
3. What were the main factors responsible for the growth of hospitals until the latter part of the 20th century?

4. Name the three main forces that have been responsible for hospital downsizing. How has each of these forces been responsible for the decline in inpatient hospital utilization?

5. What is a voluntary hospital? Explain. How did voluntary hospitals evolve in the United States?

6. Discuss the role of government in the growth, as well as the decline, of hospitals in the United States.

7. What are inpatient days? What is the significance of this measure?

8. How does hospital utilization vary according to a person's age, gender, and socioeconomic status?

9. Explain the factors that affect hospital employment.

10. Discuss the different types of public hospitals and the roles they play in the delivery of health care services in the United States.

11. What are some of the differences between private nonprofit and for-profit hospitals?

12. What is a long-term care hospital (LTCH)? What role does it play in health care delivery in the United States?

13. The table below gives some operational statistics for two hospitals located in the same community. Answer the questions following the table.

Calendar Year 2013	Nonprofit Community Hospital (A)	Proprietary Community Hospital (B)
Number of beds in operation	320	240
Total discharges	12,051	9,230
Medicare	5,130	3,876
Medicaid	3,565	2,118
Private insurance	3,356	3,236
Total hospital days	72,421	51,684
Medicare	36,935	26,359
Medicaid	23,175	12,921
Private insurance	12,311	12,404
Total inpatient revenues	$45,755,000	$35,800,000
Dollar value of community benefits	$5,000,000	$3,500,000

(a) Calculate the following measures for each hospital (wherever appropriate, calculate the measure for each pay type). Discuss the meaning and significance of each measure, and point out the differences between the two hospitals.

(1) Hospital capacity

(2) ALOS

(3) Occupancy rate

(b) Operationally, which hospital is performing better? Why?

(c) Do you think the nonprofit hospital is meeting its community benefit obligations in exchange for its tax-exempt status? Explain.

(d) Do you think the hospitals have a problem with excess capacity? If so, what would you recommend?

14. Why have physicians developed their own specialty hospitals? What legal issues can arise when physicians have an ownership interest in a hospital?

15. What criteria does Medicare use to classify a hospital as a rehabilitation hospital?

16. How do you differentiate between a community hospital and a noncommunity hospital?

17. What is a critical access hospital (CAH)? Why was this designation created?

18. What are some of the main differences between teaching and nonteaching hospitals?

19. Discuss some of the issues relative to the tax-exempt status of nonprofit hospitals. What does the Internal Revenue Service require from these hospitals in terms of documentation?

20. Discuss the governance of a modern hospital.

21. In the context of hospitals, what is the difference between licensure, certification, and accreditation?

22. What can a hospital do to address some of the difficult ethical problems relative to end-of-life treatment?

REFERENCES

American Hospital Association (AHA). 1990. *Hospital statistics 1990–1991 edition.* Chicago: American Hospital Association.

American Hospital Association (AHA). 1994. *AHA guide to the health care field 1994 edition.* Chicago: American Hospital Association.

American Hospital Association (AHA). 2008. *AHA Hospital statistics 2008.* Chicago: American Hospital Association.

Anderson, K., and B. Wootton. 1991. Changes in hospital staffing patterns. *Monthly Labor Review* 114, no. 3: 3–9.

Appleby, J. 2004. IRS looking closely at what non-profits pay. *USA Today*, September 30. p. 02b.

Arndt, M., and B. Bigelow. 2006. Toward the creation of an institutional logic for the management of hospitals: Efficiency in the early nineteen hundreds. *Medical Care Research and Review* 63, no. 3: 369–394.

Association of American Medical Colleges (AAMC). 2013. Teaching hospitals. Available at: https://www.aamc.org/about/teachinghospitals. Accessed August 2013.

Balotsky, E.R. 2005. Is it resources, habit or both: Interpreting twenty years of hospital strategic response to prospective payment. *Health Care Management Review* 30, no. 4: 337–346.

Betbeze, P. 2011. Reassessing community benefit. *Health Leaders Magazine* 14, no. 1: 50.

Centers for Medicare and Medicaid Services (CMS). 2010. *Long-term care hospital prospective payment system: Interrupted stay fact sheet.* Available at: http://www.cms.gov/MLNProducts /downloads/LTCH-IntStay.pdf. Accessed March 2011.

Clement, J.P., and K.L. Grazier. 2001. HMO penetration: Has it hurt public hospitals? *Journal of Health Care Finance* 28, no. 1: 25–38.

Congressional Budget Office (CBO). 2006. Nonprofit hospitals and the provision of community benefits. Available at: http://www.cbo.gov/sites/default/files/cbofiles/ftpdocs/76xx/doc7695/ 12-06-nonprofit.pdf. Accessed August 2013.

Coyne, J.S., et al. 2009. Hospital cost and efficiency: So hospital size and ownership type really matter? *Journal of Healthcare Management* 54, no. 3: 163–174.

Cross, G.M. 2004. What does patient-centered care mean for the VA? *Forum* (November 2004), Academy Health.

Darr, K. 1991. *Ethics in health services management.* 2nd ed. Baltimore, MD: Health Professions Press.

DelliFraine, J.L. 2006. Communities with and without children's hospitals: Where do the sickest children receive care? *Hospital Topics* 84, no. 3: 19–26.

Department of Health and Human Services (DHHS). 2002. *Health, United States, 2002.* Hyattsville, MD: National Center for Health Statistics.

Department of Health and Human Services (DHHS). 2013. *Health, United States, 2012.* Hyattsville, MD: National Center for Health Statistics.

Department of Veterans Affairs. 2013. Population tables: Nation by age/gender. Available at: http://www.va.gov/vetdata/Veteran_Population.asp. Accessed July 2013.

Feldstein, M. 1971. *The rising cost of hospital care.* Washington, DC: Information Resource Press.

Feldstein, P.J. 1993. *Health care economics.* 4th ed. Albany, NY: Delmar Publishers.

Goodman, W.C. 2006. Employment in hospitals: Unconventional patterns over time. *Monthly Labor Review, June 2006.* Washington, DC: Bureau of Labor Statistics.

Grimaldi, P.L. 2002. Inpatient rehabilitation facilities are now paid prospective rates. *Journal of Health Care Finance* 28, no. 3: 32–48.

Haglund, C.L., and W.L. Dowling. 1993. The hospital. In: *Introduction to health services.* 4th ed. S.J. Williams and P.R. Torrens, eds. Albany, NY: Delmar Publishers. pp. 135–176.

HCIA, Inc., and Deloitte & Touche. 1997. *The comparative performance of US hospitals: The sourcebook.* Baltimore, MD: HCIA Inc.

Health Forum. 2001. *AHA guide to the health care field. 2001–2002 edition.* Chicago: Health Forum.

Hilsenrath, P.E. 2006. Osteopathic medicine in transition: Postmortem of the osteopathic medical center of Texas. *Journal of the American Osteopathic Association* 106, no. 9: 558–561.

Internal Revenue Service. 2013. New requirements for 501(c)(3) hospitals under the Affordable Care Act. Available at: http://www.irs.gov/Charities-%26-Non-Profits/Charitable-Organiza-tions/New-Requirements-for-501(c)(3)-Hospitals-Under-the-Affordable-Care-Act. Accessed October 2013.

Kahl, A., and D.E. Clark. 1986. Employment in health services: Long-term trends and projections. *Monthly Labor Review* 109, no. 8: 28.

Kangovi, S., et al. 2013. Understanding why patients of low socioeconomic status prefer hospitals over ambulatory care. *Health Affairs* 32, no. 7: 1196–1203.

Kramer, M., et al. 2011. Clinical nurses in Magnet hospitals confirm productive, healthy unit work environments. *Journal of Nursing Management* 19, no. 1: 5–17.

Leonard, K. 2013. Best children's hospitals 2013-14: overview and honor roll. *U.S. News & World Report, June 11.* Available at: http://health.usnews.com/health-news/best-childrens-hospitals /articles/2013/06/11/best-childrens-hospitals-2013-14-overview-of-the-rankings-and-honor-roll. Accessed July 2013.

Mantone, J. 2005. Critical time at rural hospitals. *Modern Healthcare* 35, no. 10: 22.

Mechanic, D. 1998. Emerging trends in mental health policy and practice. *Health Affairs* 17, no. 6: 82–98.

Medicare Payment Advisory Commission (MedPAC). 2004. *New approaches in Medicare: Report to the Congress.* Washington, DC: Medicare Payment Advisory Commission.

Medicare Payment Advisory Commission (MedPAC). 2006. *Report to the Congress: Physician-owned specialty hospitals revisited.* Washington, DC: Medicare Payment Advisory Commission.

Medicare Payment Advisory Commission (MedPAC). 2012a. *Inpatient rehabilitation facilities payment system.* Washington, DC: Medicare Payment Advisory Commission.

Medicare Payment Advisory Commission (MedPAC). 2012b. *Long-term care hospitals payment system.* Washington, DC: Medicare Payment Advisory Commission.

Medicare Payment Advisory Commission (MedPAC). 2012c. *Critical access hospitals payment system.* Washington, DC: Medicare Payment Advisory Commission.

Medicare Payment Advisory Commission (MedPAC). 2012d. *Hospital acute inpatient services payment system.* Washington, DC: Medicare Payment Advisory Commission.

Muller, R.W. 2003. The changing American hospital in the twenty-first century. *Policy Brief No. 26/2003.* Syracuse, NY: Center for Policy Research, Syracuse University.

Mundy, A. 2013. Doc-owned Hospitals Prep to Fight. *Wall Street Journal U.S. Edition* May 14: B1.

Nachega, J.B., et al. 2010. Association of antiretroviral therapy adherence and health care costs. *Annals of Internal Medicine* 152, no. 1: 18–25.

Newman, J.F., et al. 2001. CEO performance appraisal: Review and recommendations. *Journal of Healthcare Management* 46, no. 1: 21–37.

Nudelman, P.M., and L.M. Andrews. 1996. The "value added" or not-for-profit health plans. *New England Journal of Medicine* 334, no. 16: 1057–1059.

O'Connell, L., and S.L. Brown. 2003. Do nonprofit HMOs eliminate racial disparities in cardiac care? *Journal of Healthcare Finance* 30, no. 2: 84–94.

Office of Inspector General. 2003. *Trends in Urban Hospital closure: 1990-2000.* Available at: http://oig.hhs.gov/oei/reports/oei-04-02-00611.pdf. Accessed August 2013.

Owens, B. 2005. The plight of the not-for-profit. *Journal of Healthcare Management* 50, no. 4: 237–250.

Paris, M. 1995. *The medical staff.* In: *Health care administration: Principles, practices, structure, and delivery.* 2nd ed. L.F. Wolper, ed. Gaithersburg, MD: Aspen Publishers, Inc. pp. 32–46.

Patrick, V., et al. 2006. Facilitating discharge in state psychiatric institutions: A group intervention strategy. *Psychiatric Rehabilitation Journal* 29, no. 3: 183–188.

Pfuntner, A., et al. 2013. Costs for hospital stays in the United States, 2010. *Statistical Brief #146, Healthcare Cost and Utilization Project.* Rockville, MD: Agency for Healthcare Research and Quality.

Raffel, M.W. 1980. *The US health system: Origins and functions.* New York: John Wiley and Sons, Inc.

Raffel, M.W., and N.K. Raffel. 1994. *The US health system: Origins and functions.* 4th ed. Albany, NY: Delmar Publishers.

Roemer, M.I. 1961. Bed supply and hospital utilization: A natural experiment. *Hospitals* 35, no. 21: 36–42.

Rosner, F. 2004. Informing the patient about a fatal disease: From paternalism to autonomy—The Jewish view. *Cancer Investigation* 22, no. 6: 949–953.

Sanofi-Aventis. 2013. *Managed care digest series: Hospital/systems digest, 2013.* Bridgewater, NJ: Sanofi-Aventis.

Shoger, T.R. 2011. Commonsense contracts. *Trustees* 64, no. 1: 6–7.

Sinay, T. 2005. Cost structure of osteopathic hospitals and their local counterparts in the USA: Are they any different? *Social Science and Medicine* 60, no. 8: 1805–1814.

Slusky, R. 2006. An investment in rural hospitals is an investment in healthier communities. *AHA News* 42, no. 5: 4–5.

Snyder, J. 2003. Specialty hospitals on rise: Facilities source of controversy. *The Arizona Republic,* February 23.

Stewart, D.A. 1973. The history and status of proprietary hospitals. *Blue Cross Reports—Research Series 9.* Chicago: Blue Cross Association.

Stranges, E., et al. 2011. Components of growth in inpatient hospital costs, 1997–2009. *Statistical Brief #123, Healthcare Cost and Utilization Project.* Rockville, MD: Agency for Healthcare Research and Quality.

Stuart, B., et al. 2006. Financial consequences of rural hospital long-term care strategies. *Health Care Management Review* 31, no. 2: 145–155.

Supreme Court of the State of Illinois. 2010. *Provena Covenant Medical Center et al. v. the Department of Revenue et al.* Docket no. 107328. Opinion filed March 18, 2010. Available at: http://www.state.il.us/court/Opinions/SupremeCourt/2010/March/107328.pdf. Accessed February 2011.

Teisberg, E.D., et al. 1991. *The hospital sector in 1992.* Boston: Harvard Business School.

Thorpe, K.E., et al. 2000. Hospital conversions, margins, and the provision of uncompensated care. *Health Affairs* 19, no. 6: 187–194.

US Census Bureau. 1985. *Statistical Abstract of the United States, 1985.* 105th ed. Washington, DC: US Government Printing Office.

US Census Bureau. 2012. *Statistical abstract of the United States, 2012.* Washington, DC: US Census Bureau.

Vogt, W.B., and R. Town. 2006. *How has hospital consolidation affected the price and quality of hospital care?* Princeton, NJ: The Robert Wood Johnson Foundation.

Weaver, C. 2010. Physician-owned hospitals racing to meet health law deadline. *Kaiser Health News*, October 28, 2010. Available at: http://www.kaiserhealthnews.org/Stories/2010 /October/28/physician-owned-hospitals.aspx. Accessed February 2011.

Wolfson, J., and S.L. Hopes. 1994. What makes tax-exempt hospitals special? *Healthcare Financial Management* 4, no. 7: 56–60.

Wood, C.A. 2011. Employment in health care: A crutch for the ailing economy during the 2007–09 recession. *Monthly Labor Review, April 2011*. Washington, DC: Bureau of Labor Statistics.

Young, G.J., et al. 2013. Provision of community benefits by tax-exempt U.S. hospitals. *New England Journal of Medicine* 368, no. 16: 1519–1527.

Chapter 9

Managed Care and Integrated Organizations

Learning Objectives

- To review the link between the development of managed care and earlier organizational forms in the US health care delivery system
- To grasp the basic concepts of managed care and how managed care organizations realize cost savings
- To distinguish between the main types of managed care organizations
- To examine the different models under which health maintenance organizations are organized and to understand the advantages and disadvantages of each model
- To understand why managed care did not achieve its cost control objectives
- To study the driving forces behind organizational integration and strategies commonly used to achieve integration
- To become familiar with highly integrated health care systems, namely, integrated delivery systems and accountable care organizations
- To learn about the provisions in the Affordable Care Act that apply to managed care and other emerging organizations

Introduction

Managed care has been the single most dominant force that has fundamentally transformed the delivery of health care in the United States since the 1990s. At first, some observers had viewed the managed care phenomenon as an aberration, but, as private employers began to realize cost savings and public policymakers and administrators saw the opportunity to slow down the growing expenditures in the Medicare and Medicaid programs, they increasingly turned to managed care. For now, managed care has become firmly entrenched in the US health care system.

As Figure 9–1 illustrates, in 2013, employer-sponsored health insurance enrolled less than 1% of employees in traditional fee-for-service plans. In recent years, high-deductible health plans (discussed in Chapter 6) have gained popularity and the share of managed care enrollment has declined proportionately, but of particular note is the almost extinction of traditional health insurance.

Although managed care originated in the United States, its tools have spread internationally. For instance, general practitioners in several European countries regulate access to specialists and have responsibility over a *per capita* annual budget (Deom et al. 2010).

In the United States, transition to managed care became necessary as employers grappled with the unaffordable excesses of unrestrained delivery of services that led to spiraling health insurance premiums. In the traditional insurance system (also referred to as fee-for-service or indemnity insurance)

Figure 9–1 Percentage of Enrollment in Health Plans, Selected Years.

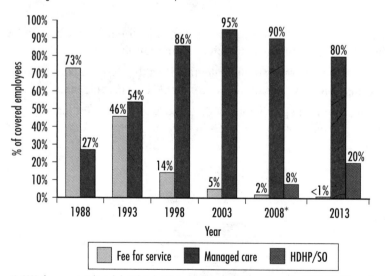

*In 2008, the survey started to include High Deductible Health Plans paired with a savings option (HDHP/SO), [discussed in Chapter 6].

Source: Data from *Employer Health Benefits: 2003 Annual Survey; Employer Health Benefits: 2013 Annual Survey,* The Henry J. Kaiser Family Foundation and Health Research and Educational Trust.

that prevailed prior to managed care, insurance companies had no incentive to manage the delivery of services and how the providers should be paid. With no controls over delivery and payment, costs got out of hand. The only way to control runaway costs was to integrate delivery and payment with the other two functions of financing and insurance. This integration of functions was accomplished through managed care.

As employers increasingly abandoned traditional insurance and switched to managed care to save on rising insurance costs, managed care started wielding enormous buying power over physicians and hospitals. Providers saw this as a threat to their independence and earnings. On the other hand, workers who had previously been able to seek any provider of their choice now had some restrictions placed on that freedom. Subsequently, there ensued what has been commonly referred to as a "managed care backlash." As a result of opposition from physicians and consumers and increased regulation from policymakers in the 1990s, managed care organizations (MCOs) were forced to relax tight controls over health care utilization and payment to providers. Some diversification within the industry also happened as more than one type of managed care plan became available. Consequently, managed care evolved as something quite different from what it was intended to be, and, eventually, had limited success in controlling health care costs.

The balancing of power on the demand and supply sides of the market led to organizational integration. Because of their erosion of marketplace power, providers began forming integrated organizations led by hospitals. Conversely, the managed care industry itself has consolidated by absorbing weaker competitors, and, more recently, joining providers in organizational integration. As a result, America's health care delivery landscape has been radically transformed.

This chapter also discusses the role of managed care and consumer oriented and operated plans (CO-OPs) under the Affordable Care Act (ACA). Managed care faces the challenge of how to further manage cost escalations in hospital care, prescription drugs, and other areas of health care. Under the ACA, it is assumed that some of these responsibilities will be shared with the newly formed accountable care organizations.

What Is Managed Care?

Managed care does not have a standard definition; its main characteristics are found in Chapter 1. In short, managed care is an organized approach to delivering a comprehensive array of health care services to a group of enrolled members through efficient management of services needed by the members and negotiation of prices or payment arrangements with providers. Managed care is generally discussed in two different contexts. First, and more common, it refers to a mechanism or process of providing health care services and has two main features: Managed care (1) integrates the functions of financing, insurance, delivery, and payment within one organizational setting (Figure 9–2) and (2) exercises formal control over utilization. Second, the term "managed care" can refer to an MCO, which can take a variety of forms discussed in this chapter. In this context, managed care is an organization that delivers health care services without using an insurance company to manage

Figure 9–2 Integration of Health Care Delivery Functions Through Managed Care.

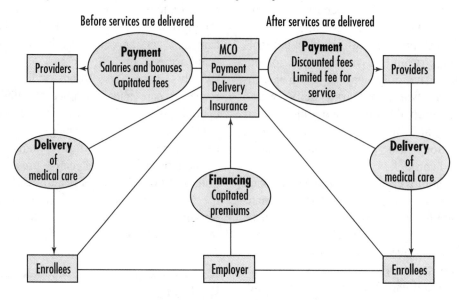

risk and without using a third-party administrator to make payments.

Financing

Premiums are based on negotiated contracts between employers and the MCO. Generally, a fixed premium per enrollee includes all health care services provided for in the contract, and premiums cannot be raised during the term of the contract.

Insurance

The MCO functions like an insurance company by assuming all risk. In other words, it takes the financial responsibility if the total cost of services provided exceeds the revenue from fixed premiums.

Delivery

In an ideal scenario, an MCO would operate its own hospitals and outpatient clinics and employ its own physicians. Some large MCOs actually do employ their own physicians on salary. Others have concluded mergers with hospitals and/or group practices. Most MCOs, however, arrange the delivery of medical services through contracts with physicians, clinics, and hospitals operating independently.

Payment

MCOs use three main types of payment arrangements with providers: capitation, discounted fees, and salaries. The three methods allow risk sharing in varying degrees between the MCO and the providers. Risk sharing puts the burden on the providers to be cost conscious and to curtail unnecessary utilization. Sometimes, a limited amount of fee for service is used for specialized services.

Capitation was discussed in previous chapters. It refers to the payment of a fixed monthly fee per member to a health care provider. All health care services are included in the one set fee so that risk shifts from the MCO to the provider.

Discounted fee arrangements can be regarded as a modified form of fee for service. After the delivery of services, the provider can bill the MCO for each service separately but is paid according to a pre-negotiated schedule called a *fee schedule*. In this case, risk is borne by the MCO, but the MCO can lower its costs by paying discounted rates. Providers agree to discount their regular fees in exchange for the volume of business the MCO brings them.

A third method of payment is salaries, often coupled with bonuses or withholdings. In this case, the provider is an employee of the MCO. The physicians, for instance, are paid fixed salaries. At the end of the year, a pool of money is distributed among the physicians in the form of bonuses based on various performance measures. From an economic perspective, the physicians are paid only partial compensation up front. The remainder is withheld and paid later on condition that the physicians meet certain performance standards. Hence, under this method of payment part of the risk shifts from the MCO to the physicians.

It is important to note that cost containment is not the only objective managed care seeks to achieve, although the potential for cost containment has been the driving force behind the phenomenal growth of managed care. A survey of physicians and employers reported consensus of the two groups on seven essential features of managed care (Business Word Inc. 1996): cost containment, accountability for quality and cost, measurement of health outcomes and quality of care, emphasis on health promotion and disease prevention, management of resource consumption, consumer education programs, and continuing quality improvement initiatives. For highly successful MCOs, pursuit of these expectations becomes perpetual. As set objectives in these areas are achieved, standards are raised higher still so that the quest for quality never ends.

Evolution of Managed Care

The concept of managed care is not new, even though the widespread application of the concept is a more recent phenomenon. The principles on which managed care is based have been around for about a century. Chapter 3 discusses the prototypes of managed care, and Exhibit 9–1 summarizes the evolutionary steps.

In retrospect, the first private health insurance arrangement (see Baylor Plan in Chapter 3) was based on capitation, in which a fixed monthly fee was paid to Baylor Hospital for every teacher who enrolled. This was done without involving an insurance company. The idea of managed care evolved from what the medical establishment pejoratively referred to as the corporate practice of medicine, referring to contract practice and prepaid group practice discussed in Chapter 3. Even before private health insurance became widespread, these practices were used sporadically as cost-effective means of providing health care services to certain groups of people. Contract practice takes the idea of capitation a step further by incorporating a defined group of enrollees. Here, an employer is the financier who contracts with one or more providers to furnish health care to a group of enrollees—the employees—at a predetermined fee per enrollee.

Exhibit 9–1 The Evolution of Managed Care

Health insurance	Capitation
	Bearing of risk by providers

Initially, health insurance combined the insurance, delivery, and payment functions of health care, as seen in the Baylor Plan, but further evolution of this initial concept was thwarted by organized medicine. Contract practice moved toward the integration of these functions, bypassing the insurance companies.

Contract practice	Defined group of enrollees
	Capitation or salary
	Bearing of risk by providers

↓

Prepaid group practice	Comprehensive services
	Defined group of enrollees
	Capitation
	Bearing of risk by providers

↓

Managed care	Utilization controls
	Comprehensive services
	Defined group of enrollees
	Capitation, discounted fees, or salary
	Limited fee for service
	Limits on choice of providers
	Sharing of risk with providers
	Financial incentives to providers
	Accountability for plan performance

Prepaid group practice goes another step further. First, it preserves the principles of capitation, bearing of risk by the provider, and a defined group of enrollees whose health care contract is financed by their employer. It then adds the delivery of comprehensive services.

The subsequent health insurance model, used by commercial insurance companies, loosely retained the insurance and payment functions but abandoned the delivery function. It let the insured decide where they would receive health services. The medical establishment, which strongly preferred the fee-for-service system, strongly influenced this fragmentation. Managed care reemerged in the 1970s with the passage of the Health Maintenance Organization Act of 1973 (see Chapter 3 for details).

Alternative Forms of Managed Care

The organization of HMOs was based on the idea of prepaid group practice.

To achieve greater cost efficiency, various utilization control measures were adopted. Management of utilization is, in essence, the "managed" part of managed care. Later, competition between HMOs and commercial insurance companies spawned other types of MCOs, notably preferred provider organizations (PPOs). Other MCO types resulted from the way they differentiated themselves, by offering enrollees greater freedom to choose their providers, adopting variations in the methods of payment to providers, and using creative means of organizing medical care providers.

Accreditation of Managed Care Organizations

The National Committee for Quality Assurance (NCQA), a private nonprofit organization, began accrediting MCOs in 1991. Accreditation began in response to the demand for standardized, objective information about the quality of MCOs. Participation in the accreditation program is voluntary, but about one-half of the plans are accredited. To be accredited, MCOs must comply with NCQA standards. Compliance is determined by a review process and evaluation by physicians and managed care experts. A national oversight committee of physicians supervises the process. Accreditation is combined with a rating system that has six status categories: excellent, commendable, accredited, provisional, interim, and denied.

Quality Assessment in Managed Care

Developed by the NCQA, Healthcare Effectiveness Data and Information Set (HEDIS) performance measures date back to 1989. Originally designed for private employers'

needs as purchasers of health insurance, HEDIS has been adapted for use by the general public, public insurers, and regulators. More than 90% of America's health plans use HEDIS measures to evaluate performance on important dimensions of care and service. These measures have also been used quite extensively to evaluate and compare the quality of care in health plans.

HEDIS 2013 contains 80 measures across five domains of care: (1) effectiveness of care (immunizations, screenings, management of chronic conditions, etc.), (2) access and availability of care (access to preventive services, treatment for alcohol and drug dependency, prenatal and postpartum care, etc.), (3) experience of care evaluated by means of client surveys, (4) utilization and relative resource use (appropriate frequency of visits, inpatient utilization, mental health utilization, relative resource use for various conditions, etc.), and (5) health plan descriptive information which includes board certification of physicians, enrollments, race/ethnic diversity of the enrolled population, etc. (NCQA 2013). The HEDIS program has been criticized because disclosure is voluntary. However, despite this concern, the overall quality of care has consistently improved among all plans reporting to the NCQA (DoBias 2008).

Growth of Managed Care

As previously mentioned, the main impetus for managed care's growth was rapid cost escalations during the 1970s and 1980s under the dominant fee-for-service system. Employers, who in many instances paid the entire cost of health insurance premiums on their employees' behalf, started switching to managed care only after they started experiencing notable escalations in premium costs. Some evidence suggests that, at least initially, managed care was also in a position to take advantage of the weakened economic position of health care providers.

Flaws in Fee for Service

Traditional fee-for-service health insurance is also referred to as *indemnity insurance*. An indemnity plan allows the insured to obtain health care services anywhere and from any physician or hospital. Indemnity insurance and fee-for-service reimbursement to providers (see Chapter 6) are closely intertwined.

Uncontrolled Utilization

In fee-for-service practice of medicine, moral hazard prevailed. In a system dominated by specialists and an absence of primary care gatekeeping, patients were free to go to any provider. Care received from specialists and utilization of sophisticated technology gave patients the impression of high quality. Competition was driven by such impressions rather than by cost or assessed quality. Physicians and hospitals competed for patients by offering the most up-to-date technologies and the most attractive practice settings (Wilkerson et al. 1997). Despite research over the years both at home and overseas, the notion of provider-induced demand (see Chapter 1) has been controversial. However, there is ample evidence that providers have an incentive to incur higher utilization in pursuit of higher revenues when there are inadequate controls over utilization (Nguyen and Derrick 1997; Rice and Labelle 1989; Yip 1998). Hence, a 10% reduction in fees, for example, will not necessarily translate

into a 10% reduction in total expenditures on physician services because physicians can, and do, generate demand in response to real fee reductions (Rice and Labelle 1989).

Uncontrolled Prices and Payment

In traditional indemnity insurance, the insurance company exercised little control over the prices providers charged or patients' utilization of services. Providers set charges at an artificially high level and billed insurance an item-by-item claim. The insurance company was merely a passive payer of claims—it paid what the providers billed, limited only by what the insurer deemed as usual, customary, and reasonable. The insurance company had little incentive to control costs because it could simply increase the premiums the following year based on utilization during the previous year.

Focus on Illness Rather than Wellness

Indemnity insurance paid for services only when a specific medical diagnosis was reported on the insurance claim. Visits for preventive checkups were not covered. The fee-for-service system presented a second and bigger problem. Indemnity insurance provided more thorough coverage when a person was hospitalized, and the physician was paid for daily hospital visits when the patient was being treated in the hospital. Thus, costly hospitalization of patients was more lucrative for the physicians.

Employers' Response to Rise in Premiums

At its inception, the concept of managed care was designed to compete against fee-for-service medicine. Up until the 1980s, HMOs were the predominant form of managed care. The price-based competition from HMOs was often referred to as "shadow pricing," in which HMOs would offer more benefits and somewhat lower premiums than indemnity plans (Zelman 1996). However, at this stage, managed care plans had limited appeal. Individuals covered by indemnity insurance saw little benefit in joining a plan that would restrict their choice of providers. Most providers also saw little benefit in contracting with MCOs that might restrict their potential income or alter their style of practice (Wilkerson et al. 1997). For the most part, employers remained passive.

Between 1980 and 1990, total cost of private health insurance went up at an average annual rate of over 12% (Figure 9–3). Economic realities forced employers to make the transition from indemnity plans to managed care. Among the US population with employer-based health insurance, the proportion of those enrolled in various managed care plans jumped from 27% in 1988 to 86% in 1998 and to 95% in 2003 (see Figure 9–1).

Weakened Economic Position of Providers

Indirectly, excess capacity in the health care delivery system may also have contributed to the growth of managed care (McGuire 1994). This was perhaps initially true because the Medicare prospective payment system, introduced in the mid-1980s, had a marked impact on hospital economics. Left with significant unused capacity in the form of empty beds, the bargaining power of hospitals substantially weakened. Physicians initially showed great resistance to managed care, but, as the financing of health care was quickly shifting toward managed care, they could no longer resist the growing momentum. In most cases, they were left with the choice of participating or being left out.

Figure 9–3　Growth in the Cost of US Health Insurance (Private Employers), 1980–1995.

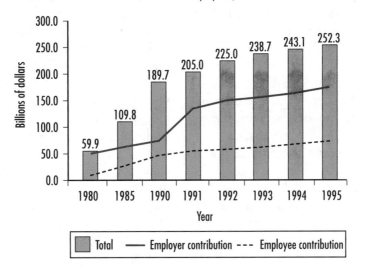

Source: Data from *Health, United States, 1998,* p. 348, National Center for Health Statistics.

Efficiencies and Inefficiencies in Managed Care

Managed care achieves efficiencies in several ways. First, by integrating the quad functions of health care delivery, MCOs eliminate insurance and payer intermediaries and realize some savings. Second, MCOs control costs by sharing risk with providers or by extracting discounts from providers. Risk sharing promotes economically prudent delivery of health care. Hence, risk sharing is an indirect method of utilization control. Third, cost savings are achieved by coordinating a broad range of patient services and by monitoring care to determine whether it is appropriate and delivered in the most cost-effective settings. For example, by emphasizing outpatient services, MCOs achieve lower rates of hospital utilization. Some evidence also suggests that HMO plans incur lower utilization of costly procedures, compared to non-HMO plans (Miller and Luft 1997). Fourth, gatekeeping reduces moral hazard. Last, a focus on preventive services saves money through illness prevention, as well as early detection and treatment of more serious illnesses.

Although many of the cost-control measures adopted by managed care have been applauded, other results have not been so commendable. Most providers find the complexity of having to deal with numerous plans overwhelming. A tremendous amount of inefficiency is created for providers, who must deal with differences in each plan's protocols and procedures. Another problem is that many contracts with providers exclude some services. For example, carving out laboratory testing services for outpatients has become a common practice. Many MCOs use one of the large national lab chains, such as Quest Diagnostics or Roche Diagnostics,

which may present certain inconveniences for both patients and providers. A third area of inefficiency is the lengthy appeals process that patients and providers must sometimes go through when an MCO denies services. In short, managed care does not always create the well coordinated, seamless system that patients and providers would like to see (Southwick 1997).

Cost Control in Managed Care

MCOs use various methods to monitor and control utilization of services. The need for utilization management emanates from the fact that, in the United States, about 10% of patients—typically those with chronic or complex medical conditions—account for 70% of overall health care spending (Berk and Monheit 2001). Utilization management requires (1) an expert evaluation of which services are medically necessary in a given case and ensure that unnecessary services are minimized, (2) a determination of how those services can be provided most inexpensively while maintaining acceptable quality standards, and (3) a review of the process of care and changes in the patient's condition to revise the course of medical treatment if necessary. Utilization management of institutional inpatient services takes priority because the cost of hospital care represents about 50% of the costs health plans pay for medical services (Melnick et al. 2011). Earlier concerns raised about the potential for negative effects of managed care's cost containment strategies on the physician–patient relationship were unfounded. Physicians seem to have managed the relationships with their patients without letting external factors compromise patient satisfaction and trust (Keating et al. 2007).

The methods commonly used for utilization monitoring and control are as follows:

- Choice restriction
- Gatekeeping
- Case management
- Disease management
- Pharmaceutical management
- Utilization review
- Practice profiling

Not all MCOs use all of these mechanisms. Traditionally, HMOs have employed tighter utilization controls than other managed care plans.

Choice Restriction

Traditional indemnity insurance gave the insured open access to any provider, whether generalist or specialist. Such indiscretion led to overutilization of services. Most managed care plans impose some restrictions on where and from whom the patient can obtain medical care. Patients still have a choice of physicians, but the choice is limited to physicians who are either employees of the MCO or have established contracts with the MCO. A physician who has formal affiliations with an MCO is said to be on the *panel* of the MCO. In a *closed-panel* (or closed-access or in-network) plan, services obtained from providers outside the panel are not covered by the plan. By contrast, an *open-panel* (or open-access or out-of-network option) plan allows access to providers outside the panel, but enrollees almost always have to pay higher out-of-pocket costs.

Because the MCO has greater control over providers who are on its panel, utilization is better managed under closed-panel plans, compared to those that allow access outside the panel. From the enrollees'

standpoint, restricted choice of providers is a trade-off for lower out-of-pocket costs. Earlier, choice restriction had caused dissatisfaction among enrollees. More recently, an increasing number of both low-income and higher income Americans have indicated their willingness to limit their choice of physicians and hospitals to save on out-of-pocket medical costs (Tu 2005).

Gatekeeping

Chapter 7 discusses primary care gatekeeping, which requires a primary care physician (PCP) to coordinate all health care services needed by an enrollee and take responsibility for managing utilization. Gatekeeping emphasizes preventive care, routine physical examinations, and other primary care services. Secondary level of services, shown in Figure 9–4, are obtained only on referral from the primary care gatekeeper. Gatekeeping strategies have been shown to result in modest cost savings (Pati et al. 2005).

Case Management

Case management is an organized approach to evaluating and coordinating care, particularly for patients who have complex, potentially costly problems that require a variety of services from multiple providers over an extended period. Examples include acquired immune deficiency syndrome (AIDS), spinal cord injury, bone marrow transplant, lupus, cystic fibrosis, and severe workplace injuries. These patients need expensive secondary and tertiary care services more often than primary care. In such circumstances, a primary care gatekeeper cannot adequately coordinate all of the patient's needs that may also frequently change. In case management, an experienced health care professional, such

Figure 9–4   Care Coordination and Utilization Control Through Gatekeeping.

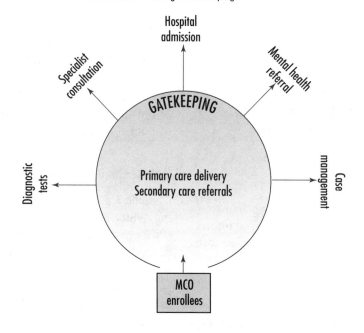

as a nurse practitioner, with knowledge of available health care resources coordinates an individual's total health care in consultation with primary and secondary care providers. Based on the patient's needs, which change over time, services are arranged so that they are delivered in the most appropriate and cost-effective settings. The delivery of services is periodically reviewed to ascertain their appropriateness and efficacy. Case managers are also frequently involved in patient and family support and advocacy. Figure 9–5 illustrates the case management model. Experience with advanced case management strategies used for high-risk populations in five states resulted in reducing the cost of health care while improving the delivery of services (Lattimer 2005). Medicare Coordinated Care Demonstration Programs have shown reductions in hospital admissions, ranging from 8% to 33%, for high-risk patients (Brown et al. 2012).

Disease Management

Whereas case management is typically highly individualized and focuses on coordinating the care of high-risk patients with multiple or complex medical conditions (Short et al. 2003), *disease management* is a population-oriented strategy for people with chronic conditions, such as diabetes, asthma, depression, and coronary artery disease. Disease management is based on well established, evidence-based treatment guidelines. After subgroups among all the enrollees in a health plan have been identified according to their specific chronic conditions, disease management focuses on patient education, training in self-management, ongoing monitoring of the disease process, and follow-up to ensure that people are complying with their medical regimens. In a nutshell, disease management can be referred to as "self-care with professional support" in which the

Figure 9–5 The Case Management Function in Health Services Utilization.

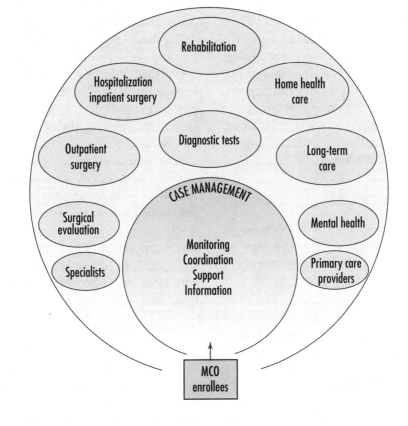

patient has significant responsibility for his or her own health.

The goal of disease management is to prevent or delay comorbidities and complications arising from uncontrolled chronic conditions. So far, cost savings from disease management programs have been uncertain. However, there is substantial evidence that disease management improves quality of care and disease control (Mattke 2008). It may also add to a person's quality of life, at least for certain chronic conditions, such as multiple sclerosis (Ng et al. 2013). Evidence from other countries shows similar results for other types of chronic diseases.

Pharmaceutical Management

In the decade of 2000–2010, expenditures for prescription drugs have risen faster than total personal health care expenditures. To manage these rising costs, health plans use three main strategies: (1) *Use of drug formularies*. A *formulary* is a list of prescription drugs approved by a health plan. Drugs not listed on the formulary are not covered by the plan. (2) *Use of tiered cost sharing*. Out-of-pocket copayments are tiered for generic drugs, preferred brand drugs, non-preferred brand drugs, and drugs in specialty tiers (Brill 2007). Specialty drugs include biologics (see Chapter 5) and other pharmaceuticals that are not only expensive, but may also need to be injected, infused, or may require special handling. Examples of common specialty pharmaceuticals include drugs for oncology and rheumatology. The lowest cost sharing applies to generic drugs. (3) *Use of pharmacy benefits management companies (PBMs)*. Because of their size and purchasing power, PBMs are able to extract discounts from pharmaceutical manufacturers. They also handle drug utilization review discussed in the next section.

Utilization Review

Utilization review (UR) is the process of evaluating the appropriateness of services provided. It is sometimes misunderstood as a mechanism for denying services, but its main objective is to ensure that appropriate levels of services are delivered, care is cost efficient, and subsequent care is planned. Hence, quality of care has become an important component of UR. Drug UR practices have also become common because of the ongoing rise in the utilization and cost of prescription drugs. Misuse of certain drugs can not only waste resources, but also harm patients. Three main types of UR are distinguished by when the review is undertaken: prospective, concurrent, and retrospective, and all three also apply to pharmaceutical management.

Prospective Utilization Review

Prospective utilization review determines the appropriateness of utilization before the care is actually delivered. An example of prospective UR is the decision by a primary care gatekeeper to refer or not refer a patient to a specialist. However, not all managed care plans use gatekeepers. Some plans require the enrollee or the provider to call the plan administrators for preauthorization

(also called precertification) of services for hospital admissions and surgical procedures. In case of an emergency admission to an inpatient facility, plans generally require notification within 24 hours. Plans use pre-established clinical guidelines to authorize hospitalization and assign an initial length of stay. In drug UR, formularies are the first step in prospective review. Subsequently, the PBM can require preauthorization for certain drugs and biologics.

In inpatient care, one objective of prospective UR is to prevent unnecessary or inappropriate institutionalization; however, it also serves other functions. It notifies the concurrent review system of a new case so that length of stay can be monitored and additional days of care be authorized when necessary.

Concurrent Utilization Review

Concurrent utilization review determines, on a daily basis, the length of stay necessary in a hospital. It also monitors the use of ancillary services and ensures that the medical treatment is appropriate and necessary. It is a critical undertaking because hospitals receive prospective reimbursement (discussed in Chapter 6) in which length of stay determines the profitability, or lack thereof, in a given case. Optimal drug therapy and management have been shown to reduce length of stay in hospitals in addition to reducing drug utilization and cost (Chen et al. 2009).

Concurrent UR is also closely linked to *discharge planning* which focuses on post-discharge continuity of care. For example, if a patient is admitted with a fractured hip, it is important to estimate whether a rehabilitation hospital or a skilled nursing facility would be more appropriate for convalescent care. If the patient requires care in a skilled nursing facility, discharge planning must find out whether the appropriate level of rehabilitation services would be available and how long the plan will pay for rehabilitation therapies in a long-term care setting. For a patient who will be discharged home, subsequent home health services and the need for durable medical equipment (DME) may be necessary. The objective is "to get all the ducks in a row" to provide seamless services at the lowest cost and in the best interest of the patient.

Retrospective Utilization Review

Retrospective utilization review refers to a review of utilization after services have been delivered. A close examination of medical records is undertaken to assess the appropriateness of care. Retrospective review may also involve an analysis of utilization data to determine patterns of overutilization or underutilization. It also allows monitoring of billing accuracy and compilation of provider-specific practice patterns which allows feedback to physicians. Such statistical data can be helpful for taking corrective action and for monitoring subsequent progress. Retrospective drug review can help reduce inappropriate use for controlled substances, for instance (Daubresse et al. 2013). It enables clinical pharmacists to intervene with the prescribing physician for therapeutic appropriateness and drug interactions which can affect future prescribing habits (Angalakuditi and Gomes 2011; Starner et al. 2009).

Practice Profiling

Also called "profile monitoring," *practice profiling* refers to the development of physician-specific practice patterns and the comparison of individual practice patterns to some norm. These may incorporate results of patient satisfaction surveys and compliance with clinical practice guidelines. Mainly, profiling is used to decide which providers have the right fit with the plan's managed care philosophy and goals. The profile reports are also used to give feedback to physicians so they can modify their own behavior of medical practice.

Physicians become understandably anxious when their practices come under scrutiny. They may think that the standards used to evaluate their work do not consider extenuating circumstances and that their fate may be decided based on sterile reports. For MCOs, the ability to report the behavior of individual physicians provides a powerful tool to discipline nonconforming physicians; however, great care must be exercised when using physician-specific reports. The administrator must look behind the data and investigate reasons for the reported performance. It is necessary to see how the norms for comparisons are established. According to one study, about one-half of all physicians affected by practice profiling viewed it positively as a useful tool to improve quality and efficiency, but 40% expressed mixed feelings (Reed et al. 2003).

Types of Managed Care Organizations

The main factors that led to the development of different types of MCOs were mentioned previously. HMOs were the most common type of MCO until, in the late 1970s, commercial insurance companies developed preferred provider organizations (PPOs) to compete with HMOs. Today, many health insurance companies in the United States offer different types of managed care plans. For example, the largest health insurers in the United States, such as United Health-care, Blue Cross/Blue Shield, Humana, and Aetna, operate both HMOs and PPOs. Moreover, many HMOs offer what is refer to as *triple-option plans*. These plans combine the features of indemnity insurance, HMO, and PPO; the insured has the flexibility to choose which feature to use when using health care services. The three main types of managed care arrangements discussed in this section are HMOs, PPOs, and point-of-service (POS) plans.

Health Maintenance Organization

An *HMO* is distinguished from other types of plans by the following main characteristics:

1. Traditional indemnity insurance paid for medical care only when a person was ill, while an HMO not only provided medical care during illness but also offered a variety of services to help people maintain their health. The ACA removes this distinction, as almost all health plans are required to provide preventive services (see Chapter 6).

2. The enrollee is generally required to choose a PCP from the panel of physicians. The PCP delivers services in accordance with the gatekeeping model discussed previously.

3. The provider receives a capitated fee regardless of whether the enrollee uses health care services and regardless of the quantity of services used.

4. All health care must be obtained from in-network hospitals, physicians, and other health care providers. Hybrid plans that have an HMO component, such as POS and triple-option plans, allow out-of-network use at a higher out-of-pocket cost.

5. Specialty services, such as mental health and substance abuse treatment, are frequently carved out. A *carve out* is a special contract outside regular capitation, which is funded separately by the HMO.

6. The HMO is responsible for ensuring that services comply with certain established standards of quality.

In the employer-based health insurance market, HMO enrollment grew rapidly in the first half of the 1990s and it peaked in 1996 (Figure 9–6). Subsequently, PPO and POS plans became more popular. HMOs fell into disfavor with enrollees because these plans were the most restrictive regarding choice of providers and utilization controls. Conversely, the majority of Medicaid and Medicare Advantage beneficiaries have been enrolled in HMO plans. Consequently, between 2006 and 2011, the number of HMO plans serving Medicaid populations increased by almost 17%; the number of HMO plans serving Medicaid Advantage enrollees increased by almost 33% (Sanofi-Aventis 2012).

There are four common HMO models—staff, group, network, and independent practice association (IPA). These models differ primarily in their arrangements with participating physicians. Some HMOs cannot be categorized neatly into any one of the four models because they may use a hybrid arrangement, referred to as a *mixed model*. An example of a mixed model is an HMO that is partially organized as a staff model, employing its own physicians, and partially

Figure 9–6 Percent of Covered Employees Enrolled in HMO Plans (Selected Years).

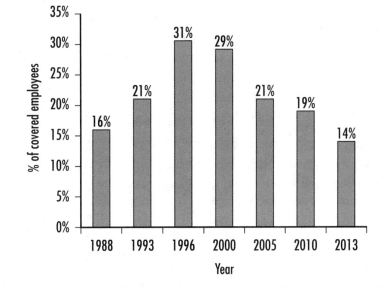

Source: Data from *Employer Health Benefits: 2013 Annual Survey,* The Henry J. Kaiser Family Foundation and Health Research and Educational Trust.

relies on the group model by contracting with a group practice.

Staff Model

A *staff model* HMO employs its own salaried physicians. Based on the physician's productivity and the HMO's performance, bonuses may be added to salary. Physicians work only for their employer HMO and provide services to that HMO's enrollees (Rakich et al. 1992). Staff model HMOs must employ physicians in all the common specialties to provide for the health care needs of their members. Contracts with selected subspecialties are established for infrequently needed services. The HMO operates one or more ambulatory care facilities that contain physicians' offices; employ support staff; and may have ancillary support facilities, such as laboratory and radiology departments. In most instances, the HMO contracts with area hospitals for inpatient services (Wagner 1995).

Compared to other HMO models, staff model HMOs can exercise a greater degree of control over the practice patterns of their physicians. These HMOs also offer the convenience of "one-stop shopping" for their enrollees because most common services are located in the same clinic (Wagner 1995).

Staff model HMOs also present several disadvantages. The fixed-salary expense can be high, requiring these HMOs to have a large number of enrollees to support operating expenses. Enrollees have a limited choice of physicians. For expansion into new markets, a staff-model HMO requires heavy capital outlays (Wagner 1995). Because of such disadvantages, the staff model has been the least popular.

Group Model

A *group model* HMO contracts with a single multispecialty group practice and contracts separately with one or more hospitals to provide comprehensive services to its members. The group practice employs the physicians, not the HMO. The HMO pays an all-inclusive capitation fee to the group practice to provide physician services to its members. The group practice may have contracts with other MCOs as well.

Large groups are usually attractive to HMOs because they deliver a large block of physicians with one contract. However, a large group contract can also be a downside for the HMO. If the contract is lost, the HMO will have difficulty meeting its service obligations to the enrollees. As for other advantages, the HMO is able to avoid large expenditures in fixed salaries and facilities. Affiliation with a reputable multispecialty group practice lends the HMO prestige and creates a perception of quality among its enrollees. Conversely, enrollees may find the choice of physicians limited.

Network Model

Under the *network model*, the HMO contracts with more than one medical group practice. This model is especially adaptable to large metropolitan areas and widespread geographic regions where group practices are located. A common arrangement in the network model is to have contracts only with primary care group practices. Enrollees may select PCPs from any of these groups. Each group is paid a capitation fee based on the number of enrollees. The group is responsible for providing all physician services. It can make referrals to

specialists but is financially responsible for reimbursing them for any referrals made. In some cases, the HMO may contract with a panel of specialists, in which case referrals can be made only to physicians serving on the panel (Wagner 1995). The network model can offer a wider choice of physicians than the staff or group model. The main disadvantage is the dilution of utilization control.

Independent Practice Association (IPA) Model

In 1954, a variant of the prepaid group practice plan was established by the San Joaquin County Foundation for Medical Care in Stockton, California. The plan was a prototype of the *IPA model* and was initiated by the San Joaquin County Medical Society (MacColl 1966). As a result of political pressures from organized medicine, this form of HMO was specifically included in the HMO Act of 1973 (Mackie and Decker 1981).

An *independent practice association* is a legal entity separate from the HMO. The IPA contracts with both independent solo practitioners and group practices. In turn, the HMO contracts with the IPA instead of contracting with individual physicians or group practices (Figure 9–7). Hence, the IPA is an intermediary representing a large number of physicians. The HMO pays a capitation amount to the IPA. The IPA retains administrative control over how it pays its physicians. It may reimburse physicians through capitation or some other means, such as a modified fee for service. The IPA often shares risk with the physicians and assumes the responsibility for utilization management and quality assessment. The IPA also carries stop-loss reinsurance, or the HMO

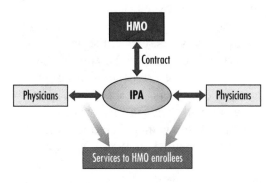

Figure 9–7 The IPA-HMO Model.

may provide stop-loss coverage to prevent the IPA from going bankrupt (Kongstvedt and Plocher 1995).

Under the IPA model, the HMO is still responsible for providing health care services to its enrollees, but the logistics of arranging physician services shifts to the IPA. The HMO is, thus, relieved of the administrative burden of establishing contracts with numerous providers and controlling utilization. Financial risk also transfers to the IPA. The IPA model provides an expanded choice of providers to enrollees. It also allows small groups and individual physicians the opportunity to participate in managed care and get a slice of the revenues. Community physicians may independently establish IPAs, or the HMO may create an IPA and invite community physicians to participate in it. An IPA may also be hospital based and structured so that only physicians from one or two hospitals are eligible to participate in the IPA (Wagner 1995). One major disadvantage of the IPA model is that, if a contract is lost, the HMO loses a large number of participating physicians.

The IPA acts as a buffer between the HMO and physicians. Hence, the IPA does

not have as much leverage in changing physician behavior as a staff or a group model HMO would have. Finally, many IPAs have a surplus of specialists, which creates some pressure to use their services (Kongstvedt and Plocher 1995). Of the four HMO models, the IPA model has been the most successful in terms of the share of all enrollments over time. Most likely, its success can be attributed to a wider choice of physicians that the enrollees have and the buffer an IPA creates between the HMO and its practicing physicians.

Preferred Provider Organization

A *PPO* is distinguished from other types of plans by the following main characteristics:

1. The PPO establishes contracts with a select group of physicians and hospitals. These providers on the PPO's panel are referred to as "preferred providers."

2. Generally, the PPO allows an open-panel option in which the enrollee can use out-of-network providers, but incurs higher cost sharing. The additional out-of-pocket expenses act largely as a deterrent to going outside the panel. If a PPO does not provide an out-of-network option, it is referred to as an *exclusive provider plan*.

3. Instead of using capitation as a method of payment, PPOs make discounted fee arrangements with providers. The discounts can range between 25% and 35% from the providers' established charges. Negotiated payment arrangements with hospitals can take any of the forms discussed in Chapter 6, such as payments based on

diagnosis-related groups (DRGs), bundled charges for certain services, or discounts. Hence, no direct risk sharing with providers is involved.

4. PPOs apply fewer restrictions to the care-seeking behavior of enrollees. In most instances, primary care gatekeeping is not employed. Prior authorization (retrospective UR) is generally employed only for hospitalization and high-cost outpatient procedures (Robinson 2002).

Insurance companies (including Blue Cross and Blue Shield), independent investors, and hospital alliances own most PPOs. Other PPOs are owned by HMOs, and some are jointly sponsored by a hospital and physicians. As a less stringent choice of managed care for both enrollees and providers, PPOs have enjoyed remarkable success. After reaching maximum enrollment of 61% in 2005 (Figure 9–8), enrollment has declined as high-deductible health plans have continued to gain enrollment in recent years.

Point-of-Service Plans

A *point-of-service plan* combines features of classic HMOs with some of the characteristics of patient choice found in PPOs. Hence, these plans are a type of hybrid plan, also referred to as open-ended HMOs. When first brought on the market, these plans had a two-pronged objective: (1) retain the benefits of tight utilization management found in HMOs but (2) offer an alternative to their unpopular feature of restricted choice. The features borrowed from HMOs were capitation or other risk-sharing payment arrangements with providers and the gatekeeping method of utilization control. The feature borrowed from PPOs was the patient's ability to choose between an in-network or out-of-network provider at the point (time) of receiving services, hence, the name "point of service." Of course, the enrollee had to pay extra for the privilege of using out-of-network providers because these providers were paid their fee-for-service charges. POS plans grew in popularity soon after they first emerged in 1988. Over time, as HMOs relaxed some of their utilization control practices and PPOs already offered a choice of providers, the need for a hybrid plan became less important to consumers. After reaching a peak in popularity in 1998 and 1999, enrollment in POS plans has continued to decline (Figure 9–9).

Trends in Managed Care

Managed care has indeed become a mature industry in the United States. In practical terms, managed care has become the only vehicle for health insurance in the private sector. States have increasingly enrolled Medicaid beneficiaries in managed care plans. Medicare beneficiaries have increasingly found value for their premium dollars by enrolling in Medicare Advantage (MA) plans.

Employment-Based Health Insurance Enrollment

Many employers offer their workers a choice of plans with level-dollar employer contribution, meaning workers pay more themselves—in premium contributions, deductibles, and copayments—if they choose a more expensive plan. In 2013, enrollment of workers was the highest in PPO plans (Figure 9–10).

Figure 9–8 Percent of Covered Employees Enrolled in PPO Plans (Selected Years).

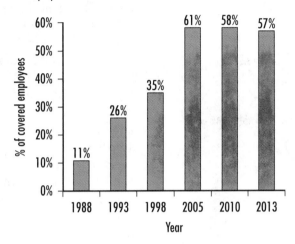

Source: Data from *Employer Health Benefits: 2002 Annual Survey; Employer Health Benefits: 2013 Annual Survey,* The Henry J. Kaiser Family Foundation and Health Research and Educational Trust.

Figure 9–9 Percent of Covered Employees Enrolled in POS Plans (Selected Years).

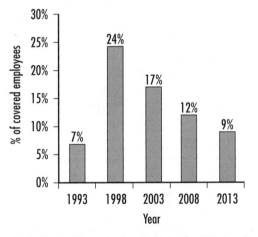

Source: Data from *Employer Health Benefits: 2002 Annual Survey; Employer Health Benefits: 2013 Annual Survey*; The Henry J. Kaiser Family Foundation and Health Research and Educational Trust.

Managed Care and Health Insurance Exchanges

Managed care is expected to be a dominant player in offering "qualified health plans" through the health insurance marketplaces (exchanges), but they must comply with ACA mandates. For example, managed care plans must include the "essential health benefits." Also, as discussed in Chapter 6, the ACA

Figure 9–10 Share of Managed Care Enrollments in Employer-Based Health Plans, 2013.

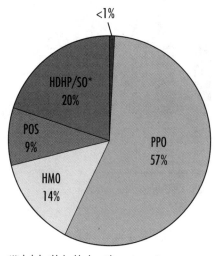

<1%

HDHP/SO*
20%

POS
9%

HMO
14%

PPO
57%

*High-deductible health plan with a savings option

Source: Data from Employer Health Benefits: 2013 Annual Survey, The Henry J. Kaiser Family Foundation and Health Research and Educational Trust.

prescribes minimum medical loss ratios in health plans to limit the percentage of premium revenue a health plan can use for administration, marketing, and profits. It is to be expected that the industry would invite further regulations should premiums rise above what the government may consider unreasonable. In addition to the MCOs that have served primarily the employer-based health insurance market, CO-OPs and Medicaid plans can also participate in the exchanges to increase competition in the hope of keeping premiums at an affordable level. What that affordable level will turn out to be will not be known for some time.

The ACA envisions that consumer operated and oriented plans (CO-OPs) would emerge, spurred by financing from the federal government. Such plans have started to emerge in small numbers. CO-OPs are nonprofit organizations modeled after an HMO or a PPO. CO-OPs are expected to be accountable to members and responsive to the specific health care needs of plan members by using profits to lower premiums, improve quality, and expand benefits or enrollment (CMS 2012). Government regulations, however, can either slow down or stifle the growth of such plans.

HMOs that already enroll Medicaid populations have been approved by several states to enroll non-Medicaid members through the exchanges (McQueen and Meyer 2013). If these HMOs participate in large numbers, attract sizable non-Medicaid members, and can maintain low premiums, they may be able to drive down overall premiums in the exchanges. However, Medicaid insurers do not always have the lowest premiums. Apart from the cost of premiums, it is unknown whether a broader segment of Americans will accept the economy-class health coverage that Medicaid beneficiaries have gotten used to. Another concern comes from providers who are anxious about payment rates that may go down as a result of large-scale participation of Medicaid HMOs in the exchanges. Low rates could discourage providers from serving millions of expected new exchange enrollees (McQueen and Meyer 2013).

Medicaid Enrollment

Waivers under the Social Security Act, particularly sections 1115 and 1915(b), allowed states to enroll their Medicaid recipients in managed care plans. The Balanced Budget Act of 1997 gave states the authority to implement mandatory managed care programs without requiring federal waivers

(Moscovice et al. 1998). Since then, enrollment of Medicaid beneficiaries in HMOs has grown rapidly, from 56% in 2000 to over 75% in 2012 (Sanofi-Aventis 2013). Most of the new Medicaid and CHIP beneficiaries under the ACA—estimated to number 7 million—are likely to be in managed care.

Some states have developed a different model of managing health care delivery, particularly in rural areas where managed care has not flourished. Medicaid *primary care case management* (PCCM) is a model that requires a Medicaid enrollee to choose a PCP, who is responsible for coordinating the enrollee's care and paid a monthly fee for doing so, on top of the payment for providing medical services. In general, all medical services are reimbursed on a fee-for-service basis. More than 30 states are using the PCCM model (GAO 2012).

Medicare Enrollment and Payment Reforms

As pointed out in Chapter 6, Medicare beneficiaries have the option to enroll in Medicare Advantage (Part C) or remain in the original fee-for-service program. Over the years, enrollments in Part C have fluctuated. Higher payments from Medicare to the MCOs have been associated with large increases in enrollment and reductions in disenrollment. Overall, a 10% increase in payment results in increased enrollment by 9.6% (Morrisey et al. 2013). Conversely, cuts in Medicare's capitation rates result in decreased enrollments as fewer MCOs are willing to participate in Part C. For example, the Balanced Budget Act of 1997 had reduced payments to HMOs. As HMOs withdrew from the Medicare program, 800,000 beneficiaries lost their HMO

coverage between 2000 and 2001 (Aventis Pharmaceuticals/SMG Marketing-Verispan LLC 2002). Enrollment in Medicare+Choice (the predecessor of Medicare Advantage) fell from 6.3 million in December 1999 to 5 million by February 2002, a decline of 21% (Thorpe and Atherly 2002). Between 2003 and 2007, the Centers for Medicare and Medicaid Services (CMS) rolled out a new payment plan that included risk adjustments based on Hierarchical Condition Categories, which represent major medical conditions that are ranked on the basis of disease severity and cost. Thus, risk-adjusted payments account for the health status of each beneficiary. Between 2009 and 2013, enrollment in MA plans grew by 10% annually, exceeding 14 million enrollees nationwide in 2013, or 28% of the total Medicare population (Gold et al. 2013). As pointed out in Chapter 6, the ACA aims to reduce payment to MA plans, which could affect MCOs' participation in Part C or raise cost sharing for enrollees.

Impact on Cost, Access, and Quality

The growth of managed care in both private and public health insurance sectors bears ample testimony to the widely held belief that managed care provides cost savings and better value for money than traditional indemnity insurance, even though any cost savings have not been quantified. Widespread use of managed care may also be a testament to few issues with access and quality. As managed care has become the primary vehicle for health insurance through employers and also to a large extent through Medicaid, Medicare still remains an open field for studying differences between managed care and indemnity insurance.

Influence on Cost Containment

Managed care has been widely credited with slowing down the rate of growth in health care expenditures during the 1990s. Between 1990 and 1998, hospitals in high managed care growth areas experienced revenue and cost growth rates 18 percentage points below hospitals in low managed care areas, but this cost containment effect reached a plateau after 1998 (Shen 2005). A backlash from both enrollees and providers prompted MCOs to back away from aggressive cost control measures. Hence, the full cost-containment potential of managed care was never realized. Ironically, alternatives for reducing spiraling health care costs in the US health care delivery system have also not been forthcoming. Future cost reductions may not be realized without tighter restrictions on utilization, particularly on the use of expensive new technology.

Impact on Access

Managed care enrollees have good access to primary and preventive care. Baker and colleagues (2004) found that timely breast cancer and cervical cancer screening was twice as likely for women receiving services in geographic areas with greater HMO market share, compared to women in areas with low managed care penetration. More recent studies report similar findings on health screenings, diabetes care, and favorable ratings of physicians by the patients (Ayanian et al. 2013). In MA plans, better access to primary care may have been responsible for lowering the risk of preventable hospitalizations. This effect was found to be particularly beneficial for ethnic/minority groups (Basu 2012).

As people's ability to obtain health care improved between 2001 and 2003, health plan–related barriers that would have led some people to delay care or go without it declined significantly (Strunk and Cunningham 2004). It perhaps reflects relaxed utilization controls adopted by health plans in the years following managed care bashing.

On a larger scale, managed care's impact on access is not known. For instance, it is not clear to what extent during the 1990s managed care might have enabled small employers to offer employees health insurance coverage by holding down premium increases. Between 1996 and 2000, the proportion of employers offering health insurance benefits increased from 59% to 67% among firms employing between 3 and 199 workers, and the most notable increase was among the smallest firms employing between 3 and 9 workers (Kaiser/HRET 2002). However, this period also saw unprecedented economic growth that may have enabled more employers to add new benefits.

Influence on Quality of Care

It is not surprising that quality varies across plans; however, overall quality of care in managed care plans has been found to be at least equivalent to that in traditional fee-for-service plans. Despite anecdotes, individual perceptions, and isolated stories propagated by the news media during the 1990s, no comprehensive research to date has clearly demonstrated that managed care's growth has been at the expense of quality in health care. Actually, available evidence points mostly to the contrary. A comprehensive review of the literature by Miller and Luft (2002) concluded that HMO and non-HMO plans provided roughly equal quality of care, as measured by a wide range of conditions, diseases, and interventions. At the same time, HMOs were found to lower the use of hospitals and other expensive resources. Hence, managed care plans have been cost effective while delivering levels of quality that are either comparable to or better than traditional indemnity plans.

Quality of health care provided by MCOs has improved over time (Hofmann 2002). Early detection and treatment are more likely in a managed care plan than in a traditional indemnity plan (Riley et al. 1999). Higher managed care penetration was associated with increased quality in hospitals when such indicators as inappropriate utilization, wound infections, and iatrogenic complications were used to assess quality (Sari 2002). A more recent national study comparing quality of care in Medicare fee-for-service and MA plans showed that the level of quality, as evaluated by breast cancer screening, quality of diabetes care, and most other HEDIS measures, was significantly higher in MA plans (Brennan and Shepard 2010). There is further confirmation that, in terms of benefits and costs, being white or a member of a minority class makes no difference for Medicare enrollees, regardless of whether they are enrolled in Medicare managed care or in the original fee-for-service program (Balsa et al. 2007).

During the 1990s, concerns were raised that risk sharing between providers and payers would influence treatment decisions made by physicians, which would result in skimping on necessary services. However, evidence suggests that financial pressures do not lead to significant changes in physician behavior, because, under capitation, a physician takes full responsibility for the patient's overall care (Eikel 2002). This is particularly true for life-saving treatment decisions, such as treatment of cancer patients (Bourjolly et al. 2004). Concerns about disparities in quality of care, based on race and socioeconomic status, are also largely unfounded (DeFrancesco 2002).

On the flip side, there is some evidence that quality of care may be lower in for-profit health plans, compared to nonprofit plans (Himmelstein et al. 1999; Schneider et al. 2005). There is also some evidence that, in MCOs serving Medicaid patients under capitation, the enrollees may not receive certain services for which the PCPs do not get additional compensation, which may have some impact on quality of care (Quast et al. 2008). After taking into account risk adjustment, enrollees in MA plans have been found to have a substantially higher likelihood of hospital readmission within 30 days of discharge compared to beneficiaries in original Medicare (Friedman et al. 2012). In Medicare Advantage Special Needs Plans (MA-SNPs discussed in Chapter 6), HEDIS measure for osteoporosis testing was worse in MA-SNPs although performance on fall risk management was better (Grace et al. 2013).

In the delivery of mental health, earlier reports suggested poorer outcomes in managed care plans (Rogers et al. 1993; Wells et al. 1989). However, later investigations concluded otherwise. In an examination of qualitative and quantitative aspects of specialty managed outpatient mental health treatment, managed care was found to achieve cost savings but not at the expense of quality of care (Goldman et al. 2003).

Managed Care Backlash, Regulation, and the Aftermath

The large-scale transition of health care delivery to managed care in the 1990s was met with widespread criticism, which turned into a backlash from consumers, physicians, and legislators. There were three main reasons behind the discontent, and widespread media reports further shaped unsympathetic public opinion toward managed care. (1) To restrain the spiraling costs of health insurance premiums, employers around the country switched to managed care by dropping, in many instances, traditional indemnity plans that allowed enrollees to choose any physician or hospital. A large number of employees experienced at least some loss of freedom and, to some extent, faced barriers to free access. (2) People did not see a reduction in their own share of the premium costs or a drop in their out-of-pocket expenses when they received health care. (3) In reaction to tight utilization management from MCOs, physicians became openly hostile toward managed care. In national surveys, managed care penetration was found to be negatively correlated with physicians' satisfaction (Landon et al. 2003). Much of this discontent arose from pressures to change the way physicians had traditionally practiced medicine with no accountability for appropriateness of utilization and costs. Physicians' vocal discontent no doubt also helped shape patients' views about managed care. Both physicians and patients perceived that managed care would drive a wedge between the patient–physician relationship. However, as the momentum continued to shift toward enrollment in managed care, physicians had little choice but to contract with managed care or lose patients. Employees had little choice but to enroll in managed care plans, or personally bear significantly higher premium costs, or go without health insurance altogether. As this drama unfolded, employers largely remained passive, as their main objective of reductions in premium costs was attained.

Regulation of Managed Care

In response to widespread complaints and negative publicity against managed care, legislators across states were prompted to take action because the state governments are primarily responsible for overseeing issues pertaining to health insurance. Hence, states passed an extensive array of anti-managed care legislation. Between 1990 and 1999, states adopted more than 1,000 distinct regulatory provisions against managed care (Kronebusch et al. 2009). Congress passed the Newborns' and Mothers' Health Protection Act of 1996, although numerous states already had laws against "drive-through deliveries." The federal law prohibits a health plan to offer less than a 48-hour inpatient maternity coverage for a mother and her child following a normal vaginal delivery and less than a 96-hour coverage following a Caesarean section.

Most states adopted legislation to limit financial incentives to physicians for curtailing utilization, to expand the rights of health care professionals, to promote continuity of care, and to give patients the right to an expeditious appeals process to review denial of services, including mandatory external reviews. States also mandated that certain benefits be included in health plans. Some examples include chiropractic services, women's health screening, diabetic supplies, and obesity care. State legislations also included provisions that gave enrollees the right to seek civil remedy in the courts for negligent actions of health plans, including the denial of services (Hurley and Draper 2002). While managed care legislation provided both consumers and providers certain protections, it also had negative implications of increasing costs.

The Aftermath

The backlash and anti-managed care laws produced their intended effects, as MCOs scaled back tight controls on utilization and took significant steps to develop better relationships with physicians and other providers. Physicians and hospitals found bargaining power shifting in their direction, mainly through organizational integration, and the providers were able to push back on MCOs by terminating contracts or negotiating more favorable payment arrangements (Short et al. 2001; Strunk et al. 2001).

The balance achieved between the bargaining powers of MCOs on the one hand and providers on the other has left the consumer in the middle. Employers had to absorb the lion's share of rising premiums and they, in turn, have passed some of those costs on to their employees through higher cost sharing. Altman and Levitt (2013) have cogently remarked, "healthcare cost spiral hasn't been cured," even though the rise in costs may have temporarily slowed because of a severe recession followed by a slow economic recovery.

The ACA was sold to the American public on the promise of lowered costs and better access. Because managed care will remain the dominant player in the health insurance arena, its future may well hinge on the triumphs or failures of the ACA's promise.

Organizational Integration

The term *integration* refers to various strategies that health care organizations employ to achieve economies of operation, diversify existing operations by offering new products or services, or gain market share. In the United States, the integration movement began with hospital mergers and acquisitions during the 1990s and early 2000s, a phenomenon that was national in scope. There can be numerous reasons behind hospital consolidation, such as technology, effects of reimbursement, and growth of services in alternative delivery settings, but the role of managed care cannot be underestimated. For instance, there is some evidence that hospitals gained increased pricing power over MCOs subsequent to consolidations (Capps and Dranove 2004). Ginsburg (2005) reached the same conclusion: "Hospitals correctly perceived that by merging with others in the same community, they would increase their leverage with health plans" (p. 1514).

Subsequent to hospital consolidations, physician groups sought to align themselves with hospitals to maintain their autonomy and find refuge from the growing influence of managed care. Hospitals saw such arrangements as mutually beneficial as more and more health care services were moving to the outpatient sector, a phenomenon discussed in Chapters 7 and 8. Large hospital systems were particularly attracted to group practices because group practices could give them a large slice of the patient market.

Later, the formation of integrated delivery systems brought about further integration to achieve *diversification*, which refers to addition of new services that the organization has not offered before. For example, a hospital may enter into post-acute long-term care services by converting an unused acute care wing into a long-term care facility or by acquiring an existing nursing home. In sprawling urban areas, integrated organizations saw the opportunity to more efficiently provide services to populations spread over large geographic areas. The highly integrated Kaiser-Permanente model, which has been in use in California since the 1940s, for example, has been known for its cost-effective care with high quality services to its enrollees. This model has even started to influence the mindsets and policy development within many

European health care systems (Strandberg-Larsen et al. 2007).

Integration Strategies

Various integration strategies are illustrated in Figure 9–11. The strategies can involve (1) outright ownership, such as through a merger or acquisition; (2) joining hands

Figure 9–11 Organizational Integration Strategies.

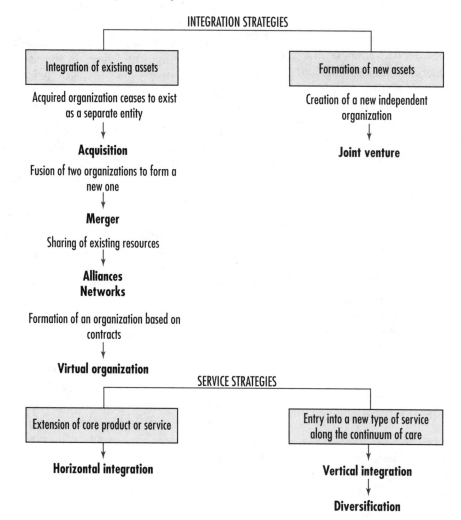

with another organization in the ownership of an entity; or (3) having a stake in an organization without owning it.

Mergers and Acquisitions

Mergers and acquisitions involve integration of existing assets. *Acquisition* refers to the purchase of one organization by another. The acquired company ceases to exist as a separate entity and is absorbed into the purchasing corporation. A *merger* involves a mutual agreement to unify two or more organizations into a single entity. The separate assets of two organizations combine, typically under a new name. Both entities cease to exist, and a new corporation forms. A merger requires the willingness of all parties, after they have assessed the advantages and disadvantages of merging their organizations.

Small hospitals may merge to gain efficiencies by eliminating duplication of services. A large hospital may acquire smaller hospitals to serve as satellites in a major metropolitan area with sprawling suburbs. A regional health system may form after a large hospital has acquired smaller hospitals and certain providers of long-term care, outpatient care, and rehabilitation to diversify its services. Multifacility nursing home chains and home health firms often acquire other facilities to enter new geographic markets.

Joint Ventures

A *joint venture* results when two or more institutions share resources to create a new organization to pursue a common purpose (Pelfrey and Theisen 1989). Each partner in a joint venture continues to conduct business independently. The new company created by the partners also remains independent.

Joint ventures are often used to diversify when the new service can benefit all the partners and when competing against each other for that service would be undesirable. Hospitals in a given region may engage in a joint venture to form a home health agency that benefits all partners. An acute care hospital, a multispecialty physician group practice, a skilled nursing facility, and an insurer may join to offer a managed care plan (Carson et al. 1995). Each participant would continue to operate its own business, and they would all have a common stake in the new MCO.

Alliances

In one respect, the health care industry is unique because organizations often develop cooperative arrangements with rival providers. Cooperation instead of competition, in some situations, eliminates duplication of services while ensuring that all the health needs of the community are fulfilled (Carson et al. 1995). An *alliance* is an agreement between two organizations to share their existing resources without joint ownership of assets.

The main advantages of alliances are: (1) They are relatively simple to form. (2) They provide the opportunity to evaluate financial and legal ramifications before a potential "marriage" takes place. Forming an alliance gives organizations the opportunity to evaluate the advantages of an eventual merger. (3) Alliances require little financial commitment and can be easily dissolved, similar to an engagement prior to a marriage.

Networks

A network is formed through alliances with numerous providers. It is built around a core organization, such as an MCO, a hospital, or a large group practice. Other, less common types of networks can also exist, such as an IPA which is a network of physicians under the umbrella of a nonphysician organization.

Virtual Organizations

Alliances and networks often involve resource-sharing arrangements between organizations. However, when contractual arrangements between organizations form a new organization, it is referred to as a virtual organization or organization without walls. The formation of networks based on contractual arrangements is called *virtual integration*. IPAs are prime examples of virtual organizations. The main advantage of virtual organizations is that they require less capital to enter new geographic or service markets (Gabel 1997). They also help bring together scattered entities under one mutually cooperative arrangement. For example, solo practitioners and small group practices can be brought under the umbrella of an IPA.

Service Strategies

Horizontal Integration

Horizontal integration is a growth strategy in which a health care delivery organization extends its core product or service. Commonly, the services are similar to or are substitutes for existing services. Horizontal integration may be achieved through internal development, acquisition, or merger. Horizontally linked organizations may be closely coupled through ownership or loosely coupled through alliances. The main objective of horizontal integration is to control the geographic distribution of a certain

type of health care service. Multihospital chains, nursing facility chains, or a chain of drugstores, all under the same management, with member facilities offering the same core services or products, are horizontally integrated. Diversification into new products and/or services is not achieved through horizontal integration.

Vertical Integration

Vertical integration links services at different stages in the production process of health care—for example, organization of primary care, acute care, postacute services, and a hospital. The main objective of vertical integration is to increase the comprehensiveness and continuity of care across a continuum of health care services. Hence, vertical integration is a diversification strategy.

Vertical integration may be achieved through acquisitions, mergers, joint ventures, or alliances. Formation of networks and virtual organizations can also involve vertical integration. Vertically integrated regional health systems may be the best positioned organizations to become the providers of choice for managed care or for direct contracting with self-insured employers (Brown 1996).

Basic Forms of Integration

The major participants in organizational integration have been physicians and hospitals. Other clinical and nonclinical entities may also be involved, as pointed out in some of the previous examples. In the past, several different types of configurations emerged; however, success of these models was spotty. Lack of experience, misplaced administrative controls, misaligned financial incentives, and unfavorable economic trends were some of the reasons many of these models failed to gain momentum. A few—namely, management services organizations and physician–hospital organizations—have survived. Provider-sponsored organizations have been greatly reduced in numbers.

Management Services Organizations

During the dominant phase of MCOs in the 1980s and early 1990s, physicians recognized that they needed management expertise to survive in the complex health care environment. In recognition of this need, management services organizations (*MSOs*) emerged to supply management expertise, administrative tools, and information technology to physician group practices. Today, MSO services are needed mainly by smaller group practices, because they find it uneconomical to employ full-time managers.

Physician-Hospital Organizations

A physician-hospital organization (*PHO*) is a legal entity that forms an alliance between a hospital and local physicians. Apart from contracting with MCOs, if a PHO is large enough, it can also contract its services directly to employers, while engaging a third-party administrator to process claims. Between 1998 and 2000, the number of hospitals associated with PHOs more than doubled. Subsequently, many failed because of poor management, undercapitalization, and federal antitrust scrutiny. Industry trends, along with rising costs and increased demand for services, continue to affect the manner in which hospitals and physicians compete or align (Sanderson et al. 2008).

Hospitals seem to be in the driver's seat as physicians increasingly turn to hospitals for financial support. There has been a growing trend of physicians leaving their practices to seek hospital employment. Some of the reasons behind this trend include declines in reimbursement, increases in practice expenses, complexities associated with newer demands such as electronic health records, and desire of younger physicians to be employees rather than owners (Jessee 2011; Minich-Pourshadi 2013).

Provider-Sponsored Organizations

A risk-bearing entity that incorporated the insurance function into integrated clinical delivery—referred to as a provider-sponsored organization (*PSO*)—emerged in the 1990s. PSOs are sponsored by physicians, hospitals, or jointly by physicians and hospitals to compete with regular MCOs by agreeing to provide health care to a defined group of enrollees under capitation. They bypass the insurance "middleman" by contracting directly with employers and public insurers. PSOs gained national attention in 1996 when Congress proposed that PSOs could legitimately participate in Medicare risk contracts. Then, the Balanced Budget Act of 1997 opened up the Medicare market to PSOs as an option to HMOs under the Medicare+Choice program. The Balanced Budget Act also required these entities to carry adequate coverage for risk protection. The initial appeal of PSOs was that they would deal with patients directly rather than through contracted arrangements as an HMO normally would do. However, after they suffered financial losses, PSOs failed in large numbers. In many instances, larger HMOs acquired PSOs. One major reason for PSO failures has been their lack of experience with risk management (the insurance function).

Highly Integrated Health Care Systems

Highly integrated systems generally include a hospital, a physician component, and at least one systemwide contract with a payer, such as Medicare or MCO. The payers may stipulate some responsibility for quality and cost.

Integrated Delivery Systems

An *integrated delivery system* (IDS), also called "integrated delivery network," may be defined as a network of organizations that provides or arranges to provide a coordinated continuum of services to a defined population and is willing to be held clinically and fiscally accountable for the outcomes and health status of the population serviced (Shortell et al. 1993). An IDS represents various forms of ownership and other strategic linkages among hospitals, physicians, and insurers. One of its objectives is to achieve greater integration of health care services along the continuum of care (Shortell and Hull 1996).

Managed care market domination prompted providers to integrate for three main reasons: (1) For MCOs, it is more cost effective to contract with organizations that offer comprehensive services to ensure a full spectrum of services to the MCO's enrollees. (2) Managed care also seeks providers who can render services in a cost-efficient manner and who will take responsibility for the quality of those services. Providers seek greater efficiencies by joining with other organizations or by diversifying into providing new services. Large organizations are in a better position to acquire up-to-date management and information systems to monitor their operations and successfully address inefficiencies. (3) Hospitals, physicians, and other providers have been concerned with protecting their autonomy. By forging linkages, these providers strengthened their bargaining power in dealing with MCOs.

Satisfaction of members enrolled in health plans that are integrated with IDSs—such as Health Alliance Plan and Kaiser Foundation Health Plan—is considerably higher than member satisfaction with plans in which the provider and payer are not part of the same organization. In addition, members enrolled in integrated plans have a better understanding of their coverage and the processes necessary to receive services (J.D. Power and Associates 2011).

A recent comprehensive review of the literature concluded that IDSs have had a positive effect on the quality of care. In some cases, IDSs lowered health care utilization, but cost savings have not materialized (Hwang et al. 2013). Some IDSs have not only failed to live up to their potential to deliver cost-efficient care, but have also experienced significant financial distress (Nader and Walston 2005). For various reasons, the number of IDSs dropped substantially from 574 in 2001 to 332 in 2012. Yet, the number of hospitals in IDSs reached an all-time high of 2,240 (43% of all hospitals) in 2012. Similarly, the number of physician practices owned or contracted by IDSs grew by 45% between 2007 and 2012 (Sanofi-Aventis 2008, 2013). Clearly, an ever-increasing number of providers have affiliated with IDSs in recent years. Although both hospitals and physicians are integrating at an accelerated pace, as past experience has demonstrated, integration alone is not the answer to the impending challenges that the US health care delivery system will face.

Accountable Care Organizations

In the ongoing pursuit for cost effectiveness and quality, recent emphasis has shifted from IDSs to accountable care organizations. In a general sense, an *accountable care organization* (ACO) describes an integrated group of providers who are willing and able to take responsibility for improving the overall health status, care efficiency, and satisfaction with care for a defined population (DeVore and Champion 2011). The concept of accountability was first associated with HMOs during the 1970s. After the HMOs were severely weakened by managed care bashing during the 1990s, IDSs emerged and carried the baton to orchestrate the formation of closely knit networks of providers in the hope of achieving the threefold objective of cost, quality, and population health. Many IDSs failed in the process.

The ACO concept evolved from CMS's demonstration projects involving hospitals and physician group practices between 2005 and 2010. In May 2010, an Accountable Care Implementation Collaborative involving 25 health systems embarked on a project to develop the key capabilities needed to operate an ACO (DeVore and Champion 2011). It is conceivable that other collaborative models involving various provider organizations, such as IPAs, multispecialty group practices, and PHOs, could emerge (Goldsmith 2011). In an attempt to realize the threefold expectation of cost, quality, and population health, ACOs use mechanisms already prevalent in managed care and IDSs—disease management, care coordination, sharing of cost savings with providers, use of information technology, etc. (Burns

and Pauly 2012). It means that the operational strategies available to ACOs are not much different from what their predecessors have used. Hence, these "new" organizations may well turn out to be nothing more than "old wine in new bottles." The evidence thus far suggests that ACOs are likely to have limited and uncertain impact, particularly on cost savings (Burns and Pauly 2012).

In one respect, however, ACO operations will go beyond the typical IDSs. The ACA authorized Medicare to establish care delivery and payment methods involving ACOs, beginning in 2012. The law specifies that the payment method must include a Shared Savings Program that authorizes Medicare to pay additional moneys to providers if an ACO achieves targeted cost savings while meeting certain defined quality objectives. The law requires ACOs that wish to participate in shared savings to enter into a contract with CMS for not less than 3 years.

There are more questions than answers about what can reasonably be expected from ACOs because they remain more of a concept than a concrete model (Foreman 2012). Their eventual success or failure will depend on how well they can control costs while improving quality. Particularly, there is lack of clarity on three main issues. (1) While hospitals and larger clinics are joining hands to form ACOs, smaller physician practices may get left out from reaping any benefits ACOs may provide. At the same time, these clinics may encounter more regulatory oversight and demands for compliance with new rules under the ACA. (2) It remains to be seen how safety-net providers, including community health centers and public hospitals—which have long experience in caring for vulnerable populations—will be included in ACOs (Witgert and Hess 2012). (3) Under certain conditions, ACOs could dominate a geographic market, reduce competition, and harm consumers through higher prices or lower quality of care. Such concerns can be addressed through existing antitrust laws. *Antitrust* policy consists of federal and state laws that make certain types of business practices illegal. The business practices prohibited or regulated by antitrust laws include price fixing, price discrimination, exclusive contracting arrangements, and acquisitions and mergers that may stifle competition. Some providers may still be able to gain pricing power over commercial insurers. Vertical integration may enable participants in ACOs to use market power to inhibit competition by monopolizing patient referrals within the ACO. Bacher and colleagues (2013) have argued that antitrust policy faces a trade-off. On the one hand, pursuit of market competitiveness would limit ACOs' size and geographic reach. On the other hand, antitrust policies may make it more difficult for ACOs to effectively integrate their operations to achieve economies and care coordination.

Payer–Provider Integration

In a radically changing health care system, payer–provider integration is on the rise. For example, insurance companies have started to acquire large physician practice groups and health systems as a strategy to gain more control over the delivery of health care (Berarducci et al. 2012).

It is too early to say, but collaboration between managed care and providers as risk-bearing entities could become the next major trend. By partnering with an entity with expertise in managing risk, these organizations would stand a much better chance to succeed than the earlier PSOs. If the trend indeed takes off, the same provider entities that had rebelled against the growing power of managed care not too long ago would now join hands with it because they would now be fearing the encroachment of a much more powerful adversary—the government.

Summary

Managed care evolved through an integration of the insurance function with the concepts of contract practice and prepaid group practice of the late 19th and early 20th centuries. Even though managed care has become the dominant medium through which the vast majority of Americans obtain health care services, its full potential to achieve cost effectiveness was thwarted by opposition from providers, consumers, and policymakers. Participation in the HEDIS program, however, has improved the quality of services provided by MCOs.

The growing power of managed care was one main factor that triggered integration among health care providers. The pace of integration between physicians and hospitals has accelerated since the passage of the Affordable Care Act. The ACA has also given a new form to an old concept by requiring Medicare contracts with accountable care organizations. Even though the exact form and function of these organizations remain unclear, these organizations are envisioned as highly integrated and responsible for achieving certain objectives regarding costs, quality, and consumer satisfaction. An ironic collaboration between managed care and providers may well become the next big trend on the American health care stage.

ACA Takeaway

- Managed care will play a dominant role in offering health insurance through the exchanges.
- ACA prescribes minimum medical loss ratios in health plans to limit the percentage of premium revenue a health plan can use for administration, marketing, and profits.
- The ACA envisions that consumer operated and oriented plans will emerge, spurred by financing from the federal government.
- Accountable care organizations are at an early stage of development. The ACA authorized Medicare to establish a Shared Savings Program for ACOs based on cost savings while meeting certain defined quality objectives.

Test Your Understanding

Terminology

accountable care
   organization
acquisition
alliance
antitrust
carve out
case management
closed panel
concurrent utilization
   review
discharge planning
disease management
diversification
exclusive provider plan
fee schedule
formulary

group model
HMO
horizontal integration
indemnity insurance
independent practice
   association
integrated delivery system
integration
IPA model
joint venture
merger
mixed model
MSO
network model
open panel
panel

PHO
point-of-service plan
PPO
practice profiling
primary care case
   management
prospective utilization
   review
PSO
retrospective utilization
   review
staff model
triple-option plans
utilization review
vertical integration
virtual integration

Review Questions

1. What are some of the key differences between traditional indemnity insurance and managed care?

2. What are the three main payment mechanisms managed care uses? In each mechanism, who bears the risk?

3. Explain how the fee-for-service practice of medicine led to uncontrolled utilization.

4. How do MCOs achieve cost efficiencies by integrating the quad functions, risk sharing with providers, and care coordination? What are some of the inefficiencies created by managed care?

5. Discuss the concept of utilization monitoring and control.

6. How does case management achieve efficiencies in the delivery of health care? How does case management differ from disease management?

7. Explain how MCOs engage in pharmaceutical management. How does utilization review apply to drug management?

8. Describe the three utilization review methods, giving appropriate examples. Discuss the benefits of each type of utilization review.

9. What is an HMO? How does it differ from a PPO?

10. Briefly explain the four main models for organizing an HMO. Discuss the advantages and disadvantages of each model.

11. What is a point-of-service plan? Why did it grow in popularity? What caused its subsequent decline?

12. What role is managed care expected to play under the Affordable Care Act?

13. To what extent has managed care been successful in containing health care costs?

14. Has the quality of health care gone down as a result of managed care? Explain.

15. What is organizational integration? What is its ultimate aim? Why did health care organizations integrate?

16. What is the difference between a merger and an acquisition? What is the purpose of these organizational consolidations? Give examples.

17. When would a joint venture be considered a preferable integration strategy?

18. What is the main advantage of two organizations forming an alliance?

19. State the main strategic objectives of horizontal and vertical integration.

20. What is antitrust policy? What type of business practices does antitrust law prohibit? How might antitrust policy play out in the formation of accountable care organizations?

REFERENCES

Altman, D., and L. Levitt. 2013. Healthcare cost spiral hasn't been cured. *Modern Healthcare* 43, no. 17: 25.

Angalakuditi, M., and J. Gomes. 2011. Retrospective drug utilization review: Impact of pharmacist interventions on physician prescribing. *Clinicoeconomics and Outcomes Research* 3: 105–108.

Aventis Pharmaceuticals/SMG Marketing-Verispan LLC. 2002. *Managed care digest series: HMO-PPO/Medicare-Medicaid digest.* Bridgewater, NJ: Aventis Pharmaceuticals.

Ayanian, J.Z., et al. 2013. Medicare beneficiaries more likely to receive appropriate ambulatory services in HMOs than in traditional Medicare. *Health Affairs* 32, no. 7: 1228–1235.

Bacher, G.E., et al. 2013. Regulatory neutrality is essential to establishing a level playing field for accountable care organizations. *Health Affairs* 32, no. 8: 1426–1432.

Baker, L., et al. 2004. The effect of area HMO market share on cancer screening. *Health Services Research* 39, no. 6: 1751–1772.

Balsa, A., et al. 2007. Does managed health care reduce health care disparities between minorities and whites? *Journal of Health Economics* 26, no. 1: 101–121.

Basu, J. 2012. Medicare managed care and primary care quality: Examining racial/ethnic effects across states. *Health Care Management Science* 15, no. 1: 15–28.

Berarducci, J., et al. 2012. New partnership opportunities for payers and providers. *Healthcare Financial Management* 66, no. 10: 58–61.

Berk, M.L., and A.C. Monheit. 2001. The concentration of health expenditures revisited. *Health Affairs* 20, 2: 9–18.

Bourjolly, J.N., et al. 2004. The impact of managed health care in the United States on women with breast cancer and the providers who treat them. *Cancer Nursing* 27, no. 1: 45–54.

Brennan, N., and M. Shepard. 2010. Comparing quality of care in the Medicare program. *American Journal of Managed Care* 16, no. 11: 841–848.

Brill, J.V. 2007. Trends in prescription drug plans delivering the Medicare Part D prescription drug benefit. *American Journal of Health-System Pharmacy* 64, Suppl. 10: S3–S6.

Brown, M. 1996. Mergers, networking, and vertical integration: Managed care and investor-owned hospitals. *Health Care Management Review* 21, no. 1: 29–37.

Brown, R.S., et al. 2012. Six features of Medicare Coordinated Care Demonstration Programs that cut hospital admission of high-risk patients. *Health Affairs* 31, no. 6: 1156–1166.

Burns, L.R., and M.V. Pauly. 2012. Accountable care organization may have difficulty avoiding the failures of integrated delivery networks of the 1990s. *Health Affairs* 31, no. 11: 2407–2416.

Business Word Inc. 1996. Physicians and employers identify seven essentials of managed care. *Health Care Strategic Management* 14, no. 12: 4.

Capps, C., and D. Dranove. 2004. Hospital consolidation and negotiated PPO prices. *Health Affairs* 23, no. 2: 175–181.

Carson, K.D., et al. 1995. *Management of healthcare organizations.* Cincinnati, OH: South-Western College Publishing.

Centers for Medicare and Medicaid Services (CMS). 2012. Health reform expands the insurance market, support consumer-governed nonprofit health plans. Available at: http://www.cms.gov/Newsroom/MediaReleaseDatabase/Press-Releases/2012-Press-Releases-Items/2012-02-21.html. Accessed September 2013.

Chen, C., et al. 2009. Evaluation of a nurse practitioner-led care management model in reducing inpatient drug utilization and cost. *Nursing Economics* 27, no. 3: 160–168.

Daubresse, M., et al. 2013. Impact of drug utilization review program on high-risk use of prescription controlled substances. *Pharmacoepidemiology and Drug Safety*, July 24.

DeFrancesco, L.B. 2002. HMO enrollees experience fewer disparities than older insured populations. *Findings Brief: Health Care Financing & Organization* 5, no. 2: 1–2.

Deom, M., et al. 2010. What doctors think about the impact of managed care tools on quality of care, costs, autonomy, and relations with patients. *BMC Health Services Research* 10, no. 331: 2–8.

DeVore, S., and R.W. Champion. 2011. Driving population health through accountable care organizations. *Health Affairs* 30, no. 1: 41–50.

DoBias, M. 2008. Uneven results. *Modern Healthcare* 38, no. 40: 12.

Eikel, C.V. 2002. Fewer patient visits under capitation offset by improved quality of care: Study brings evidence to debate over physician payment methods. *Findings Brief: Health Care Financing & Organization* 5, no. 3: 1–2.

Foreman, M. 2012. A medical neighborhood: Accountable care organizations could solve some of health care's biggest problems, but they're largely untested. *State Legislatures* 38, no.5: 22–25.

Friedman, B., et al. 2012. Likelihood of hospital readmission after first discharge: Medicare Advantage vs. fee-for-service patients. *Inquiry: A Journal of Medical Care Organization, Provision and Financing* 49, no. 3: 202–213.

Gabel, J. 1997. Ten ways HMOs have changed during the 1990s. *Health Affairs* 16, no. 3: 134–145.

Ginsburg, P.B. 2005. Competition in health care: Its evolution over the past decade. *Health Affairs* 24, no. 6: 1512–1522.

Gold, M., et al. 2013. *Medicare Advantage 2013 spotlight: Enrollment market update.* Menlo Park, CA: Henry J. Kaiser Family Foundation.

Goldman, W., et al. 2003. A four-year study of enhancing outpatient psychotherapy in managed care. *Psychiatric Services* 54, no. 1: 41–49.

Goldsmith, J. 2011. Accountable care organizations: The case for flexible partnerships between health plans and providers. *Health Affairs* 30, no. 1: 32–40.

Government Accountability Office (GAO). 2012. Report to John D. Rockefeller, IV and Henry A. Waxman on states' use of managed care. Available at: http://gao.gov/assets/600/593781.pdf. Accessed September 2013.

Grace, S.C., et al. 2013. Health-related quality of life and quality of care in specialized medicare managed care plans. *Journal of Ambulatory Care Management* 36, no. 1: 72–84.

Henry J. Kaiser Family Foundation/Health Research and Educational Trust (Kaiser/HRET). 2002. *Employer health benefits: 2002 annual survey.* Menlo Park, CA: Kaiser Family Foundation.

Himmelstein, D., et al. 1999. Quality of care in investor-owned vs not-for-profit HMOs. *Journal of the American Medical Association* 282, no. 2: 159–163.

Hofmann, M.A. 2002. Quality of health care improving. *Business Insurance* 36, no. 38: 1–2.

Hurley, R.E., and D.A. Draper. 2002. Health plan responses to managed care regulation. *Managed Care Quarterly* 10, no. 4: 30–42.

Hwang, W., et al. 2013. Effects of integrated delivery system on cost and quality. *American Journal of Managed Care* 19, no. 5: e175–e184.

J.D. Power and Associates. 2011. Press release: J.D. Power and Associates reports: Members of health plans with integrated delivery models are more satisfied than members without integrated plans. Available at: http://content2.businesscenter.jdpower.com/JDPAContent/CorpComm/ News/content/Releases/pdf/2011028-natl.pdf. Accessed September 2013.

Jessee, W.F. 2011. Is there an ACO in your future? *MGMA Connexion* 11, no. 1: 5–6.

Keating, N.L., et al. 2007. The influence of cost containment strategies and physicians' financial arrangements on patients' trust and satisfaction. *The Journal of Ambulatory Care Management* 30, no. 2: 92–104.

Kongstvedt, P.R., and D.W. Plocher. 1995. Integrated health care delivery systems. In: *Essentials of managed health care.* P.R. Kongstvedt, ed. Gaithersburg, MD: Aspen Publishers, Inc. pp. 35–49.

Kronebusch, K., et al. 2009. Managed care regulation in the states: The impact on physicians' practices and clinical autonomy. *Journal of Health Politics, Policy, and Law* 34, no. 2: 219–259.

Landon, B.E., et al. 2003. Changes in career satisfaction among primary care and specialist physicians, 1997–2001. *Journal of the American Medical Association* 289, no. 4: 442–449.

Lattimer, C. 2005. Advanced care management strategies reduce costs and improve patient health in high-risk insurance pools. *Lippincott's Case Management* 10, no. 5: 261–263.

MacColl, W.A. 1966. *Group practice and prepayment of medical care.* Washington, DC: Public Affairs Press.

Mackie, D.L., and D.K. Decker. 1981. *Group and IPA HMOs.* Gaithersburg, MD: Aspen Publishers, Inc.

Mattke, S. 2008. Is there disease management backlash? *American Journal of Managed Care* 14, no. 6: 349–350.

McGuire, J.P. 1994. The growth of managed care. *Health Care Financial Management* 48, no. 8: 10.

McQueen, M.P., and H. Meyer. 2013. A different kind of Medicaid expansion. *Modern Healthcare* 43, no. 30: 6–16.

Melnick, G.A., et al. 2011. The increased concentration of health plan markets can benefit consumers through lower hospital prices. *Health Affairs* 30, no. 9: 1728–1733.

Miller, R.H., and H.S. Luft. 1997. Does managed care lead to better or worse quality of care? *Health Affairs* 16, no. 5: 7–26.

Miller, R.H., and H.S. Luft. 2002. HMO plan performance update: An analysis of the literature, 1997–2001. *Health Affairs* 21, no. 4: 63–86.

Minich-Pourshadi, K. 2013. The drive to hire docs. *Health Leaders Magazine* 16, no. 2: 46–51.

Moscovice, I., et al. 1998. Expanding rural managed care: Enrollment patterns and prospectives. *Health Affairs* 17, no. 1: 172–179.

Morrisey, M.A., et al. 2013. Favorable selection, risk adjustment, and the Medicare Advantage program. *Health Services Research* 48, no. 3: 1039–1056.

Nader, R., and S. Walston. 2005. Transfer pricing and integrated delivery systems: The effects of interdependence and risk. *Managed Care Quarterly* 13, no. 4: 1–8.

National Committee for Quality Assurance (NCQA). 2013. *HEDIS 2013 measures*. Available at: http://www.ncqa.org/Portals/0/HEDISQM/HEDIS2013/List_of_HEDIS_2013_Measures_7.2.12. pdf. Accessed September 2013.

Ng, A., et al. 2013. Self-efficacy and health status improve after a wellness program in persons with multiple sclerosis. *Disability & Rehabilitation* 35, no. 12: 1039–1044.

Nguyen, N.X., and F.W. Derrick. 1997. Physician behavioral response to a Medicare price reduction. *Health Services Research* 32, no. 3: 283–298.

Pati, S., et al. 2005. Health expenditures for privately insured adults enrolled in managed care gatekeeping vs indemnity plans. *American Journal of Public Health* 95, no. 2: 286–291.

Pelfrey, S., and B.A. Theisen. 1989. Joint venture in health care. *Journal of Nursing Administration* 19, no. 4: 39–42.

Quast, T., et al. 2008. Does the quality of care in Medicaid MCOs vary with the form of physician compensation? *Health Economics* 17, no. 4: 545–550.

Rakich, J.S., et al. 1992. *Managing health services organizations*. 3rd ed. Baltimore, MD: Health Professions Press.

Reed, M.C., et al. 2003. Physicians and care management: More acceptance than you think. *Issue brief no. 60*. Washington, DC: Center for the Study of Health System Change.

Rice, T.H., and R.J. Labelle. 1989. Do physicians induce demand for medical services? *Journal of Health Politics, Policy and Law* 14, no. 3: 587–600.

Riley, G.F., et al. 1999. Stage at diagnosis and treatment patterns among older women with breast cancer. *Journal of the American Medical Association* 281: 720–726.

Robinson, J.C. 2002. Renewed emphasis on consumer cost sharing in health insurance benefit design. *Health Affairs Web Exclusives* 2002: W139–W154.

Rogers, W.H., et al. 1993. Outcomes for adult outpatients with depression under prepaid or fee-for-service care: Results from the Medical Outcomes Study. *Archives of General Psychiatry* 50, no. 7: 517–525.

Sanderson, B., et al. 2008. Physician integration is back—and more important than ever. *Healthcare Financial Management* 62, no. 12: 64–71.

Sanofi-Aventis. 2008. *Managed care digest series, 2008: Hospitals/Systems Digest*. Bridgewater, NJ: Sanofi-Aventis US, LLC.

Sanofi-Aventis. 2012. *Managed care digest series, 2012–2013: HMO-PPO Digest*. Bridgewater, NJ: Sanofi-Aventis US, LLC.

Sanofi-Aventis. 2013. *Managed care digest series, 2013: Hospitals/Systems Digest*. Bridgewater, NJ: Sanofi-Aventis US, LLC.

Sanofi-Aventis. 2013. *Managed care digest series, 2013: Public Payer Digest*. Bridgewater, NJ: Sanofi-Aventis US, LLC.

Sari, N. 2002. Do competition and managed care improve quality? *Health Economics* 11, no. 7: 571–584.

Schneider, E.C., et al. 2005. Quality of care in for-profit and not-for-profit health plans enrolling Medicare beneficiaries. *American Journal of Medicine* 118, no. 12: 1392–1400.

Shen, Y. 2005. *Is managed care still an effective cost containment device?* The Freeman Spogli Institute for International Studies at Stanford University. Available at http://fsi.stanford.edu /events/is_managed_care_still_an_effective_cost_containment_device. Accessed May 2011.

Short, A.C., et al. 2001. *Provider network instability: Implications for choice, costs, and continuity of care.* Community Tracking Study issue brief no. 39. Washington, DC: Center for Studying Health System Change.

Short, A.C., et al. 2003. *Disease management: A leap of faith to lower-cost, higher-quality health care.* Issue Brief No. 69 (October 2003). Washington, DC: Center for Studying Health System Change.

Shortell, S.M., et al. 1993. Creating organized delivery systems: The barriers and facilitators. *Hospital and Health Services Administration* 38, no. 4: 447–466.

Shortell, S.M., and K.E. Hull. 1996. The new organization of the health care delivery system. In: *Strategic choices for a changing health care system.* S.H. Altman and U.E. Reinhardt, eds. Chicago: Health Administration Press.

Southwick, K. 1997. Case study: How United HealthCare and two contracting hospitals address cost and quality in era of hyper-competition. *Strategies for Healthcare Excellence* (COR Healthcare Resources) 10, no. 8 (August): 1–9.

Starner, C.I., et al. 2009. Effect of retrospective drug utilization review on potentially inappropriate prescribing in the elderly. *American Journal of Geriatric Pharmacotherapy* 7, no. 1: 11–19.

Strandberg-Larsen, M., et al. 2007. Kaiser Permanente revisited—Can European health care systems learn? *Eurohealth* 13, no. 4: 24–26.

Strunk, B.C., et al. 2001. Tracking health care costs. *Health Affairs Suppl. Web Exclusives* W39–50.

Strunk, B.C., and P.J. *Cunningham. 2004. Trends in Americans' access to needed medical care, 2001–2003.* Tracking Report No. 10 (August 2004). Washington, DC: Center for Studying Health System Change.

Thorpe, K.E., and A. Atherly. 2002. Medicare+Choice: Current role and near-term prospects. *Health Affairs Web Exclusives 2002:* W242–W252.

Tu, H.T. 2005. *More Americans willing to limit physician-hospital choice for lower medical costs.* Issue Brief No. 94. Washington, DC: Center for Studying Health System Change.

Wagner, E.R. 1995. Types of managed care organizations. In: *Essentials of managed health care.* P.R. Kongstvedt, ed. Gaithersburg, MD: Aspen Publishers, Inc. pp. 24–34.

Wells, K.B., et al. 1989. Detection of depressive disorder for patients receiving prepaid or fee-for-service care: Results from the Medical Outcomes Study. *Journal of the American Medical Association* 262, no. 23: 3298–3302.

Wilkerson, J.D., et al. 1997. The emerging competitive managed care marketplace. In: *Competitive managed care: The emerging health care system.* J.D. Wilkerson et al., eds. San Francisco: Jossey-Bass Publishers.

Witgert, K., and C. Hess. 2012. Including safety-net providers in integrated delivery systems: Issues and options for policymakers. *Issue Brief—Commonwealth Fund pub. 1617,* 20: 1–18. Available at: http://www.commonwealthfund.org/~/media/Files/Publications/Issue%20Brief/2012/ Aug/1617_Witgert_including_safety_net_providers_integrated_delivery_sys_ib.pdf. Accessed September 2013.

Yip, W.C. 1998. Physician response to Medicare fee reductions: Changes in the volume of coronory artery bypass graft (CABG) surgeries in the Medicare and private sectors. *Journal of Health Economics* 17, no. 6: 675–699.

Zelman, W.A. 1996. *The changing health care marketplace.* San Francisco: Jossey-Bass Publishers.

Chapter 10

Long-Term Care

Learning Objectives

- To comprehend the concept of long-term care and its main features
- To get an overview of LTC services
- To discover who needs long-term care and why
- To become familiar with the large variety of home- and community-based long-term care services, and who pays for these services.
- To learn about long-term care institutions and the levels of services they provide
- To get an overview of specialized long-term care facilities and continuing care retirement communities
- To explore institutional trends, utilization, and costs
- To get a perspective on private long-term care insurance
- To understand application of the Affordable Care Act to long-term care

"Now, honey, where are we supposed to go from here?"

Introduction

Long-term care (LTC) is a complex subsystem within the complex American health care delivery system. It escapes a simple definition. It encompasses numerous services. Several different sources of financing are associated with the different services. The sources of public financing have their own eligibility criteria, so not everyone qualifies. Regular health insurance does not cover LTC; if it does, the coverage is limited. Private LTC insurance has made limited headway. Even many people using LTC services do not realize that they are receiving LTC, just because they are not in a nursing home.

LTC is not confined to the elderly (people age 65 and over), but the elderly are the predominant users of these services and most LTC services have been designed with the elderly patient in mind. Yet, an estimated 37% of those in need of LTC are under the age of 65 (Health Policy Institute 2003). In 2012, 44% of noninstitutionalized older persons assessed their own health as excellent or very good, compared to 64% for persons aged 18–64 years; but, compared to whites, fewer elderly African Americans, Hispanics, Asians, and American Indians/Alaska Natives rated their health as excellent or very good (Administration on Aging 2013a). Because the growing non-white elderly population is in poorer health, it is likely to face a greater need for LTC services later in life. Social and cultural factors important to each group will present new challenges in the delivery of LTC services.

According to the US government's website (http://www.longtermcare.gov), an estimated 70% of older Americans will eventually need some type of LTC, even though many may never leave their own homes. Surveys over time have shown that the vast majority of older Americans wish to stay in their own homes indefinitely. Hence, community-based services are preferred by most older people, and these services have grown more rapidly than LTC institutions. To reflect this shift, the term "long-term services and supports," has been suggested to refer to a broad spectrum of LTC options (Reinhard et al. 2011).

The clients of LTC need a variety of health care services over time. Hence, LTC cannot be an isolated component of the health care delivery system. The LTC system must interface with the rest of the system to provide ease of transition among various types of health care settings and services, both LTC and non-LTC.

LTC is associated with functional deficits arising from chronic conditions (explained in Chapter 2). Chronic conditions are the leading causes of illness, disability, and death in the United States, yet the presence of chronic conditions alone does not create the need for LTC. Almost 77% of Americans age 65 and over have at least two chronic conditions (Machlin et al. 2008). Disability and functional limitations rise dramatically among those who have multiple chronic conditions (Figure 10–1). Serious illness or injury can also lead to a rapid decline in a person's health. For certain types of disabilities, many people can maintain their independence by using adaptive devices (walkers, wheelchairs, adaptive eating utensils, etc.) to overcome their deficits and may not require any LTC services. The need for LTC services arises when an individual is no longer able to perform certain common tasks of daily living because of functional decline, and, consequently becomes

Figure 10–1 People with Multiple Chronic Conditions Are More Likely to Have Activity Limitations.

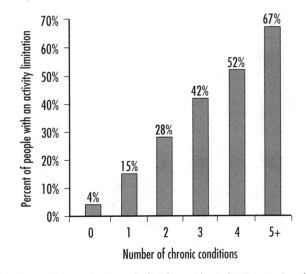

Source: *Chronic Conditions: Making the Case for Ongoing Care,* Partnership for Solutions, Johns Hopkins University, December 2002, p. 12.

dependent to carry out those functions. Without LTC intervention in this situation, the risk of further morbidity and mortality greatly increases.

Cognitive impairment also leads to functional decline. *Cognitive impairment* is a mental disorder that is indicated by a person having difficulty remembering, learning new things, concentrating, or making decisions that affect the individual's everyday life. Cognitive impairment ranges from mild to severe, and may lead to disturbing behaviors. Cognitive impairment with or without dementia contributes to neuropsychiatric symptoms and increased disability (Tabert et al. 2002).

Two common indicators used to assess functional limitations are the activities of daily living (ADLs) scale and instrumental activities of daily living (IADLs; see Chapter 2 for a description of ADLs and IADLs). As examples, ADLs include a person's ability to bathe, dress, and eat; IADLs

include a person's ability to prepare meals, do housework, and manage medication use. Limitations in ADLs indicate a more severe decline in a person's functional status than limitations in IADLs do. People receiving care in nursing homes have a greater degree of ADL decline than people who can live at home or in community housing that offers some support services (Figure 10–2).

In 2010, a person who attained the age of 65 could expect to live for another 19 years. As the elderly population in the United States continues to grow, issues related to chronic conditions, accompanying disability, and the need for LTC services will intensify. Although accurate data on LTC utilization are not available, it is estimated that approximately 9 million older Americans (22% of the elderly population) currently need LTC; this number will rise to 12 million by 2020 (21% of the elderly population). Future need for LTC services, however, will be affected by health and disease trends among the

Figure 10–2 Medicare Enrollees Age 65 and Over With Functional Limitations According to Where They Live, 2009.

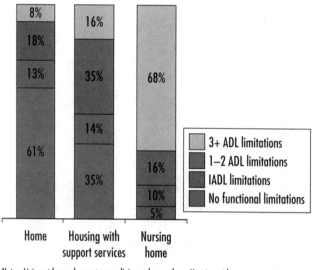

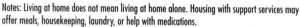

Notes: Living at home does not mean living at home alone. Housing with support services may offer meals, housekeeping, laundry, or help with medications.

Source: Federal Interagency Forum on Aging-Related Statistics. 2012. *Older Americans 2012: Key indicators of well-being.* Washington, DC: US Government Printing Office.

younger population groups. Of those who need LTC, 15.4% currently live in nursing homes (3.4% of the elderly population).* Although community-based services are more cost-effective than institutional care, the sheer volume of LTC services needed in the future will put tremendous pressures on the younger generations to shoulder the needs of a growing elderly segment of the population. The National Study of Long-Term Care Providers is a new research initiative undertaken jointly by the Centers for Disease Control and Prevention (CDC) and the National Center for Health Statistics to estimate the national supply of various kinds

of LTC services and their utilization. The first set of results is expected to be released in late 2013.

At present, the financial burden for LTC falls clearly on the shoulders of the American taxpayers. The total spending on the various types of paid LTC services, both in the community and in institutions, amounted to $203.2 billion in 2009. Two-thirds of this amount was paid by Medicaid and other public sources (National Health Policy Forum 2011).

The rest of the developed world also faces aging-related problems and challenges in providing adequate LTC services very similar to those in the United States. Actually, the elderly population as a proportion of the total population in other developed

*Data in this paragraph are retrieved from the Centers for Medicare and Medicaid Services and the U.S. Census Bureau.

countries, such as Japan, Germany, France, and Great Britain, is already higher than it is in the United States.

This chapter provides an overview of LTC, its main clients, various types of community-based and institutional services, and how these services are financed. LTC services form a continuum, from basic help to more advanced care, to address the varied needs of a heterogeneous population. Even the elderly, who are the predominant users of LTC services, are not a homogeneous group.

The Nature of Long-Term Care

Long-term care can be defined as a variety of individualized, well coordinated services that promote the maximum possible independence for people with functional limitations and are provided over an extended period of time in accordance with a holistic approach, while maximizing their quality of life. To the extent possible, the delivery of LTC should employ appropriate current technology and available evidence-based practices. LTC is unique in health care delivery, and is multidimensional.

Variety of Services

A variety of services is necessary because individual needs, as determined by health status, finances, and other factors, vary greatly among people who require LTC services. Hence, LTC services should (1) fit the needs of different individuals, (2) address their changing needs over time, and (3) suit their personal preferences.

Individualized Services

LTC services are tailored to the needs of the individual patient. Those needs are determined by an assessment of the individual's current physical, mental, and emotional condition. Other factors used for this purpose include history of the patient's medical and psychosocial conditions; a social history of family relationships, former occupation, and leisure activities; and cultural factors, such as racial and ethnic background, language, and religious practices. Information obtained from a comprehensive assessment is used to develop an individualized plan of care that addresses each type of need through customized interventions.

Well Coordinated Total Care

LTC providers are responsible for managing the total health care needs of an individual client. *Total care* requires that any health care need is recognized, evaluated, and addressed by appropriate clinical professionals (Singh 2010). Hence, LTC must interface with non-LTC services (Figure 10–3). The main non-LTC services include primary care; mental health services; acute care hospitals; and various outpatient services such as those provided by specialist physicians, dentists, optometrists, podiatrists, diagnostic labs, and imaging centers.

Patients needing LTC often require coordination among many different health care services as different needs arise over time. For most people, the myriad of health care services, eligibility requirements, and financing can be overwhelming. Hence, case management (discussed later under "Case Management") becomes an important service for many people. One key role

Figure 10–3 Key Characteristics of a Well Designed Long-Term Care System.

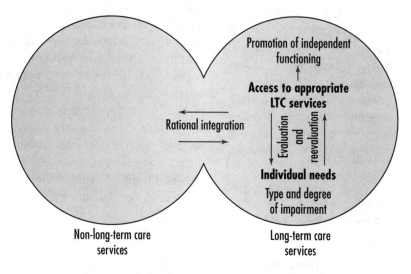

Health care delivery system

KEY CHARACTERISTICS

1. The LTC system is rationally integrated with the rest of the health care delivery system. This rational integration facilitates easy access to services between the two components of the health care delivery system.
2. Appropriate placement of the patient within the LTC system is based on an assessment of individual needs. For example, individual needs determine whether and when institutionalization may be necessary.
3. The LTC system accommodates changes in individual needs by providing access to appropriate LTC services as determined by a reevaluation of needs.
4. LTC services are designed to compensate for existing impairment and have the objective of promoting independence to the extent possible.

of case management is to match client needs with available services that are likely to best address those needs regardless of whether they are obtained within the LTC sector or from the non-LTC sector.

Maintenance of Residual Function

As a person ages, chronic ailments, comorbidity, disability, and dependency tend to follow each other. Serious physical or mental illness, accidents, severe birth defects,

and cognitive impairment may also lead to functional decline and create dependency. In some cases, the dependency is short-term. Dependency, because of a loss of ability to independently perform certain IADL and/or ADL functions, creates the need for LTC. Caregiver assistance becomes necessary when a person is either unable or unwilling to perform daily living tasks. In that case, LTC has two main goals: (1) to maintain residual function, that is, whatever ability to function a person still has, and (2) to prevent further decline. These goals are accomplished by letting the person do as much as possible for himself or herself. On the other hand, a comatose patient in a persistent vegetative state may be totally dependent on a caregiver.

Extended Period of Care

For most LTC clients, the delivery of various services extends over a relatively long period because the underlying causes of functional decline are often irreversible. In some cases, however, rehabilitation therapies or postacute convalescence may be needed for a relatively short duration, generally less than 90 days. The patient subsequently returns to independent living. People receiving community-based LTC services generally need them for a long duration to prevent institutionalization. A smaller number of LTC recipients need institutional care for an extended period of time, in some cases, indefinitely. Examples include people with severe dementia, incontinence of bowel and bladder, severe psychiatric or behavioral issues, unstable postacute conditions, or those in a comatose/vegetative state.

Holistic Care

As discussed in Chapter 2, according to the holistic model, a patient's physical, mental, social, and spiritual needs and preferences should be incorporated into medical care delivery. Holistic care becomes even more important in LTC. Connectedness not only with caregivers, but also with family, friends, and members of the faith community play an important role in overcoming social isolation and promoting well-being of the patient. A person's beliefs, values, and religious practices must be respected and incorporated in the caregiving routines.

Quality of Life

A sense of satisfaction, fulfillment, and self-worth are regarded as critical patient outcomes in any health care delivery setting. They take added significance in LTC because (1) a loss of self-worth often accompanies disability and (2) patients remain in LTC settings for relatively long periods, with little hope of full recovery in most instances.

Quality of life is a multifaceted concept that recognizes at least five factors: lifestyle pursuits, living environment, clinical palliation, human factors, and personal choices.

- Lifestyle factors are associated with personal enrichment and making one's life meaningful through activities one enjoys. Many older people still enjoy pursuing their former leisure activities, such as woodworking, crocheting, knitting, gardening, and fishing. Even those whose function has declined to a vegetative or comatose state must be engaged in something that promotes sensory awakening through visual, auditory, olfactory, and tactile stimulation.

- The living environment must be comfortable, safe, and appealing to the senses. Cleanliness, décor, furnishings, and other aesthetic features are important.

- Clinical *palliation* should be available for relief from unpleasant symptoms, such as pain or nausea, for instance, when a patient is undergoing chemotherapy.

- Human factors refer to caregiver attitudes and practices that emphasize caring, compassion, respect, and preservation of human dignity for the patient. Institutionalized patients find it disconcerting to have lost their autonomy and independence. Quality of life is enhanced when patients residing in a long-term care facility, who are often referred to as residents, have some latitude to govern their own lives, and have adequate privacy.

- Being able to make personal choices is important to most people. In nursing facilities, for example, food is often the primary area of discontentment, which can be addressed by offering a selection of menu choices. Also, the ability to set one's own schedule is important to most people. Many elderly resent being awakened early in the morning when caregivers begin their responsibilities to care for patients' hygiene, bathing, and grooming.

Use of Current Technology

Technology offers one avenue for at least mitigating the impending challenges of the growing need for LTC. Besides, technology can improve overall safety and quality of care. For example, a personal emergency response system (***PERS***) enables an at-risk elderly person living alone at home to summon help in an emergency at any time during day or night. A fall detector can be used at home or in an institution. Electronic medication dispensers are programmed to dispense pills and sound an alarm as reminders for a person to take prescribed medications. Remote monitoring technology is discussed in Chapter 5. Examples of technology for institutional settings include global positioning systems (GPS) to monitor a patient who may wander away, sensor technology to prevent and heal pressure ulcers by detecting moisture levels and length of time spent in one position, use of robotic pets, and pedometers to measure daily activity levels (Morley 2012).

Use of Evidence-Based Practices

1. ***Evidence-based care*** incorporates the use of best practices that have been evaluated for effectiveness and safety through clinical research. Best practices are often found in clinical practice guidelines (see Chapter 12), which provide directions and protocols for treatment interventions for specific health conditions. The American Medical Directors Association, for example, publishes clinical practice guidelines on important topics regarding the treatment of common clinical conditions in long term care. Evidence-based protocols are meant to be used for staff training and caregiving routines to improve quality of care. Studies show that the use of evidence-based practices in nursing homes can reduce falls (Teresi et al. 2013), prevent pressure ulcers (Niederhauser et al. 2012; Riordan and Voegeli 2009), and increase satisfaction among nurses (Barba et al. 2012).

Long-Term Care Services

The large array of LTC services can include a combination of different types of services depending on an individual's assessed needs at a given point in time, as new needs arise, and as needs change over time.

- Medical care, nursing, and rehabilitation
- Mental health services and dementia care
- Social support
- Preventive and therapeutic long-term care

- Informal and formal care
- Respite care
- Community-based and institutional services
- Housing
- End-of-life care

Medical Care, Nursing, and Rehabilitation

These services focus on three main areas: (1) postacute continuity of care, (2) clinical management of chronic illness and comorbidity, and (3) restoration or maintenance of physical function. LTC often becomes necessary after the treatment of an acute episode in a hospital. However, patients in LTC settings also encounter acute episodes, such as pneumonia, bone fracture, or stroke, and require admission to a general hospital. For the same medical conditions, the elderly are more prone to hospitalization, compared to younger age groups, who may be treated as outpatients. Nurses, rehabilitation therapists, nutritionists, and other professionals typically provide medical care in LTC settings under the direction of a physician. Preventing complications from chronic conditions (tertiary prevention) is an important aspect of LTC.

Mental Health Services and Dementia Care

It is erroneous to believe that mental disorders are a normal part of aging. Nevertheless, an estimated 25% of older adults have depression, anxiety disorders, or other significant psychiatric conditions, and mental health disorders are frequently comorbid in older adults, occurring with a number of common chronic illnesses such as diabetes, cardiac disease, and arthritis (Robinson 2010). Severe mental/cognitive disorders, such as dementias, are prevalent among 5% of the elderly population and have an unexplained predominance in women (Ritchie and Lovestone 2002). Psychiatric symptoms and cognitive decline are particularly common among nursing home residents (Scocco et al. 2006). Mental disorders range in severity from problematic to disabling to fatal. Yet, major barriers must be overcome in the delivery of mental health care. In general, assessing psychiatric illness in geriatric patients can be difficult, especially since comorbidity may obscure the diagnosis. For example, the patient with multiple chronic illnesses can display symptoms of either dementia or depression attributed to the primary medical condition rather than to an underlying psychiatric illness (Tune 2001). Hence, elderly people with mental disorders are less likely than younger adults to receive correct diagnoses and needed mental health care.

Dementia is a general term for progressive and irreversible decline in cognition, thinking, and memory. The risk of dementia increases with age. Approximately 15% of people older than 70 years of age have dementia (Hurd et al. 2013); the majority have *Alzheimer's disease*—a progressive degenerative disease of the brain, producing memory loss, confusion, irritability, and severe functional decline. Alzheimer's is the most well known form of dementia that affects roughly 5 million older Americans in the United States (Alzheimer's Association 2013). Although people with mild dementia may receive home-based care, almost 40% of people with dementia receive institutional LTC. Among institutionalized patients, almost 72% have a diagnosis of dementia, according to one study (Helmer et al. 2006).

Social Support

LTC clients need social and emotional support to help cope with changing life events that may cause stress, frustration, anger, fear, grief, or other emotional imbalances. Adaptation to new surroundings and new people becomes necessary when a patient leaves his or her own home and moves to supportive housing or a nursing home. Social support is also needed when problems and issues arise in the interactions among people within social systems. For example, conflicts may arise between what a patient wants for himself or herself and what the family may think is best for the patient. Conflicts also arise between patients and caregivers. Social services are also necessary to facilitate the coordination of total care needs. Examples include transportation services, information, counseling, recreation, and spiritual support. For people residing in LTC facilities, to remain connected with the community and the outside world is an important aspect of social support.

Preventive and Therapeutic Long-Term Care

In the context of LTC, prevention generally refers to preventing or delaying institutionalization. Various community-based LTC services have a preventive function, as long as these services include good nutrition and access to services, such as vaccinations, flu shots, and routine medical care. These services are of a long duration. Therapeutic services, such as nursing care, rehabilitation, and therapeutic diets, are specified in a plan of care under the direction of a physician. These services are of a short or long duration.

Informal and Formal Care

Contrary to popular belief, most LTC services in the United States are provided informally by family, friends, and surrogates such as neighbors and members from church or other community organizations. Informal services are not reimbursed. It is estimated that 92% of community-dwelling residents receive unpaid help (Kaye et al. 2010), from approximately 42 million informal caregivers in the United States (Feinberg et al. 2011). Family members also play an important role in managing the often critical transitions between settings of care delivery, such as between hospital and nursing home (Levine et al. 2010). Unpaid care is also the largest source of financing of LTC (Holtz-Eakin 2005). Its estimated economic value in 2009 was $450 billion, up from $375 billion in 2007 (Feinberg et al. 2011). Without informal care, a financial burden of this magnitude will fall mainly on taxpayers because many of the individuals getting informal care are economically disadvantaged; hence, the government will have to fill in the gaps. Men, minorities, married individuals, and those with less education are more likely to receive care from family and friends and are less likely to receive care in a nursing facility (Alecxih 2001).

Informal care reduces the use of formal home health care and delays nursing home entry (Van Houtven and Norton 2004). In a population of disabled elderly people, insufficient informal care is associated with overall discontinuation of living at home, all-cause mortality, hospitalization, and institutionalization (Kuzuya et al. 2011).

The pool of informal caregivers, in relation to the growing elderly population needing LTC, is going to shrink rather dramatically in the future. Various reports suggest that the number of older people who are divorced, unmarried, or without children has been on the rise.

Respite Care

Family caregivers often experience a range of physical, emotional, social, and financial problems. Negative feelings, such as anger, dissatisfaction, guilt, frustration, tension, and family conflict, are some common issues these caregivers face. Under these circumstances, caregivers experience stress and burnout. *Respite care* is the most frequently suggested intervention to address family caregivers' feelings of stress and burnout. The objective is to provide relief or assistance to caregivers for limited periods to allow them some free time without neglecting the patient. Respite care can include any kind of LTC service, such as adult day care, which allows people to work during the day, or temporary institutionalization which allows families to go on a vacation.

Community-Based and Institutional Services

For many people who need LTC, the availability of community-based services provided by formal agencies becomes an important factor in living independently. Services are brought to the patient's home or delivered in a community-based location; hence, these services are collectively referred to as home- and community-based services (HCBS). HCBS have a four-fold objective: (1) to deliver LTC in the most economical and least restrictive setting whenever appropriate, (2) to supplement informal caregiving when advanced services are needed or to substitute informal services when a person lacks a social network to receive informal care, (3) to provide temporary respite to informal caregivers, and (4) to delay or prevent institutionalization.

Institutionalization can be for a long-term or short-term duration. As can be inferred from Figure 10–2, functional deficits in 3 or more ADLs dramatically raise the probability for institutional care. The main goals for institutional care are to: (1) deliver therapeutic services in accordance with the plan of care, (2) provide professional help for ADL functions that the patient cannot perform, (3) implement measures to prevent further degeneration of remaining function, and (4) coordinate services with non-LTC providers to address the patient's total care needs.

Figure 10–4 illustrates various types of HCBS and institutional LTC settings. Types of services and financing for both are discussed later in this chapter.

Housing

Housing here refers to noninstitutional housing other than a person's own home. It includes independent living facilities and retirement living centers/communities—both private and public—that may or may not provide support services, such as meals, housekeeping, transportation, and scheduled recreational activities. Residents have their self-contained apartments or individual cottages that allow maximum privacy, and residents can come and go as they please. Occasional needs for LTC services are met by obtaining home health care through an outside agency.

Institutions, in contrast, are distinguished by services that go beyond basic support services to include therapeutic services delivered in accordance with a plan of care. Accommodations may be private or shared, but at least to some extent, privacy

Figure 10–4 Interlinkages Between Services for Those in Need of Long-Term Care.

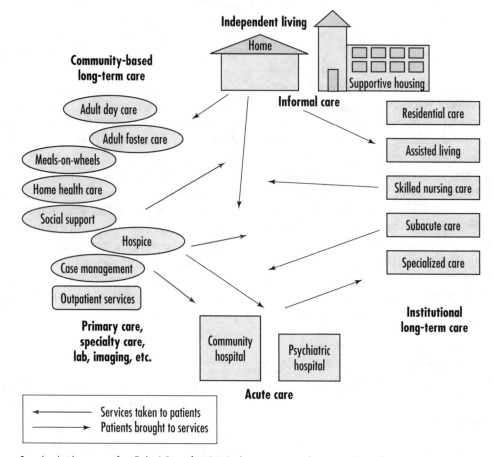

Source: Reproduced with permission from Taylor & Francis from D.A. Singh, *Nursing Home Administrators: Their Influence on Quality of Care*, p. 15, © 1997, Garland Publishing, Inc.; permission conveyed through Copyright Clearance Center, Inc.

is compromised. Individuals cannot generally leave the premises unless accompanied by an authorized person.

Housing for independent living for the elderly and disabled must support physical function and safety. Examples of supportive features include safety pull-cords to summon help in an emergency, grab bars in bathrooms to prevent falls, kitchenettes that allow the preparation of meals or snacks, railings in hallways to assist in mobility, and easy means of access to the outdoors.

Private Housing

Many upscale retirement centers abound in which one can expect to pay a fairly substantial entrance fee plus a monthly rental or maintenance fee. These complexes have various types of recreational facilities and social programs. The fees often include the evening meal. Housekeeping services and transportation may also be included.

Public Housing

More modest housing complexes provide government-assisted, subsidized housing for low-income people. The US Department of Housing and Urban Development (HUD) administers three main kinds of rent subsidy programs. These programs include federal aid to local housing agencies, which allows them to offer reduced rent to low-income tenants, vouchers that a tenant can apply toward renting housing of one's choice, and less commonly available public housing operated by the government. HUD also provides federal funds to nonprofit sponsors to construct rental housing with support services.

End-of-Life Care

Dealing with death and dying is very much a part of LTC. End-of-life care deals with preventing needless pain and distress for terminally ill patients and their families. High emphasis is placed on patient dignity and comfort.

Roughly three-fourths of all deaths occur at 65 years of age or older. Among the elderly, 28% of all deaths are related to heart disease and 22% are related to cancer (DHHS 2010). Other diseases often fatal to the elderly are stroke, chronic lower respiratory disease, Alzheimer's disease, diabetes, pneumonia, and influenza. Care professionals seem to be well positioned to provide end-of-life care in some LTC settings. In others, terminal patients are referred to hospice services (see Chapter 7). Regardless of the LTC setting, patients who suffer pain or dyspnea are more likely to be referred to a hospice service (Munn et al. 2006).

The Clients of Long-Term Care

People who need LTC services can be classified into four main categories: (1) older adults, (2) children and adolescents, (3) young adults, and (4) people with HIV/AIDS.

Older Adults

At the beginning of the 20th century, persons 65 years of age and older constituted just 4% of the population in the United States and numbered 3.1 million. In 2011, the elderly population totaled over 41 million, or 13.3% of the population (DHHS 2012). For some time now, the over-85 age group, referred to as the "oldest old," has been the most rapidly growing sector of the US population. By 2030, when all of the "baby boom generation" will have reached age 65, the elderly are expected to constitute 20% of the population, over 12% of whom would be 85 years of age and older (US Census Bureau 2012). The demographic trends have serious implications for the financing and delivery of LTC services. It is widely believed that a growing elderly population will put severe financial strains on a shrinking cohort of working taxpayers. Elderly in the lowest socioeconomic status are at the greatest risk of need for LTC and are the least able to pay for such services. Another challenge is presented by the aging of the MR/DD or IDD population (discussed in the next section). Similar to the general population, adults with IDD are living into their 70s and beyond (Robinson 2012) and present special challenges because of both low intellectual and physical function.

Children and Adolescents

In children, functional impairments are often birth related, such as brain damage, which can occur before or during childbirth. Examples of birth-related disorders include cerebral palsy, autism, spina bifida, and epilepsy. These children grow up with physical disability and need help with ADLs. The term *developmental disability* describes the general physical incapacity such children may face at a very early age. Those who acquire such dysfunctions are referred to as developmentally disabled, or DD for short. *Mental retardation* (MR), now more commonly referred to as *intellectual disability* (ID), refers to below-average intellectual functioning, which also leads to DD in most cases. Down syndrome is the most common cause of ID in America. The close association between the two is reflected in the terms mentally retarded/developmentally disabled (MR/DD) or intellectually/developmentally disabled (IDD). Approximately 14% of children in the age group 3–17 are developmentally disabled; boys are almost twice as likely as girls to have DD (Boyle et al. 2011). Those with severe ID and/or DD are also likely to have disturbing behavioral issues and usually require institutional care in specialized facilities.

Young Adults

Permanent disability among young adults commonly stems from neurological malfunctions, degenerative conditions, traumatic injury, or surgical complications. For example, multiple sclerosis is potentially the most common cause of neurological disability in young adults (Compston and Coles 2002). Severe injury to the head, spinal cord, or limbs can occur in victims of vehicle crashes, sports mishaps, or industrial accidents.

Other serious diseases, injuries, and respiratory or heart problems following surgery can make it difficult, or even impossible, for a patient to breathe naturally. Such individuals who cannot breathe (or ventilate) on their own require a ventilator. A ventilator is a small machine that takes over the breathing function by automatically moving air into and out of the patient's lungs. Ventilator-dependent patients also require total assistance with their ADLs.

MR/DD (IDD) is also prevalent among young adults who were previously housed in state-operated institutions or in nursing homes. According to the June 1999 US Supreme Court ruling in *Olmstead v. L.C.*, states must provide community-based services for MR/DD patients if treatment professionals determine that such services are appropriate and the affected individuals do not object to such placement, provided the states have the resources to offer such services. Also, states must develop a comprehensive working plan to place qualified MR/DD people in less restrictive settings. After the ruling, a serious effort began to move these people out of the institutional settings. Most adults with IDD now live in community housing with support services; a few still reside in state institutions and nursing homes.

People with HIV/AIDS

With the increased use of highly active antiretroviral therapy (HAART), AIDS has evolved from an end-stage terminal illness into a chronic condition. With reduced mortality, the prevalence of HIV in the population has actually increased, including among the elderly. People over the age of 50 are not only aging with HIV infection, but also represent a high proportion of new HIV infections (Watkins and Treisman 2012). For example, in 2007, almost 17% of new diagnoses of HIV were in individuals who were older than 50 years (Kearney et al. 2010). It is estimated that by 2015 half of all HIV-infected individuals in the United States will be over the age of 50 (Effros et al. 2008).

As HIV/AIDS patients age, they become susceptible to multiple comorbidities and cognitive impairment. Liver disease and cardiovascular disease are both associated with long-term use of HAART. HIV/AIDS patients are also at a high risk of developing various types of cancers, depression, dementia, and Alzheimer's disease (Cahill and Valadéz 2013). Older people living with HIV report lower levels of physical ability and less independence compared with younger people (Pereira and Canavarro 2011). These factors indicate a greater need of LTC services among people with HIV/AIDS. Many older adults living with HIV/AIDS are disconnected from traditional informal support networks, and rely heavily on formal care providers (Shippey and Karpiak 2005). HIV/AIDS patients have a variety of medical and social needs over time. Changing needs would require transitions between community-based services, nursing homes, and hospitals. To achieve cost efficiency, care coordination through case management or other types of care coordination approaches are common. Care coordination for HIV/AIDS patients results in fewer unmet needs for supportive services and often better utilization of services (Vargas and Cunningham 2006).

Level of Care Continuum

The importance of providing different levels of services to a heterogeneous population has given rise to a continuum of clinical categories, ranging from basic personal care to subacute care and specialized services.

Personal Care

Personal care refers to light assistance with basic ADLs. Provision of these services is largely the domain of *paraprofessionals*— personnel who provide basic ADL services, such as personal care attendants, certified nursing assistants (CNAs), and therapy aides. Personal care can be provided by informal caregivers, home health agencies, adult day care, adult foster care, and residential and assisted living facilities. Other levels of care often include a component of personal care.

Custodial Care

Custodial care is nonmedical care provided to support and maintain the patient's condition. It requires no active medical or nursing treatments. Services provided are designed to maintain rather than restore functioning, with an emphasis on preventing further deterioration. Examples are personal care with basic ADLs, range-of-motion exercises, bowel and bladder training, and assisted walking. Custodial services are rendered by paraprofessionals, such as aides, rather than licensed nurses or therapists. The settings in which custodial care is provided resemble those for personal care.

Restorative Care

Restorative care or rehabilitation involves short-term therapy treatments to help a person regain or improve physical function. It is provided immediately after the onset of a disability. Examples of cases requiring short-term restorative therapy include orthopedic surgery, stroke, limb amputation, and prolonged illness. Treatments are rendered by physical therapists, occupational therapists, and speech–language pathologists. Restorative care can be provided by home health agencies, rehabilitation hospitals, outpatient rehabilitation clinics, adult day care centers, and assisted living and skilled nursing facilities (SNFs).

Skilled Nursing Care

Skilled nursing care is medically oriented care provided mainly by a licensed nurse under the overall direction of a physician in accordance with a plan of care. Delivery of care includes assessment and reassessment to determine the patient's care needs, monitoring of acute and unstable chronic conditions, and a variety of treatments that may include wound care, tube care management, intravenous therapy, oncology care, HIV/AIDS care, and management of neurological conditions. Rehabilitation therapies often form an important component of skilled nursing care. Home health agencies and SNFs provide skilled nursing care.

Subacute Care

The term *subacute care* applies to post-acute services for people who remain critically ill during the postacute phase of illness or injury or who have complex conditions that require ongoing monitoring and treatment or intensive rehabilitation. Micheletti and Shlala (1995) suggested four categories of subacute care services: (1) extensive care (parenteral feeding, tracheostomy, etc.), (2) special care (postburn care, pressure ulcers, intravenous therapy, tube feedings, etc.), (3) clinically complex care (wound care, postsurgical care, etc.), and (4) intensive rehabilitation.

Home- and Community-Based Services (HCBS)

Financing for formal HCBS comes from a variety of sources: private out-of-pocket payments, private long-term care insurance, Medicaid, Medicare, and other public sources. Under the Older Americans Act of 1965, federal funds are granted to states for a variety of community-based services, such as nutrition programs for the elderly, case management, homemaker services, and adult day care services. The services are available to Americans aged 60 years and older, particularly those with social or economic need. The federal Administration on Aging oversees the program. Programs across the nation are carried out primarily through an administrative network of state agencies on aging, area agencies on aging, and Indian tribal organizations.

In 1981, the HCBS waiver program was enacted under Section 1915(c) of the Social Security Act. Because nursing home services are mandated under Medicaid, the 1915(c) waivers allow states to expand community-based LTC services under the Medicaid program. Services are available to those Medicaid beneficiaries who would otherwise require institutional care.

Some federal funding available to the states under Title XX Social Services Block Grants from the US Department of Health and Human Services (DHHS) may also be used for community-based LTC services when such services prevent or reduce inappropriate institutionalization. Some states also provide limited assistance with ADLs in a person's home under the Medicaid Personal Care Services program.

Even though national LTC policy has taken unprecedented steps to shift services from institutions to HBCS, researchers have identified several needs that go unmet. For example, some acute health problems and mental health issues are inadequately accommodated in HCBS. Additional unmet needs highlight an inadequate workforce, transportation barriers, and limited supportive housing options (Robison et al. 2012). It should also be noted that even though nearly all states provide HCBS to Medicaid beneficiaries, eligibility, available services, as well as the scope and extent of these services differ considerably across states and between geographical areas within states (National Health Policy Forum 2013).

Home Health Care

Chapter 7 discusses home health care and the Medicare rules for eligibility. Chapter 6 covers the prospective payment system (PPS) for home health. The organizational setup commonly requires a community- or hospital-based home health agency that sends health care professionals and paraprofessionals to patients' homes to deliver services approved by a physician. Skilled nursing care is the most common service received by home health patients (Figure 10–5).

According to the most recent Home and Hospice Care Survey (2007), the majority of home health agencies in the United States are private for profit. Of the 14,500 home health and hospice care agencies in 2007, 75% provided only home health care; 10% were mixed agencies providing both home health and hospice services (Park-Lee and Decker 2010). Medicare is the single largest payer for home health services, and Medicaid is not far behind (Figure 10–6).

Other notable facts from the 2007 survey are as follows: The mean length of service received by a patient was 315 days; nonelderly patients had a significantly longer mean length of service than elderly patients; the two most common medical

Figure 10–5 Most Frequently Provided Services to Home Health Patients.

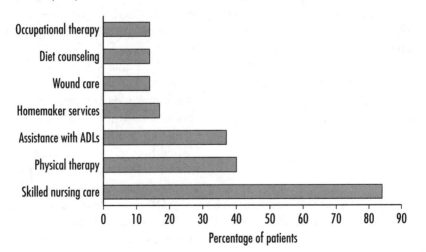

Source: Data from Jones, A.L., et al. 2012. *Characteristics and use of home health care by men and women aged 65 and over.* Hyattsville, MD: National Center for Health Statistics.

Figure 10–6 Sources of Payment for Home Health Care, 2010.

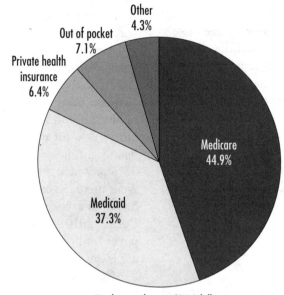

Total expenditures: $70.2 billion

Source: Health, United States, 2012, p. 326, National Center for Health Statistics.

conditions among all patients were diabetes and heart disease; 84% of the patients had at least one ADL limitation (among this group half had four or more ADL limitations); 11% of the patients had no ADL limitation; those living with others were not likely to need any ADL assistance from home health agency staff; and 21% of the patients had at least one overnight hospital stay since starting home health care (Caffrey et al. 2011).

Adult Day Care

Adult day care (ADC), also referred to as "adult day service," is a daytime group program designed to meet the needs of functionally and/or cognitively impaired adults and to provide partial respite to family caregivers so they can work during the day or pursue other responsibilities of life. ADC is designed for people who live with their families, but cannot remain alone during the day because of physical or mental conditions.

ADC centers operate programs during normal business hours 5 days a week, although some offer evening and weekend services as well. In 2012, there were an estimated 5,000 ADC centers across the United States, a 43% increase since 2006 (MetLife Mature Market Institute 2008, 2010).

ADC services have continued to evolve. In the past, ADC services could be distinguished by three models of service delivery: (1) Programs based on the health-rehabilitative model offered more intense medical, nursing, and therapy services compared to the other two, and focused on care needed after discharge from a hospital. (2) The health-maintenance model emphasized maintenance of health and function, with services that were largely preventive in nature, such as personal care and custodial care. (3) Under the specialized model, services were geared toward patients with special needs, such as Alzheimer's or IDD. Today, most ADC services are highly focused on prevention and health maintenance, with the objective of preventing or delaying institutionalization, but they also incorporate nursing care, psychosocial therapies, and rehabilitation. As such, ADC services, in many instances, have become alternatives to home health care and assisted living and/or transitional step before placement in a long-term care institution.

Nearly 80% of ADC centers have a nursing professional on staff; nearly 50% have a social work professional; nearly 60% offer case management; and approximately 50% provide physical, occupational, or speech therapy. Most provide transportation services. Group socialization, therapeutic recreational activities, and meals are included. Nearly half of the participants have dementia, and 50% of ADC centers offer specialized programs for these patients (MetLife Mature Market Institute 2010).

In 2010, on an average, an ADC served 34 participants per day, the average length of participant enrollment was 32 months, and the average daily rate was $67 (MetLife Mature Market Institute 2010). The primary sources of funding are Medicaid and private out-of-pocket payments. Medicaid provides some funding under Section 1915(c) waivers. Medicare does not pay for ADC but may cover rehabilitation services under Part B.

Adult Foster Care

Adult foster care (AFC) is a service characterized by small, family-run homes providing room, board, and varying levels of supervision, oversight, and personal care to nonrelated adults who are unable to care for themselves (AARP Studies Adult Foster Care for the Elderly 1996). Foster care provides services in a community-based dwelling in an environment that promotes the feeling of being part of a family unit (Stahl 1997). Participants in the program are elderly or disabled individuals who have a medical diagnosis, a psychiatric diagnosis, or a need for personal care. Typically, the caregiving family resides in part of the home. To maintain the family environment, most states license fewer than 10 beds per family unit.

The program differs widely from state to state and goes by several names, including adult family care, community residential care, and domiciliary care. Each state has established its own standards for the licensing of AFCs. Funding for AFCs comes from Medicaid, private insurance, or personal sources. Medicare does not pay for AFC but may cover rehabilitation services under Part B.

Senior Centers

Senior centers are local community centers for older adults where seniors can congregate and socialize. Many centers offer one or more meals daily. Others sponsor wellness programs, health education, counseling services, recreational activities, information and referrals, and limited health care services, including health screening, especially for glaucoma and hypertension. Nearly all senior centers receive some public funding. Other common revenue sources are United Way and private donations.

Home-Delivered and Congregate Meals

The elderly nutrition program (ENP) is the nation's oldest framework for providing community- and home-based preventive nutrition in the United States. The program has been in operation since 1972 for congregate meals, and since 1978 for home-delivered meals. The ENP program was authorized under the Older Americans Act, which also provides the majority of the funding. Additional funds are provided through Title XX block grants, 1915(c) waivers, and private donations.

The program provides a hot noon meal 5 days a week to Americans 60 years of age and older (and their spouses) who cannot prepare a nutritionally balanced noon meal for themselves. Home-delivered meals for homebound persons are commonly referred to as *meals-on-wheels*. Ambulatory clients are encouraged to get their meals at senior centers or other congregate settings, where they also get the opportunity to socialize. In 2010, 60% of the meals were home delivered; 40% were served in congregate settings (Administration on Aging 2013b). According to a 2009 report, the meals-on-wheels program was effective in targeting vulnerable elderly who were over 75 years old, most of whom lived alone and had some ADL deficits. Among all individuals who received meals-on-wheels, 73% were at high nutritional risk; 62% received one-half or more of their daily food intake from their home-delivered meals (Administration on Aging 2009).

It is a common practice for the Area Agencies on Aging to contract out the preparation and delivery of meals to local nursing homes, hospitals, or religious organizations. In the meals-on-wheels program, volunteers carry the meals to homebound participants. Congregate meals may be served on the premises of participating facilities, such as hospitals and nursing homes, or at local senior centers or religious establishments.

Homemaker Services

Depending on availability of funds, states provide limited housekeeping and chore services—such as essential shopping, light cleaning, meal preparation, and minor home repairs—to low-income people. Homemaker programs may be staffed largely or entirely by volunteers. The Medicaid program may pay for some homemaker services, or these services may be funded through the local seniors programs under Title XX Social Services Block Grants or the Older Americans Act. Besides the limited public funding options that help a relatively small number of people, private homemaker service agencies have sprung up across the nation.

Continuing Care at Home (CCAH)

This is a new model of home-based care that has recently emerged. Its growth has been slow because of regulatory issues at the state government level. The program is an extension of the continuing care retirement center (CCRC) model that has been in existence for a number of years. As discussed later in this chapter, CCRCs provide a continuum of housing and institutional LTC services on one campus. Therefore, CCRCs are also at the forefront of developing these home-based programs. To participate in the program, clients are required to pay an initial lump-sum fee and a monthly fee under a contract that guarantees a person's future LTC care. To qualify, a person must be in good health and not need LTC services at the time of enrollment. CCAH services typically include care coordination, routine home maintenance, home health care, transportation, meals, and social and wellness programs (Dube 2008). Most services are provided at the client's home with the objective of delaying institutionalization. When institutional services are needed, the client receives them at the CCRC's assisted living and/or skilled nursing care facilities or at subcontracted local facilities.

Case Management

Case management involves evaluating a patient's physical, medical, and psychosocial needs; preparing a plan to address those needs and identifying services that would be most appropriate; determining eligibility for services and how those services would be financed; making referrals to those services; coordinating the delivery of services; and reevaluating needs as circumstances change over time.

Three traditional models of case management in LTC have been identified: brokerage model, managed care model, and integrated care model (Scharlach et al. 2001).

Brokerage Model

In the *brokerage model*, once needs have been independently assessed, case managers arrange services through other providers. The case manager is usually a freestanding agent who is mainly responsible for linking the client with other organizations, agencies, and service providers, with no formal administrative or financial relationship with these entities. Need assessment, development of a service plan, and making referrals are the main functions of case management in this model. There is minimal coordination and monitoring of services.

In the public domain, most states have implemented preadmission screening rules. The purpose of this screening is to determine whether a Medicaid beneficiary's needs can be better met in a nursing facility or through HCBS. In addition, federal regulations require an evaluation of a patient for mental illness and/or intellectual disability before such a patient can be admitted to a Medicaid-certified nursing facility (see NF certification under "Skilled Nursing Facilities"). The process is called Preadmission Screening and Resident Review (PASRR). The purpose of this requirement is to determine whether a nursing facility is the best alternative for individuals with serious mental illness or ID or whether their needs can be adequately met in community-based settings.

Managed Care Model

This model is offered through a managed care organization (MCO), and it involves capitated financing, which places the MCO at financial risk. Professionally trained nurses and social workers are typically the case managers, who are likely to be more closely involved in the monitoring and coordination of services than is the case in the brokerage model (Scharlach et al. 2001). Delivery of services is arranged through a *social managed care plan*. The MCO operating such a plan provides the full range of Medicare benefits and additional services which include care coordination, prescription drug benefits, chronic care benefits covering short-term nursing home care, and a full range of HCBS such as homemaker, personal care, adult day care, respite care, and transportation. Other services that may be provided include eyeglasses, hearing aids, and dental benefits. Once enrolled, the beneficiaries have to obtain all covered services through the MCO.

There is some evidence that a social managed care plan may help at-risk elderly postpone long-term nursing home placement (Fischer 2003). These plans have also been shown to facilitate successful transition of short-stay nursing home patients back to the community, thus preventing these patients from becoming long-stay residents in a nursing home (Thomas et al. 2010). Despite the benefit they provide, there are only four social managed care plans participating in Medicare. They are located in Portland, Oregon; Long Beach, California; Brooklyn, New York; and Las Vegas, Nevada.

Integrated Care Model

This model exists within an interdisciplinary organizational structure that strives to provide all necessary services a client may need. Services include medical and social services, such as counseling, advocacy, and ongoing coordination and monitoring. The goal is ongoing prevention of the progression of disability (Scharlach et al. 2001). Similar to the managed care model, capitation is used as a method of payment. Services are delivered through a nonprofit health care organization. At the core of the program is ADC, augmented by home care and meals-on-wheels (Gross et al. 2004).

The Program of All-Inclusive Care for the Elderly (*PACE*) is an example of integrated case management. The PACE program was authorized under the Balanced Budget Act of 1997 after the On Lok project in San Francisco demonstrated that, in many instances, LTC institutionalization could be prevented through appropriate case management. The PACE program is available in most states to people 55 years of age and over.

PACE focuses on frail elderly who have already been certified for nursing home placement under Medicare and/or Medicaid. All medical care and social services are coordinated by a PACE team. PACE has no deductibles and copayments, which is an incentive for qualified individuals to participate. The program has been shown to result in reduced amount of hospitalizations and rehospitalizations (Meret-Hanke 2011), and substantial cost savings over other alternatives of LTC delivery (Wieland et al. 2013).

The Affordable Care Act and Community-Based LTC

The Affordable Care Act (ACA) offers some support to help states transition their LTC systems toward a better balance between institutional and community-based services:

1. The ACA offers limited financial incentives to states to enhance their HCBS programs for Medicaid beneficiaries. Options available to states are to: (a) target HCBS to particular groups of people, offer services that reach more people, or ensure the quality of services; (b) offer personal care services (referred to as "attendant services and supports") to an increased number of people, under what the law refers to as Community First Choice; (c) undertake structural reforms so that access is increased to noninstitutional services; or (d) use the existing Money Follows the Person program that allows transfer of public money previously used for nursing home care to fund HCBS when people move out of

institutions into their own homes or other community-based settings. The ACA authorized a 5-year extension, beyond 2011, of the Money Follows the Person program.

2. The Balancing Incentives Payment Program directs the greatest financial incentives to states that currently have the least balanced systems and rely more on nursing homes than on HCBS. In return for increased federal Medicaid funding, participating states must implement a single point of entry into the LTC system, conflict-free case management, and a standardized assessment instrument that is used consistently throughout the state for determining clients' eligibility for all types of LTC services (Reinhard et al. 2011).

Institutional Long-Term Care Continuum

With the expansion of HCBS, institutional LTC is more appropriate for patients whose needs cannot be adequately met in a community-based setting. Apart from a patient's clinical condition, factors such as inability to live alone or lack of social support may suggest a need to be in an institution. The institutional sector of LTC offers a continuum of services (Figure 10–4) according to the patient's level of dependency for care. On one end of the continuum, there are institutions that offer only basic personal and custodial care. At the other end, there are facilities where patients receive not only personal assistance with ADLs but also skilled nursing, subacute, or specialized services.

For institutions at the lower end of the continuum, and even in independent living

and supportive housing (discussed earlier), the concept of *aging-in-place* has become important, particularly from the viewpoint of consumer choice. It refers to older people's preference and expectation to stay in one place for as long as possible and to delay or avoid transfer to an institution where the acuity level of patients is higher. In independent and supportive housing, management often faces the dilemma of how to continue to house residents who have escalating needs for personal care and some type of coordination with the health care system (Stone and Reinhard 2007).

Most care in LTC institutions is provided by nonphysician staff, such as nurses, CNAs, dietitians, social workers, and therapists. Residents have the right to be treated by a physician of their choice, who makes periodic rounds to visit the patients. Between rounds, the professional nursing staff communicate with the physician, especially when changes in a patient's condition are observed or treatment orders are not producing the desired results. By law, a transfer agreement with a local hospital must be in place to facilitate transition between the acute care and LTC facilities. At the onset of an acute episode, such as pneumonia or severe injury from a fall, the patient is transferred to a hospital.

The different labels applied to the facilities in this section are broad and somewhat imprecise because services may overlap, especially because of the aging-in-place phenomenon. Yet, the four categories discussed in this section can be distinguished according to the level and extent of services they offer, particularly nursing care given by licensed nurses and rehabilitation services by licensed therapists. For example, residential and personal care facilities may have no licensed nurses, and the staff-to-patient ratios are higher in skilled nursing facilities than in assisted living facilities.

Residential and Personal Care Facilities

These facilities are also known as "domiciliary care facilities," "board-and-care homes," or "sheltered care facilities." Sometimes AFC homes (previously discussed) are included in this category. These facilities provide physically supportive dwelling units, monitoring and/or assistance with medications, oversight, and personal or custodial care (discussed earlier). No nursing or medical services are provided. To maintain a residential rather than an institutional environment, many such facilities limit admitting residents with severe disabilities, but some may take patients with mild levels of mental dysfunction. Services are provided by paraprofessionals rather than by licensed personnel. Minimal staffing is provided 24 hours a day for supervision and assistive purposes. More advanced services can be arranged through an external home health agency when needed.

Facilities can range anywhere from spartan to deluxe. The latter are often private pay. For people who have limited incomes, Supplemental Security Income (SSI) can be used along with other types of government assistance funds. Services include meals, housekeeping and laundry services, and social and recreational activities.

Assisted Living Facilities

An *assisted living facility* (ALF) provides personal care, 24-hour supervision, social services, recreational activities, and some nursing and rehabilitation services. These facilities are appropriate for people who cannot function independently but do not require skilled nursing care. However, ALFs are increasingly offering services for Alzheimer's/dementia care (Hoban 2013). Moreover, ALFs operate predominantly on a private-pay basis; 86% of the residents use their own financial resources (Assisted Living Federation of America 2013). To emphasize a residential environment, ALFs generally have private accommodations, as opposed to semi-private, which is common in skilled nursing facilities.

All states now regulate ALFs by requiring them to be licensed. In the absence of federal standards, regulations vary from state to state. These regulations continue to evolve in response to the rising acuity levels of residents. The typical assisted living resident is female, 87 years old, mobile, but needing assistance with two to three ADLs. The majority of these residents transfer from their homes. Approximately, 59% eventually move into a skilled nursing facility and one-third pass away (National Center for Assisted Living 2013).

Skilled Nursing Facilities

Skilled nursing facilities are the typical nursing homes at the higher end of the institutional continuum. Patients are generally transferred from a hospital after an acute episode, and the care needs of these patients have become increasingly more complex, requiring much higher levels of staffing than ALFs. Even though many nursing home residents stay for a long period of time, sometimes years, short-term stay for convalescence and rehabilitation under Medicare has become common.

The four most common conditions that patients in nursing homes suffer from are bladder incontinence, depression, Alzheimer's-type dementia, and bowel incontinence

(Figure 10–7). Various mental conditions have become increasingly more common. The prevalence of depression rose from 46.6% in 2006 to 52.3% in 2011, and the prevalence of psychiatric diagnoses rose from 19.7% to 24.8% during the same period (Sanofi-Aventis 2007, 2012). The Centers for Medicare and Medicaid Services (CMS) adopted a set of nursing home quality measures in 2002 and launched the Nursing Home Quality Initiative. Between 2006 and 2010, 12 of the 14 quality measures for chronic care residents showed consistent positive trends, indicating an improvement in quality of care. During this period, nursing homes also increased direct care nursing time per resident for licensed nurses and certified nursing assistants (CMS 2012).

Nursing home environment is generally more institutional and clinical than in ALFs. Yet, a movement, loosely referred to as "culture change," has been underway for a number of years to transform existing facilities into more homelike and vibrant living environments. Newer facilities are being built with innovative designs that offer a sense of community living; a greater degree of privacy; and enriched environments that promote physical and psychological well-being, and reduce boredom and stress (see Singh 2010, Chapter 8).

Skilled nursing facilities are heavily regulated through licensure and certification requirements. All facilities in a particular state must be licensed and, therefore, must comply with the licensing regulations, which differ considerably from state to state. Most licensing regulations establish minimum qualifications required for administrators and other staff, prescribe minimum staffing levels, establish standards for building construction, and require compliance with the national fire and safety codes. To admit patients covered under the Medicaid and/or Medicare programs, nursing homes must also be certified and must demonstrate compliance with the federal certification standards enforced by the CMS.

Until 1989, federal statutes classified nursing homes into two types: SNFs for Medicare and/or Medicaid residents and intermediate care facilities (ICFs) for those covered by Medicaid only. Patients needing

Figure 10–7 Percentage of Nursing Home Residents with Various Conditions, 2011.

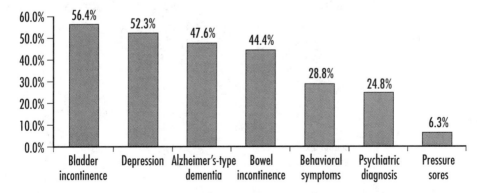

Source: Adapted from *Managed Care Digest Series: Public Payer Digest, 2012–2013*, p. 43. Bridgewater, NJ: Sanofi-Aventis.

a higher level of care were eligible for admission to an SNF, which was required to have a licensed nurse on duty 24 hours a day and a registered nurse (RN) on the day shift. By contrast, ICFs had to have a licensed nurse on duty only on the day shift.

The Nursing Home Reform Act, passed in 1987, removed differences between ICFs and SNFs on the basis of clinical acuity. The legislation created two categories for certification purposes. A nursing home certified to admit Medicare patients is called an *SNF*. This facility can be freestanding or a ***distinct part***, that is, a section of a nursing home that is distinctly separate and distinguishable from the rest of the facility. When SNF certification applies to a distinct part, Medicare patients can be admitted only to that section. A nursing home certified for Medicaid only (but not for Medicare) is called a nursing facility (*NF*). A facility may be dually certified as an SNF and an NF. Facilities having ***dual certification*** can admit Medicare and/or Medicaid patients to any part

of the facility. Hence, most nursing homes have opted for dual certification. The federal certification standards governing SNFs and NFs are essentially the same. Medicare and Medicaid patients do not receive two different levels of services; the SNF and NF categories have been created for the two distinct sources of public financing.

The term "facility" does not necessarily mean a separate physical structure. The term can be used for the facility as a whole, or, within the context of licensure and certification, it may apply more specifically to different sections or units of a building (distinct parts) with different certifications or no certification (see Figure 10–8).

A small proportion of facilities have elected not to participate in the Medicaid and/ or Medicare programs. They can admit only patients who can pay privately, either out of pocket or through private LTC insurance. These facilities are ***noncertified***; however, they must be licensed under the state licensure regulations. ***Private pay patients***—those

Figure 10–8 Distinctly Certified Units in a Nursing Home.

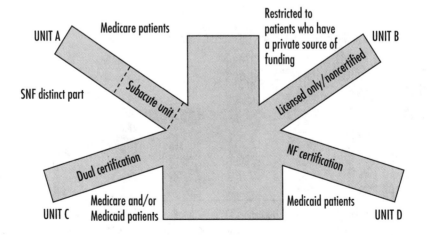

The entire facility must be licensed by the state.

not covered by either Medicare or Medicaid for nursing home care—are not restricted to noncertified facilities. These patients also may be admitted to SNF or NF certified beds. The restriction applies to Medicare and Medicaid patients who cannot be admitted to noncertified facilities.

The ACA requires that in case of an LTC facility closure, administrators of an SNF or NF must provide a written notice at least 60 days prior to closure. The administrators are also required to furnish a plan for relocating residents. To participate in Medicare and/or Medicaid, nursing facilities must also institute effective compliance and ethics programs (Farhat 2013).

Subacute Care Facilities

Subacute care became a prominent service after acute care hospitals were brought under the PPS in the 1980s. The three main institutional locations for subacute care—LTCHs (see Chapter 8), hospital transitional care units (or extended care units) certified as SNFs, or freestanding nursing homes—vary in terms of availability, cost, and quality. Selection of a setting is governed by numerous factors, both clinical and nonclinical. One main nonclinical factor is the availability of subacute care services in a given location (Buntin et al. 2005). Regarding cost, LTCHs are the most expensive. Nursing homes are often a more cost-effective alternative to LTCHs, and at least some physicians think that the level and intensity of care in the two settings are comparable (MedPAC 2004). Postacute needs can widely vary among patients, but there is no uniform system of clinical assessment and payment for subacute care. Medicare uses different payment methodologies for the different settings. For example, LTCHs are

paid according to severity-based diagnosis-related groups (see Chapter 8), and Medicare payments to hospital-based SNFs and nursing homes are based on resource utilization groups (see Chapter 6).

Specialized Care Facilities

Specialized facilities provide special services for individuals with distinct medical needs. For example, some nursing homes and subacute care facilities have specialized units for patients requiring ventilator care, wound care, intensive rehabilitation, closed head trauma care, or Alzheimer's/dementia care. Specialized facilities also exist for IDD patients who require active treatment.

Intermediate Care Facilities for Individuals with Intellectual Disabilities (ICFs/IID)

Federal regulations provide a separate certification category for LTC facilities classified as ICF/IID since 1971 (formerly known as Intermediate Care Facilities for the Mentally Retarded—ICF/MRs), when Section 1905(d) of the Social Security Act authorized Medicaid coverage for the care for IDD patients in ICF/MR facilities. Most of these patients have other disabilities in addition to IDs. For example, many of these patients are nonambulatory, have seizure disorders, behavior problems, mental illness, visual or hearing impairments, or have a combination of these conditions. The primary purpose of ICF/IID is to furnish nursing and rehabilitative services that involve "active treatment." Active treatment entails aggressive and consistent specialized programs that include skill training to help the patients function as independently as possible. Over 6,000 ICF/ IDD facilities serve over 100,000 individuals in all 50 states (CMS 2013).

Alzheimer's Facilities

For patients with dementia, informal caregivers, ADC centers, and ALFs can all play a role, but specialized Alzheimer's facilities are often needed for those who have severe dementia or when comorbid conditions are present. Modern Alzheimer's facilities have small-group living arrangements, copious use of natural lighting, pastel colors, pleasant surroundings, protected pathways for wandering, and special programming. All these features are integrated to minimize agitation, anxiety, disruptiveness, and combativeness among patients suffering from severe dementia.

Continuing Care Retirement Communities (CCRCs)

A continuing care retirement community (*CCRC*) integrates and coordinates independent living and institutional components of the LTC continuum. As a convenience factor, different levels of services are all located on one campus. Secondly, CCRCs guarantee delivery of higher level services as future needs arise. Services include independent living in cottages or apartments with or without support services, and medical and nursing care, rehabilitation, and social services in an ALF or SNF. Residents enter these communities when they are still relatively healthy.

CCRCs, for the most part, require private financing, with the exception of services delivered in a Medicare-certified SNF. Three types of CCRC contracts are common in the industry: (1) A life care or extended contract incorporates a complete package of services that includes a commitment to provide unlimited future LTC services without an increase in the monthly fee; (2) a modified contract provides for support services in independent living and includes a limited number of days of care in assisted living and SNF without an increase in the monthly fee; and (3) a fee-for-service contract which includes only support services in independent living; higher levels of services must be paid for out of pocket at the prevailing rates. There is a wide variation in entrance and monthly fees based on amenities and the type of contract. In the state of New York, for example, entrance fees begin at approximately $115,000 for a single person independent living unit; monthly fees begin at approximately $2,100 (New York Department of Health 2013). In 2009, over 1,800 CCRCs operated in the United States; most were operated by nonprofit organizations (Cackley et al. 2010).

Institutional Trends, Utilization, and Costs

With numerous community-based and institutional options for LTC that are available to people today, the industry has become increasingly more competitive. Competition is also intensifying because of the aging-in-place phenomenon whereby some of the distinctions between residential/personal care and assisted living may be narrowing. Even the first-ever National Survey of Residential Care Facilities (NSRCF) by the National Center for Health Statistics (2010) lumps together ALFs and residential care facilities, along with other types of care homes, with the exception of skilled nursing facilities. Hence, at this point, within the institutional continuum, we have a better profile of nursing homes than other types of facilities. In an effort to present at least some distinctions within the industry, Table 10–1 includes available data on the trends, capacity, utilization, and prices. Notably, the number of nursing homes and beds had continued to decrease until 2009. Since then, there has been a slight upturn. Yet, the ratio of nursing home beds per 1,000 people age 65 and over has dropped for 11 years in a row to 40.4 (Sanofi-Aventis 2012). Nursing home utilization (occupancy rates and average length of stay) also show a declining trend, reflecting an ongoing shift away from traditional nursing home services, which can again be attributed, at least partially, to people's desire to age in place.

The hospital industry has drastically cut back on the number of SNFs it operates. Starting October 2011, Medicare payments to SNFs were cut by more than 11%. Starting October 2012, Medicare started penalizing hospitals with high readmission rates for certain conditions to promote better coordination between hospitals and SNFs. This might provide an incentive for hospitals to operate their own SNFs to have better control over the coordination of services. However, the combined effect of the above two policies on whether hospitals would increase or decrease their hospital-based SNF services currently remains unknown.

ALFs have been the fastest growing segment of the institutional continuum, steadily rising until 2010, but there was a slight

Table 10–1 Trends in Number of Facilities, Beds/Resident Capacity, and Prices, Selected Years

Type of Facility	Number of Facilities	Bed Capacity	Occupancy Rate	Average Length of Stay (days)	Average Price
Nursing homes					
2006	15,174	1,699,000	84.6%	295	$62,532[a]
2009	15,007	1,649,900	84.1%	189	$66,850[a]
2011	15,020	1,670,800	83.4%	187	$70,445[a]
Hospital-based SNFs					
2006	1,025 (14.9% of hospitals)		77.1%	154.3	
2010	868 (12.3% of hospitals)		75.3%	161.9	
Assisted living facilities					
2006	13,871				$32,294[b]
2010	15,781				$38,220[b]

[a] Annual median price for a semi-private room (private-pay)

[b] Annual median price for a private one-bedroom unit (private-pay)

Source: Data from *Genworth Financial Cost of Care Surveys* for 2006, 2009, 2010, and 2011; *Sanofi-Aventis Managed Care Digest Series: Senior Care Digest* for 2007 and 2008; *Sanofi-Aventis Managed Care Digest Series: Public Payer Digest,* 2012.

decline in 2011. According to the NSRCF survey, there were 31,100 residential/personal care/assisted living facilities, with a total of 971,900 beds throughout the nation in 2010 (NCHS, 2010). By subtracting the number of ALFs in Table 10–1, we get a rough estimate of 15,300 residential/personal care facilities in the United States.

Another notable fact is the rising cost of institutional care. However, aggregate national nursing home expenditures decreased from 7.3% of total personal health care spending in 2000 to 6.5% in 2010 (DHHS 2012, pp. 325–326). Most nursing home care is financed by Medicaid (Figure 10–9). However, public policy push for the HCBS option for LTC services has been gaining popularity. Consequently, the share of total Medicaid spending for nursing home care declined from 20.5% in 2000 to 14.9% in 2009. The payment per Medicaid beneficiary receiving care in a nursing home was $29,551

in 2009 (DHHS 2012, p. 363), compared to $66,850 for private-pay (see Table 10–1). Private sources (mainly, out of pocket and private insurance) also cover a sizable portion of nursing home expenses (Figure 10–9). Total private financing, however, has been declining for a number of years. In 2010, it paid for 37.2% of total nursing home expenses, compared to 40.7% in 2000. One main reason for the decline in private spending is a rapid rise in Medicare expenditures, from 12.7% of national spending for nursing home care in 2000 to 22.3% in 2010 (DHHS 2012, p. 326). Medicare Part A provides benefits for short-stay nursing home care in an SNF, not to exceed 100 days, after a minimum of 3 consecutive days in a hospital (see Chapter 6).

Approximately 15% of the nation's ALFs are operated by the 15 largest ALF chains. The five largest ALF chains are Brookdale Senior Living (532 ALFs), Emeritus Senior

Figure 10–9 Sources of Financing Nursing Home Care (Nonhospital-based facilities), 2010.

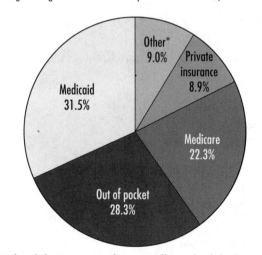

*Mainly includes Department of Veterans Affairs, other federal programs, worker's compensation, and other private funds.

Source: Data from *Health, United States, 2012,* p. 326, National Center for Health Statistics.

Living (466 ALFs), Sunrise Senior Living (269 ALFs), Assisted Living Concepts (208 ALFs), and Five Star Quality Care (159 ALFs; Sanofi-Aventis 2012).

Approximately 16% of nursing homes are operated by 15 nursing home chains. The five largest nursing home chains are Golden Living (304 facilities), Manor Care (283 facilities), Life Care Centers of America (222 facilities), Kindred Healthcare (221 facilities), and Genesis Healthcare (206 facilities; Sanofi-Aventis 2012).

Private Long-Term Care Insurance

Private LTC insurance is available in a wide range of choices regarding the extent and duration of services covered, and prices vary accordingly. In addition to nursing home care, private insurance also covers community-based services, such as home health care or ADC. In 2010, almost 9% of all nursing home expenditures were paid through private LTC insurance (Figure 10–9), about the same as in 2000. Among possible reasons are slow growth in the purchase of LTC insurance and a greater emphasis on HCBS.

Premiums depend on coverage options, such as the daily or monthly benefit amount the insurer would pay, a waiting period (also called elimination period) before benefit payments will begin, the number of years over which benefits will be paid, and inflation protection to cover rising LTC costs in the future. LTC insurance policies are particularly expensive if a plan is purchased in the later years of a person's life. People in younger age groups, for whom the cost of LTC insurance would be more affordable, face other financial priorities, such as saving for retirement, children's college education,

life insurance, and buying a home. The need for LTC in the distant future is considered a much lower priority.

In 2009, only 7 million Americans (7% of those over age 50) had coverage through LTC insurance policies (National Health Policy Forum 2011). Four main reasons can be cited for the slow growth of private LTC insurance:

1. Because of so many variables, trying to decide the right coverage can be a daunting task.

2. For most people, the premiums are unaffordable. In 2013, a 55-year-old single individual purchasing LTC insurance could expect to pay an annual premium of $2,065 for $162,000 of current benefits which would grow to roughly $330,000 at age 80, according to the American Association for Long-Term Care Insurance (2013).

3. Most people think that Medicare would pay for LTC services when needed, but Medicare covers only short-term post-acute care after discharge from a hospital. People who decide not to buy LTC insurance also tend to underestimate the potential risk of needing LTC and the cost of LTC services (AHIP 2012). Much needs to be done in educating consumers.

4. Public policy has created few incentives to spur the growth of LTC insurance. The Deficit Reduction Act of 2005 created the Long-Term Care Insurance Partnership Program, which allowed individuals who purchase private LTC insurance to shield part of their financial assets when

they became eligible to receive Medicaid benefits for LTC. This policy seems to have had only minimal effect in spurring the purchase of LTC insurance. Most Americans over the age of 50 believe that the government should provide tax incentives for the purchase of LTC insurance (AHIP 2012).

Summary

The need for LTC arises when an individual is no longer able to perform ADL and/or IADL functions because of severe chronic conditions, multiple illnesses, or cognitive impairment. These individuals need both LTC and non-LTC services on an ongoing basis. LTC is unique within health care delivery, and is multidimensional.

LTC includes medical care, nursing, rehabilitation, social support, mental health care, housing alternatives, and end-of-life care. LTC services often complement what people with impaired functioning can do for themselves. Informal caregivers provide the bulk of LTC services in the United States. Respite care can provide family members temporary relief from the burden of caregiving. When the required intensity of care exceeds the capabilities of informal caregivers, available alternatives include professional community-based services to supplement informal care. The ACA provides limited incentives to expand home- and community-based care.

Institutional services vary from basic personal assistance to more complex skilled nursing care and subacute care. Institutional care can be of long or short duration. People with severe dementia, incontinence, severe psychiatric or behavioral issues, unstable postacute conditions, or those in a comatose/vegetative state may need nursing home care for a long time. Others require short-term postacute convalescence and restorative care. A continuing care retirement community offers independent living and institution-based LTC services. Specialized institutions exist for people with Alzheimer's disease or severe IDD.

Nursing homes require federal SNF certification to admit Medicare patients and NF certification to admit Medicaid patients. Most facility beds in the United States are dually certified as both SNF and NF. Medicaid is the most common source of funding for nursing home care.

The LTC industry has become competitive as services among both community-based and institutional options have started to overlap. Within the institutional sector, the number of nursing homes and beds has seen some decline; the decline is more pronounced in hospital-based SNFs. On the other hand, ALFs have experienced remarkable growth. Costs continue to rise.

As costs in the public sector continue to rise, few people have purchased private LTC insurance. Better policies are needed to spur growth.

ACA Takeaway

- Some support through financial incentives is available to help states transition their LTC systems toward a better balance between institutional and community-based services.
- A 60-day written notice and a plan for relocating residents are required prior to the closure of an SNF or NF.
- To participate in Medicare and/or Medicaid, nursing facilities must institute effective compliance and ethics programs.

Test Your Understanding

Terminology

adult day care
adult foster care
aging-in-place
Alzheimer's disease
assisted living facility
brokerage model
case management
CCRC
cognitive impairment
custodial care
dementia
developmental disability

distinct part
dual certification
evidence-based care
intellectual disability
long-term care
meals-on-wheels
mental retardation
NF
noncertified
PACE
palliation
paraprofessionals

PERS
personal care
private pay patients
quality of life
respite care
restorative care
senior centers
skilled nursing care
SNF
social managed care plan
subacute care
total care

Review Questions

1. Long-term care services must be individualized, integrated, and coordinated. Elaborate on this statement, pointing out why these elements are essential in the delivery of LTC.

2. Age is not the primary determinant for long-term care. Comment on this statement, explaining why this is or is not true.

3. What is meant by "quality of life?" Briefly discuss the five main features of this multifaceted concept.

4. What are some of the challenges in the delivery of mental health services for the elderly?

5. Discuss the preventive and therapeutic aspects of long-term care.

6. How do formal and informal long-term care differ? What is the importance of informal care in LTC delivery?

7. What are the main goals of community-based and institution-based long-term care services?

8. What is respite care? Why is it needed?

9. Distinguish between supportive housing and institutional long-term care.

10. Why do some children and adolescents need long-term care?

11. Why has long-term care become an important service for people with HIV/AIDS?

12. Briefly discuss the three main models of case management in the delivery of long-term care.

13. What is meant by the continuum of institutional long-term care? Discuss the clinical services delivered by residential/personal care facilities, assisted living facilities, and skilled nursing facilities.

14. What is the difference between licensure and certification? What are the two types of certifications? What purpose does each serve from (1) a clinical standpoint and (2) a financial standpoint?

15. Describe a continuing care retirement community. Include in your response the financing and contractual arrangements.

16. Why has private long-term care insurance not gained popularity with consumers?

REFERENCES

AARP Studies Adult Foster Care for the Elderly. 1996. *Public Health Reports* 111, no. 4: 295.

Administration on Aging. 2009. *Fact sheet: elderly nutrition program.* Washington, DC: Department of Health and Human Services.

Administration on Aging. 2013a. *A profile of older Americans: 2012.* Available at: http://www.aoa .gov/AoARoot/Aging_Statistics/Profile/2012/14.aspx. Accessed August 2013.

Administration on Aging. 2013b. *Nutrition services (OAA Title IIIC).* Available at: http://www.aoa .gov/AoARoot/AoA_Programs/HCLTC/Nutrition_Services/index.aspx#homeAccessed August 2013.

Alecxih, L. 2001. The impact of sociodemographic change on the future of long-term care. *Generations* 25, no. 1: 7–11.

Alzheimer's Association. 2013. Alzheimer's facts and figures. Available at: http://www.alz.org /alzheimers_disease_facts_and_figures.asp#prevalence. Accessed August 2013.

American Association for Long-Term Care Insurance. 2013. 2013 long term care insurance price index published. Available at: http://www.aaltci.org/news/long-term-care-insurance-association-news/2013-long-term-care-insurance-price-index-published. Accessed August 2013.

America's Health Insurance Plans (AHIP). 2012. *Who buys long-term care insurance in 2010-2011?* Washington, DC: AHIP.

Assisted Living Federation of America. 2013. Assisted living. Available at: http://www.alfa.org /alfa/Assisted_Living_Information.asp. Accessed August 2013.

Barba, B.E., et al. 2012. Quality geriatric care as perceived by nurses in long-term and acute care settings. *Journal of Clinical Nursing* 21, no. 5/6: 833–840.

Boyle, C.A., et al. 2011. Trends in the prevalence of developmental disabilities in US children, 1997–2008. *Pediatrics* 127, no. 6: 1034–1042.

Buntin, M.B., et al. 2005. How much is postacute care use affected by its availability? *Health Services Research* 40, no. 2: 413–434.

Cackley, A.P., et al. 2010. *Continuing care retirement communities can provide benefits, but not without some risk*. Washington, DC: U.S. Government Accountability Office.

Centers for Medicare and Medicaid Services (CMS). 2012. National impact assessment of Medicare quality measures. Available at: http://www.cms.gov/Medicare/ Quality-Initiatives-Patient-Assessment-Instruments/QualityMeasures/Downloads/ NationalImpactAssessmentofQualityMeasuresFINAL.pdf. Accessed August 2013.

Centers for Medicare and Medicaid Services (CMS). 2013. Intermediate care facilities for individuals with intellectual disabilities (ICF/IID). Available at: http://www.cms.gov/Medicare /Provider-Enrollment-and-Certification/CertificationandComplianc/ICFMRs.html. Accessed August 2013.

Caffrey, C., et al. 2011. *Home health care and discharged hospice care patients: United States, 2000 and 2007*. Hyattsville, MD: National Center for Health Statistics.

Cahill, S., and R. Valadéz. 2013. Growing older with HIV/AIDS: New public health challenges. *American Journal of Public Health* 103, no. 3: e7–e15.

Compston, A., and A. Coles. 2002. Multiple sclerosis. *Lancet* 359, no. 9313: 1221–1231.

Department of Health and Human Services (DHHS). 2006. *Health, United States, 2006*. Hyattsville, MD: Department of Health and Human Services.

Department of Health and Human Services (DHHS). 2010. *Health, United States, 2010*. Hyattsville, MD: Department of Health and Human Services.

Department of Health and Human Services (DHHS). 2012. *Health, United States, 2012*. Hyattsville, MD: Department of Health and Human Services.

Dube, N. 2008. Continuing care retirement community "at home" programs. State of Connecticut Office of Legislative Research. Available at: http://www.cga.ct.gov/2008/rpt/2008-R-0110.htm. Accessed August 2013.

Effros, R.B., et al. 2008 Workshop on HIV infection and aging: What is known and future research directions. *Clinical Infectious Diseases* 47, no. 4 :542–553.

Farhat, T. 2013. Compliance clock ticks. *McKnight's Long-Term Care News* 34 (February), no. 2: 30–31.

Feinberg L., et al. 2011. Valuing the invaluable: 2011 update—the growing contributions and costs of family caregiving. AARP Public Policy Institute. Available at: http://assets.aarp.org/ rgcenter/ppi/ltc/i51-caregiving.pdf. Accessed August 2013.

Fischer, L.R. 2003. Community-based care and risk of nursing home placement. *Medical Care* 41, no. 12: 1407–1416.

Gross, D.L., et al. 2004. The growing pains of integrated health care for the elderly: Lessons from the expansion of PACE. *The Milbank Quarterly* 82, no. 2: 257–282.

Health Policy Institute. 2003. Who needs long-term care? Long-term care financing project, Georgetown University. Available at: http://ltc.georgetown.edu/pdfs/whois.pdf. Accessed August 2013.

Helmer, C., et al. 2006. Dementia in subjects aged 75 years or over within the PAQUID cohort: Prevalence and burden by severity. *Dementia and Geriatric Cognitive Disorders* 22, no. 1: 87–94.

Hoban, S. 2013. Assisted living 2013: On the upswing. *Long-Term Living: For the Continuing Care Professional* 62, no. 3: 28–30.

Holtz-Eakin, D. 2005. *CBO testimony: The cost of financing of long-term care services.* Before the Subcommittee on Health Committee on Energy and Commerce. US House of Representatives. April 27, 2005.

Hurd, M.D., et al. 2013. Monetary costs of dementia in the United States. *New England Journal of Medicine* 368, no. 14: 1326–1334.

Kaye, H.S., et al. 2010. Long-term care: Who gets it, who provides it, who pays, and how much? *Health Affairs* 29, no. 1: 11–21.

Kearney, F., et al. 2010. The ageing of HIV: Implications for geriatric medicine. *Age and Ageing* 39, no. 5: 536–541.

Kuzuya, M., et al. 2011. Impact of informal care levels on discontinuation of living at home in community-dwelling dependent elderly using various community-based services. *Archives of Gerontology & Geriatrics* 52, no. 2: 127–132.

Levine, C., et al. 2010. Bridging troubled waters: Family caregivers, transitions, and long-term care. *Health Affairs* 29, no. 1: 116–124.

Machlin, S., et al. 2008. Health care expenses for adults with chronic conditions, 2005. *Statistical Brief #203.* Rockville, MD: Agency for Healthcare Research and Quality.

Medicare Payment Advisory Commission (MedPAC). 2004. *New approaches in Medicare: Report to the Congress.* Washington, DC: Medicare Payment Advisory Commission.

Meret-Hanke, L.A. 2011. Effects of the Program of All-inclusive Care for the Elderly on hospital use. *The Gerontologist* 51, no. 6: 774–785.

MetLife Mature Market Institute. 2008. *The MetLife market survey of adult day services & home care costs.* Westport, CT: Metropolitan Life Insurance Company.

MetLife Mature Market Institute. 2010. *The MetLife national study of adult day services.* Westport, CT: Metropolitan Life Insurance Company.

Micheletti, J.A., and T.J. Shlala. 1995. Understanding and operationalizing subacute services. *Nursing Management* 26, no. 6: 49–56.

Morley, J.E. 2012. High technology coming to a nursing home near you. *Journal of the American Medical Directors Association* 13, no. 5: 409–412.

Munn, J.C., et al. 2006. Is hospice associated with improved end-of-life care in nursing homes and assisted living facilities? *Journal of the American Geriatrics Society* 54, no. 3: 490–495.

National Center for Assisted Living. 2013. Resident profile. Available at: http://www.ahcancal.org/ncal/resources/Pages/ResidentProfile.aspx. Accessed August 2013.

National Center for Health Statistics (NCHS). 2010. National survey of residential care facilities (NSRCF). Available at: http://www.cdc.gov/nchs/nsrcf.htm. Accessed January 2014.

National Health Policy Forum. 2011. *Private long-term care insurance: Where is the market heading? Forum Session, April 15, 2011.* Washington, DC: George Washington University.

National Health Policy Forum. 2013. *State variation in long-term services and supports: Location, location, location. Forum Session, July 19, 2013.* Washington, DC: George Washington University.

New York Department of Health. 2013. Continuing care retirement communities & fee-for-service continuing care retirement communities. Available at: http://www.health.ny.gov/facilities/long_term_care/retirement_communities/continuing_care. Accessed August 2013.

Niederhauser, A., et al. 2012. Comprehensive programs for preventing pressure ulcers: A review of the literature. *Advances in Skin & Wound Care* 25, no. 4: 167–188.

Pereira, M., and M.C. Canavarro. 2011. Gender and age differences in quality of life and the impact of psychopathological symptoms among HIV-infected patients. *AIDS Behavior* 15, no. 8: 1857–1869.

Park-Lee, E.Y., and F.H. Decker. 2010. *Comparison of home health and hospice care agencies by organizational characteristics and services provided: United States, 2007.* Hyattsville, MD: National Center for Health Statistics.

Reinhard, S.C., et al. 2011. How the Affordable Care Act can help move states toward a high-performing system of long-term services and supports. *Health Affairs* 30, no. 3: 447–453.

Riordan, J., and D. Voegeli. 2009. Prevention and treatment of pressure ulcers. *British Journal of Nursing* 18, no. 20: S20–S27.

Ritchie, K., and S. Lovestone. 2002. The dementias. *Lancet* 360, no. 9347: 1759–1766.

Robinson, K.M. 2010. Policy issues in mental health among the elderly. *Nursing Clinics of North America* 45, no. 4: 627–634.

Robinson, L.M. 2012. Growing health disparities for persons who are aging with intellectual and developmental disabilities: The social work linchpin. *Journal of Gerontological Social Work* 55, no. 2: 175–190.

Robison, J., et al. 2012. Transition from home care to nursing home: Unmet needs in a home- and community-based program for older adults. *Journal of Aging and Social Policy* 24, no. 3: 251–270.

Sanofi-Aventis. 2007. *Managed care digest series, 2007: Senior Care Digest.* Bridgewater, NJ: Sanofi-Aventis US, LLC.

Sanofi-Aventis. 2012. *Managed care digest series, 2012–2013: Public Payer Digest.* Bridgewater, NJ: Sanofi-Aventis US, LLC.

Scharlach, A.E., et al. 2001. *Case management in long-term care integration: An overview of current programs and evaluations.* Center for the Advanced Study of Aging Services, University of California, Berkeley, November 2001.

Scocco, P., et al. 2006. Nursing home institutionalization: A source of eustress or distress for the elderly. *International Journal of Geriatric Psychiatry* 21, no. 3: 281–287.

Shippey, R.A., and S.E. Karpiak. 2005. Perceptions of support among older adults with HIV. *Research on Aging* 27, no. 3: 290–306.

Singh, D.A. 2010. *Effective management of long-term care facilities.* 2nd ed. Sudbury, MA: Jones and Bartlett Publishers.

Stahl, C. 1997. Adult foster care: An alternative to SNFs? *ADVANCE for Occupational Therapists* September 29: 18.

Stone, R.I., and S.C. Reinhard. 2007. The place of assisted living in long-term care and related service systems. *The Gerontologist* 47, (special issue) no. 3: 23–32.

Tabert, M.H., et al. 2002. Functional deficits in patients with mild cognitive impairments: Prediction of AD. *Neurology* 58: 758–764.

Teresi, J.A., et al. 2013. Comparative effectiveness of implementing evidence-based education and best practices in nursing homes: Effects on falls, quality-of-life and societal costs. *International Journal of Nursing Studies* 50, no. 4: 448–463.

Thomas, K.E., et al. 2010. Conversion diversion: Participation in a social HMO reduces the likelihood of converting from short-stay to long-stay nursing facility placement. *Journal of the American Medical Directors Association* 11, no. 5: 333–337.

Tune, L. 2001. Assessing psychiatric illness in geriatric patients. *Clinical Cornerstone* 3, no. 3: 23–36.

US Census Bureau. 2012. National population projections: Summary tables, Table 2. Available at: http://www.census.gov/population/projections/data/national/2012/summarytables.html. Accessed August 2013.

Van Houtven, C.H., and E. Norton. 2004. Informal care and health care use of older adults. *Journal of Health Economics* 23, no. 6: 1159–1180.

Vargas, R.B., and W.E. Cunningham. 2006. Evolving trends in medical care-coordination for patients with HIV and AIDS. *Current HIV/AIDS Reports* 3, no. 4: 149–153.

Watkins, C.C., and G.J. Treisman. 2012. Neuropsychiatric complications of aging with HIV. *Journal of Neurovirology* 18, no. 4: 277–290.

Wieland, D., et al. 2013. Does Medicaid pay more to a Program of All-inclusive Care for the Elderly (PACE) than for fee-for-service long-term care? *Journal of Gerontology. Series A, Biological Sciences and Medical Sciences* 68, no. 1: 47–55.

Chapter 11

Health Services for Special Populations

Learning Objectives

- To learn about population groups facing greater challenges and barriers in accessing health care services
- To understand the racial and ethnic disparities in health status
- To get acquainted with the health concerns of America's children and the health services available to them
- To learn about the health concerns of America's women and health services available to them
- To appreciate the challenges faced in rural health and to learn about measures taken to improve access to care
- To learn about the characteristics and health concerns of the homeless population and migrant workers
- To understand the nation's mental health system
- To understand the AIDS epidemic in America, the population groups affected by it, and the services available to HIV/AIDS patients
- To point out the benefits of the Affordable Care Act for certain vulnerable groups

They all have something in common.

Introduction

Certain population groups in the United States face greater challenges than the general population in accessing timely and needed health care services (Shortell et al. 1996). They are at greater risk of poor physical, psychological, and/or social health (Aday 1993). Various terms are used to describe these populations, such as "underserved populations," "medically underserved," "medically disadvantaged," "underprivileged," and "American underclasses." The causes of their vulnerability are largely attributable to unequal social, economic, health, and geographic conditions. These population groups consist of racial and ethnic minorities, uninsured children, women, those living in rural areas, the homeless, the mentally ill, the chronically ill and disabled, and those with human immunodeficiency virus

(*HIV*)/acquired immune deficiency syndrome (*AIDS*). These population groups are more vulnerable than the general population and experience greater barriers in access to care, financing of care, and racial or cultural acceptance. After presenting a conceptual framework to study vulnerable populations, this chapter defines these population groups, describes their health needs, and summarizes the major challenges they face. The potential impact of ACA on vulnerable populations will also be discussed.

Framework to Study Vulnerable Populations

The vulnerability framework (see Exhibit 11–1) is an integrated approach to studying vulnerability (Shi and Stevens 2010). From a health perspective,

Exhibit 11–1 The Vulnerability Framework

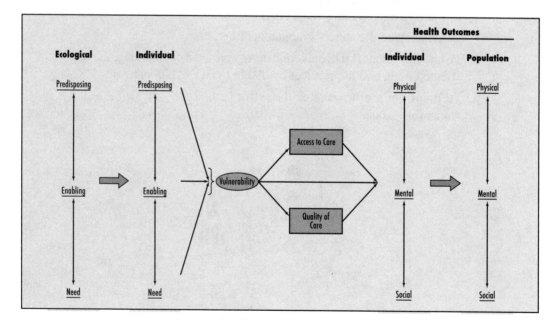

vulnerability refers to the likelihood of experiencing poor health or illness. Poor health can be manifested physically, psychologically, and/or socially. Because poor health along one dimension is likely to be compounded by poor health along others, the health needs are greater for those with problems along multiple dimensions than those with problems along a single dimension.

According to the framework, vulnerability is determined by a convergence of (1) predisposing, (2) enabling, and (3) need characteristics at both individual and ecological (contextual) levels (see Exhibit 11–2). Not only do these predisposing, enabling, and need characteristics converge and determine individuals' access to health care, they also ultimately influence individuals' risk of contracting illness or, for those already sick, recovering from illness. Individuals with multiple risks (i.e., a combination of two or more vulnerability traits) typically experience worse access to care, care of lesser

Exhibit 11–2 Predisposing, Enabling, and Need Characteristics of Vulnerability

Predisposing Characteristics
- Racial/ethnic characteristics
- Gender and age (women and children)
- Geographic location (rural health)

Enabling characteristics
- Insurance status (uninsured)
- Homelessness

Need characteristics
- Mental health
- Chronic illness/disability
- HIV/AIDS

quality, and inferior health status than do those with fewer vulnerability traits.

Understanding vulnerability as a combination or convergence of disparate factors is preferred over studying individual factors separately because vulnerability, when defined as a convergence of risks, best captures reality. This approach not only reflects the co-occurrence of risk factors, but underscores the belief that it is difficult to address disparities in one risk factor without addressing others.

This vulnerability model has a number of distinctive characteristics. First, it is a comprehensive model, including both individual and ecological attributes of risk. Second, this is a general model, focusing on the attributes of vulnerability for the total population rather than focusing on vulnerable traits of subpopulations. Although we recognize individual differences in exposure to risks, we also think there are common, crosscutting traits affecting all vulnerable populations. Third, a major distinction of our model is the emphasis on the convergence of vulnerability. The effects of experiencing multiple vulnerable traits may lead to cumulative vulnerability that is additive or even multiplicative.

Racial/Ethnic Minorities

The 2010 census questionnaire lists 15 racial categories, as well as places to write in specific races not listed on the form (US Census Bureau 2009). These are White, Black, American Indian or Alaska Native, Asian Indian, Chinese, Filipino, Japanese, Korean, Vietnamese, Other Asian, Native Hawaii, Guamanian or Chamorro, Samoan, Other Pacific Islander, or some other race. Respondents can choose more than one race.

The US Census Bureau estimated that, in 2010, over 36% of the US population was made up of minorities: Black or African Americans (12.3%), Hispanics or Latinos (16.3%), Asians (4.7%), Native Hawaiian and Other Pacific Islanders (0.2%), and American Indian and Alaska Natives (0.7%). In addition, 1.9% identified as two or more races (US Census Bureau 2010a).

Significant differences exist across the various racial/ethnic groups on health-related lifestyles and health status. For example, in 2010, the percentage of live births weighing less than 2,500 grams (low birth weight) was greatest among Blacks, followed by Asians or Pacific Islanders, American Indians or Native Americans, Whites, and Hispanics (Figure 11–1). Asians and Pacific Islanders were most likely to begin prenatal care during their first trimester, followed by Whites,

Hispanics, Blacks, and American Indians or Alaska Natives (Table 11–1). Mothers of Asian and Pacific Islander origin are least likely to smoke cigarettes during pregnancy, followed by Hispanics, Blacks, Whites, and American Indian or Alaska Natives, who have a smoking rate more than double that of any other group (19.6%) (Figure 11–2). The White adult population is more likely to consume alcohol than other races (Figure 11–3). Among women 40 years of age and older, utilization of mammography is the highest among Whites and lowest among Hispanics (Figure 11–4).

Black Americans

Black Americans are more likely to be economically disadvantaged than Whites. They also fall behind in health status, despite

Figure 11–1 Percentage of US Live Births Weighing Less than 2,500 Grams by Mother's Detailed Race.

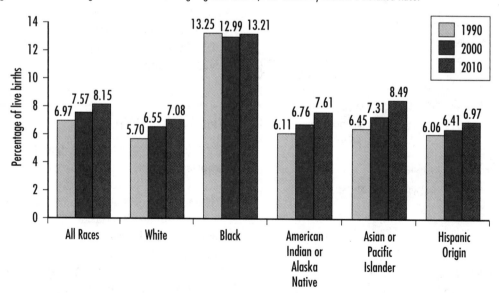

Source: Data from National Center for Health Statistics, Hyattsville, MD: Health, United States, 2012, p. 56.

Table 11–1 Characteristics of US Mothers by Race/Ethnicity

Item	1970	1980	1990	2000	2010
Prenatal care began during 1st trimester					
All mothers	68.0	76.3	75.8	83.2	83.2
White	72.3	79.2	79.2	85.0	84.7
Black	44.2	62.4	60.6	74.3	76.0
American Indian or Alaskan Native	38.2	55.8	57.9	69.3	69.5
Asian or Pacific Islander	—	73.7	75.1	84.0	84.8
Hispanic origin	—	60.2	60.2	74.4	77.3
Education of mother 16 years or more					
All mothers	8.6	14.0	17.5	24.7	26.6*
White	9.6	15.5	19.3	26.3	27.9*
Black	2.8	6.2	7.2	11.7	13.4*
American Indian or Alaska Native	2.7	3.5	4.4	7.8	8.5*
Asian or Pacific Islander	—	30.8	31.0	42.8	47.1*
Hispanic origin	—	4.2	5.1	7.6	8.7*
Low birth weight (less than 2,500 grams)					
All mothers	7.93	6.84	6.97	7.57	8.15
White	6.85	5.72	5.70	6.55	7.08
Black	13.90	12.69	13.25	12.99	13.21
American Indian or Alaska Native	7.97	6.44	6.11	6.76	7.61
Asian or Pacific Islander	—	6.68	6.45	7.31	8.49
Hispanic origin (selected states)	—	6.12	6.06	6.41	6.97

Note: Numbers are percentages.
*Data from 2003.
Source: Data from *Health, United States, 2012,* p. 144; *Health, United States, 2009,* pp. 159, 163.

progress made during the past few decades. Blacks have shorter life expectancies than Whites (Figure 11–5); higher age-adjusted death rates for a majority of leading causes of death (Table 11–2); higher age-adjusted maternal mortality rates (Figure 11–6); and higher infant, neonatal, and postneonatal mortality rates (Table 11–3). On self-reported measures of health status, Blacks are more likely to report fair or poor health status than Whites (Figure 11–7). In terms of behavioral risks, Black males

Figure 11–2 Percentage of US Mothers Who Smoked Cigarettes During Pregnancy According to Mother's Race.

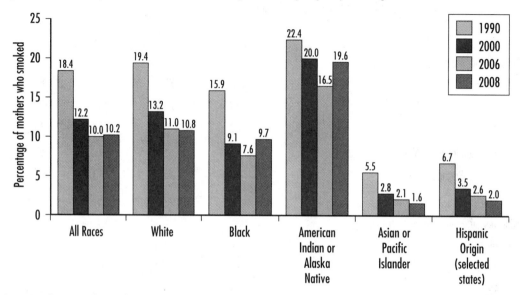

Source: Data from National Center for Health Statistics, Hyattsville, MD: Health, United States, 2011, p. 84.

Figure 11–3 Alcohol Consumption by Persons 18 Years of Age and Over.

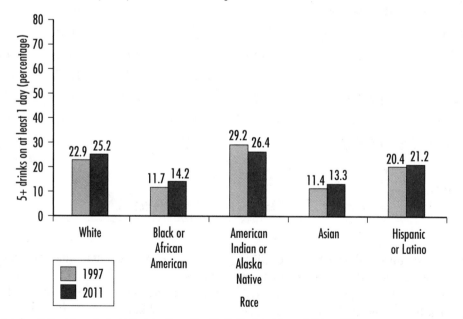

Source: Data from National Center for Health Statistics, Hyattsville, MD: Health, United States, 2012, p. 202.

Figure 11–4 Use of Mammography by Women 40 Years of Age and Over, 2008.

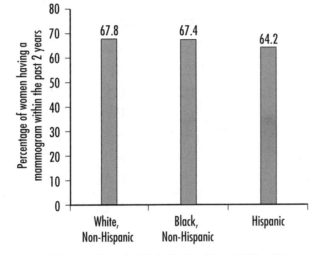

Source: Data from National Center for Health Statistics, Hyattsville, MD: Health, United States, 2012, p. 256.

are slightly more likely to smoke cigarettes than White males (23.2% versus 21.4%), but White females are more likely to smoke than Black females (17.7% versus 15.2%) (Figure 11–8), although smoking among Black females has increased. Conversely, Blacks have lower levels of serum cholesterol than Whites (Table 11–4).

Figure 11–5 US Life Expectancy at Birth, 1970–2006.

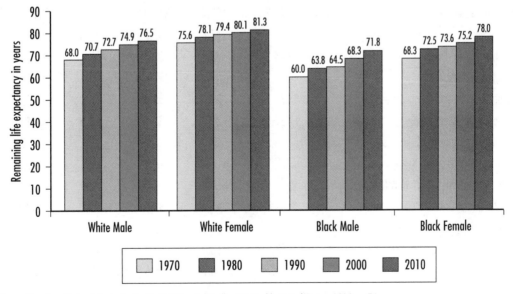

Source: Data from National Center for Health Statistics, Hyattsville, MD: Health, United States, 2012, p. 76.

Table 11–2 Age-Adjusted Death Rates for Selected Causes of Death (1970–2010)

Race and Cause of Death	1970	1980	1990	2000	2010
All persons	Deaths per 100,000 standard population				
All causes	1,222.6	1,039.1	938.7	869.0	747.0
Diseases of the heart	492.7	412.1	321.8	257.6	179.1
Ischemic heart disease	—	345.2	249.6	186.8	113.6
Cerebrovascular diseases	147.7	96.2	65.3	60.9	39.1
Malignant neoplasms	198.6	207.9	216.0	199.6	172.8
Chronic lower respiratory diseases	21.3	28.3	37.2	44.2	42.2
Influenza and pneumonia	41.7	31.4	36.8	23.7	15.1
Chronic liver disease and cirrhosis	17.8	15.1	11.1	9.5	9.4
Diabetes mellitus	24.3	18.1	20.7	25.0	20.8
Human immunodeficiency virus (HIV) disease	—	—	10.2	5.2	2.6
Unintentional injuries	60.1	46.4	36.3	34.9	38.0
Motor vehicle-related injuries	27.6	22.3	18.5	15.4	11.3
Suicide	13.1	12.2	12.5	10.4	12.1
Homicide	8.8	10.4	9.4	5.9	5.3
White					
All causes	1,193.3	1,012.7	909.8	849.8	741.8
Diseases of the heart	492.2	409.4	317.0	253.4	176.9
Ischemic heart disease	—	347.6	249.7	185.6	113.5
Cerebrovascular diseases	143.5	93.2	62.8	58.8	37.7
Malignant neoplasms	196.7	204.2	211.6	197.2	172.4
Chronic lower respiratory diseases	21.8	29.3	38.3	46.0	44.6
Influenza and pneumonia	39.8	30.9	36.4	23.5	14.9
Chronic liver disease and cirrhosis	16.6	13.9	10.5	9.6	9.9
Diabetes mellitus	22.9	16.7	18.8	22.8	19.0
Human immunodeficiency virus (HIV) disease	—	—	8.3	2.8	1.4
Unintentional injuries	57.8	45.3	35.5	35.1	40.3
Motor vehicle-related injuries	27.1	22.6	18.5	15.6	11.7
Suicide	13.8	13.0	13.4	11.3	13.6
Homicide	4.7	6.7	5.5	3.6	3.3

(*Continues*)

Table 11–2 Age-Adjusted Death Rates for Selected Causes of Death (1970–2010) (*Continued*)

Race and Cause of Death	1970	1980	1990	2000	2010
Black					
All causes	1,518.1	1,314.8	1,250.3	1,121.4	898.2
Diseases of the heart	512.0	455.3	391.5	324.8	224.9
Ischemic heart disease	—	334.5	267.0	218.3	131.2
Cerebrovascular diseases	197.1	129.1	91.6	81.9	53.0
Malignant neoplasms	225.3	256.4	279.5	248.5	203.8
Chronic lower respiratory diseases	16.2	19.2	28.1	31.6	29.0
Influenza and pneumonia	57.2	34.4	39.4	25.6	16.8
Chronic liver disease and cirrhosis	28.1	25.0	16.5	9.4	6.7
Diabetes mellitus	38.8	32.7	40.5	49.5	38.7
Human immunodeficiency virus (HIV) disease	—	—	26.7	23.3	11.6
Unintentional injuries	78.3	57.6	43.8	37.7	31.3
Motor vehicle-related injuries	31.1	20.2	18.8	15.7	10.9
Suicide	6.2	6.5	7.1	5.5	5.2
Homicide	44.0	39.0	36.3	20.5	17.7

Source: Data from *Health, United States, 2012,* Table 20, pp. 80–83, Centers for Disease Control and Prevention, National Center for Health Statistics.

Figure 11–6 Age-Adjusted Maternal Mortality Rates.

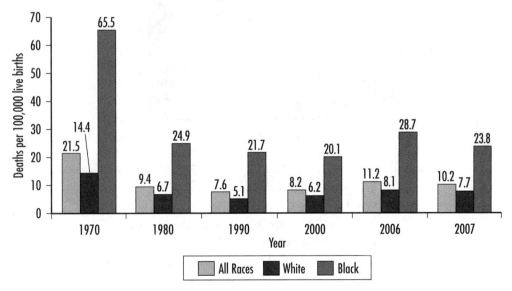

Source: Data from *Health, United States, 2010,* p. 231.

Table 11–3 Infant, Neonatal, and Postneonatal Mortality Rates by Mother's Race (per 1,000 live births)

Race of Mother	Infant Deaths				Neonatal Deaths				Postneonatal Deaths			
	1983	1990	2000	2008	1983	1990	2000	2008	1983	1990	2000	2008
All mothers	10.9	8.9	6.9	6.6	7.1	5.7	4.6	4.3	3.8	3.2	2.3	2.3
White	9.3	7.3	5.7	5.6	6.1	4.6	3.8	3.6	3.2	2.7	1.9	2.0
Black	19.2	16.9	13.5	12.4	12.5	11.1	9.1	8.1	6.7	5.9	4.3	4.3
American Indian or Alaska Native	15.2	13.1	8.3	8.4	7.5	6.1	4.4	4.2	7.7	7.0	3.9	4.2
Asian or Pacific Islander	8.3	6.6	4.9	4.5	5.2	3.9	3.4	3.1	3.1	2.7	1.4	1.4
Hispanic origin (selected states)	9.5	7.5	5.6	5.6	6.2	4.8	3.8	3.9	3.3	2.9	1.8	1.8

Source: Data from *Health, United States, 2012,* p. 66.

Figure 11–7   Respondent-Assessed Health Status.

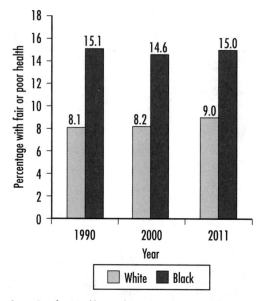

Source: Data from *Health, United States, 1995,* p. 172, Centers for Disease Control and Prevention, National Center for Health Statistics, 1996, and *Health, United States, 2012,* p. 168.

Figure 11–8 Current Cigarette Smoking by Persons 18 Years of Age and Over, Age Adjusted, 2011.

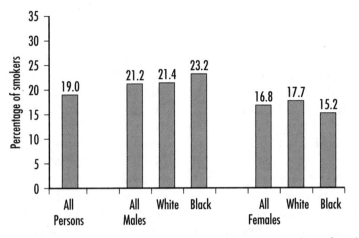

Source: Data from *Health, United States, 2012*, p. 182, Centers for Disease Control and Prevention, National Center for Health Statistics.

Hispanic Americans

The Hispanic segment of the US population is growing at a significantly higher rate than other population segments. Between 2000 and 2010, the Hispanic segment increased by 43%, compared to the 10% increase in the total population (US Census Bureau 2011, 2011b). In 2008, the Hispanic population numbered nearly 47 million and is projected to reach 57 million by the year 2015.

Table 11–4 Selected Health Risks Among Persons 20 Years and Older, 2007–2010

Sex and Race*	Percentage of Persons 20 Years of Age and Over with Hypertension	Mean Serum Cholesterol Level (mg/dl) of Persons 20 Years of Age and Over	Percentage of Overweight Persons 20 Years of Age and Over
Both sexes	30.6	196	68.5
White			
Male	31.1	193	73.6
Female	28.1	199	60.3
Black			
Male	40.5	191	70.0
Female	44.3	192	80.0

*20–74 years, age adjusted.
Source: Data from *Health, United States, 2012*, pp. 207, 211, 221, Centers for Disease Control and Prevention, National Center for Health Statistics, Division of Health Examination Statistics, 2012.

Hispanic Americans are also one of the youngest groups. In 2009, the median age among Hispanic Americans was 27.4, compared to 41.2 years for non-Hispanic Whites; 11.3% were below age 5, compared to 5.5% of non-Hispanic Whites (US Census Bureau 2012a). In 2011, 25.3% of Hispanic persons lived below the federal poverty level (FPL), compared to 9.8% of non-Hispanic White persons (US Census Bureau 2010b).

Many Hispanic Americans experience significant barriers in accessing medical care. This represents a greater problem for those from Central America (79% foreign born) and South America (75% foreign born) than those from Spain (17% foreign born) or Mexico (28% foreign born). Place of birth is also related to Hispanic people's inability to speak English, which is another factor associated with reduced access to medical services (Solis et al. 1990). Because of low education levels, Hispanic Americans have higher unemployment rates than non-Hispanic Whites (11.5% versus 7.9% in 2011; BLS 2012) and are more likely to be employed in semiskilled, nonprofessional occupations (US Census Bureau 2011a). Consequently, Hispanic Americans are more likely to be uninsured or underinsured than non-Hispanic Whites. In 2007, 30.7% of Hispanic persons were uninsured, compared to 12.8% of non-Hispanic Whites and 18.5% of non-Hispanic Blacks or African Americans (NCHS 2013). Among Hispanics, 33% of Mexican Americans were uninsured, followed by 28.1% of Cubans, 15.8% of Puerto Ricans, and 31.8% of other Hispanics (NCHS 2013).

Homicide was the seventh leading cause of death for Hispanic males in 2006. They have the highest ranking, along with Blacks, for this cause of death (NCHS 2013).

Hispanic Americans are less likely to take advantage of preventive care than non-Hispanic Whites and certain other races. Hispanic women 40 years of age or older were least likely to use mammography (64.2% versus 67.8% for non-Hispanic Whites and 67.4% for non-Hispanic Blacks; see Figure 11–4). In 2010, fewer Hispanic mothers began their prenatal care during the first trimester than mothers of other ethnic groups (77.3% for Hispanic mothers versus 84.7% for White mothers and 84.8% for Asian and Pacific Islander mothers; see Table 11–1). Among Hispanics 2 years of age and older in 2011, 57.2% had at least one dental visit during a year, compared to 69% for non-Hispanic Whites (NCHS 2013).

People of Hispanic origin also experience greater behavioral risks than Whites and certain other racial/ethnic groups. For example, among individuals 18 years of age or older in 2011, a higher proportion of Hispanics drank five or more alcoholic drinks per day than people of other ethnic origins (21.2% for Hispanics versus 14.2% for Blacks and 13.3% for Asians; see Figure 11–3). However, fewer Hispanics smoked, compared to people from other ethnic groups. In 2011, 16.4% of Hispanic males 18 years of age and older identified themselves as "current smokers," compared to 27.9% of non-Hispanic White males and 18.6% of non-Hispanic Black males (NCHS 2013). Among female adults, 9.1% of Hispanics smoked in 2011, compared to 19.4% of non-Hispanic Whites and 17.3% of non-Hispanic Blacks (NCHS 2013).

Asian Americans

Minority health epidemiology has typically focused on Blacks, Hispanics, and

American Indians or Alaska Natives because Asian Americans (AAs) have relatively small numbers. In 2009, Asians accounted for only 4.5% of the US population and numbered 14 million (US Census Bureau 2012a). To include the diversity of AAs, the National Center for Health Statistics (NCHS) has expanded the race codes into nine categories: White, Black, Native American, Chinese, Japanese, Hawaiian, Filipino, Other Asian/Pacific Islanders, and other races. But even the category of "Other Asian/Pacific Islander" is extremely heterogeneous, encompassing 21 subgroups with different health profiles.

AAs constitute one of the fastest growing population segments in the United States. The percentage of change in the Asian population was 32% between 2000 and 2009, compared to 9% for the population as a whole (US Census Bureau 2012a). The US Census Bureau (2010b) projects that the AA population will reach 16.5 million by 2015.

In education, income, and health, Asian Americans and Pacific Islanders (AA/PI) are very diverse. In 2010, 88.9% of AA/PIs 25 years of age or older had at least graduated from high school, compared with 87.6% of non-Hispanic Whites; in addition, the percentage of AA/PIs with a bachelor's degree or higher was 52.4%, compared to 30.3% for non-Hispanic Whites (US Census Bureau 2012a). Educational attainment varies greatly among the subgroups. For example, between 2007 and 2009, 94% of adults of Japanese descent had graduated from high school, whereas among Vietnamese it was 72% and only 61% among Hmong adults (US Census Bureau 2010a). In 2007, the median income for Asian males (aged 15 years and older) was $37,193, compared to $35,141 for non-Hispanic White males (US Census Bureau 2010a). In addition,

in 2010, a smaller percentage of Asians (12.1%) lived below the FPL, compared to Blacks (27.4%), and Hispanics (26.6%; US Census Bureau 2011c). One study found that Chinese, Asian Indian, Filipino, and other AA/PI children were more likely to be without contact with a health professional, compared to non-Hispanic White children. Citizenship/nativity status, maternal education attainment, and poverty status were all significant independent risk factors for health care access and utilization (Yu et al. 2004). In addition, cultural practices and attitudes may prevent AA/PI women from receiving adequate preventive care, such as Pap smears and breast cancer screening. Overall, the AA/PI population reported lower Pap smear test utilization, with a median rate of 74.4% over the course of 3 years, compared to Blacks (85%), American Indians (83.5%) and Hispanics (83.1%; CDC 2010c).

The heterogeneity of the AA/PI population is reflected in the various indicators of health status. For instance, people of Vietnamese descent are more than twice as likely to assess their own health status as fair or poor, compared to people of Korean, Chinese, Filipino, Asian Indian, and Japanese descent (NCHS 2013). The incidence of overweight and obesity varies greatly, from 47.1% among Filipinos to 24.4% among Vietnamese. Although, in the US population, overall smoking rates are the lowest among AA/PIs, 22% of Koreans are current smokers, a rate higher than that of Black (21%) and Hispanic adults (15%). Compared with Whites, Asian Indians are more than twice as likely to have diabetes (NCHS 2013). Unawareness of this heterogeneity sometimes contributes to the myth of a minority population that is both healthy and economically successful.

American Indians and Alaska Natives

More than three-quarters of the American Indian and Alaska Native (AIAN) population resides in rural and urban areas outside of reservations or off-reservation trust lands (US Census Bureau 2011d). According to the Census Bureau, the AIAN population is growing at a rate of 26.7% per year (US Census Bureau 2011d). Concomitantly, demand for expanded health care has been on the rise for several decades and is becoming more acute. The incidence and prevalence of certain diseases and conditions, such as diabetes, hypertension, infant mortality and morbidity, chemical dependency, and AIDS- and HIV-related morbidity, are all high enough to be matters of prime concern. Compared to the general US population, Native Americans also have much higher death rates from alcoholism, tuberculosis, diabetes, injuries, suicide, and homicide (IHS 2010a).

It is also no secret that Native Americans continue to occupy the bottom of the socioeconomic strata. AIANs are approximately twice as likely to be poor and unemployed (US Census Bureau 2011d). The health status of American Indians appears to be improving. For example, the mortality rate among Native American expectant mothers dropped from 28.5 per 100,000 live births in 1972–1974 to 11.1 per 100,000 live births by 2002–2004; and infant mortality declined from 25 per 1,000 births to 6.9 per 1,000 births (IHS 2009). Still, Native Americans experience significant health disparities compared to the general US population. The life expectancy of Native Americans is 4.6 years fewer than the US population as a whole (IHS 2010a). Native Americans die at higher rates than other Americans from alcohol (519% higher), tuberculosis (500% higher), diabetes (195% higher), unintentional injuries (149% higher), homicide (92% higher), and suicide (72% higher; IHS 2010a).

The provision of health services to American Indians by the federal government was first negotiated in 1832, as partial compensation for land cessions. Subsequent laws have expanded the scope of services and allowed American Indians greater autonomy in planning, developing, and administering their own health care programs. These laws explicitly permit the practice of traditional as well as Western medicine.

Indian Health Care Improvement Act

The Indian Health Care Improvement Act of 1976, and later amendments in 1980, outlined a 7-year effort to help bring American Indian health to a level of parity with the general population. Although health parity still remains unachieved, the Act has at least been successful in minimizing prejudice, building trust, and putting responsibility back into the hands of American Indians.

Indian Health Service

Chapter 6 introduced the federal program administered by the Indian Health Service (IHS). The goal of the IHS is to ensure that comprehensive and culturally acceptable health services are available to AIANs (IHS 2013). The IHS serves the members and descendants of more than 560 federally recognized AIAN tribes (IHS 2010b). However, the health care needs of a rapidly expanding American Indian population have grown faster than medical care resources, and most American Indian communities continue to be medically underserved.

IHS is divided into 12 area offices, each responsible for program operations in a particular geographic area. Each area office is composed of branches dealing with various administrative and health-related services. Delivery of health services is the responsibility of 161 tribally managed service units operating at the local level (IHS 2010b). The IHS mandate has been made particularly difficult because the locations of Indian reservation communities are among the least geographically accessible (Burks 1992).

Besides rendering primary and preventive care, special initiatives focus on areas such as injury control, alcoholism, diabetes, mental health, maternal and child health, Indian youth and children, elder care, and HIV/AIDS (IHS 1999a). Additional areas of focus include domestic violence and child abuse, oral health, and sanitation (IHS 1999b). However, despite limitations in the IHS's scope of service, many American Indians do not avail themselves of the system's services.

The Uninsured

Chapter 6 discussed the number of uninsured and the reasons why so many Americans have been without health insurance. Although uninsurance among adults has increased, lack of health insurance coverage among children declined from 13.2% in 2009 to 6.5% in 2011 (CDC 2011a), mainly because of the success of the CHIP program (see Chapter 6).

Ethnic minorities are more likely than Whites to lack health insurance. The US Census Bureau (2011e) estimated that, in 2011, 30.1% of Hispanic residents were uninsured, compared with 17.8% of Blacks, 16.2% of AAs, and 14.9% of Whites. Most of the uninsured population is comprised of young workers (O'Neill and

O'Neill 2009). Lack of coverage is also more prevalent in the South and the West of the United States, and among individuals who lack a college degree. Generally, the uninsured are in poorer health than the general population (CDC 2010a). Studies have also shown that the uninsured use fewer health services than the insured (CDC 2010a). In 2011, 53% of uninsured people reported having no regular source of health care (Kaiser 2012a). Decreased utilization of lower cost preventive services can ultimately result in an increased need for more expensive emergency health care. Even when the uninsured can access health care, they often have serious problems paying medical bills. In 2011, 30% of uninsured people postponed seeking medical care because of cost, compared to 12% of those with public insurance and 7% of privately insured people (Kaiser 2012b).

The plight of the uninsured affects those who have insurance. Medical expenditures for uncompensated care to the uninsured were estimated to be $57 billion in 2008 (Kaiser 2012b). Much of this cost was absorbed by Medicaid, federal grants to nonprofit hospitals, and charitable organizations.

Without the Affordable Care Act (ACA), the number of uninsured would be 56 million (Congressional Budget Office 2012). Yet, it is estimated that between 29.8 million and 31 million will remain uninsured after the ACA goes into effect (Nardin et al. 2013). Hence, the problem of the uninsured will continue to haunt the US health care system.

Children

In 2011, 38.2% of children under the age of 18 were covered under Medicaid and 53.7%

under private insurance (NCHS 2013). Vaccinations of children for selected diseases differ by race, poverty status, and area of residence (Table 11–5). White children have greater vaccination rates for diphtheria-tetanus-pertussis (DTP), polio, measles, *Haemophilus influenzae* serotype b (Hib), and combined series than Blacks. Children who come from families with incomes below the FPL, or who live in central city areas, have lower vaccination rates than other children.

When children have inadequate access to health care, their ability to learn is compromised. Some children stay home and miss school for long periods when they do not receive needed medical care. Some sick children go to school because of unavailability of child care or inability of working parents to get leave. Once in school, children may also expose other children to contagious illnesses (Wenzel 1996).

In 2013, the United Nations published *The State of the World's Children*, which focuses on how the health of children with disabilities is impacted by social and environmental barriers. This report suggests that greater social inclusiveness will lead to profound and positive impacts on children's health, well-being, and development (UN 2013).

Children's health has certain unique aspects in the delivery of health care. Among these are children's developmental vulnerability, dependency, and differential patterns of morbidity and mortality. *Developmental vulnerability* refers to the rapid and cumulative physical and emotional changes that characterize childhood and the potential impact that illness, injury, or disruptive family and social circumstances

Table 11–5 Vaccinations of Children 19–35 Months of Age for Selected Diseases According to Race, Poverty Status, and Residence in a Metropolitan Statistical Area (MSA), 2011 (%)

| Vaccination | Race | | | Poverty Status | | Inside MSA | |
	Total	White	Black	Below Poverty	At or Above Poverty	Central City	Remaining Areas
DTP[1]	85	85	81	81	87	86	84
Polio[2]	94	94	94	94	94	94	93
Measles containing (MMR)[3]	92	91	91	91	92	92	91
HIB[4]	80	81	75	82	76	81	80
Combined series[5]	69	69	64	64	72	70	68

[1] Diphtheria-tetanus-pertussis, four doses or more.
[2] Three doses or more.
[3] Respondents were asked about measles-containing or MMR (measles-mumps-rubella) vaccines.
[4] Haemophilus B, three doses or more.
[5] The combined series consists of four doses of DTP vaccine, three doses of polio vaccine, and one dose of measles-containing vaccine (4 : 3 : 1 : 3 : 3 : 1).
Source: Data from *Health, United States, 2012*, p. 247.

can have on a child's life-course trajectory. *Dependency* refers to children's special circumstances that require adults—parents, school officials, caregivers, and sometimes neighbors—to recognize and respond to their health needs, seek health care services on their behalf, authorize treatment, and comply with recommended treatment regimens. These dependency relationships can be complex, change over time, and affect utilization of health services by children.

Children increasingly are affected by a broad and complex array of conditions, collectively referred to as "new morbidities." *New morbidities* include drug and alcohol abuse, family and neighborhood violence, emotional disorders, and learning problems from which older generations do not suffer. These dysfunctions originate in complex family or socioeconomic conditions rather than exclusively biological causes. Hence, they cannot be adequately addressed by traditional medical services alone. Instead, these conditions require comprehensive services that include multidisciplinary assessment, treatment, and rehabilitation, as well as community-based prevention strategies.

Although serious chronic medical conditions that lead to disability are less prevalent among children, by conservative estimates, at least 3 million children 18 years of age and under are disabled, and 1 million children in the United States have a severe chronic illness. Medical problems in children are usually related to birth or congenital conditions rather than degenerative conditions that affect adults. These differences call for an approach to the delivery of health care that is uniquely designed to address the needs of children.

Oral health among children is particularly impacted by socioeconomic and demographic factors. Among Hispanic children only 46.7% are reported to have teeth in excellent or very good condition by their parents/guardians, compared to 76.4% for White children (HRSA Maternal and Child Health Bureau 2005). There is a clear relationship between family income and child oral health. At less than 100% FPL, less than half of children have teeth in excellent or very good condition, compared to 82.8% of children at 400% FPL or greater (HRSA Maternal and Child Health Bureau 2005). In addition to tooth loss, poor oral health in children can result in missed school (Gift et al. 1992), increased emergency department visits (Sheller et al. 1997), and decreased productivity and quality of life in the long term (General Accounting Office 2000).

Children and the US Health Care System

The various programs that serve children have distinct eligibility, administrative, and funding criteria that can present barriers to access. The patchwork of disconnected programs also makes it difficult to obtain health care in an integrated and coordinated fashion. These programs can be categorized into three broad sectors: the personal medical and preventive services sector, the population-based community health services sector, and the health-related support services sector.

Personal medical and preventive health services include primary and specialty medical services, which are delivered in private and public medical offices, health centers, and hospitals. Personal medical services are principally funded by private health insurance, Medicaid, and out-of-pocket payments.

The population-based community health services include community-wide health promotion and disease prevention services. Examples are immunization delivery and monitoring programs, lead screening and abatement programs, and child abuse and neglect prevention. Other health services include special child abuse treatment programs and rehabilitative services for children with complex congenital conditions or other chronic and debilitating diseases. Community-based programs also provide assurance and coordination functions, such as case management and referral programs, for children with chronic diseases and early interventions and monitoring for infants at risk for developmental disabilities. Funding for this sector comes from federal programs, such as Medicaid's Early Periodic Screening, Diagnosis, and Treatment (EPSDT) program; Title V (Maternal and Child Health) of the Social Security Act; and other categorical programs.

The health-related support services sector includes such services as nutrition education, early intervention, rehabilitation, and family support programs. An example of a rehabilitation service is education and psychotherapy for children with HIV.

Family support services include parent education and skill building in families with infants at risk for developmental delay because of physiological or social conditions, such as low birth weight or very low income. Funding for these services comes from diverse agencies, such as the Department of Agriculture, which funds the Supplemental Food Program for Women, Infants, and Children (WIC), and the Department of Education, which funds the Individuals with Disabilities Education Act (IDEA).

Women

Women are playing an increasingly important role in the delivery of health care. Not only do women remain the leading providers of care in the nursing profession, but they are also well represented in various other health professions, including allopathic and osteopathic medicine, dentistry, podiatry, and optometry (Figure 11–9).

Figure 11–9 Percentage of Female Students of Total Enrollment in Schools for Selected Health Occupations, 2006–2007.

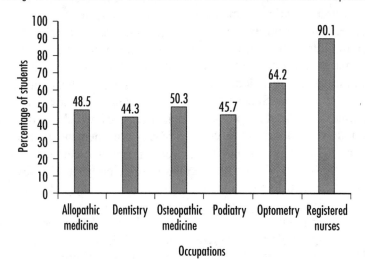

Source: Data from Health, United States, 2009, p. 383.

Women in the United States can expect to live about 4.8 years longer than men (NCHS 2013), but they suffer greater morbidity and poorer health outcomes. Morbidity is greater among women than among men, even after childbearing-related conditions are factored out. For instance, nearly 38% of women report having chronic conditions that require ongoing medical treatment, compared to 30% of men (Salganicoff et al. 2005). Women also have a higher prevalence of certain health problems than men over the course of their lifetimes (Sechzer et al. 1996). Heart disease and stroke account for a higher percentage of deaths among women than men at all stages of life. In contrast to 24% of men, 42% of women who have heart attacks die within a year (Misra 2001). Research has also demonstrated that women are more likely to experience functional limitations due to health than men (35% and 26%, respectively; NCHS 2013).

According to the 2012 Health in the United States Report, 88% of women had at least one visit to a health care provider in the previous year, compared to 80% of men (NCHS 2013). Compared to men, women have only a slightly higher mean number of specialty care visits and emergency department visits. However, women have higher annual charges than men for all types of care, including primary, specialty, emergency, and diagnostic services, which indicates that women receive more intensive services (Bertakis et al. 2000). Women are more likely to delay seeking care than men (13% compared to 9.6%, respectively; HRSA Maternal and Child Health Bureau 2011). In addition, women (9.3%) are more likely than men (7.8%) to forgo needed care (HRSA Maternal and Child Health Bureau 2011).

The differences between men and women are equally pronounced for mental illness.

For example, anxiety disorders and major depression affect two to three times as many women as men (McLean 2011). Clinical depression is a major mental health problem for both men and women; however, 4.0% or women, compared to 2.7% of men, had depression during 2006–2008 (CDC 2010b). An estimated 12% of women in the United States, compared with 7% of men, will suffer from major depression during their lifetime (Misra 2001). Certain other mental disorders also affect more women at different stages of life.

Eating disorders are among the illnesses predominantly affecting women and have been the subject of relatively little rigorous study to date. Up to 3% of women are affected by eating disorders (e.g., anorexia nervosa and bulimia), although between 29% and 38% report dieting at any given time (Misra 2001). At least 90% of all eating disorder cases occur in young women, and eating disorders account for the highest mortality rates among all mental disorders (Misra 2001).

Some disorders once thought to primarily affect men are now affecting women in increasing numbers. For example, death rates related to alcohol abuse are 50–100% higher among women than among men (Misra 2001). Compared to older men, older women are at substantially greater risk of Alzheimer's disease, a disease responsible for 60–70% of all cases of dementia and one of the leading causes of nursing home placement for older adults (Herzog and Copeland 1985).

In addition to the differences experienced in health care utilization and health outcomes between women and men there are large disparities by race and ethnicity, income, and education among women. New HIV cases are greatest among minorities.

In 2009, per 100,000 women, 47.8 Black, 13.3 Native American or Pacific Islander, and 11.9 Hispanic were newly diagnosed with HIV, compared to only 2.4 White women (HRSA Maternal and Child Health Bureau 2011). The prevalence of diabetes among women also varies, with 14% of American Indian or Alaska Natives and 11.9% of Native Hawaiian or Other Pacific Islanders, compared to only 6.4% of White women (HRSA Maternal and Child Health Bureau 2011).

Office on Women's Health

The Public Health Service's Office on Women's Health (OWH) is dedicated to the achievement of a series of specific goals that span the spectrum of disease and disability. These goals range across the life cycle and address cultural and ethnic differences among women. The OWH promotes, coordinates, and implements a comprehensive women's health agenda on research, service delivery, and education across various government agencies.

The OWH was responsible for implementing the National Action Plan on Breast Cancer (NAPBC), a major public–private partnership, dedicated to improving the diagnosis, treatment, and prevention of breast cancer through research, service delivery, and education. The OWH also worked to implement measures to prevent physical and sexual abuse against women, as delineated in the Violence Against Women Act of 1994. The OWH is also active in projects promoting breastfeeding, women's health education and research, girl and adolescent health, and heart health.

Within the Substance Abuse and Mental Health Services Administration (SAMHSA), the Advisory Committee for Women's Services has targeted six areas for special attention: physical and sexual abuse of women; women as caregivers; women with mental and addictive disorders; women with HIV infection or AIDS, sexually transmitted diseases, and/or tuberculosis; older women; and women detained in the criminal justice system. The Women's Health Initiative, supported by the National Institutes of Health (NIH), was the largest clinical trial conducted in US history, involving over 161,000 women (NIH 2002). It focused on diseases that are the major causes of death and disability among women—heart disease, cancer, and osteoporosis. In 2002, the Women's Health Initiative published a groundbreaking study, finding detrimental effects of postmenopausal hormone therapy on women's development of invasive breast cancer, coronary heart disease, stroke, and pulmonary embolism (NIH 2002).

Women and the US Health Care System

Women face a distinct disadvantage in employer-based health insurance coverage because they are more likely than men to work part time, receive lower wages, and have interruptions in their work histories. Hence, women are more likely to be covered as dependents under their husbands' plans and are at a higher risk of being uninsured. Women also place greater reliance on Medicaid for their health care coverage. In 2011, 15.6% of women were uninsured compared to 18.8% of men, while 19.3% of women compared to 16.3% of men were covered by Medicaid (NCHS 2013).

Women are more likely than men to use contraceptives (Figure 11–10), but contraceptives have been among the most poorly covered reproductive health care service in the United States. As of September 2013, 28 states required private health insurance

Figure 11–10 Contraceptive Use in the Past Month Among Women 15–44 Years Old, 2006–2010.

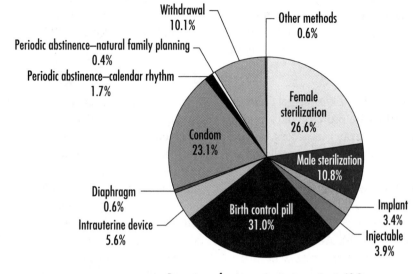

Percentage of women using contraception is 62.2.

Source: Data from National Center for Health Statistics, Hyattsville, MD: Health, United States, 2012, pp. 60–62.

plans to cover prescription contraceptives if they covered other prescription drugs (Guttmacher Institute 2013).

The ACA requires private insurance to cover, with no cost sharing, a wide variety of preventive services and additional services for women, including FDA-approved prescription contraceptives, domestic violence screening, breastfeeding supports, and human papillomavirus (HPV) testing. Although such services are not required under Medicaid, several states have started to cover all preventive services important for women with or without cost sharing (Kaiser Family Foundation 2013a).

Rural Health

For rural citizens, access to health care may be affected by poverty, long distances, rural topography, weather conditions, lack of transportation, and being uninsured. Consequently, residents of rural areas are less likely to utilize health services, and have poorer health outcomes than those in more urban areas. A greater percentage of persons residing in a rural area report being in fair or poor health compared to those in urban areas (CDC 2012a, 2012b). In addition, rural residents are more likely to report health problems, such as headaches and back and neck pain, than urban residents (17.2% compared to 14.7%, respectively; CDC 2012a, 2012b).

Among residents whose family incomes are below 100% FPL, those in rural areas are more likely than urban residents to forgo or delay care due to cost (27.1% compared to 21.4%, respectively; CDC 2012a, 2012b). Across race and ethnicity, rural residents have lower levels of insurance coverage. Among Hispanic rural residents, 48.3% do not have health insurance, compared to 42.5% of urban Hispanics. Among whites, 22.5% of rural residents were uninsured compared to 14.2% of urban residents (CDC 2012a, 2012b). The uninsured often do not have a usual source of care (Larson & Fleishman 2003).

Geographic maldistribution that creates a shortage of health care professionals in rural settings results in barriers in access to care. Reasons for the maldistribution are discussed in Chapter 4. As of January 2013, there were about 5,900 designated primary care health professional shortage areas (HPSAs), 4,600 dental HPSAs, and 3,800 mental health HPSAs (HRSA 2013b). About 21% of the US population resides in areas where primary care health professionals are in short supply (HRSA Bureau of Health Professions 2013a). More than 33 million Americans live in a non-metropolitan federally designated health professional shortage area (HRSA Bureau of Health Professions 2013a). The scarcity of health care providers encompasses a broad spectrum of professionals, including pediatricians, obstetricians, internists, dentists, nurses, and allied health professionals (Patton and Puskin 1990). Rural hospitals are often under financial strain, which results in smaller hospitals that provide fewer services than urban hospitals.

Various measures have been taken to improve access in rural America, including the promotion of the National Health Service Corps (NHSC), the designation of Health Professional Shortage Areas (HPSAs) and Medically Underserved Areas (MUAs), the development of Community and Migrant Health Centers (C/MHCs), and the enactment of the Rural Health Clinics Act. In addition, the Office of Rural Health Policy, within the Health Resources and Services Administration of the US Department of Health and Human Services (DHHS), was established in 1987 to promote better health care in rural America (HRSA Office of Rural Health Policy 2007).

The National Health Service Corps

The NHSC was created in 1970, under the Emergency Health Personnel Act, to recruit and retain physicians to provide needed services in physician shortage areas. A 1972 amendment created a scholarship program targeting HPSAs. The scholarship and loan repayment program applies to doctors, dentists, nurse practitioners, midwives, and mental health professionals who serve a minimum of 2 years in underserved areas. Since 1972, over 40,000 health professionals have been placed in medically underserved communities in hospitals and clinics (HRSA Bureau of Health Professions 2013a). Currently, nearly 10,000 health professionals are providing services under NHSC (HRSA National Health Service Corps 2013).

Health Professional Shortage Areas

The Health Professions Educational Assistance Act of 1976 provided the designation criteria for Health Manpower Shortage Areas, later renamed Health Professional Shortage Areas (HRSA Bureau of Health Professions 2007b). The act provided that three different types of HPSAs could be designated: geographic areas, population groups, and medical facilities. A geographic area must meet the following three criteria for designation as a primary care HPSA: (1) The geographic area involved must be rational for the delivery of health services. (2) One of the following conditions must prevail in the area: a) the area has a population to full-time equivalent primary care physician (PCP) ratio of at least 3,500:1, or b) the area has a population to full-time equivalent PCP ratio of less than 3,500:1 but greater than 3,000:1 and has unusually high needs for primary care services or insufficient capacity of existing primary care providers. (3) Primary care professionals in contiguous areas are overutilized, excessively distant, or inaccessible to the population of the area under consideration (HRSA Bureau of Health Professions 2007c).

A population group can be designated as an HPSA for primary care if it can be demonstrated that access barriers prevent members of the group from using local providers. Medium- and maximum-security federal and state correctional institutions and public or nonprofit private residential facilities can be designated as facility-based HPSAs. HPSAs are classified on a scale of 1 to 4, with 1 or 2 signifying areas of greatest need.

Medically Underserved Areas

The primary purpose of the MUA designation, in the HMO Act of 1973, was to target the community health center and rural health clinic programs. The statute required that several factors be considered in designating MUAs, such as available health resources in relation to area size and population, health indices, and care and demographic factors affecting the need for care. To meet this mandate, the Index of Medical Underservice was developed, comprising four variables: (1) percentage of population below poverty income levels, (2) percentage of population 65 years of age and older, (3) infant mortality rates, and (4) primary care practitioners per 1,000 population. The index yields a single numerical value on a scale from zero to 100; any area with a value less than 62 (the median of all counties) is designated an MUA.

Migrant Workers

Migrant workers are farmworkers who travel long distances from their primary residence or lack a primary residence entirely, either due to seasonal crop changes or work availability. While their exact number is difficult to assess due to citizenship issues and the transient nature of the population, it is widely accepted that there are at least 3 million migrant workers in the United States (Larson 1993; Migrant Health Promotion 2013; Rust 1990). The migrant population is largely comprised of racial and ethnic minorities. As of 2009, 72% of migrant workers were born in Mexico or Central America (US Department of Labor 2011).

The average annual income of a family in which at least one member is a migrant worker was between $17,500 and $19,999 in 2009. Furthermore, only 57% of workers were currently receiving any public assistance (US Department of Labor 2011). As of 2000, approximately 85% of migrant workers were uninsured and only 20% of all workers reported utilizing any health service within the prior 2 years (Kaiser Family Foundation 2005). Furthermore, only 42% of female migrant workers sought prenatal care during their first trimester, compared with the national average of 72% (Kaiser Family Foundation 2005). In addition to the occupational health risks that this population is exposed to, the lack of access to and utilization of health services translates to poor health outcomes.

The rate of obesity among migrant workers has risen to 81% of males and 76% of females (Villarejo et al. 2000). This rate is not found among migrant workers within their first year in the United States, therefore dietary changes in later years likely account for the rates of obesity (Ikeda 1990). In addition to higher rates of chronic conditions, migrant populations are also at greater risk for infectious disease. In part due to their living conditions, migrant workers are at greater risk of tuberculosis, with studies finding rates between 17% (McCurdy et al. 1997) and 44% (Villarino et al. 1994). The rate of HIV/AIDS is also considerably higher than in the general population, with observed rates between 5% and 13% (Organista and Organista 1997).

To address the growing health needs of this population, services have been provided to migrant workers and their families through state programs and federally through HRSA's Migrant Health Program.

Community and Migrant Health Centers (C/MHCs)

Introduced in Chapter 7, these centers provide services to low-income populations on a sliding-fee scale, thereby addressing both geographic and financial barriers to access. Although community health centers must be located in areas designated as MUAs, migrant centers must be located in "high-impact" areas, defined as areas that serve at least 4,000 migrant and/or seasonal farm workers for at least 2 months per year. For more than 4 decades, C/MHCs have provided primary care and preventive health services to populations in designated MUAs. Because of a shortage of physicians, C/MHCs heavily rely on nonphysician providers (NPPs). In 2012, C/MHCs served approximately 900,000 migrants and seasonal farm workers.

The Rural Health Clinics Act

The Rural Health Clinics Act was developed to respond to the concern that isolated rural communities could not generate sufficient revenue to support the services of a physician. In many cases, the only source of primary care or emergency services was NPPs, who were ineligible at that time for Medicare or Medicaid reimbursement. The Act permitted physician assistants (PAs), nurse practitioners (NPs), and certified nurse midwives (CNMs) associated with rural clinics to practice without the direct supervision of a physician; enabled rural health clinics (but not NPPs directly) to be reimbursed by Medicare and Medicaid for their services; and tied the level of Medicaid payment to the level established by Medicare. To be designated as a rural health clinic, a public or private sector physician practice, clinic, or hospital must meet several criteria, including location in an MUA, geographic HPSA, or a population-based HPSA. Over 3,000 rural health clinics provide primary care services to over 7 million people in 47 states (NARHC 2007).

The Homeless

Although an exact number is unknown, an estimated 3.5 million people (1.35 million of them children) are likely to experience homelessness in a given year (National Law Center on Homelessness and Poverty 2004). Nationally, approximately 1 in 200 people became homeless in 2011 (HUD 2012). Although most homeless persons live in major urban areas, a surprising 27.7% live in suburban and rural areas (HUD 2012).

The adult homeless population is comprised of 63% men and 37% women, 22.8%

are children under the age of 18, 35.8% are families with children, and 14% are veterans (HUD 2012). Homeless women in particular face major difficulties: economic and housing needs and special gender-related issues that include pregnancy, child care responsibilities, family violence, fragmented family support, job discrimination, and wage discrepancies. The economic standing of women is often more unstable than men, and women are more likely to live in poverty than men. In 2010, 17 million women were living in poverty, of which 7.5 million were in extreme poverty (National Women's Law Center 2011). The low wages and extreme poverty faced by women increases their risk for becoming homeless. In addition, domestic violence has been found to be a contributing factor to family homelessness, with 18% of families citing this as the main cause (US Conference of Mayors 2011). Amongst all homeless women, one in four state that their homelessness was a direct result of violence committed against them (Jasinski 2005). Homeless women, regardless of parenting status, should be linked with social services, family support, self-help, and housing resources. Mentally ill women caring for children need additional consideration, with an emphasis on parenting skills and special services for children. Thus, homelessness is a multifaceted problem related to personal, social, and economic factors.

The economic picture of homeless persons is dismal, as would be expected, and suggests that they are severely lacking in the financial and educational resources necessary to access health care. A majority of mothers living in poverty that have ever been homeless did not complete high school (60%; Institute for Children, Poverty, & Homelessness 2011). In addition, it is estimated that

approximately 38% of the homeless population is unsheltered (National Alliance to End Homelessness 2012). Receipt of public benefits among the homeless is low. For example, among more than 9,000 clients served by Maryland's Health Care for the Homeless, 75% were uninsured (Health Care for the Homeless 2012). These numbers remain low because of federal restrictions that prohibit federal help to those without a physical street address.

The shortage of adequate low-income housing is the major precipitating factor for homelessness. Unemployment, personal or family life crises, rent increases that are out of proportion to inflation, and reduction in public benefits can also directly result in the loss of a home. Illness, on the other hand, tends to result in the loss of a home in a more indirect way. Other indirect causes of homelessness include deinstitutionalization from public mental hospitals, substance abuse programs, and overcrowded prisons and jails.

Community-based residential alternatives for mentally ill individuals vary from independent apartments to group homes staffed by paid caregivers. Independent living may involve either separate apartments or single-room occupancy units in large hotels, whereas group homes are staffed during at least a portion of the day and traditionally provide some on-site mental health services (Schutt and Goldfinger 1996).

The homeless, adults and children, have a high prevalence of untreated acute and chronic medical, mental health, and substance abuse problems. The reasons are debatable. Some argue that people may become homeless because of a physical or mental illness. Others argue that homelessness itself may lead to the development of physical and mental disability because homelessness produces risk factors, which include excessive use of alcohol, illegal drugs, and cigarettes; sleeping in an upright position, which results in venous stasis and its consequences; extensive walking in poorly fitting shoes; and grossly inadequate nutrition. While the reasons may not be agreed upon, the outcomes are easily seen. Homeless adults typically have eight to nine medical conditions or illnesses (Breakey1989). Homeless children have a nearly doubled risk of mortality than housed children (Kerker et al. 2011).

Homeless persons are also at a greater risk of assault and victimization regardless of whether they live in a shelter or outdoors. They are also subject to exposure to extreme heat, cold, and other weather conditions. The homeless are also exposed to illness because of overcrowding in shelters and overexposure to weather.

Barriers to Health Care

The homeless face barriers to ambulatory services but incur high rates of hospitalization. A high use of inpatient services in this manner amounts to the substitution of inpatient care for outpatient services. Both individual factors (competing needs, substance dependence, and mental illness) and system factors (availability, cost, convenience, and appropriateness of care) account for the barriers to adequate ambulatory services.

Other barriers include accessible transportation to medical care providers and competing needs for basic food, shelter, and income than obtaining health services or following through with a prescribed treatment plan. Homeless individuals who experience psychological distress and disabling mental illness may be in the greatest need of health services and yet may be the least able to obtain them. This inability to obtain health care may be attributable to such individual traits of mental illness as paranoia, disorientation, unconventional health beliefs, lack of social support, lack of organizational skills to gain access to needed services, or fear of authority figures and institutions resulting from previous institutionalization. The social conditions of street life also affect compliance with medical care because of a lack of proper sanitation and a stable place to store medications. They also lack resources to obtain proper food for a medically indicated diet necessary for conditions like diabetes or hypertension.

Federal efforts to provide medical services to the homeless population are primarily through the Health Care for the Homeless (HCH) program. Community health centers supported by the 1985 Robert Wood Johnson Foundation/Pew Memorial Trust HCH program (subsequently covered by the 1987 McKinney Homeless Assistance Act) have addressed many of the access and quality-of-care issues faced by the homeless. In 2012, community health centers served approximately 1.1 million homeless patients (HRSA Bureau of Primary Health Care 2012b). A walk-in appointment system reduces access barriers at these medical facilities. Medical care, routine laboratory tests, substance abuse counseling, and some medications are provided free of charge to eliminate financial barriers.

The Mental Health Services for the Homeless Block Grant program sets aside funds for states to implement services for homeless persons with mental illness. These services include outreach services; community mental health services; rehabilitation; referrals to inpatient treatment, primary care, and substance abuse services; case management services; and supportive services in residential settings.

Services for homeless veterans are provided through the Department of Veterans Affairs (VA). The Homeless Chronically Mentally Ill Veterans Program provides outreach, case management services, and psychiatric residential treatment for homeless mentally ill veterans in community-based facilities in 45 US cities. The Domiciliary Care for Homeless Veterans Program addresses the health needs of veterans who have psychiatric illnesses or alcohol or drug abuse problems, operating 1,800 beds at 31 sites across the country (US Dept of Veterans Affairs 2006).

The Salvation Army also provides a variety of social, rehabilitation, and support services for homeless persons. Its centers include adult rehabilitation and food programs and permanent and transitional housing.

Mental Health

Mental disorders are common psychiatric illnesses affecting adults and present a serious public health problem in the United States. Mental disorders are among the leading cause of disability in the United States (WHO 2012). Mental illness is a risk factor for death from suicide, cardiovascular disease, and cancer. Suicide is currently the 11th leading cause of death in the United States and the 4th leading cause of death among persons aged 18–65 (CDC 2010e). Non-Hispanic White men 85 years of age or older have one of the highest rates of suicide, with approximately 52 suicide deaths per 100,000 (CDC 2010e). AIANs are at higher risk for suicides as well, with approximately 11 suicide deaths per 100,000 (CDC 2010e).

Mental health disorders can be either psychological or biological in nature.

Many mental health diseases, including mental retardation (MR), developmental disabilities (DD), and schizophrenia, are now known to be biological in origin. Other behaviors, including those related to personality disorders and neurotic behaviors, are still subject to interpretation and professional judgment.

National studies have concluded that the most common mental disorders include phobias; substance abuse, including alcohol and drug dependence; and affective disorders, including depression. Schizophrenia is considerably less common, with estimates ranging from 0.7% (McGrath et al. 2008) to 1.1% of the population (Regier et al. 1993).

About one in four adults suffers from a diagnosable mental disorder every year (Kessler et al. 2005). In 2009, 45.1 million adults (18 years of age or older) had a mental illness, including 11 million with severe mental illness (SMI; SAMHSA 2012a, 2012b). Among adults with any diagnosable mental disorder, 62.1% did not seek mental health treatment (SAMHSA 2012a, 2012b). Prevalence of SMI was higher among Medicaid recipients, women, and individuals in the 18–25 age group (SAMHSA 2012a, 2012b).

The mental health of children has drawn increasing concern in recent years. Approximately one in five children has a mental disorder, a similar rate to that of adults; approximately 4 million children or adolescents have a serious mental illness (DHHS 2001). Only half of those diagnosed receive mental health services (US Public Health Service 2000). If left untreated, mental health in children can lead to more severe and/or co-occuring mental illness (Kessler et al. 2005).

Most mental health services are provided in the general medical sector—a concept first described by Regier and colleagues (1988) as the de facto mental health service system—rather than through formal mental health specialist services. The de facto system combines specialty mental health services with general counseling services, such as those provided in primary care settings, nursing homes, and community health centers by ministers, counselors, self-help groups, families, and friends. Specifically, mental health services are provided through public and private resources in both inpatient and outpatient facilities. These facilities include state and county mental hospitals, private psychiatric hospitals, nonfederal general hospital psychiatric services, VA psychiatric services, residential treatment centers, and freestanding psychiatric outpatient clinics (Table 11–6). Total expenditures for mental disorders have increased since 1986, from $31 billion to $113 billion in 2005 (SAMHSA 2012a). Despite the cost of mental health care for individuals with any mental illness, only 37.9% received mental health services and only 48.5% of individuals covered under

• •

Table 11–6 Mental Health Organizations (Numbers in Thousands), 2008

Service and Organization	Number of MH Organizations
All organizations	3,130
State psychiatric hospitals	241
Private psychiatric hospitals	256
Nonfederal general hospital psychiatric services	1,292
Residential treatment centers for emotionally disturbed children	538
All other	673

Source: Data from Health, United States, 2011, p. 358.
• •

Medcaid/CHIP received care (SAMHSA 2012a, 2012b). The nation's *mental health system* is composed of two subsystems: one primarily for individuals with insurance coverage or private funds and the other for those without private coverage.

Barriers to Mental Health Care

Two main barriers to access for mental health care are commonly experienced across the United States: prohibitive costs of services and shortage of available mental health professionals. In 2009, among adults that delayed or did not seek needed mental health care, 50.1% stated that it was due to the prohibitive cost of treatment (SAMHSA 2012a, 2012b). In addition to the inability to cover the high cost of care, many individuals currently reside in a Mental Health Care Health Professional Shortage Area. A Mental Health HPSA is defined as an area in which the population to mental health profession ratio equals 6,000 people to 1 mental health professional and 20,000 people to 1 psychiatrist (HRSA Bureau of Health Professions 2013b). As of 2013, there were more than 3,700 shortage areas across the United States (Kaiser Family Foundation 2013c). This shortage translates to the available services being able to meet only 54% of need, leaving a large number of patients without needed care (Kaiser Family Foundation 2013c).

The Uninsured and Mental Health

Patients without insurance coverage or personal financial resources are treated in state and county mental health hospitals and in community mental health clinics. Care is also provided in short-term, acute care hospitals and emergency departments.

Local governments are the providers of last resort, with the ultimate responsibility to provide somatic and mental health services for all citizens regardless of ability to pay.

The Insured and Mental Health

For patients who have insurance coverage or personal ability to pay, availability of both inpatient and ambulatory mental health care has expanded tremendously. Inpatient mental health services for patients with insurance are usually provided through private psychiatric hospitals. These hospitals can be operated on either a nonprofit or a for-profit basis. There has been substantial growth in national chains of for-profit mental health hospitals. Patients with insurance coverage are also more likely to receive care through the offices of private psychiatrists, clinical psychologists, and licensed social workers. Mental health services are also provided by the VA and by the military health care system; however, access to these services is limited by eligibility.

Managed Care and Mental Health

Managed care has expanded its services into mental health delivery. State and local governments are also contracting with MCOs to manage a full health care benefit package that includes mental health and substance abuse services for their Medicaid enrollees.

Many health maintenance organizations (HMOs) contract with specialized companies that provide managed behavioral health care, an arrangement called a carve out. This is mainly because HMOs lack the in-house capacity to provide treatment. Using case managers and reviewers, most of whom are psychiatric nurses, social workers, and psychologists, these specialized companies oversee and authorize the use of mental health and substance abuse services. The case reviewers, using clinical protocols to guide them, assign patients to the least expensive appropriate treatment, emphasizing outpatient alternatives over inpatient care.

Working with computerized databases, a reviewer studies a patient's particular problem and then authorizes an appointment with an appropriate provider in the company's selective network. On average, psychiatrists constitute about 4.5% of any given provider network, psychologists constitute 17%, counselors constitute 24%, and psychiatric social workers constitute another 45% (SAMHSA 2012a).

Mental Health Professionals

A variety of professionals provide mental health services (Table 11–7), including but not limited to psychiatrists, psychologists, social workers, nurses, counselors, and therapists.

Psychiatrists are physicians who specialize in the diagnosis and treatment of mental disorders. Psychiatrists receive postgraduate specialty training in mental health after completing medical school. Psychiatric residencies cover medical, as well as behavioral, diagnosis and treatments. A relatively small proportion of the total mental health workforce consists of psychiatrists, but they exercise disproportionate influence in the system by virtue of their authority to prescribe drugs and admit patients to hospitals.

Psychologists usually hold a doctoral degree, although some hold master's degrees. They are trained in interpreting and changing the behavior of people. Psychologists cannot prescribe drugs; however, they provide a wide range of services to patients

Table 11–7 Full-Time Equivalent Patient Care Staff in Mental Health Organizations, 2000

Staff Discipline	Number	Percentage
All patient care staff	426,558	74.9
Professional patient care staff	243,993	42.9
Psychiatrists	20,233	3.6
Other physicians	2,962	0.5
Psychologists	19,003	3.3
Social workers	70,208	12.3
Registered nurses	70,295	12.4
Other mental health professionals	53,271	9.4
Physical health professionals and assistants	8,023	1.4
Other mental health workers	182,566	32.1

Source: Modified from Section V, Chapter 22, Table 19.7, *Mental Health, United States, 2004.* Ronald W. Manderscheid, Joyce T. Berry, eds. Rockville, MD: US Department of Health and Human Services, Substance Abuse and Mental Health Services Administration, Center for Mental Health Services.

with neurotic and behavioral problems. Psychologists use such techniques as psychotherapy and counseling, which psychiatrists typically do not engage in. Psychoanalysis is a subspecialty in mental health that involves the use of intensive treatment by both psychiatrists and psychologists.

Social workers receive training in various aspects of mental health services, particularly counseling. Social workers are trained at the master's degree level. They also compete with psychologists for patients.

Nurses are involved in mental health through the subspecialty of psychiatric nursing. Specialty training for nurses had its origins in the latter part of the 1800s. Nurses provide a wide range of mental health services.

Many other health care professionals contribute to the array of available services, including marriage and family counselors, recreational therapists, and vocational counselors. Numerous people work in related areas, such as adult day care (ADC), alcohol and drug abuse counseling, and as psychiatric aides in institutional settings.

The Chronically Ill

Chronic diseases are now the leading cause of death in the United States—heart disease, cancer, and stroke account for more than 50% of deaths each year. Seven out of 10 deaths each year are from chronic diseases (Kung et al. 2008). Heart disease is the number one cause of death in the United States, at 179.1 per 100,000 persons (NCHS, 2013). The prevalence of heart disease from 2010 to 2011 was 11.6%, which is equal to 36.1 million Americans (NCHS 2013). In 2010, more than one in four adults had more than one chronic illness, roughly 80 million Americans (Ward and Schiller 2013).

This large prevalence of disease results in adverse consequences such as limitations on daily living activities. Among normal weight adults with one or more chronic illnesses it is estimated that, as a result of the number of sick or unhealthy days they experience each month, the resulting cost due to loss of productivity is more than $15 billion per year (Witters and Agrawal 2011). For overweight or obese adults with one or more chronic illnesses, this loss more than doubled to $32 billion annually. Overall, the total loss due to overweight, obesity, or other chronic illnesses is estimated at more than $153 billion each year.

The loss in human potential and work days notwithstanding, chronic disease is expensive. Chronic disease places a huge economic demand on the nation. In 2010, the estimated annual direct medical expenditures for the most common chronic diseases were more than $107 billion (AHRQ 2010). In 2008, expenditures on obesity were estimated to total $147 billion (Finkelstein et al. 2009). The estimated cost to treat diabetes in 2007 totaled over $116 billion (American Diabetes Association 2008). In addition, costs related to heart disease totaled over $475 billion in 2009 (Lloyd-Jones et al. 2009).

Much of the burden of chronic diseases is the result of four modifiable risk behaviors: physical activity, nutrition, smoking, and alcohol (CDC 2010c). Only 21% of the US population met the 2008 Physical Activity Guidelines for Americans standards for aerobic and muscle strengthening (National Center for Health Statistics 2013). There has also been a decline in participation in physical education classes among high school students, from 42% in 1991 to 31% in 2011. The nation also suffers from poor nutrition. Less than 25% of adults and children eat the required five or more servings of fruit and vegetables, although the majority consumes more than the recommended amount of saturated fat (CDC 2012b).

Disability

As of 2010, approximately 56.7 million people in the United States had a disability, of which more than 38 million were severely disabled (US Census Bureau 2012b). The prevalence of disability increases with age, with 70.5% of adults aged 80 and older having a disability (US Census Bureau 2012b). The chronic conditions most responsible for disabilities are arthritis, heart disease, back problems, asthma, and diabetes (Kraus et al. 1996). The disabled tend to receive coverage from public insurance (30% by Medicare and 10% by Medicaid), compared to those who have no disabilities and are more likely to have private health insurance (US Census Bureau 2011f).

Disability can be categorized as mental, physical, or social; tests of disability tend to be more sensitive to some categories than others. Physical disability usually addresses a person's mobility and other basic activities performed in daily life, mental disability involves both the cognitive and emotional states, and social disability is considered the most severe disability because management of social roles requires both physical and mental well-being (Ostir et al. 1999).

The two commonly used measures of disability, activities of daily living (ADLs) and instrumental activities of daily living (IADLs), were covered in Chapter 2. Another tool for assessing disability is the Survey of Income and Program Participation (SIPP), which measures disability by asking participants about functional limitations (difficulty in performing activities such as seeing, hearing, walking, having one's speech understood, etc.), but ADL and IADL scales are more widely used.

Despite the availability of community-based and institutional long-term care services for people with functional limitations, many people are not getting the help they need with the basic tasks of personal care. It is estimated that approximately one in five individuals with an ADL limitation do not receive needed assistance (Newcomer et al. 2005). Furthermore, racial minorities are more likely to experience unmet personal assistance needs (Newcomer et al. 2005).

HIV/AIDS

Figure 11–11 illustrates trends in AIDS reporting. The number of AIDS cases reported increased between 1987 and 1993, decreased between 1994 and 1999, increased between 2000 and 2004, and decreased again since 2005 (US Census Bureau 2010c).

Deaths from AIDS declined 11% between 2007 and 2008 (CDC 2010d). Declines in reported AIDS cases are ascribed to new treatments; decreasing death rates may reflect the fact that benefits from new treatments are being fully realized. Consequently, the number of people living with AIDS has continued to increase. In 2010, 487,692 people were living with AIDS; in 2001, the figure was 341,332 (CDC 2011b).

For Blacks, Hispanics, and minority women, AIDS/HIV is still a major public health concern. In 2010, males and Blacks continued to have significantly higher rates of HIV/AIDS than females and Whites (Table 11–8). Also, only among Black males is HIV a leading cause of death (CDC 2012c). In 2011, rates of AIDS cases per 100,000 people were 51.3 in the Black population, 16.2 in the Hispanic population, and 4.9 in the White population, (CDC 2012d). Blacks accounted for a rate of annual diagnoses eight times greater than the rate for whites in 2009 (CDC 2013d). Racial differences in HIV/AIDS infection probably reflect social, economic, behavioral, and other factors associated with HIV transmission risks.

Figure 11–11 US AIDS Cases Reported, 1987–2008.

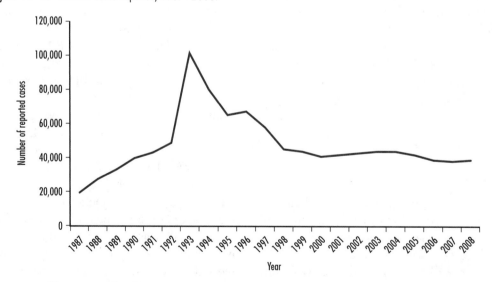

Source: Reprinted from US Centers for Disease Control and Prevention, *Statistical Abstracts of the United States, 2001,* p. 119; and *Statistical Abstracts of the United States, 2007,* p. 120; *Statistical Abstracts of the United States, 2008,* p. 121; *Statistical Abstracts of the United States, 2009,* p. 120; *Statistical Abstracts of the United States, 2010,* p. 122.; *Statistical Abstracts of the United States, 2012,* p. 125.

Table 11–8 US AIDS Cases Reported Through 2010

Characteristic	All Years		2010	
	Number	Percentage	Number	Percentage
Total	1,129,127	100.0	33,942	100.0
Sex				
Male (13 and over)	810,676	71.8	24,507	73.3
Female (13 and over)	198,544	17.6	8,242	26.6
Children under 13 years	9,209	0.8	23	0.1
Race/ethnic group				
White	429,804	38.1	8,875	26.1
Black	473,229	41.9	16,188	47.7
Hispanic	197,449	17.5	6,636	19.6
Asian	8,759	0.8	479	1.4
Native Hawaiian or other Pacific Islander	870	0.1	44	0.1
American Indian/Alaska Native	3,721	0.3	170	0.5

Source: Data from *Health, United States, 2012*, p. 140.

HIV Infection in Rural Communities

Spread of HIV in the rural United States has grown. In 2006, CDC reported 2,696 new cases of AIDS and estimated 26,154 adults and adolescents to be living with AIDS in the rural United States (CDC 2008).

Rural persons with HIV and AIDS are more likely to be young, non-White, and female and to have acquired their infection through heterosexual contact. Additionally, a growing number of these HIV-infected persons live in the rural South, a region historically characterized by a disproportionate number of poor and minority persons, strong religious beliefs and sanctions, and decreased access to comprehensive health services (CDC 1995). Trends in new cases of HIV and AIDS in rural areas indicate that poor and non-White residents are disproportionately affected (Aday 1993; Lam and Liu 1994).

HIV in Children

In the absence of specific therapy to interrupt transmission of HIV, an infected woman has a 20% chance of having a child born with HIV (Cooper et al. 2000). Building on previous success with zidovudine monotherapy in the 1990s, clinical studies established the efficacy of antiretroviral therapy on reducing the mother, 2012b to-child transmission rate when administered prenatally (Cooper 2000). Use of antiretroviral therapy resulted in a decrease of the rate of mother-to-child transmission to only 2% (Cooper 2000). Guidelines on the use of antiretroviral drugs in pregnant HIV/AIDS infected women have since been established (NIH 2012; WHO 2004). The importance of preventing perinatal transmission is underscored by the fact that 75% of all AIDS cases among US children are caused by mother-to-child transmission in pregnancy, labor, delivery, or breastfeeding (CDC 2012e). Children who are born with AIDS suffer from failure to thrive, the inability to grow and develop as healthy children. Without intervention, this failure to thrive may lead to developmental delays that can have negative lifetime consequences for the child and his or her family.

HIV in Women

Women are a rapidly growing proportion of the population with HIV/AIDS. In 2010, women made up more than one-half of HIV/AIDS cases worldwide (UNAIDS 2010). For Black US women 15 to 44 years of age and Hispanic women aged 25 to 44, HIV/AIDS was among the top 10 leading causes of death in 2010 (CDC 2013b). For women, heterosexual exposure to HIV, followed by injection drug use (IDU), is the greatest cause for exposure (US Census Bureau 2012a). Aside from the inherent risks in IDU, drug use overall contributes to a higher risk of contracting HIV if heterosexual sex with an IDU user occurs or when sex is traded for drugs or money (CDC 2013c). Black and Hispanic minority women are at particular risk. Despite representing less than one-fourth of the total US female population, Black and Hispanic

women represent more than three-fourths (79%) of all AIDS cases in women (CDC 2012c).

HIV/AIDS-Related Issues
Need for Research

HIV-related research seeks to develop a vaccine to prevent HIV-negative people from acquiring HIV. Researchers are also seeking to develop a therapeutic vaccine to prevent HIV-positive people from developing symptoms of AIDS.

People with HIV/AIDS represent a broad spectrum of social classes, races, ethnicities, sexual orientations, and genders. Behavioral intervention research, therefore, should focus particularly on populations that are most vulnerable to HIV infection and are in urgent need of preventive interventions. These populations include gay youth and young adults, especially Black and Hispanic; disenfranchised and impoverished women; heterosexual men, again, Black and Hispanic in particular; inner city youth; and out-of-treatment substance abusers and their sexual partners. Research should be aimed not only at the individual but also at the impact of broader interventions (e.g., among drug users or those involved in sexual networks or community-wide groups) that change behavioral norms and, consequently, affect individual behavior (Merson 1996).

Public Health Concerns

AIDS underscores the synergy between poverty and intravenous drug use. Further, control of the HIV epidemic among the poor is hampered by their preoccupation with other problems related to survival, such as homelessness, crime, and lack of access to adequate health care.

Additionally, a relationship exists between the current tuberculosis epidemic and HIV. Indeed, tuberculosis, an *opportunistic infection*, is the worldwide leading cause of death among HIV-infected people. Tuberculosis in HIV-infected persons is also a particular public health concern because HIV persons are at greater risk of developing multidrug-resistant tuberculosis. Multidrug-resistant tuberculosis is understandably difficult to treat and can be fatal (CDC 1999a, 1999b).

Reducing the spread of AIDS requires the understanding and acceptance of a variety of sexual issues, ranging from the likelihood that even heterosexual men may engage in anonymous homosexual intercourse to the difficulty that adolescents may have controlling their sexual urges. Prejudice against gays and lesbians is manifested as *homophobia*, a fear and/or hatred of these individuals. Homophobia explains the initial slow policy-related response to the HIV epidemic.

Unfortunately, testing for HIV may not limit its spread because many people who learn their HIV status do not change the behaviors that contribute to its spread. HIV has no cure, and current treatments do not affect the transmissibility of HIV.

Criminal law has also been used to contain the spread of HIV and to protect public health. For example, several laws nationwide require that those convicted of sex offenses be tested for HIV. Most of these laws, however, are disproportionately enforced against prostitutes. These laws suggest that those who test HIV-positive may receive greater prison sentences; however, it is questionable whether this type of punishment actually reduces the spread of HIV.

Health promotion efforts, including those used to reduce the transmission of HIV, are often hamstrung by psychosocial and other factors. For example, humans generally have difficulty changing their behaviors. Further, much human behavior is associated with functional needs (e.g., unsafe sex might fulfill a need for intimacy). The social learning theory explains that behavior change, first, requires knowledge, followed by a change of attitude or perspective.

Discrimination

HIV-positive people may experience discrimination in access to health care. The policies of various government agencies intended to help have also had a discriminatory impact on people with HIV/AIDS. For example, the Social Security Administration has not historically considered many of the HIV-related symptoms of women and IV drug users in adjudicating disability claims. Although the Department of Defense provides adequate medical care to individuals who acquire HIV in the military, recruits who test HIV-positive cannot join the military.

Provider Training

Increased knowledge about HIV and personal contact with people who have HIV have improved the attitudes of health care providers toward individuals with HIV and contributed to their willingness to care for people with HIV. Training should encompass not only medical and treatment-related information but also a range of competencies related to interpersonal skills.

In the area of psychosocial skills, the following characteristics are essential for an effectively trained provider: good communication skills (ability to establish rapport, ask questions, and listen), positive attitudes (respect, empowerment, trust), and an approach that incorporates principles of holistic care. In the area of cultural competence, essential elements include understanding of and respect for the person's specific culture; understanding that racial and ethnic minorities have important and multiple subdivisions or functional units; acknowledging the issues of gender and sexual orientation within the context of cultural competence; and respecting the customs, including modes of communication, of the person's culture. In the area of substance abuse, the following key elements are essential for primary care providers: understanding the complex medical picture presented by a person who suffers both from HIV and addiction; understanding the complicated psychosocial, ethical, and legal issues related to care of addicted persons; and being aware of the personal attitudes about addiction that may impair the providers' ability to give care objectively and nonjudgmentally (e.g., in the administration of pain medication; Gross and Larkin 1996).

Cost of HIV/AIDS

Medical care for an HIV/AIDS patient is extremely expensive. Pharmaceutical companies claim that the high prices they charge for AIDS drugs are related to their extensive investment in research and development of drugs. Medicaid covers more than 220,000 people with HIV (Kaiser Family Foundation 2013b). In fiscal year (FY) 2012, combined federal and state Medicaid spending on HIV totaled $9.6 billion, making it the largest source of public financing for HIV/AIDS care in the United States.

Of this, the federal share was $5.3 billion in FY 2012, or 55% of federal HIV care spending (Kaiser Family Foundation 2013b). Lack of insurance and underinsurance represent formidable financial barriers to HIV/AIDS care.

The US government also invests substantial amounts of money in research and development through research supported at NIH and CDC. Government programs spend money in several areas for HIV (Figure 11–12). Seventy-three percent of the cost is for antiretroviral medications, 13% for inpatient care, 9% for outpatient care, and 5% for other HIV-related medications and laboratory costs. For patients who initiate highly active antiretroviral therapy (HAART) when the CD4 cell count is 200/L, projected life expectancy is 22.5 years, discounted lifetime cost is $354,100 and undiscounted cost is $567,000 (Schackman et al. 2006). Indirect costs include lost productivity, largely because of worker morbidity and mortality. However, other factors affect cost projections associated with the HIV epidemic, including the level of employment of HIV-positive people; regional differences in the cost of care, which is often associated with the lack of subacute care in many parts of the country; and the rate at which HIV spreads.

Containment of escalating medical costs, including the coordination of medical care, is the objective of two HIV-specific efforts: the Medicaid waiver program and the Ryan White Comprehensive AIDS Resources Emergency (CARE) Act. Through the *Medicaid waiver program*, states may design packages of services to specific populations, such as the elderly, the disabled, and those who test HIV positive. At this time, it is unknown whether the program is cost effective.

Figure 11–12 US Federal Spending for HIV/AIDS by Category, FY 2011 Budget Request.

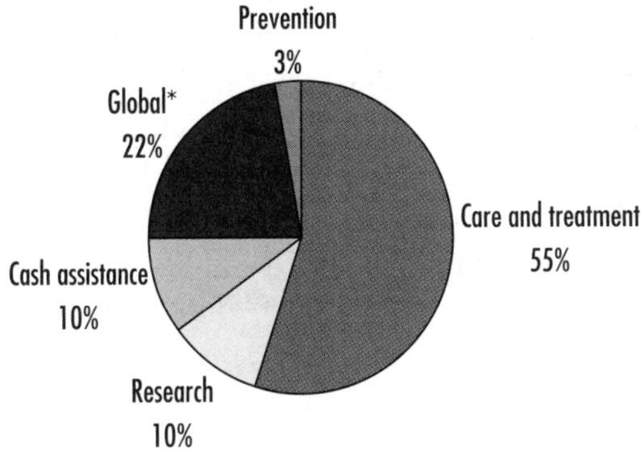

*Categories may include funding across multiple agencies/programs;
global category includes international HIV research at NIH.

Source: Adapted from Kaiser Family Foundation. US Federal Funding for HIV/AIDS: The President's FY 2011 Budget Request. HIV/AIDS Policy Fact Sheet, February 2010.

The passage of the Ryan White CARE Act in 1990 provided federal funds to develop treatment and care options for persons with HIV/AIDS (Summer 1991). Title II of this legislation is administered by states and has been used to establish HIV clinics and related services in areas lacking the resources needed to offer this specialty care. Some public health systems have used Ryan White money to provide HIV/AIDS services in rural communities in which poor or medically underserved persons lack access to adequate care. Federal spending for Ryan White was estimated to total $2.4 billion in 2012 (HRSA 2013a).

AIDS and the US Health Care System

The course of AIDS is characterized by a gradual decline in a patient's physical, cognitive, and emotional function and well-being. Such a comprehensive decline requires a continuum of care, including emergency care, primary care, housing and supervised living, mental health and social support, nonmedical services, and hospice care. The continuum can encompass elements like outreach and case finding, preventive services, outpatient and inpatient care, and coordination of private and public insurance benefits.

As HIV disease progresses, many persons become disabled and rely on public entitlement or private disability programs for income and health care benefits. These programs include Social Security Disability Income and Supplemental Security Income, administered by the Social Security Administration. Medicare and Medicaid become primary payers for health care because of the onset of disability and depletion of personal funds. Many HIV/AIDS patients are expected to gain health insurance under the ACA, which prohibits denial of health insurance because of pre-existing medical conditions.

Summary

This chapter examines the major characteristics of certain US population groups that face challenges and barriers in accessing health care services. These population groups are racial/ethnic minorities, children and women, those living in rural areas, the homeless, the migrants, the mentally ill, and those with HIV/AIDS. The health needs of these population groups are summarized, and services available to them are described. The gaps that currently exist between these population groups and the rest of the population indicate that the nation must make significant efforts to address the unique health concerns of US subpopulations.

ACA Takeaway

- The problem of the uninsured will continue to haunt the US health care system.
- The ACA requires private insurance plans to cover, with no cost sharing, a wide variety of preventive services and additional services for women, including FDA-approved prescription contraceptives, domestic violence screening, breastfeeding supports, and HPV testing.
- Many HIV/AIDS patients are expected to gain health insurance under the ACA.

Test Your Understanding

Terminology

AIDS
chronic
dependency
developmental
   vulnerability

disability
HIV
homophobia
Medicaid waiver program
mental health system

new morbidities
opportunistic infections
psychiatrists
psychologists

Review Questions

1. How can the framework of vulnerability be used to study vulnerable populations in the United States?
2. What are the racial/ethnic minority categories in the United States?
3. Compared with White Americans, what health challenges do minorities face?
4. Who are the AA/PIs?

5. What is the Indian Health Service?

6. What are the health concerns of children?

7. Which childhood characteristics have important implications for health system design?

8. Which health services are currently available for children?

9. What are the health concerns of women?

10. What are the roles of the Office on Women's Health?

11. What are the challenges faced in rural health?

12. What measures are taken to improve access to care in rural areas?

13. What are the characteristics and health concerns of the homeless population?

14. How is mental health provided in the United States?

15. Who are the major mental health professionals?

16. How does AIDS affect different population groups in the United States?

17. Which services and policies currently combat AIDS in America?

18. What is the impact of the ACA on vulnerable populations?

REFERENCES

Aday, L.A. 1993. *At risk in America: The health and health care needs of vulnerable populations in the United States*. San Francisco, CA: Jossey-Bass Publishers.

Agency for Healthcare Research and Quality. 2010. Medical expenditure panel survey. Table 3: Total expenses and percent distribution for selected conditions by type of service: United States 2010. Available at: http://meps.ahrq.gov/data_stats/tables_compendia_hh_interactive.jsp?_SERVICE=MEPSSocket0&_PROGRAM=MEPSPGM.TC.SAS&File=HCFY2010&Table=HCFY2010_CNDXP_C&_Debug=. Accessed January 2014.

American Diabetes Association. 2008. Economic costs of diabetes in the U.S. in 2007. *Diabetes Care* 31 no. 3: 1–20.

Bertakis, K.D., et al. 2000. Gender differences in the utilization of health services. *Journal of Family Practice* 49: 147–152.

Breakey, W.R., et al (1989). Health and mental health problems of homeless men and women in Baltimore. *Journal of the American Medical Association* 262 no. 10: 1352–1357.

Burks, L.J. 1992. Community health representatives: The vital link in Native American health care. *The IHS Primary Care Provider* 16, no. 12: 186–190.

Centers for Disease Control and Prevention (CDC). 1995. *Facts about women and HIV/AIDS*. Atlanta, GA: CDC.

Centers for Disease Control and Prevention (CDC). 1999a. *CDC fact sheet: Recent HIV/AIDS treatment advances and the implications for prevention*. Available at: http://www.cdc.gov/nchstp/hiv_aids/pubs/facts.htm. Accessed December 2010.

Centers for Disease Control and Prevention (CDC). 1999b. *CDC fact sheet: The deadly intersection between TB and HIV*. Available at: http://www.cdc.gov/nchstp/hiv_aids/pubs/facts.htm. Accessed December 2010.

Centers for Disease Control and Prevention (CDC). 2008. *Cases of HIV infection and AIDS in urban and rural areas of the United States, 2006.* HIV/AIDS surveillance supplemental report: 13(2). Atlanta: US Department of Health and Human Services.

Centers for Disease Control and Prevention (CDC). 2010a. Vital signs: Health insurance coverage and health care utilization, United States, 2006–2009 and January–March 2010. *Morbidity and Mortality Weekly Report* 59: 1–7.

Centers for Disease Control and Prevention (CDC). 2010b. Current depression among adults – United States, 2006 and 2008. Available at: http://www.cdc.gov/mmwr/preview/mmwrhtml /mm5938a2.htm?s_cid=mm5938a2_e%0d%0a. Accessed September 2013.

Centers for Disease Control and Prevention (CDC). 2010c. *Chronic disease and health promotion.* Available at: http://www.cdc.gov/chronicdisease/pdf/2009-Power-of-Prevention.pdf. Accessed January 2011.

Centers for Disease Control and Prevention (CDC). 2010d. Mortality slide series. Available at: http://www.cdc.gov/hiv/pdf/statistics_surveillance_HIV_mortality.pdf. Accessed September 2013.

Centers for Disease Control and Prevention (CDC). 2010e. National Center for Injury Prevention and Control (NCIP). Web-based injury statistics query and reporting system (WISQARS) . Available at: http://www.cdc.gov/injury/wisqars/index.html. Accessed September 2013

Centers for Disease Control and Prevention (CDC). 2011a. Health insurance coverage: Early release of estimates from the National Health Interview Survey, January–March 2011. Available at: http://www.cdc.gov/nchs/data/nhis/earlyrelease/insur201109.htm. Accessed September 2013.

Centers for Disease Control and Prevention (CDC). 2011b. *HIV surveillance report: diagnoses of HIV infection and AIDS in the United States and dependent areas, 2011. Vol. 23.* Atlanta, GA: US Department of Health and Human Services.

Centers for Disease Control and Prevention (CDC). 2012a. Deaths: Leading causes for 2009. *National Vital Statistics Reports* 61, no. 7.

Centers for Disease Control and Prevention (CDC). 2012b. Youth Risk Behavior Surveillance— United States, 2011. *Morbidity and Mortality Weekly Report* 61: SS–4.

Centers for Disease Control and Prevention (CDC). 2012c. HIV surveillance by race/ethnicity. Available at: http://www.cdc.gov/hiv/pdf/statistics_surveillance_raceEthnicity.pdf. Accessed September 2013.

Centers for Disease Control and Prevention (CDC). 2012d. HIV among pregnant women, infants, and children in the United States. Fact Sheet. Available at: http://www.cdc.gov/hiv/pdf/risk_WIC.pdf. Accessed September 2013.

Centers for Disease Control and Prevention (CDC). 2012e. Estimated HIV incidence among adults and adolescents in the United States, 2007-2010. *HIV Surveillance Supplemental Report 2012* 17 no. 4.

Centers for Disease Control and Prevention (CDC). 2013a. *HIV/AIDS surveillance report, 2011.* Vol. 23. Available at: http://www.cdc.gov/hiv/library/reports/ surveillance/2011/surveillance_Report_ vol_23.html. Accessed September 2013.

Centers for Disease Control and Prevention (CDC). 2013b. HIV among women. Fact Sheet. Available at: http://www.cdc.gov/hiv/pdf/risk_women.pdf. Accessed September 2013.

Centers for Disease Control and Prevention (CDC). 2013c. HIV infection among heterosexuals at increased risk – United States, 2010. *Morbidity and Mortality Weekly Report* 62 no. 10: 183–188.

Centers for Disease Control and Prevention (CDC). 2013d. Social determinants of health among adults with diagnosed HIV infection in 18 areas, 2005-2009. *HIV Surveillance Supplemental Report* 18 no. 4.

Congressional Budget Office. 2012. *Updated estimates for the insurance coverage provisions of the Affordable Care Act.* Washington, DC: Government Printing Office.

Cooper, E.R., et al. 2000. Combination antiretroviral strategies for the treatment of pregnant HIV-1–infected women and prevention of perinatal HIV-1 transmission. *Journal of Acquired Immune Deficiency Syndromes* 29, no. 5: 484–494.

Finkelstein E.A., et al. 2009. Annual medical spending attributable to obesity: Payer-and service-specific estimates. *Health Affairs* 28, no. 5: w822–w831.

General Accounting Office. 2000. Oral health: dental disease is a chronic problem among low-income populations. Report GAO/HEHS-00-72. Available at: *http://www.gao.gov/products/GAO/HEHS-00-72* Accessed January 2014.

Gift H.C., et al. 1992. The social impact of dental problems and visits. *American Journal of Public Health* 82: 1663–1668.

Gross, E.J., and M.H. Larkin. 1996. The child with HIV in day care and school. Nursing Clinics of North America 31, no. 1: 231–241.

Guttmacher Institute. 2013. Insurance coverage of contraceptives. Available at: http://www .guttmacher.org/statecenter/spibs/spib_ICC.pdf. Accessed September 2013.

Health Care for the Homeless. 2012. Client demographics. Available at: http://www.hchmd.org /demographics.shtml. Accessed September 2013.

Health Resources and Services Administration (HRSA), Maternal and Child Health Bureau. 2011. *Women's Health USA 2011*. Rockville, MD: US Department of Health and Human Services.

Health Resources and Services Administration (HRSA), Bureau of Health Professions. 2007b. Shortage designation. Available at: http://bhpr.hrsa.gov/shortage/. Accessed December 2008.

Health Resources and Services Administration (HRSA), Bureau of Health Professions. 2013a. National Health Service Corps. Available at: http://nhsc.hrsa.gov/corpsexperience/aboutus/index .html Accessed September 2013.

Health Resources and Services Administration (HRSA), Bureau of Health Professions. 2014. Shortage Designation: Health Professional Shortage Areas & Medically Underserved Areas/Populations. Available at: http://www.hrsa.gov/shortage/. Accessed January 2014.

Health Resources and Services Administration (HRSA), Bureau of Primary Health Care. 2012a. 2011 National Migrant Health Data. Available at: http://bphc.hrsa.gov/uds/view. aspx?fd=mh&year=2011. Accessed September 2013.

Health Resources and Services Administration (HRSA), National Health Service Corps. 2013. About the NHSC. Available at: http://nhsc.hrsa.gov/corpsexperience/aboutus/index.html. Accessed September 2013.

Health Resources and Services Administration (HRSA), Office of Rural Health Policy. 2007. Strategic plan 2005–2010. Available at: http://ruralhealth.hrsa.gov/policy/StrategicPlan.asp. Accessed December 2008.

Health Resources and Services Administration (HRSA), Bureau of Primary Health Care. 2012b. Special Populations. Available at: http://bphc.hrsa.gov/about/specialpopulations/. Accessed September 2013.

Health Resources and Services Administration (HRSA). 2013a. HIV/AIDS Bureau. FY2010-FY2012 appropriations by program. Available at: http://hab.hrsa.gov/data/reports/funding.html. Accessed September 2013.

Health Resources and Services Administration (HRSA). 2013b. Shortage designation: Health professional shortage areas and medically underserved areas/populations. Available at: http://www.hrsa .gov/shortage/. Accessed September 2013.

Health Resources and Services Administration (HRSA), Bureau of Health Professions. 2013b. Mental Health HPSA Designation Criteria. Available at: http://bhpr.hrsa.gov/shortage/hpsas/designationcriteria/mentalhealthhpsacriteria.html. Accessed September 2013.

Health Resources and Services Administration, Maternal and Child Health Bureau. 2005. *The National Survey of Children's Health 2003*. Rockville, MD: U.S. Department of Health and Human Services.

Herzog, D.B., and P.N. Copeland. 1985. Medical progress: Eating disorders. *New England Journal of Medicine* 313, no. 5: 295–303.

Ikeda J. 1990. *Food Habits of Farmworker Families. Tulare County. California. 1989*. Visalia, CA: Univ. Calif. Coop. Ext. Serv.

Indian Health Service (IHS). 1999a. *Fact sheet: Comprehensive health care program for American Indians and Alaskan Natives*. Washington, DC: Public Health Service.

Indian Health Service (IHS). 1999b. *A quick look*. Washington, DC: Public Health Service.

Indian Health Service (IHS). 2009. *Trends in Indian health, 2002-2003 edition*. Washington, DC: Government Printing Office.

Indian Health Service (IHS). 2010a. *Indian health disparities. IHS fact sheet*. Washington, DC: Public Health Service.

Indian Health Service (IHS). 2010b. *IHS year 2010 profile. IHS fact sheet*. Washington, DC: Public Health Service.

Indian Health Service (IHS). 2013. *Agency Overview*. Available at: http://www.ihs.gov/aboutihs/overview/. Accessed September 2013.

Institute for Children, Poverty & Homelessness. 2011. Profiles of risk: Education. Research Brief No. 2. Available at: http://www.icphusa.org/PDF/reports/ICPH_FamiliesAtRisk_No.2.pdf. Accessed September 2013.

Jasinski, J.L. 2005. The experience of violence in the lives of homeless women: A research report. Available at: https://www.ncjrs.gov/pdffiles1/nij/grants/211976.pdf. Accessed January 2014.

Kaiser Commission on Medicaid and the Uninsured (Kaiser). 2012a. *The uninsured and the difference health insurance makes*. Washington DC: Kaiser Commission on Medicaid and the Uninsured.

Kaiser Commission on Medicaid and the Uninsured (Kaiser). 2012b. *The uninsured: A primer*. Washington, DC: Kaiser Commission on Medicaid and the Uninsured.

Kaiser Family Foundation. 2005. Migrant and seasonal farmworkers: Health insurance coverage and access to care. Available at: http://kaiserfamilyfoundation.files.wordpress.com/2013/01/migrant-and-seasonal-farmworkers-health-insurance-coverage-and-access-to-care-report.pdf. Accessed September 2013.

Kaiser Family Foundation. 2013a. Health reform: Implications for women's access to coverage and care. Available at: http://kaiserfamilyfoundation.files.wordpress.com/2012/03/7987-03-health-reform-implications-for-women_s-access-to-coverage-and-care.pdf. Accessed September 2013.

Kaiser Family Foundation. 2013b. Medicaid enrollment and spending on HIV. Available at: http://kff.org/hivaids/state-indicator/enrollment-spending-on-hiv-fy2009/#notes. Accessed September 2013.

Kaiser Family Foundation. 2013c. Mental health care health profession shortage areas (HPSAs). Available at: http://kff.org/other/state-indicator/mental-health-care-health-professional-shortage-areas-hpsas/. Accessed September 2013.

Kerker, B.D., et al. 2011. A population-based assessment of the health of homeless families in New York City, 2001–2003. *American Journal of Public Health* 101, no. 3: 546–553.

Kessler, R.C., et al. 2005. Prevelance, severity, and comorbidity of twelve-month DSM-IV disorders in the National Comorbidity Survey Replication (NCS-R). *Archives of General Psychiatry* 62, no. 6: 617–627.

Kraus, L.E., et al. 1996. *Chartbook on disability in the United States, 1996. An InfoUse Report.* Washington, DC: US National Institute on Disability and Rehabilitation Research.

Kung, H.C., et al. 2008. Deaths: Final data for 2005. *National Vital Statistics Reports.* 56, no. 10.

Lam, N., and K. Liu. 1994. Spread of AIDS in rural America, 1982–1990 *Journal of Acquired Immune Deficiency Syndrome* 7, no. 5: 485–490.

Larson, A., and Plascencia, L. 1993. *Migrant enumeration study.* Washington, DC: Office of Minority Health.

Larson, S. L., & Fleishman, J. A. (2003). Rural-urban differences in usual source of care and ambulatory service use: Analyses of national data using Urban Influence Codes. *Medical care*, III65–III74.

Lloyd-Jones, D., et al. 2009. American Heart Association Statistics Committee and Stroke Statistics Subcommittee. Heart disease and stroke statistics–2009 update: A report from the American Heart Association Statistics Committee and Stroke Statistics Subcommittee. *Circulation* 119: e21–181.

McCurdy S.A., et al. 1997. Tuberculin reactivity among California Hispanic migrant farm workers. *American Journal of Industrial Medicine* 32, no. 6: 600–505

McGrath, J., et al. 2008. Schizophrenia: A concise overview of incidence, prevalence, and mortality. *Epidemiologic Review,* no. 1: 67–76.

McLean, C.P., et al. 2011. Gender differences in anxiety disorders: Prevalence, course of illness, comorbidity and burden of illness, *Journal of Psychiatric Research* 45, no. 8: 1027–1035.

Merson, M.H. 1996. Returning home: Reflections on the USA's response to the HIV/AIDS epidemic. *Lancet* 347, no. 9016: 1673–1676.

Migrant Health Promotion. 2013. Farmworkers in the United States. Available at: http://www.migranthealth.org/index.php?option=com_content&view=article&id=38&Itemid=30. Accessed September 2013.

Misra, D. ed. 2001. *Women's health data book: A profile of women's health in the United States*, 3rd ed. Washington, DC: Jacobs Institute of Women's Health and the Henry J. Kaiser Family Foundation.

Nardin, R., et al. 2013. The uninsured after implementation of the Affordable Care Act: A demographic and geographic analysis. Health Affairs Blog. Available at: http://healthaffairs.org/blog/2013/06/06/the-uninsured-after-implementation-of-the-affordable-care-act-a-demographic-and-geographic-analysis/. Accessed September 2013.

National Alliance to End Homelessness. 2012. The state of homelessness in America 2012. Homelessness Research Institute. Available at: http://b.3cdn.net/naeh/9892745b6de8a5ef59 _q2m6yc53b.pdf. Accessed September 2013.

National Association of Rural Health Clinics (NARHC). 2007. About. Available at: http://narhc.org/?page_id=1410. Accessed January 2014.

National Center for Health Statistics (NCHS). 2013. *Health, United States, 2012.* Hyattsville, MD: Department of Health and Human Services.

National Institute of Health (NIH). 2002. *News release: NHLBI stops trial of estrogen plus progestin due to increased breast cancer risk, lack of overall benefit.* Available at: http://www.nhlbi.nih.gov/new/press/02-07-09.htm. Accessed December 2006.

National Institute of Health (NIH). 2012. Guidelines for the use of antiretroviral agents in HIV-1-infected adults and adolescents. Department of Health and Human Services. Available at: http://aidsinfo.nih.gov/contentfiles/lvguidelines/AdultandAdolescentGL.pdf. Accessed September 2013.

National Women's Law Center. 2011. Closing the wage gap is especially important for women of color in difficult times. Available at: http://www.nwlc.org/resource/closing-wage-gap-especial-lyimportant-women-color-difficult-times. Accessed September 2013.

Newcomer, R., Kang, T., LaPlante, M., & Kaye, S. (2005). Living quarters and unmet need for personal care assistance among adults with disabilities. *The Journals of Gerontology Series B: Psychological Sciences and Social Sciences* 9, no. 4: S205–S213.

O'Neill, J.E. and D.M. O'Neill. 2009. *Who are the uninsured? An analysis of America's uninsured population, their characteristics and their health.* New York, NY: Employment Policies Institute.

Organista K.C., and P.B. Organista. 1997. Migrant laborers and AIDS in the United States: A review of the literature. *AIDS Education and Prevention* 9, no.1: 83–93.

Ostir, G.V., et al. 1999. Disability in older adults 1: Prevalence, causes, and consequences. *Behavioral Medicine* 24: 147–154.

Patton, L., and D. Puskin. 1990. *Ensuring access to health care services in rural areas: A half century of federal policy.* Washington, DC: Essential Health Care Services Conference Center at Georgetown University Conference Center.

Regier, D.A., et al. 1988. One month prevalence of mental disorders in the United States: Based on five epidemiologic catchment area sites. *Archives of General Psychiatry* 45, no. 11: 977–986.

Reigier, D.A., Narrow, W.E., and Rae, D.S. 1993. The de facto mental and addictive disorders service system. Epidemiologic catchment area prospective 1-year prevalence rates of disorders and services. *Archives of General Psychiatry* 50, no. 2: 85–94.

Rust, G.S. (1990). Health status of migrant farmworkers: A literature review and commentary. *American Journal of Public Health* 80, no. 10: 1213–1217.

Salganicoff, A., et al. 2005. *Women and health care: A national profile.* Menlo Park, CA: The Henry J. Kaiser Family Foundation.

Schackman, B.R., et al. 2006. The lifetime cost of current human immunodeficiency virus care in the United States. *Medical Care* 44, no. 11: 990–997.

Schutt, R.K., and S.M. Goldfinger. 1996. Housing preferences and perceptions of health and functioning among homeless mentally ill persons. *Psychiatric Services* 47, no. 4: 381–386.

Sechzer, J.A., et al. 1996. Women and mental health. New York: *Academy of Sciences.*

Sheller, B., et al. 1997. Diagnosis and treatment of dental caries-related emergences in a children's hospital. *Pediatric Dentistry* 19: 470–475.

Shi, L., and G. Stevens. 2010. *Vulnerable Populations in the United States.* 2nd ed. San Francisco, CA: Jossey-Bass Publishers, Inc.

Shortell, S.M., et al. 1996. *Remaking health care in America.* San Francisco, CA: Jossey-Bass Publishers.

Solis, J.M., et al. 1990. Acculturation, access to care, and use of preventive services by Hispanics: Findings from HHANES 1982–84. *American Journal of Public Health* 80 (Suppl): 11–19.

Substance Abuse and Mental Health Services Administration (SAMHSA). 2012a. *Mental Health, United States, 2010. HHS Publication No. (SMA) 12-4681.* Rockville, MD: Substance Abuse and Mental Health Services Administration.

Substance Abuse and Mental Health Services Administration (SAMHSA). 2012b. *Results from the 2011 National Survey on Drug Use and Health: Mental health findings,* NSDUH Series H-45, HHS Publication No. (SMA) 12-4725. Rockville, MD: Substance Abuse and Mental Health Services Administration.

Summer, L. 1991. *Limited access: Health care for the rural poor.* Washington, DC: Center on Budget and Policy Priorities.

The National Law Center on Homelessness and Poverty. 2004. *Homelessness in the United States and the Human Right to Housing*. Available at: http://www.nlchp.org/content/ pubs/homelessnessin-theusandrightstohousing.pdf. Accessed September 2013.

The United States Conference of Mayors. 2011. Hunger and Homelessness Survey. Available at: http://usmayors.org/pressreleases/uploads/2011-hhreport.pdf. Accessed September 2013.

UNAIDS. 2010. *UNAIDS report on the global AIDS epidemic 2010*. Available at: http://www .unaids.org/globalreport/Global_report.htm. Accessed December 2010.

United Nations (UN). 2013. *The state of the world's children 2013*. Available at: http://www.unicef. org/sowc2013/report.html. Accessed September 2013.

US Bureau of Labor Statistics (BLS). 2012. *Labor force characteristics by race and ethnicity*, 2011. Washington, DC: Government Printing Office.

US Census Bureau. 2009. *The 2010 census questionnaire: Informational copy*. Available at: http://2010. census.gov/2010census/pdf/2010_Questionnaire_Info_Copy.pdf. Accessed April 2009.

US Census Bureau. 2010a. *2010 Census. Profile of general population and housing characteristics*. Washington, DC: Government Printing Office.

US Census Bureau. 2010b. *Current population survey, 2010 annual social and economic supplement*. Washington, DC: Government Printing Office.

US Census Bureau. 2010c. *2007–2009 American Community Survey, 3-year estimates*. Washington, DC: Government Printing Office.

US Census Bureau. 2011a. *Overview of race and hispanic origin: 2010*. Washington, DC: Government Printing Office.

US Census Bureau. 2011b. *The Hispanic population: 2010. 2010 Census Briefs*. Washington, DC: Government Printing Office.

US Census Bureau. 2011c. *Income, poverty, and health insurance coverage in the United States: 2010*. Washington, DC: Government Printing Office.

US Census Bureau. 2011d. *The American Indian and Alaska Native population: 2010. 2010 Census Briefs*. Washington, DC: Government Printing Office.

US Census Bureau. 2011e. *Current population survey annual social and economic supplements*. Washington, DC: Government Printing Office.

US Census Bureau. 2011f. American Community Survey, American FactFinder, Table B18135. Available at: http://factfinder2.census.gov. Accessed September 2013.

US Census Bureau. 2012a. *Statistical Abstract of the United States: 2012*. Washington, DC: Government Printing Office.

US Census Bureau. 2012b. Americans with disabilities: 2010. Household economic studies. *Current Population Reports*. Available at: http://www.census.gov/prod/2012pubs/p70-131.pdf. Accessed September 2013.

US Department of Health and Human Services. 2001. *Mental health: Culture, race, and ethnicity—A supplement to mental health: A report of the Surgeon General*. Rockville, MD: U.S. Department of Health and Human Services, Substance Abuse and Mental Health Services Administration, Center for Mental Health Services.

US Department of Housing and Urban Development (HUD). 2012. *The 2011 Annual Homeless Assessment Report to Congress*. Available at: https://www.onecpd.info/resources/documents/2011AHAR_ FinalReport.pdf. Accessed September 2013.

US Department of Labor. 2011. *Changing characteristics of US farm workers: 21 years of findings from the National Agricultural Workers Survey*. Available at: http://migrationfiles.ucdavis .edu/uploads/cf/files/2011-may/carroll-changing-characteristics.pdf. Accessed September 2013.

US Department of Veteran Affairs. 2006. *Fact sheet: VA programs for homeless veterans*. Available at: http://www1.va.gov/opa/fact/hmlssfs.asp. Accessed December 2008.

US Public Health Service. 2000. *Report of the Surgeon General's Conference on Children's Mental Health: A National Action Agenda.* Washington, DC: Department of Health and Human Services.

Villarejo, D., et al. 2000. *Suffering in silence: A report on the health of California's agricultural workers*. Davis, CA: Calif. Inst. Rural Study, Calif. Endow.

Villarino, M.E., et al. 1994. Purified protein derivative tuberculin and delayed-type hypersensitivity skin testing in migrant farm workers at risk for tuberculosis and HIV coinfection. *AIDS* 8, no. 4:477–481.

Ward, B.W., and J.S. Schiller. 2013. *Prevalence of multiple chronic conditions among US adults: Estimates from the National Health Interview Survey, 2010.* Available at: http://www.cdc.gov/pcd/issues/2013/12_0203.htm. Accessed September 2013.

Wenzel, M. 1996. A school-based clinic for elementary school in Phoenix, Arizona. *Journal of School Health* 66, no. 4: 125–127.

Witters, D., and S. Agrawal. 2011. Unhealthy US worker's absenteeism costs $153 billion. Available at: http://www.gallup.com/poll/150026/unhealthy-workers-absenteeism-costs-153-billion.aspx. Accessed January 2014.

World Health Organization (WHO). 2012. Years lived with disability (YLDs) for 1160 sequelae of 289 diseases and injuries 1990-2010: A systematic analysis for the Global Burden of Disease Study 2010. *Lancet* 380: 2163–2196.

World Health Organization (WHO). 2004. Antiretroviral drugs for treating pregnant women and preventing HIV infection in infants. Guidelines on care, treatment and support for women living with HIV/AIDS and their children in resource-constrained settings. Available at: http://www.who.int/hiv/pub/mtct/en/arvdrugswomenguidelinesfinal.pdf. Accessed September 2013.

Yu, S.M., et al. 2004. Health status and health services utilization among US Chinese, Asian Indian, Filipino, and other Asian/Pacific Islander children. *Pediatrics* 113, no. 1 part 1: 101–107.

PART IV

System Outcomes

Chapter 12

Cost, Access, and Quality

Learning Objectives

- To understand the meaning of health care costs and review recent trends
- To examine the factors that have led to cost escalations in the past
- To become familiar with both regulatory and market-oriented approaches to contain costs
- To understand why some regulatory cost-containment approaches were unsuccessful
- To appreciate the framework and various dimensions of access to care
- To learn about access indicators and measurement
- To understand the nature, scope, and dimensions of quality
- To understand the difference between quality assurance and quality assessment
- To discuss the implications of the Affordable Care Act on cost, access, and quality

The health care sector of the economy is like a monster with a voracious appetite that needs to be controlled.

Introduction

Cost, access, and quality are three major cornerstones of health care delivery. For many years, employers and third-party payers in the United States have been preoccupied with controlling the growth of health care expenditures. Cost and access go hand in hand, meaning expansion of access will increase health care expenditures. This is one main reason that attempts to implement universal coverage in the United States have failed in the past and why it remains difficult even in the post-ACA era. Although cost and access have remained the primary concerns within the US health care delivery system, quality of health care has taken center stage in recent years. Cost, access, and quality are interrelated.

From a macro perspective, costs of health care are commonly viewed in terms of national health expenditures (NHE). As pointed out in Chapter 6, a widely used measure of NHE is the proportion of the gross domestic product (GDP) a country spends on the delivery of health care services. From a micro perspective, health care expenditures refer to costs incurred by employers to purchase health insurance and out-of-pocket costs incurred by individuals when they receive health care services. Improving access to health care and equal access to quality health care are contingent on expenditures at both the macro and micro levels.

High-quality care is also the most cost-effective care. Hence, cost is an important factor in the evaluation of quality. On the other hand, quality is achieved by having up-to-date capabilities, using evidence-based processes, and measuring *outcomes*. Quality goals are accomplished when the system capabilities and practices employed in the delivery of health care achieve desirable outcomes for individuals and populations.

This chapter discusses the major reasons for the dramatic rise in health care expenditures. Costs are compared with those in other countries, and the impact of cost-containment measures is examined. Dimensions of access are presented. Finally, quality of care and its measurement are discussed.

Cost of Health Care

The term "cost" can carry different meanings in the delivery of health care, depending on whose perspective is considered. (1) When consumers and financiers speak of the "cost" of health care, they usually mean the "price" of health care. This could refer to the physician's bill, the price of a prescription, or the cost of health insurance premiums. (2) From a national perspective, health care costs refer to how much a nation spends on health care, that is, NHE or health care spending. Since expenditures (E) equal price (P) times quantity (Q), growth in health care spending can be accounted for by growth in prices charged by the providers of health services and by increases in the utilization of services. (3) A third perspective is that of the providers, for whom the notion of cost refers to the cost of producing health care services. Such things as staff salaries, capital costs for buildings and equipment, rental of space, and purchase of supplies are included in the cost of production.

Trends in National Health Expenditures

Chapter 6 gave an overview of national and personal health expenditures, their composition, and the proportional share between the private and public sectors. Health care spending spiraled upward at double-digit rates during the 1970s, right after the Medicare and Medicaid programs created a massive growth in access in 1965. By 1970, government expenditures for health care services and supplies had grown by 140%, from $7.9 to $18.9 billion (DHHS 1996). During much of the 1980s, average annual growth in national health spending continued in the double digits, but the rate of increase slowed considerably (Figure 12–1). In the 1990s, medical inflation was finally brought under control, down to a single-digit rate of growth, mainly due to control over payment and utilization through managed care. The rate of growth has again started to accelerate, but at a relatively slow pace (Table 12–1).

Trends in NHE are commonly evaluated in three ways. One is to compare medical inflation to general inflation in the economy, which is measured by annual changes in the consumer price index (CPI). Except for a brief period between 1978 and 1981, when the US economy was experiencing hyperinflation, the rates of change in medical inflation have remained consistently above the rates of change in the CPI (Figure 12–2). The second method compares changes in NHE to those in the GDP. With only isolated exceptions, health care spending growth rates have consistently surpassed growth rates in the general economy (Figure 12–3). When spending on health care grows at a faster rate than GDP, it means that health care consumes a larger share of the total economic output. Put another way, a growing share of

Figure 12–1 Average Annual Percentage Growth in US National Health Care Spending During 5-Year Periods, 1960–2010.

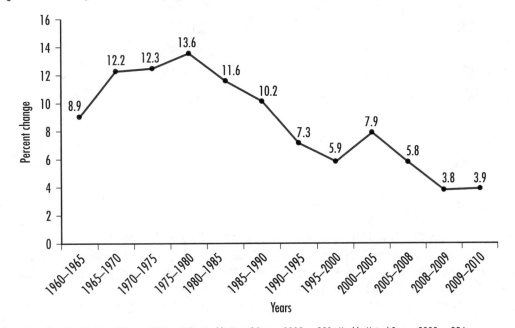

Source: Data from *Health, United States, 1995*, p. 244; *Health, United States, 2002*, p. 291; *Health, United States, 2009*, p. 396; *Health, United States, 2012*, p. 323; Department of Health and Human Services.

Table 12–1 Average Annual Percentage Increase in US National Health Care Spending, 1975–2010

Periods	% Increase	Periods	% Increase
1975–1980	13.6	1995–2000	5.9
1975–1976	14.7	1995–1996	4.6
1976–1977	13.7	1996–1997	4.7
1977–1978	11.9	1997–1998	5.4
1978–1979	12.9	1998–1999	5.7
1979–1980	14.8	1999–2000	6.9
1980–1985	11.6	2000–2005	7.9
1980–1981	16.1	2000–2001	8.7
1981–1982	12.5	2001–2002	9.3
1982–1983	10.0	2002–2003	8.2
1983–1984	9.7	2003–2004	5.9
1984–1985	9.9	2004–2005	6.5
1985–1990	10.2	2005–2010	
1985–1986	7.6	2005–2006	6.7
1986–1987	8.5	2006–2007	6.1
1987–1988	11.9	2007–2008	4.7
1988–1989	11.2	2008–2009	3.8
1989–1990	12.1	2009–2010	3.9
1990–1995	7.3		
1990–1991	9.2		
1991–1992	9.5		
1992–1993	6.9		
1993–1994	5.1		
1994–1995	4.9		

Source: Data from *Health, United States, 1995*, p. 243; *Health, United States, 1996–97*, p. 249; *Health, United States, 1999*, p. 284; *Health, United States, 2000*, p. 322; *Health, United States, 2002*, p. 288; *Health, United States, 2005*, p. 363; *Health, United States, 2006*, p. 377; *Health, United States, 2008*, p. 415; *Health, United States, 2009*, p. 396; *Health, United States, 2011*, p. 374; *Health, United States, 2012*, p. 323; K. Levit et al. Trends in US health care spending, 2003. *Health Affairs* Vol. 22, no. 1: 154–164.

Figure 12–2 Annual Percentage Change in CPI and Medical Inflation, 1975–2011.

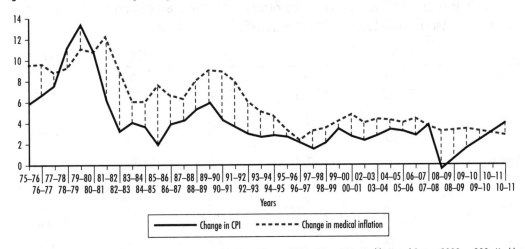

Source: Data from *Health, United States, 1995,* p. 241; *Health, United States, 1996–97,* p. 251; *Health, United States, 2002,* p. 289; *Health, United States, 2006,* p. 375; *Health, United States, 2008,* p. 413; *Health, United States, 2009,* p. 394; *Health, United States, 2010,* p. 367; *Health, United States, 2011,* p. 371; *Health, United States, 2012,* p. 321.

Figure 12–3 Annual Percentage Change in US National Health Care Expenditures and GDP, 1980–2010.

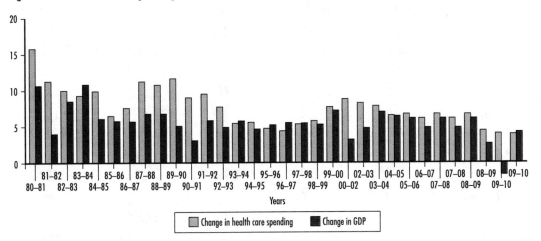

Source: Data from *Health, United States, 1996–97,* p. 249; *Health, United States, 2002,* p. 288; *Health, United States, 2006,* p. 374; *Health, United States, 2008,* p. 412; *Health, United States, 2009,* p. 393; *Health, United States, 2010,* p. 366; *Health, United States, 2011,* p. 370; *Health, United States, 2012,* p. 320.

Table 12–2 Total US Health Care Expenditures as a Proportion of GDP and Per Capita Health Care Expenditures (Selected Years, Selected OECD Countries; Per Capita Expenditures in US Dollars)

	1990	1995	2000	2005	2009
Australia	7.8	8.2	9.0	8.8	–
	$1,307	$1,745	$2,220	$2,999	–
Austria	7.0	8.0	7.6	10.3	11.0
	$1,338	$1,870	$2,184	$3,507	$4,289
Belgium	7.4	8.4	8.7	10.6	10.9
	$1,345	$1,820	$2,279	$3,385	$3,946
Canada	9.0	9.2	8.9	9.9	11.4
	$1,737	$2,051	$2,503	$3,460	$4,363
Denmark	8.5	8.2	8.4	9.5	11.5
	$1,567	$1,848	$2,382	$3,179	$4,348
Finland	7.8	7.5	6.7	8.3	9.2
	$1,422	$1,433	$1,718	$2,523	$3,226
France	8.6	9.5	9.3	11.1	11.8
	$1,568	$2,033	$2,456	$3,306	$3,978
Germany	8.5	10.6	10.6	10.7	11.6
	$1,748	$2,276	$2,761	$3,251	$4,218
Italy	7.9	7.3	8.1	8.9	9.5
	$1,391	$1,535	$2,049	$2,496	$3,137
Japan	5.9	6.8	7.6	8.2	–
	$1,115	$1,538	$1,971	$2,474	–
Netherlands	8.0	8.4	8.3	9.5*	12.0
	$1,438	$1,826	$2,259	$3,156*	$4,914
Sweden	8.4	8.1	8.4	9.2	10.0
	$1,579	$1,738	$2,273	$3,012	$3,722
United Kingdom	6.0	7.0	7.3	8.2	9.8
	$986	$1,374	$1,833	$2,580	$3,487
United States	11.9	13.3	13.1	15.2	17.4
	$2,738	$3,654	$4,539	$6,347	$7,960

*Data from 2004

Source: Data from *Health, United States, 2009*, p. 392; *Health, United States, 2011*, p. 369.

total economic resources is devoted to the delivery of health care.

International comparison is the third method. Compared to other nations, the United States uses a larger share of its economic resources for health care (Table 12–2). In addition, the United States has outpaced the growth in health care spending in other countries (Figure 12–4). Numerous reasons have been given for the growth of health care expenditures, and several initiatives have been employed over the years to prevent out-of-control spending. These topics are subsequently discussed in this chapter.

The rate of growth in health spending came down to its lowest level in 4 decades (5.7% average annual growth) between 1993

and 2000 as managed care proliferated, but the good news ended as the year 2002 recorded the fastest annual growth (9.3%) since 1992. However, the rate of growth has been slowing down each year (see Table 12–1). In 2010, the rate of growth slowed down to 3.9% over 2009. This decrease is largely attributed to the most severe recession the nation has experienced since 1933. As a result, personal health care expenditures that are paid mostly by private sources increased just 2.8%, the lowest rate since the 1990s, when managed care implemented tight cost control measures (Hartman et al. 2011). The ACA will be a major factor in determining future growth of health care expenditures. Higher utilization of health

Figure 12–4 US Health Care Spending as a Percentage of GDP for Selected OECD Countries, 1985 and 2009.

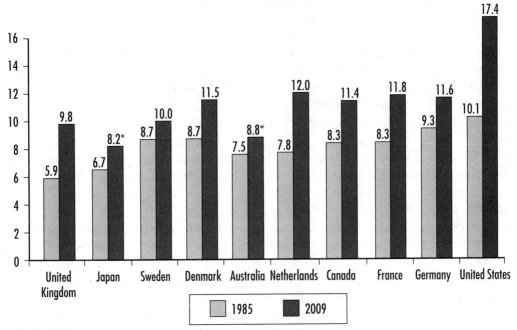

*Data for 2005.

Source: Data from *Health, United States, 2002*, p. 287; *Health, United States, 2011*, p. 368.

care services will no doubt lead to medical care cost inflation unless measures are employed to slow down the rise in P and Q.

In 2010, health care spending in the United States was $2.59 trillion, or 17.9% of GDP (DHHS 2013). According to the Congressional Budget Office, if present trends continue, health care spending will amount to 25% of GDP by 2025, 37% by 2050, and 49% by 2082 (CBO 2007). These forecasts portend that the health care sector will remain one of the fastest growing components of the US economy.

Should Health Care Costs Be Contained?

Americans view growth in expenditures in other sectors of the economy, such as manufacturing, much more favorably than expenditures on medical care. Increased medical expenditures create new health care jobs, do not pollute the air, save rather than destroy lives, and alleviate pain and suffering. Why shouldn't society be pleased that more resources are flowing into a sector that cares for the aged and the sick? It would seem to be a more appropriate use of a society's resources than spending those same funds on faster cars, fancy clothes, or other consumable items. Yet, increased expenditures for these other consumable items do not cause the concern that arises when medical expenditures increase (Feldstein 1994).

Unlike other goods and services in the economy, health care is not delivered under free market conditions (see Chapter 1). For the consumption of various other goods and services, the free market determines how much people and the nation should spend, depending on their economic capabilities. In the United States, the private sector and the government share roughly equally in the financing of health care. In a quasi-market, such as

health care in the United States, it would be almost impossible to determine how much the nation should spend. Hence, in the United States, we depend on three main sources to assess whether we spend too much:

1. The first source is international comparisons (Table 12–2), which is actually not an unbiased tool because, in these other nations, the government decides how much should be spent on health care and various rationing measures—such as supply-side controls, comparatively little spending on developing new technology, and price controls (for pharmaceuticals, for example)—are used to maintain certain levels of predetermined spending.

2. The second source is the rise in health insurance premiums in the private sector. This is what triggered private employers to abandon traditional fee-for-service insurance plans, sometime in the 1980s, and to seek employee coverage through HMO plans.

3. How much the government has to spend on health care for beneficiaries who receive health care through various public insurance programs is the third source. Concerns about the short- and long-term sustainability of the Medicare trust funds were discussed in Chapter 6.

Experts generally agree that the United States spends too much on health care, and, therefore, expenditures must be controlled. The main reasons are as follows:

1. Rising health care costs consume greater portions of the total economic output. Because economic resources

are limited, rising health care costs mean that Americans have to forgo other goods and services when more is spent on health care.

2. Limited economic resources should be directed to their highest valued uses. In a free market, consumers make purchasing decisions based on their perception of value, knowing that an expenditure on one good means forgoing other goods and services (Feldstein 1994). In health care delivery, comprehensive health insurance creates moral hazard and provider-induced demand (discussed in Chapter 1), both of which fuel inefficiencies in the consumption of resources.

3. American businesses argue that rising insurance premium costs have to be passed on to consumers in the form of higher prices, which may interfere with the ability of businesses to stay globally competitive. For example, health insurance premiums have consistently increased faster than inflation in the general economy or workers' wages in recent years. Between 1999 and 2008, the cumulative growth in health insurance premiums was 119%, whereas cumulative inflation was 29% and cumulative wage growth was 34% (Kaiser Family Foundation 2009).

4. Rising premium costs limit the ability of many employers, especially small businesses, to offer health benefits, and, when those benefits are offered, they limit the ability of some employees to contribute toward the purchase of employer-sponsored insurance coverage (Kaiser Family Foundation 2010).

5. Rising health care costs take a toll on average- and low-income Americans. The 2010 Commonwealth Fund International Health Policy Survey pointed out that affordability of health care was one of the biggest economic problems for many Americans (Health Council of Canada 2010). Only 25% of Americans were very confident in their ability to afford care in case of serious illness. Twenty-two percent of Americans (compared to an average of 8% in other countries) had a medical problem but did not visit a doctor because of cost.

6. The government has only limited ability to raise people's taxes, given that most American tax payers believe that they already pay more than their fair share of taxes. Paradoxically, as has been widely reported, half of Americans, many of whom use tax-financed health care, pay no federal income taxes (*USA Today* 2010).

Reasons for Cost Escalation

Numerous factors have been attributed to rising health care expenditures. They interact in complex ways. Hence, one cannot just point to one or two main causes. General inflation in the economy is a more visible cause of health care spending because it affects the cost of producing health care services through such things as higher wages and cost of supplies. Some of the other factors mentioned subsequently were also discussed in earlier chapters. They are

included here, along with additional pertinent details, to provide a comprehensive
picture of the reasons behind medical cost
inflation:

- Third-party payment
- Imperfect market
- Growth of technology
- Increase in elderly population
- Medical model of health care delivery
- Multipayer system and administrative costs
- Defensive medicine
- Waste and abuse
- Practice variations

Third-Party Payment

Health care is among the few services
for which a third party, not the consumer,
pays for most services used. Whether payment is made by the government or by a
private insurance company, individual
out-of-pocket expenses are far lower than
the actual cost of the service (Altman and
Wallack 1996). Hence, patients are generally insensitive to the cost of care. Introduction of prospective payment methods
and capitation has, to a large extent, minimized provider-induced demand. However, the backlash against managed care
(see Chapter 9) from consumers and providers alike has, in a sense, kept the door
open to the overuse of high-cost technologies and other services. Also, fee-for-
service reimbursement and its discounted
fee variation are still widely used in the
outpatient sector of health care delivery.
Hence, provider-induced demand has not
been expunged from the system.

Imperfect Market

Prices charged by providers for health care
services are likely to be much closer to the
cost of producing the services in a highly
regulated or highly competitive market
(Altman and Wallack 1996). Because the
US health care delivery system follows
neither the highly regulated single-payer
model nor a free market model, utilization
remains largely unchecked; prices charged
for health care services remain higher than
the true economic costs of production (Altman and Wallack 1996). A quasi-market
results in increased health care expenditures
because both Q and P remain unchecked.

Growth of Technology

The United States has been characterized as
following an early-start-fast-growth pattern
in the adoption and diffusion of intensive
procedures (TECH Research Network 2001).
Factors that drive technology innovation, diffusion, and utilization and their impact on
cost escalation were discussed in Chapter 5.
The use of advanced imaging scanning during visits to physician offices and outpatient
departments more than tripled from 1996 to
2007 (NCHS 2010a). Medicare Part B spending for imaging services under the physician
fee schedule more than doubled between
2000 and 2006, from $6.9 billion to $14.1
billion (US GAO 2008).

New technology is expensive to
develop, and costs incurred in research and
development (R&D) are included in total
health care expenditures. One reason Canada and European nations, compared to the
United States, have incurred lower costs is
that they have proportionally invested far
less in R&D.

Increase in Elderly Population

Since the early part of the 20th century, life expectancy in the United States has consistently risen (see Figure 12–5). Life expectancy at birth increased by over 30 years, from 47.3 years in 1900 to 81.0 years in 2010 (DHHS 2013). Consequently, the United States—and other industrialized nations as well—is experiencing an aging boom. Growth in the US elderly population has outpaced growth in the nonelderly population since 1900. Figure 12–6 shows changes in the makeup of the US population from 1970 to 2011. Most remarkable is the growth in the 85-and-older group, whereas

the youngest age group is shrinking. Growth of the elderly population is projected to continue through the middle of the 21st century. Between 2000 and 2030, the proportion of the US population 65 years of age and older is expected to rise from 12.4% to 20%, that is, 1 in 5 Americans will be elderly in 2030. The number in the 85-and-older category is projected to more than double.

Elderly people consume more health care than younger people. In 2009, the average medical expenses for people 65 and older were $10,082 per person, compared to $3,931 per person for those under 65 (DHHS 2013). In other words, health care costs for the elderly are 2.6 times more than those for

Figure 12–5 Life Expectancy of Americans at Birth, Age 65, and Age 75, Selected Years, 1900–2010.

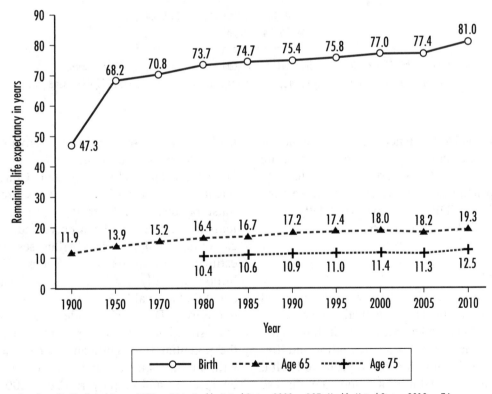

Source: Data from *Health, United States, 2002,* p. 116; *Health, United States, 2009,* p. 187; *Health, United States, 2012,* p. 76.

Figure 12–6   Change in US Population Mix Between 1970 and 2011, and Projections for 2030.

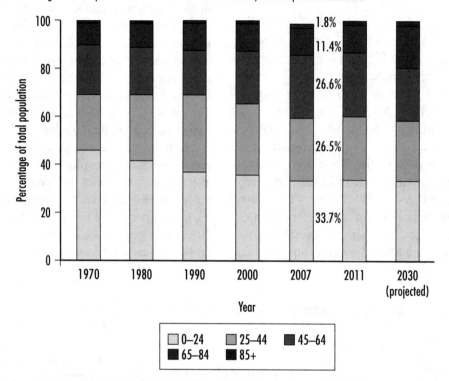

Source: Data from *Health, United States, 2012,* p. 45; National Center for Health Statistics; *Census 2000,* US Census Bureau; *Projections of the Total Resident Population by 5-Year Age Groups, and Sex with Special Age Categories: Middle Series, 2025 to 2045,* US Census Bureau.

the nonelderly. Hence, health care expenditures are sure to rise unless drastic steps are taken to curtail spending. Total Medicare expenditures are projected to increase from 2.7% of GDP in 2005 to 9% of GDP in 2050 (Van de Water and Lavery 2006).

Medical Model of Health Care Delivery

As discussed in Chapter 2, the medical model emphasizes medical interventions after a person has become sick. It does not put equal emphasis on prevention and lifestyle behavior changes to promote health. Although health promotion and disease prevention are not the answer to every health problem, these principles have not been accorded their rightful place in the US health care delivery system. Consequently, more costly health care resources must be deployed to treat health problems that could have been prevented. For example, smoking-related illnesses are estimated to cost the United States $75.5 billion annually for direct medical care and an additional $167 billion in lost productivity (CDC 2005). Evidence suggests that smoking cessation programs have the potential for significant cost savings without imposing an undue cost burden on insurers and employers (Levy 2006). Although the prevalence of cigarette smoking has been slowly declining, in 2007, 22.3% of American adult males and 17.4% of women still smoked (NCHS 2010b).

Overweight conditions and obesity have reached alarming rates in the United States and in many other developed nations. It is estimated that 68.5% of Americans age 20 and over are overweight, of which 35.3% are obese (DHHS 2013). Overweight and obesity substantially elevate the risk of heart disease, diabetes, some types of cancers, musculoskeletal disorders, and gallbladder problems. Estimates suggest that, of the total medical spending in the United States, 10% ($147 billion) could be attributed to overweight and obesity, rivaling that attributed to smoking (Finkelstein et al. 2009). Both Medicare and Medicaid spend a disproportionate share to treat overweight- and obesity-related health problems. On average, obese Medicare beneficiaries incur $600 per beneficiary per year in extra costs, compared to beneficiaries with normal weight (Finkelstein et al. 2009).

Multipayer System and Administrative Costs

Administrative costs are associated with the management of the financing, insurance, delivery, and payment functions. They include management of the enrollment process, setting up contracts with providers, claims processing, utilization monitoring, denials and appeals, and marketing and promotional expenses. The enrollment process in private, employer-financed health plans and in publicly financed Medicaid and Medicare programs includes determination of eligibility, enrollment, and disenrollment. Each activity has associated costs. Private insurers also incur marketing costs to promote and sell their plans. Providers have to deal with

numerous plans in which the extent of benefits and reimbursement is not standardized. It is difficult and costly to remain current with the numerous and changing rules and regulations. Denials of payment result in rebilling and follow-up. Denials of services result in appeals and incur costs for the insurer to review the appeals and for the provider to furnish justifications for the delivery of services. Utilization review and authorization of care incur additional costs for both payers and providers. According to the Centers for Medicare and Medicaid Services (CMS), the administrative costs, taxes, profits, and other nonbenefit expenses of private health plans have averaged about 12% of premiums (Lemieux 2005). The ACA requires health plans to standardize electronic data exchange to reduce administrative costs, although there are no specific guidelines as to how information must be transferred (Blanchfield et al. 2010). The ACA, however, addresses a minute portion of the total administrative costs; hence, its likely effects will be negligible.

Defensive Medicine

The US health care delivery system is characterized by litigation risks for providers (see Chapter 1). Fear of legal liability is one of the main reasons for carrying out unnecessary cesarean sections, for example, because it makes it easier to defend a potential birth injury case. Unrestrained malpractice awards by the courts and increased malpractice insurance premiums for physicians add significantly to the cost of health care.

Fraud and Abuse

Fraud and (system) abuse are another type of waste in health care, which were introduced in Chapter 6. *Fraud* involves a knowing disregard of the truth. It has been identified as a major problem in the Medicare and Medicaid programs. Fraud occurs when billing claims or cost reports are intentionally falsified. Fraud may also occur when more services are provided than are medically necessary or when services not provided are billed. *Upcoding* is another fraudulent practice in which a higher priced service is billed when a lower priced service is actually delivered. These practices are illegal under the False Claims Act.

Under the Anti-Kickback statute (Medicare and Medicaid Patient Protection Act of 1987), it is illegal to provide any remuneration to any individual or entity in exchange for a referral for services to be paid by the Medicare or Medicaid program. Knowingly providing such financial inducements amounts to a federal crime punishable by imprisonment. Stark Laws prohibit physician self-referral for laboratory or other designated health services (see Chapter 5).

Practice Variations

The work of John Wennberg and others brought to the fore a disturbing aspect of physician behavior, accounting for wide variations in treatment patterns for similar patients. Numerous studies in the United States and abroad have documented notable differences in utilization rates for hospital admissions and surgical procedures among different communities, as well as for the same specialties (Feldstein 1993). These practice variations are referred to as *small area variations* (SAV) because the differences in practice patterns have only been associated with geographic areas of the country. For example, in earlier studies,

variations in the rate of tonsillectomies in New England counties could not be explained by differences in the demographics or other characteristics of the populations studied (Wennberg and Gittelsohn 1973); the overall inpatient hospital utilization by an aged population in East Boston was higher than that by an equivalent population in New Haven (Wennberg et al. 1987). More recent investigations on regional differences in Medicare spending demonstrated that higher rates of inpatient-based care and specialist services were associated with higher costs but not with improved quality of care, health outcomes, access to services, or satisfaction with care (Fisher et al. 2003a, 2003b). This variation, which can be as great as two-fold, cannot be explained by age, gender, race, pricing variations, or health status (Baucus and Fowler 2002). Geographic variations, as discussed here, signal gross inefficiencies in the US health care delivery system because they increase costs without yielding appreciably better outcomes. This variation is also unfair because workers and Medicare beneficiaries in low-cost, more efficient regions subsidize the care of those in high-cost regions (Wennberg 2002). SAVs cannot be explained by demand inducement. For example, no incentives exist for physicians to induce demand in Canada or Britain, yet variations similar to those in the United States also exist in those countries. SAVs indicate that patients in some parts of the country are receiving too much treatment, whereas others may be receiving too little. Medical opinions often differ on the appropriateness of clinical interventions because physicians use different criteria for hospital admissions and surgical interventions (Gittelsohn and Powe 1995).

Cost Containment—Regulatory Approaches

Many attempts to control health care spending have been undertaken in the United States; however, most of these attempts have met with only limited success, mainly because system-wide cost controls are almost impossible to implement in a quasi-market system. Cost-containment measures in the United States have been piecemeal, affecting only certain targeted sectors of the health care delivery system at a time. So, for instance, when prices have been regulated, utilization has been left untouched; or, when capital expenditures have required preapprovals, operating costs of production have been exempted.

Single-payer systems in other industrialized nations have created national regulatory mechanisms to keep their health care spending in line with their GDPs. Many of these countries follow what is referred to as *top-down control* over total expenditures. They establish budgets for entire sectors of the health care delivery system. Funds are distributed to providers in accordance with these global budgets. Thus, total spending remains within established budget limits. The downside to this approach is that, under fixed budgets, providers are not as responsive to patient needs and the system provides little incentive to be efficient in the delivery of services. Once budget allocations are used up, providers are forced to cut back services, particularly for illnesses that are not life threatening or do not represent an emergency. This top-down approach is in sharp contrast to the "bottom-up" approach used in the United States, where each provider and MCO establishes its own fees or premiums (Altman and Wallack 1996). Competition, created by employers shopping for the best premium rates and by MCOs contracting with providers who agree to favorable fee arrangements, determines what the total expenditures will be. To some extent, the United States also uses regulatory cost control, although it is not as comprehensive as it is in countries with national health care programs.

Cost-control efforts in the United States are characterized by a combination of government regulation and market-based competition. A fragmented approach to cost control allows providers to shift costs (see Cost Shifting in Chapter 6), mainly from low payers to higher payers or from one delivery sector to another. For example, when regulatory controls are employed to squeeze costs out of the inpatient sector, providers experience reduced revenues from inpatient services. To make up for the lost revenues, they increase utilization of outpatient services if that sector is free of controls. In another scenario, when the government implements cost-control measures, providers may start charging higher prices to private payers. This practice is very common in the nursing home industry, in which reimbursement is restricted under Medicaid rate-setting criteria. In this case, nursing home administrators make a conscious attempt to make up for lost revenues by admitting more private-pay residents and by establishing higher private-pay charges.

Regulatory approaches to cost containment, in the United States and elsewhere, typically control health care supply, prices, and utilization (Exhibit 12–1). Supply-side controls (health planning) enable policy makers to limit the number of hospital

Exhibit 12–1   Regulation-Based and Competition-Based Cost-Containment Strategies

---

Regulation-Based Cost-Containment Strategies

Supply-side controls	Restrictions on capital expenditures (new construction, renovations, and technology diffusion) Example: Certificate of need
	Restrictions on supply of physicians Example: Entry barriers for foreign medical graduates
Price controls	Artificially determined prices Examples: Reimbursement formulas Prospective payment systems Diagnosis-related groups Resource utilization groups Global budgets
Utilization controls	Peer review organizations

Competition-Based Cost-Containment Strategies

Demand-side incentives	Cost sharing Sharing of premium costs Deductibles and copayments
Supply-side regulation	Antitrust regulation
Payer-driven competition	Competition among insurers Competition among providers
Utilization controls	Managed care

---

beds and diffusion of costly technology, but regulatory limits on the health care system's capacity inevitably create monopolies on the supply side. To make sure that these artificially created monopolies do not exploit their economic power, health planning is always coupled with stiff price and budgetary controls (Reinhardt 1994).

Health Planning

Health planning refers to a government undertaking to align and distribute health care resources so that, at least in the eyes of the government, the system will achieve desired health outcomes for all people. The planning function becomes critical in a centrally controlled national health care program so that the basic health care needs of the population are met and expenditures are maintained at predetermined levels.

The central planning function does not fit well in a system in which more than one-half of health care financing is in private hands and there is no central administrative agency to monitor the system. Instead, the types of health care services, their geographic distribution, access to these services, and the prices charged by providers develop independently of any preformulated plans. Levels of expenditures cannot be predetermined, and such a system is not conducive to achieving broad social objectives. Nevertheless, the United States has tried some forms of health planning on voluntary or mandated bases, but these efforts have met limited success.

Health Planning Experiments in the United States

Some of the early efforts to control health care costs in the United States took the form of voluntary health planning, with the goal of minimizing duplication of services. In the 1930s and 1940s, communitywide voluntary organizations, called hospital councils, were established by hospitals in some of the largest cities. Hospitals agreed to share or consolidate services, or they traded the closing of a service in one hospital for the expansion of another service (Williams 1995). Voluntary planning worked only on a limited basis and only in instances where participating hospitals could gain an advantage through cooperative planning. Consequently, voluntary planning contributed little to overall efficiency (Gottlieb 1974).

The federal government got involved in health planning after the passage of Medicare and Medicaid in the 1960s. Soon thereafter, recognizing the increasing dollars the federal government was putting into health care, Congress concluded that it had the right to control escalating costs (Williams 1995). The comprehensive health planning legislation of the mid-1960s mandated the establishment of local and state health planning agencies. These agencies assessed local health care needs and advocated better coordination and distribution of resources. However, the agencies had little or no actual regulatory power and were largely ineffective (Williams 1995). When these agencies were evaluated, planned and unplanned areas were found to have the same amount of duplication of facilities and services and the rate of increase in hospital costs were the same (May 1974).

Certificate-of-Need Statutes

As discussed in Chapter 5, *certificate-of-need* (CON) statutes were state-enacted legislation whose primary purpose was to control capital expenditures by health facilities. The CON process required prior approval from a state government agency for the construction of new facilities, expansion of existing facilities, or acquisition of expensive new technology. Approvals were based on the demonstration of a community need for additional services. Although the reasons given for the CON legislation were better planning of resources and control of increasing expenditures, the adoption of CON was easier in states having greater competition among hospitals (Wendling and Werner 1980), indicating that hospitals supported CON legislation when it was to their own benefit. These hospitals did not want additional capital spending on new construction and equipment by their competitors.

CON laws did not seem to lower hospital expenditures on a per patient-day basis.

CON also represented a conservative approach to containing the rise in hospital costs because it did not address reimbursement and provided no incentives to change utilization behavior in patients or physicians (Feldstein 1993). In the case of nursing homes, however, CON regulations have been used to contain Medicaid costs. In the face of a growing demand for nursing home beds, CON regulations have restricted the supply of nursing home beds that otherwise would have been utilized. More recently, the Home and Community Based Services (HCBS) waiver program—also referred to as 1915(c) waivers (see Chapter 10)—has been used to curtail nursing home utilization and costs.

Price Controls

Perhaps the most important effort to control prices of inpatient hospital care was the conversion of hospital Medicare reimbursement from cost-plus to a prospective payment system (PPS) based on diagnosis-related groups (DRGs) authorized under the Social Security Amendments of 1983 (see Chapter 6). The DRG-based reimbursement significantly reduced growth in inpatient hospital spending but had little effect on total per capita Medicare cost inflation because costs were shifted from the inpatient to the outpatient sector (Figure 12–7). As explained in Chapter 6, Medicare has implemented other price-control measures through various reimbursement methods that apply to physicians, home health care, and various inpatient service providers. These programs seem to have been successful. For example, before the implementation of the resource-based relative value scale (RBRVS) for physician payments, the per capita Medicare spending for physician

Figure 12–7   Increase in US Per Capita Medicare Spending, Selected Years, 1970–2008.

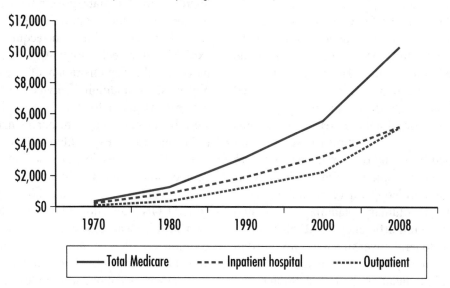

Source: Data from Health, United States, 2010, p. 402; National Center for Health Statistics.

services had increased at an average annual rate of 11.7% between 1980 and 1990. After RBRVS, per capita Medicare spending for physician services increased by only 5% annually between 1995 and 2005, based on data from the CMS. States have employed price-control measures to control their Medicaid expenditures by employing complex formulas that produce arbitrary reimbursement rates and payment ceilings.

Recent proposals are aimed to align Medicare payments with quality of care. In 2003, as part of the Medicare Prescription Drug, Improvement, and Modernization Act, the US Congress asked the Institute of Medicine (IOM) to assess the potential for implementing pay-for-performance (P4P) methods in the Medicare program (IOM 2004). The IOM found mixed evidence regarding the effectiveness of P4P payments, and it noted that unintended adverse consequences of P4P could include decreased access to care, increased disparities in care, and impediments to innovation. However, the IOM concluded that careful monitoring of P4P could minimize these adverse consequences. On the other hand, the IOM argued that, if Medicare payment structures were left unchanged, they would pose a barrier to improved quality of care.

Research to date does not show that P4P would significantly improve outcomes or control costs (Kruse et al. 2012; Ryan 2009). In longer term, improvements gained in the first few years of implementation tend to fade (Jha et al. 2012; Werner et al. 2011). Also, there is little evidence that hospitals would respond to P4P incentives (Nicholas et al. 2011). To the contrary, if P4P were to result in revenue loss for providers or cost increases for payers, there would be negative repercussions (Kruse et al. 2012). Despite the controversies, the ACA has directed the

CMS to establish a Value-Based Purchasing Program (VBP) for Medicare payments to hospitals. The law also directs the CMS to expand VBP to other areas of health care delivery, such as home health agencies and skilled nursing facilities.

The Medicare program is not alone in considering P4P strategies. As of July 2006, more than half of the states have instituted P4P in their Medicaid programs (Kuhmerker and Hartman 2007). While these programs are in the early stages of development, CMS is offering technical assistance to states for implementing and evaluating P4P. One of the largest is the MassHealth P4P program, implemented in 2008 by the Massachusetts Medicaid Program. Similar to P4P in Medicare, evaluation of this program has so far found only a limited effect on quality improvement (Ryan 2009).

There are more than 40 P4P programs in the private sector (James 2012). The California Integrated Healthcare Association's (IHA's) statewide P4P program, operated since 2003, is so far the largest and longest running private-sector P4P experiment in the United States (James 2012). However, despite the investment by health care organizations, especially for information technology (IT) adoption and data collection, no "breakthrough quality improvements" have been achieved and no evidence of "any savings or moderation in cost trends" has been found (Damberg et al. 2009).

Peer Review

The term *peer review* refers to the general process of medical review of utilization and quality when it is carried out directly by or under the supervision of physicians (Wilson and Neuhauser 1985). Based on this concept, the Social Security Amendments of 1972 required the establishment of professional standards review organizations (PSROs). These associations of physicians reviewed professional and institutional services provided under Medicare and Medicaid. The stated purpose was monitoring and control of both cost and quality. When Congress evaluated the performance of PSROs for their cost-control effectiveness, the program had not produced any net savings. Because of their questionable effectiveness, the PSROs were replaced in 1984 by a new system of peer review organizations (PROs), now called quality improvement organizations (QIOs). *QIOs* are private organizations composed of practicing physicians and other health care professionals in each state who are paid by the CMS under contract to review the care provided to Medicare beneficiaries. To control utilization, QIOs determine whether care is reasonable, necessary, and provided in the most appropriate setting.

Cost Containment—Competitive Approaches

Competition refers to rivalry among sellers for customers (Dranove 1993). In health care delivery, it means that providers of health care services will try to attract patients who can choose among several different providers. Although competition more commonly refers to price competition, it may also be based on technical quality, amenities, access, or other factors (Dranove 1993). Because competition is an essential element for the operation of free markets, competitive approaches are also referred to as market-oriented approaches. Competitive strategies fall into four broad categories: demand-side incentives, supply-side

regulation, payer-driven price competition, and utilization controls (Exhibit 12–1).

Demand-Side Incentives

The underlying notion of cost sharing is that, if consumers pay out of pocket a larger share of the cost of health care services they use, they will consume services more judiciously. In essence, cost sharing encourages consumers to ration their own health care. For example, cost sharing leads people to forgo professional services for minor ailments, but not for serious problems (Wong et al. 2001).

Cost sharing (now a common feature of almost all health plans) became popular after the Rand Health Insurance Experiment empirically demonstrated the effects of cost sharing. The most comprehensive study of its type, the experiment ran from 1974 through 1981. It enrolled more than 7,000 people into 1 of 14 different health plans. They included a free plan carrying no deductible or copayments. The other plans involved varying degrees of cost sharing. It was found that cost sharing resulted in lower costs, compared to the free plan. Coinsurance rates of 25% resulted in a 19% decline in expenditures because out-of-pocket costs reduced health care utilization. Increased coinsurance rates resulted in further declines in utilization and expenditures. Another important finding of the Rand Experiment was that lower utilization due to cost sharing did not affect most measures of health status. People enrolled in the free plan did better in three areas: vision, blood pressure, and dental health, but the average appraised mortality risk for people on the free plan was close to the risk for those with cost sharing (Feldstein 1993).

Supply-Side Regulation

As pointed out in Chapter 9, US antitrust laws prohibit business practices that stifle competition among providers. These practices include price fixing, price discrimination, exclusive contracting arrangements, and mergers the Department of Justice deems anticompetitive. The purpose of antitrust policy is to ensure the competitiveness and, thus, the efficiency of economic markets. In a competitive environment, MCOs, hospitals, and other health care organizations have to be cost efficient to survive.

Payer-Driven Price Competition

Generally speaking, consumers drive competition. However, health care markets are imperfect, and thus patients are not typical consumers in the marketplace because insured patients lack the incentive to be good shoppers and because patients face information barriers that prevent them from being efficient shoppers. Despite the information boom, it is extremely difficult for individual patients or their surrogates to obtain needed information on cost and quality. Payer-driven competition in the form of managed care has overcome the drawbacks of patient-driven competition (Dranove 1993). Payer-driven competition occurs at two different points. First, employers shop for the best value, in terms of the cost of premiums and the benefits package (competition among insurers). Second, MCOs shop for the best value from providers of health services (competition among providers).

Utilization Controls

Managed care also helps overcome some of the other inefficiencies of an imperfect health care market. The utilization controls in managed care (discussed in Chapter 9) have cut through some of the unnecessary or inappropriate services provided to consumers. Managed care is designed to intervene in the decisions made by care providers to ensure that they give only appropriate and necessary services and that they provide the services efficiently. MCOs base this intervention on information that is not generally available to consumers. MCOs thus act on the consumer's behalf (Dranove 1993).

The Affordable Care Act and Cost Containment

To keep the cost increase spiral from rising unsustainably, some cost-control measures are essential. The main cost-control measures under the ACA pertain to Medicare payment cuts to providers. Also, it is believed that competition among health plans through the exchanges would control the cost of health insurance premiums. Yet, various mandates imposed on health plans will increase premium costs, which will be borne mostly by employers who offer health insurance and their employees, because they will not get government subsidies. It is not clear whether expansion of the prescription drug benefit under Medicare Part D, by phasing out the coverage gap, is cost neutral. Another major impact on costs will come from the various new taxes imposed under the ACA. For example, excise taxes imposed on insurance companies based on their health insurance premium revenues, the 2.3% excise tax on medical devices, and taxes on pharmaceutical companies will all be passed on to consumers eventually. To assess the ACA's future impact on health care costs, it is currently unclear how the government will report health care expenditures. For example, will the government subsidies that will be paid to millions of Americans to purchase health insurance be fully captured as health care costs? What about the costs associated with the expansion of the Internal Revenue Service that are associated with the collection of the various taxes and penalties called for specifically by the ACA? On the other hand, some advocates assert that the ACA will be able to control health care costs (Kaiseredu.org 2013; Zuckerman and Holahan 2012). For now, let us hope that these advocates are right.

Access to Care

Access refers to the ability of a person to obtain health care services when needed. More broadly, access to care is the ability to obtain needed, affordable, convenient, acceptable, and effective personal health services in a timely manner. It may also refer to whether an individual has a usual source of care (such as a primary care physician), indicate the ability to use health care services (based on availability, convenience, referral, etc.), or reflect the acceptability of particular services (according to an individual's preferences and values). Access has several key implications for health and health care delivery:

- Access to medical care is one of the key determinants of health, along with environment, lifestyle, and heredity factors (see Chapter 2).
- Access is a significant benchmark in assessing the effectiveness of the

medical care delivery system. For example, access can be used to evaluate national trends against specific goals, such as those proposed in *Healthy People 2010* and *2020* (see Chapter 2).

- Measures of access reflect whether or not the delivery of health care is equitable.
- Access is also linked to quality of care and the efficient use of needed services.

Framework of Access

The conceptualization of access to care can be traced to Andersen (1968) and was later refined by Aday and Andersen (1975) and Aday and colleagues (1980). Andersen (1968) believed that, in addition to need, predisposing and enabling conditions also prompt some people to use more medical services than others. Predisposing conditions include an individual's sociodemographic characteristics, such as age, sex, education, marital status, family size, race and ethnicity, and religious preference. These factors indicate a person's propensity to use medical care. For example, holding everything else constant, elderly people are more likely to use medical care than young people. The enabling conditions are income, socioeconomic status, price of medical services, financing of medical services, and occupation. They focus on the individual's means, enabling that person to use medical care. For example, holding everything else constant, those with high incomes are more likely to use medical care than those with low incomes, particularly in countries that do not provide national health insurance.

The distinction between predisposing and enabling conditions can be applied to assess the equity of a health care system (Aday et al. 1993). To the extent that significant differences in medical care utilization can be explained by need and certain predisposing characteristics (e.g., age, gender), the delivery of medical care is considered equitable. When enabling characteristics create significant differences in medical care utilization, the delivery of medical care is considered inequitable.

This access to care model has been expanded to include characteristics of health policy and the health care delivery system (Aday et al. 1980). Examples of health policy include major health care financing initiatives (Medicare, Medicaid, and CHIP) and organization of health services delivery (Medicaid managed care, community health centers). Characteristics of the health care delivery system include availability (volume and distribution of services) and organization (mechanisms of entry into and movement within the system). Both health policy and the health care delivery system are aggregate components in contrast to the individual components of predisposing, enabling, and need characteristics. The expanded model recognizes the importance of systemic and structural barriers to access and is useful in comparing access to care among countries with different health policies and health care delivery systems.

Because of managed care's dominance in US health care delivery, the access framework was updated by Docteur and colleagues (see Figure 12–8). According to this framework, access to care is a two-stage process in a managed care environment. In the first stage, individuals select among the health plans available to them, constrained by structural, financial, and personal characteristics. In the second stage, individuals seek medical care, constrained

by both plan-specific and nonplan factors. The framework accounts for people enrolling and staying with the plan or disenrolling. It also links actual utilization with clinical and policy outcomes. Although comprehensive models are useful in conceptualizing access to care, they are difficult to test because of the range of variables and the differing levels of analysis they require.

Dimensions of Access

Penchansky and Thomas (1981) described access to care as consisting of five dimensions: availability, accessibility, accommodation, affordability, and acceptability. Availability refers to the fit between service capacity and individuals' requirements. Availability-related issues include whether primary and preventive services are available to patients; whether enabling services, such as transportation, language, and social services, are made available by the provider; whether the health plan has sufficient specialists to care for patients' needs; and whether access to primary care services is provided 24 hours a day, 7 days a week.

Accessibility refers to the fit between the locations of providers and patients. It is likely that individuals with different enabling conditions (e.g., transportation) may have different perceptions of accessibility. Accessibility-related issues include convenience (Can the provider be reached by public or private transportation?), design (Is the provider site designed for convenient use by disabled or elderly patients?), and payment options (Will the provider accept patients regardless of payment source [e.g., Medicare, Medicaid]?).

Affordability refers to individuals' ability to pay. Even individuals with insurance often have to consider deductibles and copayments

Figure 12–8 Framework for Access in the Managed Care Context.

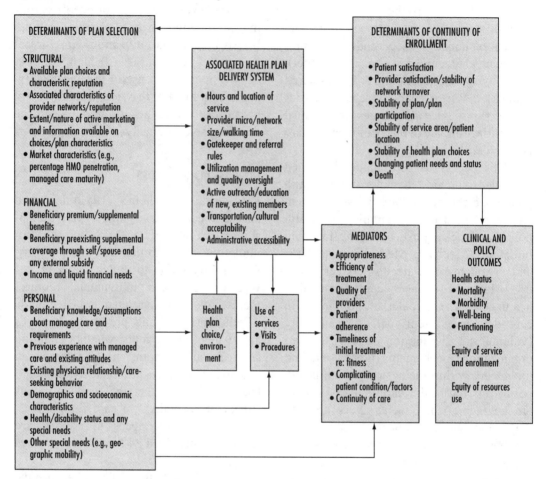

Source: Reprinted from E.R. Docteur, D.C. Colby, and M. Gold, "Shifting the Paradigm," *Health Care Financing Review* 17, no. 4 (1996): p. 12.

prior to utilization. Affordability-related questions include: Are insurance premiums too high? Are deductibles and copayments reasonable for the services covered under the plan? Is the cost of prescription drugs affordable?

Accommodation refers to the fit between how resources are organized to provide services and the individual's ability to use the arrangement. Accommodation-related questions include: Can a patient schedule an appointment? Are scheduled office hours compatible with most patients' work and way of life? Can most of the urgent cases be seen within 1 hour? Can most patients with acute, but nonurgent, problems be seen within 1 day? Can most appropriate requests for routine appointments, such as preventive exams, be met within 1 week? Does the plan permit walk-in services?

Acceptability is based on the attitudes of patients and providers and refers to the compatibility between patients' attitudes about providers' personal and practice characteristics and providers' attitudes toward their clients' personal characteristics and values. Acceptability issues include waiting time for scheduled appointments; whether patients are encouraged to ask questions and review their records; and whether patients and providers are accepted regardless of race, religion, or ethnic origin.

Types of Access

Andersen (1997) described four main types of access: potential access, realized access, equitable or inequitable access, and effective and efficient access. Potential access refers to both health care system characteristics and enabling characteristics. Examples of health care system characteristics include capacity (e.g., physician–population ratio), organization (e.g., managed care penetration), and financing mechanisms (e.g., health insurance coverage). Enabling characteristics include personal (e.g., income) and community resources (e.g., public transportation).

Realized access refers to the type, site, and purpose of health services (Aday 1993). The type of utilization refers to the category of services rendered: physician, dentist, or other practitioners; hospital or long-term care admission; prescriptions; medical equipment; and so on. The site of utilization refers to the place where services are received (e.g., inpatient setting, such as short-stay hospital, mental institution, or nursing home; or ambulatory setting, such as hospital outpatient department, emergency department, physician's office, staff-model HMO, public health clinic, community health center, freestanding

emergency center, or patient's home). The purpose of utilization refers to the reason medical care was sought: for health maintenance in the absence of symptoms (primary prevention), for the diagnosis or treatment of illness to return to well-being (secondary prevention or illness related), or for rehabilitation or maintenance in the case of a chronic health problem (tertiary prevention or custodial care).

Equitable access refers to the distribution of health care services according to the patient's self-perceived need (e.g., symptoms, pain, physical and functional status) or evaluated need as determined by a health professional (e.g., medical history, test results). Inequitable access refers to services distributed according to enabling characteristics (e.g., income, insurance status).

Effective and efficient care links realized access to health outcomes (Institute of Medicine 1993). For example, does adequate prenatal care lead to successful birth outcomes as measured by birth weight? Is immunization related to reduction of vaccine-preventable childhood diseases, such as diphtheria, measles, mumps, pertussis, polio, rubella, and tetanus? Are preventive services related to the early detection and diagnosis of treatable diseases? The concepts of effectiveness and efficiency link access to quality of care.

Measurement of Access

Using the conceptual models, access can be measured at three different levels: individual, health plan, and the delivery system. Access indicators at the individual level include (1) measures of medical services utilization relative to enabling and predisposing factors, while controlling for need for care (Aday and Andersen 1975) and

(2) the patient's assessment of the interaction with the provider. Examples include differences in physician visits by race/ethnicity, gender, age, income, and insurance. Patients' perceived level of access is closely related to patient satisfaction with care and is part of the access framework (Aday et al. 1984).

At the health plan level, indicators include (1) plan characteristics that affect enrollment, such as cost of premium, deductibles, copayments, coverage for preventive care, authorization of new and expensive procedures, physician referral incentives, and out-of-plan use; (2) plan practices that affect access, such as travel time to a usual source of care and waiting time to see a physician (accessibility), whether an appointment is necessary, hours of operation, language and other enabling services (accommodation), the content of provider–patient encounters, including tests ordered and done, and referral to specialists (contact); and (3) plan quality as measured by HEDIS (see Chapter 9) and patient satisfaction surveys.

Indicators of access at the level of the health care delivery system comprise ecological measures that affect populations rather than individuals. System indicators help study access in an environmental context, that is, how context affects the access of persons and groups. Examples of system access indicators include health policies or programs related to access, physician–population ratio, hospital beds per 1,000 population, percentage of population with insurance coverage, median household income, state per capita spending on welfare and preventive care, and percentage of population without access to primary care physicians.

Population-based surveys supported by federal statistical agencies are the major sources of data for conducting access-to-care analyses. Large national surveys, such as the National Health Interview Survey, the Medical Expenditure Panel Survey (MEPS), and the Community Tracking Survey are the leading data sources used to monitor access trends and other issues of interest. Other well known national surveys include the Current Population Survey, the National Hospital Discharge Survey, the Ambulatory Medical Care Survey, the National Nursing Home Survey, and the National Home and Hospice Care Survey. In addition, the federal government may periodically collect data on special topics, such as HIV/AIDS; mental health; health care utilization by veterans, military staff, and their dependents; patient satisfaction; and community health centers.

In addition to the federal government, states, professional associations, and research institutions also regularly collect data on topics of interest to them. Examples of state-based initiatives include state health services utilization data (all-payer hospital discharge data systems), state managed care data (managed care encounter data), and state Medicaid enrollee satisfaction data (Medicaid enrollee satisfaction surveys). Examples of association-based initiatives include data on physicians (American Medical Association's Physician Masterfile and the Periodic Survey of Physicians 1969 to present) and hospitals (American Hospital Association's Annual Survey of Hospitals 1946 to present). Examples of research institution-based initiatives include collecting data on the health care delivery system (Center for Evaluative Clinical Sciences: Dartmouth Atlas of Health Care in the United States), women's health (Kaiser Family Foundation: Women's Health Survey), minority health (Commonwealth Fund: Minority Health Survey), family health (Urban Institute National Survey of America's Families), health insurance (Commonwealth Fund Bienniel Health Insurance Survey), and access to care (Robert Wood Johnson Foundation National Access Surveys).

Current Status of Access

In the United States, barriers to access still exist at both the individual and the system levels. Many of these barriers are experienced by vulnerable population groups (discussed in Chapter 11). Access is best predicted by race, income, and occupation. These three factors are interrelated. People belonging to minority groups tend to be poor, not well educated, and more likely to work in jobs that pose greater health risks. Tables 12–3 and 12–4 summarize

physician contacts by categories of age, sex, race, income, and geographic location. Table 12–5 summarizes dental visits. These results are not adjusted for health need, however, and, therefore, are not true indicators of access. Rather, they provide utilization measures as a proxy for access.

The Affordable Care Act and Access to Care

While the ACA promises to increase access to affordable insurance coverage and supports improvements in primary care and wellness, some issues remain unaddressed. For example, more than 24 million people in the United States have limited English proficiency (Teitelbaum et al. 2012) which limits access to health care. The ACA does little to improve access for the growing number of Medicaid patients.

Table 12–3 Visits to Office-Based Physicians, 2008

Characteristic	Number of Visits (million)	Percentage Distribution	Visits per 100 Persons/Year
All visits	956.0	100.0	320.1
Age			
Under 15 years old	147.2	15.4	241.0
15–44 years old	268.5	28.1	417.2
45–64 years old	284.1	29.7	366.5
65–74 years old	127.1	13.3	639.5
75 years old and over	129.0	13.5	743.5

Source: Data from US Census Bureau. *Statistical Abstracts of the United States, 2012,* Washington, DC, p. 117.

Table 12–4 Number of Health Care Visits According to Selected Patient Characteristics, 2011

Characteristic	None	1–3 Visits	4–9 Visits	10+ Visits
Total	15.5%	46.8%	24.7%	13.0%
Sex				
Male	20.0%	47.8%	21.9%	10.3%
Female	11.0%	45.9%	27.6%	15.5%
Race and age				
White	15.2%	46.4%	25.1%	13.2%
Black	15.0%	47.6%	24.3%	13.1%
% poverty level				
Below 100%	18.9%	39.5%	24.7%	16.9%
100–200%	21.1%	42.7%	22.7%	13.5%
200% +	26.2%	99.1%	50.6%	24.1%
Geographic region				
Northeast	13.0%	47.0%	26.2%	13.8%
Midwest	13.6%	49.2%	24.2%	13.0%
South	15.4%	45.5%	25.7%	13.4%
West	19.3%	46.5%	22.7%	11.5%
Location of residence				
Within MSA	15.4%	47.4%	24.5%	12.7%
Outside MSA	15.7%	43.6%	26.2%	14.5%

Source: Data from *Health, United States, 2012,* pp. 244–246, National Center for Health Statistics, Division of Health Interview Statistics, 2013.

Models developed by six states propose increasing the availability of specialty care through telehealth, bringing specialists to primary care sites, and using physician assistants (PAs) to deliver specialty services; expanding the role of primary care providers to handle more specialized health issues through training and electronic consultations; and enhancing communication and coordination among patients, primary care providers, and specialists through broad medical home models (Felland et al. 2013).

Quality of Care

One reason the pursuit of quality in health care has trailed behind the emphasis on cost and access is the difficulty of defining and measuring quality. Since the

Table 12–5 Dental Visits in the Past Year Among Persons 18–64 Years of Age, 2011

Characteristic	Percentage of Persons
All persons	61.6
Percent of poverty level	
Below 100%	41.3
100%–199%	43.0
200%–399%	60.4
400% or more	78.9
Race and Hispanic origin	
White, non-Hispanic	62.6
Black, non-Hispanic	55.5
Hispanic	46.5
Sex	
Male	57.5
Female	65.5

Source: Data from *Health, United States, 2012,* p. 280, National Center for Health Statistics.

1990s, when cost containment became a major priority, emphasis on quality has taken center stage because of intuitive concerns that cost control may negatively impact quality. In spite of the progress made, there is still a long road ahead to specify what constitutes good quality in medical care, how to ensure it for patients, and how to reward providers and health plans whose outcomes indicate successes in quality improvement. One challenge in achieving such a goal is that patients, providers, and payers each define quality differently, which translates into different expectations of the health care delivery system and, thus, differing evaluations of its quality (McGlynn 1997).

The IOM has defined *quality* as "the degree to which health services for individuals and populations increase the likelihood of desired health outcomes and are consistent with current professional knowledge" (McGlynn 1997). This definition has several implications: (1) Quality performance occurs on a continuum, theoretically ranging from unacceptable to excellent. (2) The focus is on services provided by the health care delivery system as opposed to individual behaviors. (3) Quality may be evaluated from the perspective of individuals and populations or communities. (4) The emphasis is on desired health outcomes, and scientific research must identify the services that improve health outcomes. (5) In the absence of scientific evidence regarding two comparative measures that are widely used as proxies for medical quality, such national comparisons are debatable as to whether the US medical system should be faulted for the disparities. For example, Blum's model of health and wellness (presented in Chapter 2) clearly points to a more significant role that numerous factors other than medical care play in determining health and well-being of individuals and populations. Nevertheless, more health care expenditures do not produce better health, and high quality care must also be cost effective. The delivery of most medical care at the flat of the curve (see Chapter 5) clearly points to a greater need to incorporate cost of care into the assessment of quality.

Dimensions of Quality

Quality needs to be viewed from both micro and macro perspectives. The micro view focuses on services at the point of delivery and their subsequent effects. It is associated with the performance of individual caregivers and health care organizations. The macro view looks at quality from the standpoint of populations. It reflects the performance of the entire health care delivery system by evaluating indicators such as life expectancy, mortality rates, incidence and prevalence of certain health conditions, and so on.

The Micro View

The micro dimension of health care quality encompasses the clinical aspects of care delivery, the interpersonal aspects of care delivery, and quality of life.

Clinical Aspects

Clinical aspects of care deal with technical quality, such as the facilities where care is delivered, the qualifications and skills of caregivers, the processes and interventions used, cost efficiency of care, and the results or effects on patients' health.

One example of lack of clinical quality is medical errors. The IOM reported that 44,000 to 98,000 patients die in American hospitals each year because of medical errors, making "adverse events" the eighth leading cause of death in the United States (IOM 2000). The Agency for Healthcare Research and Quality (AHRQ) identifies four types of medical errors. Medication errors, or adverse drug events (ADEs), are errors in prescribing and administering medicines to patients. Surgical errors are errors in performing surgical operations. Diagnostic inaccuracies may lead to incorrect treatment or unnecessary testing. Systemic factors, such as organization of health care delivery and distribution of resources,

may also contribute to preventable adverse events (AHRQ 2000).

Interpersonal Aspects

When quality is viewed from the patient's perspective, interpersonal aspects of care become essential. Patients lack technical expertise and often judge the quality of technical care indirectly by their perceptions of the practitioner's interest, concern, and demeanor during clinical encounters (Donabedian 1985). Interpersonal relations and satisfaction become even more important when placed within the holistic context of health care delivery. Positive interactions between patients and practitioners are major contributors to treatment success through greater patient compliance and return for care (Svarstad 1986). Expressions of love, hope, and compassion can enhance the healing effects of medical treatments.

Interpersonal aspects of quality are also important from the standpoint of organizational management. Consumers—that is, patients and their surrogates—gain lasting impressions of organizational quality from the way they are treated by an organization's employees. Such employee–customer interactions include not just the direct caregivers but a variety of other employees associated with the health care organization, such as receptionists, cafeteria workers, housekeeping employees, and billing clerks.

To measure interpersonal aspects of quality, patient satisfaction surveys have been widely used by various types of health care organizations. Ratings by consumers provide the most appropriate method for evaluating interpersonal quality (McGlynn and Brook 1996). Satisfaction surveys have been used to give physicians feedback on important dimensions of interpersonal communication and service quality.

Quality of Life

The concept of quality of life has gained attention in recent years because patients with chronic and/or debilitating diseases are living longer but in a declining state of health. Chronic problems often impose serious limitations on patients' functional status (physical, social, and mental functioning), access to community resources and opportunities, and sense of well-being (Lehman 1995). In a composite sense, during or subsequent to disease, a person's own perception of health, ability to function, role limitations stemming from physical or emotional problems, and personal happiness are referred to as health-related quality of life (*HRQL*).

General HRQL refers to the essential or common components of overall well-being that are more broadly applicable to almost everyone. Disease-specific HRQL focuses entirely on impairments that are caused by a specific disorder and the effects and side effects of treatments for that disorder. For example, arthritis quality of life is concerned with joint pain and mobility and the side effects of anti-inflammatory agents; depression quality of life deals with the symptoms of depression, such as suicidal thoughts, and such medication side effects as blurred vision, dry mouth, constipation, and impotence (Bergner 1989); and cancer-specific HRQL may include anxiety about cancer recurrence (Ganz and Litwin 1996) and pain management.

Institution-related quality of life is also an important attribute of quality in addition to the clinical and interpersonal aspects. It refers to a patient's quality of life while confined in an institution as an inpatient. Factors contributing to institutional quality of life can be classified into three main groups: environmental comfort, self-governance, and human factors. Cleanliness, safety, noise levels, odors, lighting, air circulation, environmental temperature, and furnishings are some of the key comfort factors that are particularly relevant to the physical aspects of institutional living. Self-governance means autonomy to make decisions, freedom to air grievances without fear of reprisal, and reasonable accommodation of personal likes and dislikes. Human factors are associated with caregiver attitudes and practices. Human factors include privacy and confidentiality, treatment from staff in a manner that maintains respect and dignity, and freedom from physical and/or emotional abuse.

Quality Assessment and Assurance

The terms "quality assessment" and "quality assurance" are often encountered in literature on health care quality. Yet, these terms are not always well defined or differentiated. *Quality assessment* refers to the measurement of quality against an established standard. It includes the process of defining how quality is to be determined, identification of specific variables or indicators to be measured, collection of appropriate data to make the measurement possible, statistical analysis, and interpretation of the results of the assessment (Williams and Brook 1978). *Quality assurance* is synonymous with quality improvement. It is the process of institutionalizing quality through ongoing assessment and using the results of assessment for continuous quality improvement (CQI; Williams and Torrens 1993). Quality assurance, then, is a step beyond quality assessment. It is a system-wide or organization-wide commitment to engage in the improvement of quality on an ongoing basis. Although the two activities—quality assessment and quality assurance—are related, quality assurance cannot occur without quality assessment. Quality assessment becomes an integral part of the process of quality assurance. Conversely, it is possible to conduct quality assessment without engaging in quality assurance.

In the past, quality assurance focused on observing deviations from established standards by means of inspection techniques and was used in conjunction with punitive actions for noncompliance. The nursing home industry presents a typical case. Standards of patient care in nursing homes and the system for evaluating performance were developed mainly in conjunction with the certification of facilities for Medicare and Medicaid. Federal regulations developed by CMS are viewed as minimum standards or baseline criteria for defining quality of resident care in certified facilities. Compliance with the standards is monitored through periodic inspections of the facilities, and serious noncompliance is punishable by monetary fines and threats of expulsion from Medicare and Medicaid.

Quality assurance is based on the principles of total quality management (*TQM*), also referred to as CQI. The philosophy of TQM was developed and used in other industries before it was adapted for health care delivery. The adoption of TQM by many hospitals and health systems has streamlined administration, reduced lengths of stay, improved clinical outcomes, and produced

higher levels of patient satisfaction (HCIA Inc. and Deloitte & Touche 1997).

The Donabedian Model

In his well known model to help define and measure quality in health care organizations, Donabedian proposed three domains in which health care quality could be examined: structure, process, and outcomes.

Structure, process, and outcomes are closely linked (Figure 12–9). The three domains are also hierarchical. Structure is the foundation of the quality of health care. Good processes require a good structure. In other words, deficiencies in structure have a negative effect on the processes of health care delivery. Structure and processes together influence quality outcomes. Structure primarily influences process and has only a secondary direct influence on outcome. For improvement of quality, outcomes must be measured and compared against pre-established benchmarks. When desired outcomes are not achieved, one must examine the processes and structures to identify and correct deficiencies.

Quality of structures and processes determines quality of outcomes. Some significant initiatives toward process improvement have been undertaken, including clinical practice guidelines, cost efficiency, critical pathways, and risk management.

Processes That Improve Quality

Clinical Practice Guidelines

Clinical practice guidelines (also called medical practice guidelines) are explicit descriptions representing preferred clinical processes for specified conditions. Hence,

Figure 12–9 The Donabedian Model.

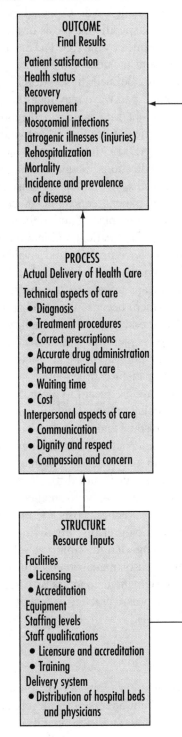

clinical practice guidelines are scientifically based protocols to guide clinical decisions. The goal is to assist practitioners in adopting a "best practice" approach in delivering care for a given health condition (Ramsey 2002). Such evidence-based guidelines provide a mechanism for standardizing the practice of medicine and improving the quality of care. Proponents believe that these guidelines simultaneously promote lower costs and better outcomes. Critics view guidelines as an administrative mechanism to reduce utilization.

One of the primary mandates of AHRQ is to build the scientific base of which health care practices work and which do not work. AHRQ has established a National Guideline Clearinghouse (NGC) in partnership with the American Medical Association (AMA) and America's Health Insurance Plans. The NGC is a comprehensive database of evidence-based clinical practice guidelines and related documents. It facilitates access to information produced by different organizations by making it all available at one site. The NGC is an Internet-based resource that enables health care professionals to compare clinical recommendations. Guidelines have been catalogued in the areas of diseases; chemicals and drugs; analytical, diagnostic, and therapeutic techniques and equipment; and behavioral disciplines and activities.

Cost Efficiency

Also referred to as cost effectiveness, *cost efficiency* is an important concept in quality assessment. A service is cost efficient when the benefit received is greater than the cost incurred to provide the service. Medical care delivered at the flat of the curve is not cost effective (see Chapter 5).

Overutilization (overuse) occurs when the costs or risks of treatment outweigh its benefits, and yet additional care is delivered. When health care is overused, its value is diluted because resources are wasted. Hence, inefficiency can also be regarded as unethical because it deprives someone else of the potential benefits of health care. *Underutilization* (underuse) occurs when the benefits of an intervention outweigh its risks or costs, and yet it is not used (Chassin 1991). Potential adverse health outcomes related to underutilization include hospitalizations that could be avoided by providing better medical access and timely care, low birth weight due to lack of prenatal care, infant mortality due to lack of early pediatric care, and low cancer survival rates due to lack of early detection and treatment.

The principles of cost efficiency indicate that health care costs can be reduced without lowering quality of care. Conversely, quality can be improved without increasing costs. A trade-off does not have to occur between cost and quality. Introduction of PPS by Medicare is an example. The resulting discharge of patients "quicker and sicker" triggered by PPS initially raised some alarm concerning decreased quality, but it was found that processes of care in hospitals actually improved and mortality rates were unchanged or lower (Rogers et al. 1990). Other potential negative health outcomes that can be avoided by curtailing overuse include life-threatening drug interactions, nosocomial infections, and iatrogenic illnesses.

Critical Pathways

Critical pathways are outcome-based and patient-centered case management tools that are interdisciplinary, facilitating coordination of care among multiple clinical departments and caregivers. A critical pathway is a timeline that identifies planned medical interventions, along with expected patient outcomes, for a specific diagnosis or class of cases, often defined by a DRG. The outcomes and interventions included in the critical pathway are broadly defined. In addition to technical outcomes, pathways may measure such factors as patient satisfaction, self-reported health status, mental health, and activities of daily living (ADLs). Interventions include treatments, medications, diagnostic tests, diet, activity regimens, consultations, discharge planning, and patient education. A critical pathway serves as a plan of action for all disciplines caring for a patient and incorporates a system for documenting and evaluating variances from the critical path plan. Critical pathways are unique to the institutions that develop them because they are based on the particular practices of that facility and its caregivers. A pathway also is customized to the patient population being served and the available patient care resources. Finally, critical pathways are meant to promote interdisciplinary collaboration within the environment of the hospital and its market. The latter occurs by making patients and families active participants in the process. For these reasons, critical pathways are difficult to replicate from one organization to another. Use of critical pathways reduces costs and improves quality by reducing errors, improving coordination among interdisciplinary players, streamlining case management functions, providing systematic data to assess care, and reducing variation in practice patterns (Giffin and Giffin 1994).

Risk Management

Risk management consists of proactive efforts to prevent adverse events related to clinical care and facilities operations and is especially focused on avoiding medical malpractice (Orlikoff 1988). In response to the threat of lawsuits, initiatives undertaken by a health care organization to review clinical processes and establish protocols for the specific purpose of reducing malpractice litigation can actually enhance quality. Because malpractice concerns also result in *defensive medicine*, risk management approaches should employ the principles of cost efficiency along with standardized practice guidelines and critical pathways.

Threat of malpractice litigation also has a downside. Fear of litigation actually leads to a reluctance by hospitals and physicians to disclose preventable harm and actual medical errors. In this respect, it is believed that fear of litigation may actually conceal problems that may compromise patient safety (Lamb et al. 2003).

Public Reporting of Quality

Public reporting on macro levels of quality expanded in the early 2000s. This section summarizes the major public reporting initiatives.

CMS Programs on Quality

CMS started launching Quality Initiatives in 2001 (CMS 2013a). The quality programs specific to Medicare include the Home Health Quality Initiative, Hospital Value-Based Purchasing Program, Hospice Quality Reporting Program, Inpatient Rehabilitation Facilities Quality Reporting, Long-Term Care Hospitals Quality Reporting, Measures Management System, Nursing Home Quality Initiative, Outcome and Assessment Information Set (OASIS), Physician Compare Initiative, ESRD Quality Incentive Program, and Post-Acute Care Quality Initiatives (http://www.cms.gov/

Medicare/Medicare.html). CMS also has initiatives to improve the quality of care provided to Medicaid and CHIP enrollees related to EPSDT (early periodic screening, diagnosis, and treatment program), dental care, obesity, maternal and infant health, home and community-based services, vaccines, prevention, health disparities, performance measurement, patient safety, external quality review, state quality strategies, and improving care transitions (http://www.medicaid.gov/Medicaid-CHIP-Program-Information/By-Topics/Quality-of-Care/Quality-of-Care.html). The following are examples of CMS's efforts to enhance quality:

- CMS began developing a large public reporting program known as Hospital Compare, which initially measured and reported process-based measures of high-quality care for acute myocardial infarction, heart failure, pneumonia, and general surgery (Ross et al. 2010). Hospital Compare has expanded beyond only 10 process measures at the beginning to include data on hospital outpatient facilities; hospital 30-day risk standardized mortality and readmission rates for acute myocardial infarction, heart failure, and pneumonia; patient satisfaction and medical imaging usage (Ross et al. 2010); and data on the new Hospital Value-Based Purchasing program under the ACA (CMS 2013b).

- CMS and AHRQ, together, developed the Hospital Consumer Assessment of Healthcare Providers and Systems (CAHPS) survey, which collects uniform measures of patient perspectives on various aspects of their inpatient care (CMS 2005). Results are publicly reported on the CMS Hospital Compare website. Results are used by health care organizations, public and private purchasers, consumers, and researchers to inform their purchasing or contracting decisions and to improve the quality of health care services (AHRQ 2010b).

- The Physician Quality Reporting System allows physicians and other eligible professions to participate by reporting quality measures to CMS about specific services provided to their Medicare patients with specific conditions. Physicians can earn incentives by reporting. (See http://www.cms.gov/PQRS.)

- Quality improvement organizations (QIOs) are contracted by CMS for each state to review medical care and help beneficiaries with concerns about quality of care. QIO contracts are 3 years in length. The core functions of the QIO program are to improve quality of care for beneficiaries, protect the integrity of the Medicare Trust Fund, and protect beneficiaries by addressing individual complaints (CMS 2013a).

- Ambulatory Surgical Center Quality Reporting is a pay-for-reporting, quality data program, where ambulatory care centers report quality of care for standardized measures to receive the full annual update to their annual payment rate, beginning with 2014 payments (CMS 2013b).

- The Electronic Prescribing (eRx) Incentive Program is a reporting program that uses incentive payments and payment adjustments to encourage electronic prescribing. Professionals and group practices that are not successful electronic prescribers will be subject to a 2.0% payment adjustment on Part B services provided beginning in 2014. This payment adjustment was 1.5% for 2013, while the incentive was 0.05% (CMS 2013c).

AHRQ Quality Indicators

Since 2003, AHRQ has published the National Healthcare Quality Report and National Healthcare Disparities Report annually (AHRQ 2012, 2013a). In identifying key measures for these reports, The Federal Interagency Workgroup focused on priority areas established in *Healthy People 2010* (AHRQ 2005). AHRQ has a set of quality indicators (QIs) that measure quality of process of care in an outpatient or an inpatient setting (Farquhar 2008). Prevention QIs identify hospital admissions that could have been avoided. Inpatient QIs and patient safety indicators both reflect quality of care inside hospitals, with the former focusing on inpatient mortality and the latter on potentially avoidable complications and iatrogenic events. Pediatric quality indicators reflect quality of care received by children inside hospitals and identify potentially avoidable hospitalizations. Current AHRQ QI modules include Prevention Quality Indicators, Inpatient Quality Indicators, Patient Safety Indicators, and Pediatric Quality Indicators. These measures expand upon Healthcare Cost and Utilization Project (HCUP) QIs and several are endorsed by the National Quality Forum. Specific information on individual quality indicators within each module can be found at http://www.qualityindicators.ahrq.gov/. Select indicators are also used by CMS's hospital compare website (http://www.hospitalcompare.hhs.gov; AHRQ 2013b; NQF 2013). Examples of ongoing AHRQ quality initiatives include the following:

- AHRQ's Patient Safety Network (PSNet) is a web-based resource that features news and resources on patient safety. The site offers updates on literature, news, tools, and meetings, and provides browsing capability and site customization (http://psnet.ahrq.gov).

- ACTION II is a model of field-based research designed to promote innovation in health care delivery by accelerating the research-to-practice path. It is a 5-year task order contract model (2011–2015), and its 17 awardees and their partnerships include over 350 collaborating organization (http://www.ahrq.gov/research/findings/factsheets/translating/action2/index.html).

- Primary Care Practice-Based Research Networks (PBRNs) initiative brings together groups of primary care clinicians and practices to answer community-based health care questions and translate research findings into practice (http://www.ahrq.gov/cpi/initiatives/pbrn/index.html).

State Public Reporting of Hospital Quality

Many states also provide data on hospital outcomes of care with focus on acquired infection, readmission rates, and mortality rates following hospitalization for the same clinical conditions reported by CMS (acute myocardial infarction, heart failure, and pneumonia). One of the advantages of state public reporting programs is that their reporting is not limited to Medicare fee-for-service beneficiaries but also includes younger adults and older adults insured through private plans and Medicaid-affiliated HMOs.

The Affordable Care Act and Quality of Care

The ACA includes some provisions for improving quality of care, through programs that link payment to quality outcomes in Medicare, strengthening of the quality infrastructure, and encouraging the development of new patient care models, such as patient-centered medical homes (see Chapter 7) and accountable care organizations (see Chapter 9).

The ACA establishes the National Quality Strategy (NQS) to set national goals to improve the quality of health care. Thus far, three objectives have been established: (1) to make health care more accessible, safe and patient-centered; (2) to address environmental, social, and behavioral influences on health and health care; and (3) to make care more affordable (RWJ 2013). One challenge that has come up thus far is the widespread use of varied measures that are not comparable, by different agencies. NQS is aiming to discontinue the use of measures that may be duplicative (AHRQ 2012). There are also challenges related to the consistency of measures, as well as a lack of robust measures (McClellan 2013). Additional challenges facing quality include issues regarding data transfer and merging across systems, and the protection of sensitive patient data.

Summary

Increasing costs, lack of access, and concerns about quality pose the greatest challenges to health care delivery in the United States. To some extent, the three issues are interrelated. Increasing costs limit the system's ability to expand access. A lack of universal coverage negatively affects the health status of uninsured groups. Despite spending the most resources on health care, the United States continues to rank in the bottom quartile among developed countries on outcome indicators such as life expectancy and infant mortality.

Nations that have national health insurance can control systemwide costs through top-down controls, mainly in the form of global budgets. This approach is not possible in the United States because it has a multipayer system. In the United States, regulatory approaches have been used to try to constrain the supply side, but the major emphasis has been on constricting reimbursement to providers. Several competitive approaches have been used, mainly through the expansion of managed care. A move toward prospective payments and the growth of managed care can be largely credited with the brakes put on rising health care spending during the 1990s.

Access to medical care is one of the key determinants of health status, along with environment, lifestyle, and hereditary factors. Access is also regarded as a significant benchmark in assessing the effectiveness of the medical care delivery system. Access is explained in terms of enabling and predisposing factors, as well as factors related to health policy and health care delivery. Access has five dimensions: availability, accessibility, accommodation, affordability,

and acceptability. Measures of access can relate to individuals, health care plans, and the health care delivery system.

Quality in health care has been difficult to define and measure, although it has received increasing emphasis. At the micro level, health care quality encompasses the clinical aspects of care delivery, the interpersonal aspects of care delivery, and quality of life. Indicators of quality at the macro level are commonly associated with life expectancy, mortality, and morbidity. Quality assessment is the measurement of quality against an established standard. Quality assurance emphasizes improvement of quality using the principles of continual quality improvement. Donabedian proposed that quality should be assessed along three dimensions: structure, process, and outcomes. These three dimensions are complementary and should be used collectively to monitor quality of care. Reliability and validity are important concepts in the measurement of quality. Since 2000, several federal and state initiatives have been implemented to report on certain macro levels of quality.

ACA Takeaway

- Cost-control measures include competition among health plans to drive down insurance costs, value-based purchasing, and reduction in Medicare payments to providers. Insurance mandates and taxes, however, will increase costs for the consumers.

- Accounting for all future health care expenditures directly tied to the ACA is currently unclear.

- While the ACA promises to increase access to affordable insurance coverage and supports improvements in primary care and wellness, some issues remain unaddressed.

- The ACA includes some provisions for improving quality of care through programs that link payment to quality outcomes in Medicare, strengthening of the quality infrastructure, and encouraging the development of new patient care models.

Test Your Understanding

Terminology

access

administrative costs

certificate-of-need

clinical practice guidelines

competition

cost efficiency

critical pathways

defensive medicine

fraud

health planning

HRQL

institution-related quality
of life

outcomes

overutilization

peer review

QIO

quality

quality assessment

quality assurance

risk management

small area variations

top-down control

TQM

underutilization

upcoding

Review Questions

1. What is meant by the term "health care costs"? Describe the three meanings of the term "cost."

2. Why should the United States control the rising costs of health care?

3. How do findings of the Rand Health Insurance Experiment reinforce the relationship between growth in third-party reimbursement and increase in health care costs? Explain.

4. Explain how, under imperfect market conditions, both prices and quantity of health care are higher than they would be in a highly competitive market.

5. What are some of the reasons for increased health care costs that are attributed to the providers of medical care?

6. What are some of the main differences between broad cost-containment approaches used in the United States and those used in countries with national health insurance?

7. Discuss the effectiveness of certificate-of-need (CON) regulation in controlling health care expenditures.

8. Discuss price controls and their effectiveness in controlling health care expenditures.

9. Discuss the role of quality improvement organizations (QIOs) in cost containment.

10. What are the four competition-based cost-containment strategies?

11. What are the implications of access for health and health care delivery?

12. What is the role of enabling and predisposing factors in access to care?

13. Briefly describe the five dimensions of access.

14. What are the four main types of access described by Andersen?

15. Describe the measurement of access at the individual, health plan, and delivery system levels.

16. What are some of the implications of the definition of quality proposed by the Institute of Medicine (IOM)? In what way is the definition incomplete?

17. Discuss the dimensions of quality from the micro and macro perspectives.

18. Discuss the two types of health-related quality of life (HRQL).

19. Distinguish between quality assessment and quality assurance.

20. What are the basic principles of total quality management (TQM; or continual quality improvement [CQI])?

21. Give a brief description of the Donabedian model of quality.

22. Discuss the main developments in process improvement that have occurred in recent years.

23. Discuss the implications of the ACA on health care access, cost, and quality.

REFERENCES

Aday, L.A. 1993. Indicators and predictors of health services utilization. In: *Introduction to health services*. 4th ed. S.J. Williams and P.R. Torrens, eds. Albany, NY: Delmar Publishers. pp. 46–70.

Aday, L.A., and R. Andersen. 1975. *Development of indices of access to medical care*. Ann Arbor, MI: Health Administration Press.

Aday, L.A., et al. 1980. *Health care in the US: Equitable for whom?* Newbury Park, CA: Sage.

Aday, L.A., et al. 1984. *Access to medical care in the US: Who has it, who doesn't?* Research Series No. 32. Chicago, IL: Center for Health Administration Studies, University of Chicago, Pluribus Press Inc.

Aday, L.A., et al. 1993. *Evaluating the medical care system: Effectiveness, efficiency, and equity*. Ann Arbor, MI: Health Administration Press.

Agency for Healthcare Research and Quality (AHRQ). 2000. *Reducing errors in health care: Translating research into practice*. AHRQ Publication No. 00-PO58, April 2000. Available at: http://www.ahrq.gov/qual/errors.htm. Accessed January 2011.

Agency for Healthcare Research and Quality (AHRQ). 2005. *National healthcare quality report: Background on the measures development process*. Available at: http://www.ahrq.gov/qual/nhqrmeasures/nhqrprelim.htm. Accessed January 2011.

Agency for Healthcare Research and Quality (AHRQ). 2010b. *Consumer Assessment of Healthcare Providers and Systems (CAHPS)*. Available at: http://www.cahps.ahrq.gov. Accessed January 2011.

Agency for Healthcare Research and Quality (AHRQ). 2012 *Annual Progress Report to Congress. National Strategy for Quality Improvement in Health Care*. Available at: from http://www.ahrq.gov/workingforquality/nqs/nqs2012annlrpt.pdf. Accessed January 2014.

Agency for Healthcare Research and Quality (AHRQ). 2013a. *National healthcare quality & disparities reports*. Available at: http://www.ahrq.gov/research/findings/nhqrdr/index.html. Accessed September 2013.

Agency for Healthcare Research and Quality (AHRQ). 2013b. *AHRQ Quality Indicators*. Available at: http://www.qualityindicators.ahrq.gov/. Accessed January 2014.

Altman, S.H., and S.S. Wallack. 1996. Health care spending: Can the United States control it? In: *Strategic choices for a changing health care system*. S. Altman and U. Reinhardt, eds. Chicago: Health Administration Press.

Andersen, R. 1968. *A behavioral model of families' use of health services*. Research Series No. 25. Chicago, IL: Center for Health Administration Studies, University of Chicago.

Andersen, R. 1997. *Too big, too small, too flat, too tall: Search for "just right" measures of access in the age of managed care*. Chicago, IL: Paper presented at the Association for Health Services Research Annual Meeting.

Baucus, M., and E.J. Fowler. 2002. Geographic variation in Medicare spending and the real focus of Medicare reform. *Health Affairs Jul–Dec, Suppl Web Exclusives*: W115–W117.

Bergner, M. 1989. Quality of life, health status, and clinical research. *Medical Care* 27, no. 3 (Suppl): S148–S156.

Blanchfield, B.B., et al. 2010. Saving billions of dollars and physicians' time by streamlining billing practices. *Health Affairs*, 29, no. 6: 1248–1254.

Centers for Disease Control and Prevention (CDC). 2005. Annual smoking-attributable mortality, years of potential life lost, and productivity losses—United States, 1997–2001. *Morbidity and Mortality Weekly Report* 54, no. 25: 625–628.

Centers for Medicare & Medicaid Services (CMS). 2005. *Costs and benefits of HCAHPS*. Available at: http://www.cms.gov/HospitalQualityInits/downloads/HCAHPSCostsBenefits200512.pdf. Accessed January 2011.

Centers for Medicaid and Medicare Services (CMS 2013a). *Quality improvement organizations*. Available at: http://www.cms.gov/Medicare/Quality-Initiatives-Patient-Assessment Instruments/QualityImprovementOrgs/index.html? redirect=/qualityimprovementorgs/. Accessed January 2014.

Centers for Medicaid and Medicare Services (CMS 2013b). *ASC Quality Reporting*. Available at: http://www.cms.gov/Medicare/Quality-Initiatives-Patient- Assessment-Instruments/ASC-Quality-Reporting/index.html. Accessed January 2014.

Centers for Medicaid and Medicare Services (CMS 2013c). *Electronic Prescribing (eRx) Incentive Program*. Available at: http://www.cms.gov/Medicare/Quality-Initiatives-Patient-Assessment-Instruments/ERxIncentive/index.html. Accessed January 2014.

Chassin, M.R. 1991. Quality of care—Time to act. *Journal of the American Medical Association* 266, no. 24: 3472–3473.

Congressional Budget Office (CBO). 2007. *The long-term outlook for health care spending*. November 2007. Available at: http://www.cbo.gov/ftpdocs/87xx/doc8758/11-13-LT-Health.pdf. Accessed January 2011.

Damberg, C.L., et al. 2009. Taking stock of pay-for-performance: A candid assessment from the front lines. *Health Affairs* 28, no. 2: 517–525.

Department of Health and Human Services (DHHS). 1996. *Health, United States, 1995*. Hyattsville, MD: National Center for Health Statistics.

Department of Health and Human Services (DHHS). 2013. *Health, United States, 2012*. Hyattsville, MD: National Center for Health Statistics.

Donabedian, A. 1985. *Explorations in quality assessment and monitoring: The methods and findings of quality assessment and monitoring*. Vol. 3. Ann Arbor, MI: Health Administration Press.

Dranove, D. 1993. The case for competitive reform in health care. In: *Competitive approaches to health care reform*. R.J. Arnould, R.F. Rich, and W.D. White, eds. Washington, DC: The Urban Institute Press. pp. 67–82.

Farquhar M. 2008. Chapter 45. AHRQ Quality Indicators. In Hughes RG (Ed.)/ Patient Safety and Quality: An Evidence-Based Handbook for Nurses. Rockville: Agency for Healthcare Research and Quality (AHRQ). www.ncbi.nlm.nih.gov/books/NBK2664/; accessed Feb. 2014.

Feldstein, P. 1994. *Health policy issues: An economic perspective on health reform.* Ann Arbor, MI: AUPHA Press/Health Administration Press.

Feldstein, P.J. 1993. *Health care economics.* 4th ed. Albany, NY: Delmar Publishers.

Felland, L., et al. (2013). Improving access to specialty care for Medicaid patients: Policy issues and options. The Commonwealth Fund. Available at: http://www.commonwealthfund.org/~/media/Files/Publications/Fund%20Report/ 2013/Jun/1691_Felland_improving_access_specialty_care_Medicaid_v2.pdf. Accessed January 2014.

Finkelstein, E.A., et al. 2009. Annual medical spending attributable to obesity: Payer- and service-specific estimates. *Health Affairs* 28, no. 5: W822–W831.

Fisher, E.S., et al. 2003a. The implications of regional variations in Medicare spending. Part 1: The content, quality, and accessibility of care. *Annals of Internal Medicine* 138, no. 4: 273–287.

Fisher, E.S., et al. 2003b. The implications of regional variations in Medicare spending. Part 2: Health outcomes and satisfaction with care. *Annals of Internal Medicine* 138, no. 4: 288–298.

Ganz, P.A., and M.S. Litwin. 1996. Measuring outcomes and health-related quality of life. In: *Changing the US health care system: Key issues in health services, policy, and management.* R.M. Andersen, et al., eds. San Francisco, CA: Jossey-Bass Publishers.

Giffin, M., and R.B. Giffin. 1994. Market memo: Critical pathways produce tangible results. *Health Care Strategic Management* 12, no. 7: 1–6.

Gittelsohn, A., and N.R. Powe. 1995. Small area variation in health care delivery in Maryland. *Health Services Research* 30, no. 2: 295–317.

Gottlieb, S.R. 1974. A brief history of health planning in the United States. In: *Regulating health facilities construction.* C.C. Havighurst, ed. Washington, DC: American Enterprise Institute for Public Policy Research.

Hartman, M., et al. 2011. Health spending growth at a historic low in 2008. *Health Affairs* 29, no. 1: 147–155.

HCIA Inc., and Deloitte & Touche. 1997. *The comparative performance of US hospitals: The sourcebook.* Baltimore, MD: HCIA Inc.

Health Council of Canada. (2010). *How Do Canadians rate the health care system?* Results from the 2010 Commonwealth Fund International Health Policy Survey. Canadian Health Care Matters, Bulletin 4. Toronto: Health Council of Canada.

Institute of Medicine (IOM). 1993. *Access to health care in America.* M. Millman, ed. Washington, DC: National Academy Press.

Institute of Medicine (IOM). 2000. *To err is human: Building a safer health system.* L.T. Kohn, J.M. Corrigan, and M.S. Donaldson, eds. Washington, DC: National Academy Press.

Institute of Medicine (IOM). 2004. *Rewarding provider performance: Aligning incentives in Medicare.* Washington, DC: National Academies Press.

James, J. 2012. Health Policy Briefs: Pay-for-Performance. Health Affairs October 11, 2012. Available at: http://www.healthaffairs.org/healthpolicybriefs/brief.php?brief_id=78. Accessed September 2013.

Jha, A.K., et al. 2012. The long-term effect of premier pay for performance on patient outcomes. *New England Journal of Medicine* 366: 1606–1615.

Kaiser Family Foundation. 2009. *Trends in health care costs and spending, March 2009*. Available at: http://www.kff.org/insurance/upload/7692_02.pdf. Accessed January 2010.

Kaiser Family Foundation, Health Research and Education Trust. 2010. *Employer health benefits 2010 annual survey*. Available at: http://ehbs.kff.org. Accessed January 2011.

Kaiseredu.org. 2013. *U.S. health care costs*. Available at: http://www.kaiseredu.org/issue-modules/us-health-care-costs/background-brief.aspx. Accessed January 2014.

Kruse, G.B., et al. 2012. The impact of hospital pay-for-performance on hospital and Medicare costs. *Health Services Research* 47, no. 6: 2118–2136.

Kuhmerker, K., and Hartman, T. 2007. *Pay-for-performance in state Medicaid programs: A survey of state Medicaid directors and programs*. Commonwealth Fund pub no. 1018. Available at: http://www.commonwealthfund.org/usr_doc/Kuhmerker_P4PstateMedicaidprogs_1018.pdf. Accessed September 2013.

Lamb, R.M., et al. 2003. Hospital disclosure practices: Results of a national survey. *Health Affairs* 22, no. 2: 73–83.

Lehman, A.F. 1995. Measuring quality of life in a reformed health system. *Health Affairs* 14, no. 3: 90–101.

Lemieux, J. 2005. *Perspective: Administrative costs of private health insurance plans*. Available at: http://www.ahipresearch.org/pdfs/Administrative_Costs_030705.pdf. Accessed March 2011.

Levy, D.E. 2006. Employer-sponsored insurance coverage of smoking cessation treatments. *American Journal of Managed Care* 12, no. 9: 553–562.

May, J. 1974. The planning and licensing agencies. In: *Regulating health facilities constructions*. C.C. Havighurst, ed. Washington, DC: American Enterprise Institute for Public Policy Research.

McClellan, M. June 26, 2013. *Testimony: Improving health care quality: The path forward*. Brookings Institute. Available at: http://www.brookings.edu/research/testimony/2013/06/26-improving-health-care-quality-mcclellan. Accessed January 2014.

McGlynn, E.A. 1997. Six challenges in measuring the quality of health care. *Health Affairs* 16, no. 3: 7–21.

McGlynn, E.A., and R.H. Brook. 1996. Ensuring quality of care. In: *Changing the US health care system: Key issues in health services, policy, and management*. R.M. Andersen, T.H. Rice, and G.F. Kominski, eds. San Francisco, CA: Jossey-Bass Publishers.

National Center for Health Statistics (NCHS). 2010a. *Health, United States, 2009: With special feature on medical technology*. Hyattsville, MD: US Department of Health and Human Services.

National Center for Health Statistics (NCHS). 2010b. *Health, United States, 2009*. Hyattsville, MD: US Department of Health and Human Services.

National Quality Forum (NQF). 2013. *Endorsed individual and composite measures*. Available at: http://www.qualityindicators.ahrq.gov/Downloads/Modules/V45/Module%20NQF%20Endorsement%20V4.5.pdf. Accessed January 2014.

Nicholas L.H., et al. 2011. Do hospitals alter patient care effort allocations under pay-for-performance? *Health Services Research* 46, no. 1: 61–81.

Orlikoff, J.E. 1988. *Malpractice prevention and liability control for hospitals.* 2nd ed. Chicago, IL: American Hospital Publishing.

Penchansky, R., and J.W. Thomas. 1981. The concept of access: Definition and relationship to consumer satisfaction. *Medical Care* 19: 127–140.

Ramsey, S.D. 2002. Economic analyses and clinical practice guidelines: Why not a match made in heaven? *Journal of General Internal Medicine* 17, no. 3: 235–237.

Reinhardt, U.E. 1994. Providing access to health care and controlling costs: The universal dilemma. In: *The nation's health.* 4th ed. P.R. Lee and C.L. Estes, eds. Boston: Jones & Bartlett Publishers. pp. 263–278.

Robert Wood Johnson Foundation (RWJ). 2013. *What is the national quality strategy?* Available at: http://www.rwjf.org/en/research-publications/find-rwjf-research/2012/01/what-is-the-national-quality-strategy-.html. Accessed January 2014.

Rogers, W.H., et al. 1990. Quality of care before and after implementation of the DRG-based prospective payment system: A summary of effects. *Journal of the American Medical Association* 264, no. 15: 1989–1994.

Ross, J.S., et al. 2010. State-sponsored public reporting of hospital quality: Results are hard to find and lack uniformity. *Health Affairs* 29, no. 12: 2317–2322.

Ryan, A.M. 2009. Effects of the Premier Hospital Quality Incentive demonstration on Medicare patient mortality and cost. *Health Services Research* 44, no. 3: 821–842.

Svarstad, B.L. 1986. Patient-practitioner relationships and compliance with prescribed medical regimens. In: *Applications of social sciences to clinical medicine and health policy.* L.H. Aikenand D. Mechanic, eds. New Brunswick, NJ: Rutgers University Press.

TECH Research Network. 2001. Technology change around the world: Evidence from heart attack care. *Health Affairs* 20, no. 3: 25–42.

Teitelbaum, J., et al. (2012). Translating rights into access: Language access and the Affordable Care Act. *American Journal of Law and Medicine* 38: 348–373.

USA Today. 2010. Our view on financing government: When 47% don't pay income tax, it's not healthy for USA. Available at: http://www.usatoday.com/news/opinion/editorials/2010-04-16-editorial16_ST_N.htm. Accessed March 2011.

U.S. Government Accountability Office (GAO). 2008. *Medicare Part B imaging services: Rapid spending growth and shift to physician offices indicate need for CMS to consider additional management practices.* Available at: http://www.gao.gov/products/GAO-08-452. Accessed January 2011.

Van de Water, P.N., and J. Lavery. 2006. Medicare finances: Findings of the 2006 trustees report. *Medicare Brief* 13: 1–8.

Wendling, W., and J. Werner. 1980. Nonprofit firms and the economic theory of regulation. *Quarterly Review of Economics and Business* 20, no. 3: 6–18.

Wennberg, J.E. 2002.Unwarranted variations in healthcare delivery: Implications for academic medical centres. *British Medical Journal* 325, no. 7370: 961–964.

Wennberg, J.E., and A. Gittelsohn. 1973. Small area variations in health care delivery. *Science* 183: 1102–1108.

Wennberg, J.E., et al. 1987. Are hospital services rationed in New Haven or over-utilized in Boston? *Lancet* 1, no. 8543: 1185–1189.

Werner, R. M., et al. 2011. The effect of pay-for-performance in hospitals: Lessons for quality improvement. *Health Affairs* 30, no. 4: 690–698.

Williams, S.J. 1995. *Essentials of health services*. Albany, NY: Delmar Publishers.

Williams, K.N., and R.H. Brook. 1978. Quality measurement and assurance. *Health Medical Care Services Review* 1: 3–15.

Williams, S.J., and P.R. Torrens. 1993. Influencing, regulating, and monitoring the health care system. In: *Introduction to health services*. 4th ed. S.J. Williams and P.R. Torrens, eds. Albany, NY: Delmar Publishers. pp. 377–396.

Wilson, F.A., and D. Neuhauser. 1985. *Health services in the United States*. 2nd ed. Cambridge, MA: Ballinger Publishing Co.

Wong, M.D., et al. 2001. Effects of cost sharing on care seeking and health status: Results from the medical outcomes study. *American Journal of Public Health* 91, no. 11: 1889–1894.

Zuckerman, S., and Holahan J. 2012. Despite criticism, the Affordable Care Act does much to contain health care costs. Available at: http://www.urban.org/UploadedPDF/412665-Despite-Criticism-The-Affordable-Care-Act-Does-Much-to-Contain-Health-Care-Cost.pdf. Accessed January 2014.

Chapter 13

Health Policy

Learning Objectives

- To understand the definition, scope, and role of health policy in the United States
- To recognize the principal features of US health policy
- To comprehend the process of legislative health policy
- To become familiar with critical health policy issues in the United States
- To discuss the passage and implementation of the Affordable Care Act from a political perspective

"Ladies and Gentlemen, to come up with a uniform health policy, we will now break up into 31 different groups."

Introduction

Even though the United States does not have a centrally controlled system of health care delivery, it does have a history of federal, state, and local government involvement in health care and health policy. Government involvement in social welfare programs can be traced back to almshouses and pesthouses, the two well known government-run institutions of the 19th century (see Chapter 3). Perhaps the most visible policy efforts, however, that continue to have repercussions and will have future implications were the social programs created under the Social Security legislation during Franklin Roosevelt's presidency in the 1940s. Amendments to the Social Security Act later created the massive public health insurance programs, Medicare and Medicaid in 1965, the Children's Health Insurance Program (CHIP) program in 1997, and the recently enacted Affordable Care Act (ACA). The government's success in bringing about social change through health policy has given the government a solid footing to engage in further expansion of tax-financed health care. Hence, the government continues to find new opportunities to mold health care delivery through health policy. This chapter defines what health policy is and explores the principal features of health policy in the United States. It describes how legislative policy is developed and provides a policy context for many past developments in health care delivery, including the recently enacted ACA.

What Is Health Policy?

Public policies are authoritative decisions made in the legislative, executive, or judicial branch of government intended to direct or influence the actions, behaviors, or decisions of others (Longest 2010). When public policies pertain to or influence the pursuit of health, they become health policies. Therefore, *health policy* can be defined as "the aggregate of principles, stated or unstated, that . . . characterize the distribution of resources, services, and political influences that impact on the health of the population" (Miller 1987).

Public policies are supposed to serve the interests of the public; however, the term "public" has been interpreted differently in the political landscape. At the most general level, the term "public" refers to all Americans. "Public" can also refer to voters or likely voters in political elections. Finally, the term can refer to only those who are politically active. The latter group consists of those Americans who communicate directly with their representatives by either writing or calling, contribute money to politicians or political groups, attend protests or other forums on behalf of a particular interest or candidate, or, in other ways, make their voices and policy preferences heard. People who are older, have more years of education, and have strong party identification are more likely to be politically active.

Legislators and policymakers tend to be responsive to the views or wishes of these active Americans, particularly when they are constituents from within their legislative districts. Conversely, politicians also tend to strongly lean toward supporting policies that agree with their own ideologies or advance their own political agendas. Because most policymakers are politicians, policymaking and politics are often closely intertwined. The danger is that policymaking often becomes highly politicized and becomes hostage to the ideologies of the political party that happens to be in power at a given time. The party in power also exerts considerable peer pressure on its own members to support policies along party lines. Also, the primary concern of most politicians is to get elected or reelected. Hence, certain policies are driven by a strong desire to keep campaign promises or to please some powerful constituent group. The policy-for-politics approach does not ask for or consider the cost-benefit of a proposed policy. Policies driven by political considerations are likely to be nearsighted. Also, party-line politics keep the American public deeply divided on major issues.

Uses of Policy

Regulatory Tools

Health policies may be used as *regulatory tools* (Longest 2010). They call on government to prescribe and control the behavior of a particular target group by monitoring the group and imposing sanctions if it fails to comply. Examples of regulatory policies are abundant in the health care system. Federally funded quality improvement organizations (QIOs, formerly peer review organizations), for instance, develop and enforce standards concerning appropriate care under the Medicare program (see Chapter 12). State insurance departments across the country regulate insurance companies and managed care organizations in an effort to protect customers from default on coverage in case of financial failure of the insurer, excessive premiums, and mendacious practices. Recently, the Department of Health and Human Services (DHHS) has been charged with the responsibility to implement many of the provisions under the ACA, whereas the Department of the Treasury, through the Internal Revenue Service (IRS), has been charged with the

responsibility to regulate the individual and employer mandates and to collect the many taxes imposed by the ACA.

Some health policies are "self-regulatory." For example, physicians set standards of medical practice, hospitals accredit one another as meeting the standards that the Joint Commission has set, and schools of public health decide which courses should be part of their graduate programs in public health (Weissert and Weissert 1996). Similarly, managed care organizations (MCOs) voluntarily collect and report on quality measures using Health Effectiveness Data and Information Set (HEDIS) data (see Chapter 9) to the National Committee for Quality Assurance, which is a voluntary, nongovernmental agency.

Allocative Tools

Health policies may also be used as *allocative tools* (Longest 2010). They involve the direct provision of income, services, or goods to certain groups of individuals or institutions. Allocative tools in the health care arena are distributive or redistributive. **Distributive policies** spread benefits throughout society. Typical distributive policies include funding of medical research through the National Institutes of Health (NIH), the development of medical personnel (e.g., medical education through the National Health Service Corps), the construction of facilities (e.g., hospitals under the Hill-Burton program during the 1950s and 1960s), and the initiation of new institutions (e.g., HMOs under the Health Maintenance Organization Act of 1973). **Redistributive policies** are designed to benefit only certain groups of people by taking money from one group and using it for the benefit of another. This system often creates visible beneficiaries and payers. For this reason, health policy is often most visible and politically charged when it performs redistributive functions. Redistributive policies include Medicaid, which takes tax revenue from the more affluent and spends it on the poor in the form of free health insurance. Other redistributive policies include CHIP, welfare, and public housing programs. Redistributive policies, in particular, are believed to be essential for addressing the fundamental causes of health disparities. Expansion of health insurance for the uninsured—proposed under the ACA—is also based on a redistributive approach.

Different Forms of Health Policies

Health policies often come as a by product of social policies enacted by the government. For example, the Social Security Act of 1935 was passed mainly as a retirement income security measure for the elderly, but it also contained the Old Age Assistance program that enabled the elderly to pay for services in homes for the aged and boarding homes. After World War II, policies that excluded fringe benefits from income or Social Security taxes and a 1948 Supreme Court ruling that employee benefits, including health insurance, could be legitimately included in the collective bargaining process (see Chapter 3) had the effect of promoting employment-based private health insurance. Consequently, employer-based health benefits grew rapidly in the mid-20th century.

The extraordinary growth of medical technology in the United States can also be traced to health policies that directly support biomedical research and encourage private investments in such research. NIH had a budget of about $10 million when the agency was established in the early 1930s. Following exponential growth, the proposed fiscal year 2014 NIH budget is $31.3 billion (NIH 2013). Encouraged by policies, such as patent laws, that permit firms to recoup their investments in research and development, private industry is the largest financier of biomedical research and development in the United States.

Health policies affect groups or classes of individuals, such as physicians, the poor, the elderly, and children. They can also affect various types of organizations, such as medical schools, HMOs, hospitals, nursing homes, manufacturers of medical technology, and employers. Examples include licensing of physicians and nurses by states; federal certification of health care institutions, enabling them to receive public funds to care for Medicare and Medicaid patients; court decisions that may prevent the merger of two hospitals on the grounds of violating federal antitrust laws; and local ordinances banning smoking in public places.

Statutes or laws, such as the statutory language contained in the 1983 Amendments to the Social Security Act that authorized the prospective payment system (PPS) for reimbursing hospitals for Medicare beneficiaries, are also considered policies. Another example is the certificate-of-need programs, through which many states seek to regulate capital expansion in their health care systems (see Chapters 5 and 12).

The scope of health policy is limited by the political and economic system of a country. In the United States, where pro-individual and pro-market sentiments dominate, public policies have been incremental and noncomprehensive. Even the massive ACA is regarded as a major incremental reform. National policies and programs are typically based on the notion that local communities are in the best position to iden- tify strategies that will address their unique needs. However, the type of change that can be enacted at the community level is clearly limited since communities are bounded by policies and regulations formulated at the national and state levels.

Principal Features of US Health Policy

Several features characterize US health pol- icy, including government as subsidiary to the private sector; fragmented, incremental, and piecemeal reform; pluralistic politics associated with demanders and suppliers of policy; decentralized role of the states; and impact of presidential leadership. These features often act or interact to influence the development and evolution of health policies.

Government as Subsidiary to the Private Sector

In much of the developed world, national health care programs are built on a consensus that health care is a right of citizenship and that government should play a leading role in the delivery of health care. In the United States, health care has not been seen as a right of citizenship or as a primary respon- sibility of government. Instead, the private sector has played a dominant role. Tradi- tionally, Americans have been opposed to any major government interventions in health care financing and delivery, except for helping the underprivileged. Because of the dominance of liberal views in the United States over the past few years, the argument that health care is a right has been put forth, and it finally became the basis of the ACA. Because not all Americans espouse liberal views, the ACA has deeply divided the nation.

A general mistrust of government by Americans goes back to the founding of this nation. The Declaration of Independence defined the new nation in a great protest over government intrusion on personal lib- erty. It outlined the individual's right to life, liberty, and the pursuit of happiness. The Constitution further limited the powers of government. The fundamental beliefs and values (see Chapter 2) that most Americans still subscribe to evolved from these earlier founding documents.

Generally speaking, the government's role in US health care has grown incremen- tally, mainly to address perceived prob- lems and negative health consequences for the underprivileged. Also, the most cred- ible argument for policy intervention in the nation's domestic activities begins with the identification of situations in which mar- kets fail or do not function efficiently. Ironi- cally, even though health care in the United States functions under imperfect market conditions (see Chapter 1), problems and issues in health care are often blamed on "the market," which prompts politicians to further regulate health care through policy interventions. For example, cost escalations in the health care delivery system were assumed to reflect on the inability of private parties to control health care costs, which paved the way for various prospective pay- ment methods. Ironically, certain policy interventions have also fueled the growth of health care expenditures, at least indi- rectly. Widespread legislation across states to rein in managed care's initiatives to con- tain escalating health care costs is a prime example. Yet, for lack of other cost-control alternatives, several states passed laws to enroll all of their Medicaid beneficiaries in managed care programs. Conversely, voluntary enrollment by Medicare enrollees in the federal Medicare Advantage (Part C) program has been less successful (see Chapter 9).

Government spending for health care has been largely confined to filling the gaps in areas where the private sector has been either unwilling or unable to address certain issues. For example, court decisions such as *Duggan v. Bowen* and *Olmstead v. L.C.* were largely responsible for promoting large-scale transfers of people with mental illness and disabilities from institutions to community-based settings across the United States. Other policy interventions include various public health measures, such as environmental protection and communicable disease control and preparedness for disasters and bioterrorism.

Fragmented Policies

Fragmentation of the government's power in the United States follows the design of the founding fathers, who developed a structure of "checks and balances" to limit government's power. Federal, state, and local governments pursue their own policies with little coordination of purpose or programs. The subsidiary role of the government and the attendant mixture of private and public approaches to the delivery of health care also resulted in a complex and fragmented pattern of health care financing in which (1) the employed are predominantly covered by voluntary insurance provided through contributions that they and their employers make; (2) the elderly are insured through a combination of private–public financing of Medicare; (3) the poor are covered through Medicaid through a combination of federal and state tax revenues; and (4) special population groups, for example, veterans, American Indians, members of the armed forces, Congress, and employees of the executive branch, have coverage that the federal government provides directly.

Incremental and Piecemeal Policies

Incremental and piecemeal health policies in the United States have been the result of compromises involving the resolution of a variety of competing interests. An example is the broadening of the Medicaid program since its start in 1965. In 1984, the first steps were taken to mandate coverage of pregnant women and children in two-parent families who met income requirements and to mandate coverage for all children 5 years old or younger who met financial requirements. In 1986, states were given the option of covering pregnant women and children up to 5 years of age in families with incomes below 100% of the federal poverty level (FPL). In 1988, that option was increased to cover families at 185% of the FPL. In 1997, under CHIP, states were allowed to use Medicaid to extend coverage to uninsured children who otherwise did not qualify for the existing Medicaid program. This illustrates how a program is reformed and/or expanded through successive legislative action achieved through compromises between the two opposite political parties. The Medicare program also expanded incrementally, at first covering only the elderly under Parts A and B in 1965.

Interest Groups as Demanders of Policy

Health policy outcomes in the United States are heavily influenced by the demands of interest groups and the compromises struck to satisfy those demands. Exhibit 13–1

Exhibit 13–1 Preferences of Selected Interest Groups

Federal and state governments
- Cost containment
- Access to care
- Quality of care

Employers
- Cost containment
- Workplace health and safety
- Minimum regulation

Consumers
- Access to care
- Quality of care
- Lower out-of-pocket costs

Insurers
- Administrative simplification
- Elimination of cost shifting

Practitioners
- Income maintenance
- Professional autonomy
- Malpractice reform

Provider organizations
- Profitability
- Administrative simplification
- Bad debt reduction

Technology producers
- Tax treatment
- Regulatory environment
- Research funding

summarizes the major concerns of dominant interest groups. Powerful interest groups involved in health care politics have historically resisted any major change (Alford 1975). Each group fights hard to protect its own best interests; however, the result for any single group is less than optimal. Well organized interest groups are the most effective "demanders" of policies. By combining and concentrating their members' resources, organized interest groups can dramatically change the ratio between the costs and benefits of participation in the political process for policy change. These interest groups represent a variety of individuals and entities, such as physicians in the American Medical Association (AMA); senior citizens allied with AARP (formerly called the American Association of Retired Persons); institutional providers, such as hospitals belonging to the American Hospital Association (AHA); nursing homes belonging to the American Health Care Association; and the companies making up the Pharmaceutical Research and Manufacturers of America (PhRMA).

Physicians have often found it hard to lobby for their interests with a single voice because they include so many specialty groups. For example, the American Academy of Pediatrics is involved in advocacy for children's health issues. Other groups include Physicians for a National Health Program, the American Society of Anesthesiologists, and the Society of Thoracic Surgeons. These groups can come together on issues that threaten the interests of the entire group, as in 1992 when Medicare decided to change the reimbursement system from fee for service to a resource-based relative value scale, although the physicians did not prevail.

The policy agendas of interest groups reflect the interests of their members. For example, the AARP advocates programs to expand financing for the elderly. It became a major advocate for prescription drug coverage for Medicare beneficiaries by supporting the Medicare Prescription Drug Improvement and Modernization Act of 2003.

Conversely, it is surprising that the "bipartisan" AARP lent its enthusiastic support to the ACA even though the law had proposed Medicare cuts, which were opposed by the elderly. It has been suggested that payment cuts to Medicare Advantage (MA) plans could trigger a withdrawal of participating insurers from MA, which would financially benefit the AARP being the largest sponsor of Medigap plans (Roy 2012). For once, this organization seems to have abandoned its primary mission to champion the interests of its elderly members. Other examples of interest groups include labor unions, which have become the staunchest supporters of national health insurance. The primary concerns of educational and research institutions and accrediting bodies are embedded in policies that would generate higher funding to support their educational and research activities.

Pharmaceutical and medical technology organizations are concerned with detecting changes in health policy and influencing the formulation of policies concerning approval and monitoring of drugs and devices. Three main factors drive health policy concerns about medical technology: (1) Medical technology is an important contributor to rising health costs, (2) medical technology often provides health benefits, and (3) the utilization of medical technology also provides economic benefits by creating jobs in health care and other sectors of the economy. These factors are likely to remain important determinants of US policies on medical technology. Another factor driving US technology policy is the policymakers' desire to develop cost-saving technology and to expand access to it. The government is spending more and more money on outcome studies and comparative-effectiveness studies to identify the value of alternative technologies that promise to provide better care at lower cost.

Business also is a major interest group, although it is split, mainly along the lines of large and small employers. American employers' health policy concerns are shaped mostly by the degree to which they provide health insurance benefits to their employees, their employees' dependents, and their retirees. Many small business owners adamantly oppose health policies requiring them to cover employees because they believe they cannot afford it. Employees also pay attention to health policies that affect worker health or the labor–management relations experienced by employers. For example, employers have to comply with federal and state regulations on employee health and well-being and on the prevention of job-related illnesses and injuries. Employers are often inspected by regulatory agencies to ensure that they adhere to workplace health and safety policies.

Other relatively newer members of the health policy community represent consumer interests. For example, the tea-party movement representing conservative Americans actively demonstrated in Washington and around the country during the passage of the ACA, even though their voices went unheard. Consumer representation on the liberal side was noticeably silent, perhaps for two main reasons: (1) It was believed that a liberal majority in Congress and a liberal president were already taking action on their behalf, and (2) the tea-party movement was extensively marginalized in the liberal news media with innuendoes based largely on false reports.

Pluralistic Suppliers of Policy

In the United States, each branch and level of government can influence health policy.

For example, both the executive and legislative branches at the federal, state, and local levels can establish health policies, and the judicial branch can uphold, strike down, or modify existing laws affecting health and health care at federal, state, or local levels. Perhaps the biggest factor is shifts in control of the presidency and the Congress that can either create or close down opportunities for reform (Oliver et al. 2004). Fundamental ideologies, leaning toward the left or the right, jump to the surface to take policy action as control passes from one political party to the other. The dominant political party often ends up sweeping its agenda through as long as there is little resistance from powerful interest groups and the American people. For either meaningful support or resistance to occur toward a proposed policy, transparency and truthful information must be made available by the policymakers, and it must be faithfully carried to the public by the news media.

All three branches of government—legislative, executive, and judicial—are suppliers of policy. Of these, the legislative branch is the most active in policy making, which is particularly evident from policies that take the form of statutes or laws. Legislators play central roles in providing policies demanded by their various constituencies.

Members of the executive branch also act as suppliers of policies. Presidents, governors, and other high-level public officials propose policies in the form of proposed legislation and push legislators to enact their preferred policies. Executives and administrators in charge of departments and agencies of government make policies in the form of rules and regulations used to implement statutes and programs. In this manner, they interpret congressional interest and, thereby, become intermediary suppliers of policies.

The judicial branch of government also is a policy supplier. Whenever a court interprets an ambiguous statute, establishes judicial precedent, or interprets the Constitution, it makes policy. These activities are not conceptually different from legislators enacting statutes or members of the executive branch establishing rules and regulations for the implementation of the statutes. All three activities concur with the definition of policy, in that they are authoritative decisions made within government to influence or direct the actions, behaviors, and decisions of others.

Decentralized Role of the States

In the United States, under the theory of federalism, political power is shared between the federal government and the governments in each state. Hence, individual states play a significant role in the development and implementation of health policies. An example is the state governments' dominant role in curtailing the influence of managed care in the delivery of health care. Other examples of states' roles include financial support for the care and treatment of the poor and chronically disabled, oversight of health care practitioners and facilities through state licensure and regulation, training of health personnel (states pay most of the costs to train health care professionals), and authorization of health services available through local governments. Exhibit 13–2 lists the arguments often cited in favor of decentralizing health programs at the state level.

Many of the incremental policy actions have originated in state governments. One action was to create a special program called an "insurance risk pool." This type of program helped people acquire private insurance otherwise unavailable to them

Exhibit 13–2 Arguments for Enhancing States' Role in Health Policy Making

- Americans distrust centralized government in general and lack faith in the federal government as an administrator in particular.

- The federal government has grown too large, intrusive, and paternalistic.

- The federal government is too impersonal, distant, and unresponsive.

- State and local governments are closer to the people and more familiar with local needs; therefore, they are more accessible and accountable to the public and better able to develop responsive programs than federal agencies.

- National standards reduce flexibility and seriously constrain the ability of states to experiment and innovate.

- States are equipped to take on such functions (i.e., they have more full-time legislators, professional staffs, and bureaucrats).

- States are more likely to implement and enforce programs of their own making.

- States have served as important laboratories for testing different structures, approaches, and programs and for providing insight into the political and technical barriers encountered in enactment and implementation.

- States respond to crises faster.

- It is easier to change a state law than a federal one.

- States are more willing to take risks.

because of the medical risks they posed to insurance companies. The program was financed by a combination of individual premiums and taxes on insurance carriers.

The ACA does away with the need for state-based risk pools under the assumption that insurers could not legally deny anyone with preexisting medical conditions, no matter how severe.

Other state-initiated programs were created to address the needs of vulnerable populations. For example, New Jersey developed a program to ensure access to care for all pregnant women. Florida set up a program called Healthy Kids Corporation, which linked health insurance to schools. Washington developed a special program for the working poor that uses HMOs and preferred provider organizations (PPOs) to provide care within the state's counties. Maine established a program, MaineCare, to offer HMO-based coverage at moderate prices to small businesses with 15 or fewer employees. Minnesota created a program, Children's Health Plan, designed to provide benefits to children up to 9 years of age who live in families with incomes below 185% of the FPL but who do not qualify for Medicaid. Two states in particular took bold policy initiatives to expand health insurance coverage. In 1989, Oregon embarked on a controversial experiment that expanded Medicaid coverage to more than 100,000 additional people, by reducing the Medicaid benefit package (Bodenheimer 1997). In 2006, Massachusetts passed a universal health insurance program based on employer and employee mandates (see Chapter 3).

There are disadvantages to the dichotomous federal–state approach to policy making. For one, it makes it difficult to coordinate a national strategy in many areas. For example, it is difficult to plan a national disease-control program if some states do not participate or if states do not collect and report data in a uniform manner. States may also interpret federal incentives in ways that jeopardize the policy's original intent. For example, many states took advantage of federal matching grants for Medicaid by including a number of formerly state-funded services under an "expanded" Medicaid program. This allowed states to gain increased federal funding, while providing exactly the same level of services they had provided before. This phenomenon, called Medicaid maximization, although pursued by only a few states, had an impact outside of those states and may have contributed to rising national health care costs in the early 1990s (Coughlin et al. 1999). Subsequent to the 2012 Supreme Court decision, states have a choice to expand or not expand their Medicaid programs, as was originally mandated by the ACA, and not risk losing federal matching funds. Under the ACA, states are promised that their additional expenses incurred as a result of Medicaid expansion would be paid by the federal government.[1] Yet, for different reasons, nearly half the states may eventually decide not to expand their existing Medicaid programs.

Impact of Presidential Leadership

To pass national policy initiatives, a strong presidential role is almost always necessary. Lyndon Johnson's role in the passage of Medicare and Medicaid, George W. Bush's role in adding prescription drug coverage to Medicare, and the more recent enactment of the ACA under Barack Obama are key examples. Presidents have important opportunities to influence congressional outcomes through their efforts to bring about compromises, to engage in political maneuvering, or to take advantage of economic

and/or political situations, particularly when policies concern their own preferred agendas. Even under the most auspicious political circumstances, presidents are often hampered from getting their agendas fully adopted by Congress, because of a number of other considerations. For example, while running for a Senate seat in Congress, candidate Obama made it clear that he was a proponent of a single-payer health care system (http://www.youtube.com/watch?v=fpAyan1fXCE, accessed October 2013). This, however, would have been opposed by hospitals, insurance companies, and the pharmaceutical industry. Only after reaching compromises with this powerful industry block, the ACA became a reality.

Ironically, presidents' political agendas often result, years later, in unintended and undesirable consequences. In 1946, Harry Truman took advantage of reports that the nation had severe capacity deficits in the hospital sector and that many Americans across the country were unable to access acute care services. Later, in 1965, Lyndon Johnson dreamed of a "great society" to push his Medicare and Medicaid agenda through Congress. These programs passed through political compromises. However, overbuilding of hospitals and unrestrained use of Medicare and Medicaid sent health care costs through an uncontrolled upward spiral. Paradoxically, just when the nation achieved its goal of 4.5 community hospital beds per 1,000 population in 1980, as envisioned under the Hill-Burton program (see Chapter 8), the government concluded that the Medicare and Medicaid programs were no longer sustainable due to the rapid rise in health care costs. Consequently, Ronald Reagan authorized the PPS method of payment to reduce hospital utilization, which started a downward trend and created a

---

[1]The federal government would pay 100% of the expenses for the first 3 years, then gradually reduce it to 90% by 2020.

glut of unoccupied hospital beds nation-wide. Rising health care costs shortly after Medicare and Medicaid were implemented also presented an economic opportunity for Richard Nixon to pass the Health Mainte-nance Organization Act in 1973. Nixon also was successful in getting the CON legis-lation enacted under the National Health Planning and Resources Development Act of 1974. This Act represented an additional effort to restrain rapidly rising health care costs by requiring approvals for new equip-ment and new hospital construction. In the 1990s, even though Bill Clinton's compre-hensive health care reform efforts failed, his incremental initiatives did succeed in the creation of CHIP and enactment of the Health Insurance Portability and Account-ability Act (HIPAA) of 1996.

Moving forward to national health care, Clinton enjoyed a relatively high level of public interest in health care reform (see Chapter 3), but his administration did not act on it quickly enough. Also, ever-chang-ing details of his proposal, which were made public, became overly complex for the people to grasp. Moreover, Americans did not want their taxes increased to pay for health care reform.

Politics of the Affordable Care Act

Prior to his election victory in 2008, there was much fanfare among Obama's support-ers, particularly at the prospect of a first black President in America who was running on a *mantra* of "hope and change." Asking any pointed questions about Mr. Obama's vision of hope and change was distorted into a racial issue by the American media. Hence, amid the excitement, no one dared raise any pertinent issues. On health care,

Obama simply stated that everyone would have health insurance. It seems that by design, however, not even a general model of the "plan" was ever made public. None-theless, Obama had overwhelming support from the members of his own party.

Instead of giving a plan, candidate Obama, and later, President Obama, repeat-edly made three promises to the American people: (1) "If you like your health plan, you will be able to keep your health care plan. Period" (Lowry 2013); (2) "Let me be clear: If you like your doctor or health care pro-vider, you can keep them" (Lowry 2013); and (3) "In an Obama administration, we'll lower premiums by up to $2,500 for a typi-cal family per year" (Conover 2013).

The enactment of the ACA became real-ity following a unique political approach that is perhaps unparalleled in the history of American policymaking. Obama used to his benefit the political opportunity of having a solid Democratic majority in both houses of Congress. He had the advantage of strong Democratic leadership of Nancy Pelosi in the House of Representatives and that of Harry Reid in the Senate. Obama used some other factors to promote his reform agenda: (1) He found a unique economic opportu-nity, as the nation was in the middle of the worst economic downturn since the Great Depression, with an unemployment rate that exceeded 10%. (2) Obama and his Demo-cratic colleagues ceaselessly bashed former President George W. Bush, laying the blame on him for every malaise that the nation was going through. (3) The insurance industry was portrayed as the villain responsible for rising health care costs. (4) Unlike Clinton in 1993, Obama and the Democrats kept the details of the ACA legislation secret from the public. Pelosi's statement in a televised speech before the Legislative Conference for the National Association of Counties makes the administration's posture quite clear when she said, "We have to pass the bill so that you can find out what is in it" (Pye 2010). However, Pelosi, only weeks earlier, had bragged "about the transparency of the process that produced the bill" (Roff 2010). During townhall meetings around the country, Obama dodged key issues and gave only vague answers about the "plan," mostly repeating the promises noted earlier. The Obama–Pelosi–Reid trio was strongly determined to pass national health care reform.

Whether there was any genuine attempt on the part of Democrats to make it a bipartisan process is debatable. During the entire process leading to the bill's passage, Republicans were marginalized and kept out of any meaningful debate on health care reform. Obama, who arranged a summit with the Republican leadership and proclaimed that he would come to the summit with an open mind, had already released the version of the legislation that had passed the Senate. As one commentator put it,

> The truth is that Democrats never had any intention of working with Republicans, except to pick off two or three Senators and calling it "bipartisanship." This worked for Democrats on the stimulus, and they had hoped to do it again on health care. In the House, three Chairmen—Charlie Rangel, Henry Waxman, and George Miller—holed up last spring to write the most liberal bill they could get through the House. Republicans were told that unless they embraced the "public option," there was nothing to discuss. (*Wall Street Journal* 2010)

The president and congressional Democrats criticized Republicans as offering only opposition and no ideas for health care reform, but the Republicans, despite the lack of media attention, had introduced three health care bills, all of which failed. In the end, the ACA passed without a single Republican vote.

Oberlander (2010) adds other factors that led to the passage of the ACA. Instead of employing different reform strategies, the House introduced a single health reform bill that combined three bills from three House committees, demonstrating greater agreement among Democrats. The final legislation also allowed certain exemptions from individual and employer mandates. Oberlander (2010) also credits weak opposition to the bill from health industry stakeholders. Instead of waging a war against the industry, Obama and congressional Democrats were willing to compromise. By promising millions of newly insured people who would use health care, they received pledges from stakeholders, including PhRMA and the AHA to support health care reform. Even the insurance industry and the AMA endorsed the legislation, although the support faded over time. Another key factor behind its success is the speedy process of pushing the reform through the legislative process. One drawback was that the general public was confused about the legislation and was not supportive (Patel and McDonough 2010). In the end, however, that did not seem to have mattered.

The Development of Legislative Health Policy

The making of US health policy is a complex process that involves private and public sectors, including multiple levels of government, and reflects (1) the relationship of the government to the private sector, (2) the distribution of authority and responsibility within a federal system of government, (3) the relationship between policy formulation and implementation, (4) a pluralistic ideology as the basis of politics, and (5) incrementalism as the strategy for reform.

The Policy Cycle

The formation and implementation of health policy occurs in a policy cycle comprising five components: (1) issue raising, (2) policy design, (3) public support building, (4) legislative decision making and policy support building, and (5) legislative decision making and policy implementation. These activities are likely to be shared with Congress and interest groups in varying degrees.

Issue raising is clearly essential in the policy formation cycle. The enactment of a new policy is preceded by a variety of actions that first create a widespread sense that a problem exists and needs to be addressed. The president may form policy concepts from a variety of sources, including campaign information; recommendations from advisers, cabinet members, and agency chiefs; personal interests; expert opinions; and public opinion polls.

The second component of policy making is the design of specific policy proposals. Presidents have substantial resources to develop new policy proposals. They may call on segments of the executive branch of government, such as the Centers for Medicare & Medicaid Services and policy staffs within the DHHS. The alternative, preferred by both Kennedy and Johnson, was the use of outside task forces.

In building public support, presidents can choose from a variety of strategies, including major addresses to the nation and efforts to mobilize their administration to make public appeals and organized attempts to increase support among interest groups. To facilitate legislative decision making and policy support building, presidents, key staff, and department officials interact closely with Congress. Presidents generally meet with legislative leaders several mornings each month to shape the coming legislative agenda and identify possible problems as bills move through various committees.

Legislative Committees and Subcommittees

The legislative branch creates health policies and allocates the resources necessary to implement them. Congress has three important powers that make it extremely influential in the health policy process. First, the Constitution grants Congress the power to "make all laws which shall be necessary and proper for carrying into execution." The doctrine of implied powers states that Congress may use any reasonable means not directly prohibited by the Constitution to carry out the will of the people. This mandate gives it great power to enact laws influencing all manner of health policy. Second, Congress possesses the power to tax, which allows it to influence and regulate the health behavior of individuals, organizations, and states. Taxes on cigarettes, for example, are intended to reduce individual cigarette consumption, whereas tax relief for employer benefits is designed to promote increased insurance coverage for working people. Third, Congress possesses the power to spend. This ability allows for direct expenditures on the public's health through federal programs, such as Medicare and the NIH, but the power to allocate resources also gives Congress the ability to induce state conformance with federal policy objectives. Congress may prescribe the terms with which it dispenses funds to the states, such as mandating the basic required elements of the federal-/state-funded Medicaid program.

At least 14 committees and subcommittees in the House of Representatives, 24 in the Senate, and more than 60 other such legislative panels directly influence legislation (Falcone and Hartwig 1991; Morone et al. 2008). The conglomeration of reform proposals that emerge from these committees face a daunting political challenge— separate consideration and passage in each chamber, negotiations in a joint conference committee to reconcile the bills passed by the two houses, and then return to each chamber for approval. In the Senate, 41 of the 100 members can thwart the whole process at any point.

Five committees—three in the House and two in the Senate—control most of the legislative activity in Congress (Longest 2010) and are subsequently discussed.

House Committees

The Constitution provides that all bills involving taxation must originate in the House of Representatives. The organization of the House gives this authority to the Ways and Means Committee. Hence, the Ways and Means Committee is the most influential by distinction of its power to tax. This committee was the launching pad for much of the health financing legislation passed in the 1960s and early 1970s under the chairmanship of Representative Wilbur Mills (D-AR). Ways and Means has sole jurisdiction over Medicare Part A, Social Security, unemployment compensation, public welfare, and health care reform. It also shares jurisdiction over Medicare Part B with the House Energy & Commerce Committee. This latter committee has jurisdiction over Medicaid, Medicare Part B, matters of public health, mental health, health personnel, HMOs, foods and drugs, air pollution, consumer products safety, health planning, biomedical research, and health protection.

The Committee on Appropriations is responsible for funding substantive legislative provisions. Its subcommittee on Labor, Health and Human Services, Education, and Related Agencies is responsible for health appropriations. Essentially, this committee holds the power of the purse. The committee and the subcommittee are responsible for allocating and distributing federal funds for individual health programs, except for Medicare and Social Security, which are funded through their respective trust funds.

Senate Committees

The Committee on Labor and Human Resources has jurisdiction over most health bills, including the Public Health Service Act; the Food, Drug and Cosmetic Act; HMOs; health personnel; and mental health legislation (e.g., Community Mental Health Centers Act). This committee formerly included a subcommittee on Health and Scientific Research, which was used by its then chairman, Senator Edward Kennedy (D-MA) as a forum for debate on whether the United States should have a national health care program. When the full committee came under Republican control in the 1980s, the subcommittee was abolished.

The Committee on Finance and its Subcommittee on Health, similar to the Ways and Means Committee in the House, have jurisdiction over taxes and revenues, including matters related to Social Security, Medicare, Medicaid, and Maternal and Child Health (Title V of the Social Security Act). It is responsible for many of the Medicare and Medicaid amendments, such as QIOs, PPS, and amendments controlling hospital and nursing home costs.

The Legislative Process

When a bill is introduced in the House of Representatives, the Speaker assigns it to an appropriate committee. The committee chair forwards the bill to the appropriate subcommittee. The subcommittee forwards proposed legislation to agencies that will be affected by the legislation, holds hearings ("markup") and testimonies, and may add amendments. The subcommittee and committee may recommend, not recommend, or recommend tabling the bill. Diverse interest groups; individuals; experts in the field; and business, labor, and professional associations often exert influence on the bill through campaign contributions and intense lobbying. The full House then hears the bill and may add amendments. The bill can be approved with or without amendments. The approved bill is then sent to the Senate.

In the Senate, the bill is sent to an appropriate committee and next forwarded to an appropriate subcommittee. The subcommittee may send the bill to agencies that will be affected. It also holds hearings and testimonies from all interested parties (e.g., private citizens, business, labor, agencies, and experts). The subcommittee votes on and forwards the proposed legislation with appropriate recommendations. Amendments may or may not be added. The full Senate hears the bill and may add amendments. If the bill and House amendments are accepted, the bill goes to the president. If the Senate adds amendments that have not been voted on by the House, the bill must go back to the House floor for a vote.

If the amendments are minor and noncontroversial, the House may vote to pass the bill. If the amendments are significant and controversial, the House may call for a conference committee to review the amendments. The conference committee consists of members from equivalent committees of the House and Senate. If the recommendations of the conference committee are not accepted, another conference committee is called.

After the bill has passed both the House and Senate in identical form, it is forwarded to the president for signature. If the president signs the legislation, it becomes law. If the president does not sign the legislation, at the end of 21 days, it becomes law unless the president vetoes the legislation. If less than 21 days are left in the congressional session, presidential inaction results in a veto. This is called a "pocket veto." The veto can be overturned by a two-thirds majority of the Congress; otherwise, the bill is dead.

Policy Implementation

Once legislation has been signed into law, it is not a fait accompli. The new law is forwarded to the appropriate agency of the executive branch, where multiple levels of federal bureaucracy must interpret and implement the legislation. Rules and regulations must be written, detailing what the entities affected by the legislation must do to comply with it. During this process, politicians, interest groups, or program beneficiaries may influence the legislation's ultimate design. Sometimes, the result can differ significantly from its sponsors' intent. The process of policy making is complex enough; its implementation can be quite daunting as well.

The agency publishes proposed regulations in the *Federal Register* and holds hearings on how the law is to be implemented. A bureaucracy, only loosely controlled by either the president or Congress, writes (publishes, gathers comments about, and rewrites) regulations. Then the program goes on to the 50 states for enabling legislation if appropriate. There, organized interests hire local lawyers and lobbyists, and a completely new political cycle begins. Finally, all parties may adjourn to the courts, where long rounds of litigation may shape the final outcome.

Implementation of the ACA

Since the signing of the ACA into law on March 23, 2010, several provisions have gone into effect, including 26 provisions in 2010, 18 in 2011, and 10 in 2012 (Kaiser Family Foundation 2013a). As of August 2013, an additional 11 provisions have gone into effect with 2013 deadlines, and 15 with 2014 deadlines (Kaiser Family Foundation 2013a). Eleven ACA provisions (deadlines vary from 2011–2018) are still pending (Kaiser Family Foundation 2013a). State take-up of the ACA provisions varies across the board. For example, only 24 states had signed Medicaid expansion legislation into effect as of mid-2013 (Kaiser Family Foundation 2013b). Seventeen states had decided to create state-based Health Insurance Exchanges as of July 2013 (Kaiser Family Foundation 2013c); the remaining are created by the federal government.

In early July 2013, the US Department of the Treasury reported that the employer mandate would be pushed back until 2015 (U.S. Department of the Treasury 2013; The White House 2013). In August 2013, the federal government also delayed, until 2015, implementation of a consumer protection mandate that places a limit on out-of-pocket costs (*New York Times* 2013). The mandate limits deductibles to $6,350 per year for individual plans, and $12,700 for family plans. The Obama administration will also delay the enforcement of the ACA's health insurance mandate, extending how long Americans may go uninsured before facing a penalty under the law.

Despite the early rollout of certain provisions, much remains to be done in implementing the full law. In October 2013, as millions of Americans tried to enroll through the Web-based exchanges, they encountered obstructions. The technical glitches would no doubt be overcome in due course. A more critical issue, however, is that most of the approximately 14 million Americans who were enrolled in individually purchased health plans "are getting or are about to get cancellation letters for their health insurance under Obamacare" (Myers and Rappleye 2013). If people lose their existing health insurance that they are satisfied with, and are forced to purchase an exchange-based plan that costs significantly more, it could result in a backlash that could impede further implementation of the ACA.

Critical Policy Issues

Most past health policy initiatives have focused on access to care, cost of care, and quality of care. Some Americans contend that they have the right (access) to the best care (quality) at the least expense (cost) despite their level of income or social class. Legislative efforts, on the other hand, have been specific to issues in access (expanding insurance coverage, outreach programs in rural areas), cost containment (PPS, RBRVS), and quality (creating the Agency for Healthcare Research and Quality [AHRQ] and calling for clinical practice guidelines; see Chapter 12).

With the publication of *Healthy People 2010* and *2020*, elimination of health disparities across sociodemographic subpopulations has emerged as a bold policy objective. Since health disparities are caused primarily by nonmedical factors (see Chapter 2), the advancement of this goal signals a new policy direction that integrates health policy with broader social policies. Although it is highly unlikely that this goal will be fulfilled within the next decade, the promotion of this policy objective reflects a significant government commitment. In the remainder of this section, the three areas of greatest health policy concerns are highlighted.

Access to Care

Underlying support for government policies that enhance access to care is the social justice principle that access to health care is a right that should be guaranteed to all American citizens. There are two variations on this argument: (1) All citizens have a right to the same level of care, and (2) all citizens have a right to some minimum level of care. Which position the United States should espouse has never been openly debated in the policy circles. In the past, access to comprehensive services was aimed primarily at the most needy and underserved populations, as was the case with Medicaid. Medicare, on the other hand, did not incorporate the same

level of access, which was limited by high deductibles and copayments and exclusion of certain services (see Chapter 6).

Providers

Policy issues include ensuring a sufficient number and desirable geographic distribution of various types of providers. The debate over the supply of physicians is an important public policy issue because policy decisions influence the number of persons entering the medical profession, and that number, in turn, has implications for policies related to access and cost. The number of new entrants into the profession is influenced by programs of government assistance for individual students and by government grants made directly to educational institutions. An increased supply of physicians, particularly specialists, may result in increased health care expenditures because of increased demand for care induced by the physicians. An increased supply of physicians, particularly primary care physicians, is necessary to provide basic health care to the newly insured under any expansion of health insurance coverage. For example, the ACA will likely remain ineffective in achieving access goals without increasing the supply of physicians.

One goal on which both Republicans and Democrats seem to agree is preserving community health centers as a safety net for the underprivileged. Consequently, federal support has been boosted. This included doubling of funding over a 5-year period under the Bush Administration and $2 billion in the American Recovery and Reinvestment Act of 2009. In addition, the ACA established the Community Health Center Fund, which will provide $11 billion in funding over a

5-year period for the expansion of health centers across the country (HRSA 2013).

Integrated Access

Access continues to be a problem in many communities, partly because health policies enacted since 1983 have focused on narrowly defined elements of the delivery system. The United States has not had a unified strategy of reforming the system based on a policy of integrated services. Despite an increased reliance on accountable care organizations proposed in the ACA, and other provisions such as integration of long-term care services, it is too early to forecast that the ACA will make a significant headway in making integrated access a reality. For example, as pointed out in Chapter 10, long-term care services need to be integrated not just within their own orbit of services, but also with the larger health care delivery system.

Access and the Elderly

Three main concerns dominate the debate about Medicare policy: (1) Spending should be restrained to keep the program viable, (2) the program is not adequately focused on the management of chronic conditions, and (3) the program does not cover long-term nursing home care. These concerns originate from the assumption that the elderly need public assistance to finance their health care. The ACA's proposed Community Living Assistance Services and Supports (CLASS) provision was repealed in 2012 due to concerns about its stability and feasibility (Colello and Mulvey 2013). While the CLASS provision will not be implemented, the requirements it established are likely to be taken into consideration by a newly

formed Commission on Long-Term Care, which aims to establish recommendations for Congress in 2013 on the development and implementation of a long-term care system (ATRA, P.L. 112-240; Colello and Mulvey 2013).

Access and Minorities

As pointed out in Chapter 11, minorities are more likely than Whites to face access problems. However, with the exception of Native Americans, no other minority population has programs specifically designed to serve its needs. Resolving the problems confronting minority groups would require policies designed to target the special needs of minorities, to encourage professional education programs sensitive to their special needs, and to develop programs to expand the delivery of services to areas populated by minorities.

Access in Rural Areas

Delivery of health care services in rural communities has always raised the question of how to bring advanced medical care to residents of sparsely settled areas. Financing high-tech equipment for a few people is not cost efficient, and finding physicians who want to live in rural areas is difficult. In the area of acute and long-term care, on the other hand, policies have been crafted in the form of the swing bed program and critical access hospitals (see Chapter 8).

Chapter 11 discussed various policy attempts that intend to alleviate shortages of health care professionals in rural areas. They include federal designation of health professional shortage areas (HPSA) and funding for the National Health Service Corps. However, the funding covers a limited period of time per physician and does not help alleviate the issue over a longer term. The ACA contains provisions to boost the supply of the health the care workforce and funding for the National Health Service Corps.

Access and Low Income

Low-income mothers and their children are likely to be uninsured. Many of them also live in medically underserved areas, such as inner cities. Pregnant women in low-income families are far less likely to receive prenatal care than women in higher income categories. The CHIP program requires periodic reauthorization, which can hamper continuity of services to those enrolled. The ACA extends the authorization of CHIP through September 30, 2015.

Access and Persons with AIDS

People with AIDS can face significant barriers in obtaining insurance coverage, and their illness can lead to catastrophic health care expenditures. The ACA makes it illegal to deny insurance coverage to people with HIV/AIDS. However, because of the many legal requirements that place increased burdens on health insurers, premiums are expected to skyrocket. If this happens, people with HIV/AIDS and others with serious preexisting conditions could well end up on Medicaid rolls.

In 2003, George W. Bush pledged $15 billion over 5 years to combat HIV/AIDS in developing countries, with a particular focus on Africa. In 2010, the White House released the National HIV/AIDS Strategy, which outlined goals for reducing infection rates, increasing access to care, and reducing the disparities experienced in receiving care (National HIV/AIDS Strategy 2010).

To support the achievement of these goals, funding for HIV/AIDS programs and policies has increased, with a proposed $29.7 billion in funding requested for fiscal year 2014 (Office of Management and Budget 2013).

Cost of Care

No other aspect of health care policy has received more attention during the past 30-plus years than efforts to contain health care costs. As pointed out in previous chapters, the government's main weapon of cost control has been payment cuts to providers. PPS has achieved success in curtailing inpatient costs, but outpatient costs have continued to escalate. Direct control over utilization has not been tried by public payers (Medicaid in the state of Oregon being one exception), but it became widely unpopular when HMOs tried it. Whether or not public policy can be used to impose explicit rationing in the United States is yet to be seen. The fragmented multipayer system does not lend itself to a centralized policy of cost containment.

Quality of Care

Along with access and cost, quality of care is the third main concern of health care policy. In March 2001, the Institute of Medicine (IOM) issued a comprehensive report, *Crossing the Quality Chasm*. Building on the extensive evidence collected by the IOM committee, the report identified six areas for quality improvement: (1) Safety—Patients should be as safe in health care facilities as they are in their homes. (2) Effectiveness—The health care system should avoid overuse of ineffective care and underuse of effective care. (3) Patient centeredness—Respect for the patient's choices, culture, social context, and special needs must be incorporated into the delivery of services. (4) Timeliness—Waiting times and delays should be continually reduced for both patients and caregivers. (5) Efficiency—Health care should engage in a never-ending pursuit to reduce total costs by curtailing waste, such as waste of supplies, equipment, space, capital, and the innovative human spirit. (6) Equity—The system should seek to close racial and ethnic gaps in health status. (Berwick 2002)

Research on Quality

Funding to evaluate new treatment methods and diagnostic tools has increased dramatically; so has funding for research to measure the outcome of medical interventions and appropriateness of medical procedures. The AHRQ is one of 12 agencies within the DHHS. Its mission is to improve the quality, safety, efficiency, and effectiveness of health care for all Americans. AHRQ fulfills this mission by developing and working with the health care system to implement information that:

- Reduces the risk of harm from health care services by using evidence-based research and technology to promote the delivery of the best possible care
- Transforms the practice of health care to achieve wider access to effective services and reduce unnecessary health care costs
- Improves health care outcomes by encouraging providers, consumers, and patients to use evidence-based information to make informed treatment decisions

Ultimately, AHRQ achieves its goals by translating research into improved health care practice and policy. Health care providers, patients, policymakers, payers, administrators, and others use AHRQ research findings to improve health care quality, accessibility, and outcomes of care (AHRQ 2013). Comparative effectiveness research (CER) is a more recent undertaking by the AHRQ (see details in Chapter 14).

Malpractice Reform

The federal government began its actions to relieve the malpractice crisis and devote greater attention to policing the quality of medical care with the Health Care Quality Act of 1986. This legislation mandated the creation of a national database within the DHHS to provide data on legal actions against health care providers. This information helps people recruiting physicians in one state know of actions against those physicians in other states. On the other hand, comprehensive tort reform, so far, has failed to materialize despite a lot of lip service from the politicians. Some states have limited damage awards in malpractice cases, but no uniform national policy has emerged. One main reason is opposition from trial lawyers and consumer groups, who contend that limiting lawsuit awards hurts victims of egregious medical mistakes and reduces incentives to protect patient safety.

Role of Research in Policy Development

The research community can influence health policy making through documentation, analysis, and prescription (Longest 2010). The first role of research in policy making is documentation; that is, the gathering, cataloging, and correlating of facts that depict the state of the world that policymakers face. This process may help define a given public policy problem or raise its political profile. A second way in which research informs and, thus, influences policymaking is through analysis of what does and does not work. Examples include program evaluation and outcomes research. Often taking the form of demonstration projects intended to provide a basis for determining the feasibility, efficacy, or practicality of a possible policy intervention, analysis can help define solutions to health policy problems. The third way in which research influences policy making is through prescription. Research that demonstrates that a course of action being contemplated by policymakers may (or may not) lead to undesirable or unexpected consequences can contribute significantly to policymaking.

Future Considerations in Health Policy

Domestic Health Policy

With the enactment of the ACA, the landscape of health policy in the United States is on the verge of undergoing significant change. While the health policy reforms under the ACA will impact access to health services, increased attention must be given to ensuring high-quality, personalized, and effective care for each and every patient. This is especially important in the area of primary and preventive health policy, which can be used as a tool to improve both health outcomes and ensure long-term cost containment. Currently, initiatives are underway to expand and evaluate primary care delivery models, such as patient-centered medical homes, that aim to provide consistent, continuous, and high-quality care.

International Health Policy

As with domestic health policy efforts, international health initiatives have faced challenges in recent years as a result of continuing attempts to reduce government spending. As a result, government spending on global health initiatives has remained largely stagnant. For example, funding for the Global Health Initiative, the umbrella of global health programs launched by President Obama in 2009, is projected to be funded at $9 billion in fiscal year 2014, a level that has remained stable since fiscal year 2010 when it was funded at $8.9 billion (Kaiser Family Foundation 2013). Within the current budget constraints, initiatives must attempt to address immediate health concerns and aid in building both the capacity of the United States and that of other countries to address evolving health issues, requiring a greater emphasis on innovation in global health policy.

Summary

The US health care delivery system is the product of many health policies, which over the years have brought about incremental changes. Health policies are developed to serve the public's interests; however, public interests are diverse. Interest group politics often have a remarkable influence on policy making. On the other hand, a complex process and divided opinions may leave the public out of even major policy decisions. Although the public wants the government to control health care costs, it also believes that the federal government already controls too much of Americans' daily lives. Presidential leadership and party politics played a major role in the passage of the Affordable Care Act. Yet, several critical policy issues pertaining to access, cost, and quality remain. Among future challenges, cost containment will be the most daunting. The political feasibility of adopting a public policy to impose explicit rationing in the United States is yet unknown.

ACA Takeaway

- The DHHS and the IRS have been charged with the responsibilities for regulating most of the ACA's provisions.
- Expansion of health insurance for the uninsured—proposed under the ACA—is based on a redistributive approach.
- The ACA is based on the liberal view that health care is a right of citizenship, but not all Americans espouse this view; hence, the nation is deeply divided over the ACA.
- The ACA became a reality only after reaching compromises with the hospital industry, insurance companies, and the pharmaceutical industry.
- The enactment of the ACA became reality following a unique political approach that is perhaps unparalleled in the history of American policy making. It was enacted by one single party with absolutely no support from the opposing party representing the other half of America.
- Despite the early rollout of certain provisions, much remains to be done in implementing the full law. In early July 2013, the US Department of the Treasury reported that the employer mandate would be pushed back until 2015. Consumer cost protection mandates are also postponed until 2015.

Test Your Understanding

Terminology

allocative tools	*health policy*	*redistributive policies*
distributive policies	*public policies*	*regulatory tools*

Review Questions

1. What is health policy? How can health policies be used as regulatory or allocative tools?

2. What are the principal features of US health policy? Why do these features characterize US health policy?

3. Identify health care interest groups and their concerns.

4. Why do you think the Clinton health reform failed but the Obama health reform succeeded?

5. What is the process of legislative health policy in the United States? How is this process related to the principal features of US health policy?

6. Describe the critical policy issues related to access to care, cost of care, and quality of care.

REFERENCES

Agency for Healthcare Research and Quality (AHRQ). 2013. *AHRQ annual highlights, 2012.* Available at: http://www.ahrq.gov/news/newsroom/highlights/highlt12.html. Accessed August 2013.

Alford, R.R. 1975. *Health care politics: Ideology and interest group barriers to reform.* Chicago, IL: University of Chicago Press.

American Taxpayer Relief Act of 2012 (ATRA). Pub. L. 112-240, Sec 643.

Berwick, D.M. 2002. A user's manual for the IOM's "Quality Chasm" report. *Health Affairs* 21, no. 3: 80–90.

Bodenheimer, T. 1997. The Oregon health plan—Lessons for the nation. *New England Journal of Medicine* 337, no. 9: 651–655.

Colello, K.J., and Mulvey, J. 2013. *Community Living Assistance Services and Supports (CLASS): Overview and summary of provisions.* CRS Report R40847. Washington, DC: Congressional Research Service.

Conover, C. 2013. Obamacare will increase health spending by $7,450 for a typical family of four [updated]. *Forbes*, September 23. Available at: http://www.forbes.com/sites/theapothecary/2013/09/23/its-official-obamacare-will-increase-health-spending-by-7450-for-a-typical-family-of-four. Accessed October 2013.

Coughlin, T., et al. 1999. A conflict of strategies: Medicaid managed care and Medicaid maximization. *Health Services Research* 34, no. 1: 281–293.

Falcone, D., and L.C. Hartwig. 1991. Congressional process and health policy: Reform and retrenchment. In: *Health policies and policy.* 2nd ed. T. Litman and L. Robins, eds. New York: John Wiley & Sons. pp. 126–144.

Heath Resources and Services Administration (HRSA). 2013. *The Affordable Care Act and health centers.* Available at: http://bphc.hrsa.gov/about/healthcenterfactsheet.pdf. Accessed August 2013.

Kaiser Family Foundation. 2013. *U.S. funding for global health: The President's FY 2014 budget request*. Available at: http://kff.org/global-health-policy/fact-sheet/u-s-funding-for-global-health-the-presidents-fy-2014-budget-request/. Accessed August 2013.

Kaiser Family Foundation. 2013a. *Health reform implementation timeline*. Available at: http://kff.org/interactive/implementation-timeline/. Accessed January 2014.

Kaiser Family Foundation. 2013b. *Status of state action on the Medicaid expansion decision, as of July 1, 2013*. Available at: http://kff.org/medicaid/state-indicator/state-activity-around-expanding-medicaid-under-the-affordable-care-act/. Accessed January 2014.

Kaiser Family Foundation. 2013c. State decisions for Creating Health Insurance Exchanges, as of May 28, 2013. Available at: http://kff.org/health-reform/state-indicator/health-insurance-exchanges/. Accessed January 2014.

Longest, B.B. 2010. *Health policymaking in the United States*. 5th ed. Ann Arbor, MI: Health Administration Press.

Lowry, R. 2013. Obama's false insurance promise. *New York Post*, October 29. Available at: http://nypost.com/2013/10/29/obamas-false-insurance-promise. Accessed October 2013.

Miller, C.A. 1987. Child health. In: *Epidemiology and health policy*. S. Levine and A. Lillienfeld, eds. New York: Tavistock Publications.

Morone J.A., et al. 2008. *Health policies and policy*. 4th ed. New York: Delmar.

Myers, L., and H. Rappleye. 2013. Obama administration knew millions could not keep their health insurance. NBC News Investigations. Available at: http://investigations.nbcnews.com/_news/2013/10/29/21222195-obama-administration-knew-millions-could-not-keep-their-health-insurance?lite. Accessed October 2013.

National HIV/AIDS Strategy for the United States. 2010. Available at: http://aids.gov/federal-resources/national-hiv-aids-strategy/nhas.pdf. Accessed August 2013.

National Institutes of Health (NIH). 2013. *Summary of the FY 2014 President's Budget*. Available at: http://officeofbudget.od.nih.gov/pdfs/FY14/FY%202014_OVERVIEW.pdf. Accessed August 2013.

New York Times. 2013. A limit on consumer costs is delayed in health care law. Available at: http://www.nytimes.com/2013/08/13/us/a-limit-on-consumer-costs-is-delayed-in-health-care-law.html?hp&_r=0. Accessed January 2014.

Oberlander, J. 2010. Long time coming: Why health reform finally passed. *Health Affairs* 29, no. 6: 1112–1116.

Office of Management and Budget. 2013. Strengthening the economy for those living with HIV/AIDS and fighting the HIV/AIDS epidemic. Available at: http://www.whitehouse.gov/omb/budget/factsheet/strengthening-the-economy-hiv-aids. Accessed August 2013.

Oliver, T.R., et al. 2004. A political history of Medicare and prescription drug coverage. *Milbank Quarterly* 82, no. 2: 283–354.

Patel, K., and J. McDonough. 2010. From Massachusetts to 1600 Pennsylvania Avenue: Aboard the health reform express. *Health Affairs* 29, no. 6: 1106–1111.

Pye, J. 2010. Pelosi: "We have to pass the bill so that you can find out what is in it." Available at: http://www.unitedliberty.org/articles/5233-pelosi-we-have-to-pass-the-bill-so-that-you-can-find-out-what-is-in-it. Accessed March 2011.

Roff, P. 2010. Pelosi: Pass health reform so you can find out what's in it. *US News and World Report: Politics*. Available at: http://www.usnews.com/opinion/blogs/peter-roff/2010/03/09 /pelosi-pass-health-reform-so-you-can-find-out-whats-in-it. Accessed March 2011.

Roy, A. 2012. How the AARP made $2.8 billion by supporting Obamacare's cuts to Medicare. Available at: http://www.forbes.com/sites/aroy/2012/09/22/the-aarps-2-8-billion-reasons-for-supporting-obamacares-cuts-to-medicare. Retrieved October 2013.

U.S. Department of the Treasury. 2013. Continuing to implement the ACA in a careful, thoughtful manner. Available at: http://www.treasury.gov/connect/blog/Pages/Continuing-to-Implement-the-ACA-in-a-Careful-Thoughtful-Manner-.aspx. Accessed January 2014.

Wall Street Journal. 2010. Republicans and ObamaCare. *Wall Street Journal-Eastern Edition* March 23: A20.

Weissert, C., and W. Weissert. 1996. *Governing health: The politics of health policy*. Baltimore: Johns Hopkins University Press.

The White House. 2013. We're listening to businesses about the health care law. Available at: http://www.whitehouse.gov/blog/2013/07/02/we-re-listening-businesses-about-health-care-law. Accessed January 2014.

PART V

System Outlook

Chapter 14

The Future of Health Services Delivery

Learning Objectives

- To identify the major forces of future change and how they will affect health care delivery
- To assess the future of the Affordable Care Act and health care reform in the United States
- To discuss the components necessary to build a delivery infrastructure for the future
- To understand the special skills needed by future nurses, physicians, and other health care workers
- To evaluate the future of long-term care
- To appreciate the role of international cooperation in dealing with global threats
- To obtain an overview of new frontiers in clinical technology
- To survey the future of evidence-based health care based on comparative effectiveness research and patient-oriented outcomes research

"Will the U.S. have a single-payer system?"

Introduction

The future outlook of health care delivery in the United States is predicated on major current developments and the course these developments might take in the foreseeable future. On the other hand, any attempts to project the future of health care provoke more questions than answers, and the future often turns out differently than people anticipate (Kenen 2011). Even though most of the provisions contained in the Affordable Care Act (ACA) went into effect in 2014, its consequences, both good and bad, will be experienced for years to come. The health care industry has so far reacted by consolidating and forming organizational alliances in which hospitals, physicians, and in many instances, managed care organizations have integrated as major partners (see Chapter 9). The insurance industry has been dropping many individual plans because they do not comply with the ACA's mandate to include essential health benefits (see Chapter 6). Many employers are trying to cope by reducing worker hours, negotiating new health plans, or sending workers to the government exchanges. By and large, the American people have remained passive, adopting a "wait and see" attitude.

When we look at health care delivery as an institution in and of itself, several external factors can be identified that would exert powerful influences for this institution to change and conform. Certain forces, such as demographic trends, project a foreseeable course, based on which some predictions can be made. For other external factors, even short-term predictions are difficult. For instance, it is impossible to predict the future course of the US economy and family incomes, both of which will affect what individual Americans and the nation may or may not be able to afford.

Future change also relies on historical precedents. Certain fundamental features of US health care delivery, such as a largely private infrastructure and the society's fundamental values, have, in the past, resisted any proposals for a sweeping transformation of health care. Yet, certain historical precedents have also been used as a springboard for current change (see Chapter 3), and they will no doubt influence future change as well.

This chapter puts the future of health care in the larger national and global context. It also assesses the likely future course of health care reform, clinical technology, and new models of delivering health care.

Forces of Future Change

The framework presented here includes 8 main forces that help us understand why certain changes have occurred in the past, and they can help inform the direction of change that might occur in the future. This framework can be used not only for viewing health care delivery and policy from a macro perspective, but it can also be used by health care executives to craft strategies for their organizations that are aligned with the changes occurring in the broader health care environment.

The 8 forces are (1) social and demographic, (2) political, (3) economic, (4) technological, (5) informational, (6) ecological, (7) global, and (8) anthro-cultural. These forces often interact in complex ways, and these interactions are generally difficult to interpret. Keen observation of these forces, however, can create opportunities for change.

How those opportunities are either garnered or forgone determines the nature of change. With the passage of time, some forces become more dominant than others. The directions of change these forces may portend have implications for cost, and hence, affordability; access to services; and power balancing within the health care system (see Chapter 1). Hence, the US health care system will continue to evolve, but nobody knows its ultimate destiny.

Another important point to bear in mind is the fact that for several decades now, the US health care delivery system has not been driven by free-market forces (see Chapter 1). Over the years, the government has become a major player that has controlled a growing segment of health care financing (see Chapter 6), and has increasingly wielded control over the private sector through its legal and regulatory powers. Yet, the government needs the private health care sector to serve its millions of beneficiaries in various public health insurance programs. At least for the foreseeable future, tension and power balancing between the private and public sectors will continue, and for better or for worse, we will see ongoing changes in the way Americans receive health care.

Another important point to keep in mind is the fact that health care encompasses almost one-fifth of the nation's economy. The ongoing ability to deliver health care is, therefore, closely tied to the nation's economic health, regardless of whether health care is delivered through private or public insurance programs.

Social and Demographic Forces

Demographically, the United States is getting bigger, older, and more ethnically diverse.

Shifts in the demographic composition of the population, cultural factors, and lifestyles affect not only the need for health care but also how those needs will be met. Demographic trends will also continue to affect a nation's ability to afford health care services.

The elderly, vulnerable populations, and people with certain health conditions all present varied needs. These groups are also among the highest cost drivers. Trends pertaining to the growing elderly population are covered in Chapter 10; almost all receive health care through Medicare, and a small proportion from both Medicare and Medicaid. Among vulnerable populations, disabled Medicare beneficiaries under the age of 65 have also been on the rise, from 13.3% of all Medicare beneficiaries in 1999 to 16% in 2009 (DHHS 2003a, 2012). During this same time period, Medicaid recipients (another vulnerable population group) increased by 56% (DHHS 2012). These expanding government programs are on an unsustainable financial path. According to the 2013 Medicare Trustees Report, the Hospital Insurance (Part A) trust fund will be insolvent in 2026 (Davis 2013). Supplementary Medical Insurance (SMI) trust fund is not projected to become insolvent simply because the government is obligated to fund the deficits from general tax revenues. In other words, general taxes must be raised or spending must be cut in other areas to keep funding SMI, which mainly covers payments to physicians (Part B) and cost of prescription drugs (Part D). Both Medicare and Medicaid face future challenges that still remain unresolved. According to the 2013 report of the Board of Trustees of the Federal Old-Age and Survivors Insurance and Federal Disability Insurance Trust Funds, retirement of the baby-boom generation—which started in 2011—will increase the number of beneficiaries much faster than the increase in the numbers of workers who will pay taxes. Cost projections by the Congressional Budget Office (CBO) estimate that Medicare, Medicaid, and Social Security will account for more than 90% of the growth in mandatory federal spending[1] between 2013 and 2022 (CBO 2012). Only after 2050 will the baby-boom generation be gradually replaced at retirement ages by historically low-birth-rate generations, causing the beneficiary-to-worker ratio to decline. Until 2050, the state of the nation's economy will be one of the key factors that will determine the future of Medicare, Medicaid, and also Social Security, the nation's retirement program funded through workers' payroll taxes, similar to Medicare.

An equally challenging factor is how population shifts affect the composition of the health care workforce, because health care delivery is labor intensive. In a free society, people choose their professions and where they work. As pointed out in Chapter 4, social and demographic factors have played a significant role in determining the number of health care professionals and their geographic distribution. Future immigration will be one factor that will affect the supply of health care professionals.

The society's cultural mix, also based on the rate and quality of immigration, will continue to slowly transform health care delivery. For example, language and other cultural barriers affect both the patient and caregiver. Language training and posting of signs in different languages are only one small piece of the more complex cultural

puzzle. Social and cultural factors affect exposure and vulnerability to disease, risk-taking behaviors, health promotion and disease prevention, and health care–seeking behavior. For example, non-Hispanic whites are more likely to visit physicians' clinics, whereas non-Hispanic blacks more frequently seek care in emergency rooms. The large number of illegal immigrants, estimated to be around 13 million (Shrestha and Heisler 2011) and not covered by any health insurance program, including the ACA, also tap into the nation's health care resources. The United States has failed to craft and pursue a well thought-out immigration policy. Hence, the effects of immigration on the economy and on health care remain unclear. Social and cultural factors also play a role in shaping perceptions of and responses to health problems.

To a large extent, population growth and aging are noncontrollable factors. Even individual responsibility for one's own health is largely beyond the control of employers and the government, except that incentives created for people to engage in healthy behaviors to prevent disease and disability can have some effect. Personal lifestyles significantly impact the future of wellness, prevention, health promotion, and the burden placed on financing and delivery of health care. Despite its heavy focus on prevention, it is not clear to what extent the ACA will successfully change individual behaviors to make any significant headway in reducing the burden of disease in society.

Economic Forces

The national debt, economic growth, and employment are major forces that will determine the availability of health care services,

---

[1]Medicare, Medicaid, and Social Security constitute more than 75% of mandatory expenditures.

their cost, and affordability. Besides employment, household income is a fundamental determinant of affordability, and both employment and personal income depend on the nation's economic health. Yet, as more and more people start depending on government handouts, it will not prove to be a recipe for economic growth, just the contrary.

On October 31, 2013 (this is just an arbitrary date), the national debt of the United States stood at $17,156,117,102,204.49—surpassing $17 trillion (Department of Treasury 2013a). This is over 100% of the nation's gross domestic product (GDP), estimated to be $16.7 trillion in 2013. The debt is the cumulative result of spending more than the revenues generated mainly through taxation. The deficit spending amounted to $1,089 billion in 2012, compared to $455 billion in 2008 (Department of Treasury 2013b). Deficit spending has to be financed by borrowing money. Whether this much debt can reach a point of crisis is a matter of controversy, but common sense suggests that all debts have to be repaid, nor can there be a default on the outstanding debt without jeopardizing the nation's economy. If the debt was not a matter of concern, the United States Treasury would need not bother publishing the extent of national indebtedness. There also would not be a need to waste public resources on publishing the trustee reports for Medicare and Social Security; in fact, there would not be a need to have trustees. So, there are obvious concerns that the public debt must be reduced. The obvious solutions are the reverse of what creates debt—a combination of spending cuts, tax increases, and economic growth. High rates of economic growth can lower the need for spending cuts and raising the tax rates.

The recession ended in June 2009, but the pace of economic recovery and employment has been slow. In 2012 alone, the before-tax median household income of Americans, adjusted for inflation, had fallen 8.3% from the prerecession level in 2007 (Center on Budget and Policy Priorities 2013). The CBO projected the economy's output to remain below its potential until the first half of 2018. Beyond that date, it is almost impossible to predict the timing or magnitude of fluctuations in the economic cycle (CBO 2012). One silver lining on the horizon is that the growth in the gross domestic product (GDP) is expected to exceed the growth in federal expenditures between 2012 and 2018 (CBO 2012). These projections assume that provisions of the Budget Control Act of 2011, which established automatic enforcement procedures to restrain both mandatory and discretionary spending, remain unchanged. In making these projections, the CBO made three main cautionary assertions: (1) Spending per enrollee for Medicare and Medicaid has generally grown faster than the GDP; if per capita costs grew just one percentage point faster per year than what the CBO has projected, spending for Medicare and Medicaid would increase by approximately $800 billion over the following 10 years. (2) The potential budgetary consequences of the ACA were uncertain. (3) According to the Sustainable Growth Rate (SGR) formula, which is part of the resource-based relative value scale (RBRVS) payment system to reimburse physicians (discussed in Chapter 6), physicians' fees were to be reduced by 27% in 2012. Each year since the SGR was made part of RBRVS reimbursement, Congress has overridden fee reductions for physicians. If physicians' fees are allowed to stay at their 2012 levels (without the reduction called for by the SGR formula), spending would increase by

$316 billion over the following 10 years. In short, a lot remains unknown about future health care spending. National health expenditures are projected to grow one percentage point above the rate of GDP growth from 2012 to 2022, reaching 19.9% of GDP by 2022, up from 17.9% in 2011 (CMS 2013).

A golden prospect that has been left out of the CBO projections, and something that even most Americans are unaware of, is the oil and gas renaissance in the United States. Thanks to new technology and private initiative, the United States has become the largest energy producer in the world. This statement may surprise some, but it is true. Declaring energy self-sufficiency at this point, however, would be like counting chickens before they hatch. Yet, to the dismay of many in the business world, the trustee of the precious energy resources, the United States, does not have an energy policy for the future. Hence, much will depend on future energy policy which can either turn an abundant God-given resource into helping Americans financially or it can turn into a self-destructive weapon that "kills the goose that lays the golden eggs." Judiciously harnessed, this one resource may well be the key to solving America's looming economic crises.

At present, it is uncertain what effects the ACA would have on employment and household incomes. According to a *CNNMoney* poll of 14 economists conducted in September 2013, 9 indicated that businesses were putting off hiring in light of health care reform, even though the employer mandate had been pushed back until 2015 (Hargreaves 2013). Small businesses, for example, could cut hiring and reduce worker hours to keep their full-time equivalent to below 50 employees. Under the ACA, employers do not have to provide health insurance to workers who work less than 30 hours a week. The nonpartisan Employee Benefit Research Institute, however, has found that the trend toward more part-time workers—and less employment-based health insurance coverage—started in 2007, well before the passage of the ACA (Fronstin 2013). If this trend continues, the ACA could be a boon for part-time workers who can get government subsidies to buy coverage through the exchanges. However, the affordability of exchange-based health insurance remains unclear. In the long run, businesses make strategic decisions in the light of the various forces discussed in this section; hence, much remains unknown about future directions in employment and household incomes.

Political Forces

Chapter 13 discusses the role of politics and its influence on health policy. As should be apparent throughout this book, policy is closely intertwined with almost all aspects of health care delivery. Policies that affect education at home, as well as immigration policies, can determine not only the number but also the qualifications needed for the future health care workforce. The history of health care in the United States and in other countries is replete with examples of major changes brought about through political will. Politics serves a nation best when it is subservient to the people's will. However, Americans remain divided on major policy issues, and health care is one such issue. It is anyone's guess whether the ACA would have passed or failed had there been adequate transparency and public debate. The nation's total economic spending and tax policies also lie in the hands of the politicians. Will they have the resolve, for example, to cut runaway government spending? Will they raise taxes to a point that severely stifles economic growth? These issues make national headlines during squabbles between the two political parties about raising the debt ceiling, meaning increasing the spending levels. Ironically, we do not hear about any collaborative efforts to reduce the debt ceiling.

Technological Forces

It is widely believed that technological innovation in medical sciences will continue to revolutionize health care. Americans strongly favor ongoing innovation, availability, and use of new technology. The high cost of research and development and subsequent costs of unrestrained use of technology, however, do raise questions about how long this can continue, given that the growth in health care spending will continue to surpass GDP growth. Yet, technologies that promote a greater degree of self-reliance and/or achieve cost efficiencies will receive much attention in the future. Nevertheless, the overall effect of technology is to increase costs unless it is accompanied by utilization control measures.

Informational Forces

Information technology (IT) has numerous applications in health care delivery, as Chapter 5 points out. IT has also become an indispensable tool for managing today's health care organizations. Garnering IT's full potential is still evolving and will continue well into the future.

Ecological Forces

New diseases, natural disasters, and bio-terrorism have major implications for public health. These factors can even have global consequences. Diseases that are communicable—such as new strains of influenza—and those related to environmental agents—such as vector-borne diseases (for example, West Nile virus and chikungunya virus)—can bring about mass hysteria, particularly in large population centers, especially when the disease remains mysterious and treatments are not readily available. *Zoonoses* refer to any diseases or infections that are naturally transmittable from vertebrate animals to humans. Growth of populations around the globe will intensify the human–animal–ecosystems interface, raising the probability of engendering diseases that are yet unknown. When a significant number of people are affected or threatened by disease, research and technological innovation go into high gear. Technologies, such as remote sensing and geographic information systems (GIS), will find ongoing applications in public health and safety.

Natural disasters disrupt not only people's daily lives, but also create conditions that pose serious health risks through contamination of food and water. Health problems and psychological distress often follow. Initiatives, such as biosurveillance and infrastructure upgrades, undertaken to cope with natural and man-made disasters are discussed in Chapter 2. The roles of the Centers for Disease Control and Prevention (CDC) and other partnering agencies will continue to evolve as new challenges emerge. On the down side, the growing need for combatting new ecological threats will divert resources from providing routine health care to patients.

Global Forces

The economies of the world are becoming progressively more interdependent.

Globalization has become an extremely complex phenomenon, because the various forces discussed here interact as this phenomenon continues to evolve (Huynen et al. 2005). For example, Rennen and Martens (2003) define contemporary globalization in terms of an intensification of cross-national cultural, economic, political, social, and technological interactions. Hence, health and health care in various countries will continue to be affected in diverse ways through multiple pathways. To give a simple example, "brain drains" of physicians, therapists, and nurses from developing countries to relieve shortages in developed countries generally occur for personal economic reasons, but social, cultural, and technological factors may pose hindrances in the full utilization of their talents and learning. Economically backward countries have received "brain gains" as the number of health professionals from developed countries on medical missions to provide care in poorer countries has grown globally (Martiniuk et al. 2012). Medical missionaries do charity work out of a sense of deeply rooted personal ethics and compassion, but cross-cultural factors have at least some diluting effects on their optimum performance.

Other signs suggest that globalization in health care will intensify. Increasingly, generic drugs are being manufactured in Asian countries for export to Europe, Canada, and the United States. This trend has made drugs more affordable in the United States, but insuring safety and adequate supplies to meet demand on a consistent basis poses major challenges for the Food and Drug Administration (FDA). Medical tourism is likely to increase if high-deductible health plans (see Chapter 6), which give greater control to the consumer on how to spend their own savings on health care, continue to grow. Given the high cost of health care services in the United States and Europe, providers from other countries are providing or will soon be able to provide lower cost, but almost identically high-quality health services, and these services often come with greater amenities (Reeves 2011). Moreover, cross-border telemedicine used in conjunction with medical tourism is becoming a rapidly developing trend (George and Henthorne 2009). In the future, we may also see foreign hospitals and clinics providing services within the United States. Countries such as Japan, Norway, Australia, and India have asked for standardization of licensing and qualification requirements in the United States and/or to allow service providers licensed in one state to practice in all states (Arnold and Reeves 2006).

Anthro-Cultural Forces

Here, by anthro-cultural we mean a society's beliefs, values, ethos, and traditions, which, in the health care context, are discussed in Chapter 2. It would also be helpful to review that the beliefs and values discussed in the previous chapters are espoused primarily by middle-class Americans. As pointed out in Chapter 3, American beliefs and values have historically acted as a strong deterrent against attempts to initiate radical changes in the financing and delivery of health care. Gallup poll results published in July 2013 showed that 52% of Americans disapproved the ACA, up from 45% in November 2012 (Gallup 2013a), as many more have learned about some of the details in this complex law. A survey in September 2013 conducted by the Pew Research Center (Pew) and *USA Today* also found that 53% of Americans disapproved of the ACA; 42% approved.

Pew commented, "opinions are now as negative as they have been [at] any point since the bill's passage" (Pew Research Center 2013). Looking ahead to the coming years, more Americans anticipate negative personal effects: 41% said the effect on themselves and their families would be negative; 25% said it would be positive, according to the Pew/*USA Today* poll. It is certainly not beyond the realm of possibility that the American public may end up deciding the final fate of the ACA.

The Future of Health Care Reform

Speculations abound that the ACA would eventually lead to a ***single-payer system***, which is a national health care program in which the financing and insurance functions are taken over by the federal government. In fact, Senator Majority Leader, Harry Reid (D), one of the chief architects of the ACA, confessed in an interview that the United States needed to work its way past an insurance-based health care system and suggested that that would absolutely happen. He further stated, "Don't think we didn't have a tremendous number of people [Democrat lawmakers] who wanted a single-payer system" (McHugh 2013). So, will the United States have a single-payer system in the future? Perhaps, yes; perhaps, no. Much will depend on the ACA's promises becoming reality, how it will affect the majority of middle-class Americans, and how the forces just discussed play out in the future. For example, if health insurance premium costs and out-of-pocket costs rise beyond what most people consider to be unaffordable, there could be a push for a single-payer system; however, it would require control of the presidency and the

Congress to be in the hands of the Democratic Party, just as it was with the passage of the ACA. Conversely, mass dissatisfaction with the ACA would kill the prospects of a single-payer system regardless of who controls the White House and Congress.

Lessons From Massachusetts

Experience in Massachusetts may provide a window into the future of the ACA, because the basic features of the federal health care reform law were patterned after the Massachusetts health plan (see Chapter 3). Hence, with some caution, lessons can be drawn regarding the future of the ACA.

The Massachusetts plan has achieved some successes, but problems with costs remain the primary issue. As was expected, health insurance coverage increased markedly in Massachusetts between 2006 (before the plan was implemented) and 2010, including for those most in need of health care, such as individuals reporting poor physical or mental health (Dhingra et al. 2013). The proportion of uninsured fell to 12-year lows, from 11.5% in 1996 to 3.5% in 2008. The overall increase in premiums between 2009 and 2011 was 9.7%, far exceeding the rate of inflation. In 2012, 59% of the total enrollment was in HMO plans (Massachusetts Center for Health Information and Analysis 2013). For health insurance offered through the exchanges (called Health Connector in Massachusetts), the state set limits on the rise in premiums (Robillard 2010). It is possible that insurance companies were able to absorb the slack through the volume of newly insured customers and by shifting costs to employer-based plans. Among Massachusetts residents, 62% had employer-based coverage (Massachusetts Center for Health Information and Analysis 2013).

Whether limits placed by the government on rises in premiums can continue in the future remains to be seen.

The overall prevalence of unmet needs because of inability to afford health care fell from 9.2% in 1996 to 7.2% in 2008. However, this was not the case for middle-income earners, Hispanics, Blacks, and those in fair to poor health (Clark et al. 2011). Although disparities may remain in some areas, for some surgical procedures racial disparities were actually reduced (Loehrer et al. 2013). The overall volume of emergency department utilization has continued to rise, with only a small decrease in the rate of low-severity visits (Smulowitz et al. 2011). The likely reason is a shortage of primary care physicians (PCPs), even though Massachusetts has a high number of PCPs and the state improved its primary care capacity by increasing the number of nurse practitioners and physician assistants. Conversely, hospitals experienced a significant decline in charity care and uncompensated care (Edwards 2010).

In the 2013 health care public opinion survey, the Massachusetts Medical Society reported 56% of those surveyed were satisfied with the health care they received. Two main concerns expressed were cost and waiting times to see a physician (Massachusetts Medical Society 2013).

The Massachusetts law focused on expanding coverage, leaving cost containment "for another day" (Mechanic et al. 2012). As time progressed, health care expenditures became the biggest challenge. After three rounds of reform legislation, a fourth round, called Chapter 224, appointed a health policy commission with a variety of regulatory powers that include limiting health care cost growth to mirror the state's economic growth and reducing Medicaid payments to providers (Barr 2013). Governor Deval Patrick also proposed an income tax hike, in addition to higher taxes on gasoline and tobacco.

Likely Experiences Under the ACA

One main caution in translating everything from Massachusetts and applying it nationally is that one state does not represent the ethos of the entire country. As pointed out earlier, before the ACA was fully implemented a significant proportion of Americans were opposed to the law. In 2011, even though 96% of physicians were accepting new patients, 31% were unwilling to accept new Medicaid patients (Decker 2012). The main reason is low reimbursement and delays in receiving payment from Medicaid after services have been delivered. To assess physician perspectives about the ACA and the future of the medical profession, a 2013 survey of US physicians conducted by the Deloitte Center for Health Solutions (Keckley et al. 2013) pointed to a relatively high level of dissatisfaction, particularly among PCPs, among whom only 59% were satisfied with their profession. Six in 10 physicians indicated that many would retire earlier than planned based on how the future of medicine was changing. Six in 10 physicians also indicated that the practice of medicine was in jeopardy. In addition, physicians thought that their take-home pay was decreasing as a result of the ACA; inadequate reimbursement in the future was one of the main concerns expressed by 90% of physicians. To address the problems in the US health care system, 44% of the physicians thought that the ACA was a good start, while 38% believed that the ACA was a step in the wrong direction. These results contradict findings from Massachusetts where a large number of physicians (70%) supported health care reform (SteelFisher et al. 2009). Of course, it is possible that negative sentiments expressed by the American public and physicians could dissipate as time progresses. For example, it is possible that as time progresses, an increasing number of people would feel like winners under the ACA. Physicians who feel like quitting may find that they have no other choice but to carry on in their chosen profession. Conversely, it is also possible that the concerns expressed could pose serious challenges to the ACA in the future. The general public and the physicians may hold the key to the future of the ACA.

Based on the experiences in Massachusetts, the ACA will decrease the number of uninsured, particularly among vulnerable and low-income population groups. However, the law fails to achieve universal coverage, leaving 25 to 30 million uninsured, even though reductions in the number of uninsured would be quite significant. Of greater concern, however, is access to health care by the 25 million newly insured between 2014 and 2023, as estimated by the Congressional Budget Office (CBO 2013). The shortage of primary care physicians (PCPs) will be a major barrier to access. The access dilemma is compounded by the fact that states with the smallest number of PCPs per capita overall, generally in the South and Mountain West, will also see the largest percentage increases in Medicaid enrollment (Cunningham 2011). Mirroring the experience in Massachusetts, the ACA presages greater government control over health care through stifling regulations, lower reimbursement for providers, higher costs, and higher taxes.

Keeping cost escalations within reasonable limits will remain the major challenge. People will negatively react to any significant increases in their out-of-pocket costs. Physicians particularly will react to cuts in their personal earnings. The ACA's effect on jobs and the economy is uncertain, although a number of employers have reduced worker hours to avoid offering health insurance. In a Gallup poll, 41% of the small business owners indicated that they had held off on hiring new employees, while others had reduced their number of employees or had reduced employee hours (Gallup, 2013b). In addition, 48% of small business owners indicated that the ACA would be bad for their business; only 9% thought that it would be good.

As stated previously, it is too early to draw definitive conclusions at this point. Yet, prevailing current negative sentiments may be difficult to overcome and may actually intensify if the promises of the ACA do not materialize. If negative sentiments intensify, the lawmakers will have no choice but to repeal the major provisions of the ACA. Can that happen? Absolutely, yes. There is precedent for it. The now-forgotten Medicare Catastrophic Coverage Act of 1988 was passed by a wide margin by both houses of Congress and was signed into law by President Reagan. In short, this law had proposed some reductions in out-of-pocket costs in both Part A and Part B, and had added prescription drug coverage beginning in January 1991. The expanded benefits would be paid for by an additional income tax to be paid by an estimated 40% of the elderly. This law became highly unpopular among the elderly, many of whom did not even understand it. Roughly 45% of the elderly had private health insurance, mainly through a previous employer, and they were satisfied with their coverage. A ground swell of negative public reaction forced Congress to repeal the legislation only 17 months after it had become law (Rice et al. 1990). Whether Republican or Democrat, politicians react to overwhelming concerns expressed by their constituents.

Finally, how much the ACA will end up costing is a major issue. Suspension of enrollment in the Pre-existing Condition Insurance Plan (PCIP–see Chapter 6) is perhaps an early warning sign of trouble ahead. On February 16, 2013, the federal government suspended acceptance of new enrollees in PCIP, even though it was a temporary measure until the mandate for insurance companies to cover all pre-existing conditions went into effect in January 2014. The explanation given by the government was that suspending further enrollment "will help ensure that funds are available through 2013 to continuously cover people currently enrolled in PCIP" (US Government 2013).

It would be fair to say that the ACA still faces headwinds, and its repeal is not completely out of the question. If a repeal should occur, however, that would not kill the prospects for future health care reform. Hence, the question, "What if?" is still a legitimate one as it could well pop up in the future.

What If?

What if the law gets repealed? Or significantly altered? Or funding to implement it gets slashed? Or it fails to deliver on its major promises (outlined in Chapter 13)? These are big questions that will be decided in the near future, most likely between 2014 and 2016. Regardless of what happens, the seeds for health care reform have already been sown, and it will no longer remain a dead issue. Any future reforms would build on rather than scrap completely some of the provisions in the ACA. For example, the exchanges established under the ACA would likely survive,

as they have been proposed by Republicans in the past. Medicaid would likely be left up to each state to deal with, although it would be difficult to scale back in states that have expanded Medicaid under the ACA. Federal subsidies, in one form or another, to assist individuals to buy health insurance would likely be retained as the Republicans in the past have proposed tax credits and vouchers to purchase health insurance. In terms of coverage, requiring health plans to cover preventive services would be retained, but other ACA mandates would be relaxed. High-deductible health plans (see Chapter 6) could play a significant role in any future health care reform. Researchers Haviland and colleagues (2012) estimated that growth of these plans from the current level of 13% to 50% would reduce annual health care spending by about $57 billion.

To reduce health insurance premiums, coverage of pre-existing conditions would likely be returned to the states who would manage their own high-risk pools as before. **High-risk pools** were created by about 35 states to make health insurance available to people who otherwise would have been uninsurable because of pre-existing health conditions. What could be repealed are the most contentious requirements of the ACA, namely, the individual mandate, the employer mandate, and the mandated essential health benefits. Other changes could include tort reform to mitigate the effects of malpractice lawsuits against physicians. Overall cost control, however, will continue to be a nagging issue for which there are no easy solutions.

Universal Coverage and Access

There is no question that the United States needs some type of universal coverage, but the nation first needs to strengthen the health delivery infrastructure. Lamm and Blank (2005) cogently stated that universal coverage is feasible, but, to financially sustain such a system, Americans will have to "give up a cherished dream: the dream of total, universal care for any ailment freely available on demand." Hence, a change in mindset will be necessary. As Paulus and colleagues (2008) have proposed, the underpinnings for a change in philosophy should be to seek value in health care. It necessitates asking the questions: What do we propose to get in return for what we pay? How much should we pay for what we should reasonably expect to get? The pillars of a value-driven system will be individual responsibility for one's own health, self-management support, patient activation, preventive services coupled with health education, and an infrastructure based on primary care. A health care system built on these pillars has the potential to return the biggest dividends in improving health at a reasonable cost.

The main barriers for moving the US health care delivery system toward an ideal state, of course, pertain to the American mindset in terms of expectations and inadequacies in the existing infrastructure that fall far short of what is necessary. Government policy that works collaboratively with private payers and providers to create strong payment incentives will be needed to tip the scale toward primary care in which both physicians and nonphysician practitioners will play mutually supportive roles. Regrettably, crafters of the ACA did not seek this type of consensus; they merely believed that creating a law with stiff mandates would automatically achieve the results most Americans would desire.

The big unknown factor is whether US medical students would react to incentives and choose to enter primary care in sufficient numbers that tip the scale. It can perhaps be achieved over time by working collaboratively with the Council on Graduate Medical Education. Immigration reform could also entice sufficient numbers of physicians to practice in the United States. These efforts, however, would take several years to achieve their goal, and may also raise concerns about the quality of care.

To get some perspective on universal coverage in the United States, Hawaii and Oregon have the longest running programs that have attempted to eliminate the uninsured in these two states. In Oregon, despite the expansion of Medicaid and rationing of care, 15.6% of the state's population was uninsured in 2006 (Office for Oregon Health Policy and Research 2007). In Hawaii, 8% of the total population was estimated to be uninsured in 2009, according to the Henry J. Kaiser Family Foundation (Kaiser 2014).

What the nation should try to achieve is a near-universal system that provides basic health care to at least 95% of the population. As described in Chapter 1, Singapore switched from a British-style government-run system to one in which the markets and people's self-reliance play a greater role and the government is responsible for providing health care only to the most needy. In the United States, high-deductible health plans with savings options, regular health insurance, defined contributions by employers toward purchase of individually desired health plans, financial contribution toward health care by everyone (with only a few exceptions), reformed Medicaid and Medicare, and charity care can all play a role in bringing about near-universal coverage and access under the umbrella of a consensus-driven government policy.

Under such a system, delivery of health care to all citizens is not the primary function of government. Experts sometimes decry the administrative costs and inefficiencies in the US health care system, but they do not take into account the inefficiencies and loss of productivity attributable to ever-increasing government regulations.

Single-Payer System

Many developed nations have been able to achieve universal coverage through a single-payer system, and their citizens have been able to accept supply-side rationing for specialty care and higher taxes. Thanks to a strong primary care system, these countries are able to provide basic services to nearly all citizens. In the United States, if this possibility exists, it appears to be far in the future.

As discussed previously in this book, despite notions to the contrary, a government-run, single-payer system does not achieve *universal access*—the ability of every, or nearly all, citizens to obtain health care when needed. This is because rationing is easier to achieve in a system financed entirely by the government.

One major advantage of a single-payer system is that all Americans and lawful residents would be entitled to some benefits. Private insurance plans and government entitlement programs (that is, Medicaid, Medicare, TriCare, and the Federal Employee Health Benefits Program) would no longer be necessary, although the market for some private insurance will remain for those desiring coverage beyond what a basic government plan might offer. Given that the United States has largely a private infrastructure for health care delivery, an American single-payer system would resemble the system in Canada (see Chapter 1). Costs would be contained through supply-side rationing, and higher taxes would be necessary to sustain the system. However, both rationing and taxes are likely to be resisted by the American public and most physicians.

Delivery Infrastructure of the Future

The future health care delivery infrastructure will evolve by incorporating the models and concepts described in this section. Some of these models and concepts are referenced in the ACA, but with little concrete proposals. They have been used on a small scale, and their widespread adoption is a few years away. Yet, some organizations have implemented the ideas presented here and have achieved positive results.

The health care infrastructure will continue to evolve, driven by an overarching concept of high-value health care focused on lowering costs, improving quality, and engaging patients in health care decisions. Yet, one model will not suffice to meet a variety of needs. Hence, many of the current structures of health care delivery will remain.

Future payment methods will also incorporate at least a value component. The evolutionary changes will also transform some of the traditional processes of health care delivery by placing an increased emphasis on evidence-based care and processes that eliminate waste. For example, improved surgical scheduling practices can reduce delays and cancellations of elective surgeries (Cosgrove et al. 2012). Redesigned workflows can improve efficiency. Cost-saving technology will play an increasing role in reformed processes of care. Finally, new approaches will be used to target programs to the needs of patients in the community who present specific health risks.

Physicians and nurses will have to be trained to practice in a wellness-oriented model of care delivery. To some extent, the delivery system will evolve to replace periodic encounters between patients and providers with an ongoing relationship that includes remote monitoring of health status and virtual consultations (Adler et al. 2009).

Implementing the Medical Home Model

The main concepts behind the medical home model are discussed in Chapter 7. Four critical issues have been identified in the implementation of this model:

1. Qualifying a physician practice as a medical home: A valid tool should capture the capabilities a medical practice should have to qualify as a medical home. This can help medical practices focus on the most important activities that would improve care. Research shows that four key primary care elements—accessibility, continuity, coordination, and comprehensiveness—positively affect health outcomes, satisfaction, and costs. An ideal qualification tool would ensure that medical homes are built on a firm foundation of these four pillars (O'Malley et al. 2008).

2. Matching patients to medical homes: For medical homes to achieve their potential to improve care, payers must link each eligible patient to a medical home practice in a way that ensures transparency, fairness, and matching of clinical needs. Equally important are adequate choice and awareness of the medical home model for patients. Also, physicians must be able to predict the additional revenue they can expect for acting as a medical home (Peikes et al. 2008).

3. Information exchange: There must be effective mechanisms for exchanging clinical information with patients and providers outside of the medical home. Adequate information exchange is necessary for care coordination across providers, care settings, and clinical conditions (Maxfield et al. 2008). This is because healing relationships grow in number and complexity when patients face serious or chronic illnesses. These patients have connections with multiple clinicians (Epstein et al. 2010). Accordingly, health care organizations should support more loosely affiliated "communities of care" besides individual clinician–patient relationships (Ubel et al. 2005).

4. Paying for medical homes: Existing payment systems do not compensate physicians for important activities such as care coordination and patient education. One major challenge is to determine an ideal array of services that result in high-quality and efficient patient care. Another challenge is that care coordination activities are difficult to itemize, may occur outside face-to-face encounters, and can vary in type and intensity across different patients. Hence, an effective payment system would require some sort of capitation or bundled fees that include an allowance for nonclinical patient care–related activities that physicians must perform.

Implementing Community-Oriented Primary Care

Community-oriented primary care (COPC) was introduced in Chapter 7. COPC would require developments on at least four fronts:

1. Primary care must take a central place in the delivery of health services. However, it will also require a refocus on how physicians are trained. Competencies needed for future practice include an understanding of the patients' community, delivery of care within rural settings, and chronic disease management (Dent et al. 2010). For example, chronic disease registries have been used in Denver to target high-impact and high-opportunity areas of focus, such as diabetes, hypertension, and cancer screening. High-risk patients are then assigned to a medical home and a PCP (Cosgrove et al. 2012).

2. The biomedical model that has dominated both research and health professionals' education must be broadened to include a stronger element of the social and behavioral sciences (Engle 1977).

3. Primary and secondary prevention (see Chapter 2) must be appropriately linked in a clinical setting with population-based health programs. Primary and secondary prevention, as well as certain aspects of tertiary prevention, are essential elements of primary care.

4. Public health functions must be strengthened as an adjunct to clinical interventions because clinicians alone cannot deal with most population-based health problems. Community organizations, such as schools, social service agencies, churches, and employers, must become partners in strengthening public health programs (Lee 1994).

Lessons From the Vermont Blueprint

In 2006, Vermont launched a program called Vermont Blueprint for Health. The pilot program has been shifting to a statewide program since the passage of the ACA. In essence, the Vermont Blueprint integrates the medical home model and COPC. It is based on a foundation of medical homes supported by community health teams and an integrated information technology infrastructure. Each community health team is staffed by five full-time equivalent employees and led by a registered nurse to serve a population of approximately 20,000. The teams offer individual care coordination, health and wellness coaching, and behavioral health counseling. For the program to be financially successful, there must be a measurable reduction in avoidable emergency department visits and hospitalizations (Bielaszka-DuVernay 2011).

The Role of Patient Activation

The choices patients make regarding daily management of their own health care profoundly affect utilization, costs, and outcomes. Many experts acknowledge that improvements in quality, cost containment, and reductions in low-value care will not occur without more informed and engaged consumers.

Patient activation refers to a person's ability to manage his or her own health and utilization of health care. Activation necessitates patients to acquire some basic knowledge and skills and to be motivated to make effective decisions about their own health in partnership with their health care providers. In addition, activation often coincides with actual changes in behavior, such as changing one's diet, engaging in physical activity, and having regular check-ups. Patient activation will continue to advance with the growth of information technology such as e-health, m-health, and the Internet become more widely used (see Chapter 5). For example, a self-management and telemonitoring program has been tried in Massachusetts to help patients with heart failure manage their health at home. The program yielded $10 million in savings and a 51% reduction in hospital readmissions (Cosgrove et al. 2012).

The challenge is that activation levels differ considerably across socioeconomic and health status characteristics. For example, among all insurance groups, people enrolled in Medicaid are the least activated (Hibbard and Cunningham 2008). Information and support may help close some of the gaps among various population groups, such as racial and ethnic minorities. Achieving this goal will require a close relationship, partnership, and mutual respect between providers and patients.

The Role of Patient-Centered Care

The IOM identified *patient-centered care* as one of the main elements of high-quality care. It defined patient-centered care as "respecting and responding to patients' wants, needs and preferences, so that they can make choices in their care that best fit their individual circumstances" (IOM 2001). Patient-centered care seeks to increase the health professionals' understanding of patients' individual needs, perspectives, and values; gives patients the information they need to participate in their care; and builds trust and understanding. Patient-centered care is also a critical element in promoting patient activation. In patient activation the patient is more actively engaged and takes a greater degree of responsibility for his or her own health compared to patient-centered care. The patient-centered approach has a positive impact on outcomes, such as patient satisfaction, adherence to treatment regimens, and self-management of chronic conditions. One of the most frequently used systems to analyze physician–patient communication is the Roter Interaction Analysis System (RIAS), which also has been used for developing training programs in patient-centered communication for practitioners in primary care settings (Helitzer et al. 2011).

Future Workforce Challenges

An adequate and well trained workforce is a critical component of the health care delivery infrastructure. Chapter 4 discusses some of the workforce-related issues and challenges. This section highlights future needs and recommendations for change.

The Nursing Profession

In 2008, The Robert Wood Johnson Foundation (RWJF) and the Institute of Medicine (IOM) launched a 2-year initiative to highlight the need to assess and transform the nursing profession. A committee was assigned the task of producing a report that would make recommendations for an action-oriented blueprint for the future of nursing. Four recommendations have been put forth (National Academy of Sciences 2010):

1. Nurses should practice to the full extent of their education and training.

Uniformity on the scope of practice for advance practice nurses, who have master's or doctoral degrees, currently does not exist across states because of varying licensing and practice rules. Also, current residency programs for nurses focus primarily on acute care. To address future needs, residency programs must be developed and evaluated in community settings.

2. Nurses should achieve higher levels of education and training through an improved education system that promotes seamless academic progression. Increased clinical demands call for higher levels of education and training. Patient needs have become more complicated, and nurses need to attain requisite competencies to deliver high-quality care. These competencies include leadership, health policy, system improvement, research in evidence-based practices, teamwork and collaboration, and competency in specific content areas, including community health, public health, and geriatrics. Nurses are also being called on to fill expanding roles and to master technological tools and information management systems, while collaborating and coordinating care across teams of health professionals.

3. Nurses should be full partners with physicians and other professionals in redesigning health care. Being a full partner involves taking responsibility for identifying problems and areas of system waste, devising and implementing improvement plans, tracking improvement over time, and

making necessary adjustments to realize established goals.

4. Effective workforce planning and policy making require better data and improved information systems. Data collection and analysis should drive a systematic assessment and projection of workforce requirements by role, skill mix, region, and demographics to inform changes in nursing practice and education.

Training of Primary Care Physicians

The shortage of PCPs and its exacerbation in the future is only one aspect of the challenge that must be addressed. Caudill and colleagues (2011) argue that the PCPs trained today will not have the requisite skills to fulfill their contemplated responsibilities because of a variety of factors. Future health care demands—mainly because of a growing number of people with complex chronic conditions—will require PCPs to function as "comprehensivists." These comprehensivists will need to be experts in (1) anticipating, preventing, and managing the progression and/or complications of common complex conditions; (2) managing complex pharmacology; (3) understanding end-of-life issues and medical ethics; (4) coordinating care; and (5) leading health care teams. Their practice environments will need to contain the elements and systems to support comprehensive care, such as advanced information systems. Comprehensivists will also need to be able to direct and coordinate a health care team that includes expertise in patient education, mental health and behavioral modification, physical and occupational therapy, pharmacy, and home health. Care delivery will have to be consistent with evidence-based medicine, while incorporating the patient's values (Caudill et al. 2011).

To train future PCPs, education must be more efficient, integrated, and longitudinal. Time must be created for medical students to learn essential elements of patient safety and quality, teamwork in the health care environment, health maintenance, and continuity of care, without sacrificing fundamental knowledge. A pay-for-educational-performance-and-outcomes model, with organizational bundling of educational costs, may need to be piloted in a similar way to the piloting of new care delivery models (Caudill et al. 2011).

Training in Geriatrics

Based on current trends, a shortage of health care professionals schooled in geriatrics is a critical challenge. Although coverage of geriatric issues at medical schools has been increasing, only about 9,000 practicing physicians in the United States (2.5 geriatricians per 10,000 elderly) have formal training in geriatrics. Without sustained efforts to improve training, this number is expected to drop to 6,000 in the future. Among nurses, fewer than 0.05% have advanced certification in geriatrics (CDC/Merck 2004). Evidence shows that care of older adults by health care professionals prepared in geriatrics yields better physical and mental outcomes without increasing costs (Cohen et al. 2002).

Current trends in the education and training of health care professionals shows that future demand will far outstrip the supply of physicians, nurses, therapists, social workers, and pharmacists with geriatrics training. This problem is compounded due to a shortage of faculty in colleges and universities who are trained in geriatrics.

Only 600 medical school faculty out of 100,000 list geriatrics as their primary specialty. Due to this and other reasons, only 3% of medical students take any elective geriatric courses. In other disciplines as well, such as nursing, pharmacy, and dentistry, the majority of educational curricula do not require geriatric training. For example, 60% of nursing schools have no geriatric faculty (CDC/Merck 2004). Health professionals prepared in geriatrics are needed not just in long-term care. Geriatrics training is also important in other types of health services, such as oncology, neurology, rehabilitation, and critical care (Kovner et al. 2002). Even though there are encouraging signs that initiatives are being taken by educational institutions in recognition of a critical deficit in geriatric training, to date few concrete efforts have been made.

The Future of Long-Term Care

Financing and delivery of long-term care will remain a major challenge. The good news is that long-term care is typically needed later in life. Even though the first wave of baby boomers started retiring in 2011, they are not likely to need professional long-term care services until 2025 or later. However, the system must be reformed before that time comes. In their report to the National Commission for Quality Long-Term Care, Miller and Mor (2006) identified six main areas of concern that must be addressed: financing, resources, infrastructure, workforce, regulation, and information technology. In addition, a "scorecard project" proposes that a high-performing long-term care system must focus on support for family caregivers, ease of access and affordability, choice of settings and providers, quality of care and life, and effective transitions and organization of care (Reinhard et al. 2011).

Financing

Most middle-class families are unprepared to meet long-term care expenses. Most people think that Medicare will pay for their long-term care needs. Medicare covers only short-term, postacute care and, for reasons discussed in Chapter 10, only a small proportion of adults have private long-term care insurance. Unless policy initiatives are established to promote long-term care insurance plans, the public sector will see its expenditures grow rapidly. The CBO (2004) recommended improving the way private markets for LTC insurance currently function. For instance, private insurance could be made more attractive to consumers by standardizing insurance policies to allow competing policies to be more easily compared. Standardized policies could also stimulate price competition among insurers and help keep premiums lower than they would otherwise be. However, reform is also needed in the public financing system.

Resources

The Home and Community-Based Services (HCBS) waiver program (see Chapter 10) has achieved some successes in moving patients out of nursing homes to receive community-based care. However, research shows that Medicaid spending, which covers a substantial share of long-term care expenses, has actually increased, not decreased. It appears that the waivers may actually induce more people to enter the Medicaid program (Amaral 2010).

Infrastructure

The institutional long-term care sector has been going through a cultural change that has led to the creation of enriched living environments in nursing homes. New architectural designs, living arrangements, and worker and patient empowerment are improving the quality of life in nursing facilities that have adopted these innovative models, such as Eden Alternative, Green House Project, and Wellspring. Over time, traditional living and care arrangements will be replaced by these and other innovative models (for an overview of these models, refer to Singh 2010). Yet, care coordination and ease of transition between various settings is essential for a high-performing system. In addition, to navigate the multitude of services, a single point of entry is recommended (Reinhard et al. 2011).

Workforce

The aging of America will shrink the overall pool of workers. Experts think that this will have a drastic effect on long-term care in particular because of low pay and hard work. Between 2000 and 2010 alone, a deficit of 1.9 million direct care workers was estimated (DHHS 2003b).

Regulation

Many experts see fundamental contradictions between the existing regulatory mechanisms that address quality issues in nursing facilities through periodic inspections and sanctioning and regulations that require the same nursing facilities to implement quality improvement programs. Also, one of the most disconcerting aspects of government regulation of long-term care is its inconsistent application, both within and across regions over time (Miller and Mor 2006). These issues need to be resolved. In addition, quality monitoring is needed in home- and community-based services.

Information Technology

Interoperable IT systems (discussed in Chapter 5) will enable providers to track patients' care across hospitals, nursing homes, home health agencies, and physicians' offices. Such systems are particularly critical in long-term care because the elderly frequently make transitions between long-term care and non-long-term care settings. Currently, such transitions rarely occur smoothly because of high rates of missing or inaccurate information (Miller and Mor 2006).

Global Threats and International Cooperation

The prevention and control of infectious diseases globally will continue to pose major challenges. Examples include natural disasters, such as the earthquake and tsunami that killed thousands in Japan in March 2011; industrial accidents, such as the oil rig explosion in the Gulf of Mexico in April 2010; and large-scale bioterrorism, which has not yet occurred, but global unrest amid the rise of extremism makes it a real possibility in the future. Often, such events occur without warning. Large-scale devastation, such as that caused by the Haiti earthquake in January 2010, can severely strain a nation's capacity to deal with mass

casualties and rebuilding efforts. Increasingly, disasters will require international assistance, cooperation, and joint efforts.

Increase in air travel resulted in the spread of severe acute respiratory syndrome (SARS) from China to Canada in 2003 and of polio virus from India to northern Minnesota in 2005 (Milstein et al. 2006). These examples highlight the importance of early identification of infectious threats and subsequent rapid response to prevent further spread, which is often difficult without international cooperation (Johns et al. 2011). Many medical advances that physicians and patients take for granted, including cancer treatment, surgery, transplantation, and neonatal care, are endangered by increasing antibiotic resistance of infectious agents and a distressing decline in the antibiotic research and development pipeline (Infectious Disease Society of America 2004). Antibiotic resistance is both a public health and security threat. Virtually all of the antibiotic-resistant pathogens that exist naturally can be bioengineered through forced mutation or cloning. Also, existing pathogens could be genetically manipulated to make them resistant to available antibiotics. Currently, international efforts, including the establishment of a Transatlantic Task Force on Antimicrobial Resistance, are under way (Hughes 2011). Efforts to strengthen global health security include disease surveillance for outbreaks of international importance and urgency, exchange of technical information on new pathogens, and early warning and control of serious animal disease outbreaks.

International cooperative efforts include the Biological Weapons Convention (BWC) and the International Health Regulations (IHR). As a treaty among participating nations, the BWC bans development, production, stockpiling, or otherwise acquiring/retaining microbial or other biological agents or toxins. It also covers weapons, equipment, or means of delivery designed to use biological agents for hostile purposes or in armed conflict. It also promotes common understanding and effective action on biosecurity, national implementation measures, suspicious outbreaks of disease, disease surveillance, and codes of conduct for scientists. The IHR constitute an international legal instrument that is binding on 194 countries. IHR's aim is to help the international community prevent and respond to acute public health risks that have the potential to cross borders and threaten people worldwide. In addition to the spread of infectious agents, the IHR can apply to other public health emergencies, such as chemical spills, leaks and dumping, or nuclear meltdowns (WHO 2008). Detecting and tracking significant public health threats that may emerge in countries that cannot or might not report such events to the global health community will be a challenge. The CDC's Global Disease Detection Program will be increasingly involved in global public health surveillance, detection, and control of emerging infectious disease and bioterrorist threats (Christian et al. 2013). Similar efforts will be undertaken by the Global Emerging Infections Surveillance and Response System operated by the US Department of Defense.

Adequate delivery of health care to millions around the world depends on an adequate and well trained workforce. Worldwide, there is a shortage of nearly 4.3 million health workers. Moreover, 57 countries, 39 of which are in Africa, have fewer than 23 health workers for every 10,000 population. Even some of Asia's burgeoning economies, such as India and Indonesia, can face a health care crisis in the event of a major disaster. The problem in many countries is compounded by an unequal distribution of workers, lack of training, and "brain drain." Also, in spite of the pivotal role that community health workers play in scaling up essential services, this workforce category does not receive adequate support in most nations (Chatterjee 2011).

New Frontiers in Clinical Technology

Despite its association with cost escalation, technological progress will continue. Increased efforts in technology assessment (see Chapter 5) will go hand in hand with new innovations. To what extent clinical decisions will be influenced mainly by cost effectiveness of technology, however, remains an open question. As cost-effectiveness research continues to advance, its use will likely find its way into health policy.

Medicine is advancing on several fronts. The future looks bright with better cures, higher quality of care, and improved quality of life. Understanding of the human genome has paved the way for a number of ways to prevent and treat disease. Future innovation and progress, however, will not come automatically. Much will depend on the future regulatory posture of the FDA.

Genetic mapping is the first step in isolating a gene. It can offer firm evidence that a disease transmitted from parent to child is linked to one or more genes. The term *genometrics* is used for the association of genes with specific disease traits. The discovery of genetic susceptibility to certain diseases will improve preventive techniques. The human genome has also opened the way for the new field of *molecular medicine*, a branch of medicine that deals with understanding the role that genes play in disease processes and treatment of diseases through gene therapy. Gene therapy is a therapeutic technique in which a functioning gene is inserted into targeted cells to correct an inborn defect or provide the cell with a new function. This technique is expected to replace treatment with medications or surgery in some areas. The future challenge in this area is to develop methods that discriminately deliver enough genetic material to the right cells. Cancer treatment is receiving much attention as a prime candidate for gene therapy since current techniques (surgery, radiation, and chemotherapy) are effective in only one-half of cases and can greatly reduce a patient's quality of life.

Personalized medicine and pharmacogenomics are relatively new fields. Pharmacogenomics is the study of how genes affect a person's response to drugs. Personal characteristics of individual patients can vary so much that not all medications work for everyone. In personalized medicine, specific gene variations among patients will be matched with responses to particular medications to increase effectiveness and reduce unwanted side effects.

Drug design and delivery: Rational design to discover new drugs will increasingly utilize multidisciplinary advances in computers, statistics, molecular biology, biophysics, biochemistry, pharmacokinetics, and pharmacodynamics. Rational drug design will shorten the drug discovery process. The chief candidates for this process are drugs to treat neurological and mental disorders and antiretroviral therapies for HIV/AIDS, encephalitis, measles, and influenza. Application of knowledge at the molecular level ultimately aims to reduce labor cost, time, and laboratory expenses in

the drug discovery process (Mavromoustakos et al. 2011). New drug delivery systems have the potential to provide more effective treatment. For example, cellular uptake of nanoparticles may efficiently translocate drug molecules into cancer tumors without damage to healthy tissues (Ding and Ma 2013). Nanotechnology also has the potential to deliver antiviral formulations to specific targeted sites and viral reservoirs in the body (Lembo and Cavalli 2010).

Imaging technologies have made one of the most dramatic advances in health care mainly because of the exponential growth in the performance of silicon devices (Busse 2006). Current research focuses on four areas: (1) finding new energy sources and focusing an energy beam to avoid damage to adjacent tissue and to minimize residual damage, (2) use of microelectronics in digital detectors and advances in the contrast media for a finer detection of abnormalities, (3) faster and more accurate analysis of images using 3-D technology, and (4) improvements in display technology to produce higher resolution displays. The rise of modern neuroscience and the rapid development of new technologies for imaging, treating, and modulating neural function are leading to an increased emphasis on the brain as the central site for medical intervention. The use of neuroimaging in understanding pain is only one area of intervention. Discovery and treatment of minor strokes and early detection of Alzheimer's are two other areas where neuroimaging will improve treatment options (Adler et al. 2009).

Minimally invasive surgery is undergoing advances that include image-guided brain surgery, minimal access cardiac procedures, and the endovascular placement of grafts for abdominal aneurysms. The overall impact of minimally invasive procedures on cost efficiency and the patients' quality of life from early recovery assures the growth of this technology and the growth of ambulatory surgicenters. The use of robotic surgery is in its early stages, and its superiority over traditional procedures has not yet been clearly demonstrated.

Vaccines have traditionally been used prophylactically to prevent specific infectious diseases, such as diphtheria, smallpox, and whooping cough. However, the therapeutic use of vaccines in the treatment of noninfectious diseases, such as cancer, has opened new fronts in medicine. At the same time, development of new vaccines for emerging infectious diseases remains on the research agenda. Making vaccines safer for wide-scale preventive use against bioterrorism in which such agents as smallpox and anthrax may be used will also be an ongoing pursuit.

Blood substitutes will likely be available one day for large-scale use. Even though the safety of blood used in transfusions has been greatly enhanced, substitutes for real blood are necessary when supplies fall short, particularly in war and in natural disasters.

Xenotransplantation, in which animal tissues are used for transplants in humans, is a growing research area. It presents the promise of overcoming the critical shortages of available donor organs. Organs from genetically engineered animals may one day be available for transplantation (Schneider and Seebach 2013).

Regenerative medicine is the first truly interdisciplinary field that utilizes and brings together nearly every field in science. This new field holds the realistic promise of regenerating damaged tissues and organs in vivo (in the living body) through reparative techniques that stimulate previously irreparable organs into healing themselves. Regenerative medicine also enables scientists to grow tissues and organs in vitro (in the laboratory) and safely implant them when the body is unable to be prompted into healing itself. This revolutionary technology has the potential to develop therapies for previously untreatable diseases and conditions. Examples of diseases regenerative medicine can cure include diabetes, heart disease, renal failure, osteoporosis, and spinal cord injuries. Virtually any disease that results from malfunctioning, damaged, or failing tissues could potentially be cured through regenerative medicine therapies (DHHS 2005).

Care Delivery of the Future

Gossink and Souquet (2006) paint a picture of what medical care in the future may look like. This will be achieved mainly through advancements in medical imaging, molecular medicine, and distant monitoring. Medical care will shift its focus from the acute phase of illness to prevention and aftercare. Lifestyle, family history, and genetic factors will be used to develop a patient's risk profile. Patients with an elevated risk profile will be regularly screened for possible onset of acute disease and to follow the course of chronic disease. Some screening will be possible at home with the patient via wireless contact with the physician. If molecular diagnosis detects disease, the extent and location of the disease will be assessed through molecular imaging. Image-guided, minimally invasive procedures will be used if surgery is recommended. Pharmaceutical treatment will be individualized. A feedback system will determine needed drug dosage by a continuous measurement of drug concentration at the targeted site in the body. Miniature implanted devices will take over damaged body functions. Regenerative medicine and cell therapy will revive organs, such as a damaged heart. If needed, complete artificial organs, such as the pancreas, liver, and even heart, could be implanted. Physicians will be able to continuously monitor the condition of elderly patients with chronic conditions and could be dispatched in case of an emergency.

The Future of Evidence-Based Health Care

Research evidence has demonstrated that high-spending providers do not necessarily deliver better outcomes. The goal of evidence-based medicine (EBM) is to increase the value of health care services. Quality of care can actually be improved while reducing costs—thus, increasing the value of medical care—by reducing misuse and overuse (Slawson and Shaughnessy 2001). The tools for the practice of EBM have been developed for several years, mainly in the form of clinical practice guidelines (see Chapter 12). Evidence-based practice guidelines are intended to represent "best practices" and "proven therapies." Halm and colleagues (2007) reported a remarkable reduction in the proportion of patients undergoing carotid endarterectomy (a surgical procedure that removes the inner lining of the carotid artery if it has become thickened or damaged by plaque) for inappropriate reasons. However, EBM's full potential has not yet been realized, and work in this area will be ongoing.

Comparative effectiveness research (CER) is a more novel concept in which a chosen intervention is guided by scientific evidence of how well it would work, compared to other available treatments. In 2009, the Institute of Medicine defined CER as:

The generation and synthesis of evidence that compares the benefits and harms of alternative methods to prevent, diagnose, treat, and monitor a clinical condition or to improve the delivery of care. The purpose of comparative effectiveness research is to assist consumers, clinicians, purchasers, and policy makers to make informed decisions that will improve health care at both the individual and population levels. (IOM 2009)

The primary agency conducting CER is the Agency for Healthcare Research and Quality (AHRQ). It is hoped that CER will answer important clinical questions about what works best for which patients. It is also hoped that delivery of care informed by CER will lead to less waste and better health outcomes (Sox 2012). The American Recovery and Reinvestment Act of 2009 allocated $1.1 billion for this type of research.

Under the ACA, the Patient-Centered Outcomes Research Institute (PCORI) has been established. According to the PCORI, *patient-centered outcomes research* "helps people and their caregivers communicate and make informed health care decisions, allowing their voices to be heard in assessing the value of health care options" (PCORI 2013). The PCORI is collaborating with other agencies, such as the AHRQ, the FDA, and the National Institutes of Health (NIH) in its research activities that involve patients and other stakeholders (Fleurence et al. 2013). It remains to be seen how these agencies will work together and move forward in a common direction. Turf protection and other conflicts, typical of government bureaucracies, will result in duplicated efforts and waste, the very problems in health care delivery that are supposed to be minimized according to the stated missions of these agencies.

While the government's efforts in promoting health services research are commendable, the question remains: Will it improve people's health and save money? Timbie et al. (2012) have concluded that despite widespread enthusiasm about the potential impact of new investments in research, recent history suggests that scientific evidence has been slow to change clinical practice. Hence, any research efforts will need to be accompanied by appropriate strategies that would motivate providers to make use of research findings. Some critical areas that will require close attention include robustness of research studies, sound interpretation of results, relevance to clinical practice, formulation of clear and specific clinical practice guidelines, performance measures, clinical decision support tools, and properly aligned financial incentives (Timbie at al. 2012).

Strategies for Evidence-Based Care

Future strategies to improve guidelines and protocols and their adherence include:

- Health care leaders must continue to emphasize the adoption of evidence-based guidelines that are revised and updated in light of new research.

- Ongoing development of computer-based models incorporating EBM will facilitate multidisciplinary caregiving based on best practices by various practitioners, including physicians and nurses.

- Robust clinical trials will be the backbone of EBM. Adherence to clinical guidelines is higher when the recommendations are supported by evidence from randomized controlled trials (Leape et al. 2003).

- Future practice guidelines must incorporate economic analysis to promote the delivery of cost-effective health care.

- Financial incentives, including provider payments and patient cost sharing, must be restructured. Reimbursement methods should focus on paying for best achievable outcomes and the most effective care over the course of treatment instead of paying for units of service (Gauthier et al. 2006).

Strategies for Comparative Effectiveness and Patient-Centered Research

The key steps involved in CER are (1) identify new and emerging clinical interventions, (2) review and synthesize current medical research, (3) identify gaps between existing medical research and the needs of clinical practice, (4) promote and generate new scientific evidence and analytic tools, (5) train and develop clinical researchers, (6) translate and disseminate research findings to diverse stakeholders, and (7) reach out to stakeholders via a citizens forum (AHRQ 2011).

Etheredge (2010) has suggested that our collective knowledge about comparative effectiveness will grow more quickly if we can draw on the voluminous information that already exists in clinical trial databases and in other research data sets, rather than on new CER studies alone. Problems of noncomparability notwithstanding, if existing information can be extracted in a meaningful way, CER could then be used to fill research gaps.

Future priorities for CER include the capacity to conduct experimental and quasi-experimental comparative studies; evaluation of broad, system-level strategies, such as benefit designs and payment reforms; focus on population subgroups, including vulnerable groups, most likely to benefit from a given intervention; dissemination of research results; and the actual use of evidence in the delivery of care (Benner et al. 2010). At present, much remains unknown about the extent to which important stakeholders, such as physicians and patients, will be involved in patient-centered research.

Americans support research that would provide information on treatment options. Conversely, public support for research is contingent upon how medical evidence will be used in practice. The public remains opposed to the use of research for allocation of resources or for mandating certain treatment decisions (Gerber et al. 2010). The public's attitudes may well become the biggest obstacle to cost-efficient delivery of health care in the future and to any attempts by the government to mandate certain types of care or to ration services.

Summary

Health care delivery in the United States and abroad will continue to change. The framework of future change presented in this chapter will help one understand the nature and direction of change. Political factors played a major role in the passage of the ACA, but the public's experiences will likely determine its eventual success or failure. In any case, the ACA is not the final word on health care reform in the United States. Major challenges will need to be addressed as time progresses. Economic challenges, in particular, will force the need for future reform.

The demographic landscape continues to change, and various models and concepts of health care delivery are at an experimental stage. Eventually, a delivery system that encompasses the best of these ideas is likely to emerge. However, an infrastructure that lacks primary care delivery presents a major obstacle to achieving this goal. The financing and delivery of long-term care will put further strains on the system.

International threats will continue to be a part of globalization. Rapid response to deal with infectious diseases that can quickly spread around the world, natural disasters, and man-made threats of terrorism will increasingly require global assistance, cooperation, and joint efforts. Besides, many developing and underdeveloped countries face critical shortages of trained health care workers.

Progress in scientific innovation and development of new technology will continue. Future emphasis will be on cost-saving technologies.

Standardized protocols for practitioners will continue to be informed by scientific evidence that will include comparative effectiveness research and patient-oriented research. Their adoption into clinical practice, however, will not be automatic. It will require strategies that include financial incentives.

ACA Takeaway

- The future of the ACA in its current form remains in doubt. There is uncertainty about its effects on future employment and household incomes. A significant number of Americans, including physicians, disapprove of the ACA.

- The ACA could be a boon for part-time workers who can get government subsidies to buy coverage through the exchanges. However, the affordability of exchange-based health insurance is unknown.

- Whether or not the ACA will lead to a single-payer system will depend on the ACA's promises becoming reality, how it will affect the majority of middle-class Americans, and how the external forces play out in the future.

- Mirroring the experience in Massachusetts, the ACA presages greater government control over health care through stifling regulations, lower reimbursement for providers, higher health care expenditures, and higher taxes.

Test Your Understanding

Terminology

comparative effectiveness
    research
genometrics
high-risk pools
molecular medicine

patient activation
patient-centered care
patient-centered outcomes
    research
single-payer system

universal access
xenotransplantation
zoonoses

Review Questions

1. Explain the eight main forces that will determine future change in health care.
2. In what way should the delivery infrastructure change to meet the needs of a larger number of insured Americans subsequent to health care reform?
3. What is patient activation? What are the main challenges in activation?
4. What recommendations have been made to transform the nursing profession?
5. What training is needed for primary care physicians to become "comprehensivists"?
6. What are some of the main reasons behind the deficits in geriatric training?
7. What are the main challenges faced by long-term care in the future?

8. Give an overview of what new technology might achieve in the delivery of health care.

9. What role does international cooperation play in globalization?

10. What can be done to achieve greater adoption of evidence-based medicine in the delivery of health care?

REFERENCES

Adler, R., et al. 2009. *Healthcare 2020*. Palo Alto, CA: Institute for the Future.

Agency for Healthcare Research and Quality (AHRQ). 2011. *What is comparative effectiveness research?* Available at: http://www.effectivehealthcare.ahrq.gov/index.cfm/what-is-comparative-effectiveness-research1/. Accessed January 2011.

Amaral, M.M. 2010. Does substituting home care for institutional care lead to a reduction in Medicaid expenditures? *Health Care Management Science* 13, no. 4: 319–333.

Arnold, P.J., and T.C. Reeves. 2006. International trade and health policy: Implications of the GATS for US health care reform. *Journal of Business Ethics* 63: 313–332.

Barr, P. 2013. Massachusetts trying to force costs lower. *Hospitals & Health Networks* 87, no. 7: 24.

Benner, J.S., et al. 2010. An evaluation of recent federal spending on comparative effectiveness research: Priorities, gaps, and next steps. *Health Affairs* 29, no. 10: 1768–1776.

Bielaszka-DuVernay, C. 2011. Vermont's blueprint for medical homes, community health teams, and better health at lower cost. *Health Affairs* 30, no. 3: 383–386.

Busse, F. 2006. Diagnostic imaging. In: *Advances in healthcare technology: Shaping the future of medical care*. G. Spekowius and T. Wendler, eds. Dordrecht, The Netherlands: Springer. pp. 15–34.

Caudill, T., et al. 2011. Health care reform and primary care: Training physicians for tomorrow's challenges. *Academic Medicine* 86, no. 2: 158–160.

Center on Budget and Policy Priorities. 2013. *Statement of Robert Greenstein on the Census Bureau's 2012 poverty, income, and health insurance data*. Available at: http://www.cbpp.org/files/9-17-13pov-stmt.pdf. Accessed October 2013.

Centers for Disease Control and Prevention/Merck Institute of Aging and Health (CDC/Merck). 2004. *The state of aging and health in America, 2004*. Available at: http://www.cdc.gov/aging/. Accessed March 2007.

Centers for Medicare and Medicaid Services (CMS). 2013. *National health expenditure projections 2012–2022*. Available at: http://www.cms.gov/Research-Statistics-Data-and-Systems/Statistics-Trends-and-Reports/NationalHealthExpendData/Downloads/Proj2012.pdf. Accessed October 2013.

Chatterjee, P. 2011. Progress patchy on health-worker crisis. *Lancet* 377, no. 9764: 456.

Christian, K.A., et al. 2013. What we are watching—five top global infectious disease threats, 2012: A perspective from CDC's Global Disease Detection Operations Center. *Emerging Health Threats Journal* 6: 20632.

Clark, C.R., et al. 2011. Lack of access due to costs remains a problem for some in Massachusetts despite the state's health reforms. *Health Affairs* 30, no. 2: 247–255.

Cohen, H.J., et al. 2002. A controlled trial of inpatient and outpatient geriatric evaluation and management. *New England Journal of Medicine* 346, no. 12: 906–912.

Congressional Budget Office (CBO). 2004. *Financing long term care for the elderly*. Washington, DC: CBO.

Congressional Budget Office (CBO). 2012. *The budget and economic outlook: Fiscal years 2012 to 2022*. Washington, DC: CBO.

Congressional Budget Office (CBO). 2013. *CBO's estimate of the net budgetary impact of the Affordable Care Act's health insurance coverage provisions has not changed much over time*. Available at: http://www.cbo.gov/publication/44176. Accessed November 2013.

Cosgrove, D., et al. 2012. *A CEO checklist for high-value health care*. Institute of Medicine. Available at: http://www.iom.edu/~/media/Files/Perspectives-Files/2012/Discussion-Papers /CEOHighValueChecklist.pdf. Accessed October 2013.

Cunningham, P.J. 2011. *State variation in primary care physician supply: Implications for health reform Medicaid expansions*. Research Brief No. 19. Washington, DC: Center for Studying Health System Change.

Cunningham, P.J., and J.H. May. 2006. *Medicaid patients increasingly concentrated among physicians*. Tracking Report No. 16. Washington, DC: Center for Studying Health System Change.

Davis, P.A. 2013. *Medicare: insolvency projections*. Congressional Research Service. Available at: http://www.fas.org/sgp/crs/misc/RS20946.pdf. Accessed October 2013.

Ding, H.M., and Y.Q. Ma. 2013. Controlling cellular uptake of nanoparticles with pH-sensitive polymers. *Scientific Reports* 3: 2804.

Keckley, P.H., et al. 2013. *Deloitte 2013 survey of U.S. physicians*. Washington, DC: Deloitte Center for Health Solutions.

Decker, S.L. 2012. In 2011 nearly one-third of physicians said they would not accept new Medicaid patients, but rising fees may help. *Health Affairs* 31, no. 8: 1673–1679.

Dent, M.M., et al. 2010. Chronic disease management: Teaching medical students to incorporate community. *Family Medicine* 42, no. 10: 736–740.

Department of Health and Human Services (DHHS). 2003. *Health, United States, 2003*. Hyattsville, MD: National Center for Health Statistics.

Department of Health and Human Services (DHHS). 2012. *Health, United States, 2012*. Hyattsville, MD: National Center for Health Statistics.

Department of Health and Human Services (DHHS). 2003. *The future supply of long-term care workers in relation to the aging baby boom generation, Report to Congress*. Washington, DC: Department of Health and Human Services.

Department of Health and Human Services (DHHS). 2005. *2020: A new vision—A future for regenerative medicine*. Washington, DC: Department of Health and Human Services.

Department of Treasury. 2013a. *The debt to the penny and who holds it*. Available at: http://www .treasurydirect.gov/NP/debt/current. Accessed October 2013.

Department of Treasury. 2013b. *Fiscal year 2012 financial report of the United States government*. Available at: http://www.fms.treas.gov/fr/12frusg/12frusg.pdf. Accessed October 2013.

Dhingra, S.S., et al. 2013. Change in health insurance coverage in Massachusetts and other New England states by perceived health status: Potential impact of health reform. *American Journal of Public Health* 103, no. 6: e107–e114.

Edwards, R. 2010. Access. *Hospitals & Health Networks* 84, no. 8: 16–19.

Engle, G.L. 1977. The need for a new medical model: A challenge for biomedicine. *Science* 196, no. 1: 127–136.

Epstein, R.M., et al. 2010. Why the nation needs a policy push on patient-centered health care. *Health Affairs* 29, no. 8: 1489–1495.

Etheredge, L.M. 2010. Creating a high-performance system for comparative effectiveness research. *Health Affairs* 29, no. 10: 1761–1767.

Fleurence, R., et al. 2013. How the Patient-Centered Outcomes Research Institute is engaging patients and others in shaping its research agenda. *Health Affairs* 32, no. 2: 393–400.

Fronstin, P. 2013. *News from EBRI*. Available at: http://www.ebri.org/pdf/PR-1026.22May13.Notes-P-T.pdf. Accessed October 2013.

Gallup, Inc. 2013a. *More Americans disapprove of the Affordable Care Act*. Available at: http://www.gallup.com/video/163328/americans-disapprove-affordable-care-act.aspx. Accessed October 2013.

Gallup, Inc. 2013b. *Half of U.S. small businesses think health law bad for them*. Available at: http://www.gallup.com/poll/162386/half-small-businesses-think-health-law-bad.aspx. Accessed October 2013.

Gauthier, A., et al. 2006. *Toward a high performance health system for the United States*. New York: The Commonwealth Fund.

George, B.P., and T.L. Henthorne. 2009. The incorporation of telemedicine with medical tourism: A study of consequences. *Journal of Hospitality Marketing and Management* 18, no. 5: 512–522.

Gerber, A.S., et al. 2010. The public wants information, not board mandates, from comparative effectiveness research. *Health Affairs* 29, no. 10: 1872–1881.

Gossink, R., and J. Souquet. 2006. Advances and trends in healthcare technology. In: *Advances in healthcare technology: Shaping the future of medical care*. G. Spekowius and T. Wendler, eds. Dordrecht, The Netherlands: Springer. pp. 1–14.

Halm, E.A., et al. 2007. Has evidence changed practice? Appropriateness of carotid endarterectomy after the clinical trials. *Neurology* 68, no. 3: 187–194.

Hargreaves, S. 2013. *Is Obamacare a jobs killer?* CNNMoney, September 30, 2013. Available at: http://money.cnn.com/2013/09/30/news/economy/obamacare-jobs/index.html. Accessed October 2013.

Haviland, A.M., et al. 2012. Growth of consumer-directed health plans to one-half of all employer-sponsored insurance could save $57 billion annually. *Health Affairs* 31, no. 5: 1009–1015.

Helitzer, D.L., et al. 2011. A randomized controlled trial of communication training with primary care providers to improve patient-centeredness and health risk communication. *Patient Education & Counseling* 82, no. 1: 21–29.

The Henry J. Kaiser Family Foundation (Kaiser). 2014. *Hawaii: Facts at-a-glance*. Available at: http://www.statehealthfacts.org/profileglance.jsp?rgn=13#. Accessed January 2014.

Hibbard, J.H., and P.J. Cunningham. 2008. *How engaged are consumers in their health and health care, and why does it matter?* Research Brief No. 8. Washington, DC: Center for Studying Health System Change.

Hughes, J.M. 2011. Preserving the lifesaving power of antimicrobial agents. *Journal of the American Medical Association* 305, no. 10: 1027–1028.

Huynen, M.M.T.E., et al. 2005. The health impacts of globalisation: A conceptual framework. *Globalization and Health* 1: 1–12.

Infectious Disease Society of America. 2004. *Bad bugs, no drugs.* Alexandria, VA: Infectious Disease Society of America.

Institute of Medicine (IOM). 2001. *Crossing the quality chasm: A new health system for the 21st century.* Washington, DC: National Academies Press.

Institute of Medicine (IOM). 2009. *Initial national priorities for comparative effectiveness research.* Washington, DC: National Academies Press.

Johns, M.C., et al. 2011. A growing global network's role in outbreak response: AFHSC-GEIS 2008–2009. *BMC Public Health* 11 (Suppl. 2): S3.

Kenen, J. 2011. Dx on the preexisting condition insurance plan. *Health Affairs* 30, no. 3: 379–381.

Kovner, C.T., et al. 2002. Who cares for older adults? Workforce implications of an aging society. *Health Affairs* 21, no. 5: 78–89.

Lamm, R.D., and R.H. Blank. 2005. The challenge of an aging society. *The Futurist* July–August: 23–27.

Leape, L.L., et al. 2003. Adherence to practice guidelines: The role of specialty society guidelines. *American Heart Journal* 145, no. 1: 19–26.

Lee, P.R. 1994. Models of excellence. *Lancet* 344, no. 8935: 1484–1486.

Lembo, D., and R. Cavalli. 2010. Nanoparticulate delivery systems for antiviral drugs. *Antiviral Chemistry & Chemotherapy* 21, no. 2: 53–70.

Loehrer, A.P., et al. 2013. Massachusetts health care reform and reduced racial disaparities in minimally invasive surgery. *JAMA Surgery* 148, no. 12: 1116–1122.

Martiniuk, A.L.C., et al. 2012. Brain gains: A literature review of medical missions to low and middle-income countries. *BMC Health Services Research* 12, no. 1: 134–141.

Massachusetts Center for Health Information and Analysis. 2013. *Annual report on the Massachusetts health care market: August 2013.* Available at: http://www.mass.gov/chia/docs/r/pubs/13/ar-ma-health-care-market-2013.pdf. Accessed October 2013.

Massachusetts Medical Society. 2013. *2013 Health Care Opinion Survey.* Available at: http://www.massmed.org/poll2013/#.UlMUuW_D-OI. Accessed October 2013.

Mavromoustakos, T., et al. 2011. Strategies in the rational drug design. *Current Medicinal Chemistry* 18, no. 17: 2517–2530.

Maxfield, M., et al. 2008. Medical homes: The information exchange challenge. In: *Making medical homes work: Moving from concept to practice.* P.B. Ginsburg, ed. Washington, DC: Center for Studying Health System Change.

McHugh, K. 2013. Reid says Obamacare will lead to a single-payer healthcare system. *The Daily Caller, August, 10.* Available at: http://dailycaller.com/2013/08/10/absolutely-yes-reid-says-obamacare-will-lead-to-a-single-payer-healthcare-system. Accessed October 2013.

Mechanic, R.E., et al. 2012. The new era of payment reform, spending targets, and cost containment in Massachusetts: Early lessons for the nation. *Health Affairs* 31, no. 10: 2334–2342.

Miller, E.A., and V. Mor. 2006. *Out of the shadows: Envisioning a brighter future for long-term care in America.* Providence, RI: Brown University.

Milstein, J.B., et al. 2006. The impact of globalization on vaccine development and availability. *Health Affairs* 25, no. 4: 1061–1069.

National Academy of Sciences. 2010. *The future of nursing: Leading change, advancing health.* Washington, DC: The Institute of Medicine.

Office for Oregon Health Policy and Research. 2007. *Profile of Oregon's uninsured, 2006.* Available at: http://www.oregon.gov/OHPPR/RSCH/docs/uninsuredprofile.pdf?ga=t. Accessed March 2011.

O'Malley, A.S., et al. 2008. Qualifying a physician practice as a medical home. In: *Making medical homes work: Moving from concept to practice.* P.B. Ginsburg, ed. Washington, DC: Center for Studying Health System Change.

Paulus, R.A., et al. 2008. Continuous innovation in health care: Implications of the Geisinger experience. *Health Affairs* 27, no. 5: 1235–1245.

Patient-Centered Outcomes Research Institute (PCORI). 2013. *Patient-centered outcomes research.* Available at: http://www.pcori.org/research-we-support/pcor. Accessed October 2013.

Peikes, D., et al. 2008. Matching patients to medical homes: Ensuring patient and physician choice. In: *Making medical homes work: Moving from concept to practice.* P.B. Ginsburg, ed. Washington, DC: Center for Studying Health System Change.

Pew Research Center. 2013. *As health care law proceeds, opposition and uncertainty persist.* Available at: http://www.people-press.org/2013/09/16/as-health-care-law-proceeds-opposition-and-uncertainty-persist. Accessed October 2013.

Reeves, T.C. 2011. Globalizing health services: a policy imperative? *International Journal of Business and Management* 6, no. 12: 44–57.

Reinhard, S.C., et al. 2011. How the Affordable Care Act can help move states toward a high-performing system of long-term services and supports. *Health Affairs* 30, no. 3: 447–453.

Rennen, W., and P. Martens. 2003. The globalisation timeline. *Integrated Assessment* 4: 137–144.

Rice, T., et al. 1990. The Medicare Catastrophic Coverage Act: A post-mortem. *Health Affairs* 9, no. 3: 75–87.

Robillard, K. 2010. A health-care showdown in Massachusetts. *Newsweek*, July 26: 8.

Schneider, M.K.J., and J.D. Seebach. 2013. Xenotransplantation literature update, July–August 2013. *Xenotransplantation* 20, no. 5: 308–310.

Shrestha, L.B., and E.J. Heisler. 2011. *The changing demographic profile of the United States.* Congressional Research Service. Available at: http://www.fas.org/sgp/crs/misc/RL32701.pdf. Accessed October 2013.

Singh, D.A. 2010. *Effective management of long-term care facilities.* 2nd ed. Sudbury, MA: Jones & Bartlett Publishers.

Slawson, D.C., and A.F. Shaughnessy. 2001. Using "medical poetry" to remove the inequities in health care delivery. *Journal of Family Medicine* 50, no. 1: 51–65.

Smulowitz, P.B., et al. 2011. Emergency department utilization after the implementation of Massachusetts health reform. *Annals of Emergency Medicine* 58, no. 3: 225–234.

Sox, H. 2012. The Patient-Centered Outcomes Research Institute should focus on high-impact problems that can be solved quickly. *Health Affairs* 31, no. 10: 2176–2182.

SteelFisher, G.K., et al. 2009. Physicians' views of the Massachusetts health care reform law—A poll. *New England Journal of Medicine* 361, no. 19: 39.

Timbie, J.W., et al. 2012. Five reasons that many comparative effectiveness studies fail to change patient care and clinical practice. *Health Affairs* 31, no. 10: 2168–2175.

Ubel, P.A., et al. 2005. Misimagining the unimaginable: The disability paradox and health care decision making. *Health Psychology* 24 (4 Suppl.): S57–S62.

US Government. 2013. *Pre-existing condition insurance plan*. The official U.S. government site for PCIP. Available at: https://www.pcip.gov. Accessed October 2013.

World Health Organization (WHO). 2008. *What are the International Health Regulations?* Available at: http://www.who.int/features/qa/39/en/index.html. Accessed March 2011.

Glossary

Academic medical center: A term commonly used when one or more hospitals organize around a medical school. Apart from the training of physicians, research activities and clinical investigations become an important undertaking in these institutions.

Access: The ability of persons needing health services to obtain appropriate care in a timely manner. Can you get medical care when you need it? If yes, you have access to medical care. Access is not the same as health insurance coverage, although insurance coverage is a strong predictor of access for primary care services.

Accountability: Refers to the respective responsibility by clinicians and patients for the provision and receipt of efficient and quality health care services.

Accountable care organization (ACO): An integrated group of providers who are willing and able to take responsibility for improving the overall health status, care efficiency, and satisfaction with care for a defined population.

Accreditation: A private mechanism designed to assure that accredited health care facilities meet certain basic standards.

Acquired immune deficiency syndrome (AIDS): The occurrence of immune deficiency caused by the HIV virus.

Acquisition: Purchase of one organization by another.

Activities of daily living (ADLs): The most commonly used measure of disability. ADLs determine whether an individual needs assistance to perform basic activities, such as eating, bathing, dressing, toileting, and getting into or out of a bed or chair. *See* **functional status** and **IADLs**.

Actuary: A person professionally trained in the technical aspects of insurance and related fields, particularly in the mathematics of insurance, such as the calculation of premiums, reserves, and other values.

Acupuncture: Use of long, thin needles passed through the skin to specific reflex points to treat chronic pain or to produce regional anesthesia.

Acute condition: Short-term, intense medical care for an illness or injury usually requiring hospitalization. *See* **subacute care**.

Adjusted community rating: Also called modified community rating, it is a method of determining health insurance premiums that takes into account demographic factors such as age, gender, geography, and family composition, while ignoring other risk factors.

Administrative costs: Costs that are incidental to the delivery of health services. These costs are not only associated with the billing and collection of claims for services delivered but also include numerous other costs, such as time and effort incurred by employers for the selection of insurance carriers, costs incurred by insurance and managed care organizations to market their products, and time and effort involved in the negotiation of rates.

Administrative information systems: Designed to assist in carrying out financial and administrative support activities such as payroll, patient accounting, materials management, and office automation.

Adult day care: A community-based, long-term care service that provides a wide range of health, social, and recreational services to elderly adults who require supervision and care while members of the family or other informal caregivers are away at work.

Adult foster care: LTC services provided in small, family-operated homes, located in residential communities, which provide room, board, and varying levels of supervision, oversight, and personal care to nonrelated adults.

Advance directives: A patient's wishes regarding continuation or withdrawal of treatment when the patient lacks decision-making capacity.

Advanced practice nurse (APN): A general name for nurses who have education and clinical experience beyond that required of an RN. APNs include four areas of specialization in nursing: clinical nurse specialists (CNSs), certified registered nurse anesthetists (CRNAs), nurse practitioners (NPs), and certified nurse midwives (CNMs).

Adverse selection: A phenomenon in which individuals who are likely to use more health care services than others due to poor health enroll in health insurance plans in greater numbers, compared to

people who are healthy. *See* **favorable risk selection**.

Affective disorders: A group of disorders characterized by severe mood changes, often accompanied by a manic or depressive syndrome.

Affordable Care Act (ACA): Shortened name for the Patient Protection and Affordable Care Act of 2010 as amended by the Health Care and Education Reconciliation Act of 2010, and also nicknamed Obamacare.

Agency for Healthcare Research and Quality (AHRQ): A federal agency within the Department of Health and Human Services whose mission is to improve the quality, safety, efficiency, and effectiveness of health care through research activities.

Agent: One of the factors of the epidemiology triangle, must be present in order for an infectious disease to occur. In other words, an infectious disease cannot occur without an agent.

Aging-in-place: Older people's preference and expectation to stay in one place for as long as possible, and to delay or avoid transfer to an institution where the acuity level of patients is higher.

AIDS: Acquired immune deficiency syndrome. The occurrence of immune deficiency caused by the HIV virus.

Alliance: A joint agreement between two organizations to share their resources without joint ownership of assets.

Allied health: A broad category that includes services and professionals in many health-related technical areas. Allied health professionals include technicians, assistants, therapists, and technologists.

Allied health professional: Someone who has received a certificate; associate's, bachelor's, or master's degree; doctoral level preparation; or post-baccalaureate training in a science related to health care and has responsibility for the delivery of health or related services.

Allocative tool: Designates a use of health policy in which there is a direct provision of income, services, or goods to groups of individuals who usually reap benefits in receiving them.

Allopathic medicine: A philosophy of medicine that views medical treatment as active intervention to counteract the effects of disease through medical and surgical procedures that produce effects opposite those of the disease. *See* **homeopathy** and **osteopathic medicine**.

Almshouse: Also a poorhouse, was an unspecialized institution existing during the 18th and mid-19th centuries that mainly served general welfare functions, essentially providing shelter to the homeless, the insane, the elderly, orphans, and the sick who had no family to care for them.

Alternative medicine: Also called "alternative and complementary medicine." Nontraditional remedies, for example, acupuncture, homeopathy, naturopathy, biofeedback, yoga exercises, chiropractic, and herbal therapy.

Alzheimer's disease: A progressive degenerative disease of the brain producing loss of memory, confusion, irritability, severe loss of functioning, and ultimately death. The disease is named after German neurologist, Alois Alzheimer (1864–1915).

Ambulatory: Refers to the ability to move about at will.

Ambulatory care: Also referred to as outpatient services. Ambulatory care includes: (1) care rendered to patients who come to physicians' offices, outpatient departments of hospitals, and health centers to receive care; (2) outpatient services intended to serve the surrounding community (community medicine); and (3) certain services that are transported to the patient.

Ancillary services: Hospital or other inpatient services other than room and board and professional medical services, such as physician and nursing care. Examples include radiology, pharmacy, laboratory, bandages and other supplies, and physical therapy.

Anesthesiology: Administration of drugs for the prevention or relief of pain during surgery.

Anorexia nervosa: A mental disturbance characterized by self-imposed starvation because the patient may claim to feel fat even when emaciated.

Antiretroviral: A drug that stops or suppresses the activity of a retrovirus, such as HIV.

Antitrust: Federal and state laws that make certain anticompetitive practices illegal. These practices include price fixing, price discrimination, exclusive contracting arrangements, and mergers among competitors.

Assisted living facility: A residential setting that provides personal care services, 24-hour supervision, scheduled and unscheduled assistance, social activities, and some health care services.

Asynchronous technology: Use of store-and-forward technology that allows the users to review the information at a later time.

Audiology: Identification and evaluation of hearing disorders and correction of hearing loss through rehabilitation and prostheses.

Average daily census: Average number of hospital beds occupied daily over a given period of time. This measure provides an estimate of the number of inpatients receiving care each day at a hospital.

Average length of stay (ALOS): The average number of days each patient stays in the hospital. For individual or specific categories of patients, this measure indicates severity of illness and resource use.

Baby boom: A sudden, large increase in the birth rate, especially that of the United States after World War II from 1946 through 1964. Baby boomers, as this generation is often referred to, comprise about 77 million adults.

Balance bill: Billing of the leftover sum by the provider to the patient after insurance has only partially paid the charge initially billed.

Beneficiary: Anyone covered under a particular health insurance plan.

Benefit period: Under Medicare rules, benefits for an inpatient stay are based on a benefit period. A benefit period is determined by a spell of illness beginning with hospitalization and ending when the beneficiary has not been an inpatient in a hospital or a skilled nursing facility for 60 consecutive days.

Benefits: Services covered by an insurance plan.

Biofeedback: A training program that uses relaxation and visualization to develop the ability to control one's involuntary nervous system as an aid to reducing stress, lowering blood pressure, and alleviating headaches.

Biologics: Biological products that include a wide range of products such as vaccines, blood and blood components, allergenics, somatic cells, gene therapy, tissues, and recombinant therapeutic proteins.

Bioterrorism: Encompasses the use of chemical, biological, and nuclear agents to cause harm to relatively large civilian populations.

Blue Cross: An independent, nonprofit membership corporation providing protection against the cost of hospital care on a service basis in a limited geographic area.

Blue Shield: An independent, nonprofit membership corporation providing protection against the cost of outpatient and surgical care on a service basis in a limited geographic area.

Board of trustees: The governing body of a hospital. It is legally responsible for hospital operations, and is charged with defining the mission and long-term direction of the hospital.

Brokerage model: A model of LTC case management in which patients' needs are independently assessed by a freestanding case manager who then arranges services through other providers.

Bulimia: A mental disturbance that leads to bouts of overeating followed by induced vomiting.

Capitation: A reimbursement mechanism under which the provider is paid a set monthly fee per enrollee (sometimes referred to as per member per month or PMPM rate) regardless of whether or not an enrollee sees the provider and regardless of how often an enrollee sees the provider.

Cardiology: Medical science pertaining to the study of the heart and its diseases.

Cardiopulmonary resuscitation (CPR): Medical procedure used to restart a patient's heart and breathing when the patient has suffered a heart failure.

Carriers: Private claims processors for Medicare Part B services.

Carve out: The assignment through contractual arrangements of specialized services to an outside organization because these services are not included in the contracts MCOs have with their providers or the MCO does not provide the services.

Case management: An organized approach to evaluating and coordinating care, particularly for patients who have complex, potentially costly problems that require a variety of services from multiple providers over an extended period.

Case mix: An aggregate of the severity of conditions requiring medical intervention. Case-mix categories are mutually exclusive and differentiate patients according to the extent of resource use.

Cases: Refers to individuals who acquire a certain disease or condition.

Catastrophic care: Medical care needed when a patient suffers a major injury or life-threatening illness that requires expensive long-term treatment.

Categorical programs: Public health care programs designed to benefit only a certain category of people.

Centers for Disease Control and Prevention (CDC): The federal public health agency of the United States.

Centers for Medicare & Medicaid Services (CMS): Federal agency that administers the Medicare and Medicaid programs.

Certificate of need (CON): Control exercised by a government planning agency over expansion of medical facilities, for example, determination of whether a new facility should be opened in a certain location, whether an existing facility should be expanded, or whether a hospital should be allowed to purchase major equipment.

Certification: Conferred by the US Department of Health and Human Services, it entitles a hospital to participate in Medicare and Medicaid. A necessary condition is for the hospital to comply with the conditions of participation.

Certified nurse midwives: RNs with additional training from a nurse-midwifery program in areas such as maternal and fetal procedures, maternity and child nursing, and patient assessment. CNMs deliver babies, provide family planning education, and manage gynecological and obstetric care. They can substitute for obstetricians/gynecologists in prenatal and postnatal care. *See* **nonphysician practitioners** (NPPs).

Charge: The amount a provider bills for rendering a service. *See* **cost**.

Chief of service: A physician who is in charge of a specific medical specialty in a hospital, such as cardiology.

Chief of staff: Also referred to as the medical director, a physician who supervises the medical staff in a hospital.

Children's Health Insurance Program (CHIP): A joint federal–state program established as Title XXI of the Social Security Act under the 1997 Balanced

Budget Act. CHIP provides health insurance for children from low-income families who do not qualify for Medicaid.

Chiropractic: A system of medicine based on manipulation of the spine, physiotherapy, and dietary counseling to treat neurological, muscular, and vascular problems. Chiropractic care is based on the belief that the body is a self-healing organism.

Chiropractor: A licensed practitioner who has completed the Doctor of Chiropractic (DC) degree. Chiropractors must be licensed to practice. Requirements for licensure include completion of an accredited program that awards a DC degree and an examination by the state chiropractic board.

Chronic: Refers to diseases or health conditions that last for significant amount of time (three months or more) and often with no complete cure or recovery.

Chronic condition (chronic disease): A medical condition that persists over time. Chronic diseases may lead to a permanent medical condition that is nonreversible and/or leaves residual disability.

Churning: A phenomenon in which people gain and lose health insurance periodically.

Claim: A demand for payment of covered medical expenses sent to an insurance company.

Clinical information systems: Involve the organized processing, storage, and retrieval of information to support patient care processes.

Clinical practice guidelines (medical practice guidelines): Standardized guidelines in the form of scientifically established protocols, representing preferred processes in medical practice.

Clinical trial: A research study, generally based on random assignments, designed to study the effectiveness of a new drug, device, or treatment.

Closed panel: Also called "closed network," "in network," or "closed access." A health plan that pays for services only when provided by physicians and hospitals on the plan's panel.

Cognitive impairment: A mental disorder that is indicated by a person having difficulty remembering, learning new things, concentrating, or making decisions that affect the individual's everyday life.

Community health assessment: A method used for conducting broad assessments of populations at a local or state level.

Community health center (CHC): Local, nonprofit, community-owned health care providers serving low-income and medically underserved communities.

Community hospital: Nonfederal (i.e., VA and military hospitals are excluded), short-term, general or special hospital whose services are available to the public.

Community-oriented primary care (COPC): Incorporates the elements of good primary care delivery and adds to this a population-based approach to identifying and addressing community health problems.

Community rating: Same insurance rate for everyone, as opposed to experience rating.

Comorbidity: Presence of more than one health problem in an individual.

Comparative effectiveness research (CER): A concept in which a chosen medical intervention is guided by scientific evidence on how well it would work compared to other available treatments.

Competition: Rivalry among sellers for the purpose of attracting customers.

Concurrent utilization review: A process that determines, on a daily basis, the length of stay necessary in a hospital. It also monitors the use of ancillary services and ensures that the medical treatment provided is appropriate and necessary.

Conditions of participation: Standards developed by the Department of Health and Human Services (DHHS) that a facility must comply with in order to participate in the Medicare and Medicaid programs.

Consumer-driven health plan: A high-deductible health plan that carries a savings option to pay for routine health care expenses.

Continuing care retirement community (CCRC): A CCRC integrates and coordinates independent living and institutional components of the LTC continuum. As a convenience factor, different levels of services are all located on one campus. Secondly, CCRCs guarantee delivery of higher-level services as future needs arise.

Continuous quality improvement (CQI): *See* **total quality management**.

Continuum: A range or spectrum of health care services from basic to complex.

Copayment (coinsurance): A portion of health care charges that the insured has to pay under the terms of his or her health insurance policy. *See* **deductible**.

Cost: What it costs the provider to produce a service. *See* **charge**.

Cost-benefit analysis: Used to evaluate benefits in relation to costs when both are expressed in dollar terms. Hence, cost benefit analysis is subject to a more rigorous quantitative analysis compared to cost-effectiveness analysis.

Cost efficiency (cost effectiveness): A service is cost efficient when the benefit received is greater than the cost incurred to provide the service. *See* **efficiency**.

Cost-effectiveness analysis: A step beyond the determination of efficacy. Whereas efficacy is concerned only with the benefit to be derived from the use of technology, cost-effectiveness evaluates the additional (marginal) benefits to be derived in relation to the additional (marginal) costs to be incurred.

Cost-plus: Reimbursement to a provider based on cost plus a factor to cover the value of capital.

Cost sharing: Sharing in the cost of health insurance premiums by those enrolled and/or payment of certain medical costs out of pocket, such as copayments and deductibles.

Cost shifting (cross-subsidizing): In general, shifting of costs from one entity to another as a way of making up losses in one area by charging more in other areas. For example, when care is provided to the uninsured, the provider makes up the cost for those services by charging more to the insured.

Cost-utility analysis: Analysis that includes the use of quality-adjusted life years.

Credentials committee: A committee that reviews qualifications of clinicians for admitting privileges.

Critical access hospital (CAH): Medicare designation for small rural hospitals with 25 beds or fewer that provide emergency medical services besides short-term hospitalization for patients with noncomplex health care needs. CAHs receive cost-plus reimbursement.

Critical pathways: Outcome-based, patient-centered case management tools that are interdisciplinary, facilitating coordination of care among multiple clinical departments and caregivers. A critical pathway identifies planned medical interventions in a given case, along with expected outcomes.

Crude rates: Measures referring to the total population; they are not specific to any age groups or disease categories.

Cultural authority: Refers to the general acceptance of professional judgment as valid. Physicians' cultural authority is reflected in the reliance placed on their evaluation of signs and symptoms, diagnosis of disease, and suggested prognosis.

Current Procedural Terminology (CPT): An accepted standard for coding physician services.

Custodial care: Nonmedical care provided to support and maintain the patient's condition, generally requiring no active medical or nursing treatments.

Days of care: Cumulative number of patient days over a given period of time.

Decision support systems: Computer-based information and analytical tools to support managerial decision making in health care organizations.

Deductible: The portion of health care costs that the insured must first pay (generally up to an annual limit) before insurance payments kick in. Insurance payments may be further subject to copayment.

Deemed status: A designation used when a hospital, by virtue of its accreditation by the Joint Commission or the American Osteopathic Association, does not require separate certification from the DHHS to participate in the Medicare and Medicaid programs.

Defensive medicine: Excessive medical tests and procedures performed as a protection against malpractice lawsuits, otherwise regarded as unnecessary.

Demand: The quantity of health care demanded by consumers based solely on the price of those services. Enabling services, such as transportation or translation services, facilitate access when an individual already has health insurance coverage.

Demand-side rationing: Refers to barriers to obtaining health care faced by individuals who do not have sufficient income to pay for services or purchase health insurance.

Dementia: A general term for progressive and irreversible decline in cognition, thinking, and memory. Alzheimer's disease is one disorder that leads to severe dementia.

Denial of claim: Refusal by a payer to reimburse a provider for services rendered.

Dental assistants: Usually work for dentists in the preparation, examination, and treatment of patients.

Dental hygienists: Work under the supervision of dentists and provide preventive dental care, including cleaning teeth and educating patients on proper dental care.

Dentist: A professional who diagnoses and treats dental problems related to the teeth, gums, and tissues of the mouth.

Department of Health and Human Services (DHHS): The principal US federal agency responsible for protecting the health of all Americans and providing essential human services.

Dependency: (1) A person's reliance on another for assistance with common daily functions, such as bathing and grooming. *See* **activities of daily living**. (2) Children's reliance on adults, such as parents or school officials, to recognize and respond to their health needs.

Dermatology: Medical science pertaining to the study of the skin and its diseases.

Developmental disability: A physical incapacity that generally accompanies mental retardation and often arises at birth or in early childhood.

Developmental vulnerability: Rapid and cumulative physical and emotional changes that characterize childhood and the potential impact that illness, injury, or untoward family and social circumstances can have on a child's life-course trajectory.

Diagnosis-related group (DRG): A diagnostic category associated with a fixed payment to an acute care hospital under the prospective payment system.

Disability: Physical or mental handicap—partial or total—resulting from sickness or injury.

Discharge: A patient who has received inpatient services. Total number of discharges indicate access to hospital inpatient services as well as the extent of utilization.

Discharge planning: Part of the overall treatment plan designed to facilitate discharge from an inpatient setting. It includes, for example, an estimate of how long the patient will be in the hospital, what the expected outcome is likely to be, whether any special requirements will be needed at discharge, and what needs to be facilitated for postacute continuity of care.

Disease management: Used primarily by health plans, this is a population-oriented strategy involving patient education, training in self-management, ongoing monitoring of the disease process, and follow-up aimed at people with chronic conditions, such as diabetes, asthma, depression, and coronary artery disease.

Disparities: Differences in the quality of health care or the health outcomes of different groups of people (e.g., racial/ethnic, socioeconomic, gender) that are not due to access-related factors or clinical needs, preferences, and appropriateness of interventions.

Distinct part: A section of a nursing home that is distinctly certified from the rest of the facility. It generally refers to an SNF distinct part.

Distributive policies: Spread benefits throughout society. Examples are funding of medical research through the NIH, the training of medical personnel through the National Health Services Corps, the construction of health facilities under the Hill-Burton program, and the initiation of new institutions (e.g., HMOs).

Diversification: Addition of new services that the organization has not offered before.

Do-not-resuscitate (DNR) orders: Advance directives telling medical professionals not to perform CPR. Through DNR orders, patients can have their wishes known regarding aggressive efforts at resuscitation.

Dual certification: Both SNF and NF certifications. Dual certification allows a facility to admit both Medicaid and Medicare patients.

Durable medical equipment (DME): Supplies and equipment not immediately consumed, such as ostomy supplies, wheelchairs, and oxygen tanks.

Durable power of attorney: A written document that provides a legal means for a patient to delegate authority to another to act on the patient's behalf, even after the patient has been incapacitated.

Effectiveness (efficacy): Health benefits of a medical intervention.

Efficiency: Provision of higher quality and more appropriate services at a lower cost, generally measured in terms of benefits relative to costs. *See* **cost efficiency**.

E-health: Health care information and services offered over the Internet by professionals and nonprofessionals alike.

E-therapy: Any type of professional therapeutic interaction that makes use of the Internet to connect qualified mental health professionals and their clients.

Electronic health records: Information technology applications that enable the processing of any electronically stored information pertaining to individual patients for the purpose of delivering health care services.

Eligibility: The process of determining whether a patient qualifies for benefits, based on such factors as age, income, and veteran status.

Emergency department: Hospital facilities for the delivery of unscheduled outpatient services to patients whose conditions require immediate care. Emergency departments must be staffed 24 hours a day.

Emergent condition: An acute condition that requires immediate medical attention.

Emigration: Means migration out of a defined geographic area.

Employer mandate: A legal requirement for employers to help pay for their employees' health insurance.

Enabling services: Services that enable people to receive medical care that otherwise would not be received despite insurance coverage, for example, transportation and translation services.

Enrollee: A person enrolled in a health plan, especially in a managed care plan.

Entitlement: A health care program to which certain people are entitled. For example, almost everyone at 65 years of age is entitled to Medicare because of contributions made through taxes. Medicaid, conversely, is a welfare program.

Environment: One of the factors of the epidemiology triangle, is external to the host. It includes the physical, social, cultural, and economic aspects of the environment.

Environmental health: The field that focuses on the environmental determinants of health.

Epidemic: An outbreak of an infectious disease that spreads rapidly and affects many individuals within a population. *See* **pandemic**.

Epidemiology: The study of the distribution and determinants of health, health-related behavior, disease, disorder, and death in a population group.

E-therapy: Any type of professional therapeutic interaction that makes use of the Internet to connect qualified mental health professionals and their clients.

Ethics committee: An interdisciplinary committee responsible for developing guidelines and standards for ethical decision-making in the provision of health care and for resolving issues related to medical ethics.

Etiology: Study of the causes of disease or dysfunction.

Evidence-based medicine (care): Delivery of health care that incorporates the use of best practices that have been evaluated for effectiveness and safety through clinical research. Best practices are often found in clinical practice guidelines.

Exclusive provider plan: A health plan that is very similar to those offered by preferred provider organizations, except that use is restricted to in-network providers.

Executive committee: A committee within the governing body that has monitoring responsibility and authority over the hospital. Usually it receives reports from other committees, monitors policy implementation, and makes recommendations. The medical staff also have a separate executive committee that establishes policy and has oversight regarding medical matters.

Experience rating: Setting of insurance rates based on a group's actual health care expenses in a prior period. This allows healthier groups to pay less. *See* **community rating**.

Family medicine: A branch of medical practice based on a core of knowledge to function as the primary provider of health care and to perform the roles of patient management, problem solving, counseling, and coordination of care.

Favorable risk selection: Also called "risk selection." A phenomenon in which healthy people are disproportionately enrolled into a health plan. *See* **adverse selection**.

Fee for service: Payment of separate fees to the providers for each separate service, such as examination, administering a test, and hospitalization.

Fee schedule: A schedule of fees for various health care services.

Fertility: The capacity of a population to reproduce.

Fiscal intermediaries: Private sector insurers, such as Blue Cross/Blue Shield and commercial insurance companies, who process provider claims under contract from Medicare and Medicaid.

First-dollar insurance: Health care coverage with no cost sharing.

Flat-of-the-curve: Medical care that produces relatively little or no benefit for the patient because of diminishing marginal returns.

Formulary: A list of prescription drugs approved by a health plan.

Fraud: Intentional filing of false billing claims or cost reports and provision of services that are not medically necessary.

Free clinic: A general ambulatory care center serving primarily the poor and the homeless who may live next to affluent neighborhoods. Free clinics are staffed predominantly by trained volunteers, and care is given free or at a nominal charge.

Free market: Characterized by the unencumbered operation of the forces of supply and demand when numerous buyers and sellers freely interact in a competitive market.

Fringe benefits: A term loosely denoting life insurance, health insurance, or pension benefits provided in whole or in part by an employer to its employees.

Functional status: A person's ability or inability to cope with the activities of daily living.

Gatekeeper: A primary care physician who functions as the provider of first contact to deliver primary care services and to make referrals for specialty care.

Gatekeeping: The use of primary care physicians to coordinate health care services needed by an enrollee in a managed care plan.

Gene therapy: A therapeutic technique in which a functioning gene is inserted into targeted cells to correct an inborn defect or provide the cell with a new function.

General hospital: A hospital that provides a variety of services, including general medicine, specialized medicine, general surgery, specialized surgery, and obstetrics, to meet the general medical needs of the community it serves. It provides diagnostic, treatment, and surgical services for patients with a variety of medical conditions.

Generalist: A physician in family practice, general internal medicine, or general pediatrics. *See* **specialist**.

Genometrics: The association of genes with specific disease traits.

Geriatrics: A branch of medicine that deals with the problems and diseases that accompany aging.

Gerontology: Study of the aging process and the special problems associated with aging.

Global budget: Allocation of pre-established total expenditures for a health care system or subsystem.

Globalization: Various forms of cross-border economic activities driven by global exchange of information, production of goods and services more economically in developing countries, and increased interdependence of mature and emerging world economies.

Gross domestic product (GDP): A measure of all the goods and services produced by a nation in a given year.

Group insurance: A policy obtained through an entity, such as an employer, a union, or a professional organization, that anticipates that a substantial number of people in the group will participate in purchasing insurance through that entity.

Group model: An HMO model in which the HMO contracts with a multispecialty group practice and separately with one or more hospitals to provide comprehensive services to its members.

Group policy: An insurance policy purchased by an organization or association as a benefit to its employees or members. Typical groups are employers, union or trade organizations, and professional associations.

Habilitation: Services that enable a person to maintain skill or function, and prevent deterioration.

Head Start: A federal government–funded program that provides child development services to children in low-income families, including services in education, health care, nutrition, and mental health.

Health care: Refers to the treatment of illness and the maintenance of health.

Health care reform: In the US context, expansion of health insurance to cover the uninsured.

Health determinants: Factors that contribute to the general well-being of individuals and population.

Health informatics: The application of information science to improve the efficiency, accuracy, and reliability of health care services. Health informatics requires the use of information technology (IT) but goes beyond IT by emphasizing the improvement of health care delivery.

Health information organization (HIO): An independent organization that brings together health care stakeholders within a defined geographic area and governs electronic information exchange among these stakeholders with the objective of improving the delivery of health care in the community.

Health maintenance organization (HMO): A type of managed care organization that provides comprehensive medical care for a predetermined annual fee per enrollee.

Health plan: The contractual arrangement between the MCO and the enrollee, including the collective array of covered health services that the enrollee is entitled to.

Health planning: Decisions made by governments to limit health care resources, such as hospital beds and diffusion of costly technology.

Health policy: Refers to public policy that pertains to or influences the pursuit of health.

Health professional shortage area (HPSA): A federal designation indicating an area has shortages of primary medical care, dental, or mental health providers. HPSAs may be urban or rural areas, population groups, or medical or other public facilities.

Health reimbursement arrangement (HRA): An account set up and funded by an employer that can be used by an employee or a retiree to pay for health care expenses.

Health-related quality of life (HRQL): In a composite sense, HRQL includes a person's own perception of health, ability to function, role limitations stemming from physical or emotional problems, and personal happiness during or subsequent to disease experience.

Health Resources and Services Administration (HRSA): A federal agency of the Department of Health and Human Services whose mission is to improve access to health care services for people who are uninsured, isolated, or medically vulnerable.

Health technology assessment: Any process of examining and reporting properties of a medical technology used in health care, such as safety, effectiveness, feasibility, and indications for use, cost, and cost effectiveness, as well as social, economic, and ethical consequences, whether intended or unintended.

Health risk appraisal: Refers to the evaluation of risk factors and their health consequences for individuals. Health risk appraisal is an important aspect of health promotion and disease prevention because it can be instrumental in developing avenues for motivating individuals to alter their behaviors to more healthful patterns.

Healthcare Effectiveness Data and Information Set (HEDIS): The standard for reporting quality information on managed care plans. The standards are developed by National Committee for Quality Assurance, a private nonprofit organization.

Hemiplegia: Paralysis of one-half of the body.

Hemodialysis: A mechanical procedure used to cleanse the blood by removing toxic chemicals in patients who have lost the function of one or both kidneys.

High-deductible health plan: A health plan that combines a savings option with a health insurance plan carrying a high deductible.

High-risk pools: State-based pools, before 2014, to make health insurance available to people who otherwise would have been uninsurable because of pre-existing health conditions.

Holistic health: Emphasizes the well-being of every aspect of what makes a person whole and complete.

Holistic medicine: A philosophy of health care that emphasizes the well-being of every aspect of a person, including the physical, mental, social, and spiritual aspects of health.

Home health care: Services such as nursing, therapy, and health-related homemaker or social services brought to patients in their own homes because such patients are generally unable to leave their homes safely to get the care they need.

Homemaker services: Nonmedical support services given to a homebound individual, for example, bathing, food preparation, house repairs, and shopping.

Homeopathy: A system of medicine based on the theory that "like cures like," meaning large doses of substances that produce symptoms of a disease in healthy people can be administered in small and diluted doses to cure the same illness. The system was founded in the late 18th century by a German physician, Samuel Hahnemann (1755–1843). *See* **allopathy**.

Homophobia: Refers to a prejudice, fear, and/or hatred of gays and lesbians. Homophobia explains the initial slow policy response to the HIV epidemic. Historically, homophobia has been supported by powerful social institutions such as religious institutions, the law, the medical profession, and the media.

Horizontal integration: A growth strategy in which an organization extends its core product or service. *See* **vertical integration**.

Hospice: A cluster of special services for the dying, which blends medical, spiritual, legal, financial, and family-support services. The venue can vary from a specialized facility to a nursing home to the patient's own home.

Hospital: A licensed institution with at least six beds, whose primary function is to deliver diagnostic and therapeutic patient services for various medical conditions. A hospital must have an organized physician staff, and it must provide continuous nursing services under the supervision of registered nurses.

Hospitalist: A physician who specializes in the care of hospitalized patients.

Host: One of the factors of the epidemiology triangle, is an organism, generally a human, who receives the agent. The host is the organism that becomes sick.

Human immunodeficiency virus (HIV): Human immunodeficiency virus. A virus that can destroy the immune system and lead to AIDS.

Hypertension: High blood pressure.

Iatrogenic illness (injury): Illness or injury caused by the process of medical care.

Immigration: Means migration to a defined geographic area.

Incidence: The number of new cases of a disease in a defined population within a specified period.

Indemnity insurance: Also referred to as fee-for-service health insurance, an indemnity plan allows the insured to obtain health care services anywhere and from any physician or hospital. Indemnity insurance and fee-for-service reimbursement to providers are closely intertwined.

Independent practice association (IPA): A legal entity that physicians in private practice can join so that the organization can represent them in the negotiation of managed care contracts.

Infection control committee: A medical committee that is responsible for reviewing policies and procedures for minimizing infections in the hospital.

Information technology (IT): Technology used for the transformation of data into useful information. IT involves determining data needs, gathering appropriate data, storing and analyzing the data, and reporting the information generated in a user-friendly format.

Informed consent: A fundamental patient right to make an informed choice regarding medical treatment based on full disclosure of medical information by the providers.

Inpatient: Services delivered on the basis of an overnight stay in a health care institution.

Inpatient day: A night spent in the hospital by a person admitted as an inpatient. It is also called a patient day or a hospital day.

Institution-related quality of life: Refers to a patient's quality of life while confined in an institution as an inpatient. Examples include comfort factors (such as cleanliness, safety, noise levels, and environmental temperature) and factors related to emotional well-being (autonomy to make decisions, freedom to air grievances without fear of reprisal, reasonable accommodation of personal likes and dislikes, privacy and confidentiality, treatment from staff in a manner that maintains respect and dignity, and freedom from physical and/or emotional abuse).

Instrumental activities of daily living (IADLs): A person's ability to perform household and social tasks, such as home maintenance, cooking, shopping, and managing money. *See* **activities of daily living (ADLs)**.

Insurance: A mechanism for protection against risk.

Insured: The individual who is covered for risk by insurance.

Insurer: An insurance agency or managed care organization that offers insurance.

Integrated delivery system (IDS): A network of organizations that provides or arranges to provide a coordinated continuum of services to a defined population and is willing to be held clinically and fiscally accountable for the outcomes and health status of the population serviced.

Integration: Various strategies that health care organizations employ to achieve economies of operation, diversify existing operations by offering new products or services, or gain market share.

Intellectual disability: *See* **mental retardation**.

Interest group: An organized sector of society, such as a business association, citizen group, labor union, or professional association, whose main purpose is to protect members' interests through active participation in the policy-making process.

Internal medicine: General diagnosis and treatment for problems involving one or more internal organs in adults.

Internal Revenue Service: The tax collection agency in the United States.

International Classification of Diseases, 9th Version, Clinical Modification (ICD-9-CM): The official system of assigning codes to diagnoses and procedures.

Investor-owned hospital: *See* **proprietary hospital**.

IPA model: An organizational arrangement in which an HMO contracts with an independent practice association for the delivery of physician services.

Joint Commission: Previously called the Joint Commission on Accreditation of Healthcare Organizations (JCAHO), it is a private, nonprofit organization that sets standards and accredits most of the nation's general hospitals and many of the long-term care facilities, psychiatric hospitals, substance abuse programs, outpatient surgery centers, urgent care clinics, group practices, community health centers, hospices, and home health agencies.

Joint venture: Creation of a new organization in which two or more institutions share resources to pursue a common purpose.

Licensed practical nurses (LPNs): Called licensed vocational nurses (LVNs) in some states. Nurses who have completed a state-approved program in practical nursing and a national written examination. They often work under the supervision of RNs to provide patient care. *See* **registered nurses**.

Licensure: Licensing of a health care facility that an organization must obtain to operate. Licensure is conferred by each state upon compliance with its standards.

Life expectancy: Actuarial determination of how long, on average, a person of a given age is likely to live.

Lifetime cap: The maximum amount of money a health insurance policy will pay over the lifetime of the insured.

Living will: A legal document in which a patient puts into writing what his or her preferences are regarding treatment during terminal illness and the use of life-sustaining technology. It is a directive instructing a physician to withhold or discontinue medical treatment when the patient is terminally ill and unable to make decisions.

Long-term care: A variety of individualized, well coordinated services that are designed to promote the maximum possible independence for people with functional limitations. These services are provided over an extended period to meet the patients' physical, mental, social, and spiritual needs, while maximizing quality of life.

Long-term care hospital (LTCH): A special type of long-stay hospital described in section 1886(d)(1)(B)(iv) of the Social Security Act. LTCHs must meet Medicare's conditions of participation for acute (short-stay) hospitals and must have an average length of stay greater than 25 days. LTCHs serve patients who have complex medical needs and may suffer from multiple chronic problems requiring long-term hospitalization.

Low birth weight: A weight of less than 2,500 grams at birth.

Magnet hospital: A special designation by the American Nurses Credentialing Center, an affiliate of the American Nurses Association, to recognize quality patient care, nursing excellence, and innovations in professional nursing practice in hospitals.

Magnetic resonance imaging (MRI): The use of a uniform magnetic field and radio frequencies to study body tissue and structure.

Maldistribution: An imbalance (i.e., surplus in some but shortage in others) of the distribution of health professionals, such as physicians, needed to maintain the health status of a given population at an optimum level. Geographic maldistribution refers to the surplus in some regions (e.g., metropolitan areas) but shortage in other regions (e.g., rural and inner city areas) of needed health professionals. Specialty maldistribution refers to the surplus in some specialties (e.g., physician specialists) but shortage in others (e.g., primary care).

Mammography: The use of breast X-ray to detect unsuspected breast cancer in asymptomatic women.

Management services organization (MSO): An MSO is an organization that brings management expertise and, in some instances, capital for expansion to physician group practices.

Managed care: A system of health care delivery that (1) seeks to achieve efficiencies by integrating the four functions of health care delivery, (2) employs mechanisms to control (manage) utilization of medical services, and (3) determines the price at which the services are purchased and, consequently, how much the providers get paid.

Margin: (Total revenues − Total costs)/ Total revenues. Generally shown as a percentage.

Market justice: A distributional principle according to which health care is most equitably distributed through the market forces of supply and demand rather than government interventions. *See* **social justice**.

Meals-on-wheels: A program of home-delivered meals for the elderly. The program is administered by Area Agencies on Aging under Title VII of the Older Americans Act.

Means test: A program in which eligibility depends on income.

Medicaid: A joint federal–state program of health insurance for the poor.

Medicaid waiver program: Enables states to design packages of services targeted at specific populations, such as the elderly, the disabled, and those who test HIV positive. The waiver is an alternative to some form of institutional care.

Medical home: Refers to the quality features of primary health care delivery in the primary care settings such as physician office or community health center.

Medical loss ratio: The percentage of premium revenue spent on medical expenses.

Medical model: Delivery of health care that places its primary emphasis on the treatment of disease and relief of symptoms instead of prevention of disease and promotion of optimum health.

Medical practice guidelines: *See* **clinical practice guidelines**.

Medical records committee: A medical committee that is responsible for certifying complete and clinically accurate documentation of the care given to each patient.

Medical technology: Practical application of the scientific body of knowledge for the purpose of improving health and creating efficiencies in the delivery of health care.

Medical tourism: Travel abroad to receive elective, non-emergency medical care.

Medical staff committee: A committee within the governing body that is charged with medical staff relations in a hospital. For example, it reviews admitting privileges and the performance of the medical staff.

Medically underserved A designation determined by the federal government. It indicates a dearth of primary care providers and delivery settings, as well as poor health indicators of the populace. The majority of this population group are Medicaid recipients.

Medically underserved area (MUA): A federal designation for a geographic area that has a shortage of personal health services for its residents.

Medically underserved population (MUP): A federal designation for a group of persons who face economic, cultural, or linguistic barriers to health care.

Medicare: A federal program of health insurance for the elderly, certain disabled individuals, and people with end-stage renal disease.

Medicare Advantage: Also called Part C of Medicare, enrollment in Medicare Advantage is an option for a beneficiary to receive all health care services through a managed care plan.

Medicare Physician Fee Schedule (MPFS): A national price list for physician services established by Medicare.

Medigap: Commercial health insurance policies purchased by individuals covered by Medicare to insure the expenses not covered by Medicare.

Mental health system: The mental health system in the United States is composed of two subsystems, one primarily for individuals with insurance coverage or money, and one for those without. Patients without insurance coverage or personal financial resources are primarily treated in state and county mental health hospitals, or in community mental health clinics. Patients with insurance coverage or the personal ability to pay receive care from both inpatient and ambulatory mental health care systems.

Mental retardation: Significantly subaverage, general intellectual functioning, existing concurrently with deficits in adaptive behavior and manifested during the developmental period.

Merger: Unification of two or more organizations into a single entity through mutual agreement.

Metropolitan statistical area (MSA): The US Bureau of Census has defined an MSA as a geographic area that includes at least (1) one city with a population of 50,000 or more or (2) an urbanized area of at least 50,000 inhabitants and a total MSA population of at least 100,000 (75,000 in the New England Census Region).

M-health: Short for "mobile health," which is the use of wireless communication devices to support public health and clinical practice.

Migration: Refers to the geographic movement of populations between defined geographic units, and involves a permanent change of residence.

Minimum data set (MDS): An assessment instrument used for determining the case mix in a skilled nursing facility.

Mixed model: An organizational arrangement in which an HMO cannot be categorized neatly into a single model type because it features some combination of large medical group practices, small medical group practices, and independent practitioners, most of whom have contracts with a number of managed care organizations.

Molecular medicine: A branch of medicine that deals with the understanding of the role that genes play in disease processes and treatment of diseases through gene therapy.

Moral agent: A person, such as a health care executive, who has the moral responsibility to ensure that the best interest of patients takes precedence over fiduciary responsibility toward the organization.

Moral hazard: Consumer behavior that leads to a higher utilization of health care services because people are covered by insurance.

Morbidity: Sickness.

Mortality: Death.

Multihospital system: Operation of two or more hospitals owned, leased, sponsored, or contractually managed by a central organization.

Nanomedicine: A new area, still in its infancy, which involves the application of nanotechnology for medical use. Nanotechnology is a cutting-edge advancement within science and engineering. It is not a single field but an intense collaboration between disciplines to manipulate materials on the atomic and molecular level (one nanometer is one-billionth of a meter).

Natality: Refers to the birth rate.

National Committee on Quality Assurance (NCQA): A private organization that accredits managed care organizations and establishes standards for reporting quality.

National health expenditures: Total amount spent for all health services and supplies and health-related research and construction activities consumed in the United States during a calendar year.

National health insurance (NHI): A tax-supported national health care program in which services are financed by the government but are rendered by private providers (Canada, for example).

National Health Service Corps (NHSC): Administered by HRSA, the NHSC recruits health professionals to work in medically underserved rural and urban communities. Education loan repayment is a major incentive for providers to join the NHSC.

National health system (NHS): A tax-supported national health care program in which the government finances and

also controls the service infrastructure (for example, Great Britain).

Naturopathy: A system of medicine based on such natural remedies as nutrition, use of herbs, massage, and yoga exercises.

Need: Need for health services (in contrast to demand for health services) is based on individual judgment. The patient makes the primary determination of the need for health care and, under most circumstances, initiates contact with the system. The physician may make a professional judgment and determine need for referral to higher-level services.

Network model: An organizational arrangement in which an HMO contracts with more than one medical group practice.

Neurology: Branch of medicine that specializes in the nervous system and its diseases.

New morbidities: Dysfunctions, such as drug and alcohol abuse, family and neighborhood violence, emotional disorders, and learning problems, from which older generations do not suffer.

Noncertified: A nursing facility that cannot admit Medicaid or Medicare patients.

Nonphysician practitioners (NPPs): Clinical professionals who practice in many areas similar to those in which physicians practice but who do not have an MD or a DO degree. NPPs are sometimes called midlevel practitioners because they receive less advanced training than physicians but more training than RNs.

Nonprofit (organization): Also called "not for profit." A private organization, such as a hospital, that operates under Internal Revenue Code, Section 501(c)(3). These organizations are tax exempt. In exchange for tax exemption, they must provide some defined public good, such as service, education, or community welfare, and not distribute profits to any individuals.

Nonurgent conditions: Do not require the resources of an emergency service, and disorder is nonacute or minor in severity.

Nosocomial infections: Infections acquired while receiving health care.

Nurse practitioners (NPs): Individuals who have completed a program of study leading to competence as RNs in an expanded role. NP specialties include pediatric, family, adult, psychiatric, and geriatric programs. The primary function of NPs is to promote wellness and good health through patient education. Their traditional nursing role has expanded to include taking patients' comprehensive health histories, assessing health status, performing physical examinations, and formulating and managing a care regimen for acutely and chronically ill patients. *See* **nonphysician practitioners (NPPs)**.

Nursing facility (NF): A nursing home (or part of a nursing home) certified to provide services to Medicaid beneficiaries. *See* **skilled nursing facility**.

Obamacare: *See* **Affordable Care Act**.

Obesity: For adults, it is defined as a body mass index (BMI) of 30 or greater. BMI is calculated by dividing a person's body weight in kilograms by the square of his or her height in meters. *See* **overweight**.

Obstetrics/gynecology: Diagnosis and treatment relating to the sexual and reproductive system of women using surgical and nonsurgical techniques.

Occupancy rate: The percentage of a hospital's total inpatient capacity that is actually utilized.

Occupational therapists (OTs): Help people of all ages improve their ability to perform tasks in their daily living and working environments. They work with individuals who have conditions that are mentally, physically, developmentally, or emotionally disabling.

Occupational therapy: Therapy to help people improve their ability to perform tasks in their daily living and working environment.

Oncology: Medical specialty dealing with cancers and tumors.

Open panel (or open-access): A plan that allows access to providers outside the panel, but some conditions apply, such as higher out-of-pocket costs.

Ophthalmology: The branch of medicine specializing in the eye and its diseases.

Opportunistic infection: An infection that occurs when the body's natural immune system breaks down.

Optometrist: A professional who possesses a Doctor of Optometry degree and has passed a written and clinical state board examination. An optometrist provides vision care—examination, diagnosis, and correction of vision disorders.

Organized medicine: Concerted activities of physicians, mainly to protect their own interests, through such associations as the American Medical Association (AMA).

Organization for Economic Cooperation and Development (OECD): A forum of approximately 30 countries, including all Western European nations, the United States, Canada, New Zealand, Australia, Japan, and others, committed to a market economy. Representatives of member nations meet and discuss global economic and social policies.

Orphan drugs: Certain new drug therapies for conditions that affect fewer than 200,000 people in the United States.

Orthopedics: Branch of medicine dealing with the skeletal system (i.e., bones, joints, muscles, ligaments, and cartilage).

Osteopathic medicine: A medical philosophy based on the holistic approach to treatment. It uses the traditional methods of medical practice, which include pharmaceuticals, laboratory tests, X-ray diagnostics, and surgery, and supplements them by advocating treatment that involves correction of the position of the joints or tissues and emphasizes diet and environment as factors that might destroy natural resistance. *See* **allopathic medicine**.

Outcome: The end result of health care delivery; often viewed as the bottom-line measure of the effectiveness of the health care delivery system.

Outliers: Unusual cases that call for additional reimbursement under a payment method. These are atypical cases requiring an exceptionally long inpatient stay or exceptionally high costs compared to the overall distribution of cases.

Out-of-pocket costs: Costs of health care paid by the recipient of care. For an individual covered by health insurance, these costs generally include the deductible, copayments, cost of excluded services, and costs in excess of what the insurer has determined to be "customary, prevailing, and reasonable."

Outpatient services: As opposed to inpatient services, outpatient services include any health care services that are not provided based on an overnight stay in which room and board costs are incurred. *See* **ambulatory care**.

Overutilization (overuse): Utilization of medical services, the cost of which exceeds the benefit to consumers or the risks of which outweigh potential benefits.

Overweight: For adults, it is defined as a body mass index (BMI) of 25 or greater. BMI is calculated by dividing a person's body weight in kilograms by the square of his or her height in meters. *See* **obesity**.

Package pricing: Bundling of fees for an entire package of related services.

Palliation: Serving to relieve or alleviate, such as pharmacologic pain management and nausea relief.

Pandemic: Relating to the spread of disease in a large segment of the population. *See* **epidemic**.

Panel: Providers selected to render services to the members of a managed care plan constitute its panel. The plan generally refers to them as "preferred providers."

Paramedic: Health care workers other than physicians who work as emergency medical technicians.

Paraprofessionals: Personnel, such as certified nursing assistants and therapy aides, who provide basic ADL assistance and/or assist licensed and professional staff.

Parenteral feeding: The full name is "total parenteral nutrition" (TPN). It infuses nutrients and water into the veins through a catheter, bypassing the gastro-intestinal tract.

Parkinson's disease: A chronic disease of the nervous system characterized by tremor and muscular debility. Named after the British physician, James Parkinson (1755–1824).

Part A of Medicare: Provides coverage for hospital care and limited nursing home care.

Part B of Medicare: Government-subsidized voluntary insurance for physician services and outpatient services.

Pathology: Study of the nature and cause of disease that involves changes in structure and function.

Patient activation: A person's ability to manage his or her own health and utilization of health care.

Patient-centered care: Delivery of health care that respects and responds to patients' wants, needs, and preferences so that they can make choices in their care that best fit their individual circumstances.

Patient's bill of rights: A document that reflects the law concerning the rights a patient has while confined to an institution such as a hospital. Some common issues addressed in the bill of rights include confidentiality, consent, and the right to make decisions regarding medical care, to be informed about diagnosis and treatment, to refuse treatment, and to formulate advance directives.

Pay for performance: A reimbursement plan that links payment to quality and efficiency as an incentive to improve the quality of health care and to reduce costs.

Payer: The party who actually makes payment for services under the insurance coverage policy. In most cases, the payer is the same as the insurer.

Pediatrics: General diagnosis and treatment for children.

Peer review: Refers to the general process of medical review of utilization and quality when it is carried out directly or under the supervision of physicians.

Per diem: A type of reimbursement mechanism for inpatient care in a health care institution. The reimbursement comprises a flat rate for each day of inpatient stay.

Per member per month (PMPM): Refers to a capitated rate. *See* **Capitation**.

Personal care: Assistance with basic ADLs.

Personal emergency response system (PERS): It provides at-risk elderly persons effective and convenient means to summon help when an emergency occurs. A transmitter unit enables the individual to activate an alarm that sends a medical alert to a local 24-hour response center.

Personal health expenditures: A portion of national health expenditures remaining after expenditures for research and construction, administrative expenses incurred in health insurance programs, and costs of government public health activities. These expenditures are for services and goods related directly to patient care.

Pesthouse: Operated by local governments during the 18th and mid-19th centuries to quarantine people who contracted a contagious disease such as cholera, smallpox, or typhoid. The primary function of a pesthouse was to protect the community from the spread of contagious disease; medical care was only secondary.

Phantom providers: Practitioners who generally function in an adjunct capacity. The patient does not receive direct services from them. They bill for their services separately, and the patients often wonder why they have been billed. Examples include anesthesiologists, radiologists, and pathologists.

Pharmaceutical care: A mode of pharmacy practice in which the pharmacist takes an active role on behalf of patients, which includes giving information on drugs and advice on their potential misuse and assisting prescribers in appropriate drug choices. In so doing, the pharmacist assumes direct responsibility collaboratively with other health care professionals and with patients to achieve the desired therapeutic outcomes.

Pharmacist: A professional who has graduated from an accredited pharmacy program that awards a Bachelor of Pharmacy or Doctor of Pharmacy degree and has successfully completed a state board examination and a supervised internship.

Pharmacology: Body of science dealing with drugs, their nature, properties, and effects.

Physical therapists (PTs): Provide care for patients with movement dysfunction.

Physical therapy: The evaluation and treatment of physical problems resulting from injury or disease, including problems with joint motion, muscle strength, endurance, and heart and lung function.

Physician assistants (PAs): Professionals who work in a dependent relationship with a supervising physician to provide comprehensive medical care to patients. The major services provided by PAs include evaluation, monitoring, diagnostics, therapeutics, counseling, and referral. *See* **nonphysician practitioners (NPPs)**.

Physician extenders: *See* **nonphysician practitioners (NPPs)**.

Physician–hospital organization (PHO): A legal entity formed between a hospital and a physician group to achieve shared market objectives and other mutual interests.

Plan: The form in which health insurance, particularly private health insurance, is obtained. The plan specifies among other details, information pertaining to costs, covered services, and how to obtain health care when needed.

Planned rationing: *See* **supply-side rationing**.

Play or pay: A type of employer mandate in which employers must choose to provide health insurance to employees ("play") or pay a penalty.

Podiatrists: Professionals who treat patients with foot diseases or deformities.

Point of service (POS) plan: A managed care plan that allows its members to decide at the time they need medical care (at the point of service) whether to go to a provider on the panel or to pay more to receive services out of network.

Population at risk: Include all the people in the same community or population group who are susceptible to acquiring a disease or a negative health condition.

Practice profiling: Use of provider-specific practice patterns and comparing individual practice patterns to some norm.

Preadmission Screening and Resident Review (PASRR): An evaluation required under federal regulations before a patient can be admitted to a Medicaid-certified nursing facility to determine whether a nursing facility is the best alternative for individuals with serious mental illness or intellectual disability or whether their needs can be adequately met in community-based settings.

Preexisting condition: A physical and/or mental condition that existed before the effective date of an insurance policy.

Preferred provider organization (PPO): A type of managed care organization that has a panel of preferred providers who are paid according to a discounted fee schedule. The enrollees do have the option to go to out-of-network providers at a higher level of cost sharing.

Premium: The insurer's charge for insurance coverage; the price for an insurance plan.

Premium cost sharing: Refers to the common practice by employers that require their employees to pay a portion of the health insurance cost.

Prepaid plan: A contractual arrangement under which a provider must provide all needed services to a group of members (or enrollees) in exchange for a fixed monthly fee paid in advance to the provider on a per-member basis (called capitation).

Prevalence: The number of cases of a given disease in a given population at a certain point in time.

Primary care: Basic and routine health care provided in an office or clinic by a provider (physician, nurse, or other health care professional) who takes responsibility for coordinating all aspects of a patient's health care needs. An approach to health care delivery that is the patient's first contact with the health care delivery system and the first element of a continuing health care process.

Primary care case management (PCCM): A managed care arrangement in which a state contracts directly with primary care providers, who agree to be responsible for the provision and/or coordination of medical services for Medicare recipients under their care.

Primary health care: Essential health care that constitutes the first level of contact by a patient with the health delivery system and the first element of a continuing health care process.

Primary prevention: In a strict epidemiological sense, it refers to prevention of disease, for example, health education, immunization, and environmental control measures.

Prior approval: A form of utilization review in which an insurance company requires a provider to get permission from the insurance company before providing care (usually surgery).

Private-pay patients: Patients not covered by either Medicare or Medicaid.

Program of All-Inclusive Care for the Elderly (PACE): An example of the integrated care model of long-term care case management for clients who have been certified as eligible for nursing home placement. It has had a high success rate of keeping clients in the community.

Proprietary hospital: Also referred to as investor-owned hospital, it is a for-profit hospital owned by individuals, a partnership, or a corporation.

Prospective payment system (PPS): Criteria for how much will be paid for a particular service is predetermined, as opposed to "retrospective payment" in which the amount of reimbursement is determined on the basis of costs actually incurred.

Prospective reimbursement: A method of payment in which certain preestablished criteria are used to determine in advance the amount of reimbursement.

Prospective utilization review: A process that determines the appropriateness of utilization before the care is actually delivered.

Provider: Any entity that delivers health care services and can either independently bill for those services or is tax supported. Common examples of providers include physicians, dentists, optometrists, and therapists in private practices; hospitals; diagnostic and imaging clinics; and suppliers of medical equipment (e.g., wheelchairs, walkers, ostomy supplies, oxygen).

Provider-induced demand: Artificial creation of demand by providers that enables them to deliver unneeded services to boost their incomes.

PSO (provider-sponsored organization, sometimes called provider service organization): A quasi-managed care organization that is a risk-bearing entity sponsored by physicians, hospitals, or jointly by physicians and hospitals to compete with regular MCOs.

Psychiatrists: Physicians who receive postgraduate specialty training in mental health after completion of medical school. They treat patients with mental disorders, prescribe drugs, and admit patients to hospitals.

Psychiatry: Branch of medicine that specializes in mental disorders.

Psychologists: Mental health professionals who must be licensed or certified to practice. Psychologists may specialize in such areas as clinical, counseling, developmental, educational, engineering, personnel, experimental, industrial, psychometric, rehabilitation, school, and social psychology.

Public health: A wide variety of activities undertaken by state and local governments to ensure conditions that promote optimum health for society as a whole.

Public hospital: A hospital owned by the federal, state, or local government.

Public policies: Authoritative decisions made in the legislative, executive, or judicial branches of government that are intended to direct or influence the actions, behaviors, or decisions of others.

Quad-function model: The four key functions necessary for health care delivery: financing, insurance, delivery, and payment.

Quality: Defined as the degree to which health services for individuals and populations increase the likelihood of desired health outcomes and are consistent with current professional knowledge.

Quality-adjusted life year (QALY): The value of 1 year of high-quality life, used as a measure of health benefit.

Quality assessment: Process of defining quality and deciding how quality is to be measured according to established standards.

Quality assurance: The process of ongoing quality measurement and using the results of assessment for ongoing quality improvement. *See* **total quality management**.

Quality improvement committee: A medical committee that is responsible for overseeing the program for continuous quality improvement.

Quality improvement organization (QIO): A private organization composed of practicing physicians and other health care professionals in each state that is paid by the Centers for Medicare & Medicaid Services under contract to review the care provided to Medicare beneficiaries.

Quality of life: (1) Quality of life refers to factors considered important by patients, such as environmental comfort, security, interpersonal relations, personal preferences, and autonomy in making decisions when institutionalized. (2) It also includes overall satisfaction with life during and following a person's encounter with the health care delivery system.

R&D: Research and development.

Radiology: The branch of medicine that involves the use of radioactive substances, such as X-rays, to diagnose, prevent, and treat disease.

Rate: The price for a healthcare service generally set by a third-party payer, whereas a charge is the price set by the provider.

Rationing: Any process of limiting the utilization of health care services. Rationing can be achieved by price, waiting lists, or deliberately limiting access to certain services.

Redistributive policies: Take money or power from one group and give it to another. Examples are the Medicaid program, which takes tax revenue and spends it on the poor in the form of health insurance.

Registered nurses: Nurses who have completed an associate's degree (ADN), a diploma program, or a bachelor's degree (BSN) and are licensed to practice.

Regulatory tools: Designate a use of health policy in which the government prescribes and controls the behavior of a particular target group by monitoring the group and posing sanctions if it fails to comply.

Rehabilitation: Therapies that restore lost functioning or maintain the current levels of functioning and prevent further decline.

Rehabilitation hospital: A hospital that specializes in providing restorative services to rehabilitate chronically ill and disabled individuals to a maximum level of functioning.

Reimbursement: The amount insurers pay to a provider. The payment may only be a portion of the actual charge.

Reinsurance: Stop-loss coverage that self-insured employers purchase to protect themselves against any potential risk of high losses.

Relative value units (RVUs): Measures based on physicians' time, skill, and intensity it takes to provide a service.

Reliability: Reflects the extent to which repeated applications of a measure produce the same results.

Residency: Graduate medical education in a specialty that takes the form of paid on-the-job training, usually in a hospital.

Resident: (1) Patient in a nursing home or some other long-term care facility. (2) Physician in residency.

Resource-based relative value scale (RBRVS): A system instituted by Medicare for determining physicians' fees. Each treatment or encounter by the physician is assigned a "relative value" based on the time, skill, and training required to treat the condition.

Resource utilization groups (RUGs): A classification system designed to differentiate nursing home patients by their levels of resource use.

Respiratory therapy: Treatment for various acute and chronic lung conditions, using oxygen, inhaled drugs, and various types of mechanical ventilation.

Respite care: A service that provides temporary relief to informal caregivers, such as family members.

Restorative care: Short-term therapy treatments to help a person regain or improve physical function.

Retrospective reimbursement: Setting of reimbursement rates based on costs actually incurred.

Retrospective utilization review: A review of utilization after services have been delivered.

Risk: The possibility of a substantial financial loss from an event of which the probability of occurrence is relatively small.

Risk adjustment: Any adjustment made for people who are likely high users of health care services, for example, adjustment of payments based on the proportion of high-risk patients.

Risk factor: An environmental element, personal habit, or living condition that increases the likelihood of developing a particular disease or negative health condition in the future.

Risk management: Limiting risks against lawsuits or unexpected events.

Risk rating: Insurance rating according to which high-risk individuals pay more than the average premium price, and low-risk individuals pay less than the average price.

Risk selection: *See* **favorable risk selection.**

Rural hospital: A hospital located in a county that is not part of a metropolitan statistical area.

Safety net: Programs, generally government financed, that enable people to receive health care services when they lack private resources to pay for them. Without these programs, many people would have to forgo the services. For example, Medicaid becomes a safety net for long-term care services once a patient has exhausted private funds. Community health centers are safety net providers for many uninsured and vulnerable populations.

Secondary care: Routine hospitalization, routine surgery, and specialized outpatient care, such as consultation with specialists and rehabilitation. Compared to primary care, these services are usually brief and more complex, involving advanced diagnostic and therapeutic procedures.

Secondary prevention: Efforts to detect disease in early stages to provide a more effective treatment, for example, screening.

Self-insured plan: A large company may act as its own insurer by collecting premiums and paying claims. Such businesses most often purchase reinsurance against unusually large claims.

Self-referral: Physicians order services from laboratories or other medical facilities in which they have a direct financial interest, usually without disclosing this conflict of interest to the patient.

Senior centers: Local community centers for older adults that provide opportunities to congregate and socialize. Many centers offer subsidized meals, wellness programs, health education, counseling, and referral services.

Short-stay hospital: A hospital in which the average length of stay is less than 25 days.

Single-payer system: A national health care program in which the financing and insurance functions are taken over by the federal government.

Skilled nursing care: Medically oriented care provided mainly by a licensed nurse under the overall direction of a physician.

Skilled nursing facility (SNF): A nursing home (or part of a nursing home) certified to provide services under Medicare. *See* **nursing facility (NF)**.

Small area variations: Unexplained variations in the treatment patterns for similar patients and medical conditions.

Smart card: A credit card-like device with an embedded computer chip and memory to hold personal medical information that can be accessed and updated at a hospital or physician's office.

Social contacts: Evaluated in terms of the number of social contacts or social activities a person engages in within a specified period of time. Examples are visits with friends and relatives, and attendance at social events, such as conferences, picnics, or other outings.

Social justice: A distribution principle according to which health care is most equitably distributed by a government-run national health care program. *See* **market justice**.

Social managed care plan: A managed care plan that provides the full range of Medicare benefits and additional services, which include care coordination, prescription drug benefits, short-term nursing home care, and a full range of home- and community-based LTC services.

Social resources: Refer to social contacts that can be relied upon for support, such as family, relatives, friends, neighbors, and members of a religious congregation. They are indicative of adequacy of social relationships.

Socialized health insurance (SHI): Health care is financed through government-mandated contributions by employers and employees. Health care is delivered by private providers (for example, Germany, Israel, and Japan).

Socialized medicine: Any large-scale government-sponsored expansion of health insurance or intrusion in the private practice of medicine.

Specialist: A physician who specializes in specific health care problems, for example, anesthesiologists, cardiologists, and oncologists. See **generalist**.

Specialty care: Tends to be limited to illness episodes, the organ system, or the disease process involved. Specialty care, if needed, generally follows primary care.

Specialty hospital: A hospital that admits only certain types of patients or those with specified illnesses or conditions. Examples include rehabilitation hospitals, tuberculosis hospitals, children's hospitals, cardiac hospitals, orthopedic hospitals, etc.

Speech therapy: Therapy focusing on individuals with communication problems, including using the voice correctly, speaking fluently, and feeding or swallowing.

Spina bifida: A deformity of the spine.

Staff model: An HMO arrangement in which the HMO employs salaried physicians.

Standards of participation: Minimum quality standards established by government regulatory agencies to certify providers for delivery of services to Medicare and Medicaid patients.

Subacute care: Clinically complex services that are beyond traditional skilled nursing care.

Subacute condition: Technically complex services that are beyond traditional skilled nursing care.

Supplemental Food Program for Women, Infants, and Children (WIC): The program was created on September 26, 1972, as an amendment to the Child Nutrition Act of 1966, with the objective of providing sufficient nutrition for pregnant women, mothers, infants, and children.

Supplemental Security Income (SSI): A federal program of income support for the disabled, including mental illness and some infectious diseases.

Supply-side rationing: Also called "planned rationing" that is generally carried out by a government to limit the availability of health care services, particularly expensive technology.

Surge capacity: The ability of a health care facility or system to expand its operations to safely treat an abnormally large influx of patients.

Surgicenter: A freestanding, ambulatory surgery center that performs various types of surgical procedures on an outpatient basis.

Swing bed: A hospital bed used for acute care or skilled nursing care, depending on fluctuations in demand.

Synchronous technology: Technology in which telecommunications occur in real time.

Teaching hospital: A hospital with an approved residency program for physicians.

Technological imperative: Implies the use of technology without cost considerations, especially when the benefits to be derived from the use of technology are small compared to the costs.

Technology assessment: See **health technology assessment**.

Technology diffusion: The proliferation of technology once it is developed.

Telehealth: Although in general the terms telemedicine and telehealth can be used interchangeably, in a stricter sense, telehealth encompasses educational, research, and administrative uses, as well as clinical applications that involve nurses, psychologists, administrators, and other nonphysicians.

Telematics: A term used to describe the combination of information and communications technology to meet user needs.

Telemedicine: Use of telecommunications technology that enables physicians to conduct two-way, interactive video consultations or transmit digital images, such as X-rays and MRIs, to other sites.

Telephone triage: Refers to a telephone call-in system staffed by specially trained nurses who receive patients' calls. Using a computer system, they can access a patient's medical history and view the most recent radiology and laboratory test results. The nurses use standardized protocols to guide them in dealing with the patient's problem and consult with primary care physicians when necessary. If necessary, the staff can direct patients to appropriate medical services such as an ED or a physician's office.

Tertiary care: The most complex level of care. Typically, tertiary care is institution-based, highly specialized, and highly technological. Examples include burn treatment, transplantation, and coronary artery bypass surgery.

Tertiary prevention: Interventions that would prevent complications from chronic conditions and prevent further illness, injury, or disability.

Third party: An intermediary between patients and providers. Third parties carry out the functions of insurance and payment for health care delivery.

Third-party administrator (TPA): An administrative organization, other than the employee benefit plan or health care provider, that collects premiums, pays claims, and/or provides administrative services.

Third-party payers: In a multipayer system, the payers for covered services, for example, insurance companies, managed care organizations, and the government. They are called third parties because they are neither the providers nor the recipients of medical services.

Title XVIII: Or more precisely, Title XVIII (18) of the Social Security Amendment of 1965 refers to the Medicare program.

Title XIX: Or more precisely, Title XIX (19) of the Social Security Amendment of 1965 refers to the Medicaid program.

Top-down control: It establishes budgets for entire sectors of the health care delivery system. Funds are distributed to providers in accordance with these global budgets. Thus, total spending remains within preestablished budget limits. The downside to this approach is that, under fixed budgets, providers are not as responsive to patient needs, and the system provides little incentive to be efficient in the delivery of services. Once budgets are expended, providers are forced to cut back services, particularly for illnesses that are not life-threatening or do not represent an emergency.

Total care: In the context of long-term care delivery, total care focuses on recognizing any health care need that may arise and ensuring that the need is evaluated and addressed by appropriate clinical professionals.

Total quality management (TQM): TQM creates an environment in which all aspects of health services within an organization are oriented to patient-related objectives and the production of desirable health outcomes. It holds the promise of not only improving quality but also increasing efficiency and productivity by identifying and implementing less costly ways to provide services. This system is viewed as an ongoing effort to improve quality. Hence, it is also referred to as continuous quality improvement (CQI).

Trauma center: An emergency unit specializing in the treatment of severe injuries.

Triage: A system of prioritizing treatment when demand for medical care exceeds supply.

Triple-option plan: A health insurance plan that combines the features of indemnity insurance, HMO, and PPO; the insured has the flexibility to choose which feature to use when using health care services.

Uncompensated care: Charity care provided to the uninsured who cannot pay.

Underinsurance: Medical insurance coverage considered inadequate to cover the costs of a major illness.

Underutilization: Occurs when medically needed health care services are withheld. This is especially true when potential benefits are likely to exceed the cost or risks.

Underwriting: A systematic technique used by an insurer for evaluating, selecting (or rejecting), classifying, and rating risks.

Uninsured: People who are without health insurance coverage.

Universal access: The ability of all citizens to obtain health care when needed. It is a misnomer because timely access to certain services may still be a problem because of supply-side rationing.

Universal coverage: Health insurance coverage for all citizens.

Upcoding: A fraudulent practice in which a higher priced service is billed when a lower priced service is actually delivered.

Urban hospital: A hospital located in a county that is part of a metropolitan statistical area.

Urgent care center: A walk-in clinic generally open to see patients after normal business hours in the evenings and weekends without having to make an appointment.

Urgent condition: Require medical attention within a few hours; a longer delay presents possible danger to the patient; and the disorder is acute but not necessarily severe.

Urology: The branch of medicine concerned with the urinary tract in both sexes and the sexual/reproductive system in males.

Utilization: Extent to which health care services are actually used.

Utilization review committee: A process by which an insurer reviews decisions by physicians and other providers on how much care to provide.

Value: Means greater benefits or higher quality at the same or lower price levels (costs).

Venous stasis: Stagnation of normal blood flow causing swelling and pain, generally in the legs.

Ventilator: A mechanical device for artificial breathing. The ventilator (or mechanical respirator) forces air into the lungs.

Vertical integration: Linking of services that are at different stages in the production process of health care. Examples include a hospital system that acquires a firm that produces medical supplies or a physician group practice or a hospital that launches hospice, long-term care, or ambulatory care services. *See* **horizontal integration**.

Virtual integration: The formation of networks based on contractual arrangements.

Virtual physician visits: Online clinical encounters between a patient and physician.

Voluntary health insurance: Private health insurance (in contrast to government-sponsored compulsory health insurance).

Voluntary hospital: A nonprofit hospital.

Voucher: The voucher approach to health insurance reform relies on individual decisions to purchase health insurance. Tax credits are issued in advance to individuals in the form of vouchers with which to offset the costs of purchasing health insurance.

Walk-in clinic: A freestanding, ambulatory clinic in which patients are seen without appointments on a first-come, first-served basis.

Welfare program: A means-tested program for which only people below certain income levels qualify. Medicaid is a welfare program. *See* **entitlement**.

Workers' compensation: Employer-paid benefit that compensates workers for medical expenses and wages lost due to work-related injuries or illnesses.

Xenotransplantation: Also called "xenografting." Transplanting of animal tissue into humans.

Yoga exercises: Using physical postures and regulation of breathing to treat certain chronic conditions and to achieve overall health benefits.

Zoonoses: Any disease or infection that is naturally transmittable from vertebrate animals to humans.

Index

Note: Page numbers followed by *t* or *f* indicate tables or figures, respectively. Page numbers in *italics* indicate exhibits.